Ending Welfare
as We Know It

Ending Welfare as We Know It

R. Kent Weaver

BROOKINGS INSTITUTION PRESS
Washington, D.C.

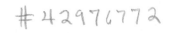

Library of Congress Cataloging-in-Publication data

Weaver, R. Kent, 1953–
  Ending welfare as we know it / R. Kent Weaver.
    p.   cm.
  Includes bibliographical references and index.
    ISBN 0-8157-9248-4 (cloth : alk. paper)—
    ISBN 0-8157-9247-6 (paper : alk. paper)
    1. Public welfare—United States.   2. Poor—Government policy—
  United States.   3. Welfare recipients—Government policy—United States.
  4. Family policy—United States.   5. United States—Social policy—1993–
  6. United States—Politics and government—1993–   I. Title.
    HV95 .W38 2000
    361.973—dc21   99-050856
                                                                        CIP

9 8 7 6 5 4 3 2 1

The paper used in this publication meets minimum requirements of the
American National Standard for Information Sciences—Permanence of Paper
for Printed Library Materials: ANSI Z39.48-1984.

Typeset in Minion

Composition by R. Lynn Rivenbark
Macon, Georgia

Printed by R. R. Donnelley and Sons
Harrisonburg, Virginia

For my teachers:

Martha A. Derthick
Hugh Heclo
Gilbert Y. Steiner

Foreword

The Personal Responsibility and Work Opportunity Reconciliation Act (PRWORA) of 1996 was a landmark in social legislation. It replaced the sixty-year-old Aid to Families with Dependent Children (AFDC) program with a new block grant program, Temporary Assistance to Needy Families (TANF). States were given substantially increased discretion over some policy choices in the new program, but they also had to meet tough new requirements on work participation rates and limitations on the period for which families could receive benefits using TANF funds. Individual entitlement to benefits was explicitly abolished under TANF. What makes this legislative event all the more remarkable is that many of the provisions enacted as part of PRWORA had only recently become part of the legislative debate on welfare reform; four or five years earlier they would have been considered far outside the mainstream of policy debate.

In this definitive study of the politics of welfare reform over the past decade, R. Kent Weaver, a senior fellow in the Brookings Governmental Studies program, sets the conflict over PRWORA in the context of immense public dissatisfaction with AFDC, a long series of failed reform initiatives (most recently, President Clinton's aborted effort of 1993–94), continued elite disagreement about the path that welfare reform legislation should take, and electoral competition between the president and a new Republican majority in Congress. Changes in this complex environment significantly lowered the longstanding barriers to passage of welfare reform legislation, notably by weakening the capacity of liberals to keep proposals to which they objected off the legislative agenda. But passage of PRWORA was by no means inevitable. Rather, any explanation of this remarkable occurrence must also incorporate relatively short-term calculations by policymakers about the range of policies that they would accept—calculations that, in turn, were strongly affected by considerations of the unity of coalitions and of the upcoming 1996 elections.

Since enactment of PRWORA, the conjunction of new welfare rules, a booming economy, and the expansion of the Earned Income Tax Credit have helped to increase the labor force participation of former welfare recipients. Weaver cautions, however, that a definitive judgment about the effects of welfare reform will have to wait until more recipients have hit TANF time limits and an economic slowdown gives some clues as to how these workers fare when jobs are scarce. Moreover, the new legislation has neither settled the direction of welfare reform nor depoliticized it. Many issues, such as work requirements, time limits, and the allocation of TANF block grant funds among states will once again be debated when the TANF program is reauthorized in 2002.

Completion of this book was aided by the many policymakers and other welfare reform participants inside and outside government who were interviewed for the study, many of them several times. All interviewees were promised anonymity, hence none is directly identified here. The author also gratefully acknowledges the tremendous assistance provided by Erica B. Baum, Ronald Haskins, Lawrence M. Mead, and R. Shep Melnick, each of whom read the entire manuscript and made extremely helpful comments. In adddition, Jeffrey Berry, Martha Derthick, David Ellwood, Mark Greenberg, Isabel Sawhill, Waltraud Schelkle, Allen Schick, Gilbert Y. Steiner, Margaret M. Weir, Joseph White, and Michael Wiseman commented on parts of the manuscript. Helpful comments were also received from participants in the Brookings Governmental Studies Research-in-Progress seminar and the Inequality and Social Policy seminar at the Kennedy School of Government.

Financial support for the author's research on welfare reform was provided by the Annie E. Casey Foundation and the Russell Sage Foundation. The author particularly wants to thank Michael Laracy and Eric Wanner for their interest in this project.

Jim Abrams, Stephanianna Lozito, Theo Noell, and Carole Plowfield provided research assistance, and Jessica Gerrity verified the factual content. At the Brookings Institution Press, Jim Schneider and Debbie Styles edited the manuscript, Carlotta Ribar proofread and Julia Petrakis indexed the pages. In the Brookings Governmental Studies program, Judith Light, Bethany

Merchant, Sherra Merchant, and Susan Stewart cheerfully provided administrative support.

The author expresses his appreciation to Ellen Broadman, who provided wise counsel and support throughout the research and writing process, and to Jeff and Danny Weaver, who provided many pleasant distractions. Finally, he would like to express his enormous gratitude to three mentors, all former senior fellows in the Brookings Governmental Studies program: Martha A. Derthick, Hugh Heclo, and Gilbert Y. Steiner.

The views expressed here are solely those of the author and should not be ascribed to any persons or institutions acknowledged above or to the trustees, officers, or other staff members of the Brookings Institution.

MICHAEL H. ARMACOST
President

July 2000
Washington, D.C.

Contents

CHAPTER ONE
*Introduction: Welfare Reform as a
Political and Policy Problem*   1

CHAPTER TWO
Welfare as We Knew It   9
Poverty and American Families   10
The Structure of American Family Support Policies   11

CHAPTER THREE
Explaining Welfare Politics: Context, Choices, Traps   23
Contextual Forces in Welfare Reform Politics   24
Analyzing Political Choice   29
Policymaking Traps in Reforming Welfare   43
Stasis and Change in Welfare Policy   52

CHAPTER FOUR
The Past as Prologue   54
Growing Controversy over AFDC   55
Nixon's Family Assistance Plan   57
Carter Tries Again   60
The Budget Blitzkrieg of 1981   66
Reagan's New Federalism   68
The Family Support Act of 1988   70

Policy Counterpoint: Expansion of the
    Earned Income Tax Credit   78
Patterns and Lessons in Welfare Reform   84
Avoiding the Welfare Reform Policymaking Traps   91
Conclusions   100

CHAPTER FIVE
Welfare Reform Agendas in the 1990s   102
Getting Politicians' Attention: The Problem Stream   103
Welfare Reform Options: The Policy Stream   106
Raising the Stakes: The Political Stream   126
Conclusions   133

CHAPTER SIX
The Role of Policy Research   135
The Boom in Policy Research   140
Uses and Limitations of Policy Research   143
Issues Surrounding Program Entry   145
From Program Exit to Self-Sufficiency   153
Conclusions: Policy Research and the
    Politics of Dissensus   160

CHAPTER SEVEN
Public Opinion on Welfare Reform   169
Public Opinion and Policy Change   169
The Importance of Elite Priming   171
Analyzing Opinion on Welfare   172
Causes of Poverty and Welfare Dependence   175
Attitudes toward Specific Reforms   177
Whom Do You Trust?   186
Conclusions and Implications   190

CHAPTER EIGHT
Interest Groups and Welfare Reform   196
Child Advocacy Groups   199
The Democratic Leadership Council   206

Intergovernmental Groups   207
Social Conservative Groups   211
Conclusions: The Ambiguous Impact of Groups   217

CHAPTER NINE
Not Ending Welfare as We Know It: The Clinton Administration's Welfare Reform Initiative   222
The Political Environment for Welfare Reform   223
A Crowded Agenda   228
Policy Choice and the Politics of Formulation   232
Coming to Closure   237
The Clinton Administration Proposal   242
The Political Feasibility of the Clinton Plan   246
Conclusions   248

CHAPTER TEN
A New Congress, a New Dynamic   252
The Electoral Earthquake   253
Initial Bids   260
Evolving Bids: Seeking a Workable Compromise
   in the House   274
Explaining the Republican Success in the House   289

CHAPTER ELEVEN
Stop and Go in the Senate   294
Setting the Stage in the Senate   295
Stop and Go   301
A Fragile Republican Coalition   303
Aftershocks   313

CHAPTER TWELVE
Endgames and Aftershocks   316
Bargaining Positions and Bargaining Rules   317
Endgame One: The Budget Process and
   Initial Vetoes   320

Endgame Two: The Senate Bill and
  Gubernatorial Intervention 321
Endgame Three: Moving a Bill 325
Provisions of the Personal Responsibility and
  Work Opportunity Reconciliation Act 328
Aftershocks 335
Conclusions 337

CHAPTER THIRTEEN
Gaining Ground? The New World of Welfare 342
Declining Caseloads 343
State Program Design 344
Welfare Offices 347
The Behavior of Welfare Recipients 350
The Long-Term Prognosis 352

CHAPTER FOURTEEN
*Welfare Reform and the Dynamics of
American Politics* 355
The Politics of Welfare Agenda Change 355
The Political Barriers to Comprehensive
  Welfare Reform 359
Enacting Welfare Reform, 1995–96 364
The Centrality of Choice 382

Notes 387

Index 465

CHAPTER ONE

Introduction

Welfare Reform as a Political and Policy Problem

BILL CLINTON'S FIRST presidential term was a period of extraordinary change in policy toward low-income families. In 1993 Congress enacted a major expansion of the Earned Income Tax Credit for low-income working families. In 1996 Congress passed and the president signed the Personal Responsibility and Work Opportunity Reconciliation Act of 1996 (PRWORA). This legislation abolished the sixty-year-old Aid to Families with Dependent Children (AFDC) program and replaced it with a block grant program, Temporary Assistance for Needy Families, or TANF, for the states that ended legal entitlement to benefits; it contained stiff new work requirements and limits on the length of time people could receive welfare benefits.

Dramatic change in AFDC was also occurring piecemeal in the states during these years. States used waivers granted by the federal Department of Health and Human Services to experiment with a variety of welfare strategies, including denial of additional benefits for children born or conceived while a mother received AFDC (known as family caps), work requirements, and time limits on receipt of cash benefits. The pace of change at the state level accelerated after the 1996 federal welfare reform legislation gave states increased leeway to design their programs.

This book analyzes how these changes in the AFDC program, particularly the national welfare reform legislation enacted in 1996, came about. To some observers the changes will seem no mystery at all. Broad social and political trends, notably concern over changes in the structure of American families and overwhelming public rejection of the existing AFDC program, helped to create a historic opening for welfare reform legislation. And candidate Clinton had promised in his 1992 election campaign to "end welfare as we know it." House Republicans included welfare reforms even more dramatic than Clinton's in their 1994 Contract with America campaign manifesto, and they controlled both chambers of Congress after the 1994 election.

These developments did not, however, make dramatic welfare reform legislation inevitable. Welfare reform raises issues of race, class, and sex (in both the gender and sexual activity senses of the word) that are as difficult and divisive as any in American politics. The dismal record of welfare reform initiatives in the United States going back more than thirty years makes it clear that getting welfare reform on the agenda and gaining support from key policymakers is far from sufficient for getting legislation passed.[1]

Given the failure of past welfare reform initiatives, expectations of many participants were low at the beginning of the Clinton administration. In the spring of 1993 when Senate Finance Committee chair Daniel Patrick Moynihan, a veteran of all the welfare reform struggles of the past quarter century and both the architect and the author of a retrospective on Nixon's Family Assistance Plan, met the cochair of the Clinton administration's new welfare reform task force, Moynihan said that he "looked forward to reading your book about why it failed this time."[2] The first three years of Clinton's first term were consistent with Moynihan's expectations: Clinton's welfare reform package was never voted on by Congress, and welfare reform legislation passed by the Republican-dominated 104th Congress was vetoed twice by the president, in December 1995 and January 1996. As late as the spring of 1996 the political epitaph of welfare reform legislation was being written by journalists and pundits, before its revival and quick passage over that summer.

If the welfare reform legislation of 1996 was not inevitable, neither was it a nearly impossible political fluke. This book examines how broad societal forces and political institutions interacted with more short-term political and policy calculations to shape decisions made by policymakers, particularly the boundaries they set on acceptable change from the status quo. Only by understanding this interaction of context and choice is it possible to explain how federal policymakers "ended welfare as we know it."

Three sets of questions about the politics of welfare reform are addressed in this book. The first involves the dismal history of comprehensive AFDC reform initiatives over the past thirty years. Why did most comprehensive initiatives fail to win enactment before 1996, while less dramatic legislation passed in 1981 and 1988? Are there common elements of the policymaking process that made welfare reform so difficult? If so, what are they? How stable are they? How have proponents of policy change attempted to avoid these barriers? Under what conditions can they be overcome?

A second set of questions concerns the dramatic changes in the welfare reform agenda in the past thirty years. Although the outcome has been similar in most rounds of welfare reform—a collapse of the initiative—the substance of what has been debated has changed dramatically. For example, President Nixon's Family Assistance Plan and President Carter's Program for Better Jobs and Incomes focused on a guaranteed income with work requirements, and President Reagan's 1982 New Federalism proposed a program swap, with the states taking control of AFDC in exchange for a federal takeover of Medicaid.

Enormous agenda change is even more evident in the two most recent rounds of welfare reform. The debate leading up to the Family Support Act of 1988 focused on training and work requirements for welfare recipients, strengthened child support enforcement, and increased discretion for the states through waivers of federal policies, granted at Washington's discretion. But providing incentives to low-benefit states to increase their benefit levels was also very much on the reform agenda in the House of Representatives in the Family Support Act round, although the incentives were not enacted. Imposing time limits on receipt of benefits, however, was not on policymakers' horizon, although there was much talk—and some action—on increasing work requirements.

By 1994 some form of time limits on receipt of cash benefits after which work would be expected was the principle from which almost all policy proposals began. Measures like family caps to discourage out-of-wedlock births were also a central element of the debate, after playing no role in 1988. What has driven these changes in the welfare reform agenda over the past quarter century? In particular, how have policy research and changing ideological debates about the causes of poverty among children and the effectiveness of various programs affected the agenda and the prospects for overcoming barriers to policy change?

The third set of questions focuses on why comprehensive welfare reform at the national level succeeded in 1996 after failing in 1993–94, in 1995, and on many previous occasions. Given the dramatic nature of the reform proposals on the agenda, in particular the high probability that those proposals would make many poor children worse off, it seemed likely that welfare reform would fail again. As noted earlier, President Clinton's 1994 initiative was not released until he had been in office for almost a year and a half, and it was never seriously considered by Congress. Republican-sponsored welfare reform legislation passed by both houses of Congress in 1995 was ultimately vetoed twice by the president before he accepted a modestly revised bill in 1996. Why did the Clinton administration's welfare reform initiative get bogged down in the formulation phase? Why did the welfare proposals passed by the Republican-controlled Congress in 1995 make it through both chambers when previous initiatives had tended to collapse at earlier stages of the policymaking process? Why did the president sign a Republican welfare bill in 1996 after two earlier vetoes?

Chapters 2 and 3 provide an introduction to these questions. Chapter 2 is a brief introduction to the problem of child poverty in the United States, as well as to Aid to Families with Dependent Children and other programs that help poor families. Chapter 3 establishes an analytical framework for understanding how policymakers make difficult choices in changing policies. The initial focus is on contextual variables (ideas, social structures, political institutions, and past policy choices) that affect welfare policy choices; it is followed by a discussion of the strategic calculations of politicians. These two frameworks are integrated in an argument that welfare reform initiatives have historically been paralyzed by distinctive traps in the design and ratification of policy change, each of which makes it almost impossible for policymakers to get something that they see as desirable without also getting something undesirable. The most fundamental trap in policymaking for low-income families is what can be called the dual clientele trap: it is impossible to take the politically popular step of helping poor children without the politically unpopular step of helping their custodial parent (or more infrequently, parents), who are mostly unmarried and therefore likely to be perceived as irresponsible, if not actively seeking welfare income. The fact that the custodial parents in AFDC/TANF families are disproportionately from racial minorities does not help either. Conversely, it is impossible to impose risks and penalties on the parents who care for poor children without also endangering their children.

AFDC policymaking is also bedeviled by the money trap: meaningful welfare reform generally requires spending more money than either politicians or the public want to spend. These and other policymaking traps show strong continuity and strength over time, and repeated failures in achieving comprehensive welfare reform can be traced to policymakers' inability to avoid these traps.

The next three chapters focus on specific elements of the social, institutional, and policy context that set the stage for the most recent rounds of welfare reform. Chapter 4 reviews the history of welfare reform initiatives, from the Family Assistance Plan of 1969 through the Family Support Act of 1988, showing how policymaking traps inhibited welfare reform. In addition, it compares the troubled history of welfare reform with the very different fate of the Earned Income Tax Credit, showing why many of the traps that make welfare reform so difficult are much weaker or do not apply at all to EITC policymaking. Finally, it explains why political learning from past rounds of welfare reform was of little importance in the passage of welfare reform legislation in 1996.

Chapter 5 outlines the factors that brought welfare reform back to the top of the public agenda in the early 1990s. The chapter focuses in particular on the role of ideas. Rather than a consensus emerging on how to reform welfare, six contending approaches to the problems of low-income families have dominated recent welfare reform initiatives. These approaches differ both in their diagnoses of the causes of poverty among families with children and in the types of solutions that flow from those diagnoses. Perceiving family poverty as resulting primarily from inadequate labor market skills, for example, produces a set of policy proposals (notably "rehabilitation" of recipients through job training) very different from those that will occur if inappropriate behavior by parents—notably out-of-wedlock births and refusal to work—is seen as the root of family poverty. Welfare reform initiatives based on any of these approaches, or some combination of them, confront major problems with one or more of the welfare policymaking traps outlined in chapter 3.

Chapters 6–8 examine three additional forces—policy research, public opinion, and interest group pressures—that shaped the choices made in the most recent round of welfare reform. I assess whether changes in these elements of the welfare reform policymaking environment can, individually or collectively, account for changes in the welfare reform policy agenda and for the success of comprehensive welfare reform legislation in 1996 after the failure of most previous initiatives.

Chapter 6 focuses on the evolution of policy research on family poverty and programs, including out-of-wedlock births, the length of "spells" of receiving AFDC, and the impact of programs intended to encourage welfare mothers to make successful transitions to work. In addition to familiarizing readers with the state of social science research on welfare issues, this chapter assesses policymakers' use of the information and the extent to which it promoted consensus among policymakers on one or more approaches to welfare reform.

Chapter 7 discusses the recent evolution of public opinion toward welfare programs and recipients, specific welfare reform proposals, and the major participants in current welfare debates. As with social science research, a clear mandate from public opinion could presumably signal which approach or approaches to low-income family policy the public supports and whom it supports to make those choices. Although the evidence suggests public ambiguity rather than a clear mandate for many items on the welfare reform agenda, it also suggests that public antipathy toward the AFDC program was so great that people would acquiesce to almost any welfare reform proposal enacted by politicians.

Chapter 8 examines the interest groups active in welfare debates, arguing that the growth of conservative groups focusing on welfare reform helped shift the balance of pressures in favor of conservative reform in the early 1990s. But these pressures were not felt evenly over time: different political parties choose which interest groups they will respond to. Thus the Republican congressional victory in 1994 and the desire of Republicans in Congress to woo groups that are socially conservative made an important contribution to the formulation and adoption of welfare reform legislation after 1994. The main lesson drawn from chapters 6–8, however, is that changes in contextual factors—policy research, public opinion, and interest group activity—shaped the agendas, bargaining positions, and agenda-setting power of the major participants in ways that created important advantages for proponents of new conservative approaches to welfare reform. But they did not, either alone or in combination, make policy change along the lines of the 1996 welfare reform bill inevitable. To close the explanatory circle, one must look at more proximate forces of bargaining position, agenda control, and choices made by the major participants.

The next four chapters of the book focus in detail on the institutional context and on policymakers' choices in what can be called the Clinton and Gingrich (or Republican) rounds of welfare reform. Chapter 9 examines the Clinton administration's efforts to develop a welfare reform proposal in 1993 and 1994. Chapters 10–12 carry the story forward into the Gingrich round, from the Republican victory in the 1994 congressional elections to Clinton's decision to accept the welfare reform legislation proposed by Congress in the summer of 1996 and the revisions to that legislation made in the 1997 budget deal. To explain these developments, I argue that Clinton's effort to reposition the Democratic party on the racially charged issue of welfare both widened the range of alternatives on the agenda for low-income families and opened the door to changes far more radical than those he initially envisioned. In the context of party polarization and competition, intense public antipathy to welfare in its current form, and budgetary constraints that limited reform options, welfare reform became the object of strategies in which the positions taken by most of the major participants were based not just on their views of the policy merits. They were also political and relational, determined in large part in relation to the positions of other participants.[3]

In trying to prove himself a New Democrat, Clinton tried to position himself between congressional Republicans and congressional Democrats ("triangulation"). But once he was in office, many moderate congressional Democrats pursued a second relational strategy: they desperately sought political cover from the charge that they were "soft on welfare" by avoiding positions to the left of the president. Thus every time that Clinton accepted Republican positions, he dragged a number of congressional Democrats with him. Congressional Republicans were torn between a desire to reach a legislative deal for which they could claim credit and a third relational strategy of "strategic disagreement," maintaining policy distance from Clinton and the Democrats so that they could continue to claim that they were the ones who were interested in real welfare reform while the president was a hypocrite who claimed to want to end welfare as we know it but was really trying to perpetuate it. The Republican strategic disagreement pulled the welfare debate to the right; Clinton's triangulation strategy led him to follow along, and congressional Democrats' desire to avoid political blame pulled many of them along as well. Having pulled the president and many congressional Democrats significantly to the right, and knowing that neither the president nor Democratic legislators wanted to be in the position of appearing to defend the status quo in the run-up to the 1996 election, congressional Republicans were in a very strong position to enact legislation on favorable terms when they switched from strategic disagreement to passing legislation in the summer of 1996. Chapter 13 briefly reviews implementation of the new welfare law.

Chapter 14 reviews the roles of context and choice in explaining passage of the 1996 welfare reform legislation and examines why welfare reform legislation passed in 1996 when most of the other domestic policy initiatives of both the Clinton administration and the Republican Revolution in the 104th Congress (1995–96) did not. More generally, I argue that the relational bargaining that characterized welfare reform is a central feature of American politics.

CHAPTER TWO

Welfare as We Knew It

MOST AMERICANS DO NOT know any welfare recipients personally or have any direct contact with the welfare system. Their views of welfare, and of welfare recipients, are likely to be shaped by what they see on television and what they read in newspapers and magazines. If they put an individual face on welfare at all as the United States debated and then carried out welfare reform in the 1990s, it may have been a face like that of Mary Ann Petri, featured in an *Oakland Tribune* series on welfare reform. Mary Ann, a forty-one-year-old mother of four children ages three to eight, lives in Alameda County, California. She has an eleventh-grade education and few job skills. When her profile was written, she had been on welfare for four years. She and her family became homeless after a recent boyfriend emptied the family bank account. She was then taking high-school equivalency classes and computer classes, which, along with child-care and transportation costs, are paid for by her local welfare agency.[1]

Welfare has many other faces as well. There is Louisa Blue, an unmarried seventeen-year-old in Boston, who had a second baby despite knowing that changes in the state welfare law meant that the new baby would not be eligible for cash welfare benefits.[2] And there is Sandi Szabrowicz, a thirty-six-year-old mother of a four-year-old son in Milwaukee. Sandi, a high-school graduate with substantial work experience but limited skills, has been struggling to attend a community college to upgrade her skills while working to meet Wisconsin's tough new work requirements for welfare recipients.[3]

Kitty Funchess, a fifty-seven-year-old grandmother living in Highland Park, Michigan, who was profiled by the *Detroit News*, is yet another face of welfare. Kitty raised four children of her own and started taking care of her grandson (now age ten) and granddaughter shortly after they were born to her daughter Donna, who was addicted to crack cocaine. Kitty used Michigan's Work First program to go back to work after seventeen years on various public assistance programs, including a decade on Aid to Families with Dependent Children (AFDC). But working and raising her grandchildren stretched her past the breaking point. She was forced to give her grandchildren up to foster care, but hopes to be able to regain custody of them once she can obtain health insurance coverage for them on her new job.[4]

There are fathers too, of course, but many are absent, and the image we get of them in media stories is often hazy at best. Mary Ann Petri's husband, we are told, beat her and used drugs heavily. The father of Sandi Szabrowicz's son, Brandon, helps with child support sometimes, but lives out of state, which makes collection more difficult. Louisa Blue's twenty-six-year-old boyfriend and the father of her infant daughter is around, but his job collecting scrap tires and iron for his uncle does not allow him to contribute much to their well-being. We learn nothing at all about the father or fathers of Kitty Funchess's grandchildren.

And then there are the children, who constitute about two-thirds of recipients of AFDC and its successor program, Temporary Assistance for Needy Families (TANF).[5] Children like Mary Ann Petri's eight-year-old daughter Rose, who helps her mother with cooking and watching the younger children, likes to read and write poetry, wants to be a veterinarian when she grows up, and says about her family's recent moves since they lost their home, "We've been to so many places, we don't know where we came from last." Children like Kitty Funchess's ten-year-old grandson Dontray, who was born with a neonatal crack addiction. Increasingly hard to control, Dontray's setting fire to a trash dumpster almost got her evicted from her town house and precipitated a chain of events that ended up with Dontray and his sister in foster care. Protecting children like Rose and Dontray who cannot provide for themselves is the reason that programs like Aid to Families with Dependent Children were established. However, debate over public assistance programs frequently concentrates on the problems of parents more than on the welfare of children.

Poverty and American Families

Statistics are part of the welfare story, too. They provide no names or faces, no hopeful stories of self-sufficiency attained or tragic stories of families left homeless. But the story they can tell is potentially just as troubling—perhaps more so because it is not "just" about a single family that a journalist has chosen to make a point or tell a story, regardless of whether it is representative of poor families overall. Statistics tell a different kind of story. They show us patterns and trends in society and how well government programs are working.

The statistics on both family structure and family poverty, like many of the individual stories of welfare recipients, make grim reading.[6] They tell us that the percentage of marriages ending in divorce more than doubled between 1950 and 1980 and has remained near that higher rate.[7] Moreover, while overall birthrates to teenage women fell through the 1970s and the first half of the 1980s, many fewer teenage mothers married, contributing to huge increases in the percentage of births that were out of wedlock.[8] By 1990 more than 20 percent of births to white mothers and 65 percent of births to African American mothers were to unmarried women.[9] As a result, a decreasing share of children in the United States are living with two parents, with dramatic differences along racial and ethnic lines. In 1992 about 77 percent of white children, but only 36 percent of African American children and 65 percent of Hispanic children in the United States were living with two parents. And 7.5 percent of black children were living with neither parent.[10]

Overall, about half of U.S. children, and a much higher percentage of African American children, are likely to spend some time in a single-parent family. Data on child poverty make it extraordinarily clear that, as Daniel Patrick Moynihan said, "Poverty is now inextricably associated with family structure."[11] Child poverty rates for white households with a male parent present in 1992 were 10.3 percent compared with 45.9 percent for those with a female head; comparable figures for black families were 19.4 percent and 67.1 percent.[12] Overall poverty rates of children in the United States rose from 15.7 percent in 1978 to 21.1 percent in 1992, with the increase due to changes in family composition, a drop in earnings among low-skilled workers, and decreases in the effectiveness of government programs aimed at reducing poverty.[13]

The Structure of American Family Support Policies

How can government help Mary Ann Petri and Kitty Funchess and others get their lives in order and move toward self-sufficiency despite tremendous obstacles? Is self-sufficiency even a realistic goal for such families? How can government stop young women like Louisa from having children as unmarried teenagers? How can it help children like Rose realize their dreams and turn around young lives like Dontray's that already seem to be going off track? And how can it keep the fathers of all of these children in their lives and get them to contribute, financially and emotionally, to their children's development? Can it, indeed, do any of these things? These are the questions that policymakers have faced as they have debated whether and how to revamp AFDC and other policies intended to assist poor families.

Policymakers rarely think about what the best plan would be if they could start from scratch, of course. Even if they did, it would make little difference because starting over is almost never an option. Instead, policymakers usually begin by confronting the most visible shortcomings of current policy and thinking about how those shortcomings can be addressed at acceptable budgetary costs and without creating such a political uproar that reform would be stopped dead in its tracks. Thus before understanding welfare reform politics, it is important to have a basic understanding of the programs and policies now in place.

Governments in the United States have tried to meet the income needs of low-income families in several ways.[14] One strategy consistent with the overall direction of U.S. social policy is the provision of *social insurance* to help families whose primary earner (usually the father) dies or is unable to work. This type of family policy is in fact built into the current Social Security system (through its components that pay benefits to disabled workers and to the survivors of deceased workers) and unemployment insurance. Social insurance avoids stigmatizing recipients because benefits have been "earned" through employee and employer contributions to the program. But this structure has distinct disadvantages and limitations. Social Security is of negligible assistance to most recipients of AFDC and TANF, for whom the problem is not a deceased parent but rather a father who is not supporting his children, whose paternity may not have been legally established, and who may have limited earnings prospects. Similarly, unemployment insurance does not provide much help to families in which parents have limited, unstable work histories, because eligibility and benefits depend on previous earnings records.

Tax expenditures represent another vehicle for helping low-income families. There are several options, with different distributive consequences. Tax exemptions like those in the current federal tax code remove a certain amount of income from taxation for each child in a family. Tax exemptions give higher benefits to wealthier taxpayers because the exempted amount would otherwise be taxed at a higher rate for people in higher income and tax brackets.[15] And exemptions provide no benefits to those who are too poor to pay income taxes.[16]

Tax credits, a flat amount per child subtracted from a taxpayer's income tax bill, avoid the problem of giving higher benefits to wealthier taxpayers. However, they benefit people whose income taxes are too low to pay income taxes only if they are refundable, that is, if any excess of the credit over tax liability is refunded to the taxpayer. The Earned Income Tax Credit (EITC) and the child and dependent care credit are the major family tax credits in use, and more will be said about the former in chapter 4. In theory, tax credits have the major advantage of ease of administration: They do not require a new bureaucracy to verify eligibility because everything is done through the existing income tax system. But this method has a number of potential disadvantages as well. Low-income taxpayers may not file for tax refunds, and if they do not, they cannot get the tax credit to which they are entitled. And tax credit benefits come as a once-a-year lump sum rather than a steady income stream throughout the year unless employers are enlisted to distribute payments along with salary and wage checks.

Means-tested or *public assistance* programs represent another mechanism to provide support to families with children. In these programs recipients receive benefits based on their income; there is often an assets test as well. This is the approach used in the AFDC and TANF programs. The earned income tax credit, which is targeted on low-income families (it increases with earnings to a specified level, then phases out as family income rises further) but delivered through the tax system, is another example of a means-tested family policy. The Supplemental Security Income (SSI) program also provides some assistance to low-income families.[17] Although SSI is targeted at low-income adults who are aged, blind, or disabled, it contains provisions giving eligibility to children with a "medically determinable physical or medical impairment of comparable severity" to that of adults.[18] A 1990 Supreme Court decision substantially increased the access of children to SSI, contributing to a tripling of the child SSI population in the early 1990s and to increasing concerns that children with behavioral disorders and children coached by parents to "act crazy" were driving up the SSI rolls.[19]

In addition to cash assistance programs, substantial assistance to low-income families is provided through means-tested nutrition programs. Indeed, most AFDC or TANF families receive benefits from one or more nutrition programs as well.[20] The largest of these, food stamps, provides federally financed vouchers to low-income households and individuals.

About 60 percent of these households in recent years have included children.[21] The school lunch and school breakfast programs subsidize free or reduced-price school meals to low-income children. And the Special Supplemental Feeding Program for Women, Infants and Children (WIC) provides nutritious foods (or, more commonly, vouchers to purchase those foods) to pregnant and postpartum women, infants, and young children. The Medicaid program also serves low-income families among other clienteles.

As these examples suggest, federal aid to families flows through a variety of programs. Some of these programs, such as the child tax exemption in the Internal Revenue Code and survivors' payments under Social Security, benefit families at many income levels. These programs have been almost invisible in debates on policy toward low-income families in recent years—Social Security survivor benefits because they are seen as earned and are a relatively small part of that very popular program, and tax exemptions because they are buried in the tax code and deliver most of their benefits to upper- and middle-income families.

Means-tested programs serving low-income families have been far more controversial and have fared unevenly. Figure 2-1 shows expenditures for major means-tested income-transfer, nutrition, and health programs with a substantial clientele of low-income families (for multiclientele programs like SSI and Medicaid, the expenditure figures shown are only those for low-income families with children). Real expenditures on these programs have grown substantially over the past twenty years, especially since the late 1980s. Most of the growth is accounted for by tremendous expenditure increases in the earned income tax credit and Medicaid. Particularly noticeable are the differing trends for the two major programs of cash support, AFDC and the EITC. In constant dollars, federal and state spending on AFDC peaked around 1976 and then declined as states began to trim the real value of benefits (for the most part by not adjusting fully for inflation) and to substitute food stamp spending for AFDC. Not until the rapid caseload increases of the late 1980s and early 1990s did AFDC expenditures again approach those peaks. EITC spending grew rapidly after 1985. Nutrition programs targeted on children have generally been politically resilient as well.

Aid to Families with Dependent Children

By the mid-1990s, Aid to Families with Dependent Children had been surpassed by both the EITC and Medicaid in outlays on families with children.

Figure 2-1. *Combined Federal and State Spending on Major Programs for Low-Income Families with Children, 1977–98*

Millions of constant 1996 dollars

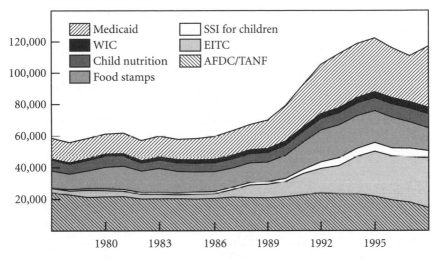

Sources: AFDC/TANF data for 1977–96 are from *1998 Green Book: Background Material and Data on Programs within the Jurisdiction of the Committee on Ways and Means*, Committee Print WMCP: 105-7, p. 412, and are net of reimbursements from child support collections. TANF data for 1997 and 1998 are from Department of Health and Human Services, Administration for Children and Families, Office of Planning, Research and Evaluation, *Temporary Assistance to Needy Families Program, First Annual Report to Congress, August 1998*, tables 1:3 to 1:5, and Department of Health and Human Services, Administration for Children and Families, Office of Planning, Research and Evaluation, *Temporary Assistance to Needy Families Program, Second Annual Report to Congress, August 1999*, tables 2:9 to 2:11. TANF data include only cash and work-based assistance expenditures under TANF and separate state programs. TANF expenditures on work activities, child care, transitional services, and so forth are excluded. Earned Income Tax Credit data are on a calendar year basis from 1977 to 1996 and fiscal year basis thereafter. EITC data for 1977–96 are from the *1998 Green Book*, p. 872; 1997 data are from *Budget of the United States Government, FY 1999 Analytical Perspectives*, p. 103; and 1998 data are from FY 2000 Budget, *Analytical Perspectives*, p. 119. Data on Supplemental Security Income spending for children are on a calendar year basis from 1977 to 1995 and a fiscal year basis thereafter, and are for federally administered payments only. They come from unpublished Social Security Administration data. Food stamp expenditures include households with children only and are from U.S. Department of Agriculture, Food and Nutrition Service, National Data Bank, "Food Stamp Program Information for FY 1980 through 1995," April 1996, and unpublished Department of Agriculture data. Child nutrition program data are from the FY 2001 Budget, *Historical Tables*, table 11-3. WIC data for 1977–96 are from the *1998 Green Book*, p. 1002; data for 1997–99 are the combined WIC Commodity Supplemental Feeding Program figure from the FY 2001 Budget, *Historical Tables*, table 11-3. Medicaid expenditures include only those for dependent children under age twenty-one and adults in families with dependent children. Data on Medicaid are from the *Health Care Financing Review*, various issues, *Social Security Bulletin Annual Statistical Supplement, 1999*, table 8.E2, plus unpublished Health Care Finance Administration data. All expenditures are deflated using the composite deflator from the *Budget of the United States Government Fiscal Year 2001, Historical Tables*, table 1.3.

However, it remained by far the best known of programs for low-income families and the one most associated in the public mind with the terms "welfare" and "welfare reform."

ORIGINS OF AFDC. Aid to Families with Dependent Children built on a variety of "mothers' pension" and "widows' pension" programs that had been enacted in forty states by 1920. These state programs were intended to ensure that the children of "decent" but destitute mothers (usually widows) could remain with their mothers rather than go into orphanages or foster care.[22] The laws generally gave counties the option to offer assistance or not. The programs suffered from unequal availability (rural counties were especially unlikely to have them in place) and underfunding. Intrusive local administration excluded many families, and all but a small number of African Americans, from receiving benefits. And because factory work was generally not deemed suitable employment for responsible mothers, recipients of mothers' pensions were forced to take the most marginal and lowest paying employment (often part-time housecleaning or laundering) to supplement their meager benefits.[23]

The modern AFDC program had its origins in the Social Security Act of 1935.[24] The program (originally called Aid to Dependent Children, or ADC; it was renamed in 1950 when benefits for the caretaking adult were added to those for dependent children) was a minor part of the Social Security Act legislative omnibus. Congress was most interested in the means-tested Old Age Assistance program, while President Franklin Roosevelt took greatest interest in the new social insurance programs, Old Age Insurance and unemployment compensation. For ADC the federal government set very broad parameters and shared the costs (originally one-third of the total). The states retained broad discretion on eligibility and benefit levels and on program administration.

AFDC AS AN AMBIGUOUS ENTITLEMENT. Social Security, Medicare, and most other federally funded income-transfer and health programs are entitlements, meaning that anyone who meets the statutory qualifications for receiving benefits (for example, the age, contribution, and retirement tests for Social Security) is legally entitled to a benefit level that is also prescribed by statute.[25] Expenditures for entitlement programs are provided with an automatic appropriation that bypasses the spending-conscious congressional appropriations committees. This has several important implications. First, spending for entitlement programs is very difficult to change in the short term because Congress and administrative agencies cannot cut benefits without changing the statutory qualifications. Persons who are denied benefits to which they are statutorily entitled can sue to receive the benefits. Second, entitlement spending is unpredictable: if a recession causes the number of persons eligible for unemployment insurance to rise, spending for that program is likely to rise as well. Spending may also be affected if a program's participation rate increases—for example because a decline in the stigma attached to receiving aid from some means-tested programs causes persons who meet eligibility standards but have not applied for them to change their minds. Third, because beneficiaries have (and perceive themselves to have) a legal right to their benefits, they cannot be denied or removed without due process; governments must establish mechanisms to adjudicate disputes over eligibility and benefits that will pass muster in the courts.

The entitlement status of AFDC was different from that for Social Security, Medicare, or other programs, however. Like those programs, the stream of federal matching funds for state AFDC programs was exempt from the appropriations process, so appropriations committees could not arbitrarily reduce funding to meet budgetary targets. Thus AFDC clearly was an entitlement *to states*. But *individual* entitlement to AFDC benefits was far more ambiguous; individual states set their own eligibility rules and benefit levels within very broad federal statutory guidelines and subject to the requirement that the plans be approved by the Department of Health and Human Services. Indeed, to the extent that the federal government was involved in approving eligibility for AFDC, it was in terms of establishing outside boundaries (notably overall limits for assets) more than minimal conditions guaranteeing eligibility.

Was AFDC an entitlement to individuals or a gratuity that states could grant or withhold as they chose? For the first thirty years of the program, states were given very broad discretion in the way that they set eligibility requirements and ran the program. There were only a few requirements, notably that the program operate statewide (although some intrastate benefit variation was permitted), that residency requirements for receipt of benefits be limited to no more than one year in duration, and that a person denied benefits have an opportunity for a fair hearing by the administering state agency.[26] Many states, especially in the South, imposed "suitable home" and "fit parent" requirements that were applied disproportionately against blacks. Federal administrators opposed these additional eligibility requirements, but had little power to block them.[27]

Things changed in the late 1960s and early 1970s when federal courts, responding to lawsuits brought largely by legal services attorneys, became more active in welfare policymaking. The U.S. Supreme Court overturned many state eligibility requirements unrelated to need, notably "man in the house" rules that terminated or reduced benefits where there was a cohabiting male resident, as well as residency requirements that restricted constitutionally protected rights to travel. State concerns about fostering immorality by mothers, the courts decided, should be dealt with using "rehabilitation" policies (notably social services casework) rather than by punishing blameless children. In addition, the courts ruled that recipients had a right to a face-to-face hearing before their benefits were terminated. In short, the courts essentially converted what had been a matching grant program into a program that gave AFDC recipients individual entitlements to the benefits laid out in state law, with both due process and substantive limits on how states could restrict access to those benefits. But the courts did allow some important limitations on welfare entitlement rights. States could, for example, require people to accept visits by welfare caseworkers and to participate in work programs as a condition of receiving benefits. In short, although the courts (and especially the Supreme Court when it was headed by the liberal Earl Warren) felt uneasy about "morality tests" for receipt of welfare, they did recognize the legitimacy of state interests in promoting work and minimal standards of parental responsibility.

If the eligibility side of rules for individual entitlement to AFDC was ambiguous, the benefit side was completely open: there was no requirement that states provide benefits at any level, let alone one of minimal adequacy. Congressional conservatives, especially those from the South, led resistance to the Roosevelt administration's 1935 proposal that public assistance payments under the Social Security Act be adequate to provide "a reasonable subsistence compatible with decency and health" and weakened federal control over state administration of the program. Scholars have variously attributed this resistance to fear of the potentially disrupting effect of such a requirement on southern labor markets and the castelike hierarchy of southern society and to the limited fiscal capacity of southern states, which made meeting such a standard impractical.[28] In fact, both considerations pushed in the same direction, while the congressional seniority of Democratic legislators from the one-party South gave them a powerful lever over the congressional agenda, allowing them to block provisions they did not like. The requirement for a "decency and health" minimum standard was not included in the final Social Security Act legislation.[29] Repeated efforts to establish minimum national payment standards in later years were invariably rejected in Congress (see chapter 4). And although court decisions substantially expanded eligibility and access to welfare in the late 1960s and early 1970s, the courts were unsympathetic to those seeking to guarantee a particular level of benefits.[30]

The AFDC benefit standards that were in place were almost meaningless. Through 1996 the federal government required that states establish a "need standard" as a measure of the costs of basic consumption items for families of varying sizes, but there was no legal requirement that states' need standards bear any relation to actual minimum living costs for a family.[31] Similarly, states were required to set a "payment standard" for AFDC families of various sizes, but this standard (set below the need standard by thirty states in 1996) did not have to meet actual living costs, either. Finally, states did not have to meet their own payment standards, and in 1996 a dozen states did not do so.[32]

In the absence of a federal statutory minimum national benefit level for AFDC recipients, benefit levels varied widely among states. In January 1996, for example, the maximum benefit for a family of three in the forty-eight contiguous states ranged from $120 in Mississippi to $703 in parts of New York State.[33] In almost all states, combined AFDC and food stamp benefits were inadequate to take a family to even 80 percent of the poverty line.[34]

Nor did states have to automatically index AFDC benefits for inflation, as is done with Social Security benefits—and none did so. Lack of indexation allowed states to let real AFDC benefits decrease without the statutory changes required to cut benefits in indexed entitlements. Federal Medicaid law did, however, prevent states from cutting their nominal AFDC benefits below the level in effect on May 1, 1988. Indeed, the combined purchasing power of food stamps and AFDC benefits for a three-person family without countable income fell 26 percent between 1972 and 1992, with the decline accounted for almost entirely by the decrease in AFDC benefits.[35] Most of this decline took place between 1972 and 1984. However, the budget shortfalls that hit the states in the early 1990s caused another round of assaults on real AFDC benefits: in 1992 only five states increased nominal benefit levels, while thirty-nine froze them and six cut them.[36]

Perhaps the most revealing aspect of the AFDC's ambiguous entitlement status, however, is its peculiar provisions for two-parent families. Although the AFDC program was designed primarily for one-parent families, an unemployed-parent (AFDC-UP) component was added in 1961 for two-parent families in which both parents are unemployed but the principal wage earner has a significant work history.[37] Until passage of the Family Support Act of 1988 (FSA), however, AFDC-UP was a state option, and only about half of the states used it.[38] Even under the FSA, states that had not previously offered AFDC-UP were only required to offer benefits to those families for six months out of every twelve-month period.[39]

A Changing Clientele

The AFDC program was revised many times in its sixty years of existence, largely on a piecemeal basis. Despite the program's unpopularity, the record of comprehensive reform initiatives in the past quarter century was largely one of failure until 1995. The fundamental character of AFDC as a shared-cost program with substantial state discretion remained intact. In the last years of the program the federal government paid between 50 and 80 percent of state benefit costs, based on a cost-sharing formula that gave a higher federal match to states with lower per capita income.

As noted earlier, the original target clientele of the AFDC program was widows with dependent children. The addition of a survivors' insurance component to the Old Age Insurance program in 1939 contributed to a widespread assumption that AFDC would wither away as more poor families were covered by social insurance benefits earned by a deceased primary breadwinner.[40] Indeed, this supplanting of means-tested payments by social insurance did take place for the elderly, as Old Age Insurance outgrew Old Age Assistance. It did not occur with AFDC, however. As more families in which the father was deceased became eligible for (usually more generous) benefits from the Social Security program, AFDC increasingly served families where the father was absent from the home because of divorce or separation or because he never had a marital tie to the mother. By the mid-1980s unwed mothers were a majority among AFDC recipients. And more than 90 percent of AFDC mothers in the early 1990s were not in the paid labor force, while a growing majority of non-AFDC mothers were working.

The number of AFDC recipients rose 50 percent between 1970 and 1981, then dropped back after cutbacks imposed by the Reagan administration. Rolls began to grow again dramatically in the late 1980s, increasing from 10.9 million children and parents in 1988 to 14.4 million in early 1994 before dropping to less than 13 million by the end of 1995.[41] Although the increase can be attributed in part to the recession at the end of the Bush presidency and to changes in AFDC policy included in the 1988 Family Support Act, the increased caseloads further undermined confidence that policymakers had a firm grip on the "welfare problem."[42]

The racial composition of the AFDC caseload gave the program a racialized cast that further contributed to its unpopularity with the public.[43] Black families were heavily overrepresented among recipients relative to their share of the population, as they are among poor families generally. In 1992 African Americans accounted for 37.2 percent of AFDC parents, about three times their share of the overall population.[44]

Critiques of AFDC

The Aid to Families with Dependent Children program faced a number of important challenges in the early 1990s. Real benefits had been falling for two decades. The more politically popular constituency among low-income families, those in which at least one parent was working (or at least working and reporting earnings) in the labor market, was increasingly excluded from AFDC benefits and was benefiting from the earned income tax credit instead.

Weak incentives for welfare recipients to enter the low-wage labor market were a particular problem with AFDC. The Reagan reforms of 1981 severely limited so-called earnings disregards that allowed welfare recipients to keep a greater share of any earnings rather than having their benefits reduced dollar for dollar by earnings. This problem was made worse because eligibility for other means-tested programs, especially Medicaid, was linked to AFDC. Thus a single mother who decided to forgo AFDC for low-wage employment with no health insurance might find herself only slightly better off in terms of cash-plus-food-stamps income and without health insurance coverage for herself and her children. This was likely to be a particularly poor trade-off if any family member suffered from a chronic illness.

Critics of the program argued that its basic incentive structure clashed with American values of work and personal responsibility for one's actions. It is no accident that both the 1994 Clinton welfare reform bill and the Republican welfare bills in 1995 and 1996 contained the words *work* and *responsibility* in their titles to emphasize their break with the status quo and their greater harmony with these core American values.

How to encourage "desirable" behavior, notably work effort and marriage by parents, without creating moral hazards—that is, inadvertently encouraging undesirable behavior such as reduced work effort, teenage pregnancies, out-of-wedlock births, family breakup, and long-term dependence on public assistance—has been a persistent problem for policymakers. For example, the provision of transitional Medicaid and child care benefits to lessen the income loss experienced by AFDC recipients who leave the program when they go into the work force may cause people who lose jobs to cycle through the program rather than go directly to another job in order to take advantage of the benefits.[45] Paternity establishment and child support enforcement may reduce incentives for fathers to work because the enforcement can dramatically reduce the percentage of their earnings that they keep, especially if they have fathered several children.[46]

Critics also charged that federal policies designed to reduce fraud and abuse in the AFDC program had caused state (or in some jurisdictions, county) welfare offices to become obsessed with ensuring that recipients did not receive higher benefits than those to which they were entitled. Welfare recipients who worked, especially in multiple jobs, or whose employment was unstable made this process of "check-writing welfare" more complicated by requiring more verification and benefit recalculations, increasing the probability of errors in calculating benefits. Critics of AFDC on both the left and the right charged that it was not surprising that most welfare offices did not strongly emphasize moving recipients into work because doing so made welfare bureaucrats' own work harder.

AFDC also spawned political critiques. Despite the fact that by the early 1990s the program represented a small share of means-tested assistance to families, it was the lightning rod around which controversy coalesced. Increasing rates of out-of-wedlock births and rising AFDC caseloads increased concern among both policymakers and the public that the existing system was a failure. Analysts and Democratic politicians often considered the program a *political* problem for the Democratic party, with the party identified "by crucial numbers of voters within the white electorate, as the party of victims, of redistribution to victims, and of a public ethos skirting the issues of individual responsibility, fiscal discipline, and social obligation."[47]

But what sorts of changes should be made that had a chance of causing a real difference in the lives of adult welfare recipients and the children they were trying to raise? And at what price? Should the welfare of children be the primary concern of policy or the behavior of adults? How much work outside the home should be expected of single mothers, especially those with young children? If they were expected to work, what policies should be used to bring it about? And what about out-of-wedlock childbearing? Should AFDC policy attempt to change this behavior, and if so, how? Should the federal government simply give up and hand the program over to the states? All these questions involved hard choices and little consensus among policymakers. Before examining those debates in detail, I turn to a more basic question: what are the forces that have constrained AFDC policymaking, and how do policymakers make welfare policy choices in the context of severe disagreements over the proper direction for policy?

CHAPTER THREE

Explaining Welfare Politics

Context, Choices, Traps

ANY ANALYSIS OF policymaking necessarily rests on a simplified model of political life. The world is such a complicated place that it is impossible to understand and explain even the simplest events without focusing on what the observer considers the most important causes while paying less attention to others.

Explaining a complex phenomenon like welfare reform requires sorting through many possible explanations, weighing the evidence for each to assess its relative importance, and, in some cases, combining two or more to create a superior explanation. For example, the potential explanations for the welfare reform legislation that was enacted in 1996, after many comprehensive initiatives had failed, range from changes in family structure and the evolution of public opinion to idiosyncratic factors such as the personality and bargaining style of individual policymakers. The number of potential explanations is so great that no analysis of less than encyclopedic length could consider them all; any analyst must make a first cut of those that seem most promising. At the same time, analysis must steer between the twin risks of making the analytic categories so specific to a policy sector that it is impossible to draw comparisons and lessons across policy sectors and making them so general that those categories disguise and distort what is unique about welfare reform or any other policy sector.

This chapter lays the analytical groundwork for the exploration of welfare reform politics in the rest of the book, built around the concepts of *context* and *choice*. The first section of the chapter sorts through explanations of stability and change in welfare policy involving broad forces such as public opinion and political institutions. These may be thought of as creating a context within which individual policymakers such as the president and collectivities of policymakers (notably Congress) confront choices and make decisions about policies toward low-income families.

The second part of the chapter moves from a discussion of context to an analysis of the substantive and strategic choices made by policymakers as they attempt to move policy toward their preferred outcomes and adjust their own positions in response to those of political competitors. The primary argument is that the prospects for policy change depend less on the policy positions that policymakers like best than on their more malleable "zones of acceptable outcomes," the range of policies that they will accept, as well as on the way that agendas are structured and the rules under which alternatives are accepted or rejected.

The third section draws on the analysis of context and choice in the first two sections to paint a more nuanced portrait of the political constraints on welfare reform. Welfare reform initiatives are made more difficult by four policymaking traps that tend to produce stalemate. These traps are neither unavoidable nor immutable, however. Understanding the contours of these constraints on policy change helps in understanding why welfare reform initiatives failed so frequently before the 1990s and why the 1996 welfare reform law succeeded in being adopted.

Contextual Forces in Welfare Reform Politics

Political scientists have looked at four clusters of contextual factors in analyzing the policymaking environment for low-income families in the United States: ideas, social structures, political institutions, and policy feedback from past choices.

Ideas

Ideas can take many different forms and play many different roles in policymaking. At the level of *public opinion* there are attitudes that persist with great stability over long periods of time and are said to form part of a country's political culture. Many analysts have, for example, emphasized the importance that Americans place on work and family and their dislike of an AFDC program that appears to reward nonwork and the formation of single-parent families as explanations for the relatively ungenerous nature of the program.[1] But another consistent attribute of American public opinion has been sympathy for poor children (see chapter 7), which has made more punitive reforms difficult. Thus the difficulty in enacting various welfare reforms can be attributed to the absence of consensus within public opinion about what should be done about welfare. Certainly the failure in the 1970s to ratify welfare reforms that smacked of a guaranteed national minimum income is consistent with public fears of undermining the work ethic. Public opinion is also subject to shifts over time, however. One plausible explanation for changing welfare agendas and for the enactment of welfare reform in 1996 is an increased emphasis placed by public opinion on work and the need to address out-of-wedlock births and long-term welfare dependency. Public rejection of the welfare status quo may have been reinforced by growing public resentment over increases in out-of-wedlock births and by rapidly growing welfare caseloads after 1989.[2]

A second idea-centered interpretation stresses the role of *policy paradigms* or approaches that are developed primarily by policy elites. The structure of the AFDC program, in this interpretation, reflects the layered accretions of different strategies for providing welfare (providing social services, imposing work requirements, and so forth) suggested by succeeding generations of "welfare experts" because earlier policies are rarely abolished entirely when new policy directions are taken. In this approach, the welfare policy agenda changes when policy intellectuals develop new approaches that offer both a compelling interpretation of the welfare problem and a set of solutions that seems both practical and politically acceptable. Policy stalemate is likely to occur when policy elites disagree among themselves, when policies fail to find politically well-placed carriers among the political class, or when there are differences between elite opinion and public opinion.[3] Dramatic reform was possible in 1996, this view would suggest, because elites reached agreement on a direction to reform and found institutional allies in the new Republican congressional majority.

The role of ideas also incorporates a third stream that interacts with the others: the influence of social science *policy research* about welfare recipients, the effects of AFDC, and various proposals for reform. Although it would be a bit far-fetched to attribute the basic structure of the program to policy research, it is much more plausible (but, as later chapters will show, not entirely correct) to argue that policy research has been important in changing the agenda of welfare reform because it showed the inadequacies of several approaches, leading to a search for new policies. Similarly, the absence of conclusive evidence about a best approach to welfare reform may hinder reform initiatives. Welfare reform may have succeeded in 1996 after past failures because policy research, especially on the effect of work-based requirements for receiving welfare, helped to create consensus on a specific direction for policy change.

Social Structures

Similarly, contextual explanations based on social structures comprise many factors ranging from deeply embedded social divisions rooted in race, ethnicity, and class to the nature of interest-group activity.

Many analysts have argued that race is critical in welfare policy: the overrepresentation of racial minorities among AFDC recipients has reinforced racial stereotypes about family structure and weak work ethics among African Americans.[4] Critics on the political left have also stressed the limited political and organizational resources of the poor, which allowed their interests to be ignored except when they were sufficiently organized to seem to pose a threat to the established political order.[5]

Certainly social divisions and the racialized nature of poverty in the United States can help to explain both the relatively ungenerous AFDC program and its decentralized character, which (especially in the early years) allowed local elites in the South to keep benefits for black families very low, if they were offered at all.[6] This suggests that changes in the welfare reform agenda reflect repeated efforts to secure social control over minority racial groups, especially African Americans, in response to changes in family structure that were felt especially among racial minorities. Comprehensive welfare reform generally failed at least in part because the attempts included improvements in benefits that were politically unacceptable because of the racial divide over welfare. Welfare reform succeeded in 1996, this perspective suggests, because the racially stereotyped image of AFDC recipients made it especially vulnerable when the 1994 elections led to an upswing in support for Republicans.

The role in welfare reform of *organized interests* partly overlaps with perspectives that focus on race and social divisions. This perspective suggests that the change in welfare reform agendas, and in particular the move toward more conservative reforms, can be traced to the decline of welfare rights groups, which enjoyed a brief surge in the late 1960s, and to the growth of socially conservative groups in the 1990s. Nevertheless, lobbies for liberal and conservative welfare reform have generally been weak, making it difficult for any initiative to overcome the hurdles in the American political process. But the close ties to the Republican majority in the 104th Congress of socially conservative groups such as the Christian Coalition gave advocates for conservative welfare reform the leverage needed to push through a package of dramatic reforms.

Political Institutions

A third set of theories focuses on political institutions as an influence on policymaking. The *fragmentation of national political institutions*—including separation of executive and legislative powers, weak legislative parties, delegation of policymaking authority within Congress to powerful standing committees, and the minority filibuster power in the Senate—all create veto points where any policy innovation can be blocked, especially if it is opposed by some powerful social interest. Thus it is not just comprehensive welfare reform initiatives that have a high mortality rate, but most major social policy initiatives.[7] The agenda of policy initiatives under active consideration by Congress is likely to change whenever party control of the presidency or of either chamber of Congress changes, as newly empowered elites try to put their political stamp on a difficult policy area. But the most controversial, divisive initiatives are likely to win adoption only in periods when one party has overwhelming control of both chambers of Congress plus the presidency: thus the concentration of American social policy initiatives in the big bangs of the New Deal and Great Society and the repeated failure of national health insurance and comprehensive welfare reforms.[8] An institutional perspective would certainly point to the Republican upsurge in Congress as a primary reason for the enactment of welfare reform legislation in 1996.

Divided party control of government is more frequently associated with policy stalemate than with the passage of major legislation, however. Institutional explanations of the passage of welfare reform legislation in 1996 could also point to changes in congressional rules (notably those governing the congressional budget process) that have given the majority party in each chamber an increased capacity to push its program through over minority opposition.

Federalism is another institutional variable that may have a powerful effect on welfare policies. State government discretion over AFDC policy increases the difficulty in setting minimum national benefits because states are usually reluctant to give up control over policy. State discretion in administering the program may also lead to competition among states to keep benefits low to avoid becoming a "welfare magnet," attracting "undesirable" beneficiaries from other states. In fact, a race to the bottom may occur even if welfare magnet effects are weak as long as politicians believe that they are real.[9] In national policymaking the representation of state interests in Congress may make legislators reluctant to vote for policy changes if they fear that home-state politicians will castigate them for imposing costs on their state. Given the diversity of state policies, virtually any proposed change from the status quo is likely to make some states feel that they are being made worse off. Federalism could have contributed to the passage of welfare reform legislation in 1996 in at least two ways: in a diffuse form, through increased support for devolution as a result of the welfare reform experiments conducted under waivers in the early 1990s; and in a more concentrated fashion, through the active political support of the nation's governors.

Policy Feedbacks

A final set of contextual factors concerns policy feedbacks—the effect that past policy choices have on later rounds of policymaking in a particular area.[10] Past decisions about how a program is to be structured may create constituencies that benefit from the structure that has been created and are likely to object to any revisions that hurt their interests. And they create sunk costs both for bureaucracies and for clienteles who adapt their behavior to existing program structures. The net result of all of these factors is to lock in current policies unless there are very strong pressures for change.

A number of such effects can be seen in the case of the AFDC program. The initial choice of a shared federal-state system for ADC in 1935, for example, made later creation of a national system of income support less likely. Failure to federalize and index AFDC benefits during a period of economic growth before the first oil shock, when many other federal benefit programs were being indexed, made it much easier for states to let AFDC benefits erode through inflation in the 1970s and 1980s. The bifurcation of family support policies into means-tested AFDC for the poor and nearly invisible tax deductions for the middle and upper classes rather than universal family allowances gave the program a narrow and weak political base of support and highlighted overrepresentation of racial minorities among its clientele. Expansion of the Earned Income Tax Credit further isolated the mostly nonworking poor clientele of AFDC.[11]

A policy feedback explanation suggests that the policy agenda for AFDC is likely to change when problems in existing policies become visible. A decentralized AFDC policy creates a diversity of state interests that promotes stalemate, making the failure of federal welfare reform initiatives more likely. But federalism also facilitated increased state experimentation with welfare programs in the early 1990s that fueled support for increased state discretion among many governors. The failures and perverse incentives in AFDC also increased political support for policy change.

Analyzing Political Choice

Analyses of societal, institutional, and past policy constraints offer a number of plausible hypotheses about the forces that have shaped, and continue to shape, welfare reform politics. Some approaches offer more plausible explanations of particular questions than of others: arguments emphasizing the importance of public opinion and expert knowledge seem particularly appropriate to explaining a changing agenda, for example, while explanations focusing on fragmented national political institutions are particularly helpful in understanding why comprehensive welfare reform initiatives have so seldom succeeded. And in some cases the explanations seem almost impossible to separate: those that stress the role of state experiments in the evolution of the welfare reform agenda and the success of welfare reform in 1996, for example, presumably draw on the intertwined effects of federalism, policy research, and policy feedback.

But although contextual explanations can tell us much about the forces acting on policymakers, it is a rare decision that can be completely explained by reference even to several factors. To gain a more complete understanding of how policy evolves, one needs to take a closer look at the microincentives and strategic options used by policymakers in making political and policy choices.[12]

These choices come in many shapes and sizes, and at all stages of the policymaking process. Some are relatively simple, clear, and visible, and are made by individuals, such as President Clinton's yes-or-no decisions to sign or veto Republican-sponsored welfare reform legislation. Other choices involve large numbers of policymakers operating under relatively clear decisionmaking rules that may empower the adherents of some positions while disadvantaging others—congressional votes on amendments to a welfare reform bill, for example. Choices made earlier in the policymaking process may also involve collectivities—formulation of the Clinton administration's welfare reform package and the welfare reform provisions of the Contract with America, for example—but they are frequently made in less formal groups that lack clearly institutionalized procedures for sorting alternatives and completing a decision.[13]

Policymakers' Objectives

What criteria do politicians and other policymakers use in making choices? Even if one assumes that they are rational—that they seek to maximize their self-interest as they perceive it—their strategic calculus is often complicated. A few basic arguments about how politicians and other policymakers (from now on I will use the encompassing term *policymakers*) make decisions provide useful building blocks for analyzing policy choice in general and welfare policy in particular.

First, although the simplest form of a choice approach views policy conflict as purely a struggle among groups of self-interested politicians to maximize their own prospects for reelection and power, this is far too simplistic.[14] Most politicians and other policymakers also have multiple objectives that go beyond electoral concerns. In particular, they are likely to have preferences for what they perceive to be good policy that are informed by ideology, experience, and factors other than the preferences of constituencies.

In addition, they are likely to value preservation of coalitional unity within their party (or in some cases a faction within the party). Coalitional unity can be important because it lowers the costs of building coalitions on specific issues where some members have a stake in a particular outcome but others do not; essentially, it serves as a "standing log-roll" across a variety of issues. On controversial issues coalitional unity can also provide safety in numbers, countering criticism that an individual coalition member's position is extreme or out of touch with the views of constituents. Thus politicians may support or oppose positions when doing so is consistent with the position taken by a majority of their party group, even when doing so is inconsistent with what they or their constituents prefer. This is especially likely if doing so is a matter of relatively modest salience (and distance) from their personal or constituency preferences. "Getting along by going along" may be part of a strategy of mutual deference: others in the party will defer on other matters about which the politician cares a great deal. Party unity also helps to foster both the public perception and the reality of a party's capacity to work effectively, which may be helpful in winning elections.[15]

Second, even within these three broad categories of electoral objectives, coalitional unity, and policy objectives, politicians often pursue multiple goals that may require difficult trade-offs. In the case of electoral objectives they may be simultaneously attempting to claim credit with some constituents or sources of campaign funds, minimize blame for actions that offend other important interests, and generate blame against political opponents. Pursuing these objectives frequently requires trade-offs: a choice that maximizes credit claiming, for example, may cut down on opportunities for blaming opponents. Politicians may also hold conflicting policy preferences, simultaneously favoring a more generous welfare system, a lower budget deficit, and greater decentralization within the federal system, that need to be sorted out in making a policy choice.

Third, although policymakers do not have a single hierarchy of objectives (for example, always placing credit claiming or other electoral objectives above policy preferences or coalitional unity), they are likely to be especially attentive to avoiding blame from constituents because voters tend to be much more sensitive to losses that have been imposed on them than to things that have been done to benefit them.[16] Politicians may have strong policy concerns; they are likely to try to claim credit with important constituencies when possible; and, recognizing the paramount importance of blame in politics, they may try to blame political opponents when they can. The relative importance of credit claiming and blame generating as well as good policy and coalitional concerns may vary among politicians and policy sectors, but for most politicians, all these concerns are likely to pale in comparison with their concern with avoiding blame. Of course, when avoiding blame is not a concern—if a politician's stance on welfare reform is of little importance to constituents, for example—policymakers can pay more attention to their other objectives. But politicians can rarely ignore the potential for blame: interest groups and political opponents may mobilize an inattentive public even around issues that had previously seemed obscure and inconsequential.[17]

Fourth, while politicians recognize the necessity of making trade-offs, they do not like to do so. Thus they are drawn to policy options that make them better off in achieving several objectives and worse off in none. A policy proposal that allows them to avoid blame but gives them few opportunities to claim credit and makes them worse off with respect to achieving some policy priorities is unlikely to be greeted with great enthusiasm. Similarly, a proposal that is consistent with a politician's policy preferences in a particular policy area but clashes with his or her overall budgetary policy objectives is likely to be viewed with some trepidation. If, however, policymakers develop or encounter an option that comes closer to their policy preferences in several ways—the specifics of policy, the size of the deficit, allocation of responsibility between the states and the federal government—

and that offers chances to claim credit while incurring little risk of blame or of splitting the party coalition, they are likely to embrace it, try to move it up on the agenda of issues being debated, and try to move it forward to adoption.[18] For Republicans in 1995, for example, pushing conservative welfare reform was a natural choice to put on the agenda: it fit with the policy and budgetary preferences of most Republican legislators, and it was seen as likely to garner much credit and little blame from their (mostly suburban and middle-class) constituents.

A fifth consideration is that policymakers are far from infallible in weighing the advantages and disadvantages of policy alternatives. They often operate with far from perfect information and must make decisions with a great deal of uncertainty, perhaps with results that are less than optimal even from their own perspective. Because the future costs and benefits of policy alternatives are uncertain and information about those costs and benefits is expensive (and sometimes impossible) to obtain, politicians are especially likely to discount potential costs and benefits that are fairly distant in time. When they are trying to get elected, they are not likely to think too hard about the risks of their election promises if polls and focus groups appear to show that a proposal works politically by appealing to swing voters. Policymakers may discount information that is uncomfortable or that does not fit with core beliefs. They are also unlikely to spend a lot of time thinking about worst-case scenarios whose probability of occurring is believed to be low. All these factors may lead them to make choices that are suboptimal with respect to their own objectives. For example, many analysts have criticized Bill Clinton's 1992 campaign pledge to "end welfare as we know it" for making AFDC even more unpopular and making it more difficult for the president and his allies to resist a Republican agenda for change after 1994 if doing so meant appearing to defend the status quo. However, because the Democrats had not lost control of the House in forty years, the idea that they might lose control of the welfare reform agenda really did not enter into their calculations until late in 1994; certainly it was not even a minor part of the campaign calculus in 1992.

Options

In a simple political world where politicians only had to worry about policy concerns and not electoral or coalitional ones, they could evaluate policy options relative to just two alternatives. The first is what can be called the default position: what policy would be in place if no policy action were taken. Usually this means continuing the status quo, although there are some exceptions (for example, when a program is about to expire under sunset provisions). They would also compare each option with what can be called their ideal points, the policies they would like to see in effect if they could simply dictate policy. They could operate according to a fairly simple decision rule: endorse any alternative that is closer to their ideal point than the default position and reject those that are further away.

In the real political world, of course, decisionmaking is far more complex, involving electoral and coalitional objectives as well as policy ones and (intertwined with the other considerations) calculations about whether an option has a significant chance of being adopted. Only when the range of options available is very limited is a politician or group of politicians likely to view a single option as superior to both the status quo and any plausible alternative—that is, as most congruent with their policy ideal points, offering greater opportunities to claim credit and generate blame against opponents than any other alternative, having little risk of incurring blame, and having the strongest prospects for surviving hurdles in the process of winning adoption. This situation of a single alternative that is clearly superior to all others, including the status quo, can be characterized as an easy choice.

In most situations the best choice is less obvious. Policymakers may consider several options to be good choices in the sense that they offer political and coalitional rewards, increased congruence with their policy preferences (that is to say, increased proximity to their ideal points relative to the status quo), and reasonable prospects for surviving the hurdles in the policymaking process.[19]

In other cases politicians and other policymakers are less fortunate: the policy agenda may be limited to undesirable alternatives, bad choices that will leave them worse off politically and meet their value preferences even less well than the status quo. Policymakers confronting this situation will probably try to retain the status quo and keep the issue off the agenda. On some occasions they may face no choice at all, with only a single option on the table that makes them worse off, either because they have been maneuvered into a situation where they must accept a fait accompli or because one option is clearly the least undesirable of a bad lot, with the status quo not a viable option. Perhaps the most common alternative, however, is what can be called hard choices, options in which some desirable attributes must be weighed against others that are undesirable. Hard choices may pit an improvement in one aspect of policy against a negative change in another— a deeply held personal political belief against the views of a constituency that is critical to that politician's reelection—or multiple constituencies against one another. Because of politicians' awareness that constituents who suffer losses are likely to be more sensitive to those losses than constituents encountering gains are appreciative of the gains, hard choices are likely to garner little more enthusiasm from politicians than bad choices.[20]

Most of the time, politicians confront a world in which several policy alternatives are on the table: some that they view as good choices, others that pose hard choices, and still others that are clearly undesirable for many reasons. Only when the range of options has narrowed substantially (for example, on a vote on final passage of legislation after all amendments have been considered) are policymakers likely to be confronted with an easy choice or no choice.

In understanding whether bargaining over policy will result in some change from the status quo, understanding politicians' ideal points is less important than recognizing what can be called their zone of acceptable outcomes, those outcomes they will accept in a choice between the default position and that alternative. This zone will generally include all alternatives on the agenda that are good choices, those that make the politician better off in electoral, coalitional, and policy terms. But because politicians set this zone based in part on electoral (especially avoiding blame) and coalitional considerations as well as policy preferences, this range may include points far from their ideal points, including options that they consider hard choices and even bad choices. Policymakers' zones of acceptable outcomes are likely to be especially broad when (as was the case with welfare reform in the 1990s) they realize that the status quo is very unpopular with their constituents and they wish to avoid being labeled defenders of the status quo.

In most political processes the zones of acceptable outcomes for many participants are fairly fluid. Participants may know even their own zones of acceptable outcomes only in fairly general terms until they are forced to accept or reject specific options. Indeed, revealing the limits of his or her zone of acceptable outcomes too early is likely to place a politician at a strategic disadvantage by making it unlikely that opponents will concede anything closer to the politician's ideal point. These zones are gradually revealed through probing by opponents and by developing packages of competing proposals on which specific positions, for or against, must be taken. And policymakers may alter their zones of acceptable outcomes during bargaining in order to hold a coalition together, facilitate or block an agreement, or avoid blame for the failure of an agreement.

Policymakers try to use their limited resources to choose among what they perceive to be good options while preventing the adoption (and preferably even the consideration) of alternatives that make them worse off on some or all criteria (bad choices) or that make them better off on some criteria and worse off on others (hard choices). Two of the most important ways of doing this are manipulating agendas and repositioning.

Manipulating Agendas

The leading analysis of agenda setting, by John Kingdon, suggests that the way issues get (and lose) the attention of politicians is fluid: they get on the agenda when there is a conjunction of what he calls *problem, policy,* and *political* streams.[21] In the problem stream, for example, increased attention may be drawn to a problem by a highly visible focusing event such as the death of a homeless family or by a newly developed indicator or an indicator that pushes through a highly visible threshold.[22]

Developments in the policy stream are also critical. Policy alternatives are usually devised by experts on a particular subject. Proposals are refined, revised, and recombined over time. They are likely to survive what is usually a long winnowing process only if they appear to be technically feasible (having some prospect of being put in place and addressing the problem without making it worse), affordable, congruent with the values of policymakers and the public, and capable of getting through legislative and other hurdles.[23]

The political stream is equally complex. Politicians are especially likely to give an issue additional attention when they sense a national mood of concern to which they feel they must respond or that offers opportunities for claiming credit. An election that brings new personnel into the White House or Congress with values, perspectives, and priorities different from those of their predecessors may also bring new issues to the fore. Other political factors, such as a need to stake out political turf (as when jurisdiction over an issue between congressional committees is ambiguous), may also cause politicians to give increased attention to an issue.

Brief opportunities to introduce change occur when the three policy streams come together and are *coupled,* often through the efforts of a skilled political entrepreneur.[24] Even if a problem is considered particularly pressing, it may not remain on the agenda long if there is no plausible policy alternative for addressing it. Issues may also fade from agendas because the public and policymakers may become inured to a situation, especially if they see it as insoluble, or they may lose interest as the memories fade of a visible event that triggered attention. Politicians may also believe that a problem has been solved after new legislation is passed; only if problems persist, or appear in a new form, will an issue reappear on the agenda.

Kingdon's analysis suggests several conclusions about policymakers' strategic choices. Those who confront an easy choice, in which one alternative to the status quo is clearly superior, are particularly likely to devote resources to getting that option on the action agenda of decisionmakers and pushing it through to adoption. But policymakers will try to keep options that are costly to themselves from being considered, so that only alternatives that they consider good choices remain. Or if they view all plausible options as less desirable than the status quo, they may try to prevent any one of them from being considered. In the U.S. political system, congressional committees are one of the most important venues where further action on a proposal that committee members oppose can be stopped, even if it enjoys wide support outside the committee.

If policymakers cannot keep undesirable options off the agenda, they may try to mitigate their negative consequences. Legislators, for example, may prevent open votes on proposals that they favor on policy or personal grounds but that they know are unpopular with the public. They may also try to put on the agenda choices that they know pose political problems (hard choices or bad choices) for their opponents (for example, requiring opponents to openly accept or reject a welfare reform proposal that is popular with constituents but inconsistent with the opponents' own preferences).

Politicians who face an agenda dominated by options they consider bad choices may also try to manipulate the range of alternatives so that the choices become hard choices or worse for their opponents. For example, opponents of change may try to attach "poison pill" provisions that are known to be anathema to the backers of a piece of legislation: proponents must then choose between accepting a legislative package they support except for one provision that they vehemently oppose or voting against the package, leaving the status quo in place.[25]

Strategic calculations by politicians about whether to try to move an issue onto the agenda are further complicated by the fact that they are simultaneously playing in multiple political and policy arenas. Each of these arenas has its own rules and political dynamics, yet choices made in them impinge on one another. The need to pay attention simultaneously to multiple arenas also limits the time and resources they can give to any one arena. For example, the substantive and strategic choices made by policymakers in creating a welfare reform proposal and developing a support coalition for legislative passage are constrained by the time, attention, and political capital that must be devoted to other policy concerns. Policymakers may decide that welfare reform does not offer sufficient political rewards or a sufficiently high prospect of political success to devise a reform initiative or to continue with one once it is under way. In 1993–94, for example, health care politics was a dominant influence on policymaking for welfare reform as the Clinton administration repeatedly put welfare reform on the back burner to avoid impinging on its top legislative priority.[26]

Repositioning

Policymakers who cannot control an agenda must use other strategies to reconcile their policy and political interests. In particular, they may change their positions on issues. Usually this repositioning does not involve altering ideal points but rather their zone of acceptable outcomes. Policymakers' reassessments of their zones are not based solely on relatively fixed calculations of the policy merits of those options; instead, choices about what positions to take are also determined in large part in relation to the positions taken by other participants.[27] Positioning relative to other participants is important because of the relatively limited information held by most constituents. As John Gilmour has noted,

> Rationally ignorant voters will not know precisely where a party stands on a particular issue, but they will be able to identify differences between parties, and know, for example, that one stands for more and the other for less. On health care issues, the Democrats want to be the party promising more than the Republicans. On crime, the Republicans want to be the party that is tougher on criminals. Exact positions in policy space are less important than relative positions because voters cannot perceive exact positions of parties, only relative ones.[28]

Politicians may engage in several different forms of relational positioning, some largely reactive and some more proactive, in trying to stake out distinctive positions of their own. And while most repositioning involves an expansion of politicians' zones of acceptable outcomes, it sometimes involves a shrinkage and rejection of positions that previously had been deemed acceptable. Among the repositioning strategies that politicians may pursue are the following (see table 3-1 for summaries).

MATCHING. Matching is a largely reactive adjustment of politicians' zone of acceptable outcomes. It is especially likely to occur when a politician's current position is relatively close to the default position (status quo) but far from that of most of his or her constituents. If the issue increases in importance to constituents, making support for the default position a

Table 3-1. *Repositioning Strategic Options*

Positional strategy	Objectives/Incentives	Conducive conditions	Countervailing conditions
Matching			
Match a move by a "benchmark" actor closer to median voter position than yours, so you at least stay even with benchmark actor, even if outside your normal range of preferences	Avoid blame as being outside political mainstream on issue	Preferences of actor pursuing strategy are relatively close to default position but far from position of median constituent; issue salient to large number of voters, making support for default position more politically risky	All credible actors have highly polarized positions distant from that of median voter; constituents highly polarized
Hand-tying			
Make firm commitment to limiting "zone of acceptable outcome" to convince others you will not be flexible	Strengthen bargaining power by limiting outcomes you will acquiesce in to those close to your ideal point	Actor pursuing strategy and constituents find default position acceptable and have similar ideal points; other actors cannot change from default position without acquiescence of actor pursuing strategy	Actor pursuing strategy and constituents disagree on ideal points or find default position unacceptable; actor pursuing strategy not needed to form winning coalition for change
Triangulation			
Position yourself between two or more competitors to appeal as "moderate" alternative	Avoid blame as being outside political mainstream on an issue; obtain credit for achieving policy change through compromise	Constituency preferences cluster toward the center	Constituency highly polarized

	Definition/Behavior	Goal	Constituency condition 1	Constituency condition 2
Strategic pursuit	Move closer to position of political opponent even if it falls outside your normal range of policy preferences	Avoid blame for failure to adjust to changing constituency preferences; avoid defection of political allies to support positions held by opponents	Constituency strongly opposes status quo	Constituency strongly opposes changes from status quo
Strategic disagreement	Maintain distance between yourself and one or more competitors even if competitor moves toward your position	Prevent compromise resulting in policy change in short term in order to preserve blame-generating opportunities or delay agreement on policy until time more propitious to move closer to your "ideal point"	Constituency strongly opposes status quo	Constituency highly satisfied with status quo
Split the difference	Policy/political opponents move to joint intermediate positions on single or multiple dimensions of policy	Move to policy position preferable to status quo; claim credit for policy change	Actors engaging in strategy share a policy space they prefer to status quo on at least some issues; differ in salience on some dimensions, facilitating trade-offs on less salient dimensions	Constituencies highly engaged in and highly polarized on all dimensions of policy under discussion

greater political risk, politicians may try to avoid blame by moving closer to the position of their median constituent, even if doing so moves them farther from their own preferred position. But because that move runs counter to their policy preferences, they will seek to move as short a distance as possible. A strategy consistent with politicians' strong emphasis on avoiding blame is to match the position taken by a respected "moderate" who is as close to their position as possible, thus providing themselves with political cover. For example, moderate Democrats in Congress may believe it politically necessary to be no further to the left on welfare reform than a Democratic president. If the president's position shifts to the right, they are likely to move their zone of acceptable outcomes to the right as well. Both before and after the president's shifts, they may view all options on the table as bad choices and prefer no change from the status quo. But if they are forced into an open choice between the unpopular status quo and a policy change that they dislike but that the president has endorsed, they may feel that they have to go along. Similar matching phenomena can be found in other contexts: for example, states may reduce their provision of social benefits to match those of neighboring states in order to avoid becoming a welfare magnet to people from other states who might be attracted by higher benefits.

HAND-TYING. Politicians may attempt to tie their own hands by announcing in advance a set of demands that define the outer boundaries of their zone of acceptable outcomes but are short of concessions deemed necessary by political competitors to reach an agreement. The objective of this hand-tying is to convince political adversaries that they cannot and will not consent to a position any further from their ideal point. If this maneuver succeeds, it narrows the number of alternatives on the table to those that are relatively close to their own ideal point and within their self-proclaimed zone of acceptable outcomes. Eventually agreeing to settle for less than those minimum conditions would presumably lead to political humiliation, a loss of credibility, and perhaps even political defeat.[29]

Of course, hand-tying strategies pose important risks as well as advantages. The most obvious risk is that political competitors will view these conditions, intended as a maximum concession, as a minimum. They may refuse to accept anything less than the outer limit of what the tied politicians have announced as their zone of acceptable outcomes while probing to see if they can get more. There are other risks as well. If the politicians or groups whose hands are tied are not necessary to build a winning coalition for policy change, they may find themselves excluded from that coalition, failing to obtain concessions that could have been won if they had used a less rigid negotiating stance. A hand-tying strategy may also result both in the failure to obtain policy change (because it increases the probability that no agreement will be reached) and in the "tied" politicians' or groups' being blamed for that failure because of their intransigence.

Hand-tying is likely to succeed (and even to be attempted) only under certain conditions. If other bargainers are able to reach an agreement without the acquiescence of the tied policymaker, for example, they have little incentive to move to that policymaker's proclaimed zone of acceptable outcomes, so there is little reason to use this strategy. If the policymaker and his or her constituents have very different ideal points, proclaiming a narrow zone of acceptable outcomes may place the policymaker and constituents at odds. Finally, because a tying strategy makes stalemate more likely, it is likely to be politically rewarding only if both policymaker and constituents find the default position—usually the status quo—acceptable. If one or both find the status quo intolerable, a hand-tying strategy has few political or policy rewards. Setting narrow bounds on acceptable change to the AFDC program when public dislike for the program is high, for example, may be perceived as intransigence by the public and punished accordingly.

TRIANGULATION. Triangulation is a somewhat more proactive form of repositioning in which a policymaker (or group of policymakers) repositions roughly midway between two or more political competitors to appeal as the "moderate" alternative. This has several potential advantages. If the policymaker's previous position is distant from that of most constituents, triangulation can help avoid blame for being outside the political mainstream on an issue. It may also allow him or her to obtain credit for achieving change through compromise. Triangulation is most likely to occur when the distribution of public preferences clusters toward the center. If constituency preferences are highly polarized, a move toward the center is likely to alienate one group of constituents while being insufficiently attractive to those at the other pole.

STRATEGIC PURSUIT. Strategic pursuit involves moving closer to the position of a political opponent even if it falls outside the politician's zone of acceptable policy outcomes. Thus it has some similarities to matching, but the repositioning involves moving closer to an actor who is usually an opponent rather than an ally or a neutral figure, and as a result it usually involves a greater move away from the politician's ideal point. Strategic pursuit is frequently motivated by changing public preferences and politicians' desire to avoid blame (for failure, for example, to adjust to an upswing in support for environmental causes). When this occurs, politicians may also engage in strategic pursuit for coalitional reasons: they may see moving part, but not all, of the way toward an opponent's position as a way to provide a defensible collective position that is closer to the opponent's position than the position they held earlier and thus prevent some of their normal political partners from defecting entirely to the opponent's camp.

STRATEGIC DISAGREEMENT.   Even if a political competitor moves substantially closer to a policymaker's ideal point through matching, strategic pursuit, or triangulation, there may be reasons to engage in what John Gilmour has labeled strategic disagreement: moving one's zone of acceptable outcomes away from the competitor to maintain the original policy distance.[30] In this circumstance the person or group moving may actually shrink the zone of acceptable outcomes, rejecting as unacceptable some of the policy space that it had previously signaled it found acceptable.

Strategic disagreement may occur for several reasons. If elections are approaching, for example, and a politician's side expects to make gains in them, it may be in his or her long-term policy and political interest to avoid an agreement now and hold out for a better deal (that is, one closer to the ideal point) later. In this situation, reaching an agreement and passing legislation have four strong disadvantages. They may decrease the probability that the issue will be revisited after the election, when the resolution would be closer to the policymaker's ideal point. They may alienate important supporters and interest groups that would view compromise as selling out. They may neutralize an issue that will benefit the politician's party in the next election, when emphasizing partisan differences would be more advantageous. And they will likely force the politician to share credit for the policy change with political adversaries.[31] Of course, strategic disagreement also carries risks: if the hoped-for electoral gains do not appear, a politician's opportunity to move closer to his or her ideal point may disappear as well. Moreover, political opponents may try to blame a legislator as politically obstructionist. And if the group making the initial move is persistent in its pursuit, a bidding war can break out that results in irresponsible legislation.[32] Overall, however, pursuit of strategic disagreement decreases the prospects for policy change.

SPLIT THE DIFFERENCE.   Policy agreement may arise not only because one person or group of political participants unilaterally decides to move its zone of acceptable outcomes much closer to the position of others (as in matching and strategic pursuit), but because two or more actors move to joint intermediate positions, thus splitting the difference. Several conditions may contribute to this outcome: if all those moving, and large shares of the public, consider the status quo unsatisfactory; if the ideal points of all those involved are fairly close; and if splitting the difference provides significant opportunities to claim credit for favoring or achieving policy change. It may also be helpful if policymakers and publics differ in the importance they ascribe to at least some of the issues being debated, facilitating trade-offs in which policymakers can make gains on issues about which they and their constituents care a great deal while making concessions on dimensions that they view as less urgent. Splitting the difference is likely to be less feasible if constituencies are highly engaged in, and high polarized on, all dimensions of policy under discussion, and a substantial portion of policymakers and their constituents view the status quo as preferable to any plausible compromise position.

Constraints on Change

This analysis of the factors constraining policymakers' strategic choices suggests that the prospects for movement away from the policy status quo are likely to be greatest under the following conditions.

—Most participants have a broad and flexible zone of acceptable outcomes, making it more likely that strategies for splitting the difference will result in some policy space that is broadly acceptable. Policymakers are most likely to have broad zones of agreement when the status quo is extremely unpopular or when the policymaker and his or her constituents consider the issue relatively unimportant.

—Crucial participants (such as the president in the U.S. system) decide to make policy change one of their priorities, placing it above the many other policy sectors that vie for their attention.[33]

—Participants with similar ideal points and political interests control which alternatives are considered and in which order at all stages in policymaking, so that one group of policymakers is less likely to succeed in using agenda limitation strategies to block a policy change that is favored by most others.

—Veto points are few and simple majorities rule at each point in decisionmaking, again making it less likely that relatively small groups of "preference outliers" will use agenda limitation to block change.

Policymaking Traps in Reforming Welfare

Analysis of the factors that shape policymakers' options and analysis of how politicians decide among options can help us to understand welfare reform politics. The substantive and strategic choices made by policymakers are inextricably intertwined with the contextual factors—ideas, social structures, political institutions, policy feedbacks—that limit the choices open to politicians, the decisions they make, and the range of outcomes.[34] Both durable national values and shifts in public opinion, for example, affect the electoral calculations of politicians. Institutional structures shape politicians' ability to manipulate agendas to their advantage, weaken the positions of rivals, and keep issues that force them to make painful choices off the agenda altogether. Policy feedbacks affect the way that groups in society organize and perceive their own interests and thus the political calculus of politicians.

Because these explanatory categories can be applied to a broad range of policy areas, they have the advantage of facilitating comparison. But they have a corresponding disadvantage: they encourage thinking of policy stability and change as resulting from values *or* social divisions *or* past policy choices *or* politicians' incentives rather than from complex interactions among these factors.

In recent years social scientists have emphasized the need to draw connections between these categories of explanation rather than thinking of them as alternatives.[35] Drawing simultaneously on several categories is especially important in thinking about welfare reform. Consider the types of choices that most AFDC reform initiatives have presented to policymakers and the constraints on those choices. Welfare reform proposals are bedeviled by zero-sum conflicts on policymaking (I will use the briefer term *traps*).[36] Each trap has a dual aspect. First, welfare reform initiatives have usually created hard choices for policymakers because they *could not increase the prospects that they would get more of something they wanted without also increasing the risk that they would get more of something that they did not want in political or policy terms*. Second, policymakers' views and constituency preferences on welfare issues are often polarized. Welfare reform initiatives have usually pitted groups of policymakers whose zones of acceptable outcomes did not overlap against one another in zero-sum conflicts: good choices for some are bad choices for others. Thus *policymakers cannot increase the prospects that they will get more of something they want without making other groups of policymakers worse off in political or policy terms*. In addition, the exact terms of each of many welfare policy trade-offs are often unknown or may change over time. This makes policymaking even more difficult because it is hard for people to calculate how much of the undesirable (child poverty, for example) they are accepting for a given amount of what they desire (greater work effort by AFDC mothers, for example).

Three things about these welfare policymaking traps should be noted at the outset and will be incorporated in the discussion of each trap. First, each trap has roots in the contextual factors outlined earlier, such as fragmented American political institutions and the tremendous conjunction of race and poverty in the United States. Second, each trap pushes some policymakers to use agenda control and repositioning strategies that make an agreement on policy change less likely. Third, individual policymaking traps may vary over time: the money trap, for example, is likely to assume greater importance when there are strong barriers against new spending programs such as the impediments imposed by the Budget Enforcement Act of 1990 and less importance when revenues are relatively flush. Although the exact nature of the traps will vary depending on the content of specific welfare reform proposals, any welfare reform package is likely to encounter several of them (table 3-2).

The Dual Clientele Trap

Perhaps the central political dilemma for American family support policy during the past quarter century has been that the AFDC program mixed together in one program two clienteles toward which policymakers and the public have strikingly different attitudes. One of AFDC's clienteles, children, is generally considered deserving of assistance, but the public has unfavorable attitudes regarding the deservingness and willingness to work of the other clients who benefit directly from AFDC: custodial parents, who are generally able-bodied but low-skilled mothers. AFDC mothers may be viewed with a mixture of resentment and sympathy, while attitudes toward noncustodial parents, especially those who do not pay child support, are limited mostly to resentment.

This then is the dual clientele trap in welfare reform: *policymakers usually cannot take the politically popular step of helping poor children without the politically unpopular step of helping their custodial parents; they cannot take politically popular steps such as increasing penalties for refusal to work or for out-of-wedlock childbearing that may hurt parents without also risking the politically unpopular result that poor children will be made worse off.*[37] Public doubts about the deservingness of adult recipients of AFDC have been reinforced in recent years as other programs, especially Social Security, have taken over the primary income support for children of widowed and disabled parents. Increasingly, AFDC recipients have been concentrated among

Table 3-2. *Policymaking Traps for Welfare Reform Initiatives*

Nature	Sources	Consequences for policy change	Factors weakening
	Dual clientele trap		
Policymakers cannot help poor children (popular) without also aiding parents (unpopular); cannot do things that make parents worse off (popular) without also risking making poor children worse off (unpopular)	Negative stereotypes of and prejudice against African Americans; strong public sympathy for poor children; concentration of clientele among very low-income single-parent families; political and social isolation of and prejudice against African Americans lead to their over-representation among AFDC clientele	Reform debates concentrate on changing behavior of adults as well as on welfare of children; impossibility of increasing both simultaneously leads first to agenda manipulation to limit change from the status quo and ultimately to stalemate	New approaches seem to improve incentives for adults without hurting children; decreased public concern over either welfare of children or behavior of adults discourages "hand-tying" and agenda limitation to prevent policy change
	Perverse incentives trap		
No plausible welfare reform can avoid creating some new perverse incentives or exacerbating some existing ones	Absence of universal health insurance and automatic eligibility of AFDC recipients for Medicaid strengthens perverse incentive to receive AFDC rather than work; weak work incentives in AFDC strengthen perverse incentive to receive AFDC rather than work	Visibility of perverse incentives may undercut support for program and for reform initiatives; efforts to weaken perverse incentives by increasing program spending and coverage require scarce resources and may cost support of conservatives	New approaches seem to improve incentives for adults without perverse incentives

Federalism trap	National policymakers cannot give states flexibility to do things they like without running risk they will also do things some national policymakers do not like; cannot strengthen national standards without undercutting flexibility some states desire and creating demand for federal compensation	Substantial autonomy of subnational governments risks race to bottom; large regional variations in income, values, and economic development strategies lead to different state policy preferences	Inability to resolve conflicting state and federal interests (or conflicts between states) leads to policy stalemate	Washington policymakers lose interest in controlling policy outcomes; new research resolves whether state discretion or nationally uniform policy is preferable
Money trap	Most welfare reform initiatives require spending more money than public thinks necessary or Congress wants to spend	Public thinks too much money spent on welfare, so reform should save money right away; budget law restrictions make spending increases more visible and procedurally difficult	Reform cannot achieve what proponents claimed at acceptable cost, encouraging policy stalemate and disillusionment with reform	New policy options seem likely to address problems without costing more money; government has bountiful revenues; government develops low-visibility mechanisms to raise funds for welfare reform initiatives

never-married mothers and racial minorities, reinforcing common stereotypes about them. Moreover, greater labor market participation by middle-
class women has coincided with changes in the rules of AFDC that have created work disincentives for recipients, further isolating them and
strengthening negative attitudes toward them.

The dual nature of the AFDC clientele has had political and programmatic consequences. If policymakers could be certain that family support
funds were spent on children and spent "wisely," the programs would be
much less controversial and might be funded more generously. This is not
possible, of course. Programmatically, the dual clientele has meant that concerns with ensuring the welfare of children have been rivaled by concerns
over the behavior (and efforts to alter the behavior) of parents and prospec-
tive parents: in particular, trying to weaken incentives to have children
(especially children out of wedlock) and ensuring that welfare does not
become an alternative to work. But requiring work is very expensive if government guarantees jobs to those who cannot find them. However, requiring the custodial parent to work to maintain benefits without providing a
job guarantee to those who cannot find or keep a job in the private sector
seriously risks the welfare of children, especially in periods of high unemployment. Significant changes in the behavior of welfare recipients are
unlikely to occur without punitive changes in incentives structures, but
these changes cannot be instituted without badly harming some recipients
(and their children) who are unable or unwilling to change their behavior.
Disagreements among policymakers on how to weigh concerns about the
welfare of children versus concerns about the behavior of adults have frequently led welfare reform initiatives to end in stalemate.

The Perverse Incentives Trap

If the dual clientele trap relates to the problems with using sticks on adult
recipients of AFDC, the perverse incentives trap deals largely with problems
in using carrots to induce increased work effort, decreased out-of-wedlock
childbearing, and so forth. The policy design problem is this: no policy
intended to help poor families can entirely avoid creating incentives for
recipients that policymakers and the public are likely to see as undesirable,
and no plausible welfare reform initiative is likely to avoid creating some new
perverse incentives or making some existing ones worse. For example, it is
difficult for policymakers to provide additional support to families in
poverty without reducing their incentives to work. Giving cash to women
who have children out of wedlock weakens incentives for them to marry or

forgo childbearing. Focusing support on single-parent families, the ones most likely to need assistance, can provide incentives to form and maintain those families rather than two-parent families. And targeting assistance to those who need it most tends to isolate recipients politically and economically while reducing relative status and economic rewards to those who are doing modestly better—especially working, two-parent families. Providing in-kind benefits (most notably Medicaid) with eligibility keyed to AFDC eligibility makes it harder for them to leave welfare for poorly paying jobs in the private sector because most of those jobs do not offer health benefits, meaning that recipients may suffer real income decreases if they leave the program to take such a job, especially if they or their children are in poor health. Providing welfare benefits independent of any obligation to society, especially the obligation to work, means that a recipient may fail to develop the sense of responsibility that is necessary for success as a worker and a citizen.

The perverse incentives trap is the political manifestation of these policy design traps: *no plausible welfare reform can avoid creating some new perverse incentives or making some existing ones worse.* If policymakers choose to ignore potential perverse incentives when they formulate a welfare reform proposal, public confidence in the initiative is likely to be threatened when critics of reform point out the problems, as they surely will. If policymakers come to grips with those consequences (for example, by expanding access to health care and child care for the working poor to reduce incentives for them to cycle through welfare) the costs of the proposal will increase.

The Federalism Trap

The federalism trap flows from the problem of how much geographic variability should be allowed in benefits, eligibility, obligations imposed on recipients, and program administration. The AFDC program allowed states substantial leeway in the benefits they paid to recipients as well as the obligations they imposed on them. In addition, states could apply for waivers that allowed them to deviate from program standards otherwise applied to all jurisdictions.

Allowing diversity across jurisdictions (usually states) has several potential advantages. State policies may be more responsive to local conditions, such as variations in unemployment rates. And state experimentation may lead to better policy designs by allowing tests of innovations such as guaranteed child support payments. It may also help answer questions about behavioral responses to innovations such as requirements that teenage mothers live with parents and that there be time limits on receipt of benefits, while decreasing the risks associated with nationwide application of untested innovations.

But allowing states to deviate from national standards may also have costs. During the welfare debates of the 1990s, liberals were particularly concerned that state discretion could lead to unequal treatment based on where recipients lived. Interstate discrepancies can in turn create "welfare magnet" effects, in which interstate migration in pursuit of higher welfare benefits is inadvertently encouraged, and movement based on pursuit of job opportunities is discouraged if it means moving to an area of lower welfare benefits.[38] State discretion may also result in a reduction of overall benefit levels due to interstate competition: even if welfare magnet effects do not occur, politicians may believe that they do, setting off a race to the bottom in benefits and eligibility restrictions as they seek to prevent immigration of AFDC recipients and to promote emigration of their own welfare recipients.[39]

Conservatives had a different set of concerns about federalism in 1990s welfare reform debates. They feared that states would not impose the mandates favored by conservatives (for example, family caps, exclusion of teenage mothers from AFDC eligibility, and strict time limits for receiving benefits) and that failure to do so would mean that community expectations would not change enough for the mandates to have their full effect on the behavior of potential and current welfare recipients. This, then, is the federalism trap: *any proposal that gives states the discretion to do things that some group of federal policymakers would like also runs the risk that states will do things that another group of policymakers (or that same group of policymakers) does not like.*

The direction and impact of state initiatives depend in part on what is happening with other policy constraints. If financial resources are tight— as they were in the early 1990s, when many states faced severe budgetary constraints caused in part by recession and exploding Medicaid expenditures—state initiatives are more likely to have a punitive cast. And the leeway that the federal government has to reject punitively oriented state initiatives is likely to be affected in part by the commitments it has made: the Clinton administration's promise to "end welfare as we know it" undercut its ability to reject state initiatives that would do exactly that by, for example, putting strict time limits on the receipt of benefits without a promise of work at the end.

The Money Trap

The money trap for AFDC can be stated simply: *most meaningful welfare reforms require spending more money than the public thinks is necessary or more than Congress wants to spend.* Because a majority of the public almost always thinks that too many people receive AFDC and too much money is being spent on it, people think that welfare reform should save money right away. But most welfare reforms require at least short-term spending increases for education, job training, or monitoring "workfare" placements. And increasing spending requires that government do one or more of three politically unpopular things: increase taxes, increase the budget deficit (or very recently, reduce the surplus), or cut other programs. Few politicians are politically brave enough to call for increasing taxes to provide more money for welfare—even a reformed welfare. Increasing the deficit diffuses the costs of welfare reform broadly, but recent changes in budgetary procedures, especially the Budget Enforcement Act of 1990, virtually eliminated this option for financing welfare reform. And cutting other programs to fund welfare reform requires finding a program that has a politically weaker clientele or is even less popular than AFDC. Because welfare is near the bottom of government programs on both counts, this leaves few options.

The difficulty of putting substantial new dollars into welfare reform means that changes to AFDC have almost always been underfunded relative to what the proposals originally promised to do and what they had any realistic prospect of doing. Proponents of the Family Support Act (FSA) of 1988, for example, argued that it would have a dramatic effect on welfare recipients while spending only an additional $3 billion over five years. Thus the FSA never came close to imposing a universal work or training mandate. Similarly, despite strong public support in the 1990s for the principle of converting AFDC into a work-based entitlement, the Clinton administration was unable to come up with a politically viable mechanism for financing it.[40]

Cross-Cutting Institutional Barriers

Because welfare reform proposals have rarely been able to draw support from across the ideological spectrum, they have usually involved delicate balances of some elements that appeal to liberals and others that appeal to conservatives. If they did not, opponents would likely block it at some point in the convoluted American policymaking process. As a result, reform initiatives have been built on fragile coalitions. American political institutions, with weak party unity and multiple veto points, aggravate this problem. When a welfare reform proposal reaches Congress, no legislative majority can be built without enlisting legislators who disagree with some elements of the package and are likely to defect if separate votes are held on individual elements. Even if the proposal can survive agenda limitation strategies from hostile political forces, elements of the package that increase spending and those that create highly visible (even if modest) perverse incentives are especially vulnerable to being peeled off. This, of course, may alienate other members of the coalition whose support is contingent on maintaining those features of the package. The risk of a collapsing coalition can be minimized if sponsors can control the agenda to reject consideration of threatening amendments. They usually cannot do so, however, especially in the Senate, where the rights of individual members and minority parties to block change are deeply entrenched.

Stasis and Change in Welfare Policy

Although each of these policymaking traps poses strong barriers to the reform of AFDC, they are neither insurmountable nor immutable. As the right-hand column of table 3-2 shows, each of the traps can be weakened under certain conditions. The dual clientele trap, for example, can be weakened if new approaches to welfare emerge that seem likely to improve the behavior of adults without hurting children, if policymakers and the public become less concerned about whether children are hurt or whether adults misbehave, or simply because the default position—keeping the status quo—becomes politically less popular. The money trap can be weakened if the federal treasury is flush and budget process rules governing new spending initiatives are eased. The federalism trap can be weakened if federal officials grow less concerned about governing or overseeing policy at the state level.

Strategic choices by policymakers can also strengthen or weaken the barriers. Policies of strategic disagreement by legislators who believe they have better prospects of obtaining welfare reform closer to their own policy ideal points after the next election clearly make it difficult to build a stable reform coalition and weaken the prospects for passage of legislation in the short term. But if proponents of reform can maintain control of the agenda and force opponents to make a public choice between going along with reform or appearing to defend an unpopular status quo, the latter may find that they have no choice but to go along.

None of these changes in the contours of individual traps is implausible. But all of them are matters of degree rather than of kind. The dual clientele or money traps, for example, may be weakened, but neither is likely to disappear altogether. This means that every welfare reform package is likely to have a fragile support coalition. As chapter 4 shows, this has also meant that welfare reform initiatives make it onto the agenda only intermittently, and once they do, some group is usually well positioned to keep them from moving forward to ratification.

CHAPTER FOUR

The Past as Prologue

"If we get into the mind-set where the good becomes the enemy of the best, we will get nothing."
—Senator Daniel Patrick Moynihan, *July 23, 1987*

"The White House wouldn't sign a bill I would vote for, and I wouldn't vote for a bill the White House would sign."
—Representative Thomas Downey, *acting chair of the House Ways and Means Public Assistance and Unemployment Compensation Subcommittee, August 1987*

THE HISTORY OF comprehensive welfare reform initiatives between 1969 and 1995 is largely a record of failure. President Nixon's Family Assistance Plan passed the House but was blocked in the Senate by an odd coalition of conservatives who believed that its income guarantees were unduly generous and liberals who felt that they were too stingy.[1] President Carter's Program for Better Jobs and Incomes (PBJI) proposal also failed to win approval from Congress.[2] Indeed, one analyst wrote of the Nixon and Carter experiences that "so many factors contributed to the collapse of welfare reform . . . that who or what to blame is almost a matter of whim."[3] President Reagan managed to push through important changes in the AFDC program as part of the Omnibus Reconciliation Act of 1981, but only one of these changes, limiting most earnings disregards for program recipients to the first four months of earnings, was really a fundamental change in the program.[4] Moreover, 1981 was the high-water mark of the Reagan administration's efforts to transform welfare. President Reagan's New Federalism proposal of 1982, which would have resulted in a federal takeover of Medicaid in exchange for giving AFDC and Food Stamps to the states, was never even introduced in Congress. Over this same period, however, the Earned Income Tax Credit program of cash assistance to low-income families that (unlike most AFDC families) have at least one worker in the labor force was repeatedly and dramatically expanded.

This chapter addresses three questions about the political history of welfare reform initiatives. First, why was welfare reform so politically difficult to achieve; why could durable majority support coalitions not be built for reform? Second, why did the Earned Income Tax Credit have such a dramatically different history from AFDC during this period? Third, how (if at all) did the past rounds of reform in policymaking toward low-income families contribute to the enactment of comprehensive welfare reform in 1996? In particular, is there evidence that policymakers engaged in political learning about the traps that had ensnared previous welfare reform initiatives and thus were better prepared to avoid them in the Clinton and Republican rounds?

Growing Controversy over AFDC

The 1960s witnessed enormous turmoil in the Aid to Families with Dependent Children program, which in turn gave rise to perceptions of a "welfare crisis" and calls for fundamental change in the program. The most obvious indicators of turmoil are data on caseloads, participation rates, and program outlays, all of which grew explosively. AFDC rolls expanded from 3 million persons (caretakers and children) in 1960 to 4.3 million in 1965 and to 10.2 million by 1971, while combined federal and state expenditures rose from barely $1 billion to $6.2 billion.[5] Participation rates (the percentage of persons theoretically eligible for benefits who actually got them) rose from 33 percent in the early 1960s to more than 90 percent in 1971.[6]

Sorting out why these changes occurred is complicated. Demographic changes such as rising rates of out-of-wedlock births and family breakup were both important. These changes were especially dramatic among black families, where the percentage of children living with only one parent rose from 21.9 to 31.8 percent between 1960 and 1970; a growing share of those parents never had married.[7] As noted in chapter 1, welfare recipients and the attorneys who worked with them increasingly challenged state rules that restricted receipt of benefits, such as the "man in the house" rule, which restricted receipt of benefits by a woman who was cohabiting with a man not legally responsible for her children, and residency requirements that required an AFDC recipient to live in the state for a substantial period before becoming eligible for benefits. Most of these rules were overturned by the courts. Other court rulings made it harder to remove AFDC recipients from the program once they began getting benefits.[8] Efforts by the short-lived National Welfare Rights Organization to organize welfare recipients and the fading stigma attached to welfare receipt both contributed to increased participation rates. So did urban unrest, especially in 1967 and 1968, which led to a fear on the part of local officials that failure to ease AFDC administration could spark civil disorder.

From all ends of the ideological spectrum there was a perception that AFDC policy had failed. Advocates for the poor objected to low payments, "dehumanizing" eligibility checks, and inequities in payments across states, with the Southern states typically having the lowest payments.[9] Daniel Patrick Moynihan and other social critics worried that the overrepresentation of African Americans on AFDC rolls would further stimulate an already growing backlash against the program. Some critics (especially conservatives) objected to a system that provided comfortable incomes to liberal social workers but paltry benefits to its alleged targets.

Congress made several responses to the increase in welfare rolls, but nothing seemed to work. In 1962 amendments to the Social Security Act approved federal funding (sharing costs with the states) to provide social services to the poor as a way to help them out of poverty. The 1962 amendments also made permanent a 1961 provision that allowed payments to two-parent households where the father was unemployed; this was an effort to end disincentives to marriage and to weaken incentives for desertion when the father became unemployed. However, this AFDC-UP (Unemployed Parent) program was only a state option, and many states, especially in the South, did not offer it.

In 1967 Congress responded to the rapid growth in AFDC rolls by simultaneously enacting liberalizing and conservatizing reforms. States were required to disregard the first thirty dollars of a recipient's earnings and one-third of all amounts above that level in calculating benefit levels, increasing incentives for recipients to go to work. At the same time, Congress created a Work Incentives Program (WIN) that required states to register for training and employment "appropriate" mothers as well as fathers receiving AFDC benefits, with penalties for those who failed to comply. But because the program lacked effective enforcement mechanisms and funding, few recipients were required to do anything beyond registering.[10] Reflecting its frustration with the increasing caseloads, Congress attempted to freeze federal spending levels for AFDC cases caused by parental desertion or children born out of wedlock. But Presidents Johnson and Nixon both refused to implement the spending freeze, and it was repealed in 1969.[11]

Nixon's Family Assistance Plan

A new approach to the problem of policy was thrown into the stew of discontent with AFDC in the late 1960s when conservative economist Milton Friedman's proposal of a negative income tax (NIT) gained popularity as a solution to the problem of poverty. The idea was conceptually simple: everyone covered by the plan (which could be everyone in a society or a smaller group, such as families with young children) would be guaranteed a minimum level of income by the government. These benefits would be taxed back at some fixed rate (for example, fifty cents on the dollar) for every dollar earned above a certain level until the benefits disappeared. Thus persons covered by the program should always be better off by working more, although an additional dollar of earnings in the income range where income subsidies were being phased out would translate into less than a full dollar of increased income. Advocates argued that a negative income tax would provide incentives to work and (because it was not limited to single-parent families) discourage family breakup or absence of marriage altogether in situations where a father's earnings potential was limited.

Negative income tax proposals had a number of problems, however, especially perverse incentives. If benefits are taxed back at a low rate, which creates a stronger incentive to work, eligibility extends far up the income scale, which both increases the costs of the program and (as conservatives tend to view it) makes more people dependent on government handouts. Moreover, any sort of income guarantee and supplement may induce people to consume more leisure and work less than they would otherwise. The interaction of an NIT with means-tested programs of in-kind benefits (notably Medicaid) may worsen "income notches," where working more means losing eligibility for Medicaid or other programs and thus being worse off.[12]

Despite these design problems, expert opinion coalesced in the late 1960s around minimum guarantees and supplements as the best way to fight poverty. More than 1,200 economists signed a manifesto supporting a negative income tax approach in 1968.[13] The Kerner Commission on Civil Disorders also urged adoption of national income supplementation as a means to attack poverty. Others saw a negative income tax as a way to move the racial composition of families receiving assistance closer to that of the general population, "deracializing" the AFDC program.[14] But the idea of a guaranteed income enjoyed little support among either the public or Congress.[15]

A negative income tax plan with a minimum income guarantee had not been a part of the Nixon campaign platform in the 1968 presidential election, and there was substantial opposition to it within the new Nixon administration when internal debate on an NIT proposal began in 1969.[16] But the proposal also had a forceful advocate in the president's assistant for urban affairs, Daniel Patrick Moynihan. President Nixon endorsed the negative income approach in an August 1969 televised address, apparently persuaded by the opportunity to put a bold Nixonian stamp on social policy, by state and local pleas for fiscal relief from the costs of welfare, and by a desire to move away from a welfare system that spent a large share of its expenditures on the salaries of "liberal" social workers.

The administration's proposed family assistance plan (FAP) would have provided a minimum income guarantee only for families with children: $1,600 for a family of four ($500 for each adult and $300 for each child). States that already had higher benefit levels than those in the plan would be required to supplement FAP benefits to ensure that some families were not made worse off. In addition, the first $720 of a family's income would be disregarded; one dollar of FAP benefits would be taken away for every subsequent two dollars of earnings until all benefits were phased out. The AFDC–Unemployed Parent (AFDC-UP) program would become mandatory for all states, and the heads of all FAP families would be subject to a work requirement. In the initial version of the FAP, the penalty for failure by a family head to accept suitable work or training to comply with work requirements was $300 per family.[17]

The president was careful to deny that FAP represented a guaranteed annual income, although of course it did. Penalties for failure to work were intended to reassure conservatives concerned about the effects of the proposal on parental work effort. From the outset, however, the dual clientele trap and the fragility of FAP's support coalition loomed large. Conservatives thought that work requirements were too weak and, if given the chance, were tempted to vote for amendments that strengthened them. Liberals thought that benefit levels were far too low to provide an adequate income for children and would try to raise them if they had the opportunity. The money trap was a problem too: the desire of the administration to limit federal spending increases on welfare while providing fiscal relief to the states and localities (which were seen as important allies in pushing the FAP through) meant that benefit levels would have to be extremely low and that benefits would have to be phased out at a high rate as earnings rose, lowering the percentage of the population covered by the FAP (and thus lowering program costs), but also lowering incentives to work among FAP families facing very high marginal tax rates. Lack of funds also meant that little funding would be available for training and child care, so that FAP's work requirement would have little practical effect. Fiscal relief was limited as well, undercutting support from states and localities.[18]

At first, prospects for congressional adoption of the family assistance plan looked bright. Wilbur Mills, chairman of the House Ways and Means Committee, shepherded it through the committee. It passed the House in April 1970 with the help of a closed rule preventing hostile amendments on the chamber floor that could siphon off support. But the bill quickly ran into trouble in the Senate. During Senate Finance Committee hearings, Senator John Williams (Republican, Delaware) and other conservatives showed that as a result of interactions of FAP, food stamps, and the income-tested Medicaid program, the plan contained "notches" in which increased earnings would actually make a family worse off. They also criticized incentives to have a first child to qualify for FAP benefits (childless couples got nothing; those with one child received $1,300) and criticized work requirements as meaningless in practice.

These highly visible perverse incentives led the Nixon administration to overhaul the proposal, including a gradual reduction of Medicaid benefits as income rose and modestly stiffer penalties for refusal to work. But Senate conservatives in both parties argued that the new bill had simply created a different set of work disincentives because it phased out benefits faster at low-income ranges.[19] Many liberal Democrats (prodded by the National Welfare Rights Organization, which opposed work requirements and favored more generous benefit levels) also opposed the bill.[20] Nor did it help that the Senate Finance Committee was, as Moynihan said, "dominated by Democrats representing Southern states, where FAP would have its greatest impact on the social order, and Republicans representing Western states, where welfare was a minimal problem and reform a marginal concern."[21]

The Family Assistance Plan failed to clear the Senate Finance Committee in 1970, and it fared little better in the next Congress. In the House the Ways and Means Committee stiffened work requirements and offered additional fiscal relief to states and localities to gain support. The bill managed to get through the House, again using a closed rule, in 1971. Once again, however, things bogged down in the Senate, where Senator Russell Long (Democrat, Louisiana) controlled the flow of welfare legislation and had a much more conservative agenda.[22]

The adoption of other legislation further weakened the prospects for building a congressional coalition for the plan. Conservatives managed to win stiffer AFDC work requirements as part of a broader Social Security bill in 1971 and had little incentive to support an FAP bill. Similarly, passage of general revenue sharing by Congress in 1972 lessened the interest of states and localities in fiscal relief offered by what was now seen as a long-shot FAP bill.[23] The president too lost interest. After the departure of the plan's chief author, Daniel Patrick Moynihan, from the White House in 1970, the bill had almost no champions there.[24] In 1972 three plans—a proposal by Senate Finance Committee chairman Russell Long to replace AFDC with guaranteed jobs at a subminimum wage, variants of the House-passed bill, and a more liberal alternative backed by Senator Abraham Ribicoff (Democrat, Connecticut)—contended in the Senate, but none could command a majority. In the end, only the adult categories of public assistance—aid to the aged, blind, and disabled—were federalized and provided a guaranteed minimum income by the Social Security Act of 1972. This provided further fiscal relief to the states, and separation out of these sympathetic (because they were not expected to work) clienteles would make it all the more difficult to provide a minimum income guarantee to the able-bodied poor in the future.

Carter Tries Again

The period from 1973 to 1976 was relatively quiet for welfare reform. Negative income tax proposals for low-income families were repeatedly floated within the Nixon and Ford administrations but never succeeded in winning White House support. There was movement outside government, however. In 1976 the American Public Welfare Association, the National Governors' Conference (predecessor to the National Governors' Association), and the Committee for Economic Development, a group of business leaders, all endorsed proposals calling for greater federal participation in setting minimum benefits in welfare programs with the objective of lowering interstate differences in benefit levels.[25]

Welfare reform gained additional momentum with the election of Jimmy Carter to the presidency in 1976. During the election campaign, a pledge to "clean up the welfare mess," had been one of Carter's major applause lines. He had never provided a clear idea of where he planned to go with his pledge, although he did express on several occasions a preference for a more uniform benefit structure and fiscal relief for states and localities.[26] And his campaign pledge did have an important effect on later events. Although warned by members of his transition staff that incremental reforms would be easier to pass than a comprehensive bill, Carter insisted that, having campaigned on the issue, he had a responsibility to propose comprehensive reforms.[27] Thus his election pledge simultaneously helped ensure that welfare would be on the new administration's agenda and raised expectations that were unlikely to be met.

After taking office, the Carter administration began to formulate a welfare reform proposal even more ambitious than Nixon's. It sought to reduce interstate disparities and differences in benefit availability for single- and two-parent families and to reduce the array of cash and near-cash (for example, food stamp) programs to make administration simpler. But the new administration sought to build a coalition from the same conflicting groups that Nixon had: liberals who sought higher benefits with national minimums, conservatives who pressed for stronger work requirements applied to a larger share of the AFDC caseload and resisted extending welfare to new groups among the working poor, and states and localities (including New York, now represented by Moynihan as chair of the newly created Senate Finance Subcommittee on Public Assistance) seeking fiscal relief. Turf battles further complicated the task: the Department of Health, Education, and Welfare and the Department of Labor battled over whether an administration plan should give higher priority to cash assistance or public service jobs, while the Departments of Agriculture and Housing and Urban Development sought to ensure that food stamps and housing subsidies were not folded into (and thus eliminated by) a single comprehensive cash grant. Recipient groups and representatives of states and localities also fought for inclusion in the planning process.[28] And as with FAP, preventing income notches' resulting from the interaction of the cash programs with Medicaid, food stamps, and housing subsidies was a difficult problem.

Compounding these problems was the money trap. There was little presidential or congressional appetite for increased spending on anything that could be labeled welfare. President Carter initially insisted that his administration's welfare reform proposal not cost the federal government more than the status quo, which risked turning welfare reform into a game in which any money provided to increase benefits in low-benefit states, fiscal relief to the states, or public sector jobs would have meant that benefits would have to be lowered for other recipients.[29] The president eventually agreed, reluctantly, to some increase in federal expenditures above the status quo. But severe cost constraints meant that any public service jobs would have to be at the minimum wage, antagonizing congressional Democrats' labor union allies, and that benefits would have to phase out quickly as earnings increased, weakening work incentives for low-income workers.

The Carter administration's welfare reform proposal, awkwardly named the Program for Better Jobs and Incomes (PBJI), was revealed in August 1977. In the administration's proposal, PBJI would replace AFDC, SSI, and food stamps with a two-tier program providing different levels of income guarantees for those expected to work and those not expected to work. The latter, a group that included single parents with children younger than age fourteen, would be guaranteed an income of $4,200 a year for a family of four, with a basic reduction rate of 50 percent for earned income. As a concession to Russell Long, mothers with children ages seven to thirteen were expected to work part time during school hours to remain in the upper tier.[30] For those expected to work (two-parent families and single-parent families with older children), the basic benefit for a four-person family was only $2,300, with a 50 percent reduction for earnings over $3,800. In practice, both benefit reduction rates and the tier structure were more complex.[31]

The biggest difference between PBJI and FAP, however, was the Carter program's much greater emphasis on public service jobs and training slots—up to 1.4 million of them at the minimum wage—that would be available to the working poor as well as welfare recipients.[32] To encourage movement out of public service jobs, the Earned Income Tax Credit was to be expanded, with eligibility limited to those in private-sector jobs. To gain support from states, each state was guaranteed at least 10 percent savings over its current welfare spending in the first year of PBJI, with fiscal relief escalating in later years. The problem of interaction with Medicaid (not only potential income notches, but a potential explosion in costs if all PBJI cash assistance recipients became eligible for Medicaid) was simply set aside with a promise that it would be addressed in a Carter administration national health insurance proposal anticipated for 1978.

Implementation of PBJI was not scheduled until 1981, moderating immediate demands on the budget so that the president could meet his objective of a balanced budget by fiscal year 1981. The initial cost of putting PBJI in place was very conservatively estimated by the administration at $30.7 billion in 1978 dollars, roughly $2.8 billion or 10 percent above the status quo.[33] However, the Congressional Budget Office later estimated that it would cost the federal government $17.4 billion more than the status quo by fiscal year 1982.[34] The much higher CBO estimates of PBJI's cost undercut the administration's credibility with legislators.[35]

The Carter administration's welfare reform initiative had several advantages over Nixon's FAP in winning adoption. The president's party had majorities in both chambers of Congress. PBJI also had a more credible work component than FAP, and the National Welfare Rights Organization was not around to pressure liberal Democrats for a more generous benefit structure. But PBJI faced serious problems, many of them familiar from the Nixon round. Concern over potential perverse incentives and their political consequences motivated many policymakers (especially conservatives) during bargaining. Long and many other conservatives still favored stronger work requirements and resisted an extension of cash assistance to a broader share of the populace, especially single people and childless couples.[36] Long also opposed any welfare reform bill that did not have work requirements for mothers of young children, at least on a demonstration basis, and he proposed that PBJI itself be field-tested before being implemented nationwide. Some conservatives, most important Al Ullman (Democrat, Oregon), chairman of the House Ways and Means Committee, thought that a cash benefit that varied with family size provided a perverse incentive for poor families to have more children.[37] And after the debacle of the FAP, many congressional leaders, including Ullman, were extremely reluctant to try another comprehensive reform initiative at all. Ullman warned HEW secretary Joseph Califano, "The liberals want too much and the conservatives want to cut back, and you can't get through the ambush. It's so complicated, whatever you do, you're going to have [income notch] situations like the ones [Republican Senator John] Williams found in FAP. All you need is one and your bill is dead."[38]

There indeed was something in the PBJI that each element of a potential coalition for welfare reform disliked. Business groups were suspicious of a larger public sector jobs program, and labor unions strongly disliked the creation of a potentially large new public service work force competing with their members at much lower cost because they were paid the minimum wage and lacked pension and health care benefits.[39] Congressional liberals and advocacy groups for the poor disliked the fact that benefit guarantees were far below the poverty line ($5,815 for a nonfarm family of four in 1977).[40] States and localities were unenthusiastic about a package that did not offer fiscal relief until 1981. The congressional agriculture committees, which regarded food stamps as part of an important log-rolling coalition to gain critical urban support for their core commodity support programs, were reluctant to see them abolished as part of Carter's consolidation proposal.[41] Moreover, welfare reform would be competing for legislative time in

Congress (and especially the House Ways and Means and Senate Finance committees) with other elements of an ambitious Carter agenda including tax reform, energy policy, a social security rescue package, hospital cost containment, and national health insurance.

Recognizing the potential for the Carter welfare reform initiative to get bogged down in Congress, House Speaker Tip O'Neill agreed to appoint a special ad hoc subcommittee made up of members from the three House committees with jurisdiction over welfare reform (Ways and Means, Education and Labor, and Agriculture). The subcommittee would try to develop a compromise plan that would be able to move quickly through all three of the parent committees.[42] But the prospects for success of this procedural maneuver were weakened both by the composition of the subcommittee (substantially to the political left both of its parent committees and of the full chamber) and by the subcommittee's inability to control the agenda: the parent committees would have the final say in rewriting the subcommittee's recommendations.[43] As was the case with FAP, the opposition of Russell Long, chairman of the Senate Finance Committee, was a strong obstacle. The Finance Committee moved forward in the fall of 1977 with a bill that provided stiffer job requirements, allowed states to require work in exchange for benefits ("workfare"), and provided more immediate fiscal relief for states and localities.[44] House liberals were just as adamantly opposed to the work requirements in the Long bill, making a compromise less likely.[45]

The special House subcommittee did succeed in voting out a bill consistent with the principles of Carter's plan on February 8, 1978, narrowly rejecting a cheaper and more incremental alternative proposed by Ways and Means chair Ullman. But with the chairs of the parent committees opposed to significant elements of the subcommittee proposal, none of the committees acted on it. With a heavy congressional agenda ahead, Senator Long signaling his opposition to crucial elements of the Carter plan (which would be sufficient to kill it in the Senate), and legislators reluctant to take on the contentious issue of welfare in an election year, it was given little chance of passage in 1978.[46] Low prospects for success further undermined already shaky presidential commitment to moving a comprehensive welfare reform package, making passage even less likely.[47]

In the late spring of 1978 there was a flurry of activity around proposals that would have adopted some of the less contentious elements of welfare reform—including fiscal relief for states and localities, simplified administration for AFDC, expansion of the Earned Income Tax Credit, and creation of a more modest number of public service jobs for welfare recipients than the Carter plan projected—as well as the more controversial requirement that all states cover unemployed two-parent families under AFDC while retaining AFDC, food stamps, and SSI as separate programs. A coalition of state and local government lobbies, concerned primarily with fiscal relief, intervened to try to broker a deal acceptable to the administration and the widely varying interests in Congress.[48] But conservatives insisted on substantially stiffer work requirements and adamantly resisted a national minimum benefit. Liberals believed that "strategic disagreement" rather than agreement to a minimal package was in their interests. They feared that a lowest-common-denominator package, containing only the elements that could pass Congress, would leave them worse off in immediate policy and make it more difficult in later years to pass a comprehensive package that included cherished goals such as a national minimum benefit.[49] In late June, O'Neill, citing both the budget-cutting mood of the House in the wake of California's Proposition 13 ballot initiative and Senate leaders' doubts that the Senate would take up any welfare reform bill passed by the House, called an end to efforts to arrive at a compromise bill.[50] Thus welfare reform died in the 95th Congress without reaching the floor of either chamber.

Welfare reform fared only a little better in the last two years of the Carter administration. Recognizing the limits on reform that had emerged in the previous Congress, proponents concentrated on more incremental and less expensive reforms, including elements that had some appeal to the various parts of a potentially broad but fragile coalition: fiscal relief, a scaled-back jobs program, and national minimum benefits. A bill containing minimum benefits and increased work incentives, but with little to appeal to proponents of stiffened work requirements, was approved by the Ways and Means Committee and passed by the House of Representatives in November 1979, but only through use of a closed rule that prevented any Republican alternatives from being considered. Republicans were nevertheless able to use the procedural gambit of a "motion to recommit with instructions" to force a vote on an alternative plan that would have turned federal AFDC payments into a fixed amount, given states added discretion to set their own work requirements, and allowed demonstrations in some states of completely state-run welfare programs. This Republican alternative failed narrowly on the House floor, 205-200.[51] Senator Long, who had backed the Republican alternative, once again refused to move welfare reform in the Senate Finance Committee in 1980, and it died.

As in the Nixon round of welfare reform, the dual clientele of AFDC forced policymakers in the Carter years to develop complex packages that bundled elements focusing on the welfare of children and responsibility for their parents. In practice these packages were prone to falling apart in the absence of very tight agenda control. Despite its meager legislative results, the Carter administration experience with comprehensive welfare reform was nonetheless important in its portents for the direction of welfare reform. It clearly suggested that guaranteed annual income plans were unlikely to be politically sellable, even if applied only to families with children.

The prospects for a guaranteed annual income plan were further dimmed by preliminary results from federally sponsored income maintenance experiments in several states that became available during this period. Although the appropriate interpretation of these results still sparks debate among experts, two findings—that guaranteed incomes could result in decreases in labor market effort and increases in family breakup—were quickly absorbed by politicians.[52] Moreover, as in the Nixon administration, the reforms in public assistance programs that were adopted in the Carter years probably made comprehensive welfare reform more difficult in the future. In particular, the Carter administration's reform that ended the purchase requirement for food stamps (adopted in 1977 and effective in 1979) led to a huge and unanticipated growth in program expenditures, making legislators even more wary of the potential costs of "reforming welfare."[53]

The Budget Blitzkrieg of 1981

The Reagan administration came to Washington with strong ideas about how to change AFDC, notably by lowering income limits for eligibility, dismantling the system of work incentives under which some of recipients' earned income was disregarded in eligibility and benefit calculations, and limiting coverage for the working poor that had been added to the program in the 1960s. Allowing workers to keep more of their earnings while continuing to receive AFDC was seen by the new administration as an ineffective mechanism for moving welfare recipients into work. As David Stockman, Reagan's first Office of Management and Budget director, said, he and the administration did not accept "the assumption that the Federal Government has a responsibility to supplement the incomes of the working poor."[54] On the contrary, the Reagan administration sought to get the ideas of a negative income tax and guaranteed income off the policy agenda, arguing that these provisions fostered dependency among groups that might otherwise avoid it.[55] The new administration's other objectives of balancing the federal budget, increasing defense spending, cutting overall domestic spending, and cutting taxes also affected its attitude toward welfare reform. Because most of the large social insurance programs were viewed as politically untouchable (as the administration learned when it floated a trial balloon on Social Security cutbacks in May 1981), and means-tested programs were viewed as problematic on other grounds, the latter emerged as an easy choice to take a disproportionate share of the domestic spending cuts.[56] Aid to Families with Dependent Children was among the most significant targets.

The Reagan administration's 1981 budget revision request, issued within two months of the president's taking office, called for important changes in the program, including a requirement that states impose work requirements (in private employment or community work experience assignments) for some AFDC recipients while restricting eligibility for those able to work.[57]

Perhaps the most striking thing about the proposals was not their substance but the vehicle used to push them through a recalcitrant Congress: reconciliation procedures established by the Congressional Budget Reform and Impoundment Control Act (CBRICA) of 1974. Although the act was originally intended as a mechanism to reconcile individual committee spending priorities with congressional spending priorities just before the beginning of a new federal fiscal year, the Reagan administration and its congressional allies used it to set and enforce spending priorities for committees much earlier in the budgetary process.[58] The Senate Budget Committee moved through its chamber reconciliation instructions to the committees that followed the president's priorities, easily defeating efforts by moderate Republicans and Democrats to restore some cuts in funding for programs targeted on the poor.[59] When the Democratic-controlled House Budget Committee took a more independent line, it was defeated on the floor by a coalition of Republicans and conservative Democrats. The same thing happened when individual authorizing committees reported back their spending cuts. Democrats in the House tried to force separate votes on the seven components of the budget-cutting package to emphasize the pain associated with specific budget cutting proposals, but Republicans and conservative Democrats rejected the attempt, winning instead approval of a straight up or down vote on the entire budget package. This procedure emphasized the budgetary aspects of the package and made the substantive cuts less visible. It, too, passed the House.

Unlike the Nixon and Carter reform proposals, which were comprehensive, most of the Reagan reforms to AFDC enacted as part of the Omnibus Budget Reconciliation Act (OBRA) of 1981 were relatively straightforward changes to specific program rules. These changes nonetheless had a significant cumulative effect on program spending and on the character of the AFDC program. Perhaps the most important was limitation of the "$30 plus 1/3 rule" for disregarding earned income in benefit calculations, which henceforth would be applied only for the first four months of employment. Deductions for work-related and child care expenditures were also reduced, and eligibility was limited to those with incomes below 150 percent of a state's standard of need. Strikers lost eligibility for AFDC benefits. The limit on assets held by AFDC families (excluding equity in a house and one car) was lowered to $1,000. States also gained increased leeway to impose community work experience (workfare) requirements as a condition for eligibility.[60] In fact, this represented a rejection by the Senate Finance Committee and the House Ways and Means Committee of the Reagan administration's proposal to *impose* workfare requirements on the states, a battle that was refought in 1988 and later rounds.[61] Overall, federal expenditures were expected to be reduced about $1.1 billion in fiscal year 1982, about a 13 percent cut, and cuts would increase in later years. Caseloads were expected to fall 10 percent immediately, with another 7 percent of recipients getting reduced benefits.[62]

Equally important from the point of view of the image of the program, however, was that AFDC receipt would increasingly be concentrated among women who did not work. Some women would lose AFDC eligibility because their earnings were too high, while others reduced their work effort to retain eligibility for AFDC and Medicaid. Thus while the trend was for more women to enter the work force, work participation by those on the AFDC caseload declined in the early 1980s, just the opposite of the message about the program that was needed to maintain its shaky political support.

Reagan's New Federalism

Even before the OBRA cuts took effect the Reagan administration was working on a follow-up round of AFDC reductions, and a second round was included in the administration's fiscal year 1983 budget proposal.[63] But these changes were overtaken by a much more dramatic proposal for change in the AFDC outlined in Reagan's 1982 State of the Union address. The New Federalism initiative proposed a program swap with the states under which the federal government would take over responsibility for the fast-growing Medicaid program and the states would take over responsibility for up to sixty-one federal grant programs, including AFDC and food stamps. A temporary federal trust fund would help the states manage the transition.[64]

The New Federalism proposal represented a dramatic reversal of the trend in the Nixon and Carter administrations toward increased federal participation in cash assistance programs. It had both long- and short-term roots. President Reagan had long been committed to shrinking the federal government's policy role generally and returning public assistance to state and local control.[65] More immediately, the Reagan administration was looking for a new theme for its 1982 agenda to dispel the public image left by the 1981 budget battles that it was interested only in cutting domestic spending.[66] Given looming budget deficits, short-term budget calculations were also important: OMB director David Stockman saw the New Federalism as a way to sell the president on increases in excise taxes that would be imposed immediately but transferred to the states only after four years, filling part of the short-term budget deficit.

At first blush, then, the New Federalism was a felicitous easy choice that married the administration's political, policy, and budgetary concerns. But conflict quickly emerged. Conservatives within the administration attacked both the federal takeover of Medicaid and the excise tax increases.[67] Just a few days before the State of the Union speech, the president reversed himself by vetoing any tax increases, weakening Stockman's enthusiasm for the proposal.[68] Governors and local officials, faced with a recession that was decimating their budgets, resisted taking over food stamps and AFDC. They disagreed with the administration's accounting, which showed the states coming out ahead in a "food stamps plus AFDC for Medicaid" swap because it assumed that Congress would make major cuts in the first two programs before turning them over to the states.[69] Moreover, even if states and localities came out even or slightly ahead in the aggregate, some states would be heavy losers while others would gain.[70] Governors also worried that the administration would use a takeover of Medicaid to make cuts in that program, eventually compelling the states to take up the slack.[71] Advocates for the poor worried that poor states, especially in the South, would engage in a race to the bottom in the absence of a national minimum benefit (anathema to the Reagan administration) or a requirement that the states at least maintain current benefit levels. And congressional leaders in the Democratic-controlled House of Representatives were largely hostile, a serious barrier since the proposal was expected to affect the jurisdiction of, and require review by, seven or more committees.[72]

Recognizing that Congress would be far more likely to adopt a package endorsed by both the Reagan administration and organizations representing states and localities, those groups entered into complex negotiations to try to reach a deal. Despite some accommodation by the Reagan administration (most notably, agreeing to keep food stamps out of the devolution package), negotiations ultimately foundered, and the New Federalism package was never introduced in Congress.[73]

Indeed, 1981 turned out to be the high-water mark for cutbacks in AFDC during the first Reagan administration. Cuts made in AFDC during 1982 were more modest than those made in 1981 and those in the administration's budget proposal.[74] The program cuts and now-standard mandatory workfare proposal that the president made in 1983 were turned down by Congress.[75] The administration continued to press an agenda that stressed the reassertion of traditional moral norms, especially relating to paternal obligation, and legislation chipped away at several court decisions liberalizing eligibility and benefit rules.[76] By 1984, however, the direction of change in AFDC policy had shifted modestly away from retrenchment, at least at the federal level. Eligibility limits and earnings disregards were both liberalized slightly.[77]

The Family Support Act of 1988

Several factors helped to put work-oriented welfare reform on the national agenda in the late 1980s. The increase in the number of middle-class mothers with young children who are in the paid labor force increased political support for requiring AFDC mothers to work. As Senator Moynihan said, "A program that was designed to pay mothers to stay at home with their children cannot succeed when we now observe most mothers going out to work."[78] In addition, the research of Charles Murray and others (discussed in more detail in chapters 5 and 6) refocused the welfare debate on issues of long-term dependency. Efforts by other social scientists to test or refute Murray's conclusions showed that while most individual welfare spells are relatively short because of cycling on and off the program, there was a substantial population of long-term dependents. Meanwhile, evaluations of state welfare reform experiments on transitions from welfare to work suggested that relatively low-cost programs could at least "modestly increase the employability of some welfare recipients."[79] All of these developments encouraged what was labeled a "new consensus" on the importance of work, including work requirements, as well as cracking down on absent fathers through stronger enforcement of child support laws.[80] Support for greater state discretion and experimentation increased as well. Although the level of consensus proved to be overstated as the discussion of details of welfare reform began, common ground among the participants in the debate increased at least slightly.

Legislation might not have moved forward, however, if President Reagan had not put welfare reform on the agenda with his 1986 and 1987 State of the Union addresses. Although the administration did not initially put forward a clear proposal, its preference was clearly for allowing states to experiment with program innovations, especially with respect to work requirements, by waiving federal statutory and regulatory requirements while not putting in any new federal money.[81] The nation's governors, who were concerned about rising AFDC costs, also stressed welfare reform.[82] Equally important, Democrats on the House Ways and Means Committee saw Reagan's speeches as an opportunity for movement on an issue that they cared about and that had been deadlocked for a number of years, and the Democratic leadership in the House saw the return of welfare reform to the agenda as an opportunity to put a Democratic stamp on important legislation.

Despite widespread agreement that something should be done about welfare reform, there was widespread disagreement about the substance of reform, reflecting traditional concerns about the program's dual clientele. Many Democrats in the House insisted that all states should be required to offer the AFDC–Unemployed Parent program, instead of having it as a state option (which only twenty-seven states offered).[83] House Democrats also wanted to require states to provide some minimum benefit level, or at least to provide incentives for low-benefit states to increase benefits, and to allow recipients who worked to keep more of their benefits. Conservatives opposed both national minimum benefits and mandatory AFDC-UP.

Another source of disagreement was whether to require states to set targets for minimum caseload participation rates in job training and community work experience programs, especially for AFDC-UP recipients. Conservatives feared that states would not require participation unless they were forced to do so and that with weak participation requirements, state officials would probably choose to help only those recipients most likely to make it off the rolls anyway (known as cream-skimming). Liberals contended that high participation rate requirements would spread resources too thinly and that work requirements would be both costly to administer and punitive, while governors worried that those requirements would require states to rush people through low-cost but not very effective programs to meet targets.[84] There was also disagreement on how generously to fund training and work programs for states—Republicans believed that expensive programs had not been proven effective.[85] Governors pressed for easier provisions for obtaining waivers allowing them to design their own program innovations and for a federal pickup of most added program costs.[86] The Reagan administration also pressed for increased waiver authority, including pooling money from AFDC, Food Stamps, Medicaid, and other programs to fund local experiments, while congressional Democrats strongly opposed tampering with the entitlement status of the programs.[87] There were also strong disagreements over which activities (education, job training, or work) should be required of recipients, whether such requirements should be applied to mothers of very young children, what services (day care, transportation, and transitional Medicaid for recipients moving into low-wage jobs) should be made available to recipients subject to work requirements and how long they should be provided, and whether public service jobs should be provided for recipients who could not find jobs in the private sector.[88]

There was little contention, however, on one issue: forcing absent fathers to pay more, and more reliably, for child support. In theory at least, child support enforcement avoids the dual clientele trap by transferring additional resources to the AFDC family unit from noncustodial parents without putting children at risk. Indeed, being tough on deadbeat dads was to prove very popular politically. Groups representing divorced fathers were the main opposition, protesting that measures such as mandatory withholding of child support payments from paychecks unfairly stigmatized fathers who were not in arrears.[89]

The early stages of policy formulation on welfare reform took place largely in Congress, especially on the Human Resources Subcommittee of the Ways and Means Committee. The entire debate, however, and especially its later stages, took place under repeated threats by the Reagan administration to veto any bill it did not like and tremendous pressures to cut costs in the era of big budget deficits and Gramm-Rudman deficit reduction legislation. As in earlier rounds, the politics of welfare reform was also complicated by jurisdictional splits, especially in the House. In addition to Ways and Means, the House Education and Labor Committee would have to approve training components in a welfare reform package, while the Energy and Commerce Committee would have jurisdiction over proposals to extend transitional Medicaid benefits to AFDC recipients moving from welfare into low-wage work (loss of health coverage was widely seen as the most formidable barrier preventing recipients from moving into private sector jobs).[90] And the agriculture committees in both chambers retained jurisdiction over the Food Stamps program. Unlike the Carter round, each committee was to develop its legislation separately, with the House Rules Committee tying the separate pieces of legislation together before the bill went to the floor.[91]

The original welfare reform bill introduced by Ways and Means Subcommittee chairman Harold Ford was clearly expansionist and expensive, $11.8 billion over five years. As in most previous packages, it combined elements designed to appeal to both liberals and conservatives, but it clearly leaned toward the liberal side.[92] However, the day before subcommittee markup, Ford announced that Ways and Means chairman Dan Rostenkowski had asked him to cut the cost of the bill in half, to $5.5 billion, to meet budget targets set by the House leadership. This was accomplished largely by delaying implementation of some parts of the bill and by forcing states to pay a bigger share. Republicans still opposed the bill, especially provisions setting minimum benefit standards for states and mandatory AFDC-UP nationwide, but they were outvoted.[93] The proposal was cut by another $1 billion at the full committee level in a bid to increase support among southern Democrats and Republicans; minimum benefit standards were dropped, but financial incentives to the states to raise benefits were retained.[94] House Republicans, meanwhile, developed their own plan, which was endorsed by President Reagan.[95]

Adding to its problems, the bill moved forward immediately after the October 1987 Black Monday stock market crash and in the midst of intense negotiations between the Reagan administration and congressional Democrats over deficit reduction. Borrowing a page from President Reagan's 1981 strategy, Democrats under Speaker James Wright tried in late October to pass their version of welfare reform as part of the reconciliation bill. Including welfare reform in the reconciliation bill had the advantages of limiting debate, eliminating coalition-shattering amendments, making the welfare provisions less visible, and putting maximum pressure on wavering conservatives within the Democratic caucus to accept provisions they did not like on a vote where partisan divisions are normally strong. But this attempt was defeated on the House floor by an alliance of Republicans and southern Democrats.[96] A separate welfare reform bill was then pulled off the floor twice because of fears it would not pass.[97]

Agenda control continued to be a critical issue in the House. Demo-crats sought to limit Republicans to a single up or down vote on the pack-age they had put together, fearing that in the prevailing antiwelfare and prodeficit reduction atmosphere, the welfare reform bill would move sig-nificantly to the right under an open rule, with work requirements being made more stringent and spending provisions stripped out. This in turn would decrease their bargaining leverage in conference negotiations with the Senate, which was expected to produce a more conservative bill than the House. The House welfare reform bill was brought up again in December under a restrictive rule that allowed only two substitutes to be considered: a Republican alternative costing $1.1 billion over five years and a Demo-cratic alternative that shaved $500 million from the committee bill and was intended to be more palatable to southern Democrats.[98] This shaved-down alternative was adopted by a vote of 230-194, largely on party lines.[99] Along with stiffened work requirements and child support enforcement, the bill retained some liberalizing elements, notably incentives for states to raise benefits, increased earnings disregards, transitional child care assistance, and substantially expanded transitional Medicaid for families leaving AFDC rolls.[100]

Action in the Senate proceeded very differently from that in the House and from past trajectories in the Senate. Senator Long, having retired in 1986, was no longer around to block reform initiatives that he did not like. Moynihan was now the acknowledged Senate Democratic leader on welfare reform, and he used his agenda-setting authority to try to promote consen-sus rather than blocking it. In particular, he and his chief staff person on welfare, Rikki Baum (who had recently completed a doctoral dissertation on the political perils of comprehensive welfare reform initiatives), pursued an incrementalist path, leaving out provisions that did not enjoy broad sup-port. Moynihan also worked very hard to make the effort bipartisan, both to ease passage though the Senate and to make sure that President Reagan would sign it. This was a tricky process because many Republican senators were reluctant to undercut the Reagan administration by signing on to an initiative that the administration was threatening to veto. And Moynihan tried to make welfare reform procedurally easier by limiting provisions to those within the jurisdiction of the Senate Finance Committee despite pres-sure to add provisions under the jurisdiction of the Labor and Agriculture Committees. This was easier in the House than in the Senate because the Senate Finance Committee also has jurisdiction over Medicaid, whereas House Ways and Means does not.

In July 1987 Moynihan introduced a bill with a much more modest price tag than its House counterpart. It had five initial Republican cosponsors, three of them members of the Finance Committee.[101] The bill did not begin to move through the full Finance Committee until 1988, however. Unlike the House sponsors, Moynihan did not even try to include a minimum benefit provision in his bill, believing that its cost and controversial nature made it a political nonstarter. The federal commitment to share costs of training and work programs was generous in its cost-sharing formula but modest and (unlike the House bill) closed-ended in its overall financing.[102] Moynihan's bill also emphasized stronger enforcement of child support laws, requiring that court-ordered child support payments be withheld from the noncustodial parent's paycheck, which Moynihan considered an engine that could pull less popular welfare reform provisions through Congress.[103] From the outset the bill gained much stronger bipartisan support than its House counterpart. It won a 17-3 victory in the Finance Committee, in part because it permitted up to fifty state and local experiments to provide alternatives to AFDC under federal waivers, a provision that reflected the Reagan administration's desire for more state discretion but sparked fears among liberals that the AFDC program might simply be experimented out of existence.[104]

Further conservative amendments were made on the floor, most notably one by Robert Dole (Republican, Kansas) that for the first time set a federal requirement (as opposed to allowing states to require) that at least one parent in AFDC-UP families participate for no less than sixteen hours a week in community work experience (workfare) programs. This amendment was approved despite strong resistance from the American Public Welfare Association, Senator Moynihan, and the nation's governors (who considered it very expensive to administer and of dubious merit in getting families off welfare). It won approval because Senate Republicans said that the Reagan administration would veto any bill that did not include it and because many Senate Democrats (especially those up for reelection in the fall) were reluctant to vote against a provision requiring able-bodied men to work a minimal number of hours in exchange for benefits. Another amendment required the states to meet specific enrollment targets for their education and job training programs.[105] The result was a somewhat more conservative bill and a stunning triumph for Moynihan's strategy of bipartisanship. The bill passed the Senate by a margin of 93-3 with its key elements—a capped entitlement for job training and education, an AFDC-UP mandate, and transitional Medicaid and child care—intact.[106]

Ways and Means Democrats initially used the language of strategic disagreement to strengthen the relatively weak bargaining leverage resulting from the much tighter margin of passage in the House. Tom Downey (Democrat, New York), acting chair of the Public Assistance and Unemployment Compensation Subcommittee, referring to the upcoming presidential election, said, "If President Reagan doesn't sign a bill, President Dukakis will. I'd rather come back next year and do a good bill than send a bad bill to the president."[107] But their bargaining leverage quickly dwindled further when the House approved a Republican-sponsored nonbinding resolution ordering its conferees to agree to a package no more expensive than the Senate bill ($2.8 billion over five years); conservatives again threatened that Reagan would veto anything more expensive.[108] Moreover, Dukakis's choice of Senate Finance Committee chairman Lloyd Bentsen (Democrat, Texas) as his vice presidential running mate gave congressional Democrats an added incentive to reach an agreement, so that the "dead cat" of blame for killing welfare reform was not laid on their (and Bentsen's) doorstep.[109] Thus House conferees were forced to begin backpedaling, agreeing to drop liberalizing elements of their bill and accede to more conservative elements of the Senate package that they did not like.[110] Reaching a conference agreement nevertheless took three months, with the final legislation much closer to the Senate bill.

Despite the grandiose claims made by its sponsors, the final version of welfare reform legislation, called the Family Support Act of 1988, was an incremental piece of legislation that was full of compromises between liberals and conservatives.[111] Most of the provisions favored by House liberals, particularly cash benefit increases, minimum national benefit standards, or incentives for states to increase cash benefits for single-parent families, were left out of the bill.[112] Nor did it provide the money that would be needed to make a major commitment to training and providing jobs for AFDC recipients. The total federal funding increase for the Family Support Act was only $3.305 billion spread over five years, of which just over $1 billion was to go to the new education, training, and work program.[113] This was certainly not an inconsequential amount in the era of Gramm-Rudman spending constraints, but it was hardly a revolutionary change, either.

The Family Support Act did include a number of steps to increase payment of child support by noncustodial parents.[114] States were also given positive and negative financial incentives to increase efforts to establish paternity. In addition, reflecting a concern that the current AFDC program was acting as a lure to teenagers to have children as a way to obtain a cash income and set up their own households, states were permitted to make living with parents or in another adult-supervised setting a condition of obtaining AFDC benefits for teenage mothers.

The strongest focus of the Family Support Act, however, was on trying to increase work effort. The politically unpopular Work Incentives program (WIN), which had always had trouble winning adequate funding from appropriators, was replaced by the Job Opportunities and Basic Skills Training program (JOBS), to be coordinated by state welfare departments. JOBS funding was provided in the form of a capped entitlement so that it could not be cut by appropriations committees. There was no direct work requirement for single-parent families. However, states were required to provide basic education, job skills training, child care, and transportation, plus two of the following four employment-oriented activities: job search, on-the-job training, work supplementation, and community work experience. The act also limited individual exemptions from JOBS, mandated state targets for both overall and targeted subgroup participation rates, and required funding to be spent on specific subgroups deemed particularly at risk of long-term dependency.[115] Overall, states were required to enroll 7 percent of their nonexempt clients in JOBS in 1990 and 1991, 11 percent in 1992, 15 percent in 1994, and 20 percent in 1995—relatively modest objectives shaped by the nation's governors, who feared that they could not meet more ambitious goals. States were required to impose a partial loss of AFDC benefits if recipients refused without good cause to participate in JOBS or to take any job that did not reduce their cash income.

Additional carrots were also provided to move AFDC recipients into the work force. Several earnings disregards were increased.[116] States were required to guarantee child care if it was required for participation in JOBS or to take a job.[117] Transitional child care assistance was to be available to those moving into employment for no more than one year (states could require parental cost sharing with payment on a sliding income-based scale). States were also required to continue Medicaid coverage for up to one year after an AFDC recipient became ineligible because of increased earnings, but the state could charge premiums or enroll recipients in a group plan after six months.[118] States were also required to pay transportation costs for JOBS participation.

The Family Support Act contained a compromise provision on the ever controversial issue of extending AFDC to unemployed parents (generally fathers) in two-parent families. All states were required to offer the program, but those that had not previously offered AFDC-UP cash benefits could limit payments to six months a year. Showing once again that extension of in-kind benefits is less controversial than cash, states were required to offer Medicaid benefits to these families even in months when they were not drawing cash benefits. As a quid pro quo demanded by the Reagan administration, states were required to make at least one parent in AFDC-UP families engage in community work experience (workfare) or another work-related activity at least sixteen hours a week. States faced increasing mandatory caseload coverage targets for the AFDC-UP work experience rule: 40 percent of caseload in fiscal year 1994, 50 percent in 1995, 60 percent in 1996, and 75 percent in 1997 and 1998.

The Family Support Act, in short, constituted an important shift toward increasing the work orientation of the AFDC program. But it also represented a compromise between contending approaches on how to achieve that goal. Welfare recipients were to be moved into the work force through a combination of carrots (increased earnings disregards, transitional child care, and Medicaid) and sticks (JOBS participation requirements for women; workfare for AFDC-UP fathers). Moreover, for single-parent families its focus was more on preparation for work through acquisition of skills than on actual work experience. And although adoption of the FSA reflects a masterful maneuvering through the welfare policy-making traps, the effects of the traps are clearly visible in the legislation. Vetoes exercised by liberals and conservatives were facilitated by the multiple veto points in the legislative process and are evident in FSA provisions such as exemptions and protections for women subject to JOBS participation requirements (the dual clientele trap), the devotion of substantial resources to lowering barriers in current policy to moving AFDC recipients into work (the perverse incentives trap), limitations on statutory waiver authority for states (the federalism trap), and the modest financing relative to the ambitions of the legislation (the money trap).

Policy Counterpoint:
Expansion of the Earned Income Tax Credit

Further insight into the policymaking traps constraining welfare reform in the quarter century before 1995 can be gained by comparing it with changes in the other program that provides cash assistance to low-income families, the Earned Income Tax Credit, over the same period. The two programs have had remarkably different politics and remarkably different histories. As noted in chapter 2, while AFDC benefits eroded and AFDC expenditures remained fairly flat in real terms, real expenditures on the Earned Income Tax Credit grew almost sixfold between 1980 and 1996. Although comprehensive welfare reform initiatives before 1996 were failing and most incentive approaches to the problems of poor families (notably a guaranteed income) were falling off the policy agenda, the EITC was thriving through incremental reforms: indeed, benefits were dramatically increased in 1986, 1990, and 1993. As Christopher Howard has pointed out, EITC expansion is all the more remarkable because it occurred during a period of economic slowdown, when politicians emphasized reducing budget deficits and created budgetary rules intended to restrain the expansion of entitlement programs. And it took place without the support of either an organized constituency or third parties (farmers for Food Stamps, providers for Medicaid).[119]

The structure of income support under the Earned Income Tax Credit is quite different from that of a guaranteed income for workers with very low earnings. Under a guaranteed income approach, income support from government is highest for families with no earnings and phases out at a steady rate (fifty cents for every dollar of earnings, for example) for every additional dollar of earnings. Under the Earned Income Tax Credit approach, families with no earnings get no benefits. For every dollar they earn, government provides a bonus (currently forty cents for every dollar of earnings for a family with two children) up to a given earnings maximum, at which point it starts to phase out like the guaranteed income. Thus at low income ranges, a worker under a guaranteed income approach might get to keep only 50 percent of earnings, while under the current EITC, workers might get 140 percent of their earnings.

The Earned Income Tax Credit had its origins in the battle over President Nixon's Family Assistance Plan. Senator Russell Long proposed the EITC in 1972 as an alternative to guaranteed income that would be targeted on the deserving poor because it only went to working parents. Benefits levels were to be modest, but would at least compensate low-income workers for rapid increases in Social Security payroll taxes. It was not adopted then, but Long continued to advocate it in following years. In 1975 Albert Ullman, the new chairman of the House Ways and Means Committee, backed it as well. Although opposed by the Ford administration, the program won approval in 1975 as part of a tax cut package that the administration and Congress both wanted.[120] Rather than the high-profile Nixon and Carter welfare reform packages that preceded and followed it, it was, as Howard has noted, "a small part of a larger revenue bill [on which] no hearings were held or votes taken specifically concerning the EITC . . . it generated little debate and reflected little input from interest groups."[121] For its first decade the EITC languished, fluctuating in its real value because the values of its phase-in and phaseout, as well as the value of the maximum credit, were adjusted for inflation on an ad hoc basis.

The expansion of the tax credit came in three steps. In 1986 Congress expanded and indexed the EITC as part of its tax reform effort; expanding the EITC helped to balance the lower tax rates enjoyed by those in higher tax brackets. The second round of expansion came in 1990 after Congress appeared to be stalemated over passage of a bill to aid state support for child care. Instead of putting most of its money into direct aid to the states for child care, most of the money was put into direct tax relief to poor families through the EITC. These successes had more to do with the politics of tax and child care policy than with the merits of the EITC. Conservatives, for example, preferred the EITC, which gave money directly to families, over funding for child care centers and for child care vouchers. But the program's growth focused the attention of academics, congressional liberals, and advocacy groups for the poor on the EITC because it was clear that, unlike comprehensive welfare reform initiatives, which were political losers most of the time, EITC expansion had real promise as a way to increase income to low-income families.[122] Thus after 1990 the EITC became a much more visible program, but without becoming a divisive lightning rod like AFDC.

It was in this more visible role that the third (and biggest) EITC expansion came as part of the Clinton administration's budget package in 1993.[123] That the administration would include an EITC initiative in its 1993 budget was a foregone conclusion. The administration's goals of expanding the Earned Income Tax Credit and increasing the minimum wage were intended to fulfill the campaign pledge to move families with one full-time worker out of poverty. In addition to that campaign commitment, EITC expansion was needed to offset for low-income families the impact of increases in energy taxes that the administration included in its 1993 budget. And it enjoyed powerful allies in the liberal advocacy community.[124] But the amount of the expansion and its targeting involved trade-offs and interactions with other administration initiatives. To lift families with more than two children out of poverty would require a larger credit, but that would interfere with the administration's deficit reduction objective, especially if the credit was implemented immediately rather than phased in. Targeting the tax effectively on the poor would require high marginal tax rates as the credit was phased out, but that would increase work disincentives. The

Senate's decision to kill a broad-based energy tax reduced the size of the credit needed to lift families out of poverty, but it also reduced the funding available for the tax credit.

The cost of an EITC expansion sufficient to move most families of four with a full-time minimum wage worker out of poverty was high: the administration's proposal to Congress was budgeted at $28.3 billion over five years. Passing such an expenditure increase independently would have been almost impossible. Meeting the provisions of the Budget Enforcement Act would have required too many cutbacks in other programs or increases in taxes. What made the Clinton administration's EITC initiative possible was its inclusion in the administration's big budget package, which involved huge offsetting revenue increases (especially on upper-income taxpayers). But because the package did contain so many unpopular measures, the relatively uncontroversial EITC measure was almost dragged down. The package passed the Senate by the narrowest possible margin (Vice President Al Gore voted to break a tie). Ultimately, Congress decided on an EITC expansion that raised expenditures on the program by $20.8 billion over five years, $7.5 billion less than the president had asked for. The credit was also introduced gradually, with full phase-in occurring in the presidential election year of 1996.

Why was the EITC able to win repeated expansion in a period when AFDC was encountering so many political difficulties? A major part of the answer can be found by comparing the traps confronting welfare reform with the policy constraints facing the EITC (table 4-1). Most obvious is the difference in the dual clientele trap. While welfare reform initiatives were constantly bedeviled by policymakers' different attitudes toward "deserving" children and "undeserving" (mostly nonworking) AFDC parents, the fact that at least one parent in every EITC family was working meant that both parents and children were likely to be perceived as deserving. Moreover, in comparison with raising the minimum wage—a primary alternative as a way to aid low-income working families—the EITC had important advantages. Unlike the minimum wage, the EITC was targeted at the constituency that policymakers thought was most in need of help rather than delivering benefits to middle-class teenagers. Because the credit uses carrots rather than sticks to secure desired parental behavior, EITC policymaking has not become bogged down in fights over how to get parents into the work force without harming children.

The EITC also enjoyed advantages over AFDC with respect to other policymaking traps. The credit does not have the perverse incentive of causing

Table 4-1. *Policymaking Traps and the Earned Income Tax Credit*

AFDC policymaking traps	Applications to EITC (before 1995)
Dual clientele trap	
Policymakers cannot help poor children (popular) without also aiding parents (unpopular); cannot do things that make parents worse off (popular) without also risking making poor children worse off (unpopular)	Less critical because EITC parents are working and thus less likely to be seen as undeserving and less concentrated in racial/ethnic minorities; effective targeting on families with children increased support for EITC
Perverse incentives trap	
No effort to help poor families can avoid creating incentives that policymakers and public are likely to see as undesirable; no plausible welfare reform can avoid creating some new perverse incentives or exacerbating some existing ones	Lack of negative impact on demand for low-income labor increased support for EITC; EITC perverse incentives significant but much less visible than those in AFDC; little empirical evidence on their magnitude available until after 1993
Federalism trap	
National policymakers cannot give states flexibility to do things they like without running the risk state policymakers will also do things some national policymakers do not like; cannot increase national standards without undercutting flexibility some states desire and creating demand for federal compensation	Not applicable; EITC based on single national standard
Money trap	
No meaningful welfare reform possible without spending more money than public thinks is necessary or Congress wants to spend	EITC expansions can be hidden in big tax bills with offsetting revenues; indexation since 1986 keeps benefit base from eroding
Cross-cutting institutional barriers	
Coalitions for welfare reform inherently fragile because no legislative majority can be built for reform without legislators who disagree with some elements of package and are likely to defect if separate votes are held on those elements	Relatively low number of program provisions and their highly technical nature lower probability of losing votes on specific provisions from political extremes; inclusion in omnibus (usually tax) legislation lowers probability that program will become focus of opposition

employers to decrease their demand for low-skilled labor that many economists associated with the minimum wage. It does, however, contain other
perverse incentives for recipients, including incentives to overstate income to
qualify for a higher EITC benefit, marriage penalties (two low-income workers may lose EITC benefits when their incomes are combined), high marginal
taxes in the phaseout range for the benefit, and incentives to fraudulently
claim nonexistent beneficiaries. But the perverse incentives in the EITC are
much less visible than those in AFDC (for example, the risk of losing
Medicaid when AFDC eligibility is lost), and their absolute size was probably
relatively modest when the EITC benefit was small. Equally important, these
perverse incentives have generally been overwhelmed by the twin messages
that the credit "makes work pay" and does not risk shrinking demand for
low-skilled workers.[125]

The EITC also enjoyed a relatively weak money trap, despite the large
spending increases involved in recent program changes. The reason is that
EITC expansions, unlike welfare reform proposals, were generally considered as part of big tax or reconciliation packages in which significant new
revenue was generated by other provisions. Thus EITC bills did not have to
identify specific revenue sources that would be used for program expansions. And the fact that benefits have been indexed since 1986 meant that
program advocates had to exert less effort simply keeping real program
spending levels stable. Because the credit was a purely federal program, it
did not become bogged down in conflicts over the proper mix of federal and
state roles and funding obligations. Because tax legislation comes before
Congress regularly, no separate legislative vehicle is required, as is the case
with welfare reform legislation. Perhaps most important, however, is the
program's weak susceptibility to the problem of fragile coalitions because of
the technical nature of the program's provisions, its inclusion in and low
visibility within bigger legislative packages, and the popularity of the concept of aiding families of the working poor.

There was more to the EITC's success relative to AFDC in the 1980s
and early 1990s than weaker traps, however. Whereas AFDC created political problems for all who tackled it, the EITC thrived because it appeared to
do the opposite: solve otherwise divisive problems for politicians in ways
that satisfied everyone. Need to raise broad-based taxes (such as an energy
or an excise tax) without appearing to hurt poor families? An expanded
EITC was the perfect solution because it could target countervailing benefits to those families. Want to help low-income families with their child care
costs in a way that skirts divisive issues of regulating child care providers

and avoids criticism by cultural conservatives who argue that subsidizing child care provides incentives to mothers to work outside the home rather than staying home to raise children? Again, the EITC can provide a way around this problem by giving cash directly to parents, who make decisions about what sort of child care provider to use or whether to forgo additional income by having a parent (usually the mother) remain home. Need to justify opposition to an increase in the minimum wage without appearing to abandon low-income families, as many moderate Republicans and "New Democrats" sought to do in the late 1980s and early 1990s? Again, support for the EITC can be just the ticket.[126] In short, supporting some level of EITC expansion became a political good choice that provided political and policy awards to legislators of a variety of political stripes and that facilitated coalition building within and across parties rather than fracturing coalitions.

The Earned Income Tax Credit is not without problems, of course. It has major shortcomings as a mechanism for delivering income supplements on a steady basis to the working poor because most recipients get it as a once-a-year lump sum rather than every month, as with AFDC. Moreover, the EITC probably reached its political limits with the 1993 expansion. In 1997 families with two or more children received a credit of 40 percent on earnings of up to $9,156 for a maximum of $3,656. EITC benefits for these families did not fully phase in until earnings reached almost $30,000.[127] Any further expansion would be extremely costly. Indeed, EITC politics since 1995 has focused primarily on program abuse and potential cutbacks rather than on further expansion.[128]

Nor does the expansion of the EITC appear to offer lessons that could have been used to make reform of AFDC less contentious, unless AFDC could somehow be transformed into a program in which most recipients worked and were perceived by politicians and the public to be working, and thus deserving. Indeed, as families of working poor increasingly received assistance from the EITC, Food Stamps, and other programs rather than AFDC, receipt of AFDC became increasingly concentrated among the poorest, least skilled, and least likely to be working.

Patterns and Lessons in Welfare Reform

The legislative history of the five rounds of welfare reform initiatives between 1969 and 1988 shows a number of recurring patterns in the way welfare reform gets on the legislative agenda and the constraints on enacting comprehensive reform. But it also shows that there is no single procedural or substantive template that successful or unsuccessful reform initiatives invariably follow.

Getting on the Agenda

In the five instances of welfare reform policymaking examined here, windows of opportunity for comprehensive reform initiatives to make it onto the agenda usually opened quickly and frequently closed just as quickly, leaving failed initiatives to die a slow, torturous death.

Developments in the problem stream appear from the cases examined here to be least helpful in understanding the timing of initiatives. Welfare was almost always seen as a problem. But that does not mean that politicians will stake a claim to addressing the problem if they do not have any proposals that have a reasonable prospect of both political and policy success. Indeed, they may have strong reasons to keep public focus away from welfare reform so that they do not reap the blame for it.

The conjunction of two factors appears to underlie most welfare reform initiatives. The first is in the policy stream: a widely held view among policy experts on a particular approach or package of approaches to reform that offers an easy choice to its proponents—that is, it at least initially appears to minimize difficult political trade-offs, perverse incentives, and threats to strongly held political values for those pushing for the reform. The negative income tax combination of income guarantees and incentives played this role for President Nixon's Family Assistance Plan, the combination of concentration on the truly needy and devolution in the first Reagan administration, and training and work requirements in the Family Support Act round.

The second major factor facilitating welfare reform initiatives is in the political stream: presidential leadership to put the issue on the agenda and put presidential credibility and prestige on the line. This does not always require a campaign commitment: neither Nixon's FAP nor the Family Support Act was the result of commitments made during a presidential campaign. But in both cases clear presidential commitments were made to reform either in the State of the Union Speech or (for FAP) in a separate, high-profile address. Presidential commitments have several important consequences: they signal the executive bureaucracy that the president thinks that the matter is important and that they should mobilize behind it; they put presidential credibility at stake, making it more difficult to back away; and they mobilize legislators and advocacy groups to support or oppose the initiative and prepare alternatives.

But consensus on a particular welfare approach and presidential commitment can dissipate quickly. Although it may initially appear to policymakers that there is an expert consensus on a particular approach to welfare reform, the approach may come under attack from threatened stakeholders or from those who see perverse incentives built into it. Cost estimates are likely to escalate as well.

Presidential commitment is just as shaky. Presidents learn quickly that although broad agendas may be helpful in getting elected, they have to choose a few priority issues on which to concentrate their limited political resources if they are to get any of their program through Congress. Presidents also learn that although welfare reform can be a popular issue in the abstract, the details are a political minefield on which there is little consensus among legislators. Presidents almost always lose control of welfare reform policymaking when Congress becomes involved. Thus presidential commitment may erode quickly if a president decides that welfare reform is far more complicated, involves unforeseen costs to other cherished policy or political objectives, or is a poorer prospect for legislative success than he originally bargained for. Support may also erode if the president sees Congress moving the substance or spending level for welfare programs in a direction of which he disapproves.

Policymaking Traps and the Enactment of Welfare Reform

Once welfare reform is on the agenda and a presidential commitment has been made, several barriers work together to prevent enactment. Indeed, each of the welfare reform policymaking traps outlined in chapter 2 appears in the cases examined here as a barrier to reform. Some appear in every round and some more intermittently (table 4-2).

The most obvious and important of these is the ubiquity of the dual clientele trap. Almost all proposals for reform are perceived by some policymakers to risk either harming innocent children or rewarding undeserving parents. What makes the trap particularly likely to lead to a collapse of welfare reform is that policymakers vary widely in the importance they place on the welfare of poor children and the behavior of adult AFDC recipients. If all members of Congress viewed such trade-offs similarly, it would be easier to assemble packages that balanced measures designed to improve the welfare of children with those designed to alter the behavior of adults (through stiffer work requirements, for example). But policymakers who care strongly about the behavior of adults and the dependency effects of welfare programs are likely to demand substantial policy changes in a conservative direction (tougher eligibility standards, work requirements, or fiscal sanctions for failure to comply) in AFDC in exchange for relatively modest changes to improve child welfare. Those who place a greater emphasis on the welfare of poor children are likely to demand the opposite trade-off. Finding a middle ground acceptable to both is extremely difficult.

The same political dynamic can be seen in the perverse incentives and federalism traps. Conservatives worry that welfare reforms that provide income guarantees will reduce the labor supply of the poor, that basing benefits on family size will encourage the poor to have more children, and that expanding the population receiving cash benefits will result in greater dependency. Liberals are far more concerned about the incentives that AFDC (and now TANF), or alternatives like Reagan's New Federalism proposal, create for states to keep benefits low. Although liberals and conservatives might concede that the concerns of the other are legitimate, they disagree strongly about how important the other's concern is relative to their own, making it difficult to split the difference and find a mutually acceptable middle ground.

The money trap has also been important in limiting prospects for comprehensive welfare reform initiatives. Because AFDC was so unpopular and policymakers (including presidents) as well as the public thought that welfare reform should reduce costs, or at worst cost no more than the status quo, getting additional money for public assistance has been very difficult. Getting money for benefit increases has been almost impossible, especially when increases foist added costs onto the states. Efforts to impose minimum benefits have always provoked not only state (and congressional) protests against the restriction of state flexibility but also state demands that the federal government foot the bill. In addition, as early as the Carter round of welfare reform, the creation of the Congressional Budget Office strengthened the money trap by making it harder to hide the increased costs associated with welfare reforms. The later imposition of budget rules that required expansionary budget initiatives to be offset by budget cuts or tax increases made it even harder to fund either liberal welfare initiatives or work-oriented packages that contained enough sweeteners on child care, AFDC-UP, and other provisions to make them acceptable to liberals.

Fragmented political institutions have worsened the problem of building a coalition among policymakers with polarized views of AFDC's two clienteles, making stalemate more likely. Because legislative initiatives can be

Table 4-2. *Policymaking Traps in Welfare Reform, 1969–88*

AFDC policymaking traps	Nixon FAP initiative	Carter PBJI initiative	Reagan 1981 initiative	Reagan new federalism initiative	Family support act round
		Dual clientele trap			
Policymakers cannot help poor children (popular) without also aiding parents (unpopular); cannot make parents worse off (popular) without also risking making poor children worse off (unpopular)	Conservatives viewed FAP income guarantees as too generous, threatening work effort, while liberals saw them as too stingy, offering inadequate protection to children; conservatives resisted extension of income support to larger segments of working poor	Conservatives viewed PBJI income guarantees as too generous, threatening work effort, while liberals saw them as too stingy, offering inadequate protection to children; conservatives resisted extension of income support to larger segments of working poor and to single adults and childless couples	Reagan administration proposals for cuts in income eligibility and earnings disregards strengthen dual clientele trap, but concentration of cutback on highest-income AFDC recipients weakens it	Potential end to entitlement to AFDC and Food Stamps heightens dual clientele trap	Dual clientele trap strengthened by conservative insistence on mandatory work requirements and liberal insistence on minimum benefits and mandatory AFDC-UP; weakened by inclusion of child support enforcement provisions, seen as helping children, lowering program costs, and hurting only "irresponsible" noncustodial parents
		Perverse incentives trap			
No effort to help poor families can avoid creating incentives policymakers and public likely to see as undesirable; no plausible welfare reform can avoid creating new perverse incentives or exacerbating existing ones	Interaction of health care and food stamps with FAP exacerbates "income notch" work disincentives, limiting conservative support for FAP and strengthening fragile coalitions trap	Perverse incentives trap strengthened by administration funding caps requiring fast phase-out of benefits, lowering work incentives, and conservative concerns that varying benefits with family size increases incentives to have children, but weakened by promise of forthcoming national health insurance initiative, which weakened debate over interaction effects of PBJI and Medicaid	Cutback of income disregards and eligibility for AFDC recipients with earnings heightened incentives to reduce work to retain Medicaid eligibility, strengthening perverse incentives trap	Depends on structure of state programs	Conservative fears that higher minimum benefits and AFDC-UP eligibility will discourage work strengthen perverse incentives trap

Federalism trap

National policymakers cannot give states flexibility to do things they like without running risk they will also do things some national policymakers do not like; cannot increase national standards without undercutting flexibility some states desire and creating demand for federal compensation	Nationalizing focus of FAP makes it difficult to keep some states from being financially worse off without spending federal money	Nationalizing focus of PBJI makes it difficult to keep some states from being financially worse off without spending federal money	Reagan administration desire to mandate work requirements for states without spending more money strengthens federalism trap	Federalism trap strengthened by fears of liberals and state officials that federal takeover of Medicaid will result in cuts, imposing costs back on states; and liberal fears that state takeover of AFDC and Food Stamps will result in race to bottom	Apparent success of states in promoting moves from welfare to work weaken federalism trap

Money trap

Most welfare reform initiatives require spending more money than public thinks is necessary or Congress wants to spend	Administration-imposed spending caps meant marginal tax rate on FAP benefits had to be high; little money available to fund work programs	Backloading of PBJI costs weakened money trap, but lack of immediate fiscal relief also weakened support from state and local governments	Absence of added costs in Reagan initiative weakens money trap	Absence of new revenues increased state fears about taking over shared-cost programs, strengthening money trap	Heavy deficit reduction pressures lowered ability to fund training and employment programs, strengthening money trap, but low expectations for increased spending weakened trap

blocked at a number of stages, the politics of comprehensive welfare reform from 1969 to 1988 was characterized primarily by a game of agenda limitation and control. Proponents of reform, usually based in the executive branch, attempted to develop and maintain support for reform packages that had enough attractive elements for liberals and conservatives that neither side would block ratification. Both conservatives and liberals in Congress sought to simultaneously give their own policy preferences privileged status and prevent alternatives from ever being considered if they are deemed to be less desirable than the status quo in one way or another.

In the Carter and Nixon rounds the most successful agenda limitation came from Senator Russell Long, who opposed anything resembling a guaranteed annual income. Indeed, Long's opposition is probably a sufficient explanation of the failure of both rounds. Liberals realized that they needed a liberal bill coming out of the House to bargain with whatever Long might agree to in the Senate, and unless they could maintain very strong agenda control, any welfare reform measure that reached the House floor was likely to be subjected to amendments that would strip away liberalizing reforms and strengthen get-tough ones. Given the blame-avoiding motivations of legislators, it is extremely difficult for them to vote against such amendments. Thus in the Nixon, Carter, and FSA rounds, liberals repeatedly sought restrictive rules that would allow them to limit the number and scope of amendments to be considered on the floor. In all three they succeeded with the cooperation of the House Democratic leadership. However, only for the FSA proposal, when Long had retired and was not around to block legislation in the Senate, did their agenda control result in the passage of legislation—and only after the legislation was further amended by the House and in conference. Agenda control was even more critical in passing the Omnibus Budget Reconciliation Act of 1981, which provided a vehicle for the Reagan administration's major welfare reform changes.

Agenda control also played an important (if less visible) role in narrowing the range of proposals that were seriously considered by Congress. Many proposals that came to the fore in the mid-1980s and 1990s (such as block grants and much stiffer work requirements) had predecessors with powerful backers as early as the Carter administration. That these precursors to the welfare reform legislation of 1996 are little remembered is less because their support was marginal than because Democratic leaders were frequently able to keep them from being explicitly considered in full chamber votes, especially in the House.

Avoiding the Welfare Reform Policymaking Traps

The rounds of AFDC and EITC policymaking reviewed in this chapter are useful for what they tell us about the constraints on policymaking for low-income families and about the usefulness of the analytic framework outlined in chapter 2. But these rounds can also directly affect the 1990s rounds discussed in later chapters in at least two ways. First, changes in policies resulting from these rounds—what in chapter 2 were labeled policy feedbacks—might strengthen or weaken policymaking traps in later rounds or offer new routes to navigate around or through them. Second, policymakers may engage in *political learning*, drawing lessons from historical experience that increases their political skill in navigating around and through the traps that remain. This chapter closes by focusing on political learning; policy feedbacks are considered in the next chapter.

Political Learning

Do past rounds of welfare reform offer politicians who may be interested in tackling the issue again consistent lessons about the political costs and benefits of such initiatives and ways to maximize success? Some lessons do indeed emerge from these experiences, although they are more in the nature of contingent hints about political probabilities than ironclad laws.[129] Perhaps the most fundamental lesson suggested by experience is that welfare reform is a high-risk proposition because the prospects for success are limited. Any option that appears to be an easy choice offering political and policy rewards across a broad spectrum of politicians is, on closer inspection, likely to be a can of worms. The main lesson that members of Congress have learned about welfare reform initiatives, according to a Democratic staff member who is a veteran of several such initiatives, is, "You engage in one of these debates, you bloody yourself trying to argue your points, and the thing fails. . . . And members [of Congress], like Pavlov's dogs, you don't have to keep sending them to be electrocuted to know that this is a painful subject, and they don't want to come back to it anytime soon."[130] Thus it is not a great surprise that there are usually several years of quiet between welfare reform initiatives and that the initiatives are usually sparked in large part by presidential actions rather than originating in Congress. Indeed, by the late 1980s advocates for the poor inside and outside government appeared to have drawn a second lesson about policymaking for low-income families: that AFDC in general and comprehensive welfare reform initiatives in particular are not a productive vehicle for helping low-income families. AFDC was such a political hot potato, and so much decisionmaking was vested at the state level anyway, that attempting to change the program was likely to be futile at best, especially as a way of achieving liberal policy objectives. Such initiatives were more likely to be counterproductive. Thus advocates for the poor shifted much of their attention to programs that were viewed with greater sympathy by politicians and the public, such as the EITC, Medicaid, and the Special Supplemental Feeding Program for Women, Infants and Children (WIC). Although many of these programs also had low benefits, overlapping benefits (receiving food stamp, school lunch, and WIC benefits that provided double coverage for some meals) provided a backdoor means to enrich them. Similarly, excluding EITC benefits from income counted in determining AFDC benefits, as the Family Support Act provided, was another backdoor vehicle for making benefit levels more generous that involved little of the risk involved in promoting AFDC reform.

Yet although the experience of the Nixon through Reagan administrations suggests that each of the policymaking traps outlined here is an important constraint on the success of welfare reform initiatives, a third political lesson is that there are at least two ways to avoid getting caught in the traps where a reform initiative may break down entirely. The first is what may be called the blitzkrieg method: AFDC cuts enacted in 1981 as part of the budget reconciliation process suggest that it is possible for temporary coalitions to ram through legislation where there is very strong disagreement. In particular, reconciliation can be a powerful mechanism for avoiding the veto points in the normal legislative process. But the more comprehensive the reform of AFDC, the greater the congressional reluctance to short-circuit debate by enacting it through reconciliation legislation. The failure of the Reagan White House to enact major reforms in later years suggests that the windows of opportunity for blitzkrieg reforms are likely to be narrow and that such changes are unlikely to occur unless mechanisms like reconciliation are available that allow coalitions to overcome the normal multiple veto points in the legislative process. The Family Support Act is an example of the second path. In this case arriving at legislation was less rushed and, in the Senate at least, more consensual. It was also fairly modest. Indeed, as noted earlier, Senator Moynihan and his staff did learn from the failure of previous welfare reform initiatives their strategy of crafting an incremental, bipartisan strategy and bill.

The Family Support Act round also suggests a fourth political lesson: reforms that are incremental and limit the number of deeply divisive issues on the agenda are more likely to win enactment than those that are com-prehensive and include dramatic structural change. Multiple veto points in the legislative process have made compromise between opposing positions and political parties an important element in enacting legislation in most rounds of welfare reform. Support coalitions for reform packages are more stable if policymakers are willing to adjust their zone of acceptable out-comes both by accepting less of what they want and by letting opponents have something of what they want. Frequently this requires simply drop-ping provisions where the gap between opposing positions is deepest and thus the prospect for overlapping zones of acceptable outcomes is lowest. Again, the Family Support Act provides a good illustration. The act involved a compromise between the Reagan administration, which sought increased freedom for state action and tougher work requirements, and congressional Democrats, who wanted mandatory AFDC-UP, more funding for training and education, and (at least among House Democrats) higher benefits. Both sides had to settle for far less than they wanted but ultimately were willing to accept what could pass and declare victory and, equally important, let the other side declare victory as well. This was possible in part because some of the most divisive issues of principle, like a guaranteed annual income, were not on the table, while other divisive issues, like the nature of work require-ments, were left to be filled in later by the states.

The cases also suggest that whether policymakers are willing to make the compromises necessary for reform initiatives to succeed may depend heavily on short-term political calculations on matters that have little to do with welfare reform. The willingness of Democrats and Republicans to split the difference on welfare reform legislation in 1988 had much to do with the politics of the approaching 1988 presidential election, although passage was also aided by the bipartisan path that Senator Moynihan had pursued with Senate legislation over the preceding two years.

Another political lesson suggested by the Family Support Act is that the chances for welfare reform are at least modestly increased if the package includes elements that weaken the dual clientele trap because they appear neither to threaten the welfare of children nor to provide unearned gains to custodial parents. In the FSA this role was played by toughened child sup-port enforcement, a provision that most liberals and conservatives could agree on and that Moynihan saw as a legislative engine around which a wel-fare reform package could be assembled. The unifying potential of such provisions should not be overstated, however. Congress may simply enact the provisions on which there is consensus and leave the others behind. As one of the participants in the Family Support Act round noted, the effect of widespread agreement on child support enforcement was that it was "largely ignored throughout the debate. We wanted it to be an 'engine,' but it proved to be a caboose."[131]

The experience of Reagan's 1981 initiative suggests a final lesson that would become relevant in the 1990s: a welfare reform package that promises to save money, while anathema to liberals, can attract strong support from conservatives because it makes them better off in two respects: draining money from a welfare system that they abhor and reducing government spending overall.

Limitations on Political Learning

Experience, in short, suggests cautionary lessons about the difficulties of reforming welfare and the necessity of compromising and seizing the moment in avoiding traps to enact meaningful, if not revolutionary, reform. These lessons were largely ignored by leading policymakers in both the Clinton and the Gingrich rounds of welfare reform, as is discussed in later chapters. Indeed, the fact that both featured welfare reform as prominent components of their platforms (the Contract with America in the case of the House Republicans) suggests that they either were not aware of or chose to ignore the low success rates of previous welfare reform initiatives. President Clinton's call to "end welfare as we know it" epitomizes the rejection of incremental reform, and the seventeen-month delay between his taking office and unveiling his final welfare plan hardly reflects an awareness of the narrow windows of opportunities for reform.

The Clinton case is particularly striking because a strong effort was made early in the administration to learn from experience. In the summer of 1993 the administration asked the Urban Institute to organize a meeting of Carter administration welfare reformers with the new welfare reform planning team to pass on their experience. But at the meeting, according to a veteran of the Carter group (and corroborated by others present):

> Most of us Carter types left the meeting feeling that they hadn't heard what we were saying. . . . [Clinton administration welfare reform task force cochair] David [Ellwood] was just ebullient: "We're going to do this, we're going to do this, we're going to do this." The Carter people kept saying, "Do you really understand the political pitfalls? Do you understand the great risks of your losing

control of this on the Hill? You think this is great politics. Do you understand that when you get to the Hill you're going to be hit by the right for not doing enough. You're going to really antagonize some of your core constituencies. You're going to lose control of the bill. It's going to go farther to the right. You're going to split the Democratic party down the middle. There's going to be blood all over the place." . . . And David and everybody just kept saying, "It's totally different now, for the following reasons: one, two, three, four. And we just kept shaking our heads. And a number of us were also saying, "Look, look at our lessons. We went for a massive bill in 1977, overhauling everything in the welfare system. We fell flat our faces." . . .

And we could kind of almost see ourselves in the early months. You come in, you know, you want to change everything. And we really felt that they did not understand what lay ahead politically. Well, they've now had a series of months where they've had the crap beaten out of them politically.[132]

Two Clinton administration officials who attended the same 1993 Urban Institute event were struck mainly by the differences in the two episodes, and agreed that they had not heard anything that was very helpful in planning this round of welfare reform. As one said:

[The Carter people] were basically saying "We tried it, couldn't get it done; you're not going to be able to do it." And we still hear that in meetings, just last week from someone from that era. And it's sort of funny, because just because it can't be done once doesn't mean that it can't be done at another point in time. But I certainly heard a lot of bitterness and a lot of regret that they couldn't get it done, therefore "we don't think they [the Clinton people] can get it done."

The other thing that I was struck by was the Labor-HEW split in that time. They started the same arguments seventeen years later. . . . They had a very severe Labor-HEW split at that point in framework and in point of view. . . . In this round . . . there certainly wasn't that much of a split in point of view. And that's a major change this time around. I came away with things they didn't intend to have as lessons. . . . It was interesting; fascinating; but not helpful.[133]

Another Clinton administration official concurred:

[Their advice was], break it in small pieces. Send one little small piece through at a time if you want to get it done. You'll never get a big bill through. [It was] pretty negative, actually, I thought. . . . Times change so much. The thinking on welfare reform at that point in time was so different from the thinking on welfare reform today, and I don't know that they incorporated those changes in their comments. They tended to think that because it couldn't be done then, it can't be done now; and they didn't think about what's changed in basic philosophical differences, and the change in attitudes out in the community.[134]

What is interesting about this incident is that people on opposite sides of the Carter-Clinton divide seem to have heard the same things at the dinner; they just disagree about what lessons could and should be drawn from them, with the Carter people stressing continuities that make their experience useful to the Clintonites and the Clintonites tending to focus on differences that make the Carter lessons less useful. Even when historical comparisons are made, policymakers tend to discount historical similarities and to overemphasize differences.

Republicans, too, overestimated the ease with which welfare could be reformed when they came to power in the 104th Congress, and thus they tended to underestimate the power of the traps and tried to achieve too much, resulting in stalemate throughout 1995. When asked how much Republicans had learned from the experience of past rounds of welfare reform, a key Republican congressional staff member interviewed in February 1996 said, "Zero." Noting that he had recently by chance sat next to a veteran of the Carter administration's welfare reform initiative at a dinner party, he noted that it was "the only conversation that I have had . . . going all the way back to right after the [1994] election . . . with someone here in Washington that was essentially historical, pointing out all the parallels and things that aren't parallel, and the general point of how hard it is to pass a welfare bill in Washington."[135]

Five interrelated factors appear to have inhibited drawing a historical lesson in the two most recent rounds of welfare reform: the ambiguity or negative character of most lessons, previous campaign commitments, poor institutional memory, distance in time, and tendencies to overestimate one's own political capacities.

Ambiguous and Negative Lessons

Perhaps the most fundamental limitation on lesson-drawing by policymakers is the ambiguity of the lessons. Past rounds of welfare reform suggest not inexorable laws but rather possibilities and probabilities. If the Reagan administration experience in 1981 suggests that a strong presidential initiative can get a controversial welfare reform proposal through Congress before opposition can be mobilized, almost all the other cases suggest the opposite. If FAP, PBJI, and the New Federalism all suggest that a drawn-out process of welfare reform inevitably collapses, the Family Support Act suggests that such an outcome is not inevitable.

Drawing lessons can also be inhibited if the lessons learned from the past are negative. When asked what lessons the Clinton administration had learned from the process of trying to pass the Family Support Act of 1988, one of the administration's policymakers stressed negative ones.

> [Major lessons are] that we need the money. That capacity is a huge issue. That full participation is an absolute fundamental. That you cannot have a program that excludes 60 percent of folks and then requires 15 percent of those after that to do something and think that you're going to [change expectations]. The program will still mostly be about writing checks. The need to do more than just place people in the first job, to have some sort of worker support, on-going support, so people can stay off welfare rather than just get off welfare.[136]

These sorts of lessons can point policymakers in later rounds in a general direction of change, but they do not provide very precise help on the specific direction of change, and they say almost nothing about how to build and maintain a coalition of support for a policy that is likely to be divisive.

Previous Commitments

Even if policymakers formulating welfare reform are aware of the risks involved in a comprehensive reform package, the political realities may clash with the desire to keep campaign promises made by their political superiors. This problem was clearly evident in the Clinton round: the incoming president had made ending welfare as we know it a central element of his platform despite recent historical experience that suggested incremental reform was most likely to make it through. As the next chapter shows, this seemed like a perfectly reasonable choice given the information at hand in 1992. It was a dramatic pledge that reflected the needs of campaigning rather than the difficulties of governing, but one that the administration believed it had to redeem to maintain its political credibility. In the 104th Congress, Republicans similarly believed they needed to live up to the promise contained in the Contract with America to bring up for a vote each of the ten planks in the Contract, including one calling for dramatic overhaul of the welfare system, in a relatively unadulterated form.

Distance in Time

The more proximate the information—in time, policy arena, and political situation—the more likely it is to be used. This is particularly true of information on politics and policymaking. Thus drawing historical lessons by the Clinton administration's planners was inhibited by the long gulf of the Reagan-Bush years. The Carter experience, the last time welfare reform was tried under unified Democratic control of the executive branch and the legislature, was sixteen years old. Lessons from the Reagan era were not deemed appropriate, and lessons from the Carter years were either unfamiliar or seen as too dated to be useful. Clinton policymakers were unlikely to draw historical lessons from more recent experiences because they had occurred under divided government, with Republicans controlling the executive branch. Even passage of the Family Support Act of 1988 did not appear to offer many lessons because, as one said, "'88 was such a Hill-driven operation. This was way different. Reagan proposed [welfare reform], but then all the work and what was in the proposal came from the Hill. So I guess it's hard for me to draw parallels because of that."[137] Ironically, congressional Republicans in the 104th Congress did not view the FSA passage as analogous either, despite the strong parallel of a Hill-dominated reform led by one party facing a president of the opposite party.

Lack of Institutional Memory

Another constraint on learning from history in the Clinton and Gingrich rounds was limited institutional memory about welfare reform among the officials charged with pushing it through Congress. The Clinton administration's top welfare policymakers were not Washington veterans. Senator Moynihan had the potential to serve as a source of political expertise for the Clinton administration, but his poor relations with it and the ambiguity of his own position on welfare reform weakened his ability to do this during the first two years of the Clinton presidency. Important Democratic staffers were still around from the time the Family Support Act passed, but only one, Wendell Primus, was important in the task force formulating the Clinton administration's welfare reform plan.

Lack of institutional memory was even more of a problem with House Republicans in the 104th Congress because of very high turnover on the Human Resources Subcommittee of Ways and Means. Very few of the key Republican legislators had been involved in the Family Support Act passage, let alone previous reforms. One reason, of course, was the influx of new Republican members to Congress and especially to the House Ways and Means Committee. But in addition, welfare is not a matter of great interest to most Republicans, and the subcommittee's Republicans tend to be those with very little seniority. They get off the subcommittee as soon as they can so they are not around when the next round of welfare reform takes place. Expertise was equally thin on the staff side: because Republicans had previously been in the minority in both chambers, they had very few staff members with substantial expertise in AFDC. Ron Haskins, who became staff director of the Human Resources Subcommittee in 1995, and Sheila Burke, chief of staff for Senate majority leader Bob Dole, were both veterans of the Family Support Act round, but beyond those two, Republican staff experience on AFDC issues was very thin.[138]

Overestimating Political Capacity

A final factor that limits lesson drawing is the natural enthusiasm of newly empowered political elites to believe that they can do anything and are not bound to repeat past failures. In particular, the massive turnover of political appointees in presidential administrations inhibits drawing lessons about the policymaking process, both because so few officials have been there for previous policymaking and because many of them are veterans of presidential campaigns: having climbed the greasy pole to win the presidency, they think that they can do anything. In short, administrations are likely to overestimate their capacity to bring about change, what might be called the Law of Initial Chutzpah.

The same pattern was initially true of the Republican majority in the 104th Congress. Having broken forty years of Democratic control of the House of Representatives, party leaders saw themselves as representing a fundamental realignment in American politics, which they needed to, and could, consolidate by delivering real policy change. Only gradually over the course of 1995 did the limits of the "Republican revolution" become clear.

Conclusions

The historical developments reviewed in this chapter suggest both continuities and evolution in the politics of welfare reform. The generally dismal
history of efforts at comprehensive welfare reform from the Nixon administration through the early 1990s reflects continuing difficulties in maneuvering around or through the four political traps and cross-cutting institutional
barriers discussed in chapter 2. In particular, policymakers repeatedly had
difficulty in bridging the gap between liberal priorities to improve benefits
and conservative priorities to increase recipients' work effort (the dual clientele trap). Because AFDC was very unpopular, committing adequate funds to
make their packages credible and politically viable (the money trap) was also
a problem. Controlling congressional agendas to get welfare reforms out of
hostile committees and hold together fragile coalitions whose members disagreed with part of the welfare package was equally difficult.

Federalism, another important attribute of the American system, offered
opportunities for compromise as well as grounds for disagreement. Although
conservatives favored national uniformity and were frustrated with state foot
dragging on some welfare provisions (for example, stricter work requirements and requirements that teenage mothers live at home), they opposed it
on others (minimum benefits standards and mandatory AFDC-UP).[139]
Allowing states varying degrees of discretion on providing parts of the AFDC
program created a way to finesse and split the difference on many issues.
However, once devolution to the states became a general approach to welfare
reform in the 1990s, its potential for blocking agreement became more serious. Both liberals and conservatives feared that giving blanket discretion to
the states on a broad array of policy matters could be used to impose policies
that they disliked or to avoid carrying out policies that they favored.

Second, the contours of each of the traps bedeviling welfare reform
were significantly weaker for the EITC than for AFDC. Indeed, EITC expansion offered policymakers opportunities to resolve quandaries in politically
rewarding ways. But while the EITC showed that getting increased assistance to low-income families was politically feasible, a short-term conse-
quence of EITC expansion was probably to further the political isolation of
AFDC recipients: increasingly, working poor families received the EITC and
not AFDC, while the nonworking (at least in the visible above-ground economy) received AFDC.

Third, important changes in both overall approaches to welfare and
specific policies did occur in this period that affected later welfare reform

policymaking in the mid-1990s. Particularly important were policies intended to increase work by custodial AFDC parents and support from noncustodial fathers. These began with increased earnings disregards and work registrations in 1967, continued with state-option workfare requirements in 1981, and included JOBS participation rate and AFDC-UP work requirements in 1988. In short, there was growing support for the idea that if AFDC receipt was a legal entitlement, it was an entitlement that also carried obligations, and this philosophy was increasingly imbedded in legislation. Chapter 5 shows that the increased discretion given to states beginning in the 1980s to experiment with welfare reform changed the incentives for politicians at both state and federal levels.

The agenda of policies under consideration shifted as well. The idea of national eligibility and benefit standards (or at least national minimums), the core of Nixon's 1969 proposal, was clearly moving to the margins of debate by the time the Family Support Act was debated. Policymakers, especially Republicans, became increasingly determined to alter the work and childbearing behavior of welfare recipients and were willing to use carrots as well as sticks to do so. Liberals grew increasingly reluctant to vote against these measures if forced to vote on them directly, making agenda control even more important.

Finally, the historical experience of reform provides some lessons that could have aided proponents of welfare reform initiatives in the most recent round to maneuver through traps and achieve their goals. But several factors—notably the ambiguity of the lessons, previous political commitments, the tendency of new regimes to overestimate their own political capacity, lack of institutional memory, and distance in time between episodes of welfare reform—interfered with the ability of reform proponents to learn and apply the lessons suggested by earlier reform efforts. Thus direct political learning from political experience with welfare reform was less important in the 1990s than in the passage of the Family Support Act and played little role in facilitating the passage of welfare reform in 1996.

CHAPTER FIVE

Welfare Reform Agendas in the 1990s

IN THE PRESIDENTIAL election year of 1992 the reforms of the Family Support Act (FSA) had been in place for only four years. Given the limited funding and (intentionally) long lead times in the FSA, many states were still in the early stages of developing and implementing the welfare-to-work programs called for by the act and trying new strategies for combating welfare dependency. Tight state budgets and rising AFDC caseloads caused by the recession also slowed the carrying out of welfare-to-work programs. In fiscal year 1992, states drew only about two-thirds of the federal JOBS matching funds to which they were entitled.[1] Moreover, President Bush had little personal interest in the issue; unlike his predecessor and his successor, he did not put welfare reform on the legislative agenda.[2] Thus it is not surprising that the welfare legislative policy front in Washington was relatively quiet during the Bush administration.

There was tremendous ferment in the world of ideas and in the states, however. This chapter outlines the forces that brought welfare reform back into national discussion in the 1990s so quickly after passage of the FSA, as well as the alternative approaches that were under discussion and the problems each alternative confronted in dealing with the welfare reform traps discussed in chapter 3. It also provides an opportunity for a preliminary assessment of one of the contextual explanations presented in chapter 3. Was the rapid shift in welfare policy agendas attributable to the development of a promising new paradigm by policy intellectuals? Was the passage of welfare reform legislation in 1996 the result of an emergent consensus among policy elites on a direction for reform and the development of effective linkages to officials with the political power to get reforms through the institutional roadblocks to enactment? John Kingdon's discussion of the problem, policy, and political streams provides a helpful framework for organizing the developments that transformed the welfare policy agenda.

Getting Politicians' Attention: The Problem Stream

Several developments in the problem stream helped put welfare reform back onto the national discussion agenda quickly after enactment of the Family Support Act. Poverty rates for American children, after increasing from less than 14 percent in 1969 to 21.8 percent in 1983, remained above 20 percent for most of the next decade, with far higher rates for single-parent and minority children.[3] Poverty rates for children in the United States are higher than for other segments of the American population and very high in comparison with other advanced industrial societies.[4]

Major indicators regarding the AFDC program and its clientele were troubling as well. The number of AFDC cases rose every month except one between August 1989 and October 1992, increasing almost 30 percent over the period.[5] The number of AFDC recipients jumped from 10.9 million in 1989 to 14.2 million in 1994, an all-time high and an increase of 30 percent in five years, before beginning a rapid decline.[6] Combined federal and state AFDC benefits topped $20 billion dollars in 1992, a figure that in inflation-adjusted dollars roughly matches the peak experienced in the mid-1970s.[7] Rates of out-of wedlock birth also increased steadily through the mid-1990s. Black out-of wedlock birthrates reached an astounding 68.7 percent in 1993, while white illegitimacy rates approached 24 percent.[8] As conservative social critic Charles Murray pointed out in an often cited *Wall Street Journal* article in March 1993, the white illegitimacy rate was close to the level that had led Daniel Patrick Moynihan to argue in the 1960s that the black family was near collapse.[9] Economists also produced evidence of "intergenerational dependency": that the daughters of women who were highly dependent on AFDC were themselves much more likely to receive AFDC as adults.[10]

Trends in work effort by AFDC recipients were alarming as well. Although women not receiving AFDC payments were working in ever increasing numbers, the percentage of AFDC families with earnings fell from 12.8 percent in March 1979 to 5.7 percent in 1983, and then stabilized around 8 percent.[11] This drop may in part be a statistical artifact: changes in

AFDC policy during the Reagan administration (more stringent income requirements for eligibility and limits on earnings disregards) removed from the rolls many recipients who had significant earnings. But those same policy changes clearly gave AFDC recipients limited incentives to work or at least report their earnings. Indeed, an ethnographic study of welfare recipients in Chicago showed that many mothers supplemented their AFDC and food stamp income with off-the-books earnings in casual employment (as well as income from absent or resident fathers), that hardly any of them reported it, and that they felt morally justified in not doing so.[12] Taken together, these patterns raised further questions about the legitimacy of the AFDC program, its effects on the behavior and values of recipients, and the need to impose work requirements to smoke out unreported work by recipients. New research on the length of spells on welfare also changed the early-1980s conventional wisdom that most recipients stayed on the rolls for a relatively brief time. By the mid-1980s research suggested that a large share of recipients stayed on welfare for long periods and many others cycled back and forth between welfare and the low-wage labor market—which was why JOBS benefits in the Family Support Act were aimed at those at risk of long-term dependency.[13]

The interpretation given to these trends was changing as well. Increasing numbers of out-of-wedlock births and increasing concern over long-term welfare receipt raised concern over welfare dependence. Dependence, rather than ensuring adequate income for poor children, became the focus of welfare debates. Critics like Charles Murray argued that the AFDC program—indeed the entire social safety net for the poor—caused more problems for poor families than it solved, encouraging out-of-wedlock births, discouraging marriage and work, and helping to create a socially and economically isolated underclass that transmitted poverty from generation to generation.[14] Murray charged that "illegitimacy is the single most important social problem of our time—more important than crime, drugs, poverty, illiteracy or homelessness because it drives everything else."[15] These conservative diagnoses and prescriptions for welfare reform were part of a broader conservative renaissance that began in the 1970s and gained momentum with the election of Ronald Reagan to the presidency in 1980. This renaissance was fueled in part by increased funding from conservative foundations, the growth of conservative think tanks, and conservative journals like the *Public Interest* that provided a visible venue and a wider audience for conservative ideas than that reached by publications like the *National Review*.[16] Conservative ideas, including those on welfare, moved from the margins of political debate to the mainstream, while liberal ideas appeared increasingly bankrupt.

Conservatives were far from united on their prescriptions for what to do about AFDC, and chapter 6 shows that conservative arguments about the incentive effects of the welfare system were disputed by advocates for the poor and by many mainstream academics. But conservatives did succeed in making the reduction of welfare dependency the focus of welfare debates in the 1990s, replacing an earlier balance between that focus and ensuring adequate income for children. This focus on dependency drew on and reinforced AFDC's underlying image as a program that primarily benefited an undeserving African American population.[17] Coverage in the media, too, emphasized adult recipients of welfare rather than the children in the program.[18] Mainstream politicians, even most Democrats, were well aware of the unpopularity of AFDC and were reluctant to defend it publicly. Concern for the well-being of children did not entirely disappear from welfare reform debates, but it became less important in designing proposals, and it was a less effective mechanism for advocates for poor children to block proposals they did not like. This redefinition of the central problem weakened the dual clientele trap: to the extent that debate centered on the behavior of adults and the reduction of parental dependency, while fear of being seen as tough on kids declined, the political barriers to enacting welfare reform diminished considerably.

Conservatives also drew attention to the cost of assistance to poor families. Traditionally welfare was identified with AFDC. Figure 2-1 in chapter 2 showed that the cost of AFDC was relatively stable in real terms through most of the 1980s. This allowed defenders of programs for poor families to argue that AFDC constituted a tiny (never more than 2 percent) part of the federal budget, downplaying the strong overall growth in spending on this group. By the early 1990s, however, it was conservatives who had gained the upper hand in choosing statistics that bolstered their arguments. They worked hard to give the welfare label to a much broader set of programs. Particularly effective was Robert Rector of the Heritage Foundation, who argued that the entire spectrum (seventy-five or more, depending on which programs are counted) of federal means-tested programs—including the gigantic Medicaid program, which gave most of its benefits to the elderly rather than to families with children, as well as job training and college aid programs intended to improve human capital—should be counted as "welfare."[19] Taken together, he argued, these programs had spent more than $5.4 trillion (in 1993 dollars) during the previous thirty years, and they represented an incredibly costly failure of the Great Society.[20] The $5.4 trillion figure was quickly picked up by leading Republican legislators as stunning evidence of a welfare state monster that had grown out of control. This more encompassing definition of welfare exacerbated concern over the fiscal dimensions of programs for low-income families among legislators (especially congressional Republicans) and the public.

Welfare Reform Options: The Policy Stream

The refocusing of the welfare debate on dependency and the behavior of parents also helped shape what policymakers saw as the relevant choices to be made in welfare reform. To be serious contenders, reform proposals would have to offer plausible answers to questions like, Which policy choices will most effectively reduce teenage pregnancy? Which policies will be most effective at moving AFDC mothers into the labor force and keeping them there? How can fathers be made to pay an increased share of the costs of raising their children? How can this reform be enacted without the perverse incentive of luring persons who are not currently receiving welfare onto the rolls? Although these questions had also been a part of previous welfare debates, the existence of several coherent reform strategies that claimed to offer plausible answers to these questions and had vigorous and well-connected policy advocates was another factor putting welfare reform back onto the agenda in the early 1990s.

Recent reform proposals can be divided roughly into six approaches that pose distinctive diagnoses of the policy problems posed by low-income families and distinctive policy prescriptions resulting from those diagnoses.[21] Three approaches (prevention and rehabilitation, incentives, and targeting within universalism) are commonly associated with liberals, and three (new paternalism, deterrence, and devolution) with conservatives. In practice, however, many proposals are consistent with several approaches, and most welfare reform packages draw on several approaches as well. Table 5-1 provides a brief overview of these approaches and the policies they suggest to confront specific problems involving program entry, moving low-income parents into the work force and promoting long-term self-sufficiency, and promoting support by noncustodial parents. Table 5-2 presents the problems that each strategy faces in trying to overcome the policy-making traps discussed in chapter 3.

None of these approaches was entirely new in the 1990s, of course. For example, Senator Russell Long was advocating increased work requirements as early as the Nixon welfare reforms, child support enforcement in the mid-1970s, and block grants in the late 1970s. The liberal approaches have antecedents that go back at least as far. What is distinctive about the early 1990s is that all of these strategies were on the agenda at the same time with highly developed intellectual critiques and strong political backers.

Incentives

Many liberal welfare reformers in the early 1990s focused on changing program incentives to "make work pay" and weaken "poverty traps" that make it difficult to exit welfare, while at the same time reducing or removing disincentives in current policies to work and form and maintain two-parent families. Proponents of an incentives approach expressed particular concern about the following.

—The absence of health benefits in most low-wage jobs. This means that women moving into the labor force and off AFDC frequently faced a decrease in real incomes as they lost eligibility for Medicaid (which comes automatically with AFDC) and greatly increased risk if they or their children became ill.

—Low returns to work effort for welfare recipients who enter the labor force. The 1981 Reagan welfare reform legislation limited provisions allowing welfare recipients to keep the first $30 plus one-third of all earnings to recipients' first four months of work, after which earnings disregards became much more limited. Thus increasing work effort could result in little income gain and drastically increased child care costs.

—Eligibility for two-parent families. Before 1988 in about half the states, two-parent families where both parents were unemployed were not eligible for AFDC benefits. Thus a family might be better off if the unemployed father left, making his family eligible for AFDC.

The 1988 Family Support Act partially addressed some of these concerns. The FSA mandated transitional Medicaid and child care assistance to welfare recipients moving into the labor force for up to twelve months. In addition, the legislation required that states make two-parent families where the primary wage earner was unemployed eligible for AFDC cash benefits at least six months out of every year (states were required to provide Medicaid and JOBS benefits even in months in which cash benefits were not being paid). The FSA also barred states from counting income received under the Earned Income Tax Credit when calculating AFDC benefit levels and eligibility, in effect reinstating a modest income disregard for people claiming the EITC. But proponents of incentive approaches argue that additional

Table 5-1. *Approaches to Welfare Reform Issues*

Issues	Targeting within universalism	Incentives	Prevention/ rehabilitation	New paternalism	Deterrence	Devolution
			Problem definitions and approaches			
Problems to address in policy change	Inadequate incomes; lack of public support for income- and race-targeted policies	Perverse incentives in government policy	Structural barriers to employment and human capital deficiencies of clientele	Behavioral deficiencies of clientele, caused or exacerbated by perverse incentives in government policy	Perverse incentives in current government policy	Federal policies too rigid and uniform and hostile to innovation
Approaches to dependency problems	Use universalistic policies to integrate poor into labor market and guarantee income floor	Provide incentives (and lower disincentives) for AFDC recipients to move to self-sufficiency	Provide services that will reduce prospects of out-of-wedlock birth and increase self-sufficiency of AFDC parents	Require behavior that will move AFDC recipients toward self-sufficiency and sanction irresponsible and self-destructive behavior	Increase disincentives (and get rid of current programmatic incentives) for behaviors likely to increase dependency	Allow states to develop and implement own approaches and programs for reducing dependency and increasing child welfare
			Program entry issues			
Prevent teen pregnancy/ illegitimacy	Avoid disincentives to marry	Provide incentives for avoiding out-of-wedlock births; avoid disincentives to marry	Provide teen pregnancy prevention and birth control programs	Sanction teen mothers who do not stay in school; require teen parents to participate in teen pregnancy prevention classes; require teen parents to live at home	Prohibit additional benefits for children born to mothers while receiving AFDC; prohibit all cash benefits to teen mothers	Allow states to set rules for program eligibility and experiment with diverse approaches to teen pregnancy prevention
Avoid lure to current nonrecipients of AFDC	Provide universal health insurance and child care for working poor	Provide universal health insurance and child care for working poor		Make program entry unattractive through work requirements	Deny AFDC recipients in work programs eligibility for EITC	Encourage states to experiment with diversion programs

Labor market entry/initial program exit issues

Move AFDC mothers into labor force	Make work pay by providing universal health insurance and increased child care support; ease labor market entry through increased job training and government acting as employer of last resort	Make work pay by easing earnings disregards for AFDC families, raising minimum wage and/or supplementing earnings of working poor with EITC; provide transitional child care and medical assistance	Provide job training programs; provide transitional child care and medical assistance	Impose work requirements on AFDC recipients with strong sanctions for noncompliance	Put time limits on cash benefits	Allow states to set own work requirements, which may draw from other approaches

Long-term self-sufficiency issues

Keep AFDC mothers in labor force	Make work pay by providing universal health insurance and increased child care support; government acts as employer of last resort	Make work pay by easing earnings disregards for AFDC families, raising minimum wage or supplementing earnings of working poor with EITC; provide transitional child care and medical assistance to avoid income notches	Provide child care and medical assistance	Impose work requirements on AFDC recipients with strong sanctions for noncompliance	Impose work requirements; put time limits on cash benefits and work slots	Allow states to set own programs, which may draw from other approaches

continued

Table 5-1. (*Continued*)

Issues	Targeting within universalism	Incentives	Prevention/ rehabilitation	New paternalism	Deterrence	Devolution
Paternal roles and child support						
Increase child support from noncustodial parents	Guarantee child support payments from state; give states added incentives to collect from absent parent	Allow AFDC mothers to keep increasing share of child support payments	Make training, job search, jobs, and counseling available to noncustodial parents	Require noncustodial parents to participate in training and work programs	Deny noncustodial parents in arrears on child support payments driver's licenses, professional licenses, or put them in jail	Allow states to devise and implement own child support strategies
Establish paternity for children born out of wedlock	Limit access to Child Support Assurance guarantee to families that have established child support orders	Reward parents and hospitals for establishing paternity; pay "bridefare" to teen AFDC parents who marry	Provide states with financial and technical assistance to establish paternity	Require establishment of paternity before paying benefits for children; penalize states and hospitals for failing to meet required percentages of paternity establishment	Require establishment of paternity before paying benefits for children; penalize states and hospitals for failing to meet required percentages of paternity establishment	Encourage states to experiment with mechanisms for paternity establishment

incentives, such as a more generous Earned Income Tax Credit, a higher minimum wage, and longer transitional assistance in child and health care were needed to promote more effective transitions into the workplace and keep workers there.

Further expansion of incentive approaches faced numerous obstacles, however (table 5-2). The reliance of the incentives approach on carrots rather than sticks to change the behavior of current and potential welfare recipients means that it does not encounter the "hurting deserving children" side of the dual clientele trap. But as noted in chapter 4, conservatives worried deeply about perverse incentives. The most intellectually sweeping critique came from Charles Murray, who argued in an extremely influential 1984 book, *Losing Ground*, that there is a "Law of Unintended Rewards" in social policy: "Any social transfer increases the net value of being in the condition that prompted the transfer."[22] The greater the package of income or services attached to being in an undesirable state, the lower the costs (or the greater the rewards) of being in that state, and the more individuals are likely to be lured into that condition by the incentives. Allowing women to keep more of their earnings, for example, may cause them to substitute leisure for work. If transitional health care and child care assistance are made available to women who leave the welfare rolls for work, it may help ease the transition for some single mothers, but it may also lead other single mothers who lose their jobs to spend some time on welfare to take advantage of those benefits rather than going directly to another job. This perverse incentive can be eased by making such benefits available more broadly to working low-income families, but only at great cost. And such provisions were unattractive to conservatives who believe that government assistance should be limited to the most needy rather than causing more and more of the populace to become dependent on government handouts. Many conservatives also argued that raising the minimum wage to make work pay would probably reduce the number of jobs available to low-skilled workers and make those with the fewest skills unable to find any job at all. For many conservatives, evidence that welfare recipients would be worse off by moving from welfare into work suggested not that wage and fringe benefits offered in the marketplace were inadequate but that welfare benefit packages (including in-kind nutritional, housing, and health benefits) were too generous.

Prevention and Rehabilitation

A strategy favored by many liberal critics of pre-1996 policies toward low-income families can be called the prevention and rehabilitation approach.

Table 5-2. *Policymaking Traps Associated with Specific Welfare Reform Approaches*

Policymaking traps	Targeting within universalism	Incentives	Prevention/ rehabilitation	New paternalism	Deterrence	Devolution
			Dual clientele trap			
Policymakers cannot help poor children (popular) without also aiding parents (unpopular); cannot do things that make parents worse off (popular) without also risking making poor children worse off (unpopular)	Increasing income guarantees increases concerns over payment of benefits to undeserving parents regardless of work effort	Increasing benefits or eligibility increases concerns about work disincentives and welfare as a lure to long-term dependency	Increasing services increases concerns about welfare as a lure	Sanctioning parents for noncompliance with new paternalism obligations also affects welfare of children	Major eligibility exclusions may cause severe hardship for affected children	States may undertake punitive initiatives that hurt children severely; race to bottom may harm children
			Perverse incentives trap			
No effort to help poor families can avoid creating incentives that policymakers and public likely to see as undesirable; no plausible welfare reform can avoid creating new perverse incentives or exacerbating existing ones	Increasing income guarantees increases prospects that AFDC parents will substitute leisure for work and encourage family breakup	Increasing eligibility and earnings disregards for welfare increases prospects that AFDC parents will substitute leisure for work; increasing minimum wage may reduce job availability for low-skill workers	Offering increased services to AFDC parents not available to others increases incentives to go onto program; providing more services may encourage passivity and dependence of clientele	Imposing work requirements for parents may cause them to abandon children on to a more expensive overburdened foster care system	Denying benefits for teen mothers and for additional children born to mothers on AFDC creates incentives for abortion; denying professional and drivers' licenses to deadbeat dads makes them less likely to be able to work and pay child support	State-level welfare experiments borrowing from other approaches may lead to perverse incentives particular to those approaches or to interstate welfare migration

Money trap						
Most welfare reform initiatives require spending more money than public thinks necessary or Congress wants to spend	Universal and means-tested programs to aid families will cost more than status quo and spark criticism that programs are poorly targeted	Increasing earnings disregards likely to cost more than status quo, at least short term	Increased services likely to cost more than status quo, at least short term	Increased work and training requirements likely to cost more than status quo, at least short term	Generally weakens money trap by reducing expenditures	Depends on level and structure of funding provided to states
Federalism trap						
National policymakers cannot give states flexibility to do things they like without running risk they will also do things some national policymakers do not like; cannot strengthen national standards without undercutting flexibility some states desire and creating demand for federal compensation	State policymakers will object unless federal government pays added program costs; states and federal policymakers may also clash over degree of uniformity required across states in program standards	State policymakers will object unless federal government pays added program costs	State policymakers will object to mandating more services unless federal government pays added program costs	Detailed federal work mandates may inhibit ability of states to respond to varying conditions and test alternative mandate structures	Liberals likely to oppose state-option deterrence policies because differences in state deterrence policies may cause welfare migration or race to bottom	Liberals likely to oppose devolution because they fear potential for inequities and race to the bottom; conservatives may oppose if new paternalism and deterrence mandates not included

Providing social services to current welfare recipients and those likely to become recipients had been a part of federal policy since the Social Service Amendments of 1962, which authorized federal matching funds for such services on a more generous matching rate than most federal grant programs.[23] Initially, the focus of service approaches was on traditional social work services provided by professional social workers. In recent years, however, emphasis has been on preventing pregnancy, promoting child development, and overcoming education and training deficiencies in low-income families and structural barriers to labor market entry by potential earners in those families. Proponents of a prevention and rehabilitation approach, such as social critic Lisbeth Schorr, argue that "intensive societal efforts can reach and help even those stuck at the bottom" through family planning, adequate pre- and postnatal care programs for high-risk children, basic education, job training, drug and alcohol prevention and treatment, preschool child development programs such as Head Start, and other services.[24] Intensive service provision is no substitute for cash assistance and special nutritional programs like the Special Supplemental Feeding Program for Women, Infants and Children (WIC). But proponents of the prevention and rehabilitation approach argue that provision of multiple services delivered in an integrated fashion and with a caring manner can help turn troubled lives around, move poor families toward long-term self-sufficiency and better health, and result in long-term savings in AFDC and Medicaid costs.[25]

By the early 1990s a prevention and rehabilitation strategy was embedded in many federal programs such as Head Start, Job Corps, and the Job Training Partnership Act, as well as pilot projects funded by governments and foundations. But the quality and availability of services varied tremendously, and no service program was an entitlement program to all poor people who needed it. Getting a commitment to a major expansion of services faced serious obstacles. Conservatives argued that providing prevention and rehabilitation services to welfare recipients offered the same sorts of perverse incentives that incentive approaches do. Social conservatives worried that a key element of most service strategies to prevent teenage pregnancy—birth control—encouraged the behavior that was at the root of the problem. Many preferred promotion of teenage abstinence from sex, which advocates of birth control criticized as unrealistic.

In addition to the perverse incentives trap, prevention and rehabilitation approaches also faced a severe hurdle in the money trap. Providing intensive services on a broad scale was likely to cost substantially more than maintaining the status quo, at least in the short run. Proponents of this strategy argue that there are likely to be significant offsetting reductions in the long run. But because these hoped-for savings are both long run and uncertain in size, they are not counted in calculations of the net budgetary impact of proposed legislation and thus cannot overcome the political and procedural obstacles to increased federal spending. Convincing evidence that these approaches are effective in reducing dependency could help over-come the money trap and skepticism caused by past overpromises about welfare reform, but as chapter 6 shows, evidence on prevention and reha-bilitation programs is often modest or ambiguous. And evidence from pilot projects encounters skepticism that projects run by enthusiastic innovators can produce similar results when enlarged. Thus the best political prospects for increased funding for prevention and rehabilitation services are proba-bly to make them part of a bigger package incorporating both liberal and conservative elements, as in the Family Support Act of 1988. The 1988 leg-islative process also showed, however, that although members of Congress may support such a package in principle, they are prone to skimping on funding, which could lead to the collapse of such a package if liberals felt that it no longer offered enough to give it their support.

Targeting within Universalism

Targeting within universalism is a third approach to welfare reform that has gained favor among many liberal intellectuals in recent years, although only bits and pieces of the strategy have made it onto the agenda of proposals seriously considered by policymakers. Proponents such as the sociologist William Julius Wilson commonly see the cause of increasing welfare case-loads in the economic devastation of inner-city neighborhoods that they contend has disrupted traditional paths to upward mobility and made mar-riage a less attractive option than welfare for young women who become pregnant.[26] Yet they also argue that programs aimed at the poor or at racial minorities are "generally underfunded, demeaning and politically unsus-tainable."[27] The War on Poverty in particular generated a political backlash among working- and middle-class families who had to pay more taxes to finance increased transfers to and services for the poor. The working class turned to Reagan, finding attacks on welfare and calls for tax cuts appealing.

Although proponents of targeting within universalism do not advocate abandoning programs explicitly aimed at the poor, they argue that the pro-grams must be complemented by policies that have broader constituencies but give disproportionate aid to those who are poor. The model for this is Social Security, which has been well funded and politically popular. It has generated a strong, broad clientele and (at least until recently) little backlash. Yet room has been made within Social Security to benefit disproportionately the less well-off through what Hugh Heclo called "helping the poor without talking about them," notably through favorable benefit and eligibility formulas.[28]

Although it is not possible to institute a comprehensive set of universal programs overnight, proponents of universal approaches to welfare reform contend that program structures consistent with broadly held values such as rewarding work need to be put in place and expanded gradually. Examples of universal programs that would be of particular assistance to low-income families include increased assistance for child care targeted on but not limited to poor families; paid parental leave for families of newborns, with unpaid leave as a first step; universal family allowances or larger refundable tax credits for families with children; increased training assistance and a national labor market system to identify places where there are jobs that are available to displaced workers and new labor market entrants; and government becoming the employer of last resort.[29]

Perhaps the top items on the universal agenda, however, are universally available health insurance and child support assurance. Health insurance is considered necessary to remove a critical barrier for low-skilled workers attempting to move from welfare to work: the fear that they will lose free Medicaid benefits when they take a low-wage job that does not provide health benefits.

Child support assurance, conceived of as an outgrowth of the current child support enforcement program for families with an absent parent, combines uniform guidelines on what noncustodial parents should pay as a percentage of their income to prevent inequities across cases and judges, automatic withholding of child support payments, and a government guarantee of a minimum payment, even if the absent parent's income is too low to provide that minimum.[30] The last component thus attempts to build on the insurance analogy that has provided such powerful support for Old Age and Survivors' Insurance and Medicare, although funding would come from general revenues rather than dedicated contributions to a trust fund.[31] Child support assurance would be universal in that all families would be potentially eligible in case of parental separation. The hope is that a program sustained by this broad clientele, including middle-class families who divorce, would reduce poor families' dependence on politically unpopular AFDC. It is thus a good example of giving the poor disproportionate benefits within programs with broader constituencies. The extent to which child support assurance would lessen AFDC dependence would depend, of course, on the minimum child support guarantee, while its cost would depend on the guarantee and government's effectiveness in collecting from noncustodial parents.

Proponents of targeting within universalism admit that the middle class would be primary beneficiaries at first of many universal initiatives, but they argue that the system would give most help to adults willing to work, and it would change attitudes of more privileged Americans toward programs that aid the poor.[32]

This approach faces many obstacles to winning adoption, however. Although its reliance on broad guarantees means that it avoids the "harming children" side of the dual clientele trap, universal approaches may also alienate groups that currently do not perceive themselves as clients of government and do not want to be (for example, noncustodial parents not subject to mandatory child support withholding and persons who have employer-provided health insurance). Providing additional cash guarantees to poor families through child support assurance raises objections among many conservatives who see it as simply a device to make AFDC transfers more politically palatable and worry that doing so would strengthen perverse incentives to have children out of wedlock and for fathers to abandon their children to the financial guarantee by government. Probably the biggest obstacle to universal strategies, however, is the money trap: even if child support assurance turned out to be relatively inexpensive (if it in fact lowered AFDC payments), providing more universal health care, training, and child care assistance most assuredly are not.

New Paternalism

A fourth approach, new paternalism, is associated with conservative writers such as Lawrence Mead, but has increasingly been advocated by "New Democrats" such as Bill Clinton. It begins with the argument that "the main problem with the welfare state is not its size but its permissiveness."[33] Mead and others argue that past antipoverty efforts "failed to overcome poverty because they largely ignored behavioral problems among the poor," notably out-of-wedlock births, criminal activity and, most important, not working.[34]

Just how grim the new paternalism diagnosis is depends on the source of these dysfunctional behaviors. If the poor suffer from a deeply ingrained and widely shared culture of poverty that does not value work and sees little hope of improving one's condition through work, the obstacles to

improving the lot of the poor are very great because the odds that these beliefs can be changed are very low. Similarly, if absence of employment
opportunities or employment discrimination are the causes of not working,
little progress toward limiting welfare dependence is likely even if beliefs
change. But Mead and others have a much more optimistic diagnosis: that
the objective barriers to employment are manageable for most of the nonworking poor and that the nonworking poor hold attitudes toward the
value of work similar to those who work—they just fail to act on their attitudes.[35] Why? Because government welfare benefits make not working an
attractive alternative to employment in the low-wage labor market.
Although the AFDC program has long had statutory work requirements for
some recipients, Mead and others have criticized those requirements as
ambiguously constructed and poorly implemented.[36] With alternative
sources of income available from government, unskilled workers "will not
work reliably unless programs require them to."[37] Thus current welfare policies that foster dependency rather than enforcing the social norms and
obligations expected of other citizens are at the root of "the welfare problem." Effective public policies must demand responsible behavior and punish irresponsible behavior with the objective of creating "for recipients
inside the welfare state the same balance of support and expectation that
other Americans face *outside* it, as they work to support themselves and
meet the other demands of society."[38] This is something that giving the poor
more income or providing them with more services cannot do. Work
requirements may also smoke out recipients who are actually working off
the books and not reporting their income.

How can the nonworking behavior of the poor be changed? Mead and
other advocates for new paternalism argue that "making work pay" through
incentives or training is not the answer; incentive approaches may in fact
reduce work effort, and training has only a limited capacity to raise earnings
of low-skilled workers.[39] The centerpiece of new paternalism welfare reform
is mandatory work requirements with assured sanctions for noncompliance. This principle of rewards and sanctions for meeting societal obligations can be applied in other ways as well. Sanctions can be applied to
younger parents, for example, by requiring unmarried teenage mothers to
live at home (a state option under the Family Support Act) and by reducing
welfare benefits for recipients who do not stay in school or do not get their
children immunized. Stepped-up child support enforcement and work
requirements for noncustodial AFDC fathers are also consistent with new
paternalism approaches to welfare reform.

Although the emphasis of new paternalism on changing the values and behavior of the nonworking poor was rejected by many liberals, it also has elements that give some conservatives pause. As Mead notes, it "assumes that government agencies can direct the lives of the disadvantaged better than they can do themselves, and perhaps even change them for the better."[40] This position, of course, is more often associated with liberals than with conservatives. Moreover, work requirements would almost certainly require at least some government-run work programs. Yet such programs, notably the Public Service Employment program under the Comprehensive Employment and Training Act, were among conservatives' top targets in the Reagan administration.

Thus despite its appeal to both conservatives and New Democrats determined to show that they were breaking with that party's past permissive policies, new paternalism approaches confront difficulties in navigating almost all of the traditional welfare reform policymaking traps. Threatening sanctions against parents who do not work or attend school inevitably raises the dual clientele trap specter of punishing innocent children for the transgressions of their parents. Increasing the size of work programs and administrative efforts to change the behavior of welfare recipients confront the money trap, especially among conservative legislators who are the natural constituency of efforts to increase work effort. Indeed, conservatives in the early 1990s were divided between those like Mead and Governor Tommy Thompson who were willing—and stated their willingness—to spend more money in the short term to promote work, and those for whom pouring more money into the welfare system was anathema.[41] The relatively modest results of past welfare-to-work initiatives (discussed in chapter 6) suggest that substantial overselling of new paternalism approaches would be required to move strong work-oriented legislation forward in Congress. Work-oriented welfare reform legislation also poses a federalism trap dilemma: how much of work requirements (participation rates, hours of work, types of sanctions) should Washington mandate, and how much should it leave to the states, in order to promote experimentation and responsiveness to local conditions?

Legislative battles over work-oriented welfare reform legislation are likely to be based on fragile coalitions. As any welfare reform package moves through Congress, conservatives and many moderate legislators are likely to support both amendments that strengthen work requirements and those that decrease federal funding levels (liberals were likely to be attracted by amendments that did the opposite on both fronts, but such amendments stand little chance of succeeding). Such amendments are likely to under-mine the workability of the legislation or to pass on the cost of work requirements as an unfunded mandate to the states. Either could cause a critical erosion of legislative support or provoke a presidential veto. In addi-tion, many family-focused conservatives have been uncomfortable with requirements that would make the mothers of very young children have to work (and thus be separated from their children), but it is difficult to exempt such mothers without giving them a perverse incentive to have more children to avoid the work requirement.

Deterrence

A fifth approach to welfare reform, deterrence, has increasingly been advo-cated by social conservatives in recent years. Proponents argue that it is not enough to provide incentives or obligations to discourage undesirable behaviors (notably out-of-wedlock childbearing and long-term dependency on AFDC); it is also necessary to provide disincentives to prevent those behaviors from occurring in the first place. Out-of-wedlock childbearing can be addressed through prohibitions on payments to mothers for children conceived while the mother was receiving AFDC (family caps) and through bans on cash payments to teenage mothers (so-called teen mother exclu-sions). Long-term receipt of benefits can be addressed by hard time limits, a set period after which recipients will be eligible neither for cash benefits nor a government-provided or subsidized job.

Predictably, the ideas of Charles Murray were at the center of debates on these measures. In *Losing Ground* he proposed ending AFDC and other public assistance programs merely as a "thought experiment." But by 1993 he was proposing that single mothers be made ineligible for AFDC, food stamps, and public housing to weaken incentives for and strengthen the social stigma (and parental pressure) against out-of-wedlock childbearing. For women and girls who continued to have children outside marriage and were unable to support them, Murray proposed steps to ease adoption and, as a last resort, that governments "spend lavishly on orphanages . . . to pro-vide a warm, nurturing environment" for those children.[42] Similarly, former education secretary William Bennett argued that "the worst problem with welfare today is not that too many unmarried women are not working; the worst problem is that too many unmarried women are having babies."[43]

These conservative critics sought to claim the moral high ground by arguing that their proposal was actually more beneficial to children than maintaining the status quo. Bennett, for example, argued that cutting off welfare and increasing use of foster care and orphanages for children taken from their mothers will lead to a lower "body count" of neglected and abused children than the current system shows.[44] Bennett argued that "the evidence is in: illegitimacy is the surest road to social decay and poverty. . . . The most humane policy is to end it [welfare] for those who have children out of wedlock." In answer to questions about whether it would be morally right to end AFDC payments to these mothers, Bennett replied that "it is morally right, because many more people would live better if we scrapped the current system, which subsidizes out-of-wedlock births. Young girls considering having a child out of wedlock would face more deterrents, greater social stigma and more economic penalties if they had babies. These strong disincentives would lead to far fewer births to unwed mothers, and far greater life opportunities for those girls."[45] As illegitimacy rates continued to rise and other solutions eluded reformers, proponents of deterrence gained increased prominence, especially within the Republican party.

Deterrence approaches faced their own political difficulties, however. To help maneuver through the dual clientele trap, proponents of deterrence-oriented policies that could harm children by limiting eligibility for AFDC would probably have to oversell the size and rapidity of change in childbearing and work behavior that such policies could be expected to produce in parents. (They would be aided, as chapter 6 contends, by the paucity of evidence on the magnitude of the behavioral effects of deterrence policies.) Exclusions of teenage mothers and family caps clearly would provide stronger incentives for many unwed mothers to have abortions, a position many social conservatives find hard to reconcile with their opposition to abortion. The abortion matter in particular has represented a potential threat to the stability of a conservative welfare reform package that included deterrence measures. More generally, the increasing commitment of many conservatives to proposals such as exclusions of teenage mothers, while liberals have continued to reject them, makes it more difficult to build a welfare reform coalition because it increases the policy distance that must be bridged in any compromise: it is easiest to reform welfare, as the 1988 experience showed, when overlapping zones of acceptable outcomes are fostered by wide agreement on the nature of the problem and the course of reform. Enacting reform is harder when policymakers are intransigent in demanding inclusion of provisions on which participants are in complete disagreement on principle, making it impossible to "split the difference."

Devolution

A final strategy for welfare reform, devolution, has been embraced most strongly by Republicans but has also gained support among New Democrats and governors—especially Republican governors. It suggests that uniform federal policies are unlikely to lead to adequate solutions to the problems of teenage pregnancy, family breakup, and getting and keeping parents in low-income families in the labor force. A better mechanism, proponents of devolution argue, would be to give additional responsibility for such policies to the states, allowing experiments from which new knowledge about which policies work effectively can emerge.[46]

In fact, a range of devolution options is possible. In the AFDC program, for example, options on the table ranged from simply allowing states to obtain additional waivers from federal requirements (allowing states to disregard additional earnings of recipients, for example, or impose stricter work requirements or family caps) under existing waiver provisions in the Social Security Act to eliminating all federal standards, with federal funds transferred to the states in a "no-strings-attached" block grant.[47]

Although the principle of encouraging experimentation in welfare policy as a way to find out "what works" enjoys broad support, there is great disagreement about the types of experimentation that should be allowed and the limitations on devolution. Liberals fear that devolution of authority to the states will lead to a loss of entitlement status in means-tested programs and a loss of federal interest—followed by a loss in federal funding—in programs in which the only remaining federal role is funneling money to the states.[48] Liberals also worry about a "race to the bottom": a competition among states to make their benefits less generous and conditions of AFDC receipt increasingly onerous to discourage immigration of potential welfare recipients from other states and encourage emigration of their own welfare recipients. Even states that do not wish to engage in such a competition would likely be forced to follow along out of fear of becoming a welfare magnet.[49] Devolution could also lead to a radical transformation of the debate away from concerns about protecting children and toward concerns with meddling by Washington. Thus devolution policies offer a way around the dual clientele trap by obscuring potential harmful effects of state initiatives on poor families. For that reason they are likely to be viewed with suspicion by liberals unless they are accompanied by substantial safeguards to protect poor families.

Although liberals have expressed the most concern about devolution of responsibility for welfare to the states, conservative proponents of new paternalism and deterrence policies express concerns of their own: that states cannot be trusted to implement tough work requirements, family caps, and time limits unless mandated by Washington. Thus not surprisingly, devolution strategies were most likely of the six approaches to welfare reform discussed here to encounter the federalism trap: a fear on the part of Washington politicians that granting states additional discretion will lead them to do things the politicians do not like as well as things they do like. This raises the specter of fragile coalitions: amendments to welfare reform legislation proposing politically popular but costly mandates on the states may cause important elements of a legislative coalition for welfare reform, such as governors, to drop their support, causing an initiative to collapse.

Selecting Alternatives

The welfare debates of the early 1990s took place in the absence of elite or mass consensus on any single definition of the policy problem posed by low-income families or a single way of addressing the problem or problems. Elements of the fragile consensus on work and welfare that had contributed to the passage of the 1988 Family Support Act, most notably twin concerns for the working poor and for moving welfare recipients into work, did survive into the 1990s. What is particularly striking about the agenda toward low-income families in the early 1990s, however, is the range of proposals put forward by policymakers, policy experts, and interest groups and the speed with which various approaches moved on and off the policy agenda. For example, when William Julius Wilson wrote in 1987 that the "laissez-faire social philosophy represented by Charles Murray is . . . too extreme to be seriously considered by most policymakers," most observers would have agreed.[50] But by 1994 many of the themes of Murray's approach, if not the immediate "cold turkey" timetable, were embodied in the Contract with America, the election manifesto of the newly elected Republican majority in Congress.

The range of welfare reform options made a consensus on policy less likely. Moreover, each of the major approaches encountered serious political obstacles, some of them obvious and some more subtle. The incentive, prevention and rehabilitation, targeting within universalism, and work-oriented new paternalism strategies all require spending more money in the short term. Many conservatives are philosophically opposed to increasing government's role in income distribution and increasing the number of persons dependent on government transfers. Deterrence runs into the most fundamental source of public ambivalence toward low-income families with children: the public wants to be tough on adult recipients whose deservingness it regards as dubious; it does not want to punish innocent children.

Despite the absence of consensus on a single approach to welfare, however, several attributes of the policy stream helped to earn welfare reform a place on policymakers' agendas. Perhaps most important, supporters of each strategy considered current welfare policies deeply flawed—not just neutral in effect but harmful. With reform proposals on the table from all points of the ideological spectrum, the current welfare system was left virtually without intellectual defenders on the political right, center, or left.

Second, and equally important, advocates of each strategy offered hope that something could be done about poverty: it was not something so deeply rooted in economic structures or the cultural attributes of recipients that changing policy was likely to have no effect. Theda Skocpol, one of the best-known advocates of targeting within universalism, argued,

> Once genuinely new and nonstigmatizing incentives, social supports, and ways of providing job opportunities were solidly in place, the example of a few go-getters who took advantage of new policies and forged better lives for themselves might well propagate among relatives, friends, and neighbors. After the word got out that work really does lead to rewards, a certain amount of the social despair that now pervades the very poor might well begin to dissipate. In a way, this could be the greatest gift that new universalistic family security policies could give to the most disadvantaged among the American poor, for it would facilitate their moral reintegration into the mainstream of national life.[51]

Although the diagnoses of the failings of current policy and the prescriptions for change are distinctive, the belief in the malleability of the behavior of the poor and the hope that behavioral change could uplift them economically and morally sounds remarkably like Mead's new paternalism or Murray's deterrence approach.

Third, all of the strategies except the universal one were at least within the range of fiscal plausibility. Of the remaining five, three (incentives, prevention and rehabilitation, and new paternalism) were likely to cost more than maintaining the status quo, at least in the short term; one (deterrence) was likely to save money; and devolution could be structured to do either or to be fiscally neutral. But even those that would cost more were not—again excepting targeting within universalism—outlandishly expensive. Equally important, none of the three were "lumpy," requiring a huge minimum investment before any positive return could be anticipated. There could be experiments at the state or substate level with further expansion or retrenchment of those initiatives made on the basis of evaluations of the experience.

In the absence of a consensus on a particular approach to welfare reform, many reform proposals drew on several strategies. Particularly influential among these mix-and-match proposals was one made by David Ellwood, an economist at Harvard's Kennedy School of Government and later cochair of the Clinton administration's welfare reform task force. In his book *Poor Support*, published in 1988, Ellwood argued for an extremely ambitious attack on poverty in American families.[52] He contended that families that were working hard to keep themselves out of poverty should be rewarded through incentives to supplement their incomes and make work pay, notably through expanding the Earned Income Tax Credit and increasing the minimum wage. Families that needed temporary assistance (as a result of family breakup, for example) could draw on cash assistance. His boldest proposal, however, was the conversion of longer-term support into a work-based entitlement on new paternalism lines: long-term recipients would be required to work at minimum wage jobs (half-time for single-parent families, full-time for one parent in two-parent families) in exchange for assistance, with government acting as provider of "last-resort" minimum wage jobs for those who could not find them in the labor market.[53] Ellwood also proposed that all Americans be guaranteed access to medical care (he was not very clear about the mechanism for providing it) to avoid the perverse incentives of welfare recipients having access to care while other low-income families did not. A uniform child support assurance system would provide additional income guarantees to low-income children. Ellwood did not include detailed cost estimates, but allowed that his proposals "may cost over $20 billion or even $30 billion to do everything right."[54]

At the time that *Poor Support* appeared, at the end of eight years of Reagan administration criticism of AFDC and in the middle of debate over what was to become the Family Support Act of 1988, the book's agenda was perceived as a bold alternative to retrenchment, informed by the latest research on what works in reducing welfare dependence. Less clear at the time was another effect of the book: it helped legitimize the idea of putting time limits on cash welfare benefits, albeit with a job or community service guarantee at the end. This distinction between "soft" and "hard" time limits would often become blurred in the welfare reform debates during the years that followed.

Raising the Stakes: The Political Stream

Developments in the political stream also helped put welfare reform back on the agenda. The low success rate of past reform initiatives had long made welfare reform a high-risk proposition. But developments outside and inside the Beltway appeared to make at least verbal support for reforming welfare more attractive and failure to do so seem risky.

The Public Mood

There was widespread agreement in the early 1990s that policies to deal with the problems of low-income families were not working well. The AFDC program in particular was unpopular with the public. As early as 1985 far more of the public (56 percent) thought that public assistance did not work well than thought it functioned well (39 percent). A majority also believed that it discouraged work.[55]

The exact dynamics of public opinion on welfare are difficult to trace consistently because of changes in the questions that pollsters ask and variations in the wording of the questions over time. Changes in economic conditions also complicate this analysis because recession tends to lead to more sympathy for welfare recipients. This ambivalence and the unfavorable connotations of welfare were evident as late as 1992 in questions about the causes of poverty. By a margin of almost two to one (52 to 27 percent) survey respondents said that "circumstances beyond his control" were more to blame than "lack of effort" when a person is poor. The results flipped around, however, when respondents in a different poll were asked whether "jobs are available for most welfare recipients who really want to work." By a margin of 64 to 33 percent, respondents said that they were.[56] By a very large margin, more respondents (74 percent) in a May 1992 poll thought that "people on welfare are so dependent on welfare that they will never get off it" rather than those (17 percent) who believed that "most people on welfare are using welfare for a short period of time and will get off it eventually."[57] Yet by a staggering 93 to 3 percent margin, respondents in a poll that same month believed that it was more important to give "poor people the skills they need to become self sufficient than to cut . . . the cost of welfare programs."[58] When asked in open-ended questions whether welfare reform was one of the top one or two most important issues facing the country, few respondents in 1991 and 1992 surveys mentioned welfare reform.[59] If, however, respondents were asked specifically if they viewed welfare as a very important issue, a majority said that they did.[60]

The Presidential Campaign

The presidential campaign of Bill Clinton clearly put welfare reform on the national political agenda in the early 1990s. The campaign picked up ideas from the work of David Ellwood: the theme of a combination of training, EITC increases, and time limits on cash benefits followed by a work requirement. Under the catchy slogans of "ending welfare as we know it" and "making work pay," welfare reform and EITC expansion became central planks of Clinton's presidential campaign.[61] Although Ellwood had been flexible about when a work requirement would kick in, the Clinton campaign specified that it would be at the end of two years. The campaign was notably vague, however, about the cost of the proposals. And unlike Ellwood, who was clear on the need for a job guarantee, the Clinton campaign was unclear on the extent to which child care and a job (as opposed to a community service requirement that would simply allow a recipient to work off current benefits) would be guaranteed. Estimates of the cost of new welfare-to-work initiatives were limited to about $4 billion a year, plus $2 billion for EITC expansion—much less than Ellwood's original proposals.[62] The Clinton forces also pledged to "revolutionize the culture of welfare offices," to convert them from bureaucracy-laden payment and enforcement centers to entrepreneurially oriented employment and training centers.

Several factors influenced the Clinton campaign's choice to make welfare reform a centerpiece of its appeal. Clinton had been cochair, along with Republican governor Mike Castle of Delaware, of the National Governors' Association task force on welfare reform during the Family Support Act round (as well as chairman of the NGA in 1987). In that role Clinton had been active in urging Congress to break its impasse over welfare reform and pass the Family Support Act of 1988. Pushing welfare reform in his presidential campaign allowed him to highlight the most prominent of his thin credentials in national policymaking. Governor Clinton also stressed his role as a welfare reformer in Arkansas, where the state had been active in promoting welfare-to-work experiments that independent evaluations had shown to be modestly effective.[63]

In addition to its policy appeals, this mixed approach to the problems of low-income families offered some potentially important political advantages in the Clinton campaign's efforts to promote, and benefit electorally from, a broader New Democratic political project. Clinton and other New Democrats argued that erosion in the party's political support could only be stopped by a new image and by new policies that would show the party to be more than an agglomeration of liberal interests (racial minorities, labor unions, feminists, homosexuals, and so forth).[64] Clinton campaign issues director (and later cochair of the administration's welfare reform task force) Bruce Reed saw "a growing consensus among Democrats that we have an obligation to end dependency and reform welfare, to move beyond the rhetoric of the right and the mistakes of the left."[65] A public philosophy that emphasized work and individual responsibility offered the Clinton campaign the opportunity to seize the moral high ground in the welfare debate, inoculate Democrats against charges that they coddle the (disproportionately minority) nonworking poor, and take away (and even turn to Democrats' advantage) one of the race-tinged wedge issues that had long alienated blue- and white-collar constituencies from the Democratic party.[66] Advocating the ideals of making work pay and ensuring that people who "work hard and play by the rules should not be poor" resonated well with constituencies who had suffered declining or stagnant real income in recent years. In short, work-oriented welfare reform offered an opportunity not only to neutralize an issue on which Democratic candidates had traditionally had to avoid blame but also to claim credit.

This approach to welfare reform also offered a good fit with other planks and themes of the Clinton platform. The need to implement universal health care as a way to avoid poverty traps in the welfare system (especially families' fear of losing health care if they moved from welfare to the low-wage labor market) obviously reinforced the administration's call for health care reform. The idea of revolutionizing the culture of welfare offices fit well with the Clinton theme that a "reinvented" government could be an effective and efficient mechanism for achieving collective objectives. The Clinton campaign's decision to emphasize a work- and responsibility-oriented welfare reform was in short a relatively easy choice, offering both political rewards and a good fit with the candidate's policy preferences. Of course, it also risked alienating traditional Democratic urban constituencies, which might make reform difficult to get through a Democratic Congress. In the short term, however, distancing candidate Clinton from those constituencies was helpful in reinforcing his credentials as a New Democrat.

President Bush did not attempt to outbid his Democratic opponent on the welfare issue in the 1992 presidential campaign.[67] The president occasionally used tough rhetoric, saying that "welfare punches a hole in the heart of the American dream," and that "we need to say [to welfare recipients] get a job or get off the dole."[68] The Bush administration did come forward with welfare proposals in July 1992 that would have given states increased flexibility to use income disregards, family caps, and other measures and allowed states to pay welfare benefits only if recipients completed mandated work or training duties.[69] But given the huge AFDC caseload increases during the Bush administration, this was widely seen as a timid response. Certainly promising increased state discretion did not match Clinton's bold promise to end welfare as we know it.

Nor did welfare become the sort of race-tinged wedge issue that crime had (with Willie Horton) in 1988, in part because challenger Clinton's rhetoric about the welfare system was not very different from Bush's. The Bush campaign instead focused on Clinton's character, widely considered the governor's most vulnerable point, and charges that he was really a traditional tax-and-spend Democrat.[70]

Clinton's more activist stance on welfare appears to have helped him at least modestly. In opinion polls he was favored by a wide margin over Bush not only on the traditional Democratic strength of "helping the poor" but also on "getting people off welfare"; 46 percent thought that Clinton would do the best job as president on this issue in a September 1992 poll, compared with only 24 percent for Bush.[71] It is unlikely that proposals for welfare reform directly moved many voters to Clinton: only 2 percent of voters supporting Clinton just before the election said that the main reason was his position on welfare reform or because he would help the poor.[72] Few voters said that welfare reform was critical to their choice on election day[73] or said that it was among the issues on which they most desired immediate action by Congress and the president.[74] But it seems fairly safe to say that the welfare issue did not hurt Clinton, and neutralizing that issue, in combination with a recession and a broad public desire for change, was enough to win Clinton the presidency with a plurality of the popular vote.

Despite the relatively limited salience of the welfare issue, the combination of Clinton's election and his bold promise to end welfare as we know it virtually ensured that the new administration would bring forward a comprehensive welfare reform package or face blame from Republicans that it had reneged on its promise. However, Clinton had not sought an electoral mandate for an *expensive* welfare reform package, which would have played into Bush campaign charges about excessive spending. Thus, although it was almost inevitable that there would be a Clinton administration welfare reform package, critical choices remained about what elements would be in the package, how expensive it would be, and how it would be paid for.

Congress

In Congress, too, being perceived as doing something about "the welfare mess" became an increasing concern. The percentage of House incumbents running in the general election who won 60 percent of the major party vote—an indicator of a relatively safe race—declined from 88.5 percent in 1988 to 76.4 percent in 1990 (it would decline another 10 percent in 1992).[75] Other forces militated against renewed congressional legislation, however. As noted earlier, states had been slow in implementing the Family Support Act of 1988; many legislators were reluctant to revisit that legislation until there was a better sense of how well it was working. Moreover, any semblance of the bipartisan consensus on welfare reform that helped pass the Family Support Act had vanished. Congressional Republicans sought to stake out positions as tougher on welfare than Democrats by demanding stiffer work requirements and a streamlining of the HHS process for consideration of state waiver requests. Congressional Democrats called for increased federal funding for the Family Support Act's JOBS program to give recession-pressed states adequate resources to do more.[76] But given the manifest unpopularity of AFDC among legislators and the public, and the fact that any welfare reform legislation would be subject to veto by President Bush, many in the Democratic congressional majorities worried that bringing up any welfare reform legislation at all would create a vehicle for punitive amendments that would be hard to oppose, with little prospect of moving forward their own policy preferences.[77] Given this political dynamic, it is not surprising that no welfare reform legislation was enacted in the 103d Congress (1991–92).[78]

Innovation in the States

Throughout most of the history of the AFDC program, states had limited discretion over how the assistance was provided. Although state politicians could bluster about being tough on welfare, their main leverage was over eligibility and benefit levels. The Work Incentives Program of 1967, the Reagan reforms of 1981, and the Family Support Act of 1988 all gave the states some additional discretion over work requirements but little money to work with.

Another avenue for increased discretion was to apply to the Department of Health and Human Services for waivers to test alternative ways of reforming welfare under section 1115 of the Social Security Act, authorized by Congress in 1962. The legislative constraints on the scope of waivers under this provision were severe, however, including a provision that any experiments be cost-neutral to the federal government. Before the late 1980s, waiver provisions were narrowly interpreted and seldom used. By 1995, however, most states had obtained waivers from Washington and were using them to test dramatic welfare reforms ranging from income disregards to family caps and time limits, without any legislative change at all by Congress.

How this policy transformation came about has been superbly told in a book by Steven M. Teles.[79] The waiver revolution began with the Reagan administration's decision to pursue a welfare policy based on giving increased discretion to the states. As noted in chapter 4, the Reagan administration pressed for incorporation of broader waiver authority into the Family Support Act but did not succeed. The administration was more successful, however, in shifting control over the waiver process to the White House and in getting more waivers approved by HHS, which retained statutory authority to approve waivers. The scope of these waivers was nevertheless fairly narrow. Moreover, new waivers virtually disappeared early in the Bush administration as states became preoccupied with implementing JOBS, the new administration showed no interest in a waivers strategy, and control over AFDC waivers drifted back to HHS.[80] But in 1992 President George Bush, faced with a serious reelection threat from Bill Clinton and sorely in need of a policy alternative to Clinton's pledge to end welfare as we know it, made clear that his administration had an open-door policy to state waiver requests. Moreover, the administration was willing to relax the traditional cost-neutrality standard to accept waiver requests that were expected to cost more up front but to save an equivalent amount of federal money in later years.[81]

As a result of this greater openness to waivers in Washington, state politicians, particularly governors, suddenly found themselves able to move beyond antiwelfare rhetoric to policy action. Equally important, action on welfare appeared to be a political winner for state politicians, stimulating imitators in other states.[82]

Early state experiments in welfare reform showed substantial diversity in both the political constellations of forces that gave rise to them and the approaches to welfare reform that they employed. Indeed, many were designed as packages that combined elements of several approaches to attract broader political support. Some of the state initiatives were prompted by a fiscal squeeze: annual state AFDC costs increased by almost $2.7 billion and Medicaid costs by more than $26 billion between 1988 and 1992, just as recession was cutting into states' revenues.[83] These pressures were particularly intense in Michigan and California, which were ranked number one and two among states in the percentage of their population receiving AFDC benefits in 1991.[84] Initiatives enacted in Wisconsin, one of the early welfare reform experimenters, were driven primarily by a Republican governor, Tommy Thompson, who used resentment against alleged welfare-induced migration from Illinois as one of the cornerstones of his initial campaign for governor. Once in office his many welfare waiver requests included earnings disregards, Medicaid extensions for families leaving the rolls (incentives), sanctions for teenage parents who did not stay in school (new paternalism), and a two-county demonstration of hard time limits (deterrence). Controversial welfare reform legislation enacted in 1992 in New Jersey was sponsored and pushed through by Assembly majority leader Wayne Bryant, an African American Democrat from Camden who likened welfare to a "modern form of slavery" that promoted the breakup of families.[85] The legislation combined earnings disregards and transitional Medicaid assistance for those who left welfare for work (the incentives approach) with family caps (deterrence) and increased funding for training programs (prevention and rehabilitation).[86] In 1991 California's Republican governor, Pete Wilson, blamed much of the state's huge budget deficit on the welfare magnet effect of the state's high AFDC benefit levels; in response he proposed an across-the-board cut in welfare benefits (with additional benefit cuts for long-term recipients and for recipients who moved to California from other states) along with expanded earnings disregards and family caps.[87] The welfare issue in California also became entangled in a growing wave of resentment against the cost of providing services to immigrants from other countries.

The initiatives in states like Wisconsin, New Jersey, and California rapidly created a bandwagon effect in other states. Not only did waiver requests appear to offer political opportunities to claim credit, they offered evidence that a governor was trying to do *something* about a welfare system that was almost universally regarded as broken, insulating them from charges by political opponents that they were indifferent to the welfare mess. The long lead times required to get a waiver request approved by a state legislature, win approval from the federal Department of Health and Human Services, undergo possible court challenges, and get evaluation results back did little to discourage waiver requests, either: the requests allowed politicians to project an image of concern about the welfare problem with a very low probability that anything with negative consequences (negative evaluation results, for example, or increased homelessness among poor families) would occur in the political near term.

Conclusions

Developments in public opinion, politics, and the world of ideas in the early 1990s not only induced policymakers to pay attention to welfare reform, but also shaped the choices that policymakers saw as relevant and the alternatives that made it onto the agenda. Four developments stand out as especially important.

First, the publication of Ellwood's *Poor Support* in 1988 legitimated among the mainstream of the welfare policy community the idea of a time limit on welfare followed by a guarantee of work accompanied by supportive services and guaranteed child support. Many moderates and almost all liberals continued to oppose some or all of these policy proposals, but they were no longer seen as outside the realm of acceptable policy discourse.

Second, the growing use of state waivers changed dramatically the political calculus in both Washington and state capitals about the political and policy potential of welfare reform without welfare reform legislation. Increasingly, state politicians came to see welfare reform as a political opportunity to be exploited and inaction on welfare reform as a potential source of political trouble. In Washington a tide of state waiver requests pushing against the limits of current policy and the increasing (and largely favorable) attention given to those requests added political weight to pro-devolution sentiment in Congress and pressure on executive agencies to approve almost any waiver request made by the states.

Third, the Clinton presidential campaign's easy choice of a welfare reform plank including time limits, with a much vaguer commitment to what would follow the time limits, ensured welfare reform a prominent place on the new administration's action agenda.

Fourth, the growth in conservative circles of support for alternative approaches, notably deterrence, meant that the Clinton administration's proposals were by no means ensured of widespread support and a speedy ticket through Congress. Indeed, the evidence for viewing the passage of welfare reform in 1996 as the result of a new policy paradigm that won the support of policy elites is mixed at best. Clearly policy intellectuals played an important role in transforming the welfare agenda, but, beyond a general agreement that government policy should promote work efforts by AFDC recipients, no consensus emerged among policy or political elites on a single approach or package of approaches to welfare reform. Rather than a consensus that makes supporting a specific welfare reform initiative an easy choice for most legislators, the array of contending strategies meant that the coalition of support for any legislative package was likely to be very fragile. Strong support for several contending approaches also meant that welfare reform could take a very different turn if the Clinton administration lost its power to set the agenda. That is of course what happened in November 1994 and beyond.

Before considering in detail how those choices emerged, however, it is helpful to consider three additional contextual explanations of the evolution of welfare policy debates and choices: policy research, public opinion, and interest group pressures. Social science evidence can influence debates and choices in several ways: evidence that welfare-to-work programs are ineffective might cause increased attention to options other than new paternalism ones, for example. Both public opinion and interest group pressures may cause politicians to move toward options more popular with the public and the groups. These factors are examined in chapters 6 through 8. Each of these factors shaped the welfare reform debates and the bargaining positions and strategies of the major participants during the first Clinton administration in important but often counterintuitive ways. However, neither individually nor collectively did they make inevitable the legislation that emerged in 1996.

CHAPTER SIX

The Role of Policy Research

"Everybody's entitled to their own statistics."
—Unidentified Democratic congressman

IN CONSIDERING CHANGES to Aid to Families with Dependent Children (AFDC) and other programs that serve low-income families, policymakers in the mid-1990s were inundated with information about the welfare "policy problem," the consequences of current policies, and the costs and benefits of potential alternatives. This information came in many forms and from many sources. Much of it was what Allen Schick calls "ordinary knowledge": information that is "unsystematic and biased . . . the perspective and attitude formed through everyday observation and interaction."[1] Policymakers read stories in the newspapers about welfare recipients who have six or seven children by different fathers, abuse drugs, and raise children who themselves go on to become welfare dependent for long periods. In September 1994, for example, many of the policymakers in the nation's capital saw a *Washington Post* series on the severely dysfunctional family of Rosa Lee Cunningham. Its saga of multigenerational welfare and drug dependence, prostitution, child abuse, and petty crime seemed a living embodiment of the statistical tale told by Charles Murray in *Losing Ground*.[2] Policymakers also heard congressional testimony from governors boasting of how successful their own state initiatives have been in moving welfare recipients into work and collecting child support payments from deadbeat dads. In addition, legislators read letters from constituents complaining about welfare fraud in their home communities. Because ordinary knowledge is gathered, interpreted, and reported informally and unsystematically, its reliability and generalizability is questionable at best. But ordinary knowledge (especially press reports) also paints a vivid portrait of real people with names and faces attached; it can seem far more real than piles of statistics, especially if it fits with and reinforces images or stereotypes that people already hold about how the world works.

The focus of this chapter is not ordinary knowledge, but a second type of information received by policymakers. This information—what Schick calls policy research—is based on the claims of those who provide it to expertise in particular policy areas. It also rests on the use of systematic social science methods in the collection, analysis, and reporting of data to ensure that findings are "objective"—not tainted by the biases of those who have generated or paid for the research.

Policy research can provide three kinds of information that may be helpful to policymakers as they seek to make more effective policy and to be taken seriously by their peers (see table 6-1 for examples). The first is of a factual, "What is happening" nature. For example, how long do welfare families receive AFDC benefits? Is AFDC receipt mostly a transitional phenomenon that occurs after the breakup of a family, or do families tend to stay on welfare for a long time? Are out-of-wedlock births increasing or decreasing? Frequently, this information is simply statistical data that establish patterns and trends in social programs, problems, and constituencies—what John Kingdon refers to as policy indicators.[3] Indicators are especially likely to be used by policymakers as a wake-up call when the conditions they measure appear to be deteriorating. If out-of-wedlock birthrates are high and rising, policymakers are likely to be far more concerned than if those rates are modest and stable. Similarly, if research suggests that AFDC receipt is mostly a long-term phenomenon that has a strong probability of being repeated generation after generation, policymakers are likely to be more concerned than if it is a short-term transitional phenomenon that occurs after family breakup, job loss, or illness of the family breadwinner.

Second, along with seeking to understand what is happening, policymakers try to make sense of these patterns by asking why they occur. Why, for example, has the percentage of out-of wedlock births expanded so much over the past thirty years? Why does it seem to be so difficult for families in single-parent households to move into private sector jobs and retain those jobs if they do get them? In short, policymakers seek analyses of time trends or cross-sectional differences that explain these patterns. As noted in chapter 5, the different approaches to welfare reform that dominated the agenda in the 1990s posed distinctive answers to each of these questions. Explanations can have an important impact on whether an issue makes it to government's agenda: if a problem is seen as resulting from forces deeply ingrained in the social order (for example, a deeply rooted "culture of poverty" that causes dysfunctional behavior by the poor), policymakers may believe there is little that they can do. If, however, a problem is considered the result of current government policies, the case for policy change is strengthened.

Third, policy research can be helpful in answering the question, "What should we do?" Can policy changes lower rates of teenage pregnancy, and at what costs to the welfare of poor children and to the taxpayers? What effects do work requirements and hard time limits on AFDC eligibility have on work effort and on the poverty status and wages of low-income workers? The primary type of policy research of interest here is evaluation studies that examine how policy changes or how experiments involving part of a population subjected to different program rules affect policy. Examples include pilot programs to move more AFDC recipients from welfare into work or to decrease rates of teenage pregnancy. Incentives, new paternalism, or other welfare reform approaches might move up on the agenda because research suggests that the proposals associated with them are effective and efficient at reducing welfare dependency. For example, if evaluation research suggests that some approaches to moving recipients from welfare into work are more successful than others (for example, emphasizing job search rather than job training), policymakers will presumably be more likely to adopt the successful approaches. Other policies could drop off the agenda if research showed them to be ineffective, too costly, or too harmful to children.

These three types of policy research can be used in several ways, which have different implications for reaching agreement on welfare policy change. Chapter 3 suggested that policymakers may use all three types of policy research in a *technocratic* fashion. In this view policy research produces an elite consensus on which of the six policy paradigms or approaches to welfare reform that were contending in this period, alone or in combination, is most efficacious and therefore should be pursued. Policymakers adjust policy accordingly. For example, if research on hard time limits demonstrated that limits had a very strong effect on work effort and a negligible effect on child welfare, presumably even many liberals would accept them; if they had the opposite effects, presumably even most conservatives would reject them. Evaluation studies of welfare experiments such as the negative income tax experiments of the late 1960s and early 1970s and the state welfare-to-work experiments in the 1980s

Table 6-1. *Policy Research Relevant to Welfare Reform*

Research area	Indicators	Explanations	Evaluation research
Program structure and federal/state roles	Interstate benefit differences	Causes of interstate benefit differences	State behavior under waivers and where given discretion under current law; experience of current block grant programs
Program entry	Caseloads; teen pregnancy and out-of-wedlock birth rates	Impact of AFDC benefits on pregnancy rates and welfare take-up and labor supply	Teen pregnancy prevention programs; family caps and teen mother exclusions; diversion effects of work requirements and time limits
Labor market entry/initial program exit	Caseloads; length of welfare spells; alternative income sources for AFDC recipients	Correlates of success in labor market entry for AFDC recipients; relative income of AFDC recipients and low-skilled workers; impact of AFDC benefits on program exit	Welfare-to-work programs; earnings disregards; transitional health and child care benefits; employer incentives to hire AFDC recipients; work requirements and soft time limits
Long-term self-sufficiency	Re-entry to AFDC and multiple spells by those who leave for employment	Correlates of long-term success in labor market for AFDC recipients	Child care, health care subsidies, and other supports for low-income families; hard time limits
Paternal roles and child support	Rates of receipt of child support; paternity establishment	Earnings potential of noncustodial fathers	Bridefare and other paternal responsibility incentives; child support enforcement programs; training and work programs for noncustodial fathers; license suspensions and other deterrence measures for deadbeat dads; child support assurance experiments

and 1990s can also raise or dampen fears about perverse incentives, the risks of state discretion (the federalism trap), and the overall effectiveness of proposed policy alternatives. Persuasive evidence that promotes elite consensus on the efficacy of particular approaches to welfare reform would presumably strengthen reform coalitions, while dissensus would make them more fragile.

Policy research could influence the prospects for welfare policy change in a more limited way, however. Policymakers may use research (and especially policy indicators) primarily as a *fire alarm*. Worrisome indicator trends would then act as a wake-up call to put an issue on the agenda, but policymakers pay less attention to explanatory and evaluation research that tells them how to respond. Instead, their responses are guided by values, political commitments, or some other source of ideas. Simple indicators showing continued increases in out-of-wedlock birthrates, for example, may weaken the dual clientele trap by increasing some policymakers' concern over the behavior of adults relative to concern over the welfare of children. If policy research operates in this way, the substance of reform—which approach or combination of approaches is pursued—is far less certain. It is likely to depend heavily on which political forces control the agenda and whether incomplete agenda control requires them to compromise with other political forces.

Policymakers may also use policy research as a *circuit breaker*. In this view they do not use explanatory analysis or evaluation research in as careful and nuanced a way as the technocratic model suggests, but if research indicates that some policy alternatives may involve high risks to the well-being of low-income families, they reject those alternatives.

Finally, policymakers may use policy research simply as *ammunition*.[4] In this model, they use policy research of all three types, but not as a source of information to affect their preferences and priorities; rather they pick and choose research that bolsters their existing (because of constituency pressures or personal values) policy preferences while rejecting and even casting doubt on research that questions those preferences.

The purpose of this chapter is to introduce the types of policy research that policymakers used in the Clinton and Republican welfare reforms and to examine how policymakers used them. Along the way I will examine what factors strengthened or limited the use of policy research. The discussion focuses on two of the major clusters of issues examined in table 5-1: entering the program (notably as a result of teenage pregnancy and illegitimacy) and getting AFDC parents (especially single parents) into the labor force and moving them to long-term self-sufficiency. The purpose is not to provide a detailed summary or critique of the policy research on these issues (a task beyond the reach of this chapter), but simply to survey the available research and assess the extent to which it settled or perpetuated policy and political conflicts among policymakers.[5]

The Boom in Policy Research

Sources of policy research on low-income families have multiplied in number and size in recent years. Policymakers receive statistics on poverty rates and the percentage of children living in single-parent families from the Bureau of the Census, on out-of-wedlock births from the National Center for Health Statistics, on changes in welfare program caseloads from the Department of Health and Human Services, and on past and projected expenditure levels from the Office of Management and Budget. Many of these data are collected, along with a narrative summary, in the *Green Book*, a thick (1,400 or more pages in recent years) paperback volume published by the House Ways and Means Committee.

Sources of explanatory and evaluation research have grown as well, ranging from the General Accounting Office, Congressional Budget Office, and other federal agencies to nonprofit public policy research organizations (popularly known as think tanks), public policy schools within universities, and contract program evaluators like the Manpower Demonstration Research Corporation. Policymakers also receive help in understanding complicated policy research from agencies like the Congressional Research Service that specialize in digesting and interpreting research for Congress.[6] Growing competition among external sources of policy advice such as think tanks has pushed them to make their research more user friendly as well.[7] For example, during the Republican round of welfare reform, both the Urban Institute and the Brookings Institution, two leading Washington think tanks, produced volumes that attempted to summarize the state of policy research on welfare issues in brief, readable essays that would be accessible to nonspecialist policymakers. Other institutions offered policy briefs that summarized policy research in predigested form.[8] The *New York Times*, the *Washington Post*, the *National Journal*, and other elite media outlets offered some coverage of welfare policy research in their news pages, and the *Times* and the *Post* featured opinion pieces based on policy research in their op-ed sections. Other publications like the *Public Interest* and the *American Prospect* also published popularized versions of policy research written by the researchers themselves.

Another potential source of information on welfare issues, especially for legislators with jurisdiction over programs, is congressional hearings. Information is available on who testified at hearings and the page length of those hearings. Of course, these measures cannot tell how many legislators and staff were actually listening (attendance by legislators at hearings is generally low, especially among senators) or whether those present absorbed or responded to the information presented, but they do suggest something about what sorts of information sources legislators value or at least believe should be provided a forum in which to express their views.

Table 6-2 provides information on the attendance at hearings held in the 103d Congress (1993–94) and the 104th Congress (1995–96) on welfare reform and related issues (child poverty, foster care, adoption, child support enforcement, and the Earned Income Tax Credit) by the two committees with jurisdiction over AFDC: the House Ways and Means Committee and the Senate Finance Committee. Hearings on welfare and related issues were far more extensive in the House, where members specialize more and have fewer committee assignments competing for their attention. Policy experts of several types are an important source of congressional testimony in both chambers, especially in the more truncated Senate hearings. But they are by no means the dominant sources of information. In the House, members of Congress (excluding members of the committee itself, who are omitted from the tabulations in table 6-2) are in fact the most common testifiers in hearings, although their testimony is frequently brief and related to specialized constituency interests. Representatives of the executive branch, while representing a relatively small percentage of those who testify, are frequently given pride of place, testifying first and most extensively. They provide an important source of information that policy researchers cannot about the administration's own proposals or its reactions to legislation being developed in Congress. Representatives of intergovernmental organizations and state and local governments, service providers (such as nonprofit job training agencies and food banks), and advocacy groups also provide a combination of political reaction about objections to proposed reforms and information about how policy changes are likely to work (or not work) in practice that are important to legislators. In the House, witness lists sometimes include a few other citizens (graduates of welfare-to-work programs, for example, or foster parents and custodial parents seeking collection of child support payments). In short, legislators seek ordinary knowledge about welfare issues as well as (but certainly not to the exclusion of) policy research.

Table 6-2. *Affiliations of Witnesses in House Ways and Means and Senate Finance Committee Hearings on Welfare Reform and Related Topics, 1993–96*

Percent unless otherwise indicated

Affiliations	103d Congress		104th Congress	
	House	Senate	House	Senate
Experts	21.05	18.75	15.09	33.87
University	7.89	0.00	5.33	11.29
Conservative think tanks	2.63	0.00	4.14	12.90
Centrist think tanks	2.63	6.25	1.18	4.84
Liberal think tanks	4.21	6.25	2.37	1.61
Policy evaluation groups	1.58	6.25	1.18	3.23
Other expert groups	2.11	0.00	0.89	0.00
Intergovernmental	19.47	56.25	18.20	20.16
Intergovernmental groups	4.74	31.25	2.37	0.00
Governors	0.53	12.50	2.37	11.29
Other state government	10.53	12.50	8.14	5.65
Local government	3.68	0.00	5.33	3.23
Federal executive	19.12	18.75	9.99	0.00
Department of HHS	4.21	18.75	3.85	3.23
Treasury Department	1.58	0.00	0.59	0.00
Other federal executive	13.33	0.00	5.56	0.00
Congress	23.16	6.25	22.49	8.06
Members of Congress	22.11	6.25	21.01	8.06
Congressional Research Service	0.53	0.00	0.59	0.00
General Accounting Office	0.53	0.00	0.89	0.00
Congressional Budget Office	0.00	0.00	0.00	0.00
Other	0.00	0.00	0.00	0.00
Advocacy groups	15.79	0.00	16.86	19.35
Liberal/child/recipient advocacy	13.68	0.00	11.24	8.06
Father avocacy groups	0.53	0.00	1.78	3.23
Social conservative groups	0.00	0.00	1.18	4.84
Other advocacy groups	1.58	0.00	2.66	3.23
Professional associations	2.63	0.00	1.92	2.42
Labor unions	0.00	0.00	0.89	1.61
Service providers	6.32	0.00	8.88	11.29
NGO service providers	5.79	0.00	7.79	11.29
Private sector providers	0.53	0.00	1.18	0.00
Everyday citizens	3.68	0.00	1.18	0.00
Total number of witnesses	190	16	338	62
Total number of hearing pages	3,130	248	4,049	1,138

Source: Congressional Information Service, *CIS Annual,* various issues.

Even within the broad category of experts there are many sources of information, as table 6-2 shows. Witnesses from nonprofit public policy research organizations testified on welfare reform issues more frequently than university-based academics. This reflects both physical proximity to Congress (most of these organizations are in Washington, allowing think tank staffers to build personal linkages and trust with legislators and congressional staff members) and the greater policy and sometimes ideological and even partisan focus of much think tank research. The think tank category spans a broad range of organizations, from "universities without students," like the Brookings Institution and the RAND Corporation, which are staffed mainly by academics and try to avoid an ideological identity, to organizations that embrace it, like the conservative Heritage Foundation. Frequently the line between children's advocacy organizations like the Children's Defense Fund and liberal think tanks such as the Center on Budget and Policy Priorities (CBPP) and the Center for Law and Social Policy is a fuzzy one, as will be discussed in chapter 8.

The information in table 6-2 also suggests that legislators' search for information is not value-free. The majority party generally is most important in formulating committee witness lists. It is not surprising, therefore, that in the 104th Congress, both conservative think tanks and social conservative organizations like the Christian Coalition and Concerned Women of America were called more frequently as witnesses than in the 103d Congress.

Uses and Limitations of Policy Research

Although many studies support the idea that policymakers pay attention to policy research in their decisionmaking, there has also been skepticism about the sources of the research and the way policymakers use it. Much of what is claimed to be policy research in fact is neither disinterested in its origins nor unbiased.[9] Andrew Rich and Kent Weaver have argued that an increasing number of think tanks are in fact "advocacy tanks," whose work may be tainted by strong ideological predispositions, and that policymakers and the public have difficulty distinguishing their work from more traditional sources of policy advice. The result, they suggest, may be a "devaluation of the currency" of policy research generally and of research from think tanks in particular.[10] Interest groups' widespread use of the techniques of social science and the resulting welter of conflicting findings may similarly cause legislators to simply dismiss all evidence that does not fit their personal or constituency preferences.[11]

On the user side, too, there are barriers to the effectiveness of policy research, especially in Congress. Legislators have incentives to gain information: a reputation for expertise in a particular policy sector can give a legislator increased influence over peers.[12] But obtaining and analyzing information is also costly, and policymakers may lower their information costs by taking cues from others rather than seeking information themselves, especially on issues of lesser importance to themselves and their constituents. In addition, legislators (and the public) may discount or ignore information that does not fit well into their existing framework of ideas, a phenomenon that psychologists refer to as cognitive dissonance. Moreover, many congressional committees are dominated by preference outliers (legislators predisposed by constituency interests to favor programs that the committee oversees), who self-select those committee assignments and may not be open to research that challenges those interests. Shortages of time and an oral culture that values the quick and clear transmission of relatively simple messages also inhibit the use of impartial policy research.[13]

Both the uses and limitations of this research can be seen in the welfare policymaking round that culminated in passage of the Family Support Act (FSA) of 1988. Several studies have concluded that policy research, especially evaluation research on work-to-welfare experiments, played an unusually strong part in shaping the act because there was a monopoly supplier of expertise on welfare-to-work experiments whom everyone had to quote: the Manpower Demonstration Research Corporation (MDRC). Equally important, the MDRC was trusted by all sides because it was not seen as having a particular ideological or policy axe to grind.[14] It also benefited from factors largely beyond its control, notably that its research fit with the "zeitgeist," in this instance a broad concern with increasing work and reducing welfare dependency.[15]

A close examination of these studies of the Family Support Act suggests that even here the effect of policy research was strongly constrained as to how much and under what conditions it was felt. Politics is likely to be more important than research on highly ideological issues where blame-generating pressures are present and where policymakers' minds are already made up. For example, the FSA compelled states to require a high percentage of AFDC-UP parents to engage in sixteen hours of community work (workfare) each week, even though research concluded that doing so would not be cost-effective.[16] Similarly, research was of little help on what constituted a decent benefit provision. Here basic value orientations of legislators and other policymakers were determinative.[17] Even if research suggests that certain policies are worth putting in place, it may be used less by policymakers in deciding how much to spend—for example, how universal to make welfare-to-work programs, and whether to focus on low-cost options like job search or more expensive but potentially more efficacious alternatives. Because of the money trap—the widespread belief that too much is already spent on welfare—policymakers may enact new programs and then underfund them, especially when they are constrained by other considerations such as budget deficits and budget rules that make spending more on a program politically or procedurally difficult.

It is also clear in retrospect that evaluation research on welfare-to-work was interpreted in an overly optimistic manner in the debate on the Family Support Act. Debate focused on the positive results rather than on the small magnitude of those results because that fit the policy and political interests of politicians. And the FSA represented a compromise between liberals and conservatives on many critical issues (for example, how much to emphasize work or training and how much discretion to grant to states) rather than an actual consensus. In short, even when policy research offers consistent findings and fosters an agreement on a particular direction to policy change, the agreement may be neither deep nor durable. In the more polarized welfare policymaking atmosphere of the 1990s, these limitations became even more pronounced. Instead of resolving disputes, policy research became contested territory.

Issues Surrounding Program Entry

No issues in the most recent rounds of welfare reform were more contentious than those surrounding program entry. Debate focused especially on conservatives' charges that the availability of benefits (AFDC alone and in combination with other programs like Medicaid to which AFDC eligibility gave automatic access) increased program entry by acting as an incentive to childbearing, discouraging marriage, and luring families onto the welfare rolls that might otherwise try to succeed in the low-wage labor market without receiving welfare.[18] Conservatives also suggested that welfare created a "culture of dependence" that was passed on from generation to generation. In addition, they argued that availability of AFDC served as a serious deterrent to work among welfare recipients and therefore to program exit, a point that will be discussed later.

Figure 6-1. *Number of AFDC/TANF Families and Recipients, 1960–99*[a]

Millions

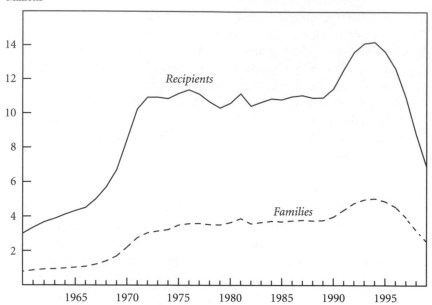

Source: "Temporary Assistance for Needy Families (TANF) 1936–1999" (www.acf.dhhs.gov/news/stats/3697.htm [April 24, 1999]).

a. All data are monthly averages except 1999, which are for June.

Indicators

Indicators produced by policy research set off fire alarms that heightened concerns about program entry in the early 1990s. One was the rapid increase in AFDC caseloads that occurred after 1988 (figure 6-1). Another was the increasing percentage of out-of wedlock births.[19] A third was a rise in the overall birthrate of teen mothers that began in the mid-1980s after having fallen for two decades. Research suggesting that children raised in single-parent families tended to fare worse scholastically and in achieving economic self-sufficiency than those raised in two-parent families (even after controlling for known educational and class characteristics of their parents) further increased concern over trends in family structure and illegitimacy.[20]

What these indicators meant and why they were taking such alarming turns was more contested, however. Simple indicators could be misleading.

Figure 6-2. *Birthrates for Teenagers Aged 15–19, by Race and Hispanic Origin of Mother, 1960–98*

Per 1,000 in specified group

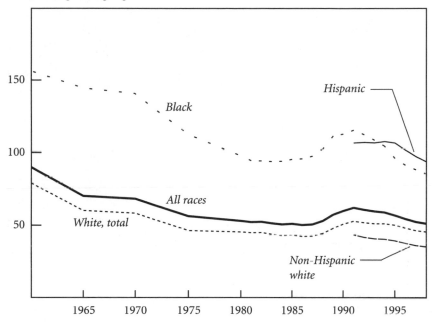

Source: Stephanie J. Ventura, T. J. Mathews, and Sally Curtin, "Declines in Teenage Birth Rates, 1991–1997: National and State Patterns," *National Vital Statistics Reports*, vol. 47, no. 12, December 17, 1998, p. 9, and Stephanie J. Ventura, T. J. Mathews, and Sally Curtin, "Declines in Teenage Birth Rates, 1991–1998: Update of National and State Trends," *National Vital Statistics Reports*, vol. 47, no. 26, October 25, 1999, p. 5. Data for 1960–75 are by race of child.

In 1992, for example, only 8 percent of AFDC families were headed by mothers younger than age twenty, suggesting (as some liberals did) that teenage pregnancy was not a big part of the AFDC problem. However, because women who had their first children as teenagers frequently stay on AFDC a long time, they constituted a very high share of AFDC recipients: 52 percent in 1992.[21]

Interpreting teenage pregnancy trends is even trickier. The overall birthrate for teenage females had fallen dramatically from the 1960s through the early 1980s before rising again, peaking in 1991, and then declining once again, though remaining above the record lows of the early 1980s (figure 6-2). Given the delay of about two years in the reporting of

Figure 6-3. *Births by Race and Hispanic Origin of Unmarried Mothers, 1970–97*

Percent of live births to unmarried mothers

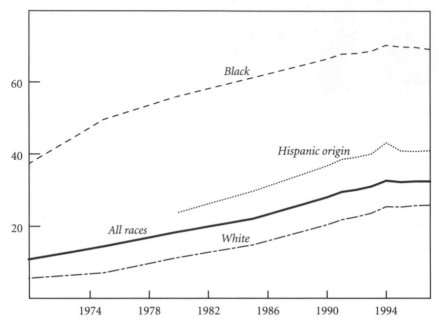

Source: National Center for Health Statistics, *Health, United States, 1999, with Health and Aging Chartbook*, Hyattsville, Md.: NCHS, 1999. Hispanic origin data are for selected states and are unavailable before 1980.

natality statistics, it was not clear in the most recent rounds of welfare reform whether a new upward trend or a short-term aberrant uptick in the birthrate to teenage mothers was under way in the 1990s.[22]

It was very clear, however, that the teenage marriage rate was declining. Shotgun weddings—indeed all weddings of teens and adults—decreased precipitously over this period, so that the share of out-of-wedlock births to teenage mothers expanded from 15 percent in 1960 to more than 70 percent in the early 1990s (figure 6-3).[23] Thus the problem was less one of increased fertility among female teenagers than of a decline of marriage among women who became pregnant—especially teenagers.

Not surprisingly, liberals and conservatives differed as to which statistics they emphasized. Conservatives highlighted the skyrocketing out-of-wedlock birthrates as a sign of a serious breakdown in societal norms and a potential future social catastrophe of fatherless children, especially fatherless males.[24] Liberals stressed the long-term decline in the overall teenage birthrate to dampen the atmosphere of social crisis and the attraction of deterrence-oriented solutions such as family caps and teenage mother exclusions that atmosphere encouraged. Indeed, some researchers said that given the limited choices available to inner-city young people, evidence suggested that the advantages to both teenage mothers and their children of delaying pregnancy were much less than the conventional wisdom suggested—certainly not enough to justify the rhetoric of a national catastrophe.[25] Those conclusions were much contested, however, and there is little doubt that the upward trend in birthrates to teenagers in the second half of the 1980s and findings on the problems associated with single parenthood put liberals on the defensive in welfare reform.

Explanations

By the early 1990s a substantial body of academic studies attempted to test conservative arguments that high welfare benefits were a lure to having illegitimate children and enrolling in AFDC. This research generally took one of two forms: longitudinal or cross-sectional studies. In longitudinal studies, links are examined between the evolution of benefit levels and various measures of out-of-wedlock childbearing or AFDC caseload changes. Longitudinal studies generally dismissed the notion of a welfare-caseload link by observing that even considering food stamps and AFDC together, real benefits had declined significantly since the 1970s (the drop was much greater if AFDC benefits are considered alone).[26] Cross-sectional studies examined variations in benefits across states and potential links to birthrates and caseloads. These studies generally found no effect or relatively modest effects that varied across ethnic groups and were generally stronger for whites.[27] Efforts to use survey research techniques to test arguments about teenage pregnancies also found that few teenage mothers cited the availability of welfare benefits as a reason for having children. Most pregnancies, these studies found, were not planned, and reasons for having children generally involved factors like a desire to hang on to a boyfriend or "have someone to love."[28] A growing number of studies also stressed the importance of culture and peer group pressure, especially among urban black males, that in the absence of promising job prospects "emphasizes sexual prowess as proof of manhood, with babies as evidence."[29] "Predation" by men who impregnated women several years younger than themselves also gained increasing attention from researchers and the press.[30]

Liberals tried to use these findings to counter conservative demands for strong deterrence measures against illegitimacy.[31] But their efforts faced three major obstacles. First, conservatives were able to argue that cross-sectional evidence of weak welfare effects was inadequate because studies simply measured variations across states, all of which had some public assistance benefits. Thus there simply were no data that tested the effect of *no* welfare benefits on out-of-wedlock childbearing.[32] And conservatives could point to research concluding that daughters of mothers who were AFDC recipients were somewhat more likely to receive AFDC later on than daughters of women who had not been recipients (even controlling for income and eligibility), suggesting that there was some intergenerational transmission of welfare dependence.[33] Liberals tried to argue that dependency effects were difficult to separate from the effects of the impoverished environments in which AFDC recipients were raised and that such effects were in any case "much less than is commonly believed."[34] Emerging research findings on intergenerational dependence nevertheless placed liberals once more on the defensive.

A second problem liberals faced was an inability to present a simple, compelling, research-supported alternative to the conservative argument about the welfare-illegitimacy link. Critics of the welfare-begets-illegitimacy argument cited a number of explanations for the increase in illegitimacy, including deterioration of the low-wage labor market in inner cities and spatial mismatch between the location of jobs and residences of urban minority groups. They argued that these factors decreased the attractiveness of marriage to low-skilled men whose earning capacity was shrinking in a "winner-take-all" economy. These critics also contended that out-of-wedlock births were increasing in all sectors of society (including the so-called Murphy Brown phenomenon), and indeed throughout the industrialized world, suggesting that a societywide decline in the stigma attached to out-of-wedlock births was involved. But most efforts to test the "marriageable male" thesis produced weak results. By the mid-1990s, William Julius Wilson and other liberal scholars were talking in terms of a complex interaction between economic opportunities and cultural norms in inner-city communities that weakened commitment to marriage, especially among young African American men.[35] This contention, whatever its theoretical and empirical merits, lacked two major political virtues: parsimony and politically viable policy prescriptions. Its lack of parsimony was ridiculed by Charles Murray, who argued that the dramatic move toward out-of-wedlock births must have a powerful force behind it and challenged liberals to identify what that "mysterious something" could be if it was not the welfare system.[36] Equally important, the policy prescriptions that liberals presented to address these problems—a broad-based attack on poverty with a special focus on inner cities—were simply not palatable to politicians in an era of chastened and budget-constrained government.

Finally and perhaps most important, conservatives could argue that explanatory research was both implausible and irrelevant. It was implausible to believe that the availability of welfare benefits had no effect on whether a couple took precautions to avoid a pregnancy, even if obtaining benefits was not the primary reason for becoming pregnant and carrying the fetus to term rather than having an abortion.[37] Conservatives contended that welfare benefits could contribute to increased illegitimacy and welfare dependency even if they were not the driving forces behind those phenomena. As former secretary of education William Bennett said in 1995 testimony before the House Ways and Means Committee, "Welfare may not cause illegitimacy, but it does make it economically viable. It sustains it and subsidizes it. And what you subsidize, you get more of. Welfare is illegitimacy's economic life-support system."[38] Moreover, to many policymakers (especially conservatives), research suggesting that welfare did not increase illegitimacy or that the social costs of teenage pregnancy were overstated was irrelevant in the sense that even if these arguments were correct, it was still wrong for the welfare system to send a signal of approval or to provide an incentive for behavior that was morally wrong.

Liberals also lacked explanations for the increase in AFDC caseloads after 1988 that could assuage concerns that the caseloads were multiplying out of control. A Congressional Research Service study attributed much of the increase to the rise in the number of families headed by never-married mothers.[39] Other research concluded that caseload increases could not be adequately explained by this factor, even in combination with other factors such as the recession in the early 1990s, policy changes made by the Family Support Act, and the crack cocaine epidemic of the late 1980s.[40] Policymakers and the attentive public were left with the image of a program with rising caseloads for which researchers had no clear explanations or solutions.

Evaluation Research

By the time that Congress began to debate welfare reform again in the Clinton administration, several experiments were under way that attempted to assess what sorts of programs would be most effective in reducing out-of-wedlock births, the most important source of entry to the AFDC program.

Various prevention and rehabilitation interventions were tested, from standard sex education to the provision of contraceptives and other services in school and special counseling for teenage mothers who already had one child to prevent second births. The results were almost universally discouraging: few programs had substantial effects in reducing pregnancies, and some even increased them.[41] Prevention measures that concentrated exclusively on promoting abstinence, the preferred approach of social conservatives, had been neither widely tried nor seriously evaluated, however.[42] Once again, the conclusions drawn from evaluation research on prevention and rehabilitation varied. Liberals generally concluded that changing the behavior of low-skilled (especially teenage) parents with few attractive career opportunities was extremely difficult and that therefore deterrence strategies such as exclusions of teenage mothers were likely to lead to a social catastrophe of massively increased deprivation among poor children. Many conservatives, starting from very different value premises, concluded that if the social catastrophe of increased illegitimacy was to be avoided, much more severe measures such as family caps and teenage mother exclusions were the only remaining hope.

Debates about deterrence measures to discourage out-of-wedlock births in the Clinton and Gingrich rounds of welfare reform took place with little direct research available. Because no state had attempted teenage mother exclusions by the time of debates on welfare during the first Clinton administration, evaluation research focused on the very limited evidence on family caps coming from New Jersey, the first state to impose them. It should be noted that the amount of money involved in the New Jersey family cap was relatively small: the benefit increase for a third birth was only $64, and one-third of the loss of this benefit increase would be offset by an increase in food stamps. The child would continue to be eligible for Medicaid.

Several questions were important in evaluating the New Jersey experience. Obviously most central was whether these provisions would reduce rates of additional out-of-wedlock births to AFDC recipients. Proponents of family caps were heartened by early studies that showed a significant decline in out-of-wedlock birthrates and then disheartened when later research did not appear to discover an effect.[43] Opponents of family caps also cited a study that suggested a 4 percent increase in abortions under New Jersey's family cap law.[44] Both positive and negative findings on family caps were cited in the Senate's September 1995 debate on an amendment to strike a mandatory family cap from the Senate's welfare reform bill, despite deep flaws in the evidence from New Jersey.[45]

Overall, the ambiguity of evaluation research on deterrence gave that approach a critical advantage over prevention and rehabilitation approaches to teenage pregnancy: there was not yet a large body of evidence from multiple sites suggesting that it did *not* work. Nor was there definitive evidence that family caps and teenage mother exclusions had harmful effects. But in evaluating whether the reforms should be adopted, policymakers had important additional *political* evidence in the form of state waiver requests about what would likely happen if family caps and teenage mother exclusions were made a state option. Many states had requested family caps, and thus that policy would likely become widespread, while only one state had requested a waiver for teenage mother exclusion. As a result, policymakers could vote for a legislative package including a state-option teen-mother exclusion knowing that the real risks that the option would be widely adopted were fairly low.

From Program Exit to Self-Sufficiency

Debates in the 1990s about the forces that prevented AFDC families from leaving the program and becoming self-sufficient through labor market income or marriage were also highly contentious. As with debates on program entry, they revolved mostly around conservative charges that the welfare system reinforced dependency and discouraged work. And once again research findings were complex and subject to differing interpretations by conservatives and liberals.

Policy Indicators

The most basic contentions on program exit involved work effort by AFDC mothers. The *1994 Green Book* reported that only 6.7 percent of unmarried parents in single-parent AFDC families reported earned income in 1992—which is not surprising considering the nearly 100 percent marginal tax rate on earned income under AFDC in this period.[46] Moreover, only one-quarter to one-half (depending on measurement methodology) of AFDC recipients who left the rolls did so because of increased earnings.[47]

The length of time that recipients remained on AFDC also raised major concerns. As Mary Jo Bane and David Ellwood wrote, "If welfare is predominantly a short-term aid . . . dependency becomes less of a worry and

policies designed to move people from welfare to work might be unnecessary, potentially even counterproductive . . . but if welfare lasts a very long
time, then the nature and the reasons for long-term use become important,
and policy responses more complex."[48]

The length of stays on welfare can be measured in several ways that give
very different assessments. Researchers found that the average length of stay
for every case that came on to the AFDC rolls appeared short: almost half of
new entrants left within two years. But this measure seriously understates the
length of time families remained on AFDC in two critical ways. First, it does
not take account of the fact that those women who do remain on welfare
rolls for a very long time compose a disproportionate share of the AFDC
caseload. Indeed, simulation studies showed that in a snapshot view of the
AFDC caseload, almost half of the women on the rolls were in the midst of
spells that would last ten years or more. Those who did not leave the rolls
within two years were particularly slow to exit thereafter.[49] Research also suggested that many AFDC recipients did not go on AFDC just once, but cycled
on and off the program when they lost (or quit) jobs. Again, the differences
between all first-time recipients and a snapshot view of the caseload is revealing. Of all women who began their first spell on AFDC, simulation studies
suggested that almost 37 percent would have a total (all spells) stay of less
than two years, and only 22 percent would have total stays totaling ten years
or more. But at any given time, the caseload composed only 8.5 percent of
persons whose total stay on AFDC would be two years or less; 56.6 percent
were expected to have a total length of stay of ten years or more.[50]

Research on length of welfare spells had several effects on policy debates.
First, increased awareness of the long length of total stays of many recipients
increased concerns over long-term dependency among many liberals as well
as conservatives. Indeed, it helped contribute to provisions in the Family
Support Act targeting the Job Opportunities and Basic Skills Training program (JOBS) on those most at risk of being long-term welfare recipients.
Second, this research increased awareness of the heterogeneous nature of the
AFDC caseload. It suggested that AFDC recipients comprised at least three
groups: short-term recipients (frequently as the result of a marital breakup),
long-term recipients, and cyclers, and that it might therefore be necessary to
treat program entrants who seemed at risk of different lengths of stay on
AFDC somewhat differently. Third, the research showed that women who
did not leave AFDC rolls within two years often stayed for a long time, raising fears that prolonged absence from labor markets made reentry more difficult.[51] This in turn undermined support for allowing women with very

young children to remain home, despite the higher costs (related in particular to child care) of moving those mothers into work. As with evidence on illegitimacy, however, this research by no means produced a consensus on the sources of long-term welfare dependency or what to do about it.

Explanatory Research

Why do mothers in poor, single-parent families have so much trouble moving into work? The different welfare reform approaches discussed in chapter 5 suggest several possibilities, from lack of education and strong labor market barriers to high benefits that made welfare a better economic deal than work. Policy research offers important evidence on a number of these points but has not led to a consensus on which explanations, alone or in combination, are most important.

LACK OF SKILLS AND NEED FOR SUPPORTIVE SERVICES. Perhaps the most obvious reason for lack of success in moving AFDC/TANF recipients into the labor force is many recipients' lack of skills. Many recipients, especially those who remain on welfare rolls the longest, have less than a high school education and fare very poorly on standardized achievement tests. Even if they are able to obtain employment, making enough to pay for child care and for support of their families is difficult. Although conservatives and liberals tend to agree that both lack of skills and costs of child care are important barriers to participation in the labor force, they frequently disagree on how serious an obstacle it is to moving recipients to work.[52]

ABSENCE OF JOBS. Another contested area is whether jobs are available to welfare recipients who seek work. Many economists contend that a spatial mismatch exists between job growth in suburban areas and the hollowed out central cities where most racial minorities live, leaving few jobs available for unskilled workers.[53] Lack of transportation and child care availability for long and odd hours increases the barriers to AFDC/TANF mothers who are making the long commutes and working the irregular hours involved in many suburban entry-level jobs. Ethnographic research suggests that within inner cities, as well, informal networks and long queues make entry-level jobs hard to come by.[54] Many conservatives argue that evidence for a spatial mismatch is mixed at best and that work is available to welfare recipients willing to work at low wages. In particular, the ability of immigrants, most of whom have poor English-language skills, to find jobs "strongly suggests that unskilled employment is plentiful in the United States."[55] These views are not entirely irreconcilable: a plausible middle position is that labor market barriers are real, but that more (but almost certainly not all) AFDC recipients and noncustodial fathers could be moved into work either by lowering the costs of working (the liberal prescription) or raising the costs of nonwork (the conservative prescription). Because evidence on labor market barriers is ambiguous and can, in any case, lead to different policy prescriptions depending on the observer's preferences for imposing costs on the poor versus on government, research in this area once again has not promoted a policy consensus.

WELFARE BENEFITS.   A standard argument made by conservatives about the failure of welfare recipients to move into low-wage work has been that welfare payments are more rewarding, especially when the costs of work are factored in. This argument is by no means a new one; it was a central argument of Charles Murray's *Losing Ground* and was contested in liberal responses to the book.[56] Policy analysts of all ideological persuasions have long noted the poverty trap faced by a single-parent family trying to leave work for a low-wage job without health benefits.[57] Work disincentives are likely to be particularly strong for families with serious health problems, where the value ascribed to Medicaid benefits (provided automatically with AFDC) is especially important.[58]

The debate over the effects of AFDC on work incentives was given heightened visibility in 1995 when the libertarian Cato Institute issued a report contending that when a variety of means-tested benefits typically available to AFDC families (notably Medicaid and Food Stamps) were taken into account, welfare benefits were far more generous than was commonly believed. Most important, the report argued, "In forty states welfare pays more than an $8.00 [an hour] job [and] in seventeen states the welfare package is more important than a $10.00 an hour job." Thus it concluded that choosing welfare over work was a rational choice for most low-skilled recipients and argued, "If Congress or state governments are serious about reducing hard-core welfare dependence and rewarding work, the most promising reform is to cut benefits substantially."[59] The Center on Budget and Policy Priorities issued a rejoinder questioning the methodology and conclusions of the Cato report.[60] Moreover, liberals could use the same empirical findings to argue for the importance of increased funding for child care and medical assistance to the non-AFDC working poor (though with limited prospects for getting them from a Republican Congress). Even many conservatives might draw different policy conclusions. For new paternalists like Lawrence Mead, for example, it suggests the need for mandating work rather than cutting benefits. But the availability of the Cato report was powerful ammunition to conservatives seeking cutbacks in spending on means-tested programs. And the perception by liberals that the public and policymakers were likely to draw conservative (cut benefits) rather than liberal (increase services) prescriptions from an analysis that welfare benefits discouraged work made liberals reluctant to acknowledge that such an effect existed.

OTHER INCOME SOURCES. Yet another possible explanation for the failure of welfare recipients to exit welfare for the low-wage labor market is that they have unreported sources of income from outside the welfare system. This might include legal but off-the-books work in providing child care, housecleaning, beauty services, and so forth, or (less frequently) illegal work such as dealing drugs or prostitution. It could also include child support income payments from noncustodial fathers that are not reported to welfare and child support authorities and assistance from friends, family, and food banks. Not surprisingly, such income is rarely reported in statistics gathered by government, such as the Panel Study of Income Dynamics. But in the early 1990s, pioneering ethnographic research by Katherine Edin and Laura Lein produced data suggesting that non-AFDC income was almost universal among AFDC recipients—indeed that they could not possibly have survived without it, given the low level of AFDC benefits.[61] The sources of this income varied across regions, however, with work income more prevalent in areas with more opportunities to hold side jobs and a lower unemployment rate.

Once again, this research did not produce a consensus on policy, but rather divergence based on differing views of the dual clientele and perverse incentives traps. For liberals, who were most concerned about providing adequate incomes to low-income families but well aware of the unpopularity of welfare benefit increases, the research suggested that a higher minimum wage, more generous earnings disregards to enable low-wage workers to combine work and welfare, child care subsidies, and increased access to medical insurance for the working poor were needed to make "aboveboard" work pay. For conservatives concerned primarily about welfare dependence, the lesson was that stiff mandatory work requirements were needed to "smoke out" welfare recipients working off the books, who would have to confess their employment to explain why they could not show up for mandated work activities. Mandating work activities for new entrants to AFDC might also "divert" many potential applicants with work-related income from ever applying for welfare benefits. Evidence from states that imposed strict work requirements and had rapidly falling caseloads, notably Wisconsin, also suggested that diversion effects could be very strong.[62]

Evaluation Research

A number of studies have taken advantage of variations in the AFDC program and of experiments at the state and local levels to evaluate different approaches to increasing work effort by welfare recipients. Research on incentive approaches that attempt to increase work by disregarding earned income and therefore lowering the benefit reduction rate of AFDC recipients have produced generally discouraging results. The reason, as economists have pointed out, is that two offsetting trends are at work. On the one hand, allowing AFDC recipients to increase their earnings does in fact produce increased work effort among this group. On the other hand, it tends to reduce work effort among women who were already working and perhaps off the rolls. The two effects largely offset one another.[63]

A second body of research focuses on welfare-to-work demonstrations based on the prevention and rehabilitation and new paternalism strategies. An overly optimistic interpretation was placed on those results by most policymakers in the 1987–88 welfare debate that culminated in passage of the Family Support Act. The act's proponents, seeking to dispel the sense that nothing works in moving recipients into jobs, emphasized that welfare-to-work programs were an efficacious mechanism for promoting work by welfare recipients. Little attention was paid to the fact that relatively few people became self-sufficient or moved out of poverty. By 1993 this optimistic interpretive gloss had been largely eroded, especially among deterrence-oriented conservatives.

A number of studies were published in the early 1990s reviewing the results of state welfare-to-work demonstration projects.[64] Reports from the General Accounting Office and congressional hearings also reviewed these experiences. The research covered a broad range of programs from low-cost "job clubs" to community work experience programs and labor-intensive (and expensive) training and education programs. The general picture that emerged was that many different approaches can have significant effects on the employment and income of AFDC recipients, but there are no magic bullets. The results were all modest, as might be expected in a population that generally has very little human capital and a lot of problems and constraints. Participants in welfare-to-work were somewhat more likely to be employed and have higher earnings than those who did not participate. But even in Riverside, California's GAIN (Greater Avenues to Independence) program, considered one of the most successful programs and the prototype of the "work first" approach with strong enforcement, participants

earned an average of only $3,113 a year, or 49 percent more than nonpar-
ticipants. As one review of the Riverside experience concluded, "More people got jobs than would otherwise have gotten them without the program,
and got them sooner, but these were usually not 'better' jobs, and families
were rarely boosted out of poverty. Thus, three years after enrolling in
Riverside GAIN, 41 percent of people were still receiving welfare benefits,
although some of them were working and receiving benefits."[65]

In general, those who were most likely to be employable (with the highest skills and education and most recent labor market participation) without program participation gained least. Potential long-term recipients benefited the most from the program, except those with the lowest skills and
longest welfare experience.[66] Welfare-to-work programs did not make a
substantial dent in lifting the recipient population out of poverty or in
reducing program cost.[67]

The studies found that a variety of program structures could yield
mildly beneficial results. The least expensive programs, which usually
focused on job search, were most beneficial in cost benefit terms, but that is
more because of their very low cost, often under $200 a person, than
because of large income gains by recipients.[68] Enforcement also made a difference, with a strong stress on finding a job and strong threats of cutting off
benefits leading to stronger earnings gains.[69] Gains were least likely to be significant, not surprisingly, in areas with high rates of unemployment such as
West Virginia and Tulare County in California. However, workfare jobs that
do not provide new skills to recipients and are most likely to be applied to
(mostly male) recipients who already have labor market experience seem to
provide the least gain in earnings. Expenditures on basic education, too,
seemed to have limited payoffs. Experiments on subsidizing employers to
hire welfare recipients suggested that they might actually have harmful
effects, apparently because they stigmatized recipients as bad workers in the
eyes of potential employers.[70]

Research on welfare-to-work programs also had several shortcomings
as a basis for extrapolating to some of the more ambitious welfare reform
initiatives proposed after 1993. As Rebecca Blank pointed out, most Manpower Development Research Corporation evaluation studies of welfare-to-
work programs were carried out with parents of older school-aged children,
and it was not clear that their effects would hold up if requirements were
extended to mothers of young children.[71] Nor was there substantial experience with the very high work participation rates (50 percent of all program
participants or more) envisioned by many policymakers in the mid-1990s.[72]

Expanding these efforts to saturation scale was likely to be particularly difficult in inner-city neighborhoods, some researchers warned.[73]

In general, the evaluation studies of welfare-to-work programs published in the 1990s were consistent with those available in the 1980s. What was different was the conclusion that many policy advocates and analysts drew from the evaluation research: that their promise is real but limited, rather than a panacea. Once again, this shared lesson allowed liberals and conservatives to draw different implications for welfare reform. To liberals it suggested that increasing successful transitions to work was likely to be a slow, arduous process, requiring multiple supportive services. If a soft time limit was imposed, after which work was required to maintain benefits, a significant share of the AFDC caseload with the lowest skills would be unlikely to get and retain private sector jobs. Thus some, perhaps as many as a quarter, would almost certainly need a fail-safe position of public sector or subsidized jobs to survive.[74] Many conservatives drew a very different conclusion: that welfare-to-work programs, even if they involved substantial new paternalist mandatoriness and sanctions, were unlikely to make a major dent in welfare dependency. More dramatic changes in incentives, involving both program entry and hard time limits, would be required to produce a significant change in behavior.

Conclusions: Policy Research and the Politics of Dissensus

Definitive conclusions about the role of policy research in the Clinton and Republican rounds of welfare reform must await the narrative history in later chapters. But the discussion in this chapter suggests some strong preliminary conclusions. An obvious first one is that research on welfare issues certainly was not unknown territory to policymaking elites (in the broad sense that incorporates specialized legislative staff), at least those most involved in devising welfare reform policy. Research findings were reported in congressional hearings, in the news and opinion pages of newspapers, and in publications that cater to policymakers. Those for whom welfare issues were less important and who were least involved in shaping policy presumably paid little attention, but it would be difficult to argue that information was not easily accessible to those most involved.

How did policymakers use policy research? Clearly they used it to sound a fire alarm in both the Clinton and Republican rounds. Concern about the nature of the welfare system and problems of dependency was increased in significant ways by social science information, by the interpretations being put on that evidence, and by the aggressive marketing of those views by conservative advocates and think tanks. The continued increases in rates of out-of wedlock births (and in welfare caseloads in the early 1990s) were visible indicators of a system that seemed to be out of control. Experts did not agree on the reasons, and in the absence of a consensus on an alternative explanation, the conservative argument that the welfare system itself was to blame gained wide support. Growing evidence that the average length of a welfare spell is very long for a substantial percentage of the AFDC caseload and that raising children in single-parent households is associated with disadvantageous outcomes became additional fire alarms for policymakers.

There is limited evidence that policymakers used research as a circuit breaker. The high risks and absence of data on the effectiveness of deterrence measures such as family caps, teenage mother exclusions, and hard time limits did not cause policymakers to wait for more complete data from experiments in the states before they considered mandating these rules nationwide. Nor did absence of evidence prevent Congress from enacting and the president from accepting family caps and teenage mother exclusions as a state option in the 1996 welfare reform legislation; however, concerns about risks to poor children may have helped prevent their being mandated to the states. Similarly, Congress mandated five-year hard time limits in 1996 despite both the absence of any direct evidence on their effect in improving either self-sufficiency or child welfare and much indirect evidence that a substantial percentage of the AFDC caseload could not become self-sufficient under that time limit. Once again, however, there was a modest circuit-breaker function because the legislation allowed states to exempt up to 20 percent of their caseloads from that time limit. The inclusion of exemptions from hard time limits in the Personal Responsibility and Work Opportunity Reconciliation Act (PRWORA) probably benefited more from lobbying by states than from its sponsors' desire for a circuit breaker, however.

Not surprisingly on such a divisive and partisan issue, the evidence suggests significant use of policy research as ammunition to defend existing value-based and coalition-based policy positions. The idea that policymakers use research in a technocratic fashion, however, enjoys limited support. Policy research did not promote a consensus on particular solutions supported by social science evidence, or even on what conclusions to draw from worrisome indicators. Several factors appear to contribute to continued dissensus.

Absent Research

In some instances relevant research results simply did not exist on the problems to which policymakers were seeking answers. This was particularly true for some of the most important new options under consideration: soft time limits followed by a work requirement, hard time limits after which no federally subsidized benefits are available, family caps, and teenage mother exclusions. State-level experiments were only starting or had not been implemented at all. Even when such evaluations did get under way, they took a long time to produce results that researchers deemed reliable. Results were frequently not available when policymakers needed to make decisions on accepting or rejecting the provisions.

The absence of definitive evaluation research seems to have had only a modest restraining effect on policy innovation, however, because the public favored change (almost any change, as the next chapter will show) and policymakers had made commitments to produce it. The combination of mixed research results and social problems that appeared to be worsening contributed to research results' having an effect on the welfare policy agenda somewhat different from that posited by Henry Aaron in his classic *Politics and the Professors*. Aaron argued that the political consequences of evaluation research are generally conservative: because results are almost always conflicting, they usually "cause action to be deferred until more evidence is available."[75] Certainly Aaron is correct that in the programs he was analyzing—negative income tax, education, and training experiments, for example—the effect of unclear evidence was that many experiments were terminated rather than turned into general policies, while additional resources were not committed to expand programmatic initiatives already undertaken. Chapter 9 shows that in the case of the Clinton welfare reform initiative the search for analytical certainty delayed action and contributed to missing a window of opportunity for policy change.

The Clinton and Republican welfare reforms also suggest, however, that the inability of evaluation research to show clear solutions to these problems may stimulate a search for new panaceas. Although evaluation research may succeed in discrediting existing strategies, it is by no means necessary to have supportive evaluation research to earn new proposals a place on the welfare agenda.[76] Partisan change in the control of Congress brought new approaches to government's action agenda that had been at the margins of debate in the welfare policy community for a number of years, notably deterrence and radical devolution through block grants. Proponents of these approaches were able to point to the failures of the status quo to justify trying new approaches.

If experimental evidence had existed on these new strategies, Republican legislators would have been forced to make explicit trade-offs: how much increase in extreme poverty, foster care caseloads, and abortions would they be willing to accept for a given reduction in out-of-wedlock births, for example. But in the absence of such data, these trade-offs could more easily be ignored.

Negative Lessons

The lessons learned from research are sometimes primarily negative, telling researchers and policymakers what does not work well and thus what *not* to do, but giving them little guidance on what they *should* do instead. Research on teen pregnancy prevention programs suggested very limited benefits. Even more important, the early and mid-1990s were a period of increasing skepticism about the value of approaches favored in the late 1980s, especially the ability of work-based approaches to solve the "welfare problem." Increasing evidence suggested that requiring work does not lift most poor families out of poverty and that many poor families would have difficulty in obtaining and maintaining employment. Requiring work remained popular with moderate and conservative policymakers and the public, but the evaporation of the fragile consensus that work-based approaches were an adequate response to welfare dependence opened up the policy agenda for new, generally untested, deterrence-oriented solutions.

Multiple Sources of Expertise

The multiplication in the 1980s and 1990s of rival sources of expertise with differing assumptions and conclusions allowed policymakers to choose ideas that suited their ideological preferences. The influence of policy research is further undercut when the purveyors of policy research are perceived as biased or interested. Except for the congressional research agencies, universally respected sources of research were hard to come by in the most recent rounds of welfare reform. A Republican congressional staffer noted that as part of the effort to increase awareness of the array of means-tested federal programs and build support for consolidating them, his committee had asked the Congressional Research Service to do a study, which showed that there were more than 300 such programs. In building a case for consolidation, "Every time we trot this thing out, and anybody who tries to say, 'Oh, that's an exaggeration,' we say, "Wait, wait. We will send you the CRS report,' because everyone trusts CRS."[77]

The highly politicized climate for welfare reform and a dearth of definitive studies by sources seen as unbiased by all sides encouraged politicians' natural tendencies to cite studies produced by researchers who supported their side while ignoring or at a minimum viewing with suspicion research produced by those with opposing views.[78] This process was accelerated by changes in the role and function of policy expertise. A number of (primarily newer) think tanks blurred the role between policy research and policy advocacy. In addition, researchers increasingly sought new outlets for their results that would be briefer and more accessible to policymakers. Although these publications may have helped to diffuse knowledge about policy research more broadly, they may also have had a less salutary effect: because many outlets (for example the liberal *American Prospect* and conservative *Public Interest*) had ideological leanings, researchers who published in them may have undermined their perceived legitimacy as objective scholars with policymakers on the other side of the growing welfare ideology divide. In short, as policy researchers sought to become more engaged in debates to inform them, policy research was unable to maintain either the appearance or the reality of neutrality and impartiality.

Differing Values

Perhaps the most important constraint on the capacity of research to produce a technocratic consensus in the most recent rounds of welfare reform was that policy research could not resolve value conflicts on fundamental issues— in particular differences on the dual clientele trap conflict over the importance of the behavior of adults versus the welfare of children. Table 6-3 summarizes some of the important matters on which liberals and conservatives largely agreed about what the policy research evidence suggested but disagreed about what policy conclusions to draw. In the case of the relatively modest effects of welfare-to-work programs, for example, liberals' concern for the welfare of children led them to favor multiple supportive services and back-up public service jobs for women who could not make it in the private labor market. For social conservatives the same evidence showed that welfare-to-work programs were not a solution to what they saw as the social catastrophe of welfare dependence. Their conclusion was that stronger deterrence measures against out-of-wedlock births and long-term welfare receipt were the only hope for reforming the system.

Table 6-3. *Conflicting Conclusions Drawn from Policy Research on Welfare Issues*

Research finding	Liberal	Conservative
Prevention/rehabilitation and new paternalism approaches to pregnancy prevention have limited effect on behavior	Efforts to change child-bearing behavior through deterrence mechanisms are unlikely to succeed and will cause major hardship for children if imposed	Only severe deterrents have any hope of changing child-bearing behavior
Benefit packages available to AFDC recipients frequently higher than income received by low-wage workers	Provide child care, health care, and earnings disregards to "make work pay"	Cut benefit packages or mandate work as condition of receiving means-tested benefits
Many welfare recipients supplement income through off-the-books work and support from others	Higher minimum wage, child care subsidies, and increased access to medical insurance for working poor needed to make work pay	Work requirements and child support must be strictly enforced to smoke out illicit work and child-support income
Welfare-to-work programs have only modest success in moving AFDC mothers into work and keeping them there, little success in moving them out of poverty	Provide multiple supportive services and backup public service employment to welfare recipients with lowest skills	Impose deterrence measures to prevent initial reliance on welfare and make long-term reliance impossible

Political Commitments

The influence of policy research is also undercut when either research findings or an absence of research findings conflicts with politicians' commitments. This is particularly evident in setting time limits. The Clinton administration came into office with a firm commitment to soft time limits (work requirements after two years) and the Republicans in 1995 with a commitment to hard time limits (a cutoff of federally subsidized AFDC cash benefits after a set period), despite the fact that there was very little evidence on the effects of either. When asked how it was possible to develop a program in the absence of such evidence, one of the Clinton administration's main welfare policymakers replied,

> First we do have . . . pretty damn good predictions, in the absence of behavioral effects, about how many people hit two years. . . . But no question about it, the hardest thing by far so far is the fact that the president has been very, very clear on "ending welfare as we know it." Very, very clear about two years. And yet, the simple reality is we don't have any time-limited welfare programs that are serious time limits. We have all kinds of things that claim to be this and that in the AFDC program. Of course we have lots of real time limited programs otherwise: UI [unemployment insurance] is a classic time limited system followed by nothing. But this particular one we don't have an example of time limits followed by a work program, especially. So, I think what we've done is try to look at what we do know from existing work programs, what we do know from [the Comprehensive Employment and Training Act]. We've spent a lot of time trying to understand the characteristics of people who hit the time limit, and what that would look like. But I think the flip side is we ended up with the view, just saying, "We need enormous flexibility in this program."[79]

This quotation suggests that technocratic values were far from absent in the minds of Clinton administration policymakers. Without direct evidence of success from the program under review, they turned to second-best evidence, drawing lessons from the most closely comparable policies and attempting implicitly or explicitly to model the behavior of the program clientele, assuming rational responses to policy change. They also sought to avoid locking in new program models prematurely. But the quotation also makes clear that the absence of such evidence is not likely to be a major barrier to policy initiatives when a presidential commitment like Clinton's pledge to end welfare as we know it is involved.

Contested Methods

The impact of policy research is also weakened when communitywide norms are expected to be affected by policy change, and changing norms in turn are expected to result in major changes in recipient behavior. Deterrence measures on program entry (family caps and teenage mother exclusions) and hard time limits are two areas where adherents of those policies expect especially strong behavioral effects from community norms about the acceptability of out-of-wedlock childbearing and prolonged receipt of AFDC. As a result, adherents of such policies tended to discount research findings from the two "second-best" methodologies that researchers used to try to test the potential effects of such policy changes before they are put in place communitywide: control group studies and simulation studies. Control group methodologies, which examine differences in behavior between a randomly assigned group subjected to the policy change (the treatment group) and a group not affected, are likely to understate the effects of policy on behavioral change no matter how they are structured. If only a small population is in the treatment group, communitywide norms are unlikely to have changed much, and the extent of policy change is likely to be understated. If all but a small control group is subjected to the policy change, the control group is likely to be affected by changing norms as well, and the measured difference in behavior (for example, additional births among AFDC mothers subjected to a family cap) is likely to be understated. In any case, this methodological difficulty compromises the ability of control group studies to produce consensus among policymakers. Discounting of any extant research is likely to be widespread by policymakers who are hostile to the research conclusions.

The problem is even greater with simulation studies of policy changes. In the absence of data from state-level experiments about the effects of deterrence measures, critics of the measures have relied on computer simulations of effects that the measures would have had if applied to the current AFDC population. Defenders of deterrence measures replied that the simulations did not take into account behavioral adaptations that would be induced by the policy change, notably reduced out-of-wedlock births and increased effort to find and retain employment. It is of course possible to make assumptions about the magnitude of such behavioral changes, but it is unlikely that proponents and opponents of teenage mother exclusions and hard time limits will agree on the magnitude of those effects.

The narrative chapters 9–13 will show that policy research was used in somewhat different ways in the two rounds of welfare reform. Technocratic concerns contributed substantially (but not exclusively) in the Clinton administration's planning for its welfare reform bill, while the formulation and later amendments to the Republicans' Personal Responsibility Act in the 104th Congress were dominated by bargaining between elements of the Republican coalition. But in both rounds the capacity of policy research to produce consensus on a particular direction for reform was undermined by factors ranging from the absence of research to different weights placed on the two main elements of the dual clientele trap. Politicians neither ignored nor relied completely on policy research about problems and programs; instead, they weighed the research against other types of knowledge and electoral and coalitional considerations.

In short, policy research did not induce a research-based consensus on a single approach or combination of approaches to welfare reform. It did, however, improve the prospects of welfare reform's being enacted in the Republican-controlled 104th Congress because

—the research heightened concern over increases in illegitimacy, long periods of welfare receipt, and intergenerational welfare dependence;

—evaluation research suggested that welfare-to-work programs alone, even if generously funded, would be inadequate to reduce welfare dependency and recidivism substantially; this in turn caused Republicans to look for alternative approaches, especially deterrence and devolution;

—explanatory and evaluation research on proposals favored by various elements of the Republican coalition was sufficiently ambiguous or incomplete in its findings that Republican elites were able to keep their coalition together by adjusting their proposals throughout the legislative process in response to pressures from multiple constituencies.

CHAPTER SEVEN

Public Opinion on Welfare Reform

PUBLIC OPINION CAN help or hinder the prospects for welfare reform initiatives in several ways.[1] Public ambivalence about the dual clientele of public assistance to poor families underlay the most fundamental of the policy-making traps that have bedeviled welfare reform initiatives over the past quarter century.[2] And shifting public opinion, like changes in social science knowledge produced by policy research, is a plausible explanation of the passage of comprehensive welfare reform in 1996 after numerous failures, including the 1993–94 Clinton initiative. This chapter outlines some hypotheses about the ways public opinion can shape welfare reform initiatives and evaluates those hypotheses by tracing the evolution of public attitudes in the early 1990s.

Public Opinion and Policy Change

Chapter 3 offered a first plausible hypothesis about the relationship between public opinion and welfare policy: that policy change directly reflects changes in public opinion on substantive issues. If the public increases its support for elements associated with specific approaches to welfare reform—deterrence or prevention and rehabilitation, for example—parties and politicians may feel compelled to adapt their positions to make them closer to those of the public. If politicians believe that welfare reform is a topic that the public views as increasingly important and on which it demands action, they are more likely to proceed with an initiative than if it is a low priority for the public. If this opinion-change hypothesis is correct, one would expect to see both a growing public consensus on the substance of welfare reform in the early 1990s and a convergence between public opinion and the policies enacted. Popular consensus on policy may facilitate welfare reform by weakening specific policymaking traps (for example, reducing concern over the welfare of children). Public agreement on the substance of policy may also prompt politicians to use repositioning strategies, such as strategic pursuit and splitting the difference, that promote accommodation with their political and policy adversaries.

An alternative argument, which can be called the elite convergence hypothesis, suggests that the public had long expressed fairly clear views about what sort of AFDC policy it wanted. In particular, people had expressed preferences for more work-based policies. However, elite dissensus had prevented policy change. As the prominence of welfare reform increased in the early 1990s, elites moved closer to this public consensus. If this hypothesis is correct, one would expect to see increased salience for welfare issues but little change in public views, with a high level of public consensus on approaches to welfare both before and during the Clinton administration.

Public opinion may affect the prospects for welfare reform in two additional ways, however, even if there is no public consensus on a particular direction for reform. If the public has a high level of trust in a particular party or politician—President Clinton or the Republicans in control of the 104th Congress, for example—to address welfare reform issues and is willing to defer to that political leadership on the details of reform, that popular leader or party may be able to use public support to win over otherwise recalcitrant politicians to the leader's own favored prescriptions about what should be done. In this public deference perspective, public support for specific political leaders may facilitate welfare reform even if the subject is not particularly prominent in voters' minds and the fit between public views and leaders' preferences on welfare issues is not close.

A final impetus for reform may arise if public discontent with AFDC is so great that the public demands change and is willing to accept virtually any modification of the status quo as an improvement (or at least believes that it could not be any worse). Political elites may then feel compelled (or may want) to respond to public discontent. But as in the third scenario, those who have control of the legislative agenda are strongly empowered vis-à-vis their policy rivals. If they can maneuver so that opposing elites, by seeking to block their proposals, are perceived as defenders of a hated status quo, they are in a strong position to enact their own policy preferences and to benefit politically from doing so. In this "public anger" scenario, it is voters' disdain for the status quo rather than support of specific leaders and their policy preferences that facilitates welfare reform.

The Importance of Elite Priming

Of course, politicians do not sit idly by and listen passively to public opinion. In the most recent rounds of welfare reform, both the Clinton administration and Republicans invested heavily in trying to influence how the public sees welfare and in trying to associate the other party with unpopular positions.[3] Republicans charged that AFDC was full of perverse incentives for parents, most notably to have children out of wedlock at government expense, and argued that "what is really cruel is the current incentive that pulls young women into the system and holds them forever in this cruel trap."[4] Congressional Democrats and children's advocacy groups contended that Republicans should not finance tax breaks to the wealthy by cutting benefits and services to poor children.[5] Both sides charged the other with being "weak on work." And both perceived the stakes to be very high: the side that was able to convince the public that its vision of welfare and its proposed solutions were the most appropriate would have an advantage in winning enactment of its proposals and perhaps in winning future electoral contests.

The crucial change in this period was in the balance of messages that Americans heard about welfare reform. The debate over welfare changed dramatically when Bill Clinton pledged in his 1992 presidential campaign to "end welfare as we know it" and to move people from income assistance to work. From both Republicans and the Clinton administration the dominant messages "priming" attitudes toward welfare reform concerned the evils of the system rather than the welfare of children. Many congressional Democrats followed the administration's rhetorical and political lead, leaving AFDC almost devoid of powerful and vocal defenders within government.

As a result the Clinton and Gingrich rounds focused on how to reform welfare, with Republicans pushing for increased responsibility for the states, increased disincentives to out-of-wedlock births, and reduced federal expenditures, while the Clinton administration stressed the need to provide additional child care and job guarantees. A stream of critiques of AFDC from both Republican and Democratic politicians contributed both to a marked increase in the prominence of welfare reform issues and to increasing dissatisfaction with the current system.[6] These factors gave a tremendous advantage to the political forces controlling the welfare reform agenda and dramatically weakened the bargaining position of those who could be presented as opposed to fundamental change in the system.

Analyzing Opinion on Welfare

A basic problem in analyzing public opinion toward welfare and welfare reform is that it may not be clear what the public means by the terms when responding to questions, because surveys often do not identify specific programs. Does the public associate welfare just with AFDC or also with Food Stamps, Head Start, Medicaid, and Supplemental Security Income? A January 1995 survey for the Kaiser Family Foundation suggests that when prompted by the names of specific programs, people who are polled identify a broad array of means-tested programs as welfare and will exclude contributory social insurance programs (Social Security and Medicare) from that definition. People also overestimate the share of the federal budget that is spent on means-tested programs.[7] It is less clear, however, whether the broad concept of welfare is triggered by general survey questions about welfare that do not include prompts about specific programs.

A second problem in analyzing public opinion on welfare stems from the phenomenon long observed by researchers that public opinion on programs for low-income Americans differs significantly depending on the precise wording of questions, most notably between questions relating to "welfare" and those relating to "programs for poor children." "Welfare" is likely to stimulate responses focusing on parents, especially on images of abuse and fraud by welfare recipients.[8] It is also likely to stimulate associations with racial minorities. The term "poor children," however, stimulates images of a sympathetic clientele that is not responsible for its own condition.[9] Thus the same surveys that show overwhelming rejection of spending on welfare also showed that many more Americans believe too little is being spent on "assistance to the poor" and "government spending on programs for poor children" than believe too much is being spent for these purposes, although support for these positions eroded significantly in the early 1990s (figure 7-1).

Most Americans—almost two-thirds in 1995 polls—think that too much is being spent on welfare. That share increased from about 40 percent of those surveyed between 1991 and 1995, after a period of stability through

Figure 7-1. *Public Opinion on Welfare Spending, 1973–93*

Percent favoring more spending minus percent favoring less spending

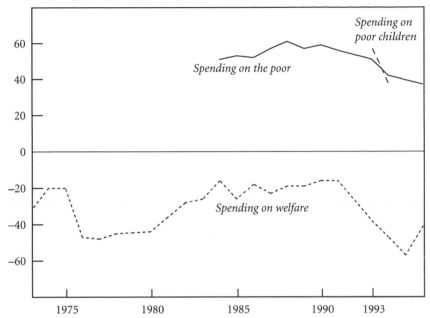

Source: All questions on welfare are from the National Opinion Research Center. The question asks, "We are faced with many problems in this country, none of which can be solved easily or inexpensively. I'm going to name some of these problems, and for each one I'd like you to tell me whether you think we're spending too much money on it, too little money, or about the right amount. First, . . . are we spending too much, too little, or about the right amount on . . . welfare?" All data on "assistance for the poor" are from the same survey. No General Social Surveys were conducted in 1979, 1981, and 1992. The 1993 data on spending for poor children are from a November Hart poll that asked, "Do you think government is currently spending too little, about the right amount, or too much on . . . poor children?" The 1994 poll on this topic is from a December CBS/*New York Times* poll that asked, "Do you think government spending on programs for poor children should be increased, decreased, or kept about the same?"

most of the 1980s and a decline after passage of the Family Support Act of 1988.[10] Part of that change is probably due to the increase in AFDC caseloads and expenditures since the late 1980s. There is also a strong relationship between the party of the incumbent president and public opinion on welfare spending. When Democrats control the presidency, some part of the public apparently assumes that governments must be spending too much on welfare. When Republicans are in control, there is a corresponding assumption that government is being too stingy.[11] But the unprecedented high levels of support by the end of 1994 for the position that too much was being spent on welfare probably reflect the combined effects of conservative arguments about bloated welfare programs and President Clinton's often repeated message that it was necessary to end welfare as we know it. Despite the president's intention to increase overall spending on poor families, the effect of this message was, not surprisingly, to increase discontent with the current welfare system among Democrats as well as Republicans.[12]

The view that the welfare system is a failure was clearly widespread in the American public by the early 1990s. Only one-sixth of Americans polled at the end of 1993 thought that the welfare system was working very well or fairly well, while 79 percent thought that it was not working very well or not well at all. This put the welfare system at the bottom of six policy sectors rated in the poll, even lower than the criminal justice system.[13] Around 80 percent of Americans polled in 1994 and 1995 thought that the welfare system was in need of fundamental rather than only minor reform.[14]

The most basic judgment that the public can make about the efficacy of a program is whether it does more harm than good. The welfare system failed this test. In an April 1995 survey 69 percent of the public agreed with the statement that "the welfare system does more harm than good, because it encourages the breakup of the family and discourages work." Only 23 percent believed that "the welfare system does more good than harm, because it provides assistance and training for those who are without jobs and are poor." This ratio does not seem to have been affected significantly by the vociferous debate in the House of Representatives and in the country in the first months of 1995.[15] By margins of more than seven to one, the public thought that the welfare system caused people to become dependent and stay poor rather than giving them a chance to stand on their own feet.[16] Both questions, it should be noted, focus primarily on the effects of the welfare system on parents rather than the protection of children, and the system is clearly judged a failure on this criterion. Much of the public was concerned that welfare benefits might be too high and that the system encouraged long-term dependence, discouraged work, and caused women to have more children than they would if they did not go on welfare.[17] Welfare, in short, was perceived as being at odds with the widely shared American belief in individualism and the work ethic. When asked in November 1993 whether "the bigger problem with the welfare system today" is that "it spends too much money" or "it spends money the wrong way," 85 percent of those surveyed argued that spending money the wrong way was the bigger problem, compared with only 4 percent for "spends too much money."[18] But although public support for cutting welfare expenditures to reduce the budget deficit has increased greatly since the late 1980s, public willingness to spend more for job training and public service jobs remained high and stable.

The most plausible explanation of these results is that much of the public was concerned with getting a welfare system more consistent with their own beliefs and values (and less ridden with fraud and perverse incentives) than with using changes in the welfare system to reduce the deficit.[19] This interpretation is supported by polls asking respondents what should be the most important goals of a welfare reform initiative. Moving welfare recipients into the work force, ending dependence on welfare as a way of life, and giving recipients skills needed to make them self-sufficient consistently ended up as top goals, while saving money for taxpayers came in near the bottom (table 7-1).

Causes of Poverty and Welfare Dependence

Too often, poll questions trying to ascertain the public's beliefs about why people are poor and become dependent on welfare programs are posed in terms of dichotomies that are too simplistic. For example, is receiving welfare more often the result of poor motivations or of circumstances beyond people's control, or of poor values or bad policies? Given these choices, the public's responses were split fairly evenly through most of the 1980s. The percentage emphasizing individual failings fell at the end of the 1980s and then rose dramatically from 1992 to 1995, no doubt reflecting both economic recovery and "priming" by politicians stressing the evils of welfare dependence (table 7-2).

Americans also believe that a large number of welfare recipients should not be receiving benefits.[20] However, when surveys offer several possible reasons for receiving welfare, large percentages of the public appear to have fairly sophisticated and complex beliefs about why people are poor or receive welfare, emphasizing both socioeconomic problems such as a shortage of jobs, poor education, breakdown in families, and individual failings such as poor motivation (table 7-3). Even many of those who believe that large segments of the poor are to blame for their condition also believe that government has a duty to care for those who cannot care for themselves, although that responsibility is not unlimited in duration.[21]

Table 7-1. Most Important Goals of Welfare Reform, 1992–95[a]

Percent unless otherwise indicated

Polling organization/ sponsor	Date	Reduce out-of-wedlock births	Help move people on welfare into work force	Make sure poor children get support	Eliminate fraud	Give people skills to be self-sufficient	End long-term dependence on welfare	Save taxpayers money, cut costs	(Volunteered) Other	(Volunteered) All	Not sure; don't know
Yankelovich Clancy Shulman for Time/CNN	3/92	...	...	...	...	90	...	5	...	3	3
Yankelovich Clancy Shulman for Time/CNN	5/92	...	...	...	...	93	...	3	...	2	2
Hart/Teeter[b]	11/93	...	52	22	28	...	29	7	...	...	1
Los Angeles Times	4/94	17	73	...	...	...	...	6	1	...	3
NBC/Wall Street Journal	3/95	15	45	17	29	...	51	...	...	9	...
Hart/Teeter for NBC/WSJ	7/95	19	62	...	...	...	...	13	...	...	6

Sources: The survey data reported in this chapter were compiled from searches of survey archives and published and unpublished sources, including the Roper Center for Public Opinion Research's on-line Public Opinion Location Library (POLL); The Public Perspective: A Roper Center Review of Public Opinion and Polling; the Inter-university Consortium for Political and Social Research (ICPSR, University of Michigan); data holdings of the Institute for Research in Social Science (IRSS, University of North Carolina); and the Times-Mirror Center for the People and the Press.

a. "What should the most important goal of welfare reform be?" Exact wording varies slightly. Where no percentage appears next to a goal, it was not included as an option in that poll.

b. Up to two responses permitted.

Table 7-2. *Public Opinion on Causes of Poverty, 1982–97*
Percent unless otherwise indicated

Polling organization/ sponsor	Date	*Circumstances*			
		Insufficient effort	*beyond control*	*Both (volunteered)*	*Don't know*
CBS/NY Times	3/82	37	39	17	7
Gallup	12/84	33	34	31	2
Gallup	7/88	40	37	17	6
Gallup	8/89	38	42	17	3
Gallup	5/90	35	45	17	3
CBS/NY Times	12/90	30	48	20	2
LA Times	1/92	27	52	18	3
Hart/Teeter/NBC/WSJ	11/93	48	33	17	2
CBS/NY Times	12/94	44	34	18	4
Hart/Teeter/NBC/WSJ	4/95	60	30	7	3
PSRA for Pew	10/97	39	44	14	3

Sources: The survey data reported in this chapter were compiled from searches of survey archives and published and unpublished sources, including the Roper Center for Public Opinion Research's on-line Public Opinion Location Library (POLL); The Public Perspective: A Roper Center Review of Public Opinion and Polling; the Inter-university Consortium for Political and Social Research (ICPSR, University of Michigan); data holdings of the Institute for Research in Social Science (IRSS, University of North Carolina); and the Times-Mirror Center for the People and the Press.

Attitudes toward Specific Reforms

Growing public unity around a particular approach to welfare reform such as how best to limit program entry or to stimulate successful transitions into the labor market might provide an impetus for policy change. A major problem with tracking public opinion on proposals for welfare reform, however, is that the terms of the debate among policymakers shifted so dramatically in the early 1990s that a long time series does not exist on many policy options: polltakers tend to ask only about proposals that are under serious discussion. In addition, when confronted with a battery of proposals for policy change about which they may know little contrasted with a program that they know they do not like, respondents may say that they are in favor of the proposal when they in fact do not have a well-defined opinion at all.

Table 7-3. *Perceived Causes of Poverty*[a]

Percent unless otherwise indicated

Cause	Mean rating	Rating 10–8	7–5	4–1	Not sure
Poor people lack motivation	6.1	29	52	18	1
Absent parents not paying child support	7.0	49	35	15	1
Increased immigration	6.3	39	35	23	3
Shortage of jobs	6.7	42	39	18	1
Welfare system	6.9	45	38	15	2
Breakdown of families and family values	7.6	60	29	10	1
Poor people receive inadequate education	6.9	46	36	16	2
Too many jobs part-time or low-wage	6.6	42	37	20	1

Source: Telephone poll conducted November 12–15, 1993, by Peter D. Hart Research Associates.

a. "For each of the following, tell me how big a factor it is in causing poverty, on a scale from 1 to 10. A rating of 1 means the item is not a cause at all; a 10 means it is a top cause of poverty; and a 5 is somewhere in the middle. Remember, you may use any number between 1 and 10, depending on how you feel. First, how big a cause of poverty is this on a scale from 1 to 10?"

Public opinion survey data show that while people detested the welfare status quo in the early 1990s, they were also hesitant to embrace whole-heartedly some of the proffered alternatives. These data also suggest that, with a few exceptions, changes in attitudes toward specific reforms were relatively modest in this period.

Program Entry Issues

Most survey research on program entry issues has focused on deterrence of out-of-wedlock births. These proposals have enjoyed mixed support. Denying an increase in benefits to mothers who bear children while on welfare is the most popular of these measures (table 7-4). Family caps enjoyed a tremendous surge in public support between 1992 and 1993. Support dropped somewhat in 1994, but most polls continued to show majority public support for the idea through 1995.

Support for related deterrence provisions—an outright ban on cash benefits to some or all unwed mothers—was significantly lower than that

Table 7-4. *Public Opinion on Family Caps*

Percent agreeing with or in favor of proposal[a]

Polling organization/ sponsor	Date of poll	Response to question
YP[b]/*Time*/CNN	3/92	39[c]
YP/*Time*/CNN	5/92	36[c]
TMLL[d]/*USNWR*	11/93	65[e]
Hart/Teeter	11/93	68[f]
LA Times	4/94	65[f]
YP/*Time*/CNN	5/94	42[c]
KRC/Harvard/Kaiser	12/94	59[g]
NY Times/CBS	4/95	56[h]
YP/*Time*/CNN	9/95	45[c]
LA Times	9/95	56[i]

Source: The survey data reported in this chapter were compiled from searches of survey archives and published and unpublished sources, including the Roper Center for Public Opinion Research's on-line Public Opinion Location Library (POLL); The Public Perspective: A Roper Center Review of Public Opinion and Polling; the Inter-university Consortium for Political and Social Research (ICPSR, University of Michigan); data holdings of the Institute for Research in Social Science (IRSS, University of North Carolina); and the Times-Mirror Center for the People and the Press.

a. Proposal was to stop giving additional money to mothers if they have another child after they go on welfare.

b. Yankelovich Partners.

c. "Here is a list of changes many people would like to make in the current welfare system. For each idea I read, please tell me whether you favor or oppose that change—End increases in welfare payments to women who give birth to children while on welfare."

d. Tarrance Group and Mellman, Lazarus and Lake.

e. "Do you favor or oppose the following suggestion to reform the welfare system?—Do not increase benefits when people on welfare have additional children."

f. "Now, here are some additional proposals related to poverty and welfare. For each one, please tell me if you would strongly favor, somewhat favor, somewhat oppose, or strongly oppose the proposal?—Stop giving extra money to mothers if they have another child after they go on welfare." (Strongly favor and somewhat favor responses are added.)

g. Women who have additional children while on welfare should not receive additional benefits for those children.

h. Would you favor or oppose denying additional benefits to unmarried mothers on welfare if they have additional children while they are on welfare?

i. "Do you favor or oppose the following welfare proposals?—Deny increased benefits to recipients who have more children."

for family caps. Table 7-5 shows the evolution of opinion on this issue, with the time dimension again flowing from left to right, and more severe provisions near the top of the table. Only the requirement that unmarried teenage mothers live with a parent or other responsible adult rather than setting up

Table 7-5. *Public Opinion on Teen Mother Exclusions*
Percent believing should not have access/should be denied

Question	4/94	12/94	2/95	3/95	4/95	9/95
Deny all benefits to a woman who has a child outside of wedlock [age not specified], even if that would create hardship for the woman and the child	26	...	...	...	...	...
"Ending welfare payments to children born of unmarried mothers"	...	36	...	...	...	...
"Ending welfare payments to unmarried mothers who have children"	...	40	...	...	...	...
Unmarried mothers under the age of 21 who have no way of supporting their children	...	20	...	...	...	...
Unmarried mothers under the age of 18[a]	...	42	...	38	...	44
Unmarried mothers under the age of 18 who have no way of supporting their children[b]	...	...	31	...	31	...
Deny teenage single parents welfare benefits unless they live with parents or another responsible adult	67	...	...	...	...	...

Source: All questions are from a Gallup poll for CNN and *USA Today*, except as noted below.
a. Yankelovich Partners for *Time*/CNN.
b. *New York Times*/CBS.

their own household (a requirement that had been a state option under the Family Support Act) garnered clear majority support (67 percent). Denial of benefits to unmarried teenage mothers attracted significant support (about 40 percent), but the support dropped substantially if the question included a clause that the mother lacked any other means of support. Support for exclusion also declined if the age of exclusion increased. Moreover, the public is uneasy, by margins of more than two to one, about proposals to ban benefits to teenage mothers if doing so would result in these children's being placed in orphanages or foster care.[22] In general, wording of questions that prime concern for the welfare of children as well as awareness of the mother reduced support for exclusionary provisions.

Table 7-6. *Public Opinion on Prevention/Rehabilitation Approaches to Labor Market Entry, 1993–95*

Percent in favor of or agreeing with option

Polling organization/ sponsor	Date	Provide job training	Provide child care[a]	Provide child care and transpor- tation[b]	Pay transpor- tation to job[c]	Provide job[d]
TMLL[e] for *USNWR*	11/93	...	...	77	...	...
Hart/Teeter	11/93	...	85	...	67	...
Gallup	4/94	94	90	...	66	60
KRC for Harvard/Kaiser	12/94	87	85	...	...	74
Hart/Teeter for *WSJ*	4/95	95	92	...	...	...

Source: The survey data were compiled from searches of survey archives and published and unpublished sources, including the Roper Center for Public Opinion Research's on-line Public Opinion Location Library (POLL); The Public Perspective: A Roper Center Review of Public Opinion and Polling; the Inter-university Consortium for Political and Social Research (ICPSR, University of Michigan); data holdings of the Institute for Research in Social Science (IRSS, University of North Carolina); and the Times-Mirror Center for the People and the Press.

a. Provide child care so a parent on welfare can work or look for work.

b. Provide child care and transportation for welfare recipients who work or are in job training or education.

c. Pay transportation or commuting costs for welfare recipients to get to their jobs.

d. Provide a job or public sector job if needed.

e. Tarrance Group and Mellman, Lazarus and Lake for *U.S. News & World Report*.

Transition to the Labor Market

Several prevention and rehabilitation approaches to moving AFDC recipients into the labor force enjoyed broad support in the period leading up to the welfare reform legislation enacted in 1996. Job training and subsidies for child care were extremely popular, receiving about 90 percent approval (table 7-6). Solid majorities of respondents also supported paying transportation costs and providing public sector jobs.

The clear public favorite among welfare reforms is work requirements, which is consistent with the new paternalism approach to reform. Indeed, a bipartisan consensus has, at least in the abstract, long favored work instead of cash welfare.[23] Table 7-7 shows opinion on a variety of work requirements, with the evolution of opinion shown from left to right and the severity of the work requirement being asked about increasing

Table 7-7. *Public Opinion on Work Requirements for Welfare Recipients*

Percent in favor of/agreeing with option

Question	5/92	11/93[a]	1/94[b]	5/94	12/94	1/95	4/95[c]	9/95[d]	10/95
"Require unemployed fathers of children on welfare to work"	...	94	...	...	...	...	...	...	...
Require fathers of children on welfare to work at public service jobs if they do not pay their child support	...	91	...	...	...	...	...	...	...
Require welfare recipients to work in exchange for their benefits	...	...	...	...	...	...	95	...	...
Limit welfare recipients to a maximum of two years of benefits, after which those who are able to work would have to get a job or do community service	...	82	89	...	...	89	...	91	...
Favor work requirements for mothers of preschool children	...	60	...	...	...	...	...	...	...
"Require all able-bodied people on welfare, including women with small children, to work or learn a job skill"	87	...	...	92	...	...	...	88	...
Favor work requirements for mothers of young children[e]	...	...	45	...	52	...	64	...	59
Favor work requirements for single parents with children under three years of age	...	57	...	...	...	...	...	...	...
Favor work requirements for mothers of infants	...	41	...	...	...	...	...	...	...
Favor work requirement for "any family where the parent has a significant physical or mental disability"	...	34	...	...	...	...	...	...	...

Source: Polls are identified in the following footnotes.

a. All questions are from a TMLL poll for *U.S. News & World Report* except for favoring work requirements for preschool children, which is a Hart/Teeter poll.

b. Limiting welfare to two years, after which work or community service is required, is from an ABC/*Washington Post* poll; favoring work requirements for mothers of young children is from a CBS/*New York Times* poll.

c. Requiring welfare recipients to work in exchange for benefits is from a Hart/Teeter poll for NBC and the *Wall Street Journal*. Favoring work requirements for mothers of young children is from a CBS/*New York Times* poll.

d. A two-year time limit after which work or community service is required is from a *Los Angeles Times* poll. Requiring able-bodied persons to work or learn a job skill is from a Yankelovich Partners poll for CNN.

e. "Do you think that women with young children should be required to work or should they stay at home and take care of their young children?"

(roughly) from the top to the bottom of the table. The public is particularly supportive of work requirements for noncustodial parents who are not paying child support and is most willing to exempt the mothers of very young children from such requirements. But support for applying work requirements even to mothers of young children also increased dramatically during the first Clinton administration. And as noted earlier, 60 percent of those surveyed claimed that they would be willing to pay more taxes to pay for additional job training and public service employment, a share that remained essentially unchanged from the beginning of 1994 through the spring of 1995.

Long-Term Self-Sufficiency

Public opinion about welfare is most ambivalent on time limits. There is widespread and apparently stable support for the principle of limiting receipt of cash welfare benefits to a few years, with the broadest support for time-limited cash benefits followed by a community service or job requirement (table 7-8). A poll taken at the end of 1993, however, suggested that most people would exempt large portions of the AFDC caseload from a time limit if that limit did not include a job guarantee. A three-to-one margin also believed that people should be able to receive benefits as long as they work for them rather than being subject to hard time limits after which no benefits would be received.[24] When asked in a December 1994 poll what should happen to those who hit a time limit, only 10 percent of respondents said that benefits should simply end; more than 81 percent favored a community service requirement or job guarantee instead.[25] Again, the implication is that the public is more concerned with responsible behavior on the part of welfare recipients, in particular engaging in work effort, than with the principle of hard time limits.

Program Structures

Some ambivalence is also evident on questions of program structure: whether AFDC should be an entitlement and whether the states should be more involved in AFDC decisionmaking. Although differences in question wording make it difficult to be certain, support for the idea of individual entitlement for AFDC benefits seems to have eroded between 1995 and 1996, while the contrasting concept of a cap on welfare program spending gained ground (table 7-9). When asked in a December 1994 poll to choose between experimenting at the state level and reform at the national level,

Table 7-8. *Public Opinion on Time Limits for Welfare Benefits*

Percent in favor of/agreeing with option

Question	11/93[a]	1/94	4/94[b]	12/94[c]	1/95	3/95	4/95	9/95
"Limit welfare benefits to two years and do not allow people to get back on welfare ever"	22	...	...	...	...	...	...	...
"Limit welfare benefits to five years and do not allow people to get back on welfare for at least five years"	50	...	...	...	...	...	...	...
"Limit to five years the amount time a welfare recipient can receive cash payments"	...	...	...	...	...	74	...	49[d]
"Limit all adults to a total of five years on welfare"	...	...	...	60	...	...	...	...
"Poor mothers should be limited to a maximum of just a few years on welfare"	...	...	...	...	...	...	61	...
"After two years, benefits would be ended for all able-bodied recipients, and the government would not provide a job"	55	...	...	...	...	...	...	...
"...cut off all benefits to people who had not found a job or become self-sufficient after two years"	...	...	67	...	...	...	...	...
"Limit welfare recipients to a maximum of two years of benefits, after which those who are able to work would have to get a job or do community service	82	89	91	...	89	...	...	...
"...welfare recipients should continue to get benefits as long as they work for them"	...	...	...	71	...	...	...	...
"If benefits are cut off after two years, should "government provide separate benefits to the children, even though their parents' benefits will have been cut off?"	...	...	78	...	...	...	...	...

Source: Polls are identified in the following footnotes.

a. All questions are from a TMLL poll for *U.S. News & World Report*, except for ending benefits for able-bodied recipients and not providing a job, which is from a Hart/Teeter poll.

b. All questions are from a Gallup poll for CNN/*USA Today*, except for limiting benefits to two years, after which a job or community service is required, which is from a *Los Angeles Times* poll.

c. Limiting all adults to five years is from a Gallup poll for CNN/*USA Today*. Allowing welfare recipients to receive benefits as long as they work for them is from a CBS/*New York Times* poll.

d. "Do you favor or oppose the following welfare proposals . . . Limit benefits to five years."

Table 7-9. *Public Support for Individual Entitlement, 1995–96*

Percent in favor of or agreeing with option

Polling organization/ sponsor	Date	Preserve entitlement; do not limit spending	Limit spending; end entitlement	Neither; other (volunteered)	No opinion; not sure; refused
CNN/NY Times[a]	4/95	47	45	...	8
Hart/Teeter for WSJ[b]	5/95	41	50	3	6
LA Times[c]	9/95	45	46	...	9
Gallup for CNN/USA Today[d]	9/96	31	55	7	7

Source: The survey data were compiled from searches of survey archives and published and unpublished sources, including the Roper Center for Public Opinion Research's on-line Public Opinion Location Library (POLL); The Public Perspective: A Roper Center Review of Public Opinion and Polling; the Inter-university Consortium for Political and Social Research (ICPSR, University of Michigan); data holdings of the Institute for Research in Social Science (IRSS, University of North Carolina); and the Times-Mirror Center for the People and the Press.

a. Currently, poor families are guaranteed welfare benefits if they qualify for them whatever the total amount of cost to the government. The Republicans in Congress are proposing limiting the amount of money for welfare benefits and eliminating the guarantee that all eligible families will receive welfare benefits. Which do you think is a better idea: guaranteeing that all eligible families receive welfare benefits whatever the cost to the government, or limiting the amount of money available for welfare benefits even if it means there might not be enough money to cover all families who qualify?

b. Which of these is the better approach for welfare and other programs for the poor? Set a limit on the amount of spending for these programs, even if it means that some people who qualify will not get benefits, or guarantee that anyone who qualifies for these programs will get benefits, even if that means spending will increase.

c. Currently, spending on welfare is determined by the number of people in the country who fall below the poverty line, and the government must spend more if additional people need help. Do you favor or oppose changing that so that the total spending on welfare would be set at a fixed amount and each welfare recipient's grant would be cut if the number of people needing benefits went up? In this poll, the total favoring includes 22 percent who favor strongly and 24 percent who favor somewhat; the total opposed includes 25 percent who oppose somewhat and 20 percent who oppose strongly.

d. Which of the following statements better represents your views about welfare: 1. Government should limit the amount of money it spends on welfare programs, even if some poor people do not receive assistance; or 2. Government should provide a basic amount of assistance to all poor people, even if there are no limits on the amount of money the government spends?

more people chose the state (52 percent) than the national (29 percent), a major increase from the previous year in support for devolution.[26] But in the same poll the public also believed by a 50 percent to 36 percent margin that the federal government should set guidelines for the states rather than allow them complete discretion.

A Fundamental Ambivalence

The public's fundamental ambivalence toward recent welfare reform initiatives and its response to nuances of questioning are clearly reflected in three polls taken over a twelve-day period in September 1995 as the Senate was completing its debate on a Republican welfare reform initiative. By margins of more than four to one, Americans polled believed that the welfare system was in need of fundamental reform, but most also believed that the Republican position represented minor rather than fundamental reform. And when asked if they were more concerned that proposed Republican reforms would go too far in denying assistance to poor families or that Democrats would not go far enough in reforms, more were concerned about going too far than in not doing enough. It is difficult to explain these results without reference to Americans' fundamental ambivalence toward the clientele of programs to aid low-income families and the deep dislike of current programs—as well as the extent to which responses are skewed by a question's wording, tapping one or another element of those complex feelings.

Expressions of public opinion on various welfare reform options suggest a number of conclusions about the structure of that opinion. First, single questions about welfare policy options are likely to provide a misleading reflection of patterns of public opinion. Because of the dual clientele of welfare, the opinion registered on specific questions can vary widely depending on whether it primarily taps opinion toward poor children, who are considered deserving of help, or their "undeserving" parents. Moreover, because of the public's overwhelming dislike of the current system, there may be a positive bias in people's response to questions that ask how they feel about specific changes to policy. But the data also suggest that the American people are much less concerned with getting people off welfare and reducing the costs of the system than they are with having recipients make an effort to help themselves.

Whom Do You Trust?

There has been far more volatility in the public's views of which political players are trusted to carry out welfare reform than in their views on specific reforms. The Clinton administration came into office with a huge advantage: the public trusted it far more than congressional Republicans to do the best job in carrying out welfare reform (figure 7-2). By the beginning of

Figure 7-2. *Public Opinion about Whether President Clinton or Republicans in Congress Will Do a Better Job of Reforming Welfare, 1993–96*

Percent

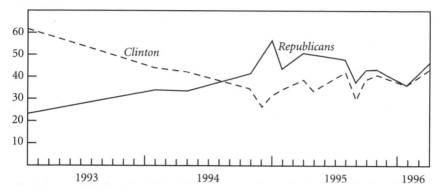

Source: Data in this figure are derived from multiple polls using slightly different wordings. Where multiple polls were available for a single month, results of the polls were averaged. Data for January 1993 are from a Greenberg/Lake poll asking, "I would like to read you a list of issues that some people from this part of the country have said are important for the federal government to deal with. Please listen as I read the list and tell me, for each one, whether you think—1) President Clinton or 2) the Republicans in Congress—could do a better job dealing with this issue . . . Reforming the welfare system." Data for January 1994 are from a Blum and Weprin poll for NBC News asking, "Who do you think would do the best job reforming the welfare system—President (Bill) Clinton or the Republicans in Congress?" Data for April 1994 and October 1994 are from a Los Angeles Times poll asking, "Who do you think can do a better job of reforming the welfare system: President (Bill) Clinton or the Republicans in Congress?" Data for August 1994 and April 1995 are from a Tarrance Group and Mellman and Lake poll asking, "Now I would like to read you a list of issues that some people from this part of the country have said are important for the federal government to deal with. Please tell me, for each one, whether you have more confidence in Bill Clinton and the Democrats in Congress or the Republicans in Congress to deal with this issue . . . Reforming the welfare system." Data for November 1994 and January 1995 are from a Hart/Teeter poll for the Wall Street Journal and NBC asking, "For each of the following issues, please tell me if you think that President (Bill) Clinton or the Republicans in Congress generally will have the better approach to this issue, or if there will not be much difference. Who do you think will have a better approach to . . . welfare reform—President Clinton or the Republicans in Congress, or do you think there won't be much difference on this issue." Data for December 1994 are from two CBS/New York Times polls asking, "Who do you think would make better decisions about reforming the welfare system—the Republicans in Congress or (President) Bill Clinton?" and "Who do you think would be more likely to make decisions about reforming the welfare system that are fair to all Americans—the Republicans in Congress or (President) Bill Clinton?" and a third poll by Princeton Survey Research Associates for Newsweek asking, "As I read off some statements, tell me whether you think each applies more to (President) Bill Clinton or more to Republican leaders in Congress. How about . . , has better ideas for reforming the welfare system." Data for February 1995 are from a similar PSRA survey. Data for January 1995 and April 1995 are from a CBS/New York Times poll asking, "Who do you think has better ideas about reforming the welfare system: President Clinton or the Republicans in Congress?" Data for March 1995 and July 1995 are from an ABC/Washington Post poll asking, "For each specific issue I name, please tell me who you trust to do a better job handling that issue—(Bill) Clinton or the Republicans in Congress."

1994, however, the administration had squandered most of its advantage as it failed to come forward with a welfare reform plan.

Meanwhile, House Republicans did bring out a plan. By the time the administration finally released its reform proposal in the middle of 1994, its advantage in public trust had turned into a deficit. After the 1994 election the deficit became deep. From January through March 1995 (when the House committee and full chamber debate on welfare reform was taking place) congressional Republicans continued to enjoy a margin of between ten and twenty points in public trust on handling welfare matters. The gap closed to six points by mid-July 1995 as the administration increased its attacks on the Republican bill, and the Republicans in the Senate became bogged down in disputes over conservative mandates and allocation of block grant funds among the states. By the fall of 1995 it had closed to a virtual tie, where it remained into 1996. Opinions on which political party voters trusted to reform welfare show a similar overall pattern, although Republicans continued to hold a modest advantage into 1996, perhaps reflecting voters' mistrust of the liberal wing of the Democratic party in Congress (table 7-10).

However, the public's ambivalence about reforming welfare if it means being "too tough on kids" appears once again in polls focusing on public confidence in politicians to handle the matter. For example, a poll released just before the full House of Representatives began debate on welfare reform in March 1995 showed that 51 percent of the public trusted the Republicans in Congress to do a better job than President Clinton of "reforming the welfare system"; 38 percent favored the president. When the issue was framed as "protecting America's children," however, the president was favored over Republicans in Congress by 49 percent to 40 percent. The president's margin of trust over congressional Republicans was even greater in terms of "helping the poor": 61 percent to 27 percent.[27] This ambivalence can also be seen in polls on perceived effects of Republican initiatives when the fate of poor families is mentioned explicitly. Only 12 percent of respondents in an April 1995 survey were concerned that Republican welfare reform initiatives went too far. But in a May 1995 poll 48 percent worried that "the Republicans will go too far in denying assistance to poor families," compared with 37 percent who thought that "the Democrats will not go far enough in making needed changes in the welfare system."[28]

Perhaps the best evidence of people's ambivalence toward political leaders on welfare issues can be found in responses to questions that did not ask which party or leader they preferred, but simply whether they approved of

Table 7-10. *In Which Political Party Do You Have Greater Confidence to Reform Welfare? 1992–97*

Percent

Polling organization/ sponsor	Date	Demo- cratic	Repub- lican	About the same; both	Neither	Not sure; don't know
Hart/Breglio for NBC/*WSJ*[a]	3/92	36	24	16	16	8
PSRA for *Times Mirror*[b]	12/93	40	30	...	11	19
Gallup[c]	12/93	47	36	...	...	17
Hart/Teeter for NBC/*WSJ*[a]	7/94	30	29	17	19	5
TMLL[d]	8/94	34	37	5	11	13
Hart/Teeter for NBC/*WSJ*[a]	10/94	28	31	12	21	8
Wirthlin[e]	11/94	45	36	4	11	3
TMLL[d]	4/95	29	50	4	9	8
Hart/Teeter for NBC/*WSJ*[a]	6/95	21	39	15	19	6
Hart/Teeter for NBC/*WSJ*[a]	12/95	31	35	13	16	5
TMLL[d]	1/96	41	42	4	8	5
Hart/Teeter for NBC/*WSJ*[a]	5/96	31	35	...	...	...
Hart/Teeter for NBC/*WSJ*[a]	9/97	32	30	15	17	6

Source: The survey data were compiled from searches of survey archives and published and unpublished sources, including the Roper Center for Public Opinion Research's on-line Public Opinion Location Library (POLL); The Public Perspective: A Roper Center Review of Public Opinion and Polling; the Inter-university Consortium for Political and Social Research (ICPSR, University of Michigan); data holdings of the Institute for Research in Social Science (IRSS, University of North Carolina); and the Times-Mirror Center for the People and the Press.

a. "When it comes to . . . reforming the welfare system, which party do you think would do a better job the Democratic party, the Republican party, neither, or are both about the same?" The order of the last two options varies across polls.

b. "Which party, Republican or Democrat, do you think can do a better job of . . . reforming the welfare system?" "Neither" response was volunteered.

c. "Do you think the Republican party or the Democratic party would do a better job of dealing with each of the following issues and problems . . . welfare reform?"

d. "Now I would like to read you a list of issues that some people from this part of the country have said are important for government to deal with. Please tell me, for each one, whether you have more confidence in the Democratic party or the Republican party to deal with this issue . . . reforming welfare." "Both equal" and "Neither; no difference" responses were volunteered.

e. "Now I'm going to read you a list of issues. This time I want you to concentrate on the two major political parties, and as I read each one, please tell me whether you think the Republican party or the Democratic party can best handle that problem . . . reforming the welfare system." "Both" and "Neither" responses were volunteered.

the handling of the welfare issue by specific leaders. The most striking pattern (table 7-11) is the frequency with which a majority expressed confidence in the leaders of neither party.

Conclusions and Implications

Like policy research, discussed in chapter 6, public opinion on welfare in the early and mid-1990s did not compel welfare policy change; that is, changes in public opinion were insufficient by themselves to force a change. But the public opinion environment was a fertile one for politicians to bring forward and move welfare reform initiatives.

Four arguments were suggested at the beginning of this chapter to explain how public opinion may weaken existing traps blocking welfare reform: increasing public consensus around a particular set of reforms; an increase in the salience of the welfare issue that forced elites to bow to an existing public consensus; an increase in public deference to a particular political elite to implement reforms of the elite's choice; and a growing antipathy toward the status quo that makes the public willing to accept almost any change. The evidence presented here suggests that the first, second, and especially the fourth of these factors were important in making welfare reform more likely in 1996.

Overwhelming public rejection of the existing system led politicians to believe that there was credit to be gained by ending it. Poll results showing that most Americans backed almost any package of reforms proposed by politicians reinforced politicians' sense of political opportunity. Thus changing public opinion supported, if it did not drive, the push to reform welfare in some direction.

But if public opinion helped push welfare reform onto the policy agenda, its role was more mixed in promoting specific solutions to the welfare problem. There was some change in attitudes during the first Clinton administration, notably an increase in the number of people who thought that too much was being spent on welfare, that the poor were primarily responsible for their own condition, and that work should be required for mothers of young children. Public support was widespread for work and training requirements for welfare mothers. Support increased for work requirements even for mothers of very young children. Strong support emerged for time limits after which work would be required, but there was less agreement on time limits without a work guarantee. The popularity of a strong work requirement could and did act as a powerful "engine" (to borrow Senator Moynihan's term from the debate on the Family Support Act) propelling a welfare reform package that contained other, more controversial provisions.

Significant disagreement remained on policies intended to curb illegitimacy, with a majority favoring family caps but much less support for an outright ban on cash benefits to teenage mothers. Overall, there was no public consensus on a single approach to welfare reform, but elements of both new paternalism and the prevention and rehabilitation strategies enjoyed broad and strong support. The final welfare legislation enacted in 1996 contained many of the provisions on which there was a strong consensus (tightened work requirements, a requirement that unmarried teenage mothers live at home, increased funding for child care), but it also had provisions, including a five-year hard time limit on federally subsidized cash benefits, on which there was no consensus.

There is little evidence to support the third argument, that the public simply trusted one political leader or another to solve the welfare problem. On the contrary, the survey evidence shows that public views on this question were quite volatile. Both President Clinton in 1993 and congressional Republicans in the 104th Congress began with strong public confidence, but this rapidly dissipated. Rather than a firm advantage for a single party on the welfare issue, poll data show a public that had high hopes and demands for reform but was quick to lose faith when politicians failed to deliver or delivered a program the public believed had serious flaws.

There is strong evidence that public support for almost any policy change as an improvement over the status quo increased the policy leeway of those who control the legislative agenda. Certainly dislike of the status quo had reached unprecedented levels. Indeed, polls showed that the public preferred almost any possible package of reforms to AFDC (table 7-12). Public opinion thus helped put welfare reform on the agenda by giving both President Clinton and congressional Republicans the sense that they could score political gains by promising a dramatic change in AFDC. People's strong negative attitudes toward the pre-1996 system and their resulting bias in favor of any reform proposals also led both the president and congressional Republicans to believe that they could sell the public on welfare reform packages close to their own policy preferences.

The remaining ambiguities and contradictions in public attitudes toward AFDC, welfare recipients, and specific reform proposals created two potential stumbling blocks for welfare reform initiatives in the 1990s. A first potential pitfall was that politicians would overestimate the public's appetite

Table 7-11. *Public Approval/Confidence in Handling of Welfare Issue by President Clinton and Selected Republicans, 1993–96*

Percent unless otherwise indicated

Polling organization/ sponsor	Date	Number surveyed	Bill Clinton		Selected Republicans	
			Approve; have confidence	Disapprove; no confidence	Approve; have confidence	Disapprove; no confidence
YP for *Time*/CNN[a]	1/93	1,000	64	30	...	...
Washington Post[b]	1/94	1,000	41	56	...	...
					Republicans in Congress	
PSRA for Times Mirror[c]	3/94	1,000	48	45	45	43
PSRA for Times Mirror[d]	7/94	1,900	38	50	...	...
					Newt Gingrich	
Gallup for CNN/*USA Today*[e]	6/95	1,005	38	52	31	47
Louis Harris[f]	9/95	1,005	47	45	...	...
					Bob Dole	
Gallup for CNN/*USA Today*[g]	1/96	1,039	40	54	37	46
Louis Harris[h]	1/96	1,005	52	45	...	...
Gallup for CNN/*USA Today*[g]	3/96	1,008	39	55	32	50

Source: The survey data were compiled from searches of survey archives and published and unpublished sources, including the Roper Center for Public Opinion Research's on-line Public Opinion Location Library (POLL); The Public Perspective: A Roper Center Review of Public Opinion and Polling; the Inter-university Consortium for Political and Social Research (ICPSR, University of Michigan); data holdings of the Institute for Research in Social Science (IRSS, University of North Carolina); and the Times-Mirror Center for the People and the Press.

a. "When it comes to each of the following, do you have a lot of confidence, some confidence, or not real confidence in Bill Clinton . . . reforming the welfare system?" "Answers combine "a lot" and "some" categories.

b. "How satisfied are you with the progress the Clinton administration has made in . . . reforming the welfare system? Are you very satisfied, moderately satisfied, not too satisfied, or not at all satisfied with the progress the Clinton administration has made in this area?" Answers combine "very/moderately satisfied" and "not too/not at all satisfied" responses.

c. "In general do you have confidence in each of the following political leaders to do or recommend the right thing to reform the welfare system? Do you have confidence in . . . President Clinton [Republicans in congress] on this issue, or not?'"

d. "I'd like you to rate the way Bill Clinton is handling his job in some specific areas. Do you approve or disapprove of the way Bill Clinton is handling . . . welfare reform?"

e. "Do you approve or disapprove of the way he [Bill Clinton/Newt Gingrich] is handling . . . welfare policy?"

f. "Overall, do you approve or disapprove of the way President Clinton is handling the following issues . . . welfare?"

g. "Now, thinking about some issues, do you approve or disapprove of the way [Bill Clinton/Bob Dole] is handling . . . welfare?"

h. "Overall, would you say you approve or disapprove of President Clinton's handling of the following issues . . . welfare?"

Table 7-12. *Public Support for Various Reform Packages, 1993–96*

Percent unless otherwise indicated

Reform package	Date	Approve; favor	Disap- prove; oppose	No differ- ence (vol- unteered)	Don't know; unsure; refused
Replacing welfare with tax credits and stronger child support enforcement[a]	11/93	67	21	1	11
Clinton's 1994 welfare reform package (details provided, but not identified with Clinton)[b]	4/94	91	7	...	2
"Swap" welfare to states for federal takeover of Medicaid[c]	12/94	58	24	...	18
House welfare reform bill pro- visions (not identified)[d]	4/95	57	34	...	9
Final welfare reform bill (identified)[e]	8/96	82	14	...	4

Source: The survey data were compiled from searches of survey archives and published and unpublished sources, including the Roper Center for Public Opinion Research's on-line Public Opinion Location Library (POLL); The Public Perspective: A Roper Center Review of Public Opinion and Polling; the Inter-university Consortium for Political and Social Research (ICPSR, University of Michigan); data holdings of the Institute for Research in Social Science (IRSS, University of North Carolina); and the Times-Mirror Center for the People and the Press.

a. "Do you favor or oppose the following suggestion to reform the welfare system: Replace welfare benefits with tax credits and strengthen child support enforcement." Tarrance Group and Mellman, Lazarus and Lake for *U.S. News & World Report.*

b. "I am going to read you some of the welfare reform proposals currently being considered. For each, please tell me if you favor or oppose that particular proposal. One proposal currently being discussed to reform welfare would require all able-bodied welfare recipients, including women with preschool children, to go to school for two years to learn a skill while receiving benefits. After that, they would be required to either get a job or take a job the government would give them and their welfare benefits would be discontinued. Childcare would be provided for the children of working mothers. Do you favor or oppose this proposal?" (If favor or oppose, ask: "Do you favor/oppose this proposal strongly or do you favor/oppose this proposal somewhat?") *Los Angeles Times.*

c. "Today the costs and responsibilities for welfare and Medicaid are shared by the federal and state governments. Recently some people have suggested dividing these responsibilities differently, with the states being in charge of welfare and the federal government taking the responsibility for paying for the health care of poor people. Do you favor or oppose this 'swap' proposal?" Harvard/Kaiser.

d. "Now I'd like to ask you about some specific proposals that have been debated by the new Congress. Do you approve or disapprove of this proposal? Reforming welfare to provide block grants to states that would end cash benefits after five years and stop cash benefits for all unmarried parents under age eighteen." Times-Mirror.

e. "As you may know, a welfare reform bill has just passed in Congress and President (Bill) Clinton said he will sign it. The legislation requires that welfare recipients work within two years of applying for benefits, it eliminates eligibility for most benefits for most legal immigrants until they become citizens, it requires able-bodied adults with no children to work 20 hours per week in order to be eligible for food stamps, and it imposes a five-year lifetime cap on welfare benefits whether or not a person can find a job. Do you favor or oppose the new welfare reform bill?" *Los Angeles Times.*

for any change that put children at risk. Surveys suggest that most Americans did not abandon their concern for poor children or their complex views of the roots of poverty; indeed, this concern continued to exist (albeit uncomfortably) alongside dislike for welfare programs and the perception that many adult welfare recipients behaved irresponsibly and unacceptably.

When conflicting beliefs coexist, which ones dominate depends heavily on whether they are primed by opinion leaders and the media.[29] Republican initiatives were aided substantially when powerful opinion leaders, Democratic as well as Republican, repeatedly expressed concerns about welfare dependence. New conservative arguments that the welfare system actually hurt children more than it helped also stimulated broad public acquiescence toward Republican initiatives. If concerns about harmful effects of welfare reform on children had been emphasized by political leaders with wide credibility, people might have expressed stronger reservations about some reform proposals as they became more aware of potential adverse consequences. But the Clinton administration raised these concerns only intermittently because it wanted to enact, and claim political credit for, welfare reform. Thus the dual clientele trap was substantially weakened in the Clinton and Republican rounds of welfare reform.

A second potential stumbling block was in the depth of public support for work guarantees. In the abstract, public support for work requirements was very strong, and it grew even stronger when proposals included a guarantee of work for those who could not find it in the private sector. But at the same time, work programs themselves have traditionally been unpopular because they have been seen as ridden with fraud, waste, and abuse. The Comprehensive Employment and Training Act (CETA) public service employment program was one of the few programs that the Reagan administration was able to kill outright in 1981. Thus a welfare reform initiative that had a strong federal work guarantee risked a strong critique from the right and an eventual erosion of public support. This stumbling block failed to materialize in the most recent round of welfare reform because the Clinton administration proposal, which did include guaranteed jobs of last resort, did not stay on the agenda long enough to undergo sustained congressional attack. Republican proposals in the 104th Congress finessed the question of work requirements and guarantees by devolving most responsibility to the states.

Given the public's intense dislike of AFDC, the critical issue for policymakers was not finding a welfare reform package that would command the support of the maximum number of voters, but rather maintaining control of the welfare reform agenda. Indeed, the Clinton administration's 1994 welfare reform proposal was probably closer to the views of the mythical "median voter" than the welfare provisions of the Contract with America. But that would be of little aid to Clinton and the Democrats after they failed to move a welfare bill before the 1994 election. Because the public demanded policy change and preferred almost any package of reforms over the status quo, whoever could control the agenda in Congress would have an important advantage in getting reform enacted on their terms. In short, public opinion ultimately worked to the benefit of the Republican welfare reform package in 1996 less because of public identification with Republican positions or deference to Republican leadership than because congressional Republicans' control of the agenda meant that President Clinton would have to choose between approving a bill written largely on Republican terms and appearing to prefer the universally maligned status quo.

CHAPTER EIGHT

Interest Groups and
Welfare Reform

ALTHOUGH THE OPINIONS of the public influence policymakers in a general way, analyses of American political life have more frequently focused on the influence of interest groups. Almost all policy areas have been analyzed as reflecting the sum of the conflicting pulls and tugs of organized groups seeking material gains for their members.

Policymaking concerning low-income families is usually one of the areas where group analysis is seen as least helpful, however. Certainly poor children, the intended beneficiaries of AFDC, have little political power. As Gilbert Steiner noted more than twenty years ago,

> Neither the traditional nor more recent styles of political action are available to children. They cannot vote, make political contributions, organize themselves to lobby in Congress or the administrative agencies, or write and speak on behalf of candidates. They are of little interest to protest organizations. As political actors, children are useless and dependent. If children are to be either advantaged or simply protected, other groups must speak and act on their behalf.[1]

But who can speak on behalf of children, especially poor children? Adult welfare recipients have generally been viewed as poorly organized and lacking the resources and capacity to form political alliances that will benefit their cause. Political science analyses of AFDC policymaking have generally focused either on the role played by race in undermining support for the program[2] or on the intermittent threat to social order posed by relatively diffuse movements of the poor,[3] rather than on the activities of organized lobbying groups. Indeed, with the exception of a brief period in the late 1960s when the National Welfare Rights Organization was active, organizations of welfare recipients have been notable primarily for their absence.[4] But at the same time AFDC has never cost so much that powerful groups were determined to kill it.

This is not the same as saying that there is no group involvement in welfare reform politics. Washington-based intergovernmental lobbies such as the National Governors' Association, the American Public Welfare Association, the National Conference of State Legislatures, the National League of Cities, and the National Association of Counties have long been involved in welfare reform politics. These organizations represent not the ultimate recipients of AFDC, but the state and local officials who develop detailed program structures, have to find funds to match (in varying degrees, depending on the wealth of the state) federal AFDC (and now TANF) funds, are responsible for implementing AFDC and its successor program, and are accountable to the federal government for meeting federal program standards and for the use of federal funds. In the 1980s, intergovernmental groups were joined by organizations such as the Center on Budget and Policy Priorities (CBPP), the Center for Law and Social Policy (CLASP), and the Children's Defense Fund (CDF), groups that combined research and advocacy functions on behalf of the poor.[5] In the 1990s the Christian Coalition and other social conservative groups also became active in welfare issues. President Clinton had close ties to a fourth interest group, the Democratic Leadership Council, and its think tank arm, the Progressive Policy Institute. Labor unions, service providers like Catholic Charities, reproductive rights groups, and right-to-life groups also became involved in specific aspects of the reform of welfare in the most recent round.

This involvement reflects changes in the interest group environment that have occurred in the past thirty years. There has been an explosion in the overall number of interest groups active in trying to influence policy formulation. Growth has been especially dramatic in the number of groups seeking policy changes that will not provide a direct material benefit to their members: a cleaner environment, eased restriction on prayer in public schools, more permissive or restrictive abortion policies, and toughened consumer protection laws.[6] Many of these "public interest" groups rely heavily on wealthy foundations and individuals for support rather than on individual members or corporations.[7] There are restrictions on how much "charitable" organizations—those to which donations are tax deductible, as recognized by section 501(c)(3) of the Internal Revenue Code—can spend on lobbying activities, and they are absolutely forbidden to engage in electoral campaign activities for public office.[8] But it is possible for them to set up non–tax deductible 501(c)(4) affiliate organizations that have more freedom to engage in lobbying activities.

Both the new "public" interest groups and the more traditional interests have expanded their repertoire of techniques beyond the traditional congressional testimony and lobbying of legislative and agency staffs to advocacy advertising in the media and "grassroots" mobilization of their membership to contact politicians.[9] Publication of "scorecards" and other types of voter guides that compare candidates' stands (or, for incumbents, their record in roll call votes) on issues of interest to the organization have proliferated as well. Voter guides can be published by tax-exempt groups as long as they do not directly recommend candidates.[10] Sometimes these ratings are linked to targeting of campaign contributions.[11]

In response to this hyperpluralism, interest groups have increasingly tried to form broad coalitions—some with a formal institutional structure, others less formal—on particular policy issues. Coalitions are beneficial to interest groups as a way to work out compromise positions, demonstrate broad support for a position, share costs, and develop an efficient division of labor.[12] At the same time, the once clear distinctions between public policy research think tanks and public interest advocacy organizations has been muddied by the growth of advocacy organizations that perform research as part of their functions and by an increase in the number of think tanks that see (and proclaim) their mission as the advancement of an ideologically driven worldview rather than as an objective search for the truth based on widely accepted norms of social science research.[13]

How did changes in the interest group environment and group strategies and resources contribute to the failure of the Clinton welfare reform package in 1994 and enactment of welfare reform legislation in 1996? In particular, how did changes in group pressures reshape the policymaking traps that have traditionally inhibited welfare reform initiatives? Generally, interest group explanations of policy change focus on the mobilization or demobilization of groups that change the balance of forces that press for policy, on changes in the resources available to groups active in a policy sector, and on changes in interest group perceptions of their interests. These general categories suggest several plausible hypotheses about how interest group politics may have reshaped AFDC politics and policy. First, liberal interest groups could have suffered decreasing resources that weakened their ability to be heard by and to gain access to political leaders after 1994. Second, existing groups may have shifted their positions on welfare issues to the right. Third, the entry of new social conservative groups and the Democratic Leadership Council into welfare policymaking might have pushed the overall balance of group pressures significantly to the right.

Child Advocacy Groups

Advocacy groups for children and families were one of the significant clusters of groups involved in the welfare debates of the first Clinton administration. To gain entrée into the policymaking process, these groups count on their policy expertise and ability to get favorable attention in the media. They rely primarily on foundations for their funding support. None has a strong mass political base, but their close links to many Democratic clienteles and legislators make them difficult for Democratic politicians to ignore. Their very closeness to Democratic politicians was, however, a liability when the Republicans took over Congress in 1994, because perceptions that they were ideological and philosophical opponents limited their access and their political clout with the new congressional majority party.

Three Washington-based organizations with differing styles and resources were at the core of the liberal advocacy groups. The Center on Budget and Policy Priorities (CBPP) was founded in 1981 by Robert Greenstein, who had headed the Food Stamp program during the Carter administration. Greenstein remained the center's most visible spokesman (and the recipient of a MacArthur Foundation "genius" award). But the center was by no means a one-man show: it had a staff of thirty-five by 1994 and a budget of almost $4 million, most of it from foundations. The center's strength is in its analytical work on policy programs relating to low-income Americans. Most of its studies are brief (five to thirty pages), easily readable reports that draw on and synthesize data on federal and state programs. The center has a strong reputation in Washington for reliable, thorough, and timely research that packs a policy punch. Its studies have become a staple for newspaper editorial writers, and they even generate news stories when they are released.[14] Equally important, although the center supports programs for low-income Americans, it has a reputation as a group that is pragmatic, conscious of budgetary constraints, and not always simply asking for more money.

During the formulation of the Clinton administration's welfare reform plan in 1993 and 1994, there were detailed formal and informal consultations between center officials and the administration, especially on financing issues. Relations were close because of a combination of mutual trust and mutual benefit. As one center official said, the center's information and suggestions were valued within the administration because of a

> perception of expertise, particularly in a lot of the areas related to financing, areas where they really thought they could use our help in figuring out what to do. . . . Certainly the belief it would be confidential [was also a factor]. There's a long standing relationship the center has with this administration, a lot of things that have been done collaboratively and where the understanding is that if we strongly disagree, we tell them that we disagree, that we don't leak it, but with them understanding that if we end up strongly disagreeing at the point when it goes public, that we're not going to be shy about saying what we think. It's not [a situation in which], because we're consulted, we're going to look the other way. It also goes to things we find out about where we're not consulted. . . . If we have a concern, we tell them the concern, we don't go outside at the point when there are internal deliberations going on and they are not yet public.[15]

Relations between the center and the Clinton administration were reinforced by personal ties. David Ellwood, cochair of the Clinton administration's welfare reform task force, had served on the center's board of directors, as had Labor secretary Robert Reich. Robert Greenstein was appointed by the Clinton administration to serve on the Kerrey-Danforth Commission on entitlement reform in 1994 and later that year was asked by the Clinton administration to become deputy director of the Office of Management and Budget, a post that he first accepted and then, after Republicans gained a congressional majority in the 1994 election, declined. In general, the center's policy recommendations focused on the incentive and prevention and rehabilitation approaches to welfare reform; indeed, Greenstein was perhaps the most forceful and visible advocate for expansion of the Earned Income Tax Credit in the 1980s and early 1990s.[16]

Not surprisingly, access by the center and other liberal advocacy groups to decisionmaking was curtailed when the Republicans won control of Congress. They still had formal access through testimony at congressional hearings and some contact with the new majority congressional staff, especially where, as with the House Agriculture Committee, they shared some objectives (in this case, opposition to conversion of Food Stamps and other nutrition programs into a block grant to the states). One CBPP official noted, comparing the new Congress with the 1987–88 round of welfare reform when the Democrats controlled Congress, that "people [from the advocacy community] weren't as involved day to day in each aspect of the legislative drafting . . . you just didn't have the same access. You didn't have the same audience on the Hill, people willing to take your suggestions."[17]

Few Republican members on the House side were receptive to working with the child advocacy groups even on issues on which there had previously been common interests, so advice was generally channeled through Democratic members, whose amendments almost always failed to win adoption. In the less partisan Senate, child advocacy groups were able to work with moderate Republican members. But even there, influence was more on the details of legislation than on broad principles. As the head of the Food Research and Action Center observed, "On the Senate side, people are willing to dance with us, but the decisions to cut have already been made. . . . We have an open invitation from the Senate staff to suggest how to cut $20 billion from nutrition programs."[18] This limited access nevertheless played to the orientation and detailed program knowledge of the CBPP. As one center official said in a 1996 interview, "This is a very pragmatic place here. So if there's even the littlest probability that you could change some little thing, you do it."[19]

The history of the Center for Law and Social Policy (CLASP), a second major advocacy organization, is different from that of the CBPP. CLASP was founded in 1969 as a nonprofit public interest law firm engaging in litigation on social, gender, and environmental issues. Like the CBPP, it is not a membership organization and has always derived almost all of its funds from foundations. When foundations (especially the Ford Foundation) phased out funding for public interest litigation in the 1980s, CLASP changed its focus to emphasize research and advocacy on behalf of the poor. In the 1990s it directed its efforts toward helping low-income families and preserving legal services for the poor. It is a much smaller organization than the CBPP, with a senior professional staff of just seven and a budget of $1.24 million in 1995.[20] Through its *CLASP Update* and policy briefs, its staff provided regular information and critiques of federal welfare reform legislation as it moved through Congress, as well as information on state actions. CLASP's Mark Greenberg was particularly visible on block grants and other devolution issues, singled out by a number of people interviewed for this study as effective because the information he provided was detailed, intelligible, and accurate and because his low-key style gave him credibility with both parties.[21]

The Children's Defense Fund (CDF), the third of the central troika of liberal child advocacy groups, is very different from the other two. It evolved in the early 1970s from the Washington Research Project Action Council, a coalition of groups interested in child development issues that had been brought together by Marian Wright Edelman.[22] Like the CBPP and CLASP, it does not take government funding and relies primarily on foundations for support, although it has also managed to develop substantial corporate support. Unlike CLASP and the CBPP, which focus primarily on research and secondarily on advocacy and are completely Washington-based, the Children's Defense Fund uses its much larger budget (almost $15 million in 1995) to fund a variety of activities such as leadership training seminars. It also has an affiliated 501(c)(4) organization that gives it more flexibility in funding lobbying activities. But the greatest difference between the CDF and the other two organizations is its public style. As one prominent child advocate observed,

> Marian has a stature and a role that carries with it obligations. She has an obligation to take moral stands at the same time that she's trying to achieve pragmatic results. There are only a handful of nonreligious leaders in this country who have moral stature. Marian is clearly one of them. You have to safeguard that authority and not throw it away to sustain it, but you also have to use it.[23]

But while the CDF continues to have high visibility and Edelman continues to win praise for her strong moral voice on children's issues, conservatives complain that the organization adhered to a 1960s ideology in a budget-driven world and that Edelman's tone of moral superiority and unwillingness to compromise leave little room for discussion or cooperation.[24]

Like the CBPP, the CDF had close ties to the Clinton administration. Hillary Clinton is a former chairman of the board of trustees, and Donna Shalala, Clinton's secretary of Health and Human Services, served on the board as well. Edelman and her husband, Peter Edelman, are long-time close friends of the Clintons. Peter Edelman was assistant secretary of Health and Human Services for planning and evaluation at the time Clinton signed welfare reform legislation in 1996 (he promptly resigned).[25]

To maximize their political leverage, children's advocacy groups worked very hard to develop coalitions. Relations between the CBPP, CLASP, and the CDF were especially close, with informal cooperation based on both functional and substantive specialization. As a CBPP official noted:

> We work most closely with CLASP. Our styles are most similar. We have a very close working relationship with CDF, but our approaches are somewhat different. We tend to do more of the analysis [and] we always tend to focus more on budget aspects of various policies. Marian speaks with a moral voice that we don't speak with. . . . Oftentimes, we find ourselves doing the analysis that other people may do more with. Also, we divide up. [The CDF] clearly has an expertise on child care and child support which we don't have. It would be the same thing with CLASP: they have child support. We have an expertise with food programs that they don't have. With the [Earned Income Tax Credit] we obviously are the lead group in town on the lobbying end, on the advocacy end, and on the policy and research end.[26]

Child advocacy groups also tried to build support among organizations for which welfare reform was a less central concern. The most striking patterns occurred in the groups' efforts to keep out of the welfare bill deterrence-oriented measures such as family caps and a ban on cash payments to teenage mothers. The child advocacy groups worked with reproductive rights and civil liberties groups, notably the National Organization of Women (NOW) Legal Defense Fund and the American Civil Liberties Union, that were mounting a court challenge to New Jersey's family cap law. But in building a broad coalition, called the Child Exclusion Task Force, to emphasize the potential harm to innocent children, child advocacy groups also worked hard to involve pro-life groups, notably the National Right to Life Committee and Catholic Charities USA, who argued that such measures would inevitably increase abortions. Sharon Daly of Catholic Charities USA, an umbrella organization for local social service agencies, often served as the liaison with conservative legislators because her organization was perceived as having more credibility with them.[27]

Once Republicans took control of the welfare reform agenda, child advocacy groups concentrated heavily on preventing the conversion of AFDC from an entitlement program into a block grant. Once that battle was lost, they tried to ensure that the block grant did not create incentives for states to withdraw their own funds from the program. They also focused on ensuring that child care funding was adequate (to make work requirements workable) and on weakening deterrence-focused illegitimacy and

Table 8-1. *Children's Advocacy Groups and Their Resources, 1992–96*[a]
Thousands of nominal dollars

	Operating expenses				
Organization	1992	1993	1994	1995	1996
CBPP	2,789	3,265	3,913	4,196	3,786
CLASP[a]	673	1,141	1,250	1,243	1,384
CDF	10,373	12,459	14,448	14,983	16,611

Source: *IRS* Form 990 for named institutions.
a. Fiscal year beginning July 1.

time limit provisions. More generally they sought to strengthen the dual clientele trap by directing attention to the potential harm to children inherent in conservative approaches to welfare reform.

In working toward these objectives the groups had important advantages, but even more critical weaknesses. Their failure to block welfare reform legislation they opposed cannot be explained by decreasing resources: they were generally gaining resources (see table 8-1). And if ever there was a period in which the so-called kids' lobby had access to a presidential administration, the Clinton administration and its many personal links with child advocacy groups should have been it. Certainly these groups had enough access to deliver a message that the welfare reform bill passed by Congress in the summer of 1996 was bad legislation. What they lacked was enough political clout to amend or block the bill before it came to President Clinton or to make him heed their opposition to that legislation.

Several problems weakened child advocacy groups, especially after the Republicans took control of Congress in the 1994 election, and the new congressional majority rather than the administration was setting the welfare reform agenda. First, their policy advice had limited value to the new congressional majority because they were considered committed to liberal policies and politically allied with the Democrats.[28] Thus they were forced largely into a reactive, defensive, and negative role. There were some exceptions: in child support enforcement, for example, child advocacy groups had more input on policy in the 104th Congress because policy perspectives were less polarized than they were on matters like illegitimacy reduction. Moreover, the child advocacy groups had strong expertise in this area, and there was little pressure from social conservative groups to move in a different policy direction.

A second critical weakness of child advocacy groups was a limited ability to mobilize grassroots support to force legislators or the president to be responsive to their views. Efforts to mobilize grassroots support take a great deal of scarce time and resources. In any case, they are likely to succeed largely among committed liberals rather than potential Republican supporters. Thus Republican legislators felt neither a political obligation nor a policy need to be responsive to their views. Nor did child advocacy organizations have the budgetary resources to mount an effective media campaign. As Jennifer Vasiloff, executive director of the Coalition on Human Needs, an umbrella group of poverty advocacy, research, and service provider organizations, said, "You have a lot of organizations that operate on a shoestring trying to get information out. This is not the health care debate, where you have moneyed interests with a stake in the outcome."[29] To get their message out, child advocacy organizations had to rely on free media, which rarely presented their message without also giving time to their conservative opponents.

Child advocacy groups were also limited in their ability to draw on partners outside the child advocacy community to help block the Republican welfare agenda. In large part this was caused by the breadth of the Republican agenda. Labor unions, women's groups, and pro-choice groups were all fighting full-time battles over issues of more immediate concern to their constituencies. Labor unions, for example, were more engaged in resisting cuts in Medicare and Medicaid, both because those issues were of more concern to their members and because the White House and congressional Democratic leadership signaled that, along with education and the environment, they were the policy sectors around which the party and its allies should circle the wagons. And to the extent that child advocacy groups broadened their coalition, it was at some cost of clarity in their message. Sharon Daly, for example, was at pains to emphasize that her organization did not "talk about a GOP war on the poor. We're not trying to defeat the GOP agenda. In fact we agree with a lot they are trying to accomplish."[30]

The most fundamental weakness of the child advocacy organizations was the lack of reliable political allies at one of the political choke points that could block a welfare reform bill. With Republicans in control of both houses of Congress, the child advocacy groups' best hope for success was to sway a Clinton White House that remained committed to "ending welfare as we know it." But the administration had a different set of political interests, was listening to a different set of voices, and was committed to a different message: that it was both possible and desirable to end welfare as we know it.

The Democratic Leadership Council

Another source of pressure on the welfare reform policy debates came from the Democratic Leadership Council (DLC) and its think tank arm, the Progressive Policy Institute (PPI). Like many of the other groups involved in the debate, the DLC was not an organization with strong grassroots. It was founded in 1985 as part of an effort by moderate and conservative Democratic politicians and activists, especially in the Sun Belt, to reorient the party after the debacle of the 1984 election, in which Walter Mondale was drubbed by President Reagan while the Republicans retained control of the Senate and picked up seats in the House. Many Southern Democrats in particular became persuaded that distancing themselves from the national party was no longer sufficient to prevent a realignment of white voters toward Republicans; only by changing the national party's image and its policies could its future be assured.[31] DLC membership was originally limited to elected officials.

After the 1988 election the DLC grew and became more institutionalized. A nominally separate think tank, the PPI, was established to serve as a source for new policy ideas, based on the principle that activist government could be a force for good, but was not itself good.[32] Disillusionment with activist government could only be countered, the DLC and the PPI argued, if Democrats abandoned support for the minimum wage, defense of affirmative action, resistance to free trade, and other policies that were outdated but beloved of liberal constituencies within the party, and if government was made to operate more efficiently.

By 1992, welfare reform had become an important feature of the "New Democratic" policies favored by the DLC. In its *Mandate for Change,* prepared for the 1993 presidential transition, the organization supported a welfare reform proposal whose main elements were almost indistinguishable from those supported by President Clinton: requiring welfare recipients to work after two years, "making work pay" through an expanded Earned Income Tax Credit, expanded access to health care for the working poor, emphasis on job placement over education and training, a national system of child support assurance, and "an intense media campaign against teenage pregnancy and out-of-wedlock births."[33]

If child advocacy groups had close personal links to the new president that allowed them to whisper in his left ear, the DLC was well placed to whisper in his right ear. Former DLC policy director Bruce Reed joined the Clinton administration as a deputy assistant to the president for domestic policy and cochair of its welfare reform planning task force, and DLC president Al From served as director of the new administration's domestic policy transition group. Elaine Kamarck and William Galston, who coauthored the chapter on family policy in *Mandate for Change*, also joined the Clinton White House. Once Clinton took office, DLC officials were critical of many of the administration's policies, especially employer mandates in health care, and pressed for speedy action on a work-oriented welfare reform package that placed as much emphasis as possible on moving AFDC recipients into private-sector jobs.[34]

The emphasis on work was reinforced after the Republicans won control of Congress in 1994. DLC policy proposals became more conservative to try to recapture the initiative on welfare from the Republicans. The PPI proposed a Work First program that, instead of a two-year time limit, would abolish any cash entitlement to AFDC and convert AFDC and JOBS into a grant to states that would require the vast majority of welfare recipients to take a job, engage in job placement activities, or perform community service almost immediately.[35] As an alternative to Republican proposals for family caps and teenage mother exclusions, the institute proposed modest federal seed money for "second chance" adult-supervised group homes for teenage mothers.[36] Above all, the DLC and the PPI pressed for maintaining the momentum for comprehensive welfare reform and not ceding the issue to Republicans, even if it meant accepting legislation largely on Republican terms. In applauding President Clinton's July 1996 decision to sign the welfare legislation passed by Congress, the DLC praised the decision as necessary, arguing that "welfare reform is a threshold credibility issue for New Democrats. If we are unwilling to radically change the most flawed and counterproductive of all paternalistic bureaucracies, then who will believe us when we call for a new, empowering form of governance in the post–big–government era?"[37]

Overall, then, the DLC-PPI contribution to the pressures on politicians was to add to pressures on Democratic politicians after 1994 to reach an accommodation with the Republican congressional majority. This pressure took indirect as well as direct forms: to the extent that President Clinton responded to New Democratic pressures to reach an agreement with the Republicans, Democratic legislators who did not wish to appear to the left of the president on welfare issues felt pressure to follow his lead.

Intergovernmental Groups

Intergovernmental lobbies have been among the most committed participants in welfare reform policymaking. As noted in chapter 4, the National

Governors' Association was instrumental in breaking the logjam that threat-ened to prevent congressional passage of the Family Support Act of 1988. The intergovernmental community in Washington consists of organizations with very different interests. There are seven large organizations of general-ist officials, known as the Big Seven: the National Governors' Association (NGA), the National Conference of State Legislatures (NCSL), the Council of State Governments, the National Association of Counties (NACo), the National League of Cities (NLC), the U.S. Conference of Mayors (USCM, an organization of larger cities), and the International City/County Manage-ment Association (ICMA).[38] In addition, the American Public Welfare Association, the association of state welfare directors, has played an impor-tant consultative role in developing welfare legislation. But because welfare directors are appointed by governors, the APWA's influence may wane if governors' interest waxes as welfare directors follow the lead of the officials who appoint them. Although all these organizations are sizable, all but the APWA cover many issues, so the resources they can devote to any particu-lar one is limited.

Many intergovernmental organizations devote significant resources to providing technical assistance and exchanging information among their members. They play a dual role in Washington, conveying information to their members about what policies are being debated and how those policies are likely to affect members and providing information to federal policy-makers about their members' views on policy options being considered. The intergovernmental groups generally have good relationships with one another and frequently work together in gathering information and influ-encing Washington policy. On the former, one association staff member observed:

> We all talk, all the state and local organizations. Our bosses meet. . . . That happens all the time on any piece of legislation. . . . We all try to . . . share information with each other because we get different kinds of information. We all [have] different contacts. We have different constituents with different connections to different members [of Congress]. So we all use those, obviously, to maxi-mize our coverage. . . . We don't agree on everything, but we can agree on a lot of things. And . . . what we try to do for the most part is just inform our constituents about what [is] going on.[39]

A similar sort of cooperation and division of labor based on organiza-tional expertise takes place in trying to influence policymaking, although this is clearly more difficult when the interests and views of the organizations differ, and it is most difficult with the big-city mayors, who have the most distinctive problems and interests.

The most formal way intergovernmental organizations try to influence federal policymaking is to adopt organizational policy positions. For both the NGA and the NCSL, these positions are approved at member conferences. They require a supermajority of support to ensure some measure of bipartisanship, and they cease to be valid after some defined period unless they are reratified (sunset provisions). For example, the National Governors' Association requires approval by two-thirds of its members to take an organizational position, with a sunset after two years.[40]

Because agendas can change rapidly and formal policies frequently deal in generalities, formal policy positions must be supplemented by other interactions such as letters to congressional committees considering legislation, testimony by association leaders and staff before those committees, and informal discussions with agency and congressional committee staffs. In the details of legislative drafting, association staff members may have to act in the absence of clear policy direction from the organization's elected leaders.

For both policy and political reasons, intergovernmental groups generally have good access to federal policymakers. They are viewed as useful conduits for expertise from state and local officials who will implement or otherwise be affected by changes made by policymakers at the federal level. Listening to state and local officials now may help to avoid programmatic and political problems later. Politically, state and local officials are respected in Washington for having good links to the grassroots and constituent concerns that also are important to federal legislators. State legislators, mayors, and governors are also of a kind with federal legislators: they hold the offices that many federal legislators have held in the past or aspire to hold in the future.

Neither the policy functions of intergovernmental groups nor the access they enjoy is fixed. Like other organizations, these lobbies must be careful what they say and how they say it if they want to preserve their access to federal policymakers. A staff member of one of the large intergovernmental groups noted in an interview as the House of Representatives was just finishing passage of Contract with America legislation in March 1995:

> there is a lot of pressure right now on Republicans from top to
> bottom—whether it's Republican local government officials or

federal officials, congressmen, state legislators—to not do anything to change what's going to happen in the first one hundred
days [of the Republican-controlled Congress]. . . . And I've certainly had [members of the association] tell me off the record that
they want me to be out there raising these issues of cost shifts and
of mandates and so forth; they're not going to raise them. . . . I
think that's where the association is helpful sometimes, in express-
ing concerns that the members themselves can't raise for political
reasons. . . .

[In setting our lobbying priorities] we understood that
[AFDC] cash assistance was going to be block granted and that we
would be out of the debate if we opposed—or actively opposed—
capping the cash assistance block grant. . . . I never would have
been meeting with [House Majority Leader Richard] Armey's
office and others if we had taken that position.[41]

The NGA and the NCSL try to preserve a bipartisan—as opposed to
nonpartisan—character by rotating their top officers between Republicans
and Democrats each year and ensuring that there is bipartisan participation
in all major issue areas. But the requirement for supermajorities to reach
organizational positions also means that intergovernmental organizations
may be on the sidelines when there are deep partisan or ideological divisions among their members. It is fairly easy, for example, for the NGA and
the NCSL to take consistent positions in support of additional flexibility in
shared-cost programs—allowing state options rather than mandating specific work requirements or deterrence measures under the TANF program,
for example. A consensus is also easy to achieve in resisting unfunded mandates such as requirements that the states pay for the education of illegal
immigrants. But it is much harder to reach bipartisan agreement on a particular approach to welfare such as converting AFDC entitlement into a
block grant or imposing hard time limits.

The risk and reality of stalemate in the intergovernmental lobby were
defining characteristics of the most recent round of welfare reform. If the
intergovernmental lobby—particularly the NGA, the most visible of the
intergovernmental lobbies—could reach a unified position in favor of devolution, it could have had a major impact in weakening the federalism trap.
Certainly President Clinton, chair of the NGA when the Family Support Act
of 1988 was passed, could be expected to be sympathetic to pleas from his
former colleagues for more autonomy in setting AFDC policy.

An even greater impetus for a devolutionary approach to welfare reform was supplied by the 1994 election, when devolution-oriented Republicans took control of Congress and gained control of thirty governorships, although they were still short of the supermajority that the NGA required to adopt an official policy. There were four possible outcomes in this situation: (1) the NGA could be sidelined during welfare reform debates or confined to advising on relatively technical, nondivisive issues; (2) Republican governors could build alliances on their own with their partisan compatriots in Congress, bypassing the NGA; (3) the NGA could be co-opted into participating in the welfare reform debate largely on Republican terms; or (4) a bipartisan approach to welfare reform could develop among the governors, as in 1988. As later chapters show, 1995 was characterized largely by the first two possibilities, and 1996 by the second and third.

Social Conservative Groups

In the 1990s yet another set of groups—conservative pro-family organizations such as the Christian Coalition, the Family Research Council, the Eagle Forum, and the Traditional Values Coalition—became engaged in welfare reform.[42] Several of these groups had links to leaders in the evangelical Christian community.[43] The Christian Coalition, for example, was founded by televangelist-businessman (and former presidential candidate) Pat Robertson.[44] The Family Research Council, then headed by former Reagan administration official Gary Bauer, is an outgrowth of (although formally separate from) radio psychologist and lay leader James Dobson's Colorado-based Focus on the Family.[45] Concerned Women of America is led by Beverly LaHaye, wife of evangelist Tim LaHaye. The Eagle Forum was founded by long-time conservative activist Phyllis Schlafly. The Traditional Values Coalition was founded by California-based minister Louis Sheldon.[46] Although most of the leaders, and followers, of these organizations come from conservative Christian backgrounds, the groups prefer the collective label pro-family, which emphasizes values that are widely shared with Americans outside their base of support and minimizes the fears that a suspicious secular society associates with terms like "the religious right."[47]

There are important differences among the organizations in structure, strategy, and issue emphasis. The Christian Coalition has a strong organizational base in state and local chapters. Under former executive director Ralph Reed it argued in favor of a more pragmatic political strategy for evangelical groups. Reed also called for broadening the group's appeals beyond decrying abortion and endorsing school prayer to issues that would have broad appeal to middle-income families, such as non-means-tested tax credits for families with children.[48] Focus on the Family and the Family Research Council have bitterly opposed any compromise or softening of Republican positions on abortion and other moral concerns and have criticized the Republican leadership in the 104th Congress for focusing on economic issues to the detriment of social and moral concerns.[49]

What unites the social conservative groups is their alienation from Washington and their concerns about the moral state of America. As James Dobson of Focus on the Family said,

> People inside the Beltway are not aware of the multiple millions of Americans out there who believe things differently than is perceived in Washington and have different aspirations for their lives. . . . They're very concerned about what they consider to be a moral free fall occurring, a moral meltdown in this country. They're worried about their children and what they're exposed to on television and MTV and what Hollywood produces. They're very concerned about safe-sex ideology and what [their kids are] being taught in school.[50]

Thus social conservative organizations were attracted to welfare policy both by their concern about the breakdown of two-parent families and by their desire to broaden their appeal.

Social conservative groups have a diagnosis of the welfare problem that is very different from that of liberal advocacy groups. They have focused on the corrosive effects of out-of-wedlock births. They see the welfare system as contributing to a broader process of social decay in America. The conversion of these groups to deterrence-oriented solutions favored by Charles Murray and other conservative writers was not immediate, however. In his 1993 manifesto calling on Christian conservatives to "cast a wider net" with their issue agenda, Ralph Reed called for a devolutionary approach emphasizing waivers to the states and "additional funding to states willing to experiment with welfare reform." He argued that "pro-family activists should use the states as laboratories, and legislate at the federal level only the reforms that work."[51] By 1994, however, most of the social conservative groups had united around a deterrence-focused approach centered on reducing out-of-wedlock births and preventing long-term dependence. Many of these groups also argued for an increased role for private charities in providing social services to the poor, believing that only private charities can offer the individually tailored programs and the moral regeneration that are needed for truly changing the lives of the spiritually as well as economically impoverished.[52]

Focusing on welfare reform was not a completely easy choice for Christian conservative groups. Deterrence strategies such as family caps and teenage mother exclusions carry with them a risk that mothers will choose abortion to terminate pregnancies if no government financial assistance is available to raise those children. Opposition to abortion has long been a strong issue for Christian conservatives. Indeed, the National Right to Life Committee opposed both family caps and teen mother exclusions and scored the provisions in its House and Senate 1995 roll call vote guides. But the more broadly focused social conservative groups stuck together and worked together in favoring strong illegitimacy and teenage mother exclusion provisions in the welfare bill.

Perhaps the most important factor explaining the pro-family groups' strong and cohesive support for pro-family deterrence strategies was the very effective leadership provided by Robert Rector, a welfare policy analyst at the Heritage Foundation, the conservative Washington-based think tank. So intense in manner that even Heritage colleagues refer to him as a "pit bull," Rector contributed to the cause by providing a steady stream of critiques of the current welfare system, building coalitions among groups, drafting legislation, and working with individual legislators and committee staffs. As noted in chapter 5, Rector's work broadening the definition of welfare programs and asserting that they had been a $5.4 trillion failure was an important part of the conservative assault on the system. Perhaps most important of his attributes, however, were his energy and his willingness to engage in the legislative process. Unlike Charles Murray, Rector sought out legislative allies, especially among freshman members of the House and Senate, and became actively involved in political mobilization. He built links not only with the social conservative groups but also with junior Republican legislators who pressed for deterrence-oriented welfare reform within the Republican congressional caucuses.[53]

Finally, Rector was an effective advocate for the position that deterrence-oriented solutions in fact constituted the moral high ground in the welfare reform debate. He argued that "spiritual poverty" is more important than material poverty in determining children's achievement.[54] Child advocacy groups, Rector claimed, should be referred to as the "single mothers' lobby," and the policies they advocated, because they increased spiritual poverty, amounted to "throwing acid into children's faces."[55] To the extent that these claims were widely accepted, conservatives would make major progress in weakening the dual clientele trap, the most fundamental barrier toward adopting conservative approaches to welfare reform.

The social conservative groups depended heavily on Rector and were inclined toward coalition, in part because their own expertise on welfare issues was thin, especially in comparison with that of the liberal advocacy groups specializing in policy toward low-income families. Most of the social conservative groups had very small Washington offices that attempted to cover a range of issues. The Traditional Values Coalition, for example, had a Washington staff of around five people during the welfare reform debate. A majority of the pro-family organizations had no more than one or two staff people who spent all their time working on welfare issues and had a full mastery of the details of the programs; in fact, most had no full-time staff devoted to welfare issues. Even the most active could not hope to do a lot of original research on welfare or any other issue. Instead, they found their niches elsewhere. Gary Bauer, president of the FRC, said, "There is a lot of social science research out there that supports our agenda, and it tends to get lost. What we do is take that and put it in layman's language, put it in language that even members of Congress can understand, and circulate it around."[56] The FRC published a steady stream of short (generally one to five pages) policy briefs throughout 1995 with titles such as "A Pro-Life Defense of the Family Cap," "Family Cap Talking Points," "Responses to Liberal Scare Tactics," and "The Update on New Jersey: Beware a Rush to Judgment" (the last a response to data that appeared to show an increase in abortion rates after New Jersey imposed a family cap).[57] They were intended less to win over uncommitted legislators or opponents of measures to reduce illegitimacy than to give nervous Republican legislators fearful of offending pro-life groups the information and intellectual ammunition they could use to justify supporting those measures.

The FRC also commissioned a national poll on the family cap in October 1995. Framing the question in a way that was most likely to draw support for the measure (asking if those surveyed favored "increasing a welfare mother's monthly welfare check if she has another child out of wedlock"), the poll indeed found overwhelming support for a cap. In reporting the results, the FRC argued that they should "allay any doubts congressional Republicans may have about whether the public supports their 'family cap' proposal" and argued that "support for the family cap among rank-and-file pro-lifers is at least as strong as support from other Americans."[58] In short, the FRC's information was designed to appeal to the blame-avoiding instincts of Republican legislators fearing flak from one of their key constituencies.

Social conservative groups brought some important resources to the conflict over welfare reform. Most of them have a mass base: Focus on the Family claimed a mailing list of 3.5 million people; the Christian Coalition claimed a membership of 1.7 million in 1995, with 1,700 local chapters and a record of distributing 45 million voter guides in the 1994 election cycle.[59] Although some claims were almost certainly inflated, Christian conservative groups nevertheless had a much stronger mass base than liberal advocacy groups focusing on children's issues.[60]

Whether the grassroots of the social conservative groups could be mobilized to support family caps and teenage mother exclusions to the same extent that they could for abolishing abortion and urging school prayer is far from clear. But the use of voter guides by social conservative groups—some groups distribute guides through local chapters or churches—offers a mechanism to influence legislators on issues of interest to organizational leaders even when the commitment of the grassroots is dubious.[61] Groups often announce in advance when they will be scoring a roll-call vote and which position they support, and they frequently choose votes on amendments and procedural motions that would otherwise be obscure but have a major effect on the direction of a bill. Inclusion in an advocacy group's scorecard can dramatically raise the stakes for legislators because they suddenly must weigh the cost of casting a "negative" vote that will be scored and broadcast to the legislator's constituents, even if those constituents do not view the specific issue as particularly important.

Social conservative groups were also aided in building a coalition on welfare reform because they had compatible views and a history of working together on issues of common concern (the National Right to Life Committee, which was opposed to mandates for reducing illegitimacy, did not participate in welfare reform meetings held by social conservative groups, however). Although the collaboration was more ad hoc than that among liberal advocacy groups, social conservative groups did meet together informally and try to arrive at common positions and strategies, especially when important roll-call votes were approaching in the 104th Congress. This collaboration took several forms. As the head of the Washington office of one group described the activity before a vote, if we have one hundred members we have to call . . . I might say, "Okay, I'll take the first ten. Eagle Forum take the next ten. But then I might say, "I'll take these ten, plus I know this person on Eagle Forum's list. I'll call them, too." . . . Sometimes we'll all send individual letters to members. Sometimes we'll send a group letter. Group letters are effective because then they know all the family groups [are] for this, [that] this is important. That's very helpful.[62]

In addition to their outside-the-Beltway political base and ability to work together, social conservative organizations had additional advantages that became evident when the Republican party took control of Congress in 1994. First, they were well connected with the Republican leadership, especially in the House. Relations with the Senate leadership were more strained, especially with Majority Leader Bob Dole, whom many of the leaders of the social conservative groups viewed as more committed to pragmatic legislating than to their principles.[63] In addition, as chapter 10 shows, they had leverage in the House: Republican leaders in that chamber "owed" them because their core concerns, school prayer and right to life, were not included in the Contract with America.

In lobbying for strong deterrence provisions in a welfare reform bill, Rector and the social conservatives also benefited from the fact that their agenda did not conflict with that of other important allies of the new Republican majority, especially big business and small business. Some policy sectors have experienced strong conflict between the agendas of the business community and of social conservatives, notably in dividing tax cuts between individuals and businesses and in linking trade and commerce with human rights and family planning policies.[64] On welfare reform, business organizations generally kept a low profile and were concerned primarily with welfare-to-work provisions; they did not take a position on illegitimacy reduction initiatives.[65]

The goals of the social conservative groups did clash with the desire of Republican governors for more flexibility in welfare policy. Thus in seeking to solidify support among social conservative groups, Republicans in Congress were pulled by those groups toward a mandatory deterrence-based welfare reform, especially for reducing illegitimacy. Meanwhile, liberal child advocacy groups were pulling Democratic politicians to the left, and Republican governors were pushing for a devolution (no federal mandates from the left or right). Thus the prospects for finding a middle-ground consensus solution to welfare reform were slim indeed. Any move to find a middle ground would offend important constituencies, making any welfare reform coalition in Congress very fragile.

Conclusions: The Ambiguous Impact of Groups

This sketch of interest groups concerned with welfare issues suggests that several changes improved the prospects for substantial welfare reform from 1993 to 1996. But although there is some truth to each of the interest-centered hypotheses posited at the outset of this chapter, they are not very helpful in explaining welfare policy change unless reformulated.

Liberal advocacy groups were as strong as ever in financial resources in the 1990s, and they had close links to officials in the Clinton administration. But they were clearly on the defensive after the Republicans won control of Congress in 1994 and took control of the welfare reform agenda. They had little direct access to and influence on the formulation of new welfare reform legislation, except in the area of child support enforcement. They could work with Democrats and moderate Republicans to try to pose alternatives to Republican proposals, and they could lobby the Clinton administration to veto whatever a Republican Congress came up with. But President Clinton, having promised to "end welfare as we know it," had a very different set of interests from theirs.

Intergovernmental organizations and the Democratic Leadership Council did shift their positions to the right, but this was in many respects a response to rather than a cause of changing policy debates in Washington. Moreover, as chapter 10 will show, it was the immobilization of the National Governors' Association, more than any policy shift by any intergovernmental group, that helped move welfare reform forward in 1995. For the first year of the new Republican majority Congress, a small group of Republican governors replaced intergovernmental lobbies as the key bargaining partner of Republican leaders in Congress.

The third argument, concerning the growing importance of social conservative groups, is undoubtedly true, but as with liberal groups and intergovernmental lobbies, the influence of these groups depends as much on the gatekeeping power of elected officials in Washington as on changes in group involvement and group power. Social conservative groups were gaining in strength, but they had little influence other than working with Republican legislators to press conservative alternatives in the first two years of the Clinton presidency. In the 104th Congress they were only one of several interests (albeit an important one) trying to grab the attention of a

Republican leadership that grew increasingly concerned with preserving its congressional majority rather than pleasing core electoral constituencies as the 1996 elections approached. Conservative pro-family groups were successful in helping move political debate to the right and weakening the dual clientele trap by focusing public debate on the costs of illegitimacy rather than the potential costs to children of welfare reform and by defending Republican legislators against criticism by right-to-life groups. Less clear through most of the 104th Congress was their effect on efforts to build a Republican-centered coalition for welfare reform. If pro-family groups held firm to their support for family caps and teenage mother exclusions, they had the potential to sink welfare reform by removing support of Republican conservatives for a bill that had weak provisions (or none) in those areas. As chapter 12 shows, pro-family groups eventually proved willing to compromise, endorsing welfare reform legislation that did not mandate either family caps or teenage mother exclusions but did permit states to impose both measures. The legislation also contained less obtrusive provisions (funds for abstinence education and rewards to states that succeeded in reducing illegitimacy without increasing abortion rates) designed to placate social conservative groups.

What emerges, in short, is a picture not of interest groups driving the welfare policymaking process, but of organizations very dependent on building alliances with policymakers in Congress and the executive branch who set the welfare reform agenda and exercised critical veto power. Indeed, despite its idiosyncrasies, the welfare reform case also suggests some general conclusions about the influence of interest and advocacy groups in contemporary American politics. It certainly suggests, for example, that interest groups have responded to the hyperpluralism of American politics in part by forming coalitions of varying formality with like-minded groups. Both liberal and social conservative groups formed coalitions, which facilitated a division of labor and, more important, conveyed an image of additional political clout on issues where a panoply of voices were striving to be heard.

Welfare reform also suggests important lessons about the power that interest groups wield and the limitations of that power. Rather than simply reflecting changes in resources, the influence that interest groups exercise in welfare reform or any other policy sector depends on complex attributes of the groups, of politicians, and of the issue itself.

—*Individual interest groups have more power when they are internally united.* This was clearly a problem for the National Governors' Association in the first year of the 104th Congress (1995), when the governors were unable to arrive at a position and press for it because of their super-majority decision rules. Because of the NGA's bipartisan nature, it was likely to have a major influence only if it could arrive at a genuine consensus or if it could be coopted by activists within its ranks. But because partisan divisions on welfare reform were deep, the NGA was throughout 1995 stalemated and sidelined on major issues, reduced to a consultative role on the details of reform packages.

—*Politicians have substantial leeway in choosing the interests to which they respond.* Hyperpluralism may allow policymakers to choose among several putative representatives of a broad interest and claim they have responded to the concerns the group represents. When the National Governors' Association was deadlocked in 1995, Republican congressional leaders turned to the Republican Governors' Association as a negotiating partner, and most voters could not tell the difference.

—*Interest group influence on policymaking may depend as much on whether a sympathetic political party is in power as it does on group resources.* Politicians are likely to respond to interest groups that are closely linked to core constituencies of their own party (Christian conservatives for the Republicans, environmentalists and feminist organizations for the Democrats) because members of these groups often furnish the activists for political campaigns, a solid voting base, and an important source of campaign contributions for the party. Offending these interests may alienate and demobilize them. Interests closely associated with the other party may have limited access or no access at all.[66] Thus different groups may have varying degrees of influence at different points in the policymaking process (one chamber of Congress, for example), reflecting the relative power of their policymaker allies at that point in the process.

—*Interest group power is maximized when a group can pose a plausible threat of withholding valued resources.* Although groups that build close alliances with one of the two political parties have important advantages in political access, groups at the political extremes also risk being taken for granted by their policymaker allies. Because the positions of these groups tend to be very far from the other party's positions, there is little risk that they or their supporters will defect. Moreover, politicians who "pander" too much to these constituencies may turn off voters whose positions are closer to the middle and spark charges that they are captives of special or extreme interests. Thus politicians may be tempted to ignore these interests if they think that they can do so without suffering political losses.

Indeed, the common problem faced by both liberal child advocacy groups and social conservative pro-family groups is that both are farther from the positions of median voters than are the parties to whose leaders they appeal. They can threaten to use negative publicity to weaken the support of their sympathizers among party activists in the Democratic and Republican political parties. But this is in large measure a hollow threat, for doing so would only weaken their natural allies and benefit their opponents. Indeed, the reluctance of many liberal advocates to criticize Bill Clinton on welfare is probably attributable in part to their experience of twelve years in a row of Republican presidents. Clinton, if not a reliable ally, at least provided them with good access to the administration and claimed to be sympathetic to their concerns. It was a better deal than they had received from Republican presidents, and they had no desire to undermine him if that meant a return to the bad old days. Thus when politicians choose to alienate their party's core constituencies—as Nixon did when he went to China, George Bush when he backed away from his pledge of no new taxes, and Bill Clinton when he signed a Republican-oriented welfare reform bill—constituency leaders not only have little recourse to change the policies, they may also have to bite their tongues to limit criticism of their political "allies."

Groups with strong grassroots support face particularly complex challenges. They must simultaneously (1) convince their supporters that they are not compromising on principles while (2) avoiding the appearance of dictating to the party, which may alienate mainstream voters; and (3) avoid alienating their politician allies and convincing them that their proposals are not too far outside the political mainstream. These patterns were all in evidence when the Christian Coalition unveiled its Contract with the American Family in May 1995, shortly after the new Republican Congress had passed most elements of the House Republicans' Contract with America. The Family Contract was clearly structured after the earlier contract and was intended to pressure Republican leaders to move social issues up on their policy agenda. But in announcing it, Ralph Reed also emphasized that the document represented "ten suggestions, not the Ten Commandments," and stressed that polling and focus groups had shown its provisions were supported by a majority of the American public.[67] Despite these efforts, little progress was made on the provisions of the Christian Coalition's contract, and tensions between leaders of the social conservative groups and the Republican party remained high.[68]

Interest groups, in short, had an ambiguous impact on the politics of welfare reform from 1992 to 1996. The growth of new social conservative groups and the DLC clearly helped focus attention on the behavior of adult AFDC recipients, weakening the dual clientele trap and making conservative approaches to welfare reform more likely to become policy. The fact that different groups also viewed different issues as important—governors focusing on the structure of block grants, New Democrats and some social conservatives on work requirements, and pro-family groups on illegitimacy provisions and time limits—made a compromise, if not a consensus, more feasible. A conservative welfare reform could at least make it through Congress if each constituency got most of what it wanted and was willing to defer to the others on issues about which they cared less. But if each constituency and the policymakers allied with it were intransigent in demanding all of what it wanted and opposing the demands made by others, a coalition for reform could easily unravel.

CHAPTER NINE

Not Ending Welfare as We Know it

The Clinton Administration's Welfare Reform Initiative

"The bargain on welfare reform is going to have to persuade liberals to force people to work and persuade conservatives to spend more money for programs. This is not going to be easy."
—Will Marshall, *Progressive Policy Institute*

"The financing [of a Clinton welfare reform proposal] has been really problematic. There are no good choices."
—Clinton administration official

"You let loose a lot of forces when you say, 'End welfare as we know it,' which is why I never said any such thing. We may look back and say, 'What in the name of God have we done?'"
—Senator Daniel Patrick Moynihan

PREVIOUS CHAPTERS HAVE suggested that the prospects for welfare reform depend critically on constraints imposed by the social and political environment within which policymakers work. These forces shape the policymaking traps through which any reform proposals must pass, the content of the reform proposals, and the weights policymakers give to various factors in their decisionmaking.

Although the policymaking environment constrains choices, it rarely if ever eliminates discretion entirely. New presidential administrations in particular can be particularly powerful in shaping welfare reform initiatives. This chapter focuses on the formulation of the Clinton administration's welfare reform proposals in 1993–94 and the reasons the initiative collapsed without making it out of the House Ways and Means Committee.

The policymaking environment, agenda, and debate surrounding welfare reform in the first two years of the Clinton presidency were dramatically different from those surrounding the Family Support Act debates of 1987–88. Issues that had been important in the FSA debates (at least in the House of Representatives), such as minimum benefit standards or incentives to the states to increase benefits, essentially disappeared. Other issues, such as the importance of work requirements, grew in importance. New subjects such as immigration began to intrude into welfare reform debates. But above all, a new, powerful, and essentially untested idea—time limits—dominated debates.

The Political Environment for Welfare Reform

The previous three chapters traced factors in the environment outside government that shaped and constrained policymaking in the first Clinton administration. But factors within government, such as more stringent federal budget rules and a crowded administration agenda, also shaped policymaking in critical ways. The most important was the election of Bill Clinton to the presidency of the United States on a platform that prominently featured a commitment to "end welfare as we know it."

A Presidential Commitment to Change

As noted in chapter 5, the intellectual foundations of the Clinton administration's pledge to "end welfare as we know it" can be found in David Ellwood's proposals for putting time limits on AFDC benefits without work, after which half-time work would be expected. Ellwood also proposed an expanded Earned Income Tax Credit, universal health care, and increased support for child support assurance, child care, and other services to move welfare recipients into the labor force and allow them to stay there. But the Clinton administration's initial campaign proposal differed from Ellwood's in important ways. The campaign platform was clearer than Ellwood had been about how long the time limit for welfare without work should be: two years. But in most other ways it offered few details. Would everyone who hit the time limit be offered a job forever? Would half-time work be sufficient to meet the work requirement, as suggested in Ellwood's proposal? Would some mothers (those with very young children, for example) be exempted from work requirements, and if so, which ones and for how long? Would time spent in education and training be counted toward meeting a work requirement, and if so, for how long?

The Clinton administration's efforts to construct a new Democratic policy toward poor families had important implications for welfare policy-making traps. First, although the administration avoided most of the harsh rhetoric of the conservative critics of welfare, packaging its proposal under the slogan "ending welfare as we know it" implicitly reinforced the wholesale condemnation of AFDC—and the notion that nothing could be worse for poor children than the status quo—of conservative critiques.[1] Criticizing AFDC was part of an overall strategy to weaken the dual clientele trap for welfare reform on the new administration's terms by convincing the public that the Clinton administration's approach neither put children unduly at risk nor coddled their parents. This ultimately would place the administration at a severe bargaining disadvantage with a Republican-controlled Congress.[2] Having wholeheartedly condemned the status quo and focused public attention on the behavior of parents rather than the welfare of children, President Clinton would be in the very awkward position of implicitly defending the status quo if he vetoed Republican-inspired welfare reform legislation. This was not a concern at the time that the pledge was made, of course: candidate Clinton was understandably concentrating on the grand strategic game of realigning the image of the Democratic party on welfare issues rather than on the serious legislative bargaining that might follow his election. Nor could he anticipate the Republican takeover in Congress that would seize control of the welfare reform agenda and force him into a defensive posture on welfare.

The president's rhetorical flourish may also have strengthened the money trap. In public perceptions, ending welfare as we know it is likely to be interpreted as something more akin to ending welfare than to dramatically increased expenditures for training, child care, and jobs in the short term to reduce welfare dependence in the long term. Why, many policymakers and members of the public wondered, was it necessary to spend more money on welfare if we were supposed to be ending it?[3] And if we were spending a lot more money, didn't that support Republican charges that the administration was made up of the same old tax-and-spend Democrats rather than New Democrats who were going to transform the way that government worked?

The Clinton campaign's bold pledge also posed a risk that the administration might not be able to keep the promise it had made. The pledge was made without seriously considering either the costs or potential implementation difficulties.[4] Once in office the administration was almost certain to confront a classic case of overselling. Transforming AFDC in a way that does not simply cut off recipients is a complex and very expensive process. But having made the commitment to end welfare as we know it, the administration risked being politically hammered by the Republicans if it did not come up with a proposal that could plausibly be portrayed as doing so. Indeed, postelection research by the new administration's pollsters showed that welfare reform ranked third on the list of the administration's most important promises.[5]

Finally, the administration's acceptance of AFDC time limits followed by a work requirement pushed Republicans to pursue strategic disagreement using deterrence approaches (notably time limits with no work guarantee) that would differentiate them from the Democrats as tougher on welfare to win back an issue the president appeared to be taking away from them. All these processes threatened to push the welfare debate further to the right.

Strains in the Democratic Coalition

The new administration's policies toward low-income families also posed potential problems in relations with traditional Democratic constituencies, especially organized labor. The administration's proposals for an expanded Earned Income Tax Credit and an increase in the minimum wage were both popular with organized labor. But the proposal to dramatically increase the scope of public service employment programs risked alienating public service employee unions, an important Democratic constituency that feared their members would be replaced by minimum wage "workfare" recipients.[6] The welfare issue could also hurt the administration with liberal advocacy groups: if the administration moved too far to the right in its welfare proposals—by endorsing hard time limits and teenage mother exclusions, for example—those groups could turn their formidable publicity powers against the administration. Nor did welfare reform offer promising opportunities for creating effective new links with the social conservative pro-family groups, which had close ties to the Republican party and advocated deterrence-oriented strategies that were unacceptable to core Democratic constituencies.

The prospects for using welfare policy to revitalize Democratic coalitions in Congress were also problematic. The potentially punitive aspects of the Clinton administration's welfare proposals were anathema to liberal Democrats in Congress and to the Congressional Black Caucus. But breaking with the president would not be easy, either. As an important Democratic House staff member said in an April 1994 interview, "Democrats are now finally realizing that even though they dislike the fact that he proposed [welfare reform], they love the fact that he got elected. Now he has to fulfill his promises, and that's one of them. They're going to have to find a way to go along with it, or they will damage him politically."[7] And if congressional liberals did not support the administration's welfare initiatives, they might bring on an outcome that they liked even less, for Clinton would then have to attract some Republican votes to pass welfare reform, and the Republican asking price would probably be high. In short, welfare reform risked shattering rather than strengthening the Democratic coalition in Congress as well as in the electorate.[8]

New Budget Rules

Congressional efforts to deal with the ballooning budget deficits of the 1980s also had important implications for the administration's welfare reform initiative. Especially important were the reforms enacted as part of the Budget Enforcement Act of 1990. The BEA replaced overall deficit targets enacted as part of the Gramm-Rudman-Hollings Act of 1985 with mechanisms that are more focused on expenditures. So-called discretionary spending, where benefit levels are not mandated by law, is subject to a spending cap.[9] Social Security, Aid to Families with Dependent Children, Food Stamps, Medicare, and most veterans' benefits are treated differently. Here the BEA rule is that any legislated changes that increase spending in a program need to be offset by cuts in that program or in other entitlements or by raising additional revenue.[10]

The Budget Enforcement Act procedures had two major effects on the prospects for welfare reform, both exacerbating the money trap. First, the zero-sum nature of budgeting was intensified. Given the reluctance of the administration to propose tax increases and the vehement opposition of congressional Republicans and conservative Democrats to such increases, cuts in other entitlement programs were the most likely source of funds for the additional costs associated with child care, transportation assistance, training, subsidized work slots, and other expected expenses of moving welfare recipients into work. But which programs could be cut to offset the added costs of welfare reform? Social Security? Programs for disabled veterans? Medicare? It did not take much imagination for the administration's welfare policymakers to imagine the headlines and the uproar from affected groups if they appeared to be taking resources from one of these constituencies to give to welfare mothers. The central political challenge for the administration, then, was to come up with entitlement programs to cut that were less popular than AFDC. But few entitlements fit that description. As a result, the search for offsetting entitlement cuts increasingly came to focus on unpopular clienteles within entitlement programs (immigrants, for example, and persons receiving disability payments in part because of drug and alcohol addiction) and on entitlements targeted on the poor. A second, related effect was to add to the secrecy of welfare policymaking. With very few politically viable sources of increased revenue available, any hint that a proposal to cut a weak program was under consideration might set off a competitive scramble with other policy entrepreneurs to reserve those cuts for their own proposals: act too slowly and the potential cut might get taken by someone else.

The administration could have adapted to the BEA budget rules in two ways, but each had its problems. The first was to use the administration's widely anticipated 1993 initial budget package to finance welfare reform. The package would involve significant tax increases that could be used to offset the added costs associated with welfare reform. Including a welfare proposal in the package, as the expansion of the Earned Income Tax Credit was, would avoid its being pitted directly against other programs and clienteles for funds. Using this route had two problems, however. The budget package was on a fast track, with the administration hoping to complete action within the first one hundred days after coming into office. And ending welfare as we know it requires extraordinarily detailed legislation; it is a far more complex legislative (and administrative) task than expanding the EITC. Coming up with a detailed proposal required consultation with the states (who would have to carry out its directives) and advocacy groups. And given the controversial nature of AFDC, including welfare reform in the budget package risked bogging the budget down and giving it a less popular political face. In addition, "deficit hawks" within the administration and Congress were determined to use the budget package to reduce the deficit and wanted to reserve as much as possible of the increased revenue for that purpose. As a result, welfare reform was dropped from the administration's 1993 budget package.[11]

A second option was to evade the Budget Enforcement Act's pay-as-you-go strictures by phasing in the program expansion and the increased spending on child care, work, and so forth, after the five-year window in which any increased program costs must be balanced by increased funding or cuts in other programs. As is discussed later in this chapter, the administration did indeed do this with its phase-in of work requirements for younger mothers. But a slow phase-in creates problems. The administration would appear not to be keeping its promise to end welfare as we know it within its first term in office. Indeed, the House Republicans' welfare reform bill in the 103d Congress, unveiled seven months before Clinton's, put tougher work requirements in place more quickly while still cutting overall expenditures. The Republicans were able to do this largely because they were willing to be much tougher on restricting benefits to immigrants than the administration was willing to be and to cap expenditure growth in many means-tested programs.

A Crowded Agenda

Far more issues come to policymakers' attention than they can possibly devote substantial time to. Issues at the top of their lists will receive substantial attention. Items lower on the agenda may be raised for discussion, but are less likely to have significant resources devoted to them. Items still lower are likely to receive occasional lip service but little more. Items at the bottom are unlikely to receive even lip service. Setting priorities is especially important for elected politicians because failure to concentrate on the few that have some prospect for success is likely to result in wasted effort, little policy movement, little political credit from the public, and weaker prospects for reelection.[12] Although the multiple venues for policymaking in the United States allow simultaneous processing of many issues, only the president and a few powerful legislators can put items on the agenda if others have no interest in them. Moreover, there are many bottlenecks, especially in the legislative process, where proposals can become clogged and the process may break down.[13]

Welfare reform was just one element of a broader agenda for change that the Clinton administration promised. Health care reform, deficit reduction, introduction of national service, community empowerment, and improved school-to-work transitions were among the most important initiatives vying for attention and requiring decisions in a White House known for its long meetings, tangled lines of authority and decisionmaking, and seeming inability to come to closure on important issues.[14]

The most important and prominent element on the administration's agenda was the promise to make affordable, secure health care available to all Americans. Health care reform had several implications for the prospects of welfare reform. First, it promised to address a key element of the perverse incentives trap in AFDC: recipients' fear of losing Medicaid benefits when they took a low-paying, insecure job with no health benefits. This fear is particularly important for those families in which a family member has a chronic illness. The administration's pledge to introduce universal health insurance promised to reduce the relative attractiveness of welfare by extending health insurance to the working poor, thus easing the way for AFDC recipients to leave welfare for low-paying jobs and ending the lure of AFDC as a way to get health coverage. Universal health insurance would lower the costs of welfare reform by decreasing the number of persons who went on welfare and of those who were likely to need publicly provided or subsidized jobs after benefits ran out.

The interaction of health care reform and welfare reform also created problems for welfare reform, however. The first was scheduling. Many of the entities involved in shaping and approving the two proposals were the same, notably the Department of Health and Human Services, the Office of Management and Budget, and the domestic policy staff in the White House. Because executive agencies were preoccupied with developing an administration health care package by the spring of 1993, as the president had promised, they could not turn their full attention to making the many decisions involved in creating a welfare reform package. Certainly it would be difficult to have a fully developed package by the time the administration's 1993 budget package was debated in Congress.

The same sorts of bottlenecks were likely to recur in Congress, where both health care reform and welfare reform would have to pass through the House Ways and Means and Senate Finance committees. As the administration's schedule for health care reform fell further behind, welfare risked getting pushed back even further. When the health care initiative got into trouble and ultimately collapsed, there was increased pressure within the Clinton administration and among congressional Democrats to enact some kind of welfare reform before the 1994 election to show that they had accomplished something, even if the bill was not particularly to the administration's liking. The long, torturous death of health care reform did not allow the Clinton administration to mount a salvage operation for welfare reform before it lost control of Congress.

A second problem caused by the interaction of health care reform and welfare reform was that the rules for budgetary scorekeeping also suggested delaying welfare reform, because health care reform was supposed to reduce the projected costs and caseload estimates for welfare reform by making entry into the low-wage labor market more attractive. This meant adopting welfare reform either concurrently with health care reform or after it. But health care reform was likely to be politically dicey enough without making it into a single package with the always controversial welfare reform. As opponents to the Clinton health care package mobilized, health care reform looked even more unlikely. And without universal health coverage, the working poor with incomes just above those of welfare recipients were likely to remain uncovered, leading these workers to rely at least intermittently on AFDC as a gateway to Medicaid.

New Issues

Another factor shaping the Clinton administration's welfare reform initiative was the growth in importance of immigration, especially illegal immigration, as a policy issue. The issue has been particularly important in California, Texas, and Florida, which were disproportionately affected by immigration in the 1990s.[15] In September 1993, for example, 86 percent of Californians polled by the *Los Angeles Times* called illegal immigration a major or moderate problem for the state.[16] Illegal immigrants are not eligible for AFDC, Medicaid, and Food Stamps, although they are eligible for the special supplemental food program for women, infants and children (WIC) and Head Start, as well as many services for which the states bear the primary financing responsibility, especially public education and emergency health services. Indeed, growing resentment against immigrants was fueled in part by state politicians who argued that state budgets were being devastated by the cost of services provided to immigrants. California governor Pete Wilson asserted that services to illegal immigrants cost his recession-racked state $3 billion a year, more than 10 percent of the state budget.[17] Several state governments sued the federal government to force it to pay more for services to illegal aliens.[18] Groups in California organized to force a statewide referendum to ban virtually all social services, including education, for illegal immigrants; emergency medical care would be the only exception. The initiative passed by a three-to-two margin in the November 1994 election and was immediately challenged in the courts.[19]

Complaints from the states also helped increase awareness of the costs of services to *legal* immigrants. In the early 1990s the news media, scholars, government research agencies, and congressional committees all took up the problem of benefits' being provided, sometimes fraudulently, to noncitizens.[20] Although illegal immigrants were not eligible for AFDC benefits, their children born in the United States are automatically citizens and do qualify. In addition, legal immigrants were eligible for AFDC, although those who were brought in as "sponsored aliens" (usually by family members) were subject to a three-year period during which the income of U.S.

residents who sponsored them was deemed available for their support in calculating eligibility (after that time, these sponsored aliens could become eligible for AFDC based on their incomes). Overall, noncitizens increased from 5.5 percent of AFDC adult recipients in 1983 to 9.3 percent in 1993.[21] The growth in benefits was much higher in the federal Supplemental Security Income program, which provides means-tested assistance to citizens and legal immigrants who are aged, blind, or disabled. By 1994 noncitizens constituted 30 percent of the aged portion of the national SSI caseload and a far higher percentage in California.[22]

Sentiment against perceived abuses of welfare programs by legal and illegal immigrants had several effects on welfare reform debates. On the one hand, it raised the prospect of providing money for welfare reform by cutting benefits to noncitizen immigrants; after all, they cannot vote, although they may have family members who do. This could weaken the welfare reform money trap by providing a clientele to hurt that is as unpopular as AFDC recipients. But if the Clinton administration proposed cutting immigrant benefits, it would also threaten an already fragile coalition for reform. It would certainly threaten support from the Hispanic Caucus, a significant element of the Democratic party in the House, which opposed the proposals because many of the immigrants affected are from Latin America. Jewish groups also opposed cutbacks in benefits to legal immigrants because Jewish refugees from the former Soviet Union were also heavily represented among immigrant recipients of means-tested assistance.[23] Cutting federal benefits could also arouse opposition from state governors, who feared that they would inherit the costs of caring for poor immigrants if the federal government withdrew benefits.

A Fractious Congress

The political environment for welfare reform in Congress also contained several question marks that could affect prospects for passage. The indictment of Ways and Means Committee chairman Dan Rostenkowski on May 31, 1994, meant that he had to step down from the chairmanship. The second ranking committee member, Sam Gibbons of Florida, replaced him, but Gibbons was known neither as a welfare expert nor as a deal maker who could deliver his committee for a piece of legislation.[24]

Leadership on the Human Resources Subcommittee was another question mark. The chair, Harold Ford of Tennessee, was an experienced member of the subcommittee and had been chair from 1981 through the early stages of the 1987–88 round before he had to step down because of an indictment for bank fraud. He had only recently been cleared of charges and resumed the chairmanship and an active role in the committee.[25] Although Ford pledged to work with the administration, his position on welfare was far to the left of the Clinton administration's.[26] The president might talk the language of broad bipartisan compromise, but that was not the pattern of welfare reform legislation on Ways and Means. Instead, the pattern even in 1987–88 had been one of intense interparty competition for the votes at the margin that would allow Democratic or Republican bills to prevail.

Prospects in the Senate were even more unpredictable. The close partisan alignment on the Senate Finance Committee (Democrats held a one-seat majority) made bipartisanship a necessity, as did the ability of the minority party to filibuster any legislation that could not muster sixty votes on the chamber floor to break the filibuster. In addition, Lloyd Bentsen's departure to become secretary of the Treasury had made Daniel Patrick Moynihan, chief author of Nixon's Family Assistance Plan and one of the primary architects of the 1988 Family Support Act, head of the Senate Finance Committee. There was little doubt that Moynihan would make his voice heard on social policy. Early in 1994, for example, he asserted, "We don't have a health crisis in this country. We do have a welfare crisis. And we can do both." He accused the administration of using welfare as "boob bait for Bubbas" and threatened obliquely to hold up health care reform if a welfare reform proposal was not forthcoming.[27] But Moynihan was not clear about what he wanted a welfare bill to include, and he had several reasons to avoid taking the lead in proposing his own welfare bill. He believed that the president should be given the opportunity to lead. As the primary mover behind the 1998 Family Support Act, he also complained repeatedly that his legislation had been given neither the time nor the financing to work properly and that it should be given both before further changes were made. And Moynihan was facing a 1994 primary challenge from black activist Reverend Al Sharpton, who attacked him from the left as racially insensitive.[28] Although there was almost no prospect that Moynihan would lose his Senate seat, deferring to presidential leadership on this controversial legislation was the easiest choice on all grounds.

Policy Choice and the Politics of Formulation

As the Clinton administration sought to transform into legislation its pledges to make work pay, to end welfare as we know it, and to move above the poverty line all families with parents who work full time, it faced critical strategic choices and challenges on issues such as timing, packaging, and presenting its proposals.[29] But the fate of welfare reform would depend even more on the substantive choices the administration made in developing its proposal. How should the plan be financed? What should happen to people who reached the two-year time limit? Should that limit be a lifetime limit, or should the clock start over for women who went off the rolls and then returned, perhaps years later? Should there be a time limit on job slots, and if there was, what should happen to the persons who reached it? Strong divisions were certain to arise on each of these questions both within the administration and within Congress.

To develop its proposal, the administration appointed an interagency task force with three cochairs and thirty-two members, drawing on the major departments concerned with poverty policy. One cochair was David Ellwood, the author of *Poor Support* and the new assistant secretary for planning and evaluation in the Department of Health and Human Services. The second was Mary Jo Bane, Ellwood's collaborator on much of the pathbreaking research on welfare spells while both were on the faculty of Harvard's Kennedy School of Government. Bane had only recently begun serving as the commissioner of social services for New York State in the Cuomo administration. Key administration decisionmakers were thus well acquainted with the research on AFDC and welfare-to-work programs.[30]

The third cochair was Bruce Reed, who represented the New Democrat strand in Clinton's thought. Only thirty-three years old when the administration came into office, he was a quintessential Clintonite. He had been a Rhodes scholar, worked for Al Gore when Gore was a senator, and followed with a stint as policy director at the Democratic Leadership Council. He had served as deputy campaign manager for policy in Clinton's presidential campaign, where he coined the "ending welfare as we know it" catchphrase.[31] Reed came to the White House as one of two deputy assistants to the president for domestic policy.

Although these three brought great intellectual ability to the welfare reform initiative, they brought limited Washington experience: only Reed had worked in the federal government before, and that in a Senate staff position. The three also brought differing views, with Reed the most conservative. Moreover, these divisions extended to other important members of the administration: both Secretary of Health and Human Services Donna Shalala and the president's wife, Hillary Rodham Clinton, were former chairs of the Children's Defense Fund, an advocacy organization that was firmly opposed to many of the president's welfare initiatives that the CDF believed inevitably harmed children.

Differences in basic value positions among administration decision-makers and differences in attentiveness to political considerations were real problems. As one administration policymaker observed,

> The things we disagree on are really quite fundamental, and they inevitably do not involve empirical results. They involve philo-sophical beliefs. Part-time workers are the perfect example of that. Limiting the work program in some fashion is [another]. Can you ever say to someone, "We've done enough, it's time for you to find some support on your own." Or do you have an obligation so long as someone had played by the rules all along to keep providing it, no matter how long it goes, no matter what happens, recognizing that you may not have been very strict about the rules or you may not have had a good system in place? . . . Those are two examples where in the end it isn't science.[32]

Indeed, putting time limits on the WORK program and how to treat part-time work by welfare recipients proved to be two of the hardest issues to resolve because the cochairs disagreed on these basic values and on the politics that surrounded them. Reed—the campaign veteran, New Demo-crat, and White House representative—was more concerned than the other cochairs with the importance of appearing to "end welfare as we know it" in the administration's proposal.

Coming to closure on any of these issues was made more complicated by a decisionmaking process with multiple layers and unclear lines of authority.[33] At the center of the process were Ellwood, Bane, and Reed, whose thirty-two member task force drew from Health and Human Services, Agriculture, and Housing and Urban Development as well as the White House (notably the Office of Management and Budget and the Domestic Policy Council). But the task force proved an unwieldy body whose members were busy with their departmental responsibilities and who varied tremendously in their institutional stake and personal interest in wel-fare reform. The group met only a few times, mainly to serve as a sounding board for ideas developed in less formal bodies.

The three cochairs were at the center of this less formal process, but they also worked closely with a somewhat larger group that included Wendell Primus, the Health and Human Services deputy assistant secretary for human resources and a long-time veteran of the Democratic staff on the House Ways and Means Committee; Isabel Sawhill, the associate director of the Office of Management and Budget for Human Resources; and Kathi Way from the White House Domestic Policy Council. Underneath these in the hierarchy was an interagency group that met at 7:30 most workday mornings to have an informed debate, discuss options, and eventually develop detailed specifications for welfare reform legislation. The flow of paper was managed primarily by Primus. Meetings were generally organized by topic, and attendance varied by topic, but generally fifteen to twenty people, about half of whom were civil servants (mostly from HHS) and half political appointees, attended.[34] The civil servants rarely spoke, however, especially on matters in which they knew that their opinions differed from those of Bane and Ellwood. In retrospect, many of the participants viewed the process as flawed. Although observing that the process led to a full debate on the issues, one important participant noted, "The disadvantage was that it was slow, it was frustrating because there wasn't one person running the train and calling the shots, and there was a tendency for decisions to kind of get half-made and then come unraveled."[35]

The cochairs' decisions could be appealed to a group of the cabinet secretaries directly concerned with welfare reform and ultimately to the president. But appealing decisions caused problems. Because the White House was constantly preoccupied with the budget, the crime bill, and health care, meetings with the president were difficult to obtain, and even when they occurred, they did not always resolve differences. As one of the central participants in the Clinton welfare reform effort said, "The president never weighed in on something in a totally clean way." Reflecting the well-known Clinton practice of wanting to seem to agree with those he was talking to, even when they disagreed among themselves, a presidential intervention usually involved "a meeting in which he said various things that people interpreted in various ways."[36] Thus even after the president made his views known, the leaders of the welfare task force were frequently left once again with finding a compromise that everybody could live with.

Incomplete Agenda Control

The administration's calculations were also influenced by planners' realization that they did not have complete control over the legislative agenda. Republicans in Congress, seeking to share in any credit for welfare reform and to push the administration in the direction of their own policy preferences, had several bills in the hopper before the administration was ready with its own plan. The main Republican bill, H.R. 3500, put together by a fourteen-member welfare reform task force, was actually more expensive than the eventual Clinton bill in providing $10 billion for child care and work programs because Republicans had fewer compunctions about cutting means-tested benefits to finance AFDC work programs.[37] H.R. 3500 imposed a two-year time limit (a lifetime limit), for receipt of AFDC benefits without work. After that, recipients had to be working thirty-five hours a week in either subsidized private sector or public sector jobs. It prescribed tough sanctions for those who failed to comply with state requirements. States were also allowed, but not required, to impose hard time limits for removal of all aid after a recipient had been engaged in the work component of the program for no less than three years. The bill moved strongly in the direction of deterrence measures to reduce illegitimacy, with states required to impose family caps and deny benefits to minor parents unless the state passed legislation explicitly exempting itself from such requirements.

H.R. 3500 was a precursor of the Republican themes of spending reductions and devolution that would come to the fore in the 104th Congress. The bill was expected to produce substantial savings by capping the aggregate growth of most cash means-tested programs (including the recently expanded Earned Income Tax Credit) at inflation plus 2 percent. Nutrition programs, including Food Stamps, school lunch, and WIC, would also have been combined into a single block grant with total spending reduced. Means-tested benefits would have been all but eliminated for most legal immigrants who had not yet become citizens. States also would have been given the option of converting their AFDC funding into a fixed block grant. Thus, despite increased spending on aiding transitions to work, the bill was expected to produce savings of $19.5 billion over five years.[38]

H.R. 3500 was most important, however, not for its specific provisions, but for the fact that it gave the Republicans something to rally around. And they did: 160 of 176 House Republicans had signed on as cosponsors when the bill was introduced. Thus the Republicans served notice that with many liberal Democrats unlikely to back the administration's welfare plan, the White House would have to move toward Republican positions if it were to build a winning coalition. To add to the pressure, Republicans tried to attach their welfare proposal during a House Budget Committee markup of the House Budget resolution in March, where it lost by a 22-21 vote as four Democrats defected to support the provision.[39] Republicans also threatened to use the arcane House procedure called a discharge petition to force the release of their bill from the Ways and Means Committee to the House floor for consideration.[40] As a result, the administration welfare reform planning group was playing defense even during its planning stages, trying to style specific provisions in its own bill that could beat H.R. 3500 counterparts in a committee legislative markup or floor amendment battle and to create an overall bill that would beat H.R. 3500 when Republicans offered it as a substitute in committee and on the floor.

There were also divisions within Republican ranks, however, that would become much more prominent as the House members developed the welfare reform provisions of the Contract with America. Conservative Republicans considered H.R. 3500 too close to the middle ground sought by the Clinton administration rather than staking out a distinctive and more deterrence-focused Republican position.[41] In April 1994 two relatively junior Republicans, James Talent (Missouri) in the House and Lauch Faircloth (North Carolina) in the Senate, introduced a bill pushed by the new Republican think tank Empower America and by Heritage Foundation welfare analyst Robert Rector. The most controversial provision of the bill, modestly titled The Real Welfare Reform Act of 1994, would have banned benefits to all mothers younger than age twenty-one (or a higher age at state option), with any savings given back to the states to run alternative centers such as orphanages and group homes for mothers and children. It also would have forbidden states from choosing not to impose family caps and teenage mother exclusions, forced a much faster phase-in of work requirements, and capped welfare expenditures.[42] Once again, the threat that conservatives and liberals might jointly sink welfare loomed large.

Coming to Closure

Given the complexity and lack of clear hierarchy or decision rules in the Clinton administration's welfare reform decisionmaking process, it should not be surprising that critical decisions on the administration's plan were made in different venues, at different times, and with different dominating motivations. Those that appeared to policymakers to be easy choices—not posing tough choices among values, costs, ease of implementation, or factional support—were made earlier and at lower levels in the fuzzy hierarchy than when only "hard" or "bad" choices were available.

Phasing In Work Requirements

One choice that was a relatively easy and early one was the decision on how to phase in work requirements for welfare recipients. Providing jobs, even low-skilled jobs, takes lots of money for administration, transportation, and child care. Providing jobs to all AFDC parents could cost more than $20 billion a year. Senator Moynihan had earlier estimated added costs at up to $30 billion a year.[43] Phasing a work program in gradually was dictated by budgetary constraints: the administration was unwilling, in the face of tight new spending rules imposed by the Budget Enforcement Act, to propose new taxes to finance welfare reform, and it was unable to come up with enough politically acceptable cuts in other entitlement programs to fund a large welfare reform package.

One phase-in option was simply to give states a lot of discretion in implementing work requirements, but this was considered unacceptable on both programmatic and political grounds: if work was not seen as truly mandatory for a group, it was unlikely that members of the group would change their childbearing, family formation, and educational and labor market behavior. Nor would this be perceived as ending welfare as we know it. But how should scarce resources for imposing work requirements be targeted first: toward young mothers, mothers of older children, or perhaps state by state? Each approach had problems. Research suggesting that mothers with very young children are the most difficult clientele to move into jobs could have provided a cost-effectiveness rationale for focusing first on mothers of older children, who are generally older mothers. But some policymakers feared that starting work requirements with mothers of older children might encourage them to have more children to avoid those requirements. Implementing work requirements a few states at a time might encourage welfare migration to avoid the work requirement. It would also create political problems in Congress (few legislators would want their states excluded) and would not appear to the public to be changing the status quo.

The catalyst for a decision on targeting phase-ins was a January 1994 *New Republic* article by Paul Offner, the top welfare policy analyst for Senator Moynihan, suggesting that the administration "Target the Kids"— concentrate on teenage parents, because "It is the teen mothers who are most at risk of being permanently trapped in poverty."[44] Despite the problems of moving these mothers into jobs, targeting young mothers was an easy choice. It offered an opportunity to send a strong signal to potential mothers and to voters that the administration really was ending welfare as we know it. Its connection to Moynihan, with whom the administration had recently had stormy relations over welfare (Offner's article appeared less than two weeks after Moynihan's "welfare crisis" remark) also did not hurt. One of the administration's key planners recalled later that "David [Ellwood] got very enamored with it and basically sold that idea to the rest of the group. It basically got ratified."[45]

Hard Time Limits

Time limits were far more controversial. Conservatives and New Democrats within the Clinton administration advocated limits on both cash benefits and subsidized jobs to send a firm message to welfare recipients and because they believed it was politically necessary to redeem the president's pledge.[46] Liberals in Congress, on whom the administration would depend to pass its welfare package, opposed both kinds of time limits, especially those affecting recipients who had played by the rules but were still unable to find steady work, leaving them without either cash benefits or a job guarantee.[47] In the end the president rejected inclusion of hard time limits.

Discouraging Teenage Pregnancy

The most concrete manifestation of the dual clientele trap in the Clinton welfare reform occurred in the debate over deterrence-focused proposals to decrease out-of-wedlock births through teenage mother exclusions and family caps. Excluding teenage mothers from benefits never had strong support within the administration. But compelling them to live at home rather than set up an independent household enjoyed broad support in the administration and the public and was already a state option under the Family Support Act.

Whether to include mandatory family caps in the administration's welfare reform proposal was a far more contentious question and was resolved relatively late. Some of the administration's planners, notably Mary Jo Bane, were strongly opposed to family caps on moral grounds. Social science evidence also weighed in: some administration planners thought it foolish to mandate to the states a requirement that had not been proven to reduce out-of-wedlock births. Strategic arguments were also made against including a mandatory family cap in the administration's bill. Leaving family caps out of the bill and being reversed by Congress could placate conservatives in Congress by giving them a great victory; conceding it at the outset would require conceding even more once the bill reached Congress.

Several financial and political factors supported the caps, however. Imposing mandatory family caps would reduce benefit payments and thus count as a reduced AFDC program expenditure that could be used to offset increased expenditures for work and other elements of the Clinton reform proposal. Moreover, family caps were growing in popularity, and it was thought that Congress might impose them no matter what the adminis-tration proposed. As one administration planner recalled, "We thought that there was a 99 percent chance the Hill was going to [impose family caps]. . . . So if that was going to happen, since it generated some savings, that was kind of an argument for including it in the bill in the first place."[48] The president had also given a signal in an early meeting that some sort of compromise was in order when, as one top welfare planner recalled, "The president indicated personal discomfort [with family caps] but reiterated his view that we've got to let the states do some things that we're not com-fortable with."[49] The decision came back to Clinton near the end of the welfare proposal process, and his desire to let the states have options was a critical factor in proposing to allow them to impose family caps if they desired.

Child Care Funding

How much to spend on child care, and for whom, illustrated the potential perverse incentives attached to a prevention and rehabilitation strategy. Many of the administration's planners believed that substantial spending on child care was required not just to allow welfare recipients to move into work but also to help the working poor. If the working poor were not cov-ered, they might be lured onto AFDC to take advantage of child care bene-fits. The major problem with providing more funding for child care, how-ever, was its cost. Providing more funding for child care for the working poor was hard to justify politically when work requirements for welfare recipients were being phased in much more slowly than the president's pledge to "end welfare as we know it" had implied. Ultimately, funding for child care was determined not by the preferences of the welfare planners but by limitations on the funding that they were able to raise for their overall project. In short, child care suffered from its status as a second-order goal and an expensive one.[50]

Financing Welfare Reform

The biggest hurdle in developing the Clinton plan was money. In his first meeting with David Ellwood after the young man came to Washington, Senator Moynihan clearly stated his perception that Congress was unwilling to provide money and his skepticism that the administration could over-come the money trap. "There simply is no money. None," he told Ellwood. "So what are you going to do?"[51]

The administration had committed itself to trying to fund welfare reform without raising taxes. Institutional rivalries, the relatively insulated nature of the planning, and the low priority given to welfare reform within the administration hurt as well. The initial development of targets for raising funds was run out of HHS as part of the welfare reform planning process with help from the Office of Management and Budget (OMB). As one White House player observed, "Treasury wasn't dying to come up with money for us . . . the tax people tended to want to keep their cards pretty close to their chest and their money in their own vaults."[52] But the administration's desire to avoid tax increases meant that there were few acceptable options for raising funds. Most proposals to fund welfare reform by cutting other entitlements—reducing veterans' benefits, reducing food stamp benefits to those who receive housing assistance, and taxing other means-tested program benefits—also failed to survive the trial balloon stage, most often because they raised adamant opposition from liberal Democrats in Congress and their allies in the liberal advocacy community.[53]

In the high-stakes political atmosphere of 1993—Clinton's budget package passed only because Vice President Al Gore broke a tie vote in the Senate, and an equally close and tough vote was anticipated shortly on health care reform—individual legislators who were willing to play a hostage-taking game gained enormous power. One or a few legislators who were considered swing votes on health care could virtually rule out any revenue increase. This had a spillover effect on welfare reform. When the administration considered imposing a tax on gambling to finance welfare reform, for example, Senator Harry Reid of Nevada threatened, "I will become the most negative, the most irresponsible, the most obnoxious person of anyone in the Senate."[54] With Reid's vote considered crucial to the passage of health care reform, it is not surprising that the administration backed down on a gambling tax. The administration's own political commitments limited the search for revenue by keeping off the agenda proposals to crack down on abuse in the Earned Income Tax Credit. As one of the administration's planners said:

> We were convinced that the Earned Income Tax Credit was paying out a lot of benefits to people who were not eligible for it. And we had some evidence of that. And we wanted to reform [it]. Not reform so much; we wanted to remove the abuse. . . . But there was a concern. The administration had put a lot of political capital into the Earned Income Tax Credit, and coming out then a year later

saying "This program has some abuse that needs to be curtailed" was not exactly a winning message in some people's minds.[55]

Ultimately, the search for funding was taken over by Budget director Leon Panetta after the HHS-led process failed to identify enough politically viable targets. But the OMB-led search fared little better, resulting in a welfare reform proposal far less ambitious than most of the planners wanted.

The Clinton Administration Proposal

The administration ended its long process of deliberation and planning when it unveiled its proposal on June 14, 1994.[56] As with health care reform, the administration was not content to outline reform principles and allow Congress to fill in the details. On June 21 it unveiled its draft legislation, 464 pages of new programmatic language and amendments to existing laws. The themes the administration wished to highlight were in the title of the proposed bill, The Work and Responsibility Act of 1994.[57]

Facilitating the Transition to Work

Title I of the proposed Work and Responsibility Act focused on changes in the JOBS program and in the philosophy of AFDC. Mothers born after 1971 would be subject to a work requirement after receiving two years of AFDC benefits. At the time of the bill's introduction, this group constituted about one-third of the AFDC caseload. The states could expand the new requirements to additional groups if they chose. Two-thirds of the adult caseload was expected to be covered by work requirements by 2004.[58]

New signals were to be sent to all AFDC recipients and to welfare caseworkers from the time of application for assistance. The initial signal was a requirement that applicants and state agency representatives sign a "personal responsibility agreement" at the time of application acknowledging that cash benefits were limited in duration and pledging that both parties would work to "enable the individual to achieve maximum economic independence and self-sufficiency." There were to be mutual obligations: agency representatives would pledge to provide the services (especially education and job training) needed by the recipient to attain that economic independence, and applicants would pledge to participate in those activities. For recipients, these conditions were intended to demonstrate that welfare was not to be a permanent way of life; for welfare workers the pact was to demonstrate that their institutional culture should be reoriented from checking on eligibility toward helping people gain job skills and find work.

State agencies would be required to assess the needs and resources of the applicant and to develop an employability plan for each person within ninety days of the beginning of assistance payments.[59] Those who refused to sign a plan would lose their own benefits, but not benefits for children in their care. Beginning no later than forty-five days before the end of the two-year time limit (and before receiving a work assignment), recipients would be required to engage in job search. Younger recipients judged ready to work would be required to engage in job search as soon as their applications for assistance were approved.

After two years, recipients subject to the work requirement who had not found private sector jobs were to take community service jobs in a pro gram called WORK (which, unlike JOBS, was not an acronym: it is just the word "work" capitalized). Those in WORK would be paid only for the hours they worked.

Some provisions of the bill were intended to ease the concerns of various groups about the WORK program. To placate public sector unions, states were required not to use WORK slots to displace existing workers, replace strikers, or replace directly employed workers with contractors. States had to establish grievance procedures to deal with complaints from employees and their union representatives that such displacement had in fact occurred.[60] As an additional safeguard against displacement, employers were required to pay the higher of the federal or state minimum wage or the rate paid by the employer to workers doing similar work, with the same length in the job. But to make WORK assignments less attractive than alternative sources of employment, payments under the WORK program were not to be eligible for supplementation by the Earned Income Tax Credit. In addition, no WORK assignment was to last more than a year.

These new work obligations were to be phased in gradually, beginning with mothers born after 1971 and with numerous exemptions. By 1999 fewer than 170,000 out of almost 5 million AFDC parents were expected to be at work in government-provided or government-subsidized jobs. The slow phase-in was a bow to the budgetary reality that it is cheaper to pay benefits than to provide jobs and support services such as child care and transportation. The phase-in held down costs in the five years counted under the Budget Enforcement Act. It had the additional advantage of giving the states more time to build up their administrative capacity to manage very large job, training, and child care initiatives. But it had the strong

political disadvantage of not appearing to end welfare as we know it immediately. The image that the administration sought to project to the public
was that of an income transfer program's being transformed into a work
program. But the reality would have been different: many welfare mothers
would not have been expected to work because they were born in 1971 or
earlier, were caring for infants, or were seriously disabled or caring for children who were disabled. Indeed, to Republican critics, it appeared to be
"more welfare as we know it": substantial new expenditures with little
immediate increase in work.

Flexible Time Limits

In general, all recipients born after 1971 were to be subject to the twenty-
four-month time limit for receiving cash benefits without working. This
limit was ostensibly a lifetime limit. However, several provisions in the
administration's bill allowed extensions. And recipients could "earn back" a
month of eligibility for cash benefits for every four months that they
received neither cash benefits nor payment for a WORK assignment, but
they could not earn back months until they had drawn down their
"account" to six months of remaining benefits, and they could never earn
back more than six months of remaining eligibility for such benefits.[61]

Child Support and Paternity Establishment

The administration's welfare reform bill also contained initiatives to establish paternity and to enforce child support payments. Most of these provisions built on elements in the Family Support Act of 1988 and elicited far
more interparty agreement than other provisions of the Clinton bill. States
were required to initiate programs to establish paternity for children born
out of wedlock; states that failed to meet increasingly stringent targets for
establishing paternity were to be sanctioned by having their AFDC grants
reduced. Mothers who did not cooperate in establishing paternity (with
cooperation to be judged by child support workers rather than welfare case
workers) were to be denied all access to AFDC.[62]

Child support enforcement measures were also stiffened. States were
required, for example, to establish procedures giving the state authority to
withhold or restrict driver's licenses, occupational licenses, and even recreational licenses for persons in arrears in child support payments.[63] They
were also required to report to credit agencies those noncustodial parents
who were more than one month overdue in child support payments and to
place liens on the auto titles of parents who were more than two months in

arrears in their support payments.[64] Those who were more than $5,000 in arrears were to be denied new passports and could have existing passports revoked or limited.[65]

In a modest bow to the targeting-within-universalism approach to welfare reform, the bill included funding for child support assurance demonstrations in three states for durations of seven to ten years. These provisions were more controversial than those on child support enforcement because many conservatives regarded child support assurance as simply a way to make AFDC more politically palatable.[66]

Discouraging Teenage Pregnancy

In addition to the paternity establishment and child support reforms, the administration also attempted to send more direct messages to discourage out-of-wedlock births and especially teenage pregnancies, drawing primarily on the prevention/rehabilitation and new paternalism approaches. Modest new funding was provided to underwrite teenage pregnancy reduction demonstration projects. Following the new paternalism strategy, the bill required teenage mothers to live with their parents in most circumstances rather than setting up new households. But it did not require states to implement family caps or teenage mother exclusions, the favorite reforms of deterrence advocates. Both measures had strong opponents within the administration. The bill allowed family caps as a state option, but retained the ban on teenage mother exclusions.

Funding

The size of the administration's reform package was ultimately determined in large part by difficulties in finding politically acceptable financing mechanisms. The administration was able to come up with only $9.3 billion over five years, almost three times the level in the Family Support Act of 1988, but with goals far more ambitious than those of the FSA.[67] Indeed, *no new tax revenues were included* in the package. Although 20 percent of the funding was raised by extending currently expiring revenue provisions (most from the Superfund), these were essentially an accounting gimmick because their extension had always been planned.

Much of the financing came from restrictions on other entitlement programs. Almost 40 percent of the $9.3 billion ($3.7 billion) was to come from restricting benefits to immigrants. The bulk of that savings came from making permanent the extension of the period for which sponsors' incomes would be deemed available to support sponsored aliens from three to five years in the SSI program and by matching that period in the AFDC and Food Stamp programs.[68] Another one-sixth of the funding was projected to come from capping the rapidly growing program of emergency assistance to the states. The purpose of the program was to meet emergency needs of the poor and keep them off welfare, but the administration believed that states had been abusing the program because of its loose criteria to fund services that the states should properly have been paying for themselves. Another 9 percent of funds were to be raised by limiting SSI benefits for individuals who were receiving them as a result of drug or alcohol addictions—who, like immigrants, constituted a very unpopular clientele. Smaller amounts were to be raised by restricting payments for meals in family day care homes (a program that had been criticized even by poverty advocates for its poor income targeting), restricting farm support payments to people with very high nonfarm incomes, and denying payment of the Earned Income Tax Credit to taxpayers who do not reside in the United States.

The Political Feasibility of the Clinton Plan

The administration proposal closely reflected the positions of median voters. It emphasized work and child support enforcement, which were strongly supported by the public, allowed a state option on the family cap, over which the public was fairly evenly divided, and rejected most of the contentious deterrence-oriented proposals for reform (teenage mother exclusions and hard time limits after which no federal cash assistance would be available).

The Clinton plan also had enormous problems, however. The major funding mechanisms—restrictions on benefits to aliens, on emergency assistance to the states, and on benefits to persons with drug and alcohol addictions, which in the aggregate constituted two-thirds of the $9.3 billion— were all areas in which the states feared that federal cutbacks would simply lead to costs being transferred to them.

Clinton's coalition was fragile in other ways. The major strategic challenge facing the administration was to ensure that during the committee mark-ups and floor amendments a balance of carrots and sticks and adequate financing remained in the welfare package, rather than having both liberalizing elements and financing stripped away. Certainly there was something in the package for almost everyone to dislike. Child advocacy groups feared the plan would deprive many families of cash benefits without guaranteeing a job or adequate child care. Republicans and conservative Democrats disliked the plan's slow phase-in of work requirements, and the

Hispanic Caucus objected to its financing provisions. Public sector unions worried that a large public jobs program would displace their workers.[69] Conservatives feared that WORK could turn into another Comprehensive Education and Training Act Public Service Employment Program. State-option family caps were opposed by right-to-life groups, who feared it would encourage abortions. Social conservatives were uneasy about child care assistance for the working poor, which they felt skewed incentives toward mothers working outside the home rather than those staying with their children. These conflicting pressures could have provided ample reason for many wavering legislators to oppose welfare reform. Neither a very generous nor a highly punitive version of reform was likely to command a congressional majority, but it is far from clear whether there was an adequate middle ground for significant reform.

All these considerations about building a centrist political coalition turned out to be moot. In the end welfare reform in 1994 was derailed more by short-term political calculations made by the administration, House Democrats, and House Republicans. The administration's repeated delays in getting a package to Congress and unclear signals about how quickly it wanted action once the package was released (caused in part by a desire to keep the decks clear for health care reform) meant that there were only a few months left between the June 1994 public unveiling of the package and the November election. Nor was there a "must pass" legislative vehicle to which welfare reform could be attached to push it through Congress quickly and with a minimum of potentially unraveling amendments.

Democratic members in the House, especially those on the Ways and Means Committee, were crucial in killing welfare reform once the package was released. Poll numbers suggesting there would be more Republicans in the 104th Congress were an argument in favor of the Democrats' pushing for quick action. But many House Democrats also faced a different, decidedly short-term decisionmaking calculus, and they viewed House consideration of welfare reform in 1994 as a potential political disaster in the November election. Many came from moderate to conservative districts that were less liberal than they were. They knew that the Democratic leadership lacked effective control of the House floor. For these Democrats, committee markup and floor debate on welfare reform legislation posed a series of threatening "bad choices" on amendments that the Republicans were certain to propose (and conservative Democrats were certain to vote for). They could vote their conscience and risk losing their seats (and larger overall losses to the Republicans) or vote for provisions that would make the bill far more conservative than the original package and thus even further from their preferred policy positions.

Two options potentially available to policymakers for whom the only change options are bad choices are to defend the status quo and to use agenda control to prevent adoption of changes to the status quo. President Clinton's repeated attacks on AFDC had made the former strategy untenable for all except those with enormous political courage or very liberal districts. Simply not moving the legislation was much easier. Although the House Ways and Means Committee held hearings on the Clinton proposal in the summer of 1994, it kept the bill bottled up in committee, never proceeding to mark it up (that is, vote on amendments) in committee, let alone report it to the full chamber.

Nor did congressional Republicans have an incentive by the late summer of 1994 to facilitate quick passage of welfare reform. They were anticipating substantial gains in the fall election, so delaying consideration of welfare until the new Congress would increase the prospects of getting a reform package closer to the median preferences of Republican legislators. Equally important, delay would deny the president a legislative victory and the credit that would accrue to him, and it would allow Republican candidates to continue to use the welfare issue that was working very well for them in the election campaign.[70] It is thus not surprising that welfare reform in the 103d Congress died not with a bang but with a whimper.

Conclusions

The failure of welfare reform proposals to make significant headway before the Republican takeover of Congress in 1995 raises two questions about the Clinton administration's strategy of making health care and deficit reduction its top domestic policy priorities and putting welfare reform on a stop-and-go schedule to make sure that it did not get in the way of health care reform. The first question is about policy. Would putting welfare first have resulted in a reform outcome closer to the administration's policy preferences than what eventually resulted? The second question is about politics. Would a harder push on welfare have had strong political payoffs, perhaps even helping to avoid the Republican victory in the 1994 elections?

Mickey Kaus, a writer for the *New Republic* and author of *The End of Equality*, has made a strong affirmative response to both questions. Kaus argued immediately after the 1994 election that the administration's failure to move more swiftly to develop and pass a welfare reform package in the first two years of its term was "the fundamental strategic mistake of the Clinton presidency. . . . If President Clinton had pushed for welfare reform rather than health care reform in 1994, we would now be talking about a great Democratic realignment, rather than a great Republican realignment."[71]

Attempting to evaluate such claims requires delving into the speculative realm of counterfactual history. There are strong reasons for doubting Kaus's claims, however. Certainly the timing is problematic. We can never know whether inclusion of welfare reform in the spring 1993 Clinton budget would have smoothed the passage of reform by removing the revenue constraint, sunk the Clinton budget, or had little impact because a Congress intent on reducing the budget deficit would have simply stripped out the welfare provisions and devoted the "reserved" funds to deficit reduction. But the most likely candidate is probably much closer to the last than to the smooth passage of welfare reform.[72] The deficit-cutting mood in both the administration and Congress was simply too strong.

Similarly, it is doubtful that welfare reform could have been passed after the budget but before health care reform. The administration needed comprehensive health care reform to keep the costs of the proposed welfare package down to politically plausible levels (because health care reform was expected to remove many recipients from welfare rolls). And the tricky politics of welfare reform made many in the White House reluctant to put it first, fearing that it could endanger their higher priority.[73]

Revisiting history is even more speculative in assessing the prospects for political realignment. Clearly presidential candidate Bill Clinton believed that giving the Democratic party a new image vis-à-vis welfare would provide an opportunity to counteract the hemorrhage of working class whites from the party. But it is far from clear that passage of a reform package by the Clinton administration would have transformed the image of the Democratic party in the minds of voters. It is far more likely that a prolonged congressional debate in the 103d Congress would have fractured the Democratic party publicly, as it did less publicly in the formulation stage of the administration's proposal. Indeed, it is far from clear that the administration could have passed a welfare reform plan even if it had made doing so a top priority, just as it failed to pass a "top priority" health care plan.

Even if the administration had managed to legislate welfare reform more or less on its terms, this might not have served as a realigning issue for the Democrats. First, welfare was only one of several targets (of which crime was probably the most salient) on which the Democrats were seen as coddling disfavored groups. And removing one issue on which the public has a negative attitude is unlikely to be sufficient grounds for a voter realignment. Second, welfare reform was most likely to contribute to a voter realignment favoring the Democratic party if a Democratic administration was seen as solving the welfare problem. But because very deeply rooted social problems underlie the working of the welfare system and the modest scope of the administration's proposal, the public perception (let alone the reality) of policy success would have been unlikely to be realized. As long as the welfare problem did not go away, many Democratic politicians would probably continue to criticize whatever policies were in place as too harsh, and many Republican politicians would criticize them as too lenient. Thus, rather than leading to and solidifying a realignment, a Clinton success in reforming welfare would more likely have prevented the solidification of new partisan alignments because it would allow both sides to call up and reinforce unfavorable attitudes that many voters have about both parties—Democrats as coddling the shiftless and irresponsible and Republicans as favoring the rich at the expense of the helpless.

Rather than providing a simple lesson about a faulty political strategy, the Clinton administration's welfare reform initiative instead suggests more complex lessons about the interaction of constraints and choices in a divisive policy sector. The three constraints that were the focus of chapters 6 through 8—social science research, public opinion on welfare issues, and group pressures—clearly helped shape the welfare reform policymaking traps, the agenda, the timing, eventual content, and demise of the administration's welfare plan. Research and public opinion were particularly important influences on the decisions made by administration policymakers, but they by no means determined those decisions alone. Critical strategic and substantive choices made by policymakers involved complex trade-offs involving political, moral, scientific, and strategic judgments. Different participants within the administration gave varying weight to these criteria.

The four most important factors shaping outcomes in the Clinton welfare reform were probably (in roughly declining order of importance) Clinton's triangulating campaign promise to "end welfare as we know it," the budget neutrality provisions of the Budget Enforcement Act, the decision to make health care reform the administration's priority, and the decision not to include welfare reform in the 1993 budget package. What is striking about this list is that all but the second are decisions that had to be made by policymakers in a very uncertain situation. The decisions were, to be sure, all influenced by deeper structural features like public opinion and the multiple veto points in Congress. They also are consistent with the pat-

tern of policymakers' objectives discussed in chapter 3: simultaneous attention to advancing political and policy interests while taking account of
external constraints. Ultimately they came down to policymakers' doing
what they are elected and appointed to do: making choices, some hard and
some easy.

Another striking feature of the factors constraining administration policymakers is how their interaction strengthened rather than weakened the
traps in welfare policymaking. The combination of extravagant promises
and constraints on financing led to a particularly vicious form of the money
trap: the administration could not raise enough money to plausibly redeem
its promise, and the money that it did raise came from some of the Democratic party's core constituencies in Congress. Fragmented American political institutions made it impossible for the administration to control the
legislative agenda and would have given legislators to the left and right of
the administration (which was itself far from united) many opportunities to
block or alter the package if it had proceeded through Congress. The result,
as in several past rounds of welfare reform, was an initiative that never got
off the ground. Equally important, the administration's initiative sparked a
strategic disagreement response from congressional Republicans that
pushed the welfare reform debate further to the right. This would have even
more dramatic consequences after November 1994, when the administration lost its weak "positive" agenda control (ability to set the terms of the
debate on welfare issues) and congressional Democrats lost their "negative"
agenda control (ability to block open votes on alternatives they saw as bad
or hard choices).

CHAPTER TEN

A New Congress, a New Dynamic

"We're pulling up the current welfare system by its roots and throwing it away so it can never grow back."
  —Bill Archer, *House Ways and Means Committee chair,*
  March 3, 1995

"They're hurting 15 million infants and children by this legislation. To do what? To pay for that notorious, lousy, stinking tax cut bill."
  —Sam Gibbons, *House Ways and Means Committee ranking*
  minority member, March 22, 1995

ON NOVEMBER 8, 1994, Americans elected a new Congress, with the first Republican majority in both chambers since the 80th Congress of 1947–48. The prospects for welfare reform were suddenly very different from just a few months earlier. Before the election the Republican leadership in the House of Representatives had offered voters a Contract with America, comprising ten propositions that Republicans signing the contract—more than 350 House Republican incumbents and candidates for election—agreed to bring up for a vote (but not necessarily vote for) in the first hundred days after a Republican-majority Congress began meeting.[1] The contract included a brief section on welfare that was fleshed out in a bill entitled the Personal Responsibility Act.

The enormous publicity surrounding the contract and the House Republicans' new leader, Newt Gingrich, ensured that the program would occupy center stage in the first half-year of the new Congress and that, unlike the Clinton welfare plan of 1994, some welfare reform package would indeed make it to the floor of the House of Representatives. Republican control of Congress meant that this package would reflect Republican values—and that it would be exceptionally difficult for the Clinton administration to win back control of the agenda.

Welfare reform had been a relatively easy choice to become a significant item on the Republican political agenda because it appeared to offer a mixture of political and policy gains.[2] It offered Republicans the political opportunity to regain from President Clinton the political initiative on welfare that they had lost in 1992. In policy terms, limiting expenditures on AFDC, along with bigger reductions in other means-tested programs (especially cuts in nutrition programs and eligibility for noncitizens), offered an opportunity to finance tax cuts and deficit reduction.

The Republicans shared with the Clinton administration a new paternalist emphasis on work, but sought to push it earlier and much more firmly. The new Republican leadership also put more emphasis on deterrence and devolutionary approaches in its welfare reform initiative than the Clinton administration had and much less on incentives and prevention and rehabilitation. Issues such as block grants, hard time limits on federally subsidized benefits, "orphanages" for the children of young unwed mothers, family caps, and a prohibition on cash benefits to teenage mothers took center stage. Moreover, whereas the Clinton administration had proposed spending more to reduce welfare dependency, the Republicans proposed spending less.

Republicans were far from united over which approach or package of welfare reform approaches to emphasize, however. Even before the new Congress met, the deterrence and work elements embedded in the Contract with America were challenged by an activist group of Republican governors who favored a devolution of power to the states. In attempting to enact welfare reform proposals, the Republican majorities in Congress confronted the same basic traps that had bedeviled the previous Congress. The contours of these traps were altered somewhat with the Republican takeover of both houses: the nature of the proposals, the coalition of support that needed to be built, and the institutional obstacles to enacting legislation all changed. But the traps initially were almost as vexing for the new congressional majority as they had been for the Clinton administration and its allies in the previous Congress.

The Electoral Earthquake

Little evidence suggests that welfare and welfare reform were prominent factors in voters' decisions to give Republicans control of Congress for the first time in almost a half century, but clearly discontent with welfare and hopes that Congress would do something about "the welfare mess" were high. In a *Wall Street Journal*/NBC poll taken shortly after the new Congress began meeting, welfare reform was identified as an issue that needed to be addressed by more of those polled than any other issue, although that prominence in the public mind may have been primed by very public squabbles over welfare during the period the poll was being conducted.[3] Although putting welfare reform on the agenda had been a relatively easy choice for Republican leaders, many obstacles remained to reaching agreement on a substantive package and developing a strategy to push legislation toward ratification.

Polarization and Political Uncertainty

One important effect of the election was a further polarization of party caucuses in Congress, especially in the House. The reduced Democratic contingents were concentrated in the party's liberal wing, while Republicans were more homogeneously conservative. The reduction in the ranks of moderates in both parties who were willing to accept political compromise made a broad bipartisan compromise similar to the one achieved in 1988 in the Senate extremely unlikely. It posed particular problems for Democratic leaders in attempting to prevent the conservative members of their caucus, especially those from the South, from defecting to support Republican proposals that were likely to be closer to their own preferences than to alternatives favored by their liberal Democratic colleagues. The desire of the Clinton administration and Democratic leaders to maintain at least the appearance of party unity meant that they might move their zone of acceptable outcomes quite far to the right to accommodate the conservative members of the caucus.

Even if a bill made it through the House, the ultimate course of welfare reform would depend in large part on political dynamics that would only gradually be established in the 104th Congress, and in which welfare would play only a relatively minor part. Three intertwined dynamics were especially important in determining the prospects for ratification of welfare reform. A first was that between the House Republicans and the Senate Republicans. Although the House Republicans came into power with a more clearly defined agenda, it was by no means certain that Senate Republicans would defer to the policy preferences of their House colleagues. Indeed, both history and the differing rules of the two chambers suggested that they would not. But history would not necessarily repeat itself: if the Contract agenda proved popular and the House Republicans were able to claim that passing it intact was critical to the electoral prospects of all

Republicans in 1996, Senate Republicans might feel obliged to follow the policy lead of the House. If the Senate passed a bill substantially less conservative than its House counterpart, would House Republicans insist on provisions of their bill at the risk of losing the momentum gained in the 1994 election, or would they expand their zone of acceptable outcomes to achieve an agreement between the chambers?

A second critical dynamic, to be discussed more fully in the next chapter, was that between Senate Republicans and Senate Democrats. The Senate is generally a less partisan institution than the House, and Senate rules reinforce tendencies toward bipartisanship. Would Senate Republicans cooperate in drafting a bipartisan welfare reform document, as they had in 1988, or would they try to use their slender majority to push through a bill with little or no Democratic support? Or could they pick off enough Democrats to push through a bill that reflected Republican priorities? If they chose the first strategy, would they be able to reach an agreement with their House colleagues?

A third dynamic was that between the White House and Congress. Would the White House actively pose alternatives to the Republicans, and if so, how successful would they be? Would the administration be in a position to veto a strong deterrence-focused bill if Congress passed one, or would it feel trapped by the president's pledge to "end welfare as we know it" and sign virtually anything that Congress passed in order to maximize Clinton's own prospects for reelection? Again, the popularity of the Contract and the president's own popularity were likely to be critical determinants of the administration's strategic choices and its ultimate bargaining leverage. But the apparent political weakness of the administration also posed risks for the Republicans, namely that conservatives would push the party to overplay its hand by forcing the welfare bill far to the right and provoking a veto, risking passage of welfare reform for the electoral opportunity to present the president as a hypocrite who was not really committed to welfare reform.

An Ambitious Agenda

The Contract with America, the House Republicans' blueprint for action in the 104th Congress, was a clear effort to articulate an overarching philosophy and a coherent and politically attractive set of programs consistent with that philosophy that would build a new majority coalition among the electorate. Several themes were particularly important to policy toward low-income families: a smaller role for Washington, devolution of program authority to the states, a balanced budget, and an emphasis on strengthening two-parent families. The contract's welfare provisions were intended both to reduce spending in the short term and to ensure lower spending in the long term by putting a firm cap on funds for AFDC and other means-tested programs rather than preserving them as open-ended entitlements. They thus contributed to the contract's extremely ambitious goals of simultaneously reducing taxes and balancing the budget.

The contract's welfare provisions also reflected an ideological commitment to shrinking the welfare state and returning power to the states, reducing the power held in Washington—which many Republican leaders saw as dominated by a coterie of liberal interest groups, bureaucrats, and legislators that sustained the welfare state.[4] As with the Clinton administration's New Democratic political project, however, the Republicans' efforts to articulate an attractive and coherent public philosophy and to create a new majority electoral coalition were not without tensions and contradictions. Perhaps the greatest conflict involved the amount of flexibility to be given to states in reforming welfare. Some conservatives argued that getting Washington out of the welfare business and ending individual entitlement to benefits were crucial to reform.[5] But many activists, notably Robert Rector of the Heritage Foundation, contended that it was irresponsible to give states money without mandating deterrence provisions—family caps, a ban on benefits to teenage mothers, hard time limits—that states might not adopt on their own.[6]

Deterrence-oriented strategies for welfare reform offered a real opportunity for Republicans to solidify links with conservative pro-family groups. Alliance with these groups, however, ran the risk that the groups' reluctance to sacrifice some of their most firmly held objectives could sink efforts at enacting compromise legislation. Given that some deterrence measures (notably family caps and teenage-mother exclusions) were likely to encourage an increase in abortions, the Republican agenda also risked splitting the pro-life constituency that was an increasingly important part of the Republican political base.

While deterrence-oriented approaches to welfare reform energized a core group of Republican members of the House and Senate, especially the newer and more conservative members, devolution of policymaking authority to the states without mandates offered an opportunity to gain support from governors for otherwise unpopular cutbacks in federal funds. Governors were likely to endorse such a trade-off, however, only if it was favorable to their interests. Given the deficit and tax reduction goals in the Contract and pressure for deterrence and work mandates in welfare reform, being able to develop an attractive package was by no means a sure thing. Cutting back on AFDC and other grants to the states also raised the specter of formula fights over how to allocate the pain of cutbacks. Because these matters tend to divide congressional delegations on the basis of state population, wealth, and population growth rates (all of which may enter into grant allocation formulas) rather than ideology, they posed special dangers for keeping the Republican coalition together.

In specific policies as well as coalitional politics, House Republicans set themselves an extraordinarily ambitious agenda, but one that did not necessarily add up. Most important, Republican tax reduction pledges made in the Contract with America were estimated to cost $196 billion over five years; the popular proposal for a refundable tax credit of $500 per child for families with incomes under $200,000 was estimated to cost $124.1 billion over that period.[7] Under current budget rules the tax cuts would have to be offset by expenditure reductions. Welfare policymaking was thus increasingly driven by the search for money. Because using Social Security funds was politically out of bounds, there were few opportunities, especially within the portfolio of the tax-writing House Ways and Means Committee, for offsetting expenditure reductions. If a bidding war erupted between the president and congressional Republicans over a tax cut, it would increase the pressure for a welfare reform package that produced large savings from welfare. Indeed, the commitments made in the Contract with America to simultaneously cut taxes and balance the budget would eventually drive the Republicans to make cuts not just in AFDC but also in popular programs like Medicare and Medicaid that had not originally been targeted for cuts in the Contract with America.[8]

The availability of the budget reconciliation process provided the new Republican majority with an important procedural advantage in pushing welfare reform and the rest of its ambitious agenda through Congress, however. Rolling welfare reform into a reconciliation bill offered several benefits for the Republicans in avoiding the institutional barriers to welfare reform. One advantage was the incentives that reconciliation would create for Republican unity. As with the 1981 Reagan budget cuts, folding a vote on welfare reform into an omnibus bill covering dozens or hundreds of programs makes the elements of the welfare reform bill with which individual legislators disagree relatively less prominent than they would be if welfare were being considered separately. Second, because seriousness about deficit reduction was a major part of congressional Republicans' political message, there would be a strong incentive for Republican legislators to make sure that the reconciliation package passed. For both these reasons, Republican party unity on the reconciliation bill was likely to be strong; whatever qualms legislators might have about individual provisions of the welfare bill, they were likely to hold their noses and vote yes.[9] But if welfare reform and most other spending initiatives were rolled into a single budget package as a way to push through unpopular measures, the president might veto it, using the most unpopular provisions as a justification. The Republicans' entire legislative program could be dragged down by its least popular elements.[10]

The States as Laboratories and Lobbyists

The 1994 elections brought extraordinary success to Republicans at the state level as well as in Congress. After the election they controlled thirty governorships, up from nineteen. They also controlled the most important governors' posts: of the nine states with the largest populations, only Florida had a Democratic governor. Sitting Republican governors such as Tommy Thompson in Wisconsin, John Engler in Michigan, William Weld in Massachusetts, and Pete Wilson in California, who had been aggressive in their own welfare initiatives, were reelected.

Even before the electoral earthquake, significant policy change was occurring in many states.[11] The national and state processes were not just parallel, however. They were also deeply intertwined with each other, as the Reagan, Bush, and Clinton administrations encouraged state experimentation through federal waivers. Once the welfare reform bandwagon began to roll in the states in the early 1990s, many other states joined Wisconsin, New Jersey, and Michigan, the early leaders. But the process was not one of states' emulating successful state innovations that has long been described by political scientists.[12] Instead, states often adopted innovations before their efficacy in changing behavior or incomes had been demonstrated. The process was politically driven; politicians quickly absorbed lessons about the *politics* of welfare reform without formal evaluations of policy impacts. As one astute observer said, "No state wants to be left behind in the welfare reform sweepstakes. No governor wants to be perceived as doing nothing. Neither political party want to be perceived as soft on welfare."[13] As in Washington, state actions were driven at least as much by fear of political blame as by hopes of political credit. But it was a process in which Democrats and advocates for welfare recipients repeatedly found themselves at a disadvantage. Democrats' attempts to jump on the welfare reform bandwagon were usually matched, and often outbid, by Republican competitors. This became evident early in Wisconsin, where Democratic state legislators attempted to call Republican governor Tommy Thompson's bluff by including in their welfare reform legislation provisions that would abolish AFDC entirely by 1998. Thompson signed the bill, including the AFDC sunset provisions, and used Wisconsin's unusually powerful legislative veto to alter the legislation further to his liking.[14]

A strong desire on the part of states to reduce the massive caseload run-ups experienced between 1989 and 1994 also stimulated state innovation. By early 1996 twenty states had imposed family caps, and twenty-two had imposed some time limit on receipt of cash benefits after which work would be required or benefits reduced or both. Thirty-two states had also eased earnings disregards or lowered asset limits.[15]

As the use of waivers increased, their purpose evolved. The original purpose was to allow states to experiment, to create a knowledge base that could then be applied in other states. Requirements that states obtain federal waivers could in theory have been used by the federal government to ensure that variation in experiments and ability to evaluate their effects were maximized. In practice the states drove the waiver process from the beginning, and waiver requests often involved so many elements that a careful evaluation of the effects of individual components was difficult if not impossible. Demands from the Department of Health and Human Services (HHS) that states provide program designs that were easier to evaluate were likely to spark complaints of interference with states' efforts to be innovative, so HHS was reluctant to make such demands. Indeed, during the Clinton administration HHS officials believed they had to walk a very thin line in negotiating state waiver requests to preclude states' appealing over their heads to the White House. As one top HHS official recalled:

> The basic message we got from the White House, though it wasn't always wildly explicit . . . was, approve waivers. The basic message we got from the White House was, we're in favor of state flexibility, and we want you to do [waivers] fast, and we want you to do them. My general strategy with the waiver process was to try to keep the decisions from getting to the level where the White House would get a call from the governor and tell us to approve the waiver, because my general read of the politics over there was that if a governor called up and said, "I'm not getting my waiver," we'd be told to [grant it] pretty much no matter what it was.[16]

The waiver process was also frustrating for the states, however, because it involved lots of negotiations and no clear rules. As HHS expanded what it would allow states to do to show that the department was not obstructionist, a state might find that a waiver request similar to one HHS had forced it to whittle back a few months before was now being approved for another state. One child advocate later compared the process, and the reaction it engendered in the states, with the frustration and anger felt by used car buyers who can never be sure that they received the best possible deal.[17]

The Republican takeover of Congress in 1994 dramatically strengthened the states in their relations with Washington. The Clinton administration sought to show that it was just as committed to welfare reform as the Republicans. The president even pledged to "end welfare one state at a time" through the waiver process if Congress failed to pass comprehensive welfare reform legislation. The administration's determination not to appear soft on welfare severely compromised its ability to veto waiver requests that it did not like, because doing so would add credence to the Republican governors' and congressional leaders' charges of obstruction. Administration reluctance to appear soft on welfare also gave Republican governors incentives to make increasingly bold waiver requests that would allow their Republican congressional allies to portray the administration as obstructionist. This political dynamic is particularly evident in increasing requests for hard time limits (no cash benefit after a certain period even if a recipient participated in a work program), and the administration began approving them, albeit with the proviso that an exception be made for families in which the custodial parent complied fully with program rules but was unable to find a job.[18] The political dynamics of the 104th Congress encouraged states to seek maximum discretion and weakened the Clinton administration's ability to veto state initiatives. Congressional Republicans, in short, had critical allies in the states for promoting policy change, but also important rivals who preferred state discretion to deterrence-oriented mandates.

Initial Bids

The 1994 election expanded the number of protagonists in welfare reform and forced on them difficult strategic choices as they looked toward the presidential election year of 1996.

A First Republican Bid: The Contract with America

The main policy and political objectives of the new House Republican leadership can be summarized succinctly. They hoped to use control of the

House to push through a thoroughgoing transformation of welfare that emphasized work requirements and deterring out-of-wedlock births and long-term welfare receipt. Many members also pushed for devolution of authority to the states. In addition, they sought to reduce expenditures in means-tested programs to pay for the tax cuts promised in the Contract with America. Politically their objectives were to prove their effectiveness at governing by enacting as much of the Contract with America as possible and to force President Clinton to choose between signing a Republican-inspired welfare reform initiative and appearing to betray his campaign promise.

The most critical choice facing House Republicans when they began formulating the Contract with America in the summer of 1994—long before it seemed likely that they would win control of Congress in the fall election—was how radical a path of welfare reform to attempt. Clay Shaw (Republican, Florida), Nancy Johnson (Republican, Connecticut), and other Republican moderates on the Ways and Means Committee's Human Resources Subcommittee preferred building on H.R. 3500, the House Republican task force bill developed as an alternative to Clinton's (then unreleased) package in the fall of 1993. They had already moved quickly and far to the right of positions they had taken just two years earlier.[19] Social conservatives, meanwhile, argued that the bill sponsored by Jim Talent (Republican, Missouri) and Senator Lauch Faircloth (Republican, North Carolina) was closer to the conservative mainstream of the party and posed a much starker symbolic difference between the two parties. But the Talent-Faircloth bill, with its strong emphasis on deterrence measures, could bring to the fore the sensitive issue of encouraging abortion, an issue Gingrich had explicitly decided to avoid in the Contract because it divided Republican candidates, constituencies, and voters.[20] Thus pursuing either action threatened to reveal fissures within the Republican party.

The electoral, policy, and coalitional calculus if the Republicans did win control of Congress was also murky. A bill like H.R. 3500 would certainly pass a Republican-controlled House and would be unlikely to fall victim to a filibuster or Republican defections in the Senate or to a presidential veto. This strategy would be consistent with the House Republican leadership's pledge to deliver real change, showing that the Republicans could govern effectively. However, the strategy might also give the president too much credit for whatever welfare reform was eventually adopted. Moreover, party conservatives led by Talent and Tim Hutchinson (Republican, Arkansas) and the social conservative groups allied with them might refuse to support a bill like H.R. 3500, meaning that welfare reform would require some Democratic votes and would need a more bipartisan cast.

Alternatively, Republicans could try to pass legislation closer to the preferences of conservatives (including most party leaders) in the House, daring the president either to sign it and deeply offend the Democratic party's political base or to veto it and allow the Republicans to claim that he had betrayed his 1992 electoral pledge. Indeed, Talent, the sponsor of the conservative Republican alternative to H.R. 3500 in 1994, argued during the 1994 campaign that he hoped that Clinton would "get trapped by his own rhetoric" and veto welfare reform.[21] But if stalemate occurred, Republican pledges of dramatic change promised in their 1994 campaign might be perceived in 1996 to have resulted in "stalemate as usual" in Washington. That outcome could also reinforce public impressions that the Republican party was a party that favored the rich at the expense of the poor.

All these conflicts were evident in the development and evolution of the House Republicans' initial bid in the welfare debates of the 104th Congress, the Personal Responsibility Act, included in the Contract with America. Participants almost universally described this process in retrospect as "nasty," "unpleasant," and leaving "blood on the floor." In drafting the Contract during the summer of 1994 the House Republican leadership decided that revisions that would move H.R. 3500 in a more conservative direction did indeed need to be made. Drafting the specific contract provisions was entrusted to Dick Armey of Texas, chairman of the House Republican Conference and a prominent conservative within the party. Armey in turn appointed a six-person working group to reach agreement on the welfare provisions. The working group was chaired by Dave Camp of Michigan, a relatively new member of the Ways and Means Committee. There were two other Ways and Means members (Rick Santorum of Pennsylvania and Nancy Johnson of Connecticut) as well as the two most prominent conservatives (Jim Talent and Tim Hutchinson) and a leading Republican moderate, Mike Castle of Delaware, who as governor of Delaware had cochaired the National Governors' Association task force on welfare reform with Bill Clinton in 1987–88.

The initial mandate to the working group was murky, however, and not put in writing. Three points in particular were to cause trouble. The first was whether H.R. 3500 was to be used as the "base bill." This seemingly mundane consideration was in fact very important. If H.R. 3500 was the base bill, provisions of that bill that were not explicitly revised by the working group would be included in the bill announced in the Contract with

America. Provisions of the Talent-Faircloth bill would be included only if the working group could reach an agreement on them. But if there was no base bill, the provisions of the two bills would enjoy equal standing in case of conflict, and if Talent-Faircloth had a provision on which H.R. 3500 was silent, there would be a strong presumption that the provision should be in the merged bill.

The second murky area was how decisions were to be made within the working group. The mandate from the leadership was to work out a compromise, which suggests consensual decisionmaking. But a consensus requirement means that a bargainer who is most willing to hold out rather than compromise does best, because all other bargainers must move toward his or her position to reach an agreement.

The third murky area was whose decisions would be final and how the bill would come to closure. If the Republican leadership had ultimate authority to overrule the working group at will, that created a back channel available to interests who believed that the working group had not done well enough. And given the preferences of the leadership, notably Armey, the appeals channel would be open mostly to the conservatives. Armey was determined that the welfare provisions of the bill be tough ones, in part because Gingrich had insisted on leaving out of the Contract with America any provisions on eliminating abortion and reintroducing school prayer, ideas that energized the party's political base among religious conservatives but divided Republican legislators and candidates.[22] Armey later argued that those omissions "made the welfare provisions tougher and more imperative because we had a very, very important, significant part of our base already disappointed."[23]

The implications of the back channel became clear when Armey called a meeting of social conservative groups in August to review the draft legislation prepared by the working group. The groups were critical. In response to their criticism, Armey agreed to include several provisions from the Talent-Faircloth bill, and he later requested additional changes.[24]

The Personal Responsibility bill included in the Contract with America was indeed more conservative than H.R. 3500.[25] It capped the growth of spending in AFDC, Child Support Enforcement, and SSI and converted a number of nutrition programs, including Food Stamps, into a block grant. None of these programs would have entitlement status any longer. It also allowed the states to convert their AFDC grants from the federal government into block grants with which they could design their own programs to serve low-income families with children, allowing them to avoid most federal regulations, including the new ones included in the proposed Personal Responsibility Act.[26]

In addition, the bill contained deterrence-focused innovations in AFDC, generally splitting the difference between the H.R. 3500 and Talent-Faircloth provisions.[27] In particular, it excluded from AFDC eligibility almost all children for whom paternity had not been established; all children born to mothers under age eighteen, unless the mother married someone who assumed legal responsibility for such children (states had the option of increasing this to mothers younger than twenty-one at the time of their child's birth); and children born to mothers who received AFDC at any time during that pregnancy.[28] Abortion counseling was forbidden as a concession to social conservative groups.

The Personal Responsibility Act also contained tough work provisions. It required single parents receiving AFDC to work at least thirty-five hours a week if they had been receiving assistance under the program for at least two years in order to continue receiving help. States were required to have an unprecedented percentage of their caseload in work activities or face financial penalties.

The Personal Responsibility bill made the most dramatic changes in setting time limits, outstripping both earlier Republican bills.[29] It set a five-year lifetime hard time limit for all AFDC aid and allowed states to terminate aid for anyone who had received aid for as little as twenty-four months if the aid included at least twelve months under the work program. To prevent people from migrating in search of higher welfare benefits, the proposed bill allowed states to use the eligibility and benefit standards that would have been used in the new migrant's former state of residence for up to twelve months after the migration.

The Personal Responsibility Act produced fiscal good news: it was estimated that it would produce net savings of about $40 billion over five years, giving the Republicans a lot of room for both reducing the deficit and paying for a possible "middle-class tax cut." Most of these savings were produced by ending eligibility of almost all legal immigrants who had not become citizens for sixty means-tested programs, including Medicaid, Supplemental Security Income, and the Job Training Partnership Act.[30]

The Personal Responsibility Act posed some real problems for the Republican party, however. Controlling the agenda to keep the various elements of the Republican coalition united was a particular source of concern for party leaders. The act contained provisions with which various factions within the party were unhappy. As the welfare reform bill moved through Congress, elements of the coalition would be tempted to defect if presented with preferred alternatives on at least some issues.

Republican moderates were one potential source of dissension. Even before the new Congress met, some of the figures who would take leading roles in shepherding the legislation through Congress expressed reservations about the proposed act. Two leading Republican moderates on the Ways and Means Committee, Clay Shaw of Florida, the new chair of the Subcommittee on Human Resources that would have initial jurisdiction over the legislation, and Nancy Johnson of Connecticut, criticized on grounds of both equity and constitutionality the provision that would permanently deny AFDC benefits to unmarried teenage mothers. A memo by the Congressional Research Service had already raised questions about whether such a provision might violate the equal protection clause of the Constitution. Shaw even threatened to break with Republican ranks by not using the Contract's provisions as the basis for subcommittee debate on welfare reform—a position from which he quickly retreated after Ways and Means Committee chair Bill Archer threatened him with the loss of his subcommittee chairmanship.[31]

Members with strong "right to life" positions were also possible defectors. Although most of the social conservative groups supported the act's provisions on family caps and denial of benefits to teenage mothers, the National Right to Life Committee had not. How would individual members resolve this hard choice between two constituencies? Republican governors, meanwhile, would be likely to exert pressure to provide states with more flexibility and to alter costly mandates on work. Indeed, on September 27, the day before the Contract with America was to be unveiled, Nancy Johnson warned her Republican colleagues: "Unlike when we introduced . . . H.R. 3500, we have solicited no comments from Republican Governors' offices on the impact of this proposal. Given what their staffs have stated in the past, however, there is not a doubt that they would condemn our latest proposal as unworkable and out-of-touch."[32]

Enter the Governors: A Second Republican Bid

In the afterglow of the November 1994 Republican electoral triumph, Republican governors did not condemn the Contract with America welfare bill. They did something far more important: they set out to revise it. In so doing, they brought to the fore the elements of the federalism trap implicit in the act: states were being asked to take on many more responsibilities, including what Republicans had taken to calling unfunded mandates, without being given any more money.

There was a fundamental difference within the Republican coalition on this point. Social conservatives like Robert Rector of the Heritage Foundation favored mandating deterrence measures as well as stiff work requirements, but Republican governors favored block grants with as few strings attached as possible. As Governor John Engler of Michigan pronounced, "Conservative micromanagement is just as bad as liberal micromanagement."[33] Many House Republicans felt, as one key aide said in January 1995, that "what some of the governors want is for us to put the federal money on a stump in the middle of a forest in the dead of night."[34]

Republican governors recognized that the Republican congressional victory meant their strategic calculus must change; simple opposition was unlikely to be effective. As an aide to one of the most influential Republican governors described the situation:

> There was . . . a realization that this new [Republican congressional] majority also wanted to try to balance the budget. . . . If you're going to balance the budget, it means everyone's going to take a cut: every single interest group, every state. And the worst case scenario is if you were to just take a 15 to 20 percent cut across the board, but keep in place every single string [or] mandate that went with all the programs.[35]

A Republican congressional staffer echoed, "The governors, they knew the business here [in Congress] was cutting money. And I think that they believed that no matter what happened, Republicans were going to seriously cut money, and that they were—you know, it's [Lyndon] Johnson's old thing about, 'Would you rather have them in the tent pissing out or outside pissing in?' They decided they wanted to be in the tent."[36]

Although the Personal Responsibility Act component of the Contract—given the bill number H.R. 4 when it was introduced in Congress—did eliminate many existing strings, in other ways it was close to being the governors' worst nightmare. It reduced and capped federal AFDC funding, reduced state discretion with a number of new mandates (while ending others), and imposed very tough (and costly) work requirements. It also had the potential to transfer entirely to the states the obligations to support legal immigrants and poor families who had hit time limits. Thus the governors' incentive to try to push welfare reform in a different direction was very strong indeed.

Although the Republican governors initially signaled their willingness to give up some federal funding in exchange for increased flexibility in using the remaining federal funds, fears about the fiscal impact on their states of the various components of the contract, including a federal balanced budget amendment to the Constitution, were not long in coming to the surface.[37]

But the Republican governors faced important obstacles in building a coalition of support for a proposal that reflected their interests. The first was that they could not develop a united bipartisan front, as they had during the 1987–88 welfare reform, by acting through the National Governors' Association (NGA). For while the Republican governors who were most interested and involved in welfare reform endorsed devolution, most Democratic governors would not go along, objecting in particular to the "threshold issue" of loss of individual entitlement to AFDC benefits. As noted in chapter 8, the NGA is a bipartisan organization. To safeguard that bipartisanship, it requires approval by three-quarters of its member governors on an organizational position. Republicans, despite their gains in the November elections, controlled only thirty governors' offices. When the governors met at the end of January, a group of activist Republican governors spearheaded by John Engler of Michigan, Tommy Thompson of Wisconsin, and William Weld of Massachusetts could not muster the needed supermajority to gain the organization's endorsement for their ideas.[38] Throughout his tenure as chairman of the NGA, Democrat Howard Dean of Vermont was one of the most persistent and vocal critics of the Republican governors' welfare reform proposals.[39]

Unable to take a position either favoring or opposing the Republican welfare reform initiatives, the NGA was largely sidelined during the 1995 debates. As a result, Republican governors simply bypassed the organization. The activist Republican governors who sought transformation of AFDC into a block grant with minimal mandates were able to dominate both public and private debates as representatives of the states by using the Republican Governors' Association as their vehicle.[40] This of course was a symbiotic relationship: congressional Republicans had a strong interest in promoting as the sole voice of the states a group of Republican governors whose political and policy interests were closer to their own than was the NGA average; the activist Republican governors hoped to use their leverage to tailor the combination of reforms and cutbacks they saw as inevitable in a way that gave them maximum freedom and minimum federal mandates.

In early January 1995 Speaker Newt Gingrich and other Republican congressional leaders negotiated with four Republican governors the outlines of a new welfare reform deal.[41] Representatives of other intergovernmental groups were excluded from these negotiations. Contact between the activist governors' group and the House leadership and committees remained close during the early months of 1995, both in public testimony during committee hearings and in almost constant behind-the-scenes negotiations between the Ways and Means Committee and governors and their staffs. This was especially true of Governor Engler of Michigan, who was chair of the Republican governors' welfare reform task force, and Gerald Miller, the head of Michigan's Social Services Department, who handled much of the day-to-day negotiations for the Republican governors.

The new proposal agreed to by the House Republicans and the Republican governors would turn AFDC, Food Stamps, and a number of other programs into three capped block grants for child cash assistance, nutrition, and child care. Thus states would gain increased freedom to use the funds, especially in work programs, but, as in the Contract bill, AFDC recipients would lose their entitlement to benefits.

Although the Republican governors' agreement with Gingrich did prescribe a number of principles for using the block grants, many important issues were left unresolved. These included some of the core concerns of the Talent-Hutchinson wing of the party—issues where hard battles had recently been fought within Republican ranks during the development of the Personal Responsibility Act. Such questions included whether there would be mandatory family caps, exclusion of teenage mothers, time limits, and—most critical for the governors because of the costs—stiff work requirements.[42]

Converting AFDC and other means-tested programs into block grants offered a number of potential political advantages to the new Republican majority in the House. The action certainly would constitute the dramatic change that the Republicans had promised in the election. Moreover, because the grants would be frozen in nominal dollars for five years, they would save lots of federal money unless caseloads declined significantly. Changing AFDC and related programs into block grants also potentially weakened the dual clientele trap by moving the welfare reform debate away from concerns about protecting children and toward concerns about meddling by Washington and making government more responsive by giving increased responsibility to the states. If critics charged that Washington was abandoning poor children, defenders of block grants could ask in response why critics thought that state governors would be any less willing to defend children than politicians in far-off Washington.[43]

Perhaps the biggest advantage offered by the block grant concept was the opportunity for finessing the federalism trap conflict between the pro-devolution governors and the deterrence-oriented social conservatives. Because the flow of federal funds under a fixed-fund block grant no longer depended on the size of caseloads, imposing time limits and child exclusions would not affect the flow of funds to the states, even if those policies caused case loads to fall.[44] If deterrence-oriented provisions were written so that they applied only to the federal funds in the block grant, governors would be less likely to object because they could still use state funds to serve teenage mothers and families subject to a benefit time limit, although they might have to jump through some bureaucratic hoops (for example, setting up separate, parallel programs financed entirely by state funds) to do so. Thus Republican governors were ultimately willing to concede on several matters of importance to social conservatives, facilitating an agreement. Conceding on these matters (especially when states retained discretion to use their own funds) to stay in the bargaining game was very much on the mind of one of the governor's chief negotiators during an interview in 1995:

> As far as the family cap [goes], I think the debate is headed that way. We will still say today it should be up to the states, but if you have to deal something away in the end, you deal that away. Cutting benefits off to minor moms—it is federal benefits. How we resolved it in the end is, if we weren't going to win, then just don't prohibit [in federal legislation] any funds [going to the families of teenage mothers], so that we can still provide state funding to those populations.[45]

In short, block grants allowed social conservatives to claim a symbolic victory and permitted them to argue that they had sent a powerful message to current and potential recipients about the transformed nature of the welfare system. At the same time it gave the governors additional discretion, leaving the actual policies that would confront poor mothers and children subject to future politics in individual states.

Despite its several advantages, Speaker Gingrich's January deal with the governors put the House Republicans in an awkward position. Their leadership had agreed to two distinct and incompatible deals on welfare reform: the deterrence and new paternalism approach of the original Personal

Responsibility Act and the devolution approach negotiated with the governors. The later deal had the advantage of being given the imprimatur of the Speaker as having superseded the original act. But the Personal Responsibility Act was closer to the preferences of many House Republicans, and the governors' bargaining leverage inevitably weakened as legislation moved from backroom negotiations into House committees and onto the floor, where the governors were no longer directly at the table. It was Republican House members, not the governors, whose support would be critical as welfare reform legislation moved through the House.

Declining to Bid: The Clinton Administration

If the Republicans' problem at the beginning of the 104th Congress was two incompatible bids, the Clinton administration's problem was its inability to come to an agreement on even one. Indeed, the administration was reduced to playing defense on welfare reform throughout the early part of 1995 without being clear about what it was trying to achieve.

The 1994 election demonstrated the president's political weakness and weakened him further. Clinton seemed to have attained the worst of all political worlds. Economic growth weakened the appeal of the president's 1992 slogan—"It's the economy, stupid"—but the president and his party received little credit for the recovery. Instead, voters' attention shifted to social matters, especially crime and welfare. Surveys conducted at the time of the election showed that President Clinton was unpopular, particularly with white male voters.[46] Indeed, after the 1994 Republican triumph some politicians and analysts began to question whether he should seek renomination—and whether he was assured renomination if he did so.[47] There was no obvious best political course for the administration in this situation. A political move to the right could disillusion the party's political base and provoke a primary challenge from the left, most likely from the Reverend Jesse Jackson. There were fewer obvious primary challengers if the president moved to the left. But a leftward shift promised to provoke continued sniping from the president's own political base, notably the "New Democratic" Democratic Leadership Council, and seemed likely to lead to political irrelevance in the short term and electoral disaster for both the president and his party in 1996.[48]

The election also changed the legislative opportunities that seemed open to the Clinton administration. With a Republican majority in the 104th Congress, there was virtually no chance that the administration would make major progress on comprehensive health care reform, which had been its major domestic priority during its first two years. If the administration was to build any record of accomplishment in the period leading up to President Clinton's reelection bid in 1996, welfare reform was one of a relatively short list of items on which some compromise with the Republican majorities in Congress might be possible. But the Clinton administration's strong focus on prevention/rehabilitation and new paternalism approaches in its 1994 welfare reform package was quite different from the thrust of Republican proposals. Moreover, the administration's package cost more money than the status quo, while both the House Republican plan and the Republican governors' plan saved money. The election also meant that some items dropped from the president's 1992 platform after his election, notably a middle-class tax cut, might have to be resurrected to add some spice to an administration program notably lacking in vote-winning initiatives in Congress or with the public. But giving more to the middle class would make it even harder to find funding for the jobs, training, and child care components of the administration's welfare reform initiative than it had been in 1994.

The administration's main problem, however, was its extremely weak bargaining position at virtually every stage of the policymaking process. Republican majorities in both houses of Congress would make it difficult to give administration proposals visibility and credibility. Indeed, the administration's initial challenge in 1995 was to demonstrate its continued policymaking relevance in the midst of what seemed to be a Republican revolution.

The fact that the administration was internally divided on both the substance and the strategy of welfare reform did not help in seeking to reassert its relevance. As one top administration official put it:

> The basic tension that probably underlay the whole period was between the folks in the Administration who more or less desperately wanted a welfare reform bill, and the folks in the Administration who didn't; i.e., who thought that the bill that was coming out of the Republican Congress, and anything that we were going to get passed would be a bad bill. . . . And that tension underlay all the strategy problems, because it's hard to develop a consistent strategy when you've got people with very different goals.[49]

This internal administration conflict generally pitted policy experts at the Department of Health and Human Services, hoping for no bill, against political operatives like Bruce Reed and Rahm Emmanuel at the White

House, but it followed ideological as well as institutional lines. One administration official summarized the conflict as follows:

> I think there evolved sort of a bunker mentality among David and Mary Jo and the folks [at HHS] in the sense of, "Oh, my goodness. We lit this fuse and now it's burning out of control. We've got to move to sort of a containment strategy. Where we've been the promoter in welfare reform, now we've got to make sure that the Republicans don't take us too far." I think Bruce on the other hand perceived it as sort of a liberating experience, in the sense that the Republicans were offering us an opportunity to get this done, sort of free from the shackles of traditional liberal dogma about how much Democrats could support.
>
>   There was also a very different view of the President's political situation. The predominant White House view was, you need to find a way to be for welfare reform in the end, and our job as staff was to get enough changes in the underlying bills that he could declare victory and be for it. I think the David and Mary Jo view was basically, "Yeah, let's get as many changes as we can. But, in the end, we can't be afraid to say no." And indeed, there may be some political benefits in saying no, from the perspectives of the base constituencies, standing up for principle in the public eye, et cetera.[50]

While this internal conflict did not lead to paralysis—proponents of enacting welfare reform legislation always held the upper hand within the administration—it did lead to a great deal of mistrust, miscommunication, and difficulty in agreeing on a proactive, rather than a reactive, strategy on the part of the administration.

The administration was divided on the fundamental strategic issue of whether it should even make an opening bid by reintroducing its 1994 welfare reform bill or some variant of that bill. Those counseling against reintroduction argued that it would save the Clinton administration the embarrassment of having its proposal declared "dead on arrival" in the Republican-controlled House of Representatives. But the failure to introduce a new bill also meant that Democrats in Congress did not have a plan around which they could try to unite, and it sent confusing signals about just what (if anything) the administration really wanted on welfare reform.

Ultimately the administration did refuse to make an opening bid, or even to state a firm bargaining position. The Clinton administration's Fiscal

Year 1996 budget, released in February 1995, highlighted problems of welfare dependency and called for cooperative action with congressional Republicans on a welfare reform bill that emphasized work and making AFDC parents responsible for their actions.[51] But the administration neither sent a welfare reform bill to Congress nor included specific cost estimates for welfare reform in the budget. This strategy was predicated on the calculation that the Republicans' efforts to hold together their coalition, and in particular to reach an agreement with governors, would fail. The great risk associated with this strategy was that the Republican coalition would hold and that Democrats in Congress would essentially face a choice between voting for the hugely unpopular status quo and voting for the Republican bill. Given that choice, there is little doubt that many Democrats, especially conservative Southerners, would vote with the Republicans, giving their bill an overwhelming victory and perhaps a veto-proof margin in the House. Thus in the event that the Republican coalition did hold together through the early stages of House consideration of welfare reform, House Democrats would be left scrambling for an alternative vehicle that could hold their troops together at the end.

The administration's main weapon was likely to be the veto, or the threat of a veto. Veto threats could be used to try to moderate Republican initiatives. But it was unclear whether a veto threat would be plausible. If the Republicans crafted a welfare reform bill that appealed to many conservative Democrats, a veto-proof majority coalition could develop. This was especially likely in the case of a veto override vote, where the effective choice for legislators would be between the highly unpopular status quo and some change from that status quo. Thus there was a strong risk that the president could be portrayed as having been reduced to either a "me too" or an obstructionist role in welfare reform.

The weakness of the administration's bargaining position was clearly evident in December of 1994 when it proposed a working session on welfare reform that would bring together leading members of Congress, governors, mayors and the administration to try to work toward a bipartisan agreement on welfare reform.[52] The proposal originated in the White House as a way of trying to bring the president back into the dialogue on welfare reform to which he increasingly appeared irrelevant. But neither the new congressional majorities nor the activist Republican governors had any incentive to deal with the Clinton administration, and the administration was rapidly reduced to lowering expectations. Not surprisingly, the bipartisan session yielded no agreement.[53]

Evolving Bids: Seeking a Workable Compromise in the House

The House Republicans had a number of advantages in controlling the agenda and building coalitions to advance their objectives. First and foremost, their majority control of the House of Representatives meant that as long as they remained fairly united, they would set the agenda and control debate at all stages of the process. This would be particularly important in determining which amendments would be considered on the floor of the House of Representatives. Second, the inclusion of welfare reform as part of the Contract with America meant that it would be on a fast-track schedule. Thus the House would act before the Senate, at least in part setting the agenda for the other chamber. Perhaps most important, inclusion of welfare reform in the Contract with America also had advantages in building and maintaining a majority coalition for their bill. In particular, it gave all House Republicans a stake in passing legislation, since Republicans' success at "governance"—breaking gridlock to enact real change—would be judged by their ability to enact the components of the contract.

Orphanages: The Rise and Fall of an Issue

While welfare reform legislation was being renegotiated behind closed doors in discussions between House Republicans and Republican governors, it was also playing out on another, far more public, stage. Politicians from both parties engaged in a process of "framing and blaming" on the welfare issue to try to influence how the public saw the welfare issue and to associate the other party with unpopular positions.[54] These framing and blaming initiatives inevitably reflected the most fundamental of all welfare reform traps, the dual clientele trap. On each of the two parts of trap—the unpopularity of giving assistance to able-bodied adults and the unpopularity of hurting children, Republicans and Democrats offered both old refrains and new riffs. Republicans continued to charge that the existing system was full of perverse incentives for parents—most notably the incentive to have children out of wedlock at government's expense. But they also argued, "What is really cruel is the current incentive that pulls young women into the system and holds them forever in this cruel trap,"[55] and they characterized the current welfare system as "systematic child abuse." Democrats and children's advocacy groups opposed this rhetoric with arguments that Republicans should "pick on someone your own size" rather than financing tax breaks for the wealthy by cutting benefits and services to poor children.[56]

The first major public skirmish on welfare revolved around the issue of orphanages. "If mothers are unable to support their children, what happens to the kids?" is one of the key questions posed by the dual clientele trap. The very strong deterrence measures proposed in the original Contract with America version of the Personal Responsibility Act—especially time limits and child exclusions—posed this question starkly. These measures were criticized by child advocacy groups and Democratic politicians as saving money for the federal government (which would no longer have to provide matching grants for state AFDC expenditures for these children) at the direct expense of innocent children who were born into circumstances over which they had no control.

Conservatives who favored deterrence initiatives were aware of both the political and the social problems their initiatives presented, but thought that they had at least a partial answer. In the version of the Personal Responsibility Act included in the Contract with America, states were to be given grants equal to the amount that federal expenditures were reduced by the prohibition of cash benefit payments for children born to teen mothers.[57] States could use these funds "to establish and operate orphanages" and "to establish and operate closely supervised residential homes for unwed mothers," among other things. On the surface the proposal—particularly the orphanage provisions—appeared to be a political plus. It inoculated the Republicans against charges that they were balancing the budget by hurting poor children, and it appeared to offer a solution to the dual clientele trap as well: if (politically popular) poor children were physically separated from (politically unpopular) welfare mothers, the mothers could be cut off and the children helped.

For several weeks at the end of 1994 and beginning of 1995, orphanages dominated the welfare debate, even appearing as the cover story in *Newsweek*.[58] Experts and pundits debated the efficacy, limitations, and costs of orphanages; they also discussed in what situations children would be better off living in group homes than with their parent or parents. In December, First Lady Hillary Rodham Clinton ridiculed "the unbelievable and absurd idea of putting children into orphanages because their mothers couldn't find jobs." Speaker Gingrich issued a spirited reply on "Meet the Press," arguing, "We are allowing a brutalization and a degradation of children in this country, a destructiveness. We say to a thirteen-year-old drug addict who is pregnant, you know, put your baby in a dumpster, that's O.K., but we're not going to give you a boarding school, we're not going to give you a place for that child to grow up."[59] He suggested that the president and first lady watch the old Spencer Tracy–Mickey Rooney movie "Boys Town" to learn about the advantages of orphanages.

The orphanage appeal did not play well with the public, however, and Republicans quickly began to back away from a focus on orphanages, arguing that group homes where mothers and children would live together would be a preferred option in most cases.[60] Rising awareness of the high cost of residential facilities for children also dampened their enthusiasm. By mid-January, rather than trumpeting the uniqueness of their approach, House Republicans were maneuvering in a House Ways and Means Committee hearing to force Donna Shalala, the Clinton administration's secretary of Health and Human Services, to admit that some children could end up in orphanages under the Clinton administration's welfare proposals, too, if their parents refused to work.[61]

By late January the orphanage issue had largely played itself out. Republicans, including Speaker Gingrich, were heeding the advice of pollster Frank Luntz to avoid mentioning orphanages.[62] With no fresh defenses from the Republicans to serve as a foil, Democrats moved on to other themes in bashing Republican cruelty. By the time the House Ways and Means Committee began marking up welfare reform legislation in February, orphanages were essentially a dead issue. Thus while the orphanage issue ultimately proved to be a sideshow in the 1995 welfare reform debate, it sent an important initial message to Democrats that charging the Republican welfare bill was "tough on kids" could resonate with the public.

Evolution of a Bill in Ways and Means

The beginning of detailed consideration of welfare reform legislation by congressional committees in February of 1995 rejoined the public "framing and blaming" and behind-the-scenes negotiating streams that had been largely separated for the previous two months. The huge scope of the Personal Responsibility Act proposal meant that its provisions were parceled out to committees with jurisdiction over specific programs, with a final bill to be reassembled once those committees finished writing detailed legislation. Some provisions went to the Agriculture Committee, and others to the Economic and Educational Opportunities Committee (under the Democrats, it had been called Education and Labor). But the core of the bill, including reform of AFDC, provisions on child care and child protection (foster care), enforcement of child support, reform of Supplemental Security Income, and most provisions restricting benefits to immigrants, went to the House Ways and Means Committee.

The extraordinarily broad jurisdiction of the Ways and Means Committee meant that many other provisions of the new Republican agenda, including tax cuts and Medicare reform, also would be considered by the Ways and Means Committee. In many ways, means-tested programs like AFDC and SSI, as well as Unemployment Compensation, were the poor stepchildren of Ways and Means. They fell under the jurisdiction of the Subcommittee on Human Resources, a subcommittee of low salience for most members, which served as a first port of call for new committee members who did not have enough seniority to get assignments on more prestigious and powerful subcommittees like Trade.[63] This was especially true for Republican members of Ways and Means, most of whom did not have the constituency concerns on poverty issues that some Democrats did.[64]

The effects of low issue salience were compounded by the crushing schedule required to complete the Contract with America and the inexperience of many new Republican members—even on the Ways and Means Committee, which traditionally has been a committee assignment given primarily to senior members from relatively safe districts. Because Ways and Means has, since 1975, given "two-thirds plus one" of seats to the majority party in the House, there was a huge influx of new members to the committee at the beginning of the 104th Congress—ten of twenty-one Republicans were new to the committee, and three were new to the Congress.[65] Representative John Ensign (Republican, Nevada) noted that he and Jon Christensen (Republican, Nebraska), both newcomers to Congress and to Ways and Means, often felt overwhelmed by the complexity of the issues facing them on the committee: "Sometimes we'll lean over to each other and say 'What does that mean.' And he'll say, 'I was going to ask you.'"[66] The relative inexperience and indifference of many Ways and Means Republicans on welfare issues had some advantages for the Republican congressional leadership, however. In particular, it increased leadership bargaining discretion. They were able to change the previously agreed-on Contract provisions to broaden the coalition for reform by bringing Republican governors aboard without getting huge disagreement from most of their members.

The new welfare reform package unveiled by the Ways and Means' Human Resources Subcommittee on February 13 as it began to mark up (that is, consider amendments to) the bill was indeed quite different from the original H.R. 4 in the Contract with America, reflecting two months of negotiations with the Republican governors (see table 10-1). The most dramatic changes were in funding structure. As in the Contract with America bill, the new package provided no individual entitlement to benefits, but

Table 10-1. *The Evolution of Selected Provisions of the Personal Responsibility Act in the House of Representatives, 1995*

Policy issue	Previous law	Personal Responsibility Act (Contract with America version)	Original Ways and Means Subcommittee draft (governors' agreement)	House-passed legislation
		Program structure, entitlement status, and financing		
Entitlement status	AFDC was open-ended entitlement to states and indirectly to recipients, but states' benefit levels varied widely	Converts AFDC, SSI, Food Stamps, and other means-tested programs into capped grants; allows states to opt out of AFDC program and receive fixed block grant funds	Converts AFDC into fixed (in nominal dollars) block grant of $15.355 billion for FY 1996–2000; no state matching or maintenance of effort requirements; individual entitlement eliminated	Converts AFDC into fixed (in nominal dollars) block grant of $15.355 billion for FY 1996–2000; no state matching or maintenance of effort requirements; individual entitlement eliminated
Responsiveness to economic conditions	Spending rose automatically if recession made more people eligible for benefits	Caps program spending (adjusted for inflation and poverty rates); no provision for rainy day fund	Allows states to carry over unspent block grant funds in rainy day fund and transfer those funds to general revenues when they reach 120 percent of annual block grant expenditures; states may borrow from $1 billion federal government rainy day fund in periods of recession	States allowed to carry over unspent block grant funds in rainy day fund; states may borrow from $1 billion federal government rainy day fund in periods of recession
Responsiveness to changes in population size	Spending increased automatically if income-eligible population increased	No provision	No provision	States growing faster than average may share in $100 million per fiscal year fund

Interprogram transfers	…	…	States may move up to 30 percent of family assistance block grant funds to three other block grants	States may move up to 30 percent of funds from one block grant to another
			Program entry and pregnancy prevention	
Family caps	No provision	Prohibits use of additional benefits for children born to mothers while receiving AFDC in most circumstances	Prohibits states from using federal block grant funds to pay cash benefits for children born to mothers who received AFDC at any time during ten-month period before birth; continues Medicaid and Food Stamps	Prohibits states from using federal block grant funds to pay additional benefits for children born to mothers who received AFDC at any time during ten-month period before birth; continues Medicaid and Food Stamps
Restrictions on benefits to teen mothers	No provisions	Permanently prohibits states from paying cash benefits on behalf of children born to unmarried mothers who gave birth before age eighteen (twenty-one at state option); continues Medicaid	Permanently prohibits states from using federal block grant funds to pay cash benefits on behalf of children born to unmarried mothers who gave birth before age eighteen; continues Medicaid and Food Stamps	Prohibits use of federal block grant funds to pay *cash* benefits to unmarried teen mothers until they reach age eighteen, but allows payment of noncash assistance; continues Medicaid and Food Stamps

continued

Table 10-1. (*Continued*)

Policy issue	Previous law	Personal Responsibility Act (Contract with America version)	Original Ways and Means Subcommittee draft (governors' agreement)	House-passed legislation
Other provisions		Establishes block grant to provide noncash services for teen mothers and their children, with prohibition on funding for abortions and abortion counseling	No provision	Provides additional block grant funds to states that lower ratio of out-of-wedlock births plus abortions to live births
		Labor market entry/initial program exit		
Individual work requirements	Parent with no child under age three (one at state option) had to participate in JOBS; parents of children under age six exempt unless child care guaranteed and participation limited to twenty hours a week	Imposes minimum thirty-five hours/week work/ job search requirements on AFDC single parent recipients (forty hours for two-parent families) who have received cash benefits for at least two years	Imposes work activity (defined by states) requirement on those who have received cash benefits for at least two years; no federal requirement on hours per week to meet participation requirement	Requires at least one AFDC parent in family to participate in work activities within two years. Must participate 20 hours by 1996, 35 by 2003 to count toward participation requirement.

Work participation rate requirements for states	Twenty percent of nonexempt caseload had to participate in JOBS in FY 1995; at least 50 percent of AFDC-UP parents had to participate in workfare or other work program	States must move 2 percent of caseload into work program by 1996, rising to 50 percent by 2003	Requires states to move 2 percent of caseload into work activities (defined by states) by 1996 and 20 percent by 2003	Requires states to move 4 percent of caseload into work activities by 1996 and 50 percent by 2003; two-parent families required to reach 50 percent by 1996 and 90 percent by 1998

Long-term self-sufficiency

Hard time limits	No provision; time limits implicitly forbidden without waiver	Five-year limit on receipt of benefits	Five-year lifetime limit on receiving benefits from block grant funds (up to 10 percent of state's caseload may receive hardship exemption)	Five-year lifetime limit on receiving benefits (up to 10 percent of state's caseload may receive hardship exemption)

Paternal responsibility

Establishing paternity for children born out of wedlock	Applicant had to cooperate in establishing paternity for children born out of wedlock	Paternity must be established before benefits paid for children; states required to establish paternity for children in 90 percent of AFDC cases	If paternity not established, benefits reduced by no more than $50 or 15 percent of benefits for minimum of three months and maximum of six months	If paternity not established, benefits reduced by no more than $50 or 15 percent of benefits for minimum of three months and maximum of six months; forbids payment to family where any individual not cooperating in establishing paternity for child of that individual

continued

Table 10-1. (*Continued*)

Policy issue	Previous law	Personal Responsibility Act (Contract with America version)	Original Ways and Means Subcommittee draft (governors' agreement)	House-passed legislation
		Other means-tested programs		
Legal immigrant benefits	Provisions vary, but some restrictions in AFDC, Food Stamps, Medicaid, and certain other programs	Bars legal immigrants from sixty means-tested programs, with SSI exception for individuals in country more than five years and over age seventy-five	Bars legal immigrants from approximately thirty-five means-tested programs not opportunity-oriented; makes sponsor's pledge of support legally binding, with SSI exception for individuals in country more than ten years and over age seventy-five	Bar legal immigrants from approximately thirty-five means-tested programs not opportunity-oriented; make sponsor's pledge of support legally binding, with SSI exception for individuals in country more than ten years and over age seventy-five
Net budget cost	Not applicable	Republicans' estimate: $40 billion in net savings over five years	Not available	Approximately $35 billion in savings for programs under Ways and Means jurisdiction only; about $66 billion for all provisions

Source: Provisions of the original Ways and Means subcommittee draft are from House Ways and Means Committee, Subcommittee on Human Resources, "Markup Documents for Welfare Reform," February 13, 1995. Provisions of prior law and House-passed legislation are from House Report 104-430, *Personal Responsibility and Work Opportunity Act of 1995*, December 20, 1995

the funding stream was different. States were promised a fixed amount of money—$13.35 billion a year for five years (the level of AFDC and JOBS funding in 1994)—with money allocated among the states based on past expenditure levels.[67] The package made no adjustment for inflation or changes in population and economic conditions (a modest loan fund was established that states could draw upon in times of recession). Gone as well was the $9.9 billion over five years in additional funding that Republicans had pledged in the Contract with America (and the earlier H.R. 3500) to facilitate work by providing child care, transportation subsidies, and so forth. States would not be required to match federal funding to receive their block grant funds. Indeed, they were not required to spend any of their own money at all on poor families, and states that were highly successful in reducing expenditures were even allowed to transfer excess federal block grant funds to their general funds.[68]

The other main change in the subcommittee bill was much weaker work requirements than the Contract bill. Recipients had to engage in work activities after two years, but states got to define what is meant by "work activity" and the number of hours devoted to those activities and had to meet only minimal participation rate requirements (20 percent of the caseload by fiscal year 2003). Moreover, there were no penalties for failing to meet even these weak requirements.[69] In short, the money trap was reasserting itself: House Republicans' need to make the budget numbers in their proposals "add up" now that they were in power led them to back down substantially on the work objectives of the Contract in exchange for budgetary savings.

Bans remained on payment of cash benefits to teen mothers (without the state option to raise the age limit above eighteen); family caps and a sixty-month (consecutive or nonconsecutive) hard time limit remained as well. But these spending exclusions applied only to federal funds, and, unlike the Contract bill, states were allowed to exempt up to 10 percent of their caseload from the sixty-month hard time limit. Restrictions on benefits to legal immigrant noncitizens were also eased slightly.[70] However, access to SSI for disabled children was dramatically restricted, responding to criticisms that access had been made too broad—and was sometimes obtained through fraud—in recent years.

While HHS Secretary Donna Shalala and others at HHS opposed substituting a block grant for individual entitlement, the White House refused to oppose it, believing that the issue had little resonance with voters.[71] The administration chose to concentrate most of its rhetorical effort on the choicer target of Republican cuts in child and school-based nutrition programs that were moving through the Opportunities Committee at the same time the welfare reform bill was moving through Ways and Means.[72] Within the House Representative Charles Rangel, the ranking Democrat on Ways and Means, conceded, "We don't have the votes to keep entitlements" for AFDC. Individual entitlement for benefits was an issue about which liberals cared deeply, but many members (and Democratic leaders) saw it as both a lost cause and a political loser with the electorate—especially if President Clinton provided no leadership.[73] House Democrats, seeking a consensus position around which members of their badly divided caucus could unite, decided, in coordination with the Clinton administration, to focus on criticizing the Republican bill as "weak on work" as the only position that could prevent massive defections to the Republican bill.[74] Ironically, they were joined in these criticisms by social conservatives. Robert Rector of the Heritage Foundation blasted the subcommittee bill as a "very, very modest step forward . . . in some respects no better than the status quo" because of its weak work requirements and criticized the governors as "with very few exceptions, . . . obstacles to reform rather than engines of reform."[75] Once the markup began, debates frequently turned highly acrimonious and partisan. Democrat Harold Ford (Tennessee) charged that Republicans were engaging in "an experiment that uses America's children as crash-test dummies"; Human Resources Subcommittee chair Clay Shaw retorted that Democrats were defending "the last plantation" of the federal welfare system.[76] The subcommittee nevertheless moved briskly: action on the huge bill was completed in three days, and almost all Democratic amendments—including those to stiffen work requirements—were rejected on eight-to-five party-line votes.[77]

New problems in keeping the Republican coalition together kept arising in the multi-front Contract with America war, however. Food Stamps emerged as a particular problem at the end of February. Farm-state Republicans seeking to retain the program as a federal entitlement argued that doing so was a critical part of a "log-roll" with urban legislators needed to pass commodity price-support programs, while Republican governors argued that they needed the flexibility of a block grant of Food Stamp funds to make up for expected overall budget cuts in means-tested grant programs. Underscoring the frenzied pace of Contract with America policymaking, Republican leaders reversed themselves twice on a Food Stamp block grant in less than a week. They unveiled a new deal on Food Stamps designed as a compromise between farm state interests and Republican governors on the second day of markup of the welfare reform bill by the full Ways and Means Committee.[78]

The markup in the full Ways and Means Committee, which began on February 28, also showed the effects of strains within the coalition—notably charges by social conservatives (and Democrats) that the bill approved by the Human Resources subcommittee was "soft on work." Rather than simply incorporating changes made during the subcommittee markup, the new "Chairman's Mark" (the rough outline of a bill from which any amendments would be made in the full committee) contained a number of new provisions. Most prominent were far more detailed and strict work requirements than had been in the bill reported out by the subcommittee. States now had to place an escalating share of their caseload in work (reaching 50 percent by 2003); they had less flexibility in defining work activities; and hours of work that a recipient could count toward meeting participation requirements were stiffened, rising to thirty-five hours a week by fiscal year 2002.[79] To compensate, the states were allowed to count toward meeting the work participation rate requirements declines in their overall caseload. But this last change illustrated the difficulty of avoiding perverse incentives. Activist Republican governors argued that giving states credit for caseload declines was fair because it avoided penalizing states for being successful in moving households off welfare entirely and into work, but child advocates responded that it gave states incentives to kick recipients off the rolls regardless of whether they had found employment.

Similar problems with perverse incentives arose with new provisions intended to deter illegitimacy. To appease pro-life forces that feared that the lifetime ban on cash benefits to teen mothers and their offspring would lead to increased abortions, that ban was made temporary rather than lifetime, as in the subcommittee bill. Both mothers and children could now receive cash benefits once the mother turned eighteen. To compensate pro-deterrence forces for this change, a new provision was added that would reward states for reducing the total number of out-of-wedlock births plus abortions in their state.[80] Putting abortions in the equation was seen as necessary by social conservatives because they feared that simply rewarding states for reducing out-of-wedlock births might lead them to encourage abortions. But this in turn made prochoice legislators unhappy, because it could reward states for reducing abortions (for example, by reducing access to clinics), which is probably easier to do than reducing out-of-wedlock births.[81] This problem, which apparently had not been foreseen by authors of the provision, was addressed by a successful committee amendment that made the formula more "abortion-neutral."[82] It was one of the few amendments considered by the full committee that was adopted.

Overall, action at the full committee level was similar to that in the subcommittee: rapid, rancorous, and partisan. Democrats proposed amendments intended to win the support of moderate Republicans; or, if that failed, to show that Democrats valued work and compassion for poor families over concessions to governors; and above all, to show that Democrats were not just defenders of the status quo. Thus they proposed amendments that would, for example, have compelled states to make child care available to parents participating in work and training programs; required states to provide services such as training and substance abuse counseling before terminating families from cash welfare assistance; and required states to maintain their existing level of spending on services to poor families. They also proposed an amendment to toughen the bill's recently added provisions on child support enforcement by requiring states to suspend or restrict driver's and professional licenses for parents who failed to meet their child support obligations.[83] All were defeated.[84] The committee's bill, including not only the welfare block grant but equally controversial cuts in access to Supplemental Security Income for disabled children, conversion of federal child protection funds into a block grant, and cuts in eligibility of noncitizens for means-tested programs, left the committee with the support of all Republicans and a single Democrat.[85]

The president, meanwhile, sent ambiguous messages, alternately lambasting failures of the Republican bill (for example, providing incentives for states to meet work requirements by cutting recipients off, and failing to provide additional resources for child care and transportation to facilitate moving AFDC mothers into work) and saying that the two parties could and should work together to produce a better bill. Equally important was what he did not say: he did not propose a specific alternative bill, he did not threaten a veto, and he did not say that he would veto a bill that abolished individual entitlement to AFDC benefits or contained hard time limits. On the contrary, he called, at least rhetorically, for an end to requirements that states obtain waivers before engaging in future experiments, a move that could eventually dismantle the existing AFDC program just as much as the Republican bill.[86]

Republicans did not feel that they had to make many concessions to avoid a presidential veto, however. The GOP believed that it held the strategic high ground because a presidential veto would leave the widely despised status quo in place and could be portrayed by Republicans as such. Indeed,

Clay Shaw predicted immediately after the full committee approved the welfare bill that the president would not dare veto it because doing so would represent "nothing less than an endorsement of the existing system," while the administration tried just as hard to make clear that it was not defending the status quo.[87]

From Committee to House Passage

In the rush to meet the hundred-day deadline for consideration of the Contract with America, floor debate on the welfare reform bill was scheduled for the week after the three House committees of jurisdiction—Ways and Means, Economic Opportunities, and Agriculture—finished consideration of their bills. The Rules Committee had to meld the three pieces of legislation and decide which amendments, and substitutes for the entire bill, would be in order. The House Rules Committee was flooded with more than 150 proposed amendments. The Republican leadership was extremely effective in using the House Rules Committee to control which alternatives would be considered in floor amendments, rewarding those interests that cooperated, while keeping issues that were likely to split their coalition off the agenda.[88] As a House Republican leadership aide put it:

> We literally went over amendment by amendment and said, . . . "Is this . . . something that the bill can survive and have that [amendment] pass? Is there any reason why we should or should not allow this amendment to be offered?" [We were] trying to be as fair as possible, but don't sink the bill. That was the bottom line. Nothing that could definitely sink the bill.[89]

For example, representatives allied with right-to-life groups and Roman Catholic bishops were given an opportunity to present floor amendments, supported by the leadership, that allowed states to use federal funds to give vouchers to teen mothers excluded from cash benefits and those affected by a family cap who would no longer be eligible for federal funding for cash benefits.[90] Moderate Republican leader Nancy Johnson was allowed to offer an amendment that increased funding for child care for mothers subject to the work requirement.[91] But amendments that threatened to split the Republican coalition were not permitted on orders of the House leadership. Thus the rule did not allow a vote on an amendment eliminating the block granting of school lunches. Nor was there to be a vote on deleting financial incentives to states to reduce out-of-wedlock births—a provision unpopular with Republican moderates, right-to-life groups, and reproductive rights groups on the left, but critical to retaining support from the "Rector block" of Republican social conservatives.[92] Nevertheless, fifteen Republicans, mostly allied with right-to-life causes or with Cuban-American interests concerned about the immigrant provisions of the bill, voted against the rule for debate of the House bill—a vote that usually follows party lines very closely. It survived only by the extraordinarily close margin of 217 to 211, and only because three Democrats defected to vote for it.[93]

Meanwhile, House Democrats, who had been playing defense all spring and were very badly split on AFDC reform, faced a terrible strategic dilemma on the House floor: if they failed to unite around an alternative, moderate and conservative Democratic members, given nothing to support but the status quo, would vote for the Republican bill. And that in turn would give the Republicans a massive majority that would increase their bargaining leverage with the Senate in an eventual conference committee and, more important, make it difficult for the president to veto whatever bill eventually emerged. But in order to attract moderate and conservative Democrats (and in the most optimistic scenario, enough moderate Republicans to defeat the Ways and Means Committee bill on the House floor and substitute for it), a Democratic alternative bill would have to be very conservative indeed—far more conservative than liberal Democrats could feel comfortable with. Given the strong incentives for coalitional unity, Democrats did rally around a Democratic alternative sponsored by a soon-to-be Republican, Representative Nathan Deal of Georgia, and backed by the White House.[94] The Deal bill was, for House Democrats, an extraordinarily conservative measure. It continued assistance to poor families as a "conditional entitlement" rather than a block grant, provided a child care guarantee to those in its "Work First" Program, and maintained current school nutrition programs. But it also contained a four-year hard time limit (with some exemptions), outbidding the Republicans. In addition, it allowed family caps and teen mother exclusions as a state option and set state work participation rates that once again slightly outbid the Republicans (52 percent by 2003).[95]

The House Rules Committee allowed two Democratic substitute bills to come to a vote on the floor of the House. The more liberal alternative, sponsored by Representative Patsy Mink (Democrat, Hawaii), was overwhelmingly defeated. Democrats gave solid support to the Deal bill, but it attracted only one Republican member and lost by a margin of 228-205.[96] Only nine House Democrats supported final House passage of the Republican bill; it passed on a nearly party-line vote of 234-199.[97]

Thus the House debate contained both good news and bad news for Republicans. The critical good news was that President Clinton had backed the Deal bill despite the fact that it contained hard time limits, something the administration had ultimately backed down from including in its own welfare package the previous June. Thus the "zone of acceptable outcomes" of the president and House Democrats had been pushed substantially to the right, giving the Republicans additional leverage to insist on hard time limits in a final welfare reform package. But on the negative side, the unity of the Democrats in the House in opposing the Republican welfare reform bill in the vote on final passage suggested that it might be hard to gain Democratic support for a Republican bill in the Senate where, given that body's nonmajoritarian procedures, help from some members of the minority party would be needed.

The bill passed by the House bequeathed some additional problems, moreover. Including measures such as conversion of the school lunch program from an entitlement into a block grant gave critics of the bill a target and a potent symbol with which to attack it. These measures also created a politically viable excuse for the president to veto the bill. Indeed, both President Clinton and White House chief of staff Leon Panetta raised the specter of a veto immediately after the House passed its bill, with objections to school lunch provisions as their main point of attack.[98] Even Speaker Gingrich conceded that the Democrats had gotten the better of the rhetorical battle on school lunches.[99] Finally sensing a viable line of attack against the Republican juggernaut, the Clinton administration made the notion that Republican bills were "tough on kids" a consistent theme in its attacks on the party throughout the spring and summer of 1995.[100]

Explaining the Republican Success in the House

The bill that passed the House and was sent on to the Senate was an enormous legislative achievement in a highly contentious policy arena. Even if substantially modified by the Senate, it set out a strong bargaining position for House negotiators in the conference committee between the House and Senate; showed that a common "zone of acceptable outcomes" between the diverse elements of the Republican coalition could be established; and showed that the "zone of acceptable outcomes" for both the Clinton administration and House Democrats could be moved quite far to the right if choices were posed in terms of change versus a highly unpopular status quo. This Republican success occurred despite the fact that the policy traps that had inhibited welfare reform in the past were by no means uniformly weak-ening. The appearance of deterrence measures on the agenda clearly had the potential to strengthen the dual clientele trap, for example, while the clash between the desire of conservative Republicans for tougher work requirements clashed with the preferences of Republican governors for more flexibility, strengthening the federalism trap. And the money trap was strengthened by the push to produce big savings through cuts in means-tested programs, which meant that Republicans could not easily buy the support of disgruntled elements of their coalition by adding spending on programs that those groups favored.

Nevertheless, the overall trend was clearly toward a weakening of each of the major traps. Particularly critical in this regard was President Clinton's "end welfare as we know it" pledge, which weakened the dual clientele trap by focusing attention on the behavior of adults rather than the welfare of children. Also critical was the Republican electoral victory in 1994, which gave Republicans a common agenda requiring substantial budget cuts (which means-tested programs were to help provide), an empowered lead-ership, and a sense of shared political destiny and political interests—all of which made the Republican reform coalitions less fragile.

The most important challenge that had confronted House Republican leaders in overcoming the welfare policymaking traps was to find compro-mises that would hold together Republican moderates and conservatives, especially on the "conservative mandate" issues, while preserving an alliance with the leading Republican governors and neutralizing the intergovern-mental lobby. At the same time, Republican leaders had to prevent defec-tions by their own special constituency-oriented members, notably those with a strong right-to-life orientation. That they succeeded in doing so is a tribute to an extraordinarily effective Republican leadership, which central-ized authority over political and policy deal-making, thus weakening the impact of fragmented political institutions and multiple veto points. But it also reflects strong individual and collective incentives for the coalition partners to hold together and to try to pass a compromise that they all could live with as well as an astute use of the House Rules Committee to prevent challenges likely to sink the bill.

The most obvious collective incentive for Republican legislators was the desire to show Republican unity—and in particular to demonstrate that the Republicans could govern effectively and end gridlock. In addition, there was a desire to avoid losing the welfare issue back to the Democrats. Presi-dent Clinton had used the issue of welfare reform effectively in the 1992 election, but the House Republicans, with their very aggressive stance, had regained the initiative and public confidence (see figure 7-2 in chapter 7) in 1994. The Republicans had no desire to cede it back. And while there were deep substantive divisions among House Republicans on some elements of the Personal Responsibility Act, virtually none of them wanted a stalemate to ensue, a stalemate that would likely result in the policy status quo's remaining in place. Another important impetus for the Republicans to hang together and pass welfare reform was that they needed the savings to meet the extremely ambitious deficit and tax reduction targets they had set. The Congressional Budget Office provided new estimates that the House-passed bill would produce more than $76 billion in expenditure reductions in its first five years.[101]

The timing of House consideration of welfare reform was also helpful. It came at the end of the "One Hundred Days" in which the new majority had pledged to hold votes on all provisions of the Contract with America. Republican members were under enormous pressure to vote for the bill to "complete the Contract." There was, in addition, enormous exhaustion on the part of House GOP members (and Democrats as well). Both of these conditions conferred an advantage on the party leadership. Finally, the Republican leadership benefited from the fact that most Republican members, excepting only a few (for instance, Cuban American representatives from Florida, whose constituents would be disproportionately affected by the immigrant provisions of the Personal Responsibility Act), did not have a strong constituency interest in resisting the cutbacks to means-tested programs contained in the Personal Responsibility Act.

Each of the partners in the House Republican coalition also had strong incentives to go along with the welfare reform package negotiated in the House. GOP conservatives, who gained most of what they wanted in the House bill, had perhaps the greatest incentive to agree. But GOP moderates who had reservations about the bill could be comforted by the idea that this was not the final word on welfare reform. As Representative Jim Greenwood of Pennsylvania, put it, "I don't have to condition my support on perfection in the House vehicle. . . . We all know the Senate will look at it closely."[102] Moreover, the already marginal position of GOP moderates within the party caucus (as well as access to perquisites such as assignments to choice committees) would be even more tenuous if they abandoned their leaders on such an important vote. Even Republican moderates wanted change from the status quo—and keeping the process moving was the way to get it. For them, voting for the welfare reform bill was a hard choice, rather than an easy one. But given the array of coalitional and policy incentives they faced (as well as last-minute leadership concessions on issues such as child care funding), it is hardly surprising that they supported final passage of the welfare reform bill overwhelmingly.

Perhaps the greatest success was keeping Republican governors on board for a bill that was expected to dramatically reduce funding from the federal government and might also result in increased state costs over time. There were some complaints from the governors: Christine Todd Whitman of New Jersey, for example, stated her opposition both to an exclusion of benefits to teen mothers and to a cutoff of benefits to legal immigrants; George Voinovich of Ohio complained about the formula for allocating funds to states, the failure to provide significant funding in case of a recession, and numerous data-reporting requirements in the House bill. But both backed the basic concept of a block grant to the states, and neither opposed the bill during House consideration.[103]

Republican governors had numerous incentives to stay on board in the House initiative. In policy terms, the activist Republican governors, who had lost ground as the bill moved through the House, were more likely to advance their interests by retaining what they could in the House bill through being supportive while recognizing that they would have another opportunity to reshape the bill when it went to the Senate. If they had been uncooperative, it is likely that the House Republican bill would have been even less responsive to their objectives. Better to gain 40 percent of what they wanted in the House, try for 80 percent in the Senate, and compromise at 60 percent in the conference committee than to deal yourself out in the House and get only 20 percent in the House and have to win back all that ground in the Senate.

Republican governors also had political incentives to cooperate. All had an interest in conveying an image of party unity: if voters saw Republicans as effective promoters of policy change, leading to a Republican realignment, the governors' boats, too, would rise on the tide. National political ambitions also played a role for at least some governors. Republican prospects for winning the presidency in 1996 looked very good indeed in early 1995. A number of governors (including Engler, Thompson, and Weld) had been mentioned as possible vice-presidential nominees, and one governor, Pete Wilson of California, was inching closer to running for president himself.[104]

Just as striking as the Republicans' feat in keeping their coalition together was their ability to move congressional Democrats, and President

Clinton, so far to the right. The idea that virtually all congressional Democrats would unite in extending their "zone of acceptable outcomes" to a proposal as conservative as the Deal bill would have been unimaginable just six months earlier. It reflects the political maneuvering of a disparate and desperate legislative minority faced with nothing but bad choices.

The unity of House Democrats in supporting the Deal bill was of course a facade. It reflected the convergence of electoral, coalitional, and policy concerns that resulted in "strategic pursuit" (of Republicans in their move to the right) and "matching" of the positions staked out by conservative Democrats. The desire to establish a politically defensible position to avoid blame as a defender of the status quo was critical to this repositioning. Establishing a position that had some popular elements in it (for instance, child care guarantees and a preservation of the status quo on child nutrition programs) also provided a mechanism to generate blame against Republicans and to try to drive a wedge within the Republican coalition, with the larger political goal of stalling an important part of the Republican Contract with America juggernaut. To limit defections in a situation where conservative Democrats had maximum bargaining leverage and felt (because most of them came from very conservative districts) maximum pressure to go along with Republican welfare proposals, the rest of the Democratic caucus essentially had to "match" the positions of the conservatives within their party. In purely policy terms, almost all Democrats saw the Deal bill as preferable to the Republican bill and as the only alternative to that bill that could conceivably emerge from the House.

Of course, House Democrats would not necessarily feel bound to support a bill like the Deal bill in the future, when welfare came back to the House from the Senate. Many of them assuredly would not do so if they had any politically plausible alternative. In future bargaining, however, it would be politically much harder for President Clinton to back away from his endorsement of Deal bill provisions such as hard time limits without appearing to be a hypocrite and an opportunist.

CHAPTER ELEVEN

Stop and Go
in the Senate

WHILE THE HOUSE TOOK center stage in Congress on welfare reform in the spring of 1995, events on the Senate side were much quieter. The Senate Finance Committee held a series of informational hearings in March.[1] But by the time the House completed action on a welfare reform bill in late March, neither the Finance Committee Republicans, headed by Bob Packwood of Oregon, nor the Democrats, under ranking minority member Daniel Patrick Moynihan of New York, had introduced a bill as a starting point for debate in that chamber. Indeed, by the time the House passed its bill, Senate Finance Committee chairman Bob Packwood had not decided whether to use the House bill as a starting point or to begin with a new bill. Nor had he foreclosed the option of working with Moynihan to fashion a bipartisan bill. However, Packwood announced at the end of March that he favored moving to a block grant approach because the existing federal-state partnership had failed and the "time has come to let the states take a whirl at whether or not they can administer these programs better than we can if we give them flexibility."[2] This appeared to shut the door on a bipartisan approach, since Moynihan vehemently opposed de-entitling AFDC.

A block grant with maximum flexibility for states had strong attractions for Republican leaders in the Senate: it might allow them to dodge many of the most difficult and contentious policy issues surrounding welfare reform, such as work participation rates, time limits, and measures to reduce illegitimacy by leaving them up to the states. At the same time, a block grant with minimal strings fit with Republicans' general orientation toward moving more responsibilities out of Washington and back to the states.[3] But it also raised the specter of the federalism trap in a very stark form: did federal legislators really trust the states to use their discretion wisely, or would they prefer to mandate certain policy preferences to the states?

Packwood's endorsement of block grants also caused liberal advocacy groups to alter their strategy. With Packwood favoring block grants, the chances that a Senate bill would maintain individual entitlement to AFDC benefits were minimal. Recognizing that entitlement was probably a lost cause, child advocacy groups shifted their efforts to focus on inclusion of a "state maintenance of effort" requirement in the Senate bill. Under AFDC, federal funds were provided as a match to state expenditures on the program. If states reduced their expenditures, they would lose federal funds. But under the House welfare reform bill, states could potentially phase out their own expenditures and rely solely on the federal block grant to fund a smaller program for poor families, while reaping a fiscal dividend. The response favored by liberal advocacy groups was to cut block grant funds if states fell below some fixed percentage of their previous spending effort for AFDC. This argument was almost certain to strike a sympathetic chord in federal legislators, who were quite familiar with state efforts in other programs (notably Medicaid) to manipulate federal grants to their own advantage. But it was strongly opposed by the activist Republican governors, who argued that it would penalize the states that were most successful in moving recipients off welfare and into work.

Setting the Stage in the Senate

The slower course of action on the Senate side, and the greater proclivity toward bipartisanship, had several roots. The House leadership's deadline for enacting the Contract with America helped speed action in the House, as did greater member and staff expertise on welfare issues in the new Republican majority. In addition, different procedures, traditions, and the size of the respective chambers made building a winning coalition for passage of legislation much more difficult in the Senate than in the House. The Senate Finance Committee had only a narrow margin—11-9—of Republicans over Democrats, and two of those Republicans, Chairman Packwood himself and John Chafee of Rhode Island, were among the Senate's most liberal Republicans on social issues (two other Republican moderates on Senate Finance, David Durenberger and John Danforth, had retired at the end of the 103d Congress).[4] If Packwood were to take a more partisan approach, he would have to be sure either that he could hold Chafee or that he could woo Democrats over to the Republican side.

Packwood also faced constraints of a more personal nature. Just days after he was reelected to the Senate in 1992, charges surfaced that the senator had repeatedly engaged in sexual harassment of congressional staff and campaign workers throughout much of his twenty-four years in the Senate and had solicited lobbyists to provide jobs for his former wife. By the time Packwood finally held Finance Committee markup sessions on a welfare bill at the end of May 1995, the Senate Ethics Committee had already accused him not only of these ethics charges but also of altering his diaries when it became clear that they would be subpoenaed as evidence against him.[5] Thus, rather than mastering the details of a welfare reform package and attempting to build a compromise, Packwood would be spending much of his time preparing his legal and political strategy to retain his seat. The prospect that Packwood would pursue a maverick course on welfare reform was further weakened by the fact that he would depend on the support of his party colleagues, and the party leadership, to defend him against any movement to censure him or to expel him from the chamber.[6]

Other Republican moderates, both on the Senate Finance Committee and outside it, also had constraints on how far they could buck their party colleagues on welfare reform. Senators have limited political capital, and expending resources on welfare reform might risk retaliation from their party colleagues in other policy sectors that might be higher on their list of priorities. Senator Chafee, for example, had already been dropped as chair of the Senate Republican Conference in 1990 because of his relatively liberal views, and some Republicans had proposed stripping him of his status as ranking Republican on the Environment and Public Works Committee after he supported the Clinton administration's crime bill in 1994.[7] His top priorities were in the Environment and Public Works Committee (of which he became chairman in 1995) and, within the Finance Committee, protecting the Medicaid program, the children's SSI program (reflecting his long-time interests in health care and disability issues), and child welfare programs. Thus while Chafee—and other moderates on the floor—might propose moderating amendments and back some offered by Democrats, they were unlikely to vote for a Democratic substitute bill, and they would go a long way in accommodating conservatives to avoid voting against a Republican bill.[8]

The most serious constraints on Republican welfare reform legislation—and thus the greatest incentives to bipartisanship—in the Senate would occur on the chamber floor.[9] In the Senate, unlike the House, the Rules Committee does not act as a powerful gatekeeper to limit the time for debate and the number of amendments. A determined minority can extend debate almost indefinitely, unless the majority can win the votes needed to impose cloture on debate. But cloture requires sixty votes rather than a simple majority for most pieces of legislation. Even with two Democratic defections early in the 104th Congress, the Republicans had only fifty-four (fifty-three after Packwood's resignation from the Senate in September). Thus on welfare reform, and a number of other issues, the White House and Democratic congressional leaders saw the Senate as the place where, as presidential advisor George Stephanopoulos put it, Republicans "don't have the votes to beat back our hard priorities."[10] Less clear, however, was whether the White House would see AFDC as a "hard priority" and what its policy bottom line on welfare would be.

Budget Politics

Budget politics and procedures affected welfare reform policymaking in the Senate in a number of important ways. The budget reconciliation package, which attempts to bring spending in line with the priorities laid out in Congress's budget resolution, is the main route around the nonmajoritarian procedural obstacles (notably the threat of filibuster) on the Senate floor. The budget reconciliation bill is usually passed during the summer, with final agreement between the two chambers in September. Senate debate on reconciliation is limited to twenty hours.[11] Tucking welfare reform into a reconciliation package could thus provide a mechanism to ensure that welfare reform was brought to a final vote. Including welfare reform in reconciliation would also discourage defection by Republican moderates since any objectionable welfare provisions would be less salient in a big package, and moderates would not want to risk sinking a reconciliation bill since their party had such a big stake in it.[12]

As with the Clinton administration's strategy in 1993, using the budget bill as a vehicle for welfare reform had disadvantages in addition to attractions—notably the risk that it might drag down a reconciliation bill that was already bound to be highly contentious.[13] Moreover, as budget politics became increasingly weighed down with contentious issues like Medicaid and Medicare reform during 1995, an omnibus reconciliation bill began to seem like less of a "sure thing." Enacting such an important piece of legislation with minimal debate—welfare reform would undoubtedly be allocated only a small share of the twenty hours of debate on the reconciliation bill—would give the Democratic minority in the Senate ammunition to criticize the Republican majority as both undemocratic and callous in their treatment of poor families.[14] Thus the best outcome

Republicans could hope for was that the threat of including welfare reform in reconciliation would force Democrats to eschew procedural obstacles and agree to time limits on separate welfare reform legislation—but that was likely to happen only if Democrats took seriously the threat of including welfare in reconciliation.

The Senate debate was affected by budget politics in another way: as in the House, the need to produce savings to meet budget and tax reduction targets meant that reduction in expenditures would drive much of the debate on welfare reform. Any efforts to lubricate the legislative process by allocating additional funds to address the concerns of specific groups or senators would run into these budget constraints.

Presidential Politics

Political calculations on welfare reform in the Senate were also complicated by the presidential ambitions of Senate Majority Leader Bob Dole of Kansas. Dole's personal policy preferences suggested a bipartisan approach to welfare. Although far from a liberal on most social issues, Dole had generally been supportive of nutrition programs and might be expected to resist pressures to convert them into block grants, as the House-passed bill proposed.[15] In January he criticized the evolving House Republican bill on welfare reform—and in particular its ban on cash benefits to young mothers—as too radical.[16]

Dole faced four conflicting pressures on welfare reform. First, as the only Republican presidential contender in a congressional leadership position, Dole needed to show that he was an effective leader in getting legislation passed—never an easy task in the fractious and individualistic Senate. This consideration suggested building a winning coalition for welfare reform through bipartisanship.

A second pressure acting on the majority leader was to increase his appeal to conservative activists (including the social conservative groups that were increasingly uniting around deterrence approaches to welfare reform), who tend to vote disproportionately in those primaries. Dole faced competition in the Republican primaries from competitors placing themselves to his right. He had to increase his appeal to these conservatives without creating a record that would make him appear to the general electorate as an extremist if he won the Republican presidential nomination.[17] Given the sequencing of the primary and general elections, most of Dole's early moves were to the right. As the House was considering welfare reform legislation, Senator Dole issued a sharp critique of affirmative action, and he promised to bring up before the Senate a repeal of the assault weapons ban enacted in 1994. Both of these steps represented reversals of positions he had previously held and were widely seen as efforts to appeal to conservative Republican primary voters.[18] In addition, Dole signed the Americans for Tax Reform's "no-new taxes" pledge he refused to sign in his 1988 presidential campaign.[19]

Third, Dole also faced criticism from his Senate party colleagues—especially more junior (and generally more conservative) Republicans—about the Senate's slow pace in enacting the provisions of the Contract with America. One early Republican presidential contender, Governor Pete Wilson of California, referred to the Senate as the "graveyard" for Contract with America provisions.[20] Although the Contract originated in the House, many of these Senators worried that the Senate too would be judged on its success in passing legislation based on its provisions. As one Republican senator put it, "Most newspapers now run a daily chart showing action on Contract issues—lots of check marks in the House, almost none in the Senate."[21] In March the Senate under Dole's leadership fell one vote short of approving the Balanced Budget Amendment; if Dole pushed for a consensus version of welfare reform, he would unquestionably face further criticism from the conservative wing of his own party. Conservative Republican senators, led by Senator Lauch Faircloth of North Carolina and Senator Phil Gramm of Texas, a rival presidential aspirant, could deny Dole and Packwood a majority for a welfare bill if they were able to hold together in resisting a bill that they viewed as not conservative enough.

Fourth, Dole and his Senate colleagues were under intense pressure from House Republicans to support both a balanced budget and significant tax cuts.[22] Doing so, however, would require large cuts in social programs and make a bipartisan approach to welfare reform—or even buying the votes of a few Democrats by giving extra funds for their home states or provisions close to their hearts (such as child care)—far more difficult. In short, if Dole was to achieve all of his political objectives, he would need to use all of his skills as a legislative compromiser, without appearing to be a compromiser, and with very limited use of one of the main tools of compromise: using additional funding to buy the support of wavering senators on particular provisions of a bill.

Given these conflicting pressures, the Senate Republican leadership faced a set of hard choices in deciding whether to follow the lead of House Republicans or to fashion a bipartisan agreement with Democrats, as in 1988. Clearly there were strong incentives to wait and see both what came out of the House and how popular the House Republican agenda was. If the Contract agenda was popular, if Senate Republicans saw their political fates tied to the success of the Contract with America agenda, and if it appeared that substantial numbers of Senate Democrats were likely to defect to support Republican initiatives in order to protect themselves politically, then incentives to build a bipartisan agreement on welfare reform were minimized. If the House Republicans produced a bill that seemed too punitive and was unpopular with the public, however, the incentives for a bipartisan course would be much stronger.

Democrats in Disarray

Senate Democrats also had incentives for delay and even stronger incentives for bipartisanship. Democratic Senators felt some unease about being constantly on the defensive—as one key staffer put it, they wanted to be "for something." But attempting to stake out a partisan Democratic position early made little strategic sense. It risked torpedoing any prospects for bipartisanship on the Senate Finance Committee, where the Senate Democrats had their best chance of shaping the course of welfare reform legislation. Democratic senators' position on welfare reform would also depend heavily on what came out of the House, what seemed politically feasible in light of public reactions to the House bill, and the signals the president sent about what kind of welfare bill he was willing to sign.

In a body as small and personalistic as the Senate, prospects for passage of a welfare bill with bipartisan support also depend on key individuals. As the Senate welfare reform debate began in the 104th Congress, the key individual for the Democrats was Senator Daniel Patrick Moynihan of New York. Recognized as the Senate's leading expert on welfare, Moynihan was also the primary author of the Family Support Act of 1988. Moynihan made it clear that he did not think the Family Support Act had been given enough time or funding to be abandoned. He was publicly critical not only of Republican approaches to welfare, but also of the Clinton administration, which he felt had opened the door to cataclysmic cuts in welfare programs through the campaign pledge to "end welfare as we know it," and its unwillingness to fight to preserve entitlement status for AFDC. Moynihan charged that the administration had forfeited leadership on welfare, health, and other issues in a cynical political calculation that the president's chances for reelection would be maximized if the administration simply would "cease all initiatives and say [to the Republicans], 'All right, you're so smart, you fix it.'"[23] Moynihan's strong resistance to many of the key elements in

Republican approaches—block grants, time limits, and stiff work requirements—which President Clinton had already signaled he might accept, further lowered prospects for a bipartisan approach to welfare reform in the early stages of the Senate debate. Why should the Republicans compromise with Moynihan if they could get a better deal from many rank-and-file Senate Democrats and from the president, who was refusing to give firm backing to Moynihan's stands?[24] Moynihan's isolation also moved the center of Democratic response to Republican welfare initiatives in the Senate away from the Finance Committee and toward the Democratic leadership in the chamber. This paralleled the movement of policymaking from Packwood to Dole on the Republican side.

Stop and Go

As they had in the House just after the 1994 election, activist Republican governors intervened at an early point in the Senate legislative process to try to push the welfare debate toward block grants, but without the "conservative mandates" in the House Republican bill. Here the governors had a temporary advantage over their uneasy coalition partners, the conservative House Republicans, in trying to win back some of the flexibility they had lost between their January agreement with Gingrich and the final House version of the welfare reform bill. Governors could lobby hard for their positions in the Senate without offending institutional prerogatives of that chamber; House members could not so easily do this. The governors needed to gain as much as possible in the Senate because they would not have a seat at the conference table when the bill came before the House-Senate conference committee at the end of the legislative trail.

Attempting to make use of this temporary advantage, Republican governors Tommy Thompson of Wisconsin, John Engler of Michigan, and Jim Edgar of Illinois met with Packwood and other senators during the final House floor debate on welfare reform. Shortly thereafter Packwood and a number of other Finance Committee Republicans announced that they would be supporting a block grant approach—at least for AFDC—with maximum state flexibility, while Moynihan announced that he would fight to preserve AFDC's entitlement status.[25] Throughout April and early May, negotiations took place between Senate Republicans and their staff members and Republican governors, with the governors increasingly critical of the House bill. The Republican governors sought a relaxation of "conservative mandates" (including participation targets for work programs) and additional federal funding protection in recessionary periods. They also sought replacement of the Food Stamp program with a block grant to the states, which the House had refused to accept.[26]

When the Senate Finance Committee finally did act, it did so swiftly, and the results were largely consistent with the governors' wishes. In mid-May Packwood announced that his welfare bill would "give the states as much flexibility as I have the votes to give them." Echoing a refrain heard often in the House debate, Packwood admitted that his approach was not without risks, but that the status quo was simply unacceptable: "Can I guarantee that states will be successful? No. Some will, some won't. Is it worth the risk of trying? Yes."[27]

Packwood's bill had a number of similarities to the House-passed bill. States were to be given a fixed-sum block grant based on 1994 spending rather than an open-ended grant based on caseload trends. There would also be a revolving fund (slightly larger than in the House bill) from which states could borrow during economic downturns. The bill had no provision to award extra funds to states with rapidly growing populations. States were not required to maintain their existing level of spending effort for poor families or to match federal expenditures. Soft and hard time limits remained in place, too. Individuals had to participate in "work-related" activities after two years on the program and were to be limited to no more than five years in benefits financed by the new Temporary Family Assistance Grant; states were permitted to implement a stricter hard time limit. But states could exempt up to ten percent of the caseload from the five-year limit, and families who hit the limit could continue to get food stamps and Medicaid after that period.

Other provisions gave the states more flexibility than the House bill, however. Rather than requiring the states to meet narrowly defined work participation targets, the bill set escalating participation requirements in the JOBS program (which was abolished in the House-passed bill). This gave the states more options about whether to channel recipients into work, training, or education than did the House bill. The Senate bill was also silent on the issues of family caps, prohibition of cash benefits to unmarried teen mothers, and exclusion of noncitizens from eligibility, neither forbidding nor requiring states to impose such restrictions.[28] In addition, the Senate bill required states to provide child care assistance to mothers of children under age six engaged in JOBS activities. Unlike the House bill, Packwood's bill did not convert child protection/foster care programs into a capped block grant. This position reflected intense lobbying by child welfare advocates and threats by Republican Senator John Chafee to jump ship if the programs were converted.[29] The bill was estimated by the Congressional Budget Office to save $41 billion dollars over seven years, somewhat less than the comparable provisions of the broader House bill.[30]

After the long delay, committee action was swift, and Packwood proved to be a good vote counter: the Finance Committee approved Packwood's bill on May 26 after less than three days of debate. The committee did adopt without objection an amendment increasing the exemption from the five-year time limit to 15 percent of the caseload. But the committee turned down most of a series of liberalizing amendments and substitutes offered by Democrats, including a substitute offered by Senator Moynihan that would have retained entitlement status for AFDC and expanded the JOBS program, largely following party lines.[31] Packwood retained the support of all committee Republicans and one Democrat on final committee passage of the legislation.[32] He promised to bring the bill to the full Senate quickly and predicted that it would pass with at least sixty votes.[33]

A Fragile Republican Coalition

External signs about the prospects for the Packwood welfare reform bill were mixed, however. Signals from the administration were guardedly positive: White House officials did not respond to pleas from Finance Committee Democrats that the president lead a strong defense of entitlement status for AFDC. During and immediately after the Senate Finance Committee markup, the administration sent signals that the president would not veto the Packwood bill.[34] During the Finance Committee hearings, for example, Moynihan had tried to pin down an HHS official about whether the administration would veto a bill that ended AFDC entitlement. When the official gave an evasive answer, Moynihan turned to Packwood and said scornfully, "Thank you, Mr. Chairman, that's all you'll get [out of them]."[35] One administration official—understandably under the cloak of anonymity—told a reporter that AFDC was "the bone the Clinton White House can throw to the hounds at the door."[36]

There were signs on a number of other fronts that maintaining the coalition for welfare reform could grow more difficult at later stages in the Senate, however. The day that the Finance Committee passed the welfare reform bill, the Congressional Budget Office estimated that forty-four states would not be able to meet the bill's work requirements unless they devoted a majority of their federal grant to spending on job training, work placement, and other services rather than to paying cash benefits. Given the relatively modest penalties for noncompliance with work requirements, however, most states were likely not to comply and simply take the penalty.[37] Thus the administration had an opening to attack the Packwood bill as "weak on work" if it chose to do so.

There were also troubles among Republicans. A group of four conservative Republicans, including Dole's presidential rival Phil Gramm, backed a competing bill modeled after the House-passed measure and vowed to oppose a bill that did not include measures to combat illegitimacy.[38] Senator Faircloth even vowed to lead a filibuster of the Finance Committee bill unless provisions to reduce illegitimacy were added.[39] He argued at a Republican caucus meeting on June 14th that ten to fifteen Republican senators would demand illegitimacy-reducing provisions, and asked, "How do you pass a welfare bill if you have fifteen Republicans against it?"[40] Social conservative groups such as the Christian Coalition, the Family Research Council, and the Traditional Values Coalition also lobbied heavily for those provisions.[41] But Republican moderates resisted moving further to the right: at the end of June, seven moderate Republican senators also went public with strenuous objections to including illegitimacy provisions in the Senate bill.[42] If both sides held firm, the Packwood bill would probably lose on the Senate floor. Conservatives—especially Gramm—had little incentive at this point to back down and acquiesce in a Dole bill that did not fit their policy preferences and would give a political boost to Dole.[43] But would they, and their moderate opponents, be willing to take responsibility for sinking welfare reform when push came to shove, or would they back down? The question was particularly relevant for Gramm, who would not want to be seen as culpable for the failure of Congress to pass any welfare reform bill, leaving himself vulnerable to charges by Dole that Gramm would be a president who would be so isolated in his pursuit of ideological purity that he would not be able to accomplish any real policy change.

In addition, several Republican governors criticized the fixed nature of the block grant, which would require them to borrow money from the federal government to pay for increased welfare caseloads in times of recession. Ohio's George Voinovich said that he would ask Ohio's senators to vote against the bill in its current form.[44] But none of the GOP governors supported Democratic efforts to preserve AFDC's entitlement status.[45] The governors remained largely split along partisan lines, preventing their acting as a catalyst for bipartisan reform, as they had in 1988.

Yet another potential complication concerned the Packwood bill's funding formula. Like the House bill, the Finance Committee bill based family assistance block grant allocations for individual states on federal AFDC fund allocations to those states in 1994. Just before the Senate Finance Committee markup, Senator Kay Bailey Hutchinson (Republican, Texas) sent a letter to Packwood signed by a bipartisan group of thirty senators, mostly from the sunbelt (and again including Gramm), charging that their states would be subject to a double penalty under this system.[46] First, using historical allocations would lock in a pattern that had lost its policy rationale (rewarding extra state effort for poor families) with a move to a fixed sum grant. Because northern states had tended to spend more per child under AFDC, those states would receive more per child in block grant funds. Second, many sunbelt states were growing rapidly in population, but the fixed pot of funds in the block grant made no adjustment for such growth, and could do so only by taking away money from low-growth states (mostly in the north) or putting in new funds. A plan sponsored by Senator Hutchinson would have based allocations primarily on the number of poor children in a state, with a bonus to states with small populations (a political plus in the Senate, where states with small populations are represented equally with large states). Understandably, northern senators did not want to give up funding to their states from the fixed pot of available funds. Those losses would have been considerable in some states. Under the Hutchinson plan, New York would have lost $749 million annually, or almost one-third of the allocation it would have received under the Finance Committee bill. California would have lost $805 million; Michigan, Wisconsin, and Massachusetts, the home states of the activist Republican governors most involved in welfare reform, would all have lost as well.[47] Texas, however, would have gained $254 million a year.[48] Overall, thirty-six states—and 72 of 100 senators—would have been better off under the Hutchinson allocation formula. Making the stakes even higher was the expectation that any change in the allocation for the family assistance block grant would set a precedent for what was expected to be an even bigger fight over converting the much larger Medicaid program into a block grant later in 1995.[49] An obvious solution to the formula fight was to put more funds in the pot, but the Senate Republican leadership, already hard pressed to keep up with the House in deficit reduction, did not want to put in new funds that would limit its ability to meet deficit reduction targets.

Senators Gramm, Faircloth, and some other conservative Republican senators proposed an alternative solution to the funding fight: turning more programs—notably Food Stamps and the school lunch program—over to the states. This would help to even out the per capita funding disparity in the family assistance block grant, since Food Stamps—a much larger program in federal dollars than AFDC—convey greater benefits per capita in poorer, low-benefit states. Converting Food Stamps into a block grant also had some appeal to the states, since it would transfer to the states substantial control over funds for a program in which benefits are currently 100 percent financed by the federal government. But making a block grant of the Food Stamp program probably would constrict its growth during recessions, an advantage for those trying to bring the federal budget under control, but not for governors. Moreover, block granting Food Stamps had already failed to win the endorsement of the Senate Agriculture Committee.[50]

A final threat to the Packwood bill emerged from the Senate Democratic leadership. On June 8 Minority Leader Tom Daschle unveiled the outlines of a Democratic alternative welfare reform bill called "Work First." Two senators who were members of the Democratic leadership and represented opposite ends of the party's ideological spectrum—John Breaux of Louisiana and Barbara Mikulski of Maryland—also played principal roles in shaping the legislation, using as their political ideal the near unanimity among Democrats achieved by the Deal bill in the House. As might be expected from a bill designed to hold conservative Democrats and appeal to moderate Republicans, the bill contained much that made liberal Democrats—and Senator Moynihan—unhappy. Although the bill preserved individual entitlement, the new Transitional Employment Assistance (TEA) that would replace AFDC was "a conditional entitlement of limited duration." It would be made available only to those who signed a contract establishing a plan to move them from welfare to work. Moreover, all families would have to have a family member working (not in education or training) after two years. States were required to meet work participation requirements that rose to 50 percent of the caseload by the year 2000, and those that were most successful in moving recipients into work would be awarded bonus funding. The bill set an overall lifetime time limit of five years for receiving benefits under TEA, but provided a number of exemptions from the time limit and provided for continued payment through vouchers of a child's portion of the benefit.[51] To help encourage a move into work, eligibility for transitional Medicaid and child care was extended to two years after leaving TEA. And the JOBS program would be replaced with a more work-focused "Work First" block grant. But the Democratic leaders were vague on the details of the bill—they did not release a text until August—and on how they would pay for it.

Though Democratic leaders initially had little hope that the Daschle bill could beat Packwood's bill in a straight up or down contest, the bill did give Senate Democrats something to rally around besides a status quo that was perceived as indefensible—it allowed them to be "for something"—and it won the endorsement of President Clinton. This could help to prevent substantial Democratic defections to the Packwood bill on the Senate floor. Thus Senate Democrats could pursue a dual strategy. First, if an unamended Packwood bill appeared likely to pass by a narrow margin, they could use the threat of a presidential veto of that bill (assuming Clinton eventually proved willing to make such a threat) to try to compel Senate Majority Leader Dole to pursue a more bipartisan approach. At the same time, they could try to peel off enough moderate Republicans uncomfortable with the Finance Committee bill to support some elements of the Daschle bill offered as separate amendments. In short, they could try to build what they considered a better block grant requiring that states "maintain effort" (not cut their own spending) if they were to receive their full complement of block grant funds.

The bill also created internal problems for Senate Democrats, however. It committed the Senate Democratic leadership to positions on issues such as time limits that would have been unthinkable a year earlier, risking open fissures among the Democratic caucus and alienating Senator Moynihan, who, as ranking minority member of Senate Finance, would be the Democrats' floor leader when welfare reform came to the Senate floor.[52] In strategic terms, the Daschle bill (like the Deal bill in the House) ensured that any splitting of the difference between Democratic and Republican positions in the Senate would take place from a position near the right of the Democratic caucus.

It was Republican infighting that had the greatest effect on the path of welfare reform legislation, however. Most important, GOP bickering forced Senate majority leader Dole to scrub floor debate on the welfare bill originally scheduled for mid-June. It also increased efforts to find a middle ground across party lines, especially on provisions requiring state maintenance of effort.[53] It even resulted in highly personal attacks on Majority Leader Dole's chief of staff, Sheila Burke, by social conservative groups such as the Traditional Values Coalition, which accused Burke of pushing Dole into liberal positions on welfare reform.[54] Meanwhile, the Senate Budget Committee ordered the Finance Committee in early July to come up with an additional $25 billion in cuts to low-income programs to help achieve a balanced budget in seven years—making it even more difficult to resolve the formula fight by adding more money.[55]

President Clinton, attempting to take advantage of Republican divisions, stepped up his praise for the Daschle bill, chided the Republican majority in Congress for failing to send him a welfare reform bill, and reiterated his hope for a bipartisan approach to welfare reform. The president's criticism of Republican welfare reform efforts focused on insufficient funding for child care and teen mother exclusions—provisions that the polls showed were relatively unpopular (see chapter 7)—while reiterating support for time limits. The president avoided mentioning entitlements rather than block grants, once again implying that he would sign something close to the Packwood bill as long as it did not move significantly further to the right.[56] And he pledged to continue unilateral reform of welfare, with or without congressional legislation, through his administration's policy of approving more state waiver requests "in two and a half years than in the past twelve years combined."[57] Henceforth, certain types of welfare waiver requests were to be on a "fast track," getting a decision from Washington within thirty days of a state request.

Negotiations among Senate Republicans and their staffs took place through most of the early summer of 1995. To increase pressure for a settlement, Senator Dole threatened to keep the Senate in session through its usual August recess to consider welfare reform legislation. He also threatened to attach welfare legislation to the budget reconciliation bill if a freestanding bill seemed unlikely to pass.[58] Dole took over the central role in developing a leadership substitute that would build on but replace the Senate Finance Committee bill, occupying the middle political ground between the Gramm-Faircloth bill and the Democrats' Daschle bill.

In developing his substitute, Dole was able to patch up the formula fight temporarily by promising more money for states that had both high-growth rates and low benefits while protecting high-benefit states against cuts in the nominal (that is, not adjusted for inflation) value of their block grants.[59] Broadening the scope of the block grant to include other means-tested programs was also finessed by allowing, but not compelling, states to convert their participation in the Food Stamp program into a block grant, with expanded options (notably using up to 25 percent of nutrition block grant funds to employers as wage subsidies) for states that chose block grants.[60] The bill also imposed tough new work requirements on Food Stamp recipients. Dole's bill provided additional state flexibility by consolidating the JOBS program and most other training programs into a single block grant. It dropped the requirement in the Senate Finance Committee bill that parents of children under age six be provided with child care, antagonizing moderates. As a further concession to conservatives, the state option to impose teen mother exclusions, family caps, and exclusion of noncitizens that was implicit in the Finance Committee bill was made explicit in the Dole substitute.

Dole could not achieve a partisan consensus on some key issues, however. The "conservative mandates" were the most contentious. Conservative proposals to include teen mother exclusions and family caps but allow states to opt out were rejected by Packwood and other moderates.[61] Gramm, Faircloth, and conservative groups such as the Traditional Values Coalition denounced his bill as inadequate, and Faircloth threatened—but did not promise—a filibuster.[62] Some moderate Republicans, on the other hand, favored guarantees of child care for those required to work and state "maintenance of effort" requirements, which were opposed by both conservatives and the activist Republican governors. But the true "zone of acceptable outcomes" of both groups remained in doubt: neither group firmly tied its hands to reject packages with provisions it disliked. Though both conservative and moderate Republican senators could threaten to vote against a bill backed by their party's leadership and most other Republican senators, would they really do so?

Democrats had their own problems. Although President Clinton pledged his support for the Daschle bill and criticized Senator Dole's bill, administration spokespeople also sent signals that President Clinton might sign the Dole bill if some modifications were made.[63] Thus Senate Democrats who opposed the Dole bill risked being portrayed as being to the left of the president if he ended up signing a modified Dole bill passed mostly with Republican support.

Senator Dole called welfare reform up for Senate debate in early August, at a point when the Senate would normally be breaking for a summer recess. Without the agenda control afforded by the House rules process, it appeared that consideration of amendments to the welfare reform bill would be a lengthy process that would simply delay essential consideration of other legislation and highlight divisions among Republicans, with little prospect of coming to a successful resolution. With limited leverage to compel the other camps to follow his lead, and little prospect that adjusting his own position would produce a majority (even if a filibuster by conservatives could be avoided), Dole's effort to push through welfare reform before the August recess collapsed before voting on any amendments began. Senator Dole pulled the bill from the Senate floor on August 8 after less than two days of debate, with a pledge to bring it up again as soon as the Senate reconvened in September—and a threat to roll it into the budget reconciliation bill if a bill did not pass the Senate at that time.

To assemble a winning coalition for a welfare bill the next time, Dole needed to make changes in the bill that would solidify his Republican base and compel at least a few Democrats to go along. Although divisions among Republicans were deep, Dole had three things working for him. First, a large share of the Senate Republican caucus did not care deeply about the details of welfare reform and would likely follow the leadership whatever it chose. To this core of support, Dole needed to add three groups of Republicans: about twenty conservatives, seven moderates, and the Republican governors. A second advantage Dole had was that there were some differences among these three non-core groups in the areas they cared most about. Thus Dole might succeed if he could add provisions attracting moderates on issues that they cared about most (such as state maintenance of effort and child care) without alienating conservatives, while appealing to conservatives on issues of greatest concern to them (notably illegitimacy provisions) in ways that would not drive away moderates—and all the while keeping the Republican governors on board. This would be easiest in areas where the differences across the camps in issue salience were highest, where there were not big differences in principle (such as child care, where moderates cared deeply and conservatives cared less), and where differences could be ameliorated by adding more dollars. It would be far more difficult in areas where there were major differences of principle, like illegitimacy provisions. Even here there were some possibilities for compromise, such as imposing a requirement that states have family caps and teen mother exclusions, but allowing states to explicitly opt out of those provisions if they chose to do so.

A final advantage that Dole had was that none of the Republican groups wanted to be seen as blocking welfare reform, and none liked the status quo or wanted to be perceived as defending it. Thus, if it could be demonstrated through an open vote on the chamber floor that their position could not command a majority in the Senate as a whole, they probably would support final passage of a bill without the provisions they favored. This in turn meant that moderates were in a better bargaining position to get their positions adopted than either conservatives or the Republican governors: they could draw on Democratic votes to support their positions on the floor, while the other groups generally could not. Liberal Democrats were then forced to consider a classic strategy for those for whom all of the plausible options to the status quo are "bad choices." They could support "killer" amendments posed by conservatives that would make the bill less attractive to moderates in the hope that doing so would make the overall bill unappealing to conservative Democrats and moderate Republicans. The problem with this strategy, however, was that supporting "killer" amendments would likely alienate both their own supporters and the "swing" senators whose support they needed to block the bill.

Behind-the-scenes negotiations began at once. Before adjourning in August, Dole succeeded in getting key Republican governors to agree to a requirement that states maintain 75 percent of their previous spending level for the first two years of the block grant in order to receive their full complement of block grant funds. Liberal groups quickly pointed out, however, that because the Dole bill allowed a wide variety of expenditures (notably the fast-growing Medicaid program) to count toward maintenance of effort, the maintenance of effort requirement was close to meaningless.[64]

These changes in the bill were packaged with other changes designed to appeal to conservatives—for example, addition of a requirement that states be ranked annually on their success in reducing the rate of out-of-wedlock births among welfare recipients and a requirement that the Department of Health and Human Services eliminate most of the Washington-based jobs of bureaucrats responsible for overseeing family assistance payments to the states.[65] To increase the appeal of the bill to the states, various job training programs were consolidated and handed over to the states—giving the states a bigger pot of money to meet their welfare reform work participation rates, but raising charges from Democrats that the changes would placate governors at the expense of promises made to workers dislocated by free trade agreements and imports or by closings of military bases.[66]

Dole did indeed enjoy greater success on welfare reform in September, despite his inability to arrive at a Republican consensus on illegitimacy provisions of the bill. Dole's strategy was simply to allow the unsettled arguments to be settled in floor votes on amendments to his welfare bill, while getting his colleagues to agree not to block final passage of the bill.[67] In a week-long debate that was dramatically interrupted by Senator Bob Packwood's announcement that he would resign from his Senate seat, Dole demonstrated once again how he earned his reputation as a legislative tactician, smoking out the center of policy gravity in a series of votes, then building a Senate majority and coopting the White House into the process of reform on largely Republican terms. Daschle's Democratic alternative preserving entitlement status for welfare payments was first defeated on a near-party-line vote.[68] Dole then introduced another package of amendments that once again attempted to move simultaneously right and left. A mandatory family cap and bonuses to states that reduced out-of-wedlock births were added in an effort to gain conservative support. To appeal to moderates, the new bill had a firmer (though short-term) maintenance of effort requirement and a provision prohibiting states from cutting off benefits to women with children under age six if they refused to work because of a lack of appropriate or affordable child care.[69] Senators from both parties filed more than 200 amendments to the bill, threatening yet another stalemate.[70]

When voting on amendments began in earnest, the Republican majority was able to defeat most of the proposed revisions to the bill. Two votes revealed, however, that the ideological center in the Senate was still to the left of the Dole bill: a Democratic initiative to expand child care assistance dramatically fell short by only two votes, and another amendment to require states to maintain 90 percent of their current spending levels for five years failed by a single vote—and then only after Republican leaders agreed to back an 80 percent state "maintenance of effort" requirement. Republican senator Pete Domenici then led an effort to make family caps a state option; it passed by an overwhelming margin, 66-34. A series of Faircloth amendments to exclude teen mothers from benefits financed by the federal government were defeated later the same day by even greater margins.

When the Senate broke for the weekend, it appeared that Dole was well on the way to producing a strong Senate majority for a welfare reform bill. Dole's initiative received an even bigger boost over the weekend. On that Friday President Clinton received a draft report from HHS secretary Donna Shalala arguing that the Senate welfare bill would push more than a million more children into poverty. He nevertheless used his weekly Saturday radio address to give the Senate bill an endorsement in principle, while warning that if the bill moved further to the right in conference negotiations with the House, he would veto it.[71] The president's endorsement made it politically much more difficult for Senate Democrats to oppose the bill, for in so doing they could appear to be to the left of the president if he went ahead and signed the legislation. Political expediency suggested matching the president's expanded "zone of acceptable outcomes."

Final passage came swiftly the following week. With the two main deterrence-oriented illegitimacy proposals (family caps and teen mother exclusions) clearly established as minority positions and therefore excluded from the bill, Dole offered a package of amendments intended to solidify the support of a broad coalition of moderate Republicans and Democrats. These amendments included more money for child care and for states facing economic downturns. Conservative Republicans were isolated and decisively outvoted, mustering only eleven votes in opposition to Dole's package. They were joined by only one Democrat: Senator Moynihan, who, having decided that the bill was an abomination that would lead to a major increase in poverty and homelessness for children, refused to back amendments that would increase its prospects for passage. In the vote on final Senate passage of the revised Dole bill, liberal Democrats were isolated on the losing end of an 87-12 vote.[72]

Several factors contributed to Dole's ability to build a huge bipartisan coalition after several false starts. Probably the most important was the desire of both the White House and many Senate Democrats to avoid being perceived as obstructionist holdouts against welfare reform. Also important was the decision of conservative senators like Gramm and Faircloth not to carry out filibuster threats if the bill failed to include anti-illegitimacy provisions that they wanted. Ultimately, they recognized that their chances of obtaining their policy preferences would be improved by carrying the bill forward to a conference with the House (where the bill did contain those measures) rather than by blocking it.

Aftershocks

The passage of the Senate welfare reform bill with a quasi-endorsement from the president and the support of an overwhelming majority of Democratic senators is perhaps the most important single event in the history of the legislation; it fundamentally altered the nature of subsequent bargaining over welfare reform. The president shifted his "zone of acceptable outcomes" even further to the right than the Deal bill in the House, accepting an end to individual entitlement to AFDC benefits. Most Senate Democrats, pursuing a matching strategy, also moved far to the right. Moreover, both had their room for future maneuver dramatically constricted. Having already endorsed the Senate bill, President Clinton could not later refuse to back a bill with similar provisions without being vulnerable to Republican charges that he was not really interested in reforming welfare. The majority of Senate

Democrats who had voted for the legislation (and who did not in any case want to take a position to the left of the president) were in the same boat: they, too, would have problems backing away from the Senate legislation.

Republicans gained critically on both individual components of welfare reform and in more general bargaining leverage. Since the president and most Democratic senators had already conceded an end to individual AFDC entitlement and the imposition of hard time limits in signing on to the Senate welfare reform bill, there was no reason for Republicans to make concessions on those issues in future negotiations. Passage of the Senate bill allowed Republicans to try to push welfare reform further to the right while setting a minimum gain—a new default position—to which Republicans could return at any time if negotiations with the administration broke down. In effect, the Senate bill became the most liberal possible outcome if any welfare legislation was to be enacted.

Thus from September 1995 on, welfare reform negotiations would not be driven by whether the president would assent to some Republican-sponsored welfare reform package. His endorsement in principle of the Senate bill answered that question. Instead, three other issues became critical. First, how much further could the administration be pushed to the right? Second, could House and Senate Republicans reach an agreement among themselves and their outside support coalition on a welfare reform package near or somewhat to the right of the Senate bill? Third, and somewhat related to the second question, would the Republicans put a higher priority on passing legislation (while sharing some of the credit with the President) or on having an election issue—the president's unwillingness to agree on welfare reform legislation—with which they could bash the president?

Passage of the Senate bill also energized child advocacy groups and intensified conflict within the Democratic camp—both within the administration and between the administration and congressional Democrats. Within the Clinton administration there was, as noted earlier, a "basic tension . . . between the folks in the administration who more or less desperately wanted a welfare reform bill, and the folks in the administration who didn't."[73] In the immediate aftermath of Senate passage of the Dole package, this conflict focused on release of the administration's estimates of the impact on poverty of the Senate welfare reform bill. Although White House officials had initially leaked news that those estimates existed in order to demonstrate that the president could stand up to pressure from liberals within his own party, they were reluctant to release the actual figures for fear that they would embarrass the president. Liberal Democrats, led by Senator

Daniel Patrick Moynihan, put pressure on the White House to release the estimates, viewing them, as one HHS official put it, as "a way of just putting into a ten-second sound bite the pain of the bill." After initially denying that reliable estimates existed, the White House eventually had to release the numbers, just as the conferees were working on the welfare bill.

Child advocacy groups also began to challenge President Clinton more openly. On November 3, after President Clinton had indicated that he might sign the Republican-sponsored welfare reform bill that had passed the Senate with a bipartisan majority, Children's Defense Fund head Marian Wright Edelman published a blistering "open letter to the president" in the *Washington Post*, demanding that he veto it. She argued that both the Senate bill and its more conservative House-passed counterpart "are morally and practically indefensible. . . . Both are fatally flawed, callous, anti-child assaults. Both bills eviscerate the moral compact between the nation and its children and its poor." It would, she argued, "be a tragic irony . . . for this regressive attack on children and the poor to occur on your watch. For me, this is a defining moral litmus test for your presidency."[74] Clinton was reported to have told acquaintances that he was feeling "huge heat" over the welfare reform bill from congressional Democrats and advocacy groups.[75] As the next chapter will show, President Clinton did veto the welfare bill that emerged from the conference committee in the fall of 1995. But he did not alter his fundamental objective of achieving an accommodation with the Republican-controlled Congress and seeing welfare reform enacted.

CHAPTER TWELVE

Endgames and Aftershocks

PASSAGE OF THE Dole welfare reform bill in the Senate, with the support of the president and the votes of many Senate Democrats, showed that it was possible to obtain presidential approval for a Republican-oriented welfare reform package significantly more conservative than President Clinton's own 1994 proposal. It essentially created a new bargaining game in which the potential outcomes ranged from the Senate-passed bill on the liberal end of the spectrum to the House-passed bill on the conservative end, plus the possibility that the status quo could remain in place if the process broke down through Republican "strategic disagreement" or a presidential veto. Furthermore, it dramatically strengthened Republicans' bargaining leverage vis-à-vis the president and congressional Democrats.

Passage of the Senate welfare bill did not make enactment of welfare reform a sure thing, however. It was by no means clear that the coalition that supported the Senate bill would move much further to the right unless the president moved too, or that House Republicans and their allies among the conservative pro-family groups would agree to drop many of their favored provisions from the House bill. House Republicans could certainly be expected to probe to see how much further President Clinton could be pushed to the right. The result was yet another process of stop-and-go policymaking.

In the end it took eleven months, and three distinct "subrounds" of policymaking, after passage of the Senate welfare bill in September 1995 to enact welfare reform legislation. Each of the first two subrounds altered the contours of legislative bargaining in later rounds. Republicans tried both using an omnibus reconciliation bill and passing a separate welfare bill to gain presidential assent, but both initiatives ended in presidential vetoes. When these strategies failed, they considered simply passing the Senate bill President Clinton had tentatively endorsed in September, but this option was overtaken when the nation's governors jump-started the process yet again. When this process stalled as well, bringing welfare reform to closure required both a clear decision by Republican leaders to pass legislation rather than pursuing strategic disagreement with the president and a continuation of the administration's strategy of seeking accommodation with the Republicans.

Bargaining Positions and Bargaining Rules

Even if the provisions on which the welfare reform bills passed by the House and Senate were in agreement had been enacted, it would have constituted a remarkable transformation of federal policy toward low-income families. Both bills retained "state entitlement" status for the AFDC program for the states: that is, block grant funds to the states would not have to be appropriated, but would be guaranteed to the states. "Individual entitlement" was ended in both bills, however: poor children and their families would no longer have a legal claim on funds if they met state eligibility criteria. Both bills required adult recipients of block grant funds to work within two years of receiving family assistance block grant funds and placed a five-year overall lifetime limit on federally subsidized benefits.

Important differences remained between the House and Senate welfare reform bills, however, reflecting the greater leverage of Republican moderates and Democrats in the Senate.[1] These differences were especially evident in the bills' deterrence provisions. The House bill mandated that states both adopt a family cap and deny cash benefits for teen mothers; the Senate bill contained neither mandate. The Senate bill allowed states to exempt a higher percentage of their caseloads (20 percent versus 10 percent) from the five-year lifetime "hard" time limit. The Senate bill required the states to maintain 80 percent of their previous spending level (maintenance of effort) in spending on low-income families or suffer financial penalties, and it was more generous in the activities it counted toward meeting state work participation rates.

The non-AFDC portions of the welfare reform bill contained important differences as well. The House bill converted the school lunch and child protection (foster care) programs into capped block grants, while the Senate bill did not. And the House bill made deeper cuts in Supplemental Security

Income benefits for disabled children and benefits for immigrants. Overall the Congressional Budget Office estimated the House bill would save $62.1 billion over five years and $102 billion over seven years—substantially more than the Senate figures of $38.6 billion and $65.8 billion.[2]

While the Senate roll calls had demonstrated that the House bill could not pass the Senate, it was not clear how far the Senate bill could move toward the House position in negotiations on a conference bill and still command a Senate majority, let alone gain the signature of the president, who became even more elusive about his own policy bottom line than he had been throughout most of 1995.[3] On the surface, there was a straightforward way to resolve differences over welfare. Since the president had already indicated that he found the Senate bill acceptable, but would tolerate very little in the way of additional deterrence-oriented provisions from the House bill, the House could simply accept the provisions from the Senate bill, send that bill to the president, and attempt to claim that they, not the president, were really responsible for "ending welfare as we know it." Attempting to get more than those provisions might simply lead to a stalemate.

For the House members to fold, however, they had to believe several things: that the president was sincere in his statements that he would not sign a bill significantly closer to the conservatives' proposal; that he would sign something close to the Senate bill; and that enacting the Senate bill was a more desirable outcome than the risk of having no bill at all—especially since a presidential veto would give the Republicans a chance to castigate Clinton as hypocritical in his professed desire to end welfare as we know it.

Whether the president would stand by his pledge to veto a bill that contained many of the House provisions that he disliked seemed open to question. President Clinton warned the Republicans that if they strayed too far from the Senate bill by passing "a bill that is weak on work and tough on children," he would veto it and pursue a process of welfare reform through waivers to individual states. He also sought, in the words of a *New York Times* story, to "rebut conventional wisdom that says he will sign almost any welfare bill sent to him by Congress," and argue that Congress would be to blame for the failure of welfare reform if they did not compromise.[4] Predictably Republican leaders like House Ways and Means subcommittee chair Clay Shaw sought to toss the blame right back, accusing the president of "looking for reasons to veto the bill" and "caving in to the liberal wing of the Democratic party," while arguing that if the president failed to sign welfare reform legislation passed by Congress, it would constitute "a breach of faith with the American people."[5] Having navigated this far through the multiple welfare policymaking traps, the major remaining risks to passage of welfare reform were that Republicans would overplay their hand for the sake of political gain, risking passage of welfare reform for the electoral opportunity to present the president as a hypocrite who was not really committed to welfare reform, or that conservatives in the House would refuse to go along with a compromise bill that lacked many of the anti-illegitimacy provisions that they sought.

Groups on the outside of government also attempted to influence the process. The National Governors' Association, the most important intergovernmental lobby, was able to break its prolonged stalemate long enough to agree that any welfare bill should provide more money for child care and additional protection against recessions and that conservative as well as liberal mandates (for example, teen mother exclusions and family caps) should be minimized.[6] Groups representing local governments—the National League of Cities, the National Association of Counties, and the U.S. Conference of Mayors—endorsed many elements of the Senate bill, notably state maintenance of effort requirements, because they feared that cutbacks at the state level would lead to increased demand for locally funded services. The U.S. Catholic Conference urged caution on provisions that might encourage abortions.[7] Liberal advocacy groups and some congressional Democrats, meanwhile, tried to strengthen the dual clientele trap by pressing the White House to release an administration report stating that an additional 1 million children would be pushed into poverty by the Senate welfare reform plan, and an even higher number by the House welfare bill.[8]

Although far from a sure thing, a welfare reform bill largely consistent with Republican preferences nevertheless appeared to have good prospects for final passage. The apparently weak bargaining position of the president gave Republicans an important advantage. Republicans knew that President Clinton, having pledged to end welfare as we know it, would be hard pressed to veto any welfare reform proposal (whether as a separate piece of legislation or as part of a budget reconciliation bill) that did just that by converting it from an entitlement into a block grant and imposing stiff work requirements. Indeed, the administration resisted efforts to tie the president's hands to a bottom line of what he would not accept, in part because of fears that the Republicans would come right up to that point—that is, that whatever minimum conditions he specified would become the Republican's minimum from the other direction.

Endgame One: The Budget Process and Initial Vetoes

Reconciling the House and Senate versions of the welfare reform bill ultimately took more than three months, with much of the delay concerning not AFDC but rather a dispute about whether the school lunch program should be turned over to the states in a block grant. Conferees finally agreed in December on a bill turning AFDC into a block grant that would remain essentially fixed in nominal terms–and thus decline in real dollar value—for five years. (Minor funding adjustments were allowed for states growing rapidly in population, and for those undergoing recession.) Thus the block grant would freeze the current interstate distribution of funds that confers advantages on wealthier states—largely because any attempt to change that distribution would inevitably create visible winners and losers among states, reducing the prospects for congressional passage of legislation.

The conference agreement would also have imposed some new specific policy mandates on the states, generally splitting the difference between the House and Senate bills. States would be prohibited from using federal funds to provide assistance to individual families for more than sixty months, consecutively or nonconsecutively. States could exempt up to 15 percent of their caseloads from this limit, a compromise between the House and Senate positions. And states would have to meet tough targets for moving recipients from welfare into work or face losing 5 percent of their federal funding. On the anti-illegitimacy mandates, there was a classic congressional compromise, splitting the difference: states could choose to opt in to teen mother exclusions, but they did not have to do so. States would have to impose family caps, however, unless the state legislature explicitly voted to opt out.

The conference agreement was sent to President Clinton for his signature twice. In December it was included in a congressionally passed reconciliation bill that included unpopular cuts in the Medicare and Medicaid programs, and the president vetoed it. Congress then sent a separate welfare package to the president, this time without the health care cuts. But the bill still contained other controversial cuts and structural changes in the Food Stamp and School Lunch programs and immigrant benefits, and the president focused on those provisions in vetoing welfare reform again, arguing that the welfare bill "was designed to meet an arbitrary budget target rather than to achieve serious reform."[9]

Endgame Two: The Senate Bill and Gubernatorial Intervention

As a result of these vetoes and the failure of budget negotiations between the president and Republican congressional leaders, the Republican deficit reduction and devolution agendas both appeared to be in a shambles at the beginning of 1996. Congressional Republicans briefly considered a strategy of embarrassing the president by passing the Senate welfare reform bill that he had indicated he would support the previous September and forcing him either to veto it or to sign it. But this strategy was superseded in February of 1996 by yet another intervention from the governors. At their winter meeting in Washington the governors, who had been unable the previous year to arrive at a bipartisan agreement, now proposed a package of reforms to both Medicaid and cash welfare programs that won the unanimous support of all fifty governors.

Rather than a new piece of legislation, the governors' package was a sketchy set of proposed modifications to the Republican welfare conference bill vetoed by the president in January. Not surprisingly, the governors' modifications focused on areas where Democratic as well as Republican governors had common interests: increasing funding to the states (most notably an additional $4 billion in entitlement funds for child care—with no requirement for a state match—and an additional $1 billion in contingency funds), as well as increased flexibility for the states (for example, higher allowable caseload exemptions to the five-year time limit and making family caps a state option rather than a mandate with state opt-out) and easing the work participation rate requirements.[10] Medicaid provisions suggested in the governors' package also included fiscal relief and additional flexibility for the states. Overall, the Congressional Budget Office estimated that the governors' proposal would reduce non-Medicaid savings from about $60.4 billion over seven years in the conference agreement to about $43 billion—that is, by almost a third.[11]

Why did the governors agree to back such a package after more than a year of stalemate? Several forces were at work. Part of the answer lies in states' need to be able to plan budgets that meet state balanced budget requirements. Governors in several states, including California and New York, were relying on increased flexibility to reduce AFDC and Medicaid expenditures and a change in the Medicaid funding formula included in the Republican budget reconciliation bill that would benefit wealthier states to help balance their state budgets. The collapse of budget talks between President Clinton and congressional Republicans appeared to sink this possibility—and with it the budget savings those governors had counted on.[12] For all governors, prolonged uncertainty meant that their own state budgets would be based on guesswork.[13] Moreover, as the waiver process moved forward, more governors became comfortable with increased flexibility in the use of state funds. With AFDC entitlement seen as a dead letter anyway, additional flexibility to use federal money for child care and work programs was increasingly attractive, even to many Democrats.

In addition, it was clear by early 1996 that AFDC caseloads were declining in most states—and in some states quite dramatically. For those states a block grant based on earlier years' spending levels offered not only more flexibility but also more money in the near term than they would get under AFDC. Reaching a bipartisan NGA agreement also offered a way to give state concerns more leverage in a welfare reform legislative process that was likely to move forward with them or without them. Finally, organizational leadership mattered: Howard Dean, an implacable foe of welfare reform focused on devolution, was replaced as chair of the NGA by Tommy Thompson, Wisconsin's Republican governor, one of its primary proponents.

Once again, however, the problem was how to develop a package that contained terms of devolution that were simultaneously acceptable to all the political forces that would have to approve it. These disputes centered on issues of mandates and the extent of deficit reduction. Conservatives in the House insisted on mandates to reduce illegitimacy and tight limits on exemptions to the five-year time limits.[14] As a key Republican staffer put the problem:

> We could put this on the president's desk, bipartisan, except that we're going to have to change the governors' proposal, because they [conservative groups] definitely would sink it. . . . They'll make it a key vote [in their voter guides]. If it doesn't have a family cap, any Republican who votes yes is making a key vote against the Christian Coalition. That will cost us a good forty to fifty votes [in the House].[15]

Republican moderates in the Senate as well as governors and the White House resisted those mandates and sought additional federal funds for child care. The White House also insisted on vouchers to protect children whose parents hit the five-year time limit on welfare benefits.[16] Congressional budget committees had a different objective: additional budget savings. Republican governors insisted on linking welfare reform with Medicaid reforms—a much bigger item in state budgets, where they hoped for substantial savings and flexibility—but the White House repeatedly insisted that Republican Medicaid cuts were unacceptable. Indeed, the president repeatedly dared Republicans to send him a separate welfare bill stripped of Medicaid provisions.

Further complicating congressional reactions to the governors' February welfare reform initiative was the evolving race for the Republican presidential nomination. Phil Gramm, one of the leading Senate advocates of the deterrence approach, stumbled badly in the early Republican caucus states of Louisiana and Iowa. He withdrew from the race before the New Hampshire primary, endorsing Robert Dole. After some problems of his own in the first Republican primaries, Dole emerged as the clear frontrunner for the Republican presidential nomination in early March. Even Speaker Gingrich, who years earlier had derided Dole as the "tax collector for the welfare state," began to urge other Republican presidential candidates to withdraw so that the party could focus on attacking Clinton.

Republicans in the Dole presidential campaign and on Capitol Hill faced not only conflicting pressures on specific provisions of the welfare reform bill, but also the classic strategic question of whether it was better to have a bill or an issue.[17] Some Republicans, such as Ways and Means subcommittee chair Clay Shaw, wanted to get a welfare reform bill through that would be enacted. Others wanted to keep sending the president welfare bills that he was likely to veto in order to paint the president as hypocritical in his pledge to reform welfare. Still others wanted to do nothing, arguing that two vetoes were enough to run against the president and fearing that if the Republican Congress sent the president a bill that was even partially acceptable, the president would sign it and get most of the public credit for ending welfare as we know it.[18] But doing nothing also had costs as long as Dole remained in the Senate (he resigned in mid-May), because the president could blame Dole for not moving a welfare bill.

Congressional Democrats also faced a political dilemma that revolved around avoiding blame. Liberal Democrats were certain to oppose any bill the Republicans might bring forward, and some conservative Democrats were almost equally certain to back a Republican bill. But many moderate Democrats were on the fence: they had deep policy reservations about elements in the Republican bill, but they did not want to end up on the wrong side of a popular legislative initiative. In short, they would set their "zone of acceptable outcomes" based on the amount of cover provided by other policymakers, especially President Clinton. But those zones of acceptable outcomes were likely to be very wide if the only alternative to supporting a

Republican bill was a vote for the status quo. The endorsement of a welfare reform package by the National Governors' Association made resistance to welfare reform even more difficult, since the NGA endorsement had made welfare reform appear more bipartisan. From the Democratic legislators' perspective, the worst case scenario would be to vote against a Republican welfare bill that passed anyway and was then signed by the president: to do so would play right into the hands of Republican accusations that they were "too liberal" in the upcoming elections.[19]

Thus Democratic opponents of welfare reform on Republican terms were trapped in a Catch-22: in deciding how hard to resist Republican welfare reform initiatives, they were constantly looking over their shoulders for assurances that the president would provide them with political protection. What they saw was not very reassuring. Democratic legislators could not help but be aware that one of the president's chief political advisors, Dick Morris, was pushing a "triangulation" strategy in which the president positioned himself ideologically between congressional Republicans and Democrats, confronting the new congressional majority on issues such as opposition to cuts in Medicare and Medicaid, where the Democratic position had broad popular support, but working with Republicans on issues like balancing the budget, where Republican positions were more popular.[20] The unpopularity of welfare reform made it a poor candidate for presidential confrontation. And the president's repeated pleas that the Republicans send him a clean welfare bill undercut his leverage to veto such a bill if he got one. The president was likely to veto a congressional welfare reform only if it had encountered solid Democratic opposition to that bill in Congress, but his own unclear signals were making that much less likely.[21]

As Republicans blasted presidential obstructionism on welfare, President Clinton used several strategies to inoculate himself against those charges. He signed executive orders forcing states to implement tougher rules on keeping teen mothers in school and requiring AFDC mothers to cooperate in locating their children's fathers.[22] He trumpeted his record in granting state waivers and promising to end welfare one state at a time through waivers if the Republicans failed to pass acceptable legislation. President Clinton also publicly praised a dramatic welfare plan submitted for federal approval by Wisconsin's Republican governor, Tommy Thompson—and then more quietly backed away from his endorsement, while Republicans tried to make sure that he in fact approved it.[23]

Endgame Three: Moving a Bill

House and Senate Republicans introduced their revised welfare proposals in May 1996 as Republican rather than bipartisan bills. While the bills contained many of the welfare reform proposals endorsed by the NGA, other provisions were closer to the Republican congressional bills of 1995. Moreover, the bills proposed cutting $10 billion more than the NGA proposal and linked welfare and Medicaid reform. Democratic governors and the administration pronounced several of the provisions unacceptable. It appeared that no compromise could be worked out that would allow welfare reform to move forward. This raised hopes among liberal Democrats in Congress that the impasse might last through the 1996 election, with no welfare reform legislation enacted.[24]

The outlook for enacting welfare reform legislation remained uncertain as the Republicans moved their bills through committees largely on party-line votes, because the Republicans could modify their bill and split off the Medicaid provisions at any time if they decided that they wanted to have a statute rather than an issue. Republicans also had the advantage of a procedural ace-in-the-hole that increased their bargaining leverage if they decided to move a separate welfare bill quickly. Because they had designated the welfare reform bill as a deficit-reducing reconciliation bill, they had reduced the prospects that it could be subject to procedural delays and multiple amendments—and even filibuster—in the Senate. Republican efforts were also aided by the refusal of the Clinton administration (which sought to keep open the president's option to sign a welfare bill) to prepare estimates of how many additional children would be put into poverty if the new Republican welfare bills passed—information that had helped liberal advocacy groups mobilize opposition to Republican welfare bills in the fall of 1995.[25]

As long as welfare reform remained linked to politically unpopular Medicaid reform, the stalemate between the Republican Congress and President Clinton was unlikely to be broken. But a changing mood among Republican members in the House eroded their commitment to this linkage. Polls in the early summer of 1996 showed voters favoring Democratic candidates over Republicans by a substantial margin, indicating that the Republicans might lose control of Congress in the upcoming election.[26] These polls served as a dual wake-up call to Republicans. First, if members hoped to get reelected, they should enact welfare reform so that they would not be vulnerable to Democratic charges that their revolutionary fervor had resulted in little legislation.[27] Second, if they might lose control of Congress in the fall, they should act quickly to end welfare as we know it on Republican terms. In June two junior Ways and Means Committee Republicans circulated a letter that asked Speaker Gingrich and new Senate Majority Leader Trent Lott to separate welfare reform and Medicaid reform as a necessary prelude to enacting the former. They gathered almost 100 signatures from House Republicans.[28] Congressional Democrats, meanwhile, moved in the opposite direction: six of nine Democrats on the Senate Finance Committee voted against an amendment to strip Medicaid provisions from the welfare bill because they feared that many Democrats in Congress would not vote against, and the president would not veto, a "clean" welfare bill with provisions that they found unacceptable.[29]

On July 11, 1996, Republican leaders in Congress announced that they were delinking Medicaid and welfare reform. As Ways and Means Committee chair Bill Archer put it, "Mr. President, we are calling your bluff. It's time to either put up or stop the rhetoric."[30] Sending the president a separate welfare reform bill, Republicans hoped, would force the president either to veto it, dividing the Democratic party on the eve of his renominating convention, or reveal his promise to end welfare as we know it as hypocrisy.[31] The president tried to improve his bargaining position by demanding additional changes in the bill, but administration officials also undercut the administration's ability to get more changes by avoiding direct veto threats and sending signals that he would sign whatever the Republicans sent.[32] Indeed, in order to produce additional savings, House Republicans passed an amendment on the House floor to significantly stiffen the bill's work requirements for adult food stamp recipients who have no dependents. Despite the White House's urging that House Democrats vote against the bill to gain additional leverage in conference negotiations, the bill passed the House with almost solid Republican support and thirty Democrats defecting to back the bill. Moreover, House and Senate Republican negotiators began working on a final joint bill even before either chamber voted on the bill.[33]

Five days after House action, the Senate approved a slightly softer Senate bill with nearly solid Republican support and half of Democratic senators voting in favor. While the White House called for additional concessions in conference committee, it did not say that it would veto the bill if they were not made.[34] Nor did the administration prepare and release, as it had in 1995, estimates of how many children would be moved into poverty by the welfare reform legislation; indeed it sought to squelch such estimates and cast doubt on their validity. The numbers were released anyway by the Urban Institute, the Washington think tank that had prepared the original poverty estimates for the administration. They showed that more than a million additional children were likely to be moved into poverty.[35]

Sensing that their nightmare was about to occur, advocacy groups for children mobilized to press for a veto.[36] But their leverage with the president remained weak. The Children's Defense Fund (CDF) had already organized a massive "Stand for Children" March in Washington, held in June 1996. While the CDF managed to attract a broad array of groups as sponsors for the event, it was able to do so only by muting the political tone of the event. Moreover, media coverage nevertheless gave prominent coverage to conservative organizations' denunciations of the event as a campaign for a failed liberal agenda.[37] In any case, it appears to have had little effect on the Clinton administration or other policymakers.

While the president's advisors continued to threaten a veto if further movement toward the president's position did not occur in the conference committee, many Republican leaders in Congress believed that Clinton would sign virtually anything that he was sent.[38] The prospects for major concessions by the Republican majority in conference were further limited by the rules of conference committees, which ostensibly prohibit reopening issues on which the House and Senate bills agree or adding new provisions, and by more informal conference norms, which generally limit the scope of change to somewhere between the House and Senate provisions rather than something outside their scope.[39] Both conference rules and norms can be violated when there is a strong agreement among conferees that doing so is desirable and necessary to enact legislation. But where that agreement is absent—as it was on the welfare bill—opponents of concessions have strong bargaining leverage to resist moving too far toward the president's position.

Conferees moved quickly, seeking to head off the mobilization efforts of liberal advocacy groups and to force the president to declare before the Democratic convention whether he would sign a final welfare bill. In their accord, conferees moved toward Senate positions on a number of provisions but did not go as far as the president had requested. As the Republicans moved to bring the conference report up for final passage in the House the day after reaching an agreement, Democrats sought a strong signal from the president about his intentions. In the words of Representative Robert Matsui (Democrat, California), "Most members would like to know what he is going to do. If the president supports it, they will support it. . . . A lot of members just don't want to be to the left of the president on welfare."[40] The morning of the scheduled House vote, the president held a long meeting with his cabinet and top political advisors. Health and Human Services secretary Donna Shalala, Treasury secretary Rubin, Chief of Staff Leon Panetta, and others urged a veto, while Bruce Reed, presidential political advisor Rahm Emmanuel, and Commerce secretary Mickey Kantor urged that he sign it. Presidential pollster Dick Morris, although not present at the meeting, sent a warning that failure to veto the bill could turn a projected fifteen-point Clinton victory over Dole in the fall presidential election into a three-point loss.[41] After meeting privately with Panetta and Vice President Al Gore, the president announced that he would sign the bill and work for revisions (mostly in non-AFDC provisions) in the next Congress. Both chambers quickly passed the welfare bill by overall margins of more than three to one, with Democrats almost evenly split.[42]

Provisions of the Personal Responsibility and Work Opportunity Reconciliation Act

The legislation signed by the president, the Personal Responsibility and Work Opportunity Reconciliation Act of 1996 (PRWORA), makes dramatic changes in family assistance and other means-tested programs (table 12-1). The AFDC and JOBS programs were abolished, replaced by a block grant to the states, Temporary Assistance to Needy Families (TANF). Individual entitlement to family assistance benefits under federal law was ended.[43] Individual entitlement could still exist under state law, and welfare recipients would still be able to sue in state courts for benefits promised under state law. But welfare clients and advocates and Legal Services lawyers would henceforth have few claims in *federal* court.[44]

TANF funds are provided as a block grant that is an essentially fixed sum in nominal terms, based on the total amount being spent at the time of the legislation by the federal government on AFDC and AFDC administration, JOBS, and Emergency Assistance. Thus TANF funds would decline in real terms over time, with faster declines if inflation is high. Federal outlays on TANF would no longer play a countercyclical role, rising as unemployment increased welfare rolls. On the other hand, if TANF caseloads fall rapidly, the states enjoy a fiscal windfall, since their funding remains fixed through fiscal year 2002.

The thorny political question of how to distribute funds among the states was resolved by basing each state's share of the block grant on that state's historical spending on AFDC. To resolve conflicts between states that had already reduced their caseloads substantially (and therefore would be penalized if their most recent year's spending was used as the benchmark) and those that had not, states were allowed to choose the most favorable of three benchmark periods. Limited contingency funds were also provided for periods of recession. Given the healthy U.S. economy and immense declines in caseloads that had already begun by 1996 and accelerated under TANF, states have in fact gotten more funds from TANF than they would have received under the old AFDC program. States are required to maintain 80 percent of their own previous AFDC spending to draw down their full share of federal block grant funds, however. States that meet work requirements need only maintain 75 percent effort.

Specific features of the new TANF program reveal many compromises and trade-offs between differing approaches to welfare reform. On issues of illegitimacy and of program eligibility and entry, proponents of deterrence approaches enjoyed limited success. Teen parents were required to live with parents or in an adult-supervised setting—a provision that the Clinton administration had also endorsed. No requirements for family caps or exclusions for teen mothers were included in PRWORA, but states were implicitly allowed to impose those restrictions themselves if they chose to do so. To placate social conservatives on the loss of illegitimacy mandates in the House bill, PRWORA had a provision for competitive bonuses of up to $20 million a year for each of up to five states that were most successful in reducing illegitimacy.

Competition between congressional Republicans and the Clinton administration to appear "tough on work" led to strict, escalating work requirements, with rising penalties for states that did not meet the requirements, but a lot of discretion for the federal Department of Health and Human Services to impose those penalties. By 2002 states will be required to have 50 percent of their caseloads in work activities—at least thirty hours a week by the year 2000—with higher requirements for two-parent families. The act provides additional funding for child care over that anticipated under the pre-1996 law, but no entitlement to that care. Families of children under age six are protected from a benefit cutoff if they cannot find child care. PRWORA also allowed states to pursue much more generous "incentive-oriented" policies if they chose to do so by ending federal restrictions on earnings disregards.

Proponents of deterrence approaches enjoyed greater success in imposing hard time limits to avoid long-term dependence on federal TANF funds.

Table 12-1. Selected Changes in Federal Law toward Low-Income Families Effected by the Personal Responsibility and Work Opportunity Reconciliation Act of 1996

Aid to Families with Dependent Children (AFDC)	Personal Responsibility and Work Opportunity Reconciliation Act of 1996 (PRWORA)
Program structure and financing	
ENTITLEMENT	
States legally entitled to AFDC funds according to funding formula in federal law; individual recipients legally entitled based on eligibility and benefit criteria established in state law (following federal guidelines)	States legally entitled to funds based on formula in federal block grant; individuals have no legal entitlement to benefits
FUNDING ALLOCATION FORMULA TO STATES	
Federal government matches state AFDC benefit and administrative expenditures on open-ended basis, with higher match rates for poorer states; JOBS is capped entitlement requiring state match	Federal payments to states are largely fixed in nominal terms for five years, with some relief for rapidly growing states and in the event of inflation; individual state TANF allocations based on AFDC allocations in previous years (states can choose from three benchmark periods)
SUPPLEMENTAL AND CONTINGENCY FUNDS	
No provision, since federal funding adjusts automatically to program population	$2 billion contingency grant and $1.7 billion loan funds established for recessionary periods, with an additional $800 million grant fund for use in high-growth states with low benefit levels
MAINTENANCE OF EFFORT	
Federal funding depends on state expenditure based on matching formula	States must maintain 80 percent of their historic state fund spending levels (75 percent if they meet work participation requirements) or face dollar-for-dollar loss of federal TANF funds[a]

continued

PROGRAM FLEXIBILITY

States can shift up to 30 percent of TANF funds to Child Care block grant and Social Services block grant, with some restrictions

No switching funds between programs permitted

Program entry issues

FAMILY CAPS AND TEEN MOTHER EXCLUSIONS

States allowed to impose family caps (no increase in benefits if an additional child is born outside marriage while mother is receiving benefits) and deny assistance to unmarried teen mothers without federal permission in TANF

No provision on family caps and teen mother exclusions in AFDC (states could apply for waivers)[b]

TEEN PARENTS

Almost all teen parents required to live with parents or other responsible adults rather than setting up their own households

States have option to require AFDC teen mothers to live at home; no federal requirement

ILLEGITIMACY REDUCTION BONUS

$100 million per year in 1999–2002 awarded to up to five states that succeed in reducing out-of-wedlock births without increasing abortions

No provision.

RESIDENCY REQUIREMENTS

States allowed to restrict welfare recipients to benefits they would have received in former states for up to twelve months after moving

State residency requirements prohibited in AFDC

MEDICAID ELIGIBILITY

States generally prohibited from tightening income and resource eligibility standards above those in place for AFDC on 7/16/96, adjusted for inflation, with some exceptions

AFDC families automatically eligible for Medicaid

Table 12-1. (*Continued*)

Aid to Families with Dependent Children (AFDC)	*Personal Responsibility and Work Opportunity Reconciliation Act of 1996 (PRWORA)*
Labor market transition issues	
WORK REQUIREMENTS	
AFDC single parents with child under age three (age one at state discretion) exempted from JOBS participation requirement; others theoretically required to participate	Adult recipients required to engage in work after two years of receiving AFDC/TANF
STATE WORK PARTICIPATION RATES	
In FY 1995, 20 percent of nonexempt adult AFDC recipients required to engage in education, work or training in single-parent families (50 percent in two-parent families)	States required to meet escalating work participation rate requirements (30 percent of families at least twenty hours a week in 1998; 50 percent working thirty hours a week by 2002, with higher rates for two-parent families), with credit permitted for most caseload reductions. Escalating penalties (beginning at 5 percent of TANF block grant funds and rising to maximum of 21 percent) for states that fail to meet work participation rates and performance bonuses for most successful states
EARNINGS DISREGARDS	
States could "disregard" first $30 plus one-third of earnings only for first four months of AFDC receipt, after which earnings disregards much more limited	Federal government no longer regulates earnings disregards for TANF recipients

CHILD CARE FUNDING	
Child care provided under several funding streams (AFDC Child Care, At-Risk Child Care, Transitional Child Care, and Child Care and Development Block Grant	Child care funding consolidated under capped Child Care and Development Block Grant, with funding in part as state entitlement and remainder requiring state match at Medicaid rate
CHILD CARE GUARANTEE	
Child care guaranteed for young children of AFDC recipients working or in JOBS or other approved training; parents with no child care exempted from JOBS participation requirement; states required to provide Transitional Child Care Assistance with sliding scale fee structure to AFDC recipients entering work force	No child care guarantee to TANF recipients or transitional child care guarantee; single parents with children under age six who cannot find child care cannot be sanctioned for failure to participate in work activities, but that period counts against hard time limits
Medicaid transition benefits	
Families who lose Medicaid eligibility due to increased earnings eligible for one year of transitional Medicaid benefits	Same as previous law, except that eligibility for Medicaid transitional benefits now linked to income rather than receipt of AFDC/TANF
Long-term self-sufficiency	
Hard time limits in AFDC prohibited without federal waiver	No more than 20 percent of clients in state caseload can be in receipt of federally funded TANF benefits (including compensation for work) for more than sixty months over their adult lifetime, even if working while receiving benefits; shorter time limits permitted at state discretion; states cannot use federal funds to provide vouchers for children reaching sixty-month time limit

continued

Table 12-1. (Continued)

Aid to Families with Dependent Children (AFDC)	Personal Responsibility and Work Opportunity Reconciliation Act of 1996 (PRWORA)
	Paternity and child support
	PATERNITY ESTABLISHMENT
No provision	Parent who refuses to cooperate in paternity establishment must have benefit reduced by at least 25 percent and may have benefit terminated entirely; state can exempt parents from benefit cuts for good cause
	CHILD-SUPPORT PASS-THROUGH
States required to "pass through" to AFDC families first $50 in child support received	States have option of eliminating $50 pass-through to TANF families
	LICENSE SUSPENSIONS
No requirement regarding professional licenses of noncustodial parents	States required to establish procedures giving themselves authority to suspend driver's, professional, occupational, and recreational licences of noncustodial parents with overdue child support

Sources: Jeffrey L. Katz, "Welfare Overhaul Law, *Congressional Quarterly Weekly Report*, September 21, 1996, pp. 2696–2705; Mark Greenberg and Steve Savner, *A Detailed Summary of Key Provisions of the Temporary Assistance for Needy Families Block Grant of H.R. 3734, The Personal Responsibility and Work Opportunity Reconciliation Act of 1996* (Washington: Center for Law and Social Policy, August 13, 1996); David A. Super and others, *The New Welfare Law* (Washington: Center on Budget and Policy Priorities, August 13, 1996); Jodie Levin-Epstein, *Teen Parent Provisions in the Personal Responsibility and Work Opportunity Reconciliation Act of 1996* (Washington: Center for Law and Social Policy, November 1996).

a. To be able to draw down federal contingency funds during an economic downturn, states must maintain 100 percent of their historic effort in the year that they drawn down funds.

b. States could limit the number of children for whom an increased benefit was paid, but could not discriminate between children conceived based on the marital status or AFDC recipiency status of the mother in awarding benefits.

PRWORA puts a sixty-month lifetime limit on adults' receipt of cash assistance using federal TANF funds, and states can set lower limits if they choose. Nor can federal TANF funds be used for vouchers for those who have exhausted the time limit. States can, however, exempt up to 20 percent of their caseload from time limits, and they can use their own state revenues to provide benefits to families after those limits are reached.

Overall, PRWORA was estimated to save about $54 billion through fiscal year 2002 over provisions in earlier law.[45] The family assistance and child care provisions taken together do not save money over current law in that period. In fact, the Congressional Budget Office estimated that they would result in a net increase in outlays of about $3.8 billion over the period from 1997 through 2002, largely because of funding increases for child care. Advocates for the poor pointed out, however, that the new welfare law also dramatically increased the need for child care over earlier law because of its much stiffer work requirements; thus child care funding might actually be less adequate to demand than under the old law.[46] The big savings in PRWORA come from cutting benefits to legal immigrants and other changes in the Food Stamp and Supplemental Security Income programs, including stricter definitions of disability for children receiving SSI benefits.

In short, PRWORA represented major gains for proponents of new paternalist and deterrence approaches to welfare reform. But the increased discretion granted to states under TANF meant that the on-the-ground mixture of approaches to welfare reform confronting current and potential TANF recipients would depend heavily on state decisions. That mix could vary substantially across states, and could change within states over time, especially if a race to the bottom broke out. Would states, for example, impose time limits of less than five years? Would they allow more generous earnings disregards to help make work pay for TANF recipients? How would limited child care funds be allocated? Would states create public service job slots for recipients who could not find work in the private sector? And would states use their own funds to help families who hit TANF hard time limits? Until states answered these and many other questions, the real face of the new welfare law would remain unclear.

Aftershocks

President Clinton's decision to sign the welfare bill had limited political fallout. Three of the administration's top welfare officials in the Department of Health and Human Services resigned in protest over the president's decision to sign the bill—Deputy Assistant Secretary for Human Resources Wendell Primus left immediately and Mary Jo Bane and Peter Edelman (who had succeeded David Ellwood as assistant secretary for planning and evaluation) after a short interval.[47] But HHS secretary Shalala, who had opposed that decision as well, stayed on. The public signaled its approval of the legislation by a wide margin, although when asked directly, as a CBS/*New York Times* poll did, if they knew enough about the bill to say, 44 percent of respondents said that they did not. For most respondents, the fact that both the president and congressional Republicans said that it would end welfare as we know it was good enough (table 12-2). However, the people surveyed were cynical about the president's motives in signing it: 52 percent thought that he had done so mostly to win votes, while only 33 percent thought he did so because he thought it would change welfare for the better.[48]

The months after passage of the PRWORA saw further maneuvering and posturing on welfare reform. In the 1996 presidential election contest, President Clinton tried for the political equivalent of having his cake and eating it, too. He tried simultaneously appealing to conservative and moderate voters by claiming credit for ending welfare as we know it and arguing to liberals that if reelected he would fix a flawed welfare law. The president's priorities for change focused on immigrant and food stamp provisions of PRWORA more than on the new TANF program, however, and they explicitly did *not* include trying to restore individual entitlement to AFDC, now recognized by all sides as a lost cause.

Republican leaders in Congress, meanwhile, vowed to block substantial changes in the new law until it had been given a chance to work.[49] Congressional Democrats, still fearing the appearance of being to the left of the president on welfare issues and well aware that the prospects for a rollback of the statutory transformation of AFDC was a political nonstarter, were content to let the president take the lead on welfare. Republican governors pressed for easing of PRWORA's immigrant provisions, which they feared would leave them to pick up the tab in caring for those groups. But, under pressure from Republican leaders in Congress who feared erosion of PRWORA budget savings and the creation of an opening for Democratic pressure to reverse many PRWORA statutory changes, Republican governors also insisted that they did not want a major reopening of debate on the TANF provisions of welfare reform.[50]

The prospects that Clinton would be able to make major changes in the TANF provisions of the 1996 welfare reform law were further limited when Republicans retained control of both chambers of Congress in the 1996 election. The president's only vehicle to force the Republican Congress to act on welfare legislation now was the balanced budget bill under negotiation between the White House and congressional leaders through the first seven months of 1997. These negotiations naturally focused on spending provisions rather than the statutory changes (loss of entitlement, time limits, work requirements) that were at the heart of PRWORA provisions on low-income families. Short-term pressures for changing PRWORA were also minimized by the slow phase-in of its work requirements and hard time limits and by the relatively flush financial condition of the states caused by a combination of a rebounding economy, falling TANF caseloads, a fixed TANF block grant that provided most states with more funds than they would have received under the old caseload-sensitive AFDC law, and added child care funding.

The Balanced Budget Act (BBA) of 1997, passed in August of that year, made a number of changes in the 1996 welfare reform statute. Substantial additional funding was provided for immigrant benefits and a bit more for food stamps. The provisions regarding low-income families were changed only modestly. Additional federal funds ($3 billion over two years) were provided to the states for welfare-to-work activities, but the new grants would "sunset" at that time. At the urging of the Clinton administration, a temporary tax credit was also provided to employers who hired long-term welfare recipients, despite evidence that similar programs in the past had proven ineffective in increasing employment among those recipients.[51] The BBA also reaffirmed earlier Department of Labor regulations requiring states to meet federal minimum wage law requirements in workfare assignments—a requirement that had been strongly advocated by public sector unions and vehemently opposed by many governors and congressional Republicans.[52]

At the same time, however, the act stipulated that workfare "earnings" would not count for the purpose of receiving the Earned Income Tax Credit, making private sector earnings relatively more attractive to welfare recipients as an income source than workfare. The new act also lessened HHS's discretion to exempt states from penalties for failing to have a required share of their caseload in work activities.

Conclusions

The struggle over welfare reform legislation in the eleven months after September 1995 was an incredible roller-coaster ride. Enactment was seen

Table 12-2. *Public Opinion on 1996 Welfare Reform Bill*
Percent unless otherwise indicated

Questions and survey data	Hart/Teeter for NBC/Wall Street Journal[a]	CBS/New York Times[b]	Los Angeles Times[c]	Gallup for CNN/ USA Today[d]	CBS/New York Times[e]	Los Angeles Times[f]
Month of poll	8/96	8/96	8/96	8/96	1/97	2/97
Support/favor/right thing	73	47	82	68	53	75
Oppose/wrong thing	19	7	14	15	16	22
Mixed opinion	...	...	...	3[g]	...	...
Don't know enough/ haven't heard about it	...	44	...	7[g]	11[g]	...
Not sure/don't know	8	2	4	3	20	3

Source: DIALOG File 468: Public Opinion, Roper Center for Public Opinion Research, 1996.

a. As you may know, Congress recently passed a bill that makes changes in the way the nation's welfare programs are run and reduces funding for some programs, and President (Bill) Clinton has said he will sign the bill. Do you strongly favor, somewhat favor, somewhat oppose, or strongly oppose this welfare reform bill? Thirty-five percent said strongly favor and 38 percent said somewhat favor; 11 percent said somewhat oppose, and 8 percent strongly oppose.

b. This week, Congress passed legislation to change the welfare system and President (Bill) Clinton agreed to sign it. Do you think that President Clinton did the right thing in agreeing to sign this legislation, or the wrong thing, or don't you know enough about this welfare legislation to say?

c. As you may know, a welfare reform bill has just passed in Congress and President (Bill) Clinton said he will sign it. The legislation requires that welfare recipients work within two years of applying for benefits, it eliminates eligibility for most federal benefits for most legal immigrants until they become citizens, it requires able-bodied adults with no dependent children to work twenty hours per week in order to be eligible for food stamps, and it imposes a five-year life-time cap on welfare benefits whether or not a person can find a job. Do you favor or oppose the new welfare reform bill?

d. Turning now to the welfare bill passed by Congress last week—would you say you generally favor or oppose the changes which will be made to the wel-fare system under the new law?

e. Do you approve or disapprove of the welfare reform bill passed last summer?

f. As you may know, a welfare reform bill was signed last year by President (Bill) Clinton that requires welfare recipients to work within two years of apply-ing for benefits, it eliminates eligibility for most federal benefits for most legal immigrants until they become citizens, it requires able-bodied adults who do not have dependent children to work twenty hours per week in order to be eligible for food stamps, and it imposes a five-year lifetime cap on welfare benefits whether or not a person can find a job. Do you favor or oppose the new welfare reform bill?

g. Volunteered.

as almost a foregone conclusion in the fall of 1995. Early in 1996 welfare reform was viewed as an apparent dead letter, and it went through additional ups and downs before the White House signing ceremony in August of that year.

That comprehensive welfare reform legislation was enacted depended on the weakening of a number of the policymaking traps that had traditionally bedeviled welfare reform initiatives. In most cases, the weakening of the trap resulted from a complex mixture of social and institutional changes and the preferences and strategic calculations of policymakers. This interaction is particularly evident in weakening of the dual clientele trap. The biggest single factor weakening this trap was certainly the decision of Democrat Bill Clinton in 1992 to condemn the existing AFDC system in very harsh terms, and to pledge, ambiguously, to "end welfare as we know it." Clinton's decision to press for a work-based welfare reform, in turn, was made much easier by the fact that it simultaneously provided an opportunity for credit-claiming, fit with Clinton's personal values on welfare, and offered an opportunity to escape voters' long-standing disapprobation of Democrats' "coddling" of welfare recipients.

Equally important was the Republican endorsement of block grants as a vehicle for welfare reform. Once again, block grants appeared to satisfy several objectives common among Republicans, offering an opportunity to curb overall spending (at least in the long run), more flexibility to the states, and the possibility of both obscuring any negative consequences of welfare reform and shielding congressional Republicans from direct blame for those consequences. Especially important was the agreement in principle of the group of activist Republican governors to accept a fixed block grant in exchange for increased flexibility as the best deal they could get from a Republican-controlled Congress.

The availability of the congressional budget reconciliation process was a major aid in avoiding the multiple veto points in the U.S. legislative process. The budget process provided a handy mechanism for Republican leaders to set targets for deficit reduction, push forward their agenda, and package their cuts in a way that would keep wavering Republican moderates on board in the name of party unity. That the Republicans should choose this device should not be surprising: few alternatives would overcome procedural obstacles in the Senate and at least partially shield members from unpopular votes on cutbacks. Moreover, President Reagan had already shown in 1981 that reconciliation can be a powerful tool in changing policy priorities.

Reconciliation proved to be a double-edged sword in the welfare reform legislative process, however. Reconciliation cannot work effectively if those who are opposed to change control at least one of the three constitutional entities (the House, the Senate, and the presidency) that need to approve reconciliation legislation and are willing to use their blocking power. If proponents of change cannot bully or badger their recalcitrant partner into going along, the result is likely to be stalemate. Ultimately, public resentment of federal government shutdowns and proposed cuts in Medicare and Medicaid included in the 1995 Republican budget reconciliation bill, as well as doubts about the terms of devolution in other components of the Republican initiative, gave President Clinton sufficient political cover to reject both the budget reconciliation bill sent to him by Congress in 1995 and a separate welfare reform bill in January 1996. Because President Clinton chose to veto those packages, most of a year's worth of Republican efforts resulted in no statutory change at the end of 1995. But once Republicans settled on a strategy of passing legislation rather than strategic disagreement in the summer of 1996, they were able to use the reconciliation process to get the legislation to the president quickly, making impossible dilatory tactics in the Senate that might have succeeded in blocking the bill. Facing an imminent election, the president was unwilling to use his blocking power.

Although the policymaking traps for welfare reform had weakened substantially by 1996, however, they were not eliminated entirely. As with earlier stages in the process, choices by politicians played a critical role in moving welfare reform legislation forward and in getting it back on track when it seemed to have derailed. Four decisions in particular were critical: the governors' decision to jump-start welfare reform in February 1996; President Clinton's decision to challenge Republicans to put forward a welfare reform bill throughout the first half of 1996; the decision of congressional Republican leaders to choose passing legislation over having an election issue in the summer of 1996; and President Clinton's decision to sign the bill passed by the Republicans. While none was an obvious easy choice, each decision appeared likely to satisfy a combination of political and policy motivations in an uncertain political environment. The NGA's agreement on a welfare reform package was aided by a complex mixture of budgetary imperatives and a desire to increase state leverage in the legislative process. Clinton's combination of ambiguity on his policy bottom line and his daring Republicans to send him a separate welfare bill seemed to provide maximum flexibility. More important, it protected the president in an election year against charges that he was trying to sabotage welfare reform.

The Republicans' decision to drop Medicaid reform and to proceed with welfare reform similarly reflected their best guess about what was likely both to increase their chances of retaining their majority and to fix their policy preferences in place if they did not, at a time when their future majority status seemed very much in doubt. President Clinton's decision to sign the bill, over the objections of many of his policy advisors, offered the president both an opportunity to redeem his promise to end welfare as we know it and, most important of all, to avoid blame for sinking welfare reform.

CHAPTER THIRTEEN

Gaining Ground?

The New World of Welfare

REPLACEMENT OF Aid to Families with Dependent Children (AFDC) with a new program, Temporary Assistance for Needy Families (TANF), was intended to provide a new set of incentive structures that would move welfare recipients toward self-sufficiency. Because both AFDC and TANF are run by the states, however, changes in federal legislation can work only indirectly by affecting the structure of state programs, their implementation by "street-level bureaucrats" in welfare offices, and ultimately the behavior of welfare recipients and potential recipients. Actions at each link in this "chain" must be altered if there is to be a "new world of welfare."[1]

These changes in incentive structure take several different forms:

—*increased freedom* to undertake actions that previously were prohibited or required approval from Washington;

—*mandates* to take actions that were previously optional or forbidden;

—*prohibitions* against actions that were previously optional or required;

—*changed financial incentives* to undertake or forbear certain actions. For example, state program managers and their political masters are given more freedom to design programs that respond to local needs, and they have financial incentives to move welfare recipients into employment quickly. States were also required to impose a minimum set of sanctions on TANF recipients who failed to meet TANF requirements or to cooperate with child support enforcement, and they were given discretion to impose additional sanctions as well.[2] States also face financial penalties for failing to meet new federal standards on work participation rates or to enforce program time limits.

Imposing penalties for states that fail to meet work requirements means that the performance of local welfare offices at moving recipients into the labor force (or at least off welfare rolls) is likely to be monitored more closely. TANF recipients face stronger incentives to prepare for work, identify the fathers of their children, move off welfare rolls quickly, and (if states impose family caps) have fewer children. The eventual result of these changes, proponents of the Personal Responsibility and Work Opportunity Reconciliation Act of 1996 (PRWORA) argue, will be lower rates of out-of-wedlock births and lower welfare dependency. Critics of PRWORA foresee a very different future, with increased poverty and homelessness and poverty among poor families and a race to the bottom on the part of the states in terms of eligibility and benefits.

Declining Caseloads

The easy availability of TANF caseload data and the desire of federal and state politicians to use caseload declines as an indicator of the effectiveness of their policies have made caseloads the dominant subject of welfare debates in the implementation phase of the new welfare reform law. Welfare rolls are unquestionably down dramatically. AFDC rolls peaked at 14,225,591 in 1994. By June 1999 there were just under 6.9 million TANF recipients, a decline of more than 51 percent since January 1994.[3]

Caseload declines across the states have been very uneven, however. The number of AFDC/TANF recipients has declined in every state, but ranges from an astounding 89 percent since January 1993 in Wisconsin and 91 percent in Wyoming to a still substantial 18 percent in Rhode Island, 15 percent in New Mexico, and 28 percent in California.[4] These variations in caseload decline across states reflect both differences in economic conditions across states and differences in state policy decisions. In most states, caseload declines have also been more rapid among whites than among African-Americans and Hispanics. Thus TANF caseloads have increasingly concentrated among racial minorities. By mid-1998 blacks and Hispanics together outnumbered whites among TANF recipients by more than two to one.[5] TANF recipients are also increasingly concentrated in central cities.[6]

Clearly economic expansion and a tight labor market have been a major factor in this caseload decline, helping former welfare recipients to move into employment.[7] Work requirements have reduced welfare rolls both by accelerating exits and by reducing take-up: they have "smoked out" some recipients who were already working but not reporting their income. In other cases recipients who would otherwise have gone onto welfare rolls have been "diverted" into the regular work force without going onto welfare.[8]

Although a declining caseload is good news in the short term for state officials, because it means lower TANF obligations and thus more money to spend on remaining recipients or other purposes, it does not necessarily mean that poor families have moved toward greater self-sufficiency; it could simply mean that more are desperately poor. But there is no question that huge welfare caseload declines, and the absence of either compelling data or media-hyped anecdotes suggesting that welfare reform has caused great suffering among poor children, have been the fundamental *political* facts in the early implementation of PRWORA. These central political facts have allowed state and federal politicians to boast of their success and made it harder for liberal child advocacy groups to argue that welfare reform has caused widespread harm. The risk of an overwhelming focus on caseload declines, of course, is reinforcing pressure on politicians and program managers to avoid being seen as laggards in the sole easily available metric of program "success," even if doing so endangers children or fails to improve poor families' long-term prospects for self-sufficiency.

State Program Design

The substantial discretion that PRWORA gives the states means that the mixture of deterrence, incentives, new paternalist and prevention/rehabilitation approaches experienced by welfare recipients and applicants may vary dramatically across states and even localities, at least in the short term. How have states responded to the new incentives and increased discretion?

In the short term, no states chose radical paths of reform (such as entirely doing away with cash benefits). A few states have taken extraordinarily restrictive approaches: Idaho cut its caseloads by 79 percent between January 1993 and June 1999, in part with major restrictions on eligibility and benefits.[9] In some states, legislatures have given increased responsibility (backed by incentives and penalties) to county governments to design their own programs—a move that critics fear will intensify a "race to the bottom" as county governments try to make their programs less attractive than those of their neighbors.[10]

What can broadly be called "program entry" issues (denial of benefits to teen mothers, family caps, and residency requirements for interstate migrants) are among the program attributes in which states gained the greatest additional discretion under TANF. Twenty-three states had imposed some form of family cap provisions by mid-1999.[11] The main regional clustering of family caps is in the politically conservative South, where almost all states have adopted this provision, rather than among states with contiguous major population centers.[12] The movement toward family caps had essentially stopped by 1997, however: nineteen of the twenty-three states that now have family caps had received permission to adopt them using waivers before PRWORA was passed, and only one state added them after October 1997.[13] This suggests that the spread of family caps owes more to a combination of intra-state *political* incentives than to a "race to the bottom." Moreover, no states have adopted the "teen mother exclusion" that was implicitly made optional under PRWORA, perhaps reflecting low popular support for this measure. And while fourteen states had by 1998 imposed provisions treating immigrants from other states differently, these limitations were overturned by the Supreme Court in the summer of 1999.

The area where the most—and most diverse—state innovation has occurred under PRWORA involves encouraging transitions to the labor market. Even in states with politically liberal traditions, changing to a welfare system oriented toward moving recipients into work as soon as possible generally encountered little resistance. This transition was aided by a combination of high demand for workers, research suggesting that employment and training approaches were not efficacious, and awareness that states would soon face sanctions for failing to meet increasingly stiff work participation rates.[14]

States have varied in the approaches they have used to promote labor market attachment, however. Changes have been especially evident in what can broadly be termed "incentive" approaches. By June 1998, forty-two states treated earned income more generously than under the old AFDC system.[15] In addition, forty-three states had by 1999 also eased the strict asset limits ($1,000 in countable assets) for program eligibility that existed under AFDC.[16] Similarly, recognizing that a reliable automobile is necessary if many TANF recipients are going to be able to work, all states had by 1999 loosened or eliminated limits on the value of a car owned by welfare recipients. States have also given attention to transitional services as well, with twelve states extending transitional Medicaid and thirty-three states allowing transitional child care for more than a year.[17]

States have also embraced new paternalism approaches to welfare reform with enthusiasm. While PRWORA mandated that the states require TANF recipients to begin working within twenty-four months of receiving benefits, twenty states have chosen to impose immediate work requirements.[18] Almost all states have also chosen sanctions policies toward non-compliance with work requirements more severe than the TANF minimums, with fifteen states imposing the most stringent sanctions policies allowed (full-family sanctions for the first and repeated offenses). There has been a modest trend toward increased severity in 1998 and 1999.[19] States have been less adventurous, however, in the types of services they use to encourage labor market entry. Most states have increasingly focused on short-term job search activities and job readiness training (such as how to write a résumé and how to dress and behave on the job) rather than basic skills or longer-term vocational training.[20]

It is also clear that there are major differences across states in the resources available for moving poor families from welfare to work. These differences result from the combined effects of historical differences in state spending levels, the TANF funding allocation mechanism (which allocates current block grant amounts based on historical spending levels regardless of changes in caseload), and differences across states in the recent falloff in welfare caseloads. The fiscal dividend from caseload declines has varied dramatically; states that have cut their caseloads most deeply from a high initial expenditure level have enjoyed the most resources for assisting the remaining caseload.[21] Texas and Mississippi, for example, received less than $2,500 per TANF family in federal TANF funds for fiscal 1997, while Michigan and Connecticut got about twice as much per family and Oregon three times as much.[22] States with higher funding levels will have far greater capacity to provide expensive services like child care than poor states and thus may be less tempted simply to cut recipients off.[23]

The ultimate deterrent to long-term welfare dependence under PRWORA is a sixty-month lifetime time limit. However, states can exempt 20 percent of their caseload from the hard time limit. They also have the option of setting a shorter limit, and they can use state funds to help families after they hit the five-year limit. Early evidence suggests that states are taking deterrence seriously: by 1999, twenty-seven states were using the sixty-month standard, while eight had shorter limits, and a number of states had intermittent time limits (for example, only twenty-four months out of any sixty-month period) in addition to the overall sixty-month limit. States with stricter time limits are heavily concentrated in the South. Only a few states, notably Michigan and Rhode Island, have announced that they will use state funds to avoid the sixty-month time limit.[24]

Overall, there does not appear to be a single pattern or motivation for all states in setting policy under TANF. Some states, like New Jersey and Wisconsin, have tried a wide variety of policy changes drawn from both conservative and liberal approaches to welfare reform; others, such as Missouri and West Virginia, for example, have chosen an incremental approach, with minimal policy change. A few states, like Vermont and Maine, can be categorized as liberals, and a few others (Idaho and Indiana, for example) appear to be relying almost exclusively on deterrence and new paternalist policies or have expenditure minimization as their sole objective. Southern states are especially likely to choose conservative "packages" of TANF policies.

There does not appear to be a race to the bottom in the early phase of PRWORA implementation. Instead, after an initial rush of legislation to bring state programs into compliance with the PRWORA, there has been a legislative lull, as states absorbed and implemented earlier policy changes. The absence of an immediate race to the bottom should not come as a surprise for at least two reasons. First, flush state budgets, new federal funds, falling caseloads, and maintenance of effort requirements have all weakened fiscal pressures to engage in a race to the bottom. Second, for the most part, state politicians do not yet appear to see actions of neighboring states as leading to their own state's becoming a welfare magnet. If the U.S. economy turns sour in the future, however, it is possible that welfare migration, and pressures for a race to the bottom could grow.

On the negative side, the recent legislative lull suggests that there is limited learning from "best practices" of other states. Instead, rapidly falling caseloads seem to have two effects on state attitudes toward TANF. First, if "it's not broke, we don't need to fix it." Second, it is difficult for state policymakers to figure out what are the "best practices" in other states that they are supposed to emulate because (1) caseloads—the most easily measurable outcome—are falling everywhere; (2) most states have tried multiple innovations whose effects are difficult to separate; and (3) most evaluations of state experiences are incomplete or evaluations are not being performed at all.

Welfare Offices

In the early 1990s the need to alter the priorities and behavior of street-level bureaucrats was symbolized by the Clinton administration's pledge to "revolutionize the culture of welfare offices," orienting them more toward helping recipients move into work rather than simply filling out forms and checking information to establish recipients' eligibility for the program.[25] The new TANF program emphasizes the work goal, but it also complicates the administrative burden for states in numerous ways. Eligibility and benefit rules have become much more time-consuming to administer as a larger share of benefit recipients begin working, especially when their earnings are irregular. In addition to more complex eligibility and benefits calculations, states are supposed to track the number of months that beneficiaries receive assistance against federal time limits—and in many cases against state time limits (frequently based on different criteria) as well.[26]

Both research and anecdotal evidence in news reports suggest the complex ways in which state welfare offices are changing and coping. It seems clear that most state welfare offices are sending much clearer messages to adult recipients that they are expected to begin work immediately rather than first undergoing additional training or basic education. A recent Rockefeller Institute of Government study of nineteen states found that explanation of work requirements and time limits generally occurred near the beginning of the application process, frequently followed by a requirement for independent job search and a review for diversion assistance (small grants that allow recipients to avoid receiving TANF), before applicants could qualify for benefits.[27] Similarly, a General Accounting Office study of seven states found that almost all had increased the percentage of their caseload required to engage in some sort of work-related activity. Moreover, all seven states had increased the share of participants in work-related activities who are assigned to job placement activities while cutting the percentage assigned to education and training activities.[28] Some states (for example, Connecticut, Louisiana, and Wisconsin) are also relying increasingly on community work experience (workfare) programs.

In some states, where applicants are required to engage in job search before their TANF applications are processed, this new bureaucratic hurdle has had the effect of administratively depriving low-income people not only of TANF benefits, but also of Food Stamps, Medicaid, and other benefits to which they are legally entitled. The most notorious example is New York City, where both advocates for welfare recipients and regional Food Stamp administrators complained that the city's new job centers had systematically discouraged applicants from applying for cash assistance, Food Stamps, and Medicaid by requiring them to undergo multiple interviews and appointments plus a job search process before they were allowed to file an application for benefits—a complaint that was upheld by a U.S. District Court.[29]

The existence of differences in the behavior of local welfare offices, usually in response to signals from state policies, was also confirmed in the Rockefeller Institute's ambitious multistate implementation study. It found that roughly 40 percent of local sites were strongly oriented toward both work and welfare avoidance through techniques such as up-front diversion, strong signals in orientation meetings, and frequent recertifications. In these offices, "Local officials and workers view state officials as wanting to see, above all else, lower caseloads." An approximately equal number of their sites, mostly in Northern states, place a much stronger emphasis on labor market entry than on avoiding welfare per se. In these states (such as Michigan and Kansas) "the 'packaging' of cash benefits and earnings is perfectly acceptable."[30] In a smaller (and shrinking) share of sites, the old AFDC "eligibility/compliance" mentality was still dominant. In these sites, eligibility workers were generally still the dominant bureaucratic force, and they were under substantial pressure to reduce their error rates in Food Stamp eligibility and benefits, where a quality control system remains in place.

States have also varied dramatically in the frequency with which they apply sanctions and the severity of those sanctions.[31] States clearly vary substantially in their attitude toward benefit termination. In assessing early state experiences with benefit termination, the General Accounting Office noted in a 1997 report:

> Some states continued to assume primary responsibility for ensuring that recipients complied with program requirements and viewed benefit termination as a failure of their programs to work as intended. These states established a rigorous process to keep the number of terminations low. In contrast, other states sought to shift primary responsibility for compliance to recipients and viewed benefit termination as a needed strengthening of their sanctions to enforce recipients' obligation toward self-sufficiency.[32]

In sanctioning decisions as well as diversion, there is some evidence of erring on the side of severity, especially when those behaviors are encouraged or incentivized by agency management. In Milwaukee County, Wisconsin, for example, the GAO found that "44 percent of termination notices through August of 1996 were subsequently reversed because county officials determined that program requirements had been met or the sanctions had been based on inaccurate data."[33]

Differences among states are also evident in implementing "hard time limits" where states with short time limits already have a significant share of their clients approaching those limits. In most of these states, the recipients least willing to work or to prepare for work have already been removed from the rolls for noncooperation with work requirements. Some states, like Connecticut, have accommodated most of those who ask for extensions. Other states, like Arizona and Virginia, have not.[34]

The news about change in welfare offices, in short, is a mixed bag. The good news from welfare offices is that case workers in most states seem to have clearly gotten the message that it is a new world of welfare, and they seem highly responsive to the mix of signals sent by higher-ups in their individual states about the relative importance of labor market entry, welfare avoidance, family self-sufficiency, and accuracy in benefit determination. In some states, however, the new message they have received appears to be less about getting recipients into sustainable employment than reducing caseloads at any cost. And caseworkers in many states remain overwhelmed by huge caseloads that make the more active case management called for by PRWORA almost impossible.

The Behavior of Welfare Recipients

Welfare reform is also based on the assumptions that welfare recipients try to maximize their well-being and that changing the incentive structure in the AFDC system was critical to lessening welfare dependence and, ultimately, to making poor families more self sufficient. Paternity establishment and enhanced enforcement of child support are intended to increase the perceived liability of fathers for out-of-wedlock births, causing them to become more responsible in their sexual behavior. Family caps, which are a state option under PRWORA, are likewise intended to change potential mothers' calculus about the costs and benefits of childbearing. Time limits after which work is required and lifetime time limits after which no TANF benefits can be received (five years, or less at state discretion) are both intended to give recipients a stronger incentive to move into the labor market and remain there rather than receiving welfare benefits. Have welfare recipients, potential recipients, and noncustodial parents in fact altered their behavior in the intended directions? Not surprisingly, the evidence is somewhat mixed.

Clearly there have been substantial increases in the number of mothers working in recent years. Between 1994 and 1997 the number of single, divorced, and never-married mothers holding jobs increased by 837,000 in the United States.[35] This trend began before welfare reform legislation passed in 1996 and is probably due to a combination of an improving job market, changes in the Earned Income Tax Credit, and changes in welfare reform experiments in the states. Studies of women who have left welfare rolls suggest that between 60 and 80 percent are employed at any given point in time, with lower rates for those who leave as a result of sanctions. However, most of those who leave welfare do not earn enough to escape poverty.

Given the multiple policy changes enacted simultaneously by PRWORA and by the states, it is unclear which policy changes have been most important in leading to single mothers' increased participation in the labor force. Is it work requirements, hard time limits, or services and incentives, or some combination? The Manpower Demonstration Research Corporation (MDRC) found that in group discussions with Family Transition Program (FTP) recipients in Florida who had used up half of their twenty-four-month time limit, "Many recipients were focused on day-to-day problems, and saw the time limit as a distant concern."[36] If that is true, it suggests that new paternalist "soft time limits" (after which work is required) may produce most of the increased work effort sought by policymakers without the need for hard time limits (after which no cash benefits may be received).

The record in the area of reproductive behavior is much murkier. PRWORA included several measures intended to reduce illegitimacy. In addition to the previously discussed state-option family cap, it required teen mothers receiving TANF funds to live with a parent or other responsible adult(s) rather than setting up an independent household except in individual circumstances (for example, where there was parental sexual abuse).[37] As noted in chapter 5, there has been a substantial drop in teen birth rates since 1991, antedating PRWORA and most state waivers. Thus, while the effect sought by PRWORA is occurring, linking that effect to a particular cause has proven much more difficult.[38]

The Welfare of Low-Income Children and Families

The political nightmare for backers of PRWORA was a spate of horror stories that would capture the imagination of the public and turn people against the legislative changes made in 1996. For the most part, proponents of reform got their wish. Most media portrayals have shown some cases of significant hardship, but not the sort of vivid tragedies that capture the public's imagination and transform public opinion. There has also been little evidence thus far of changes in "fire alarm" indicators of most severe forms of child distress, such as the number of cases in foster care, although there has been a dramatic increase in child-only TANF cases. There is also some evidence of increased use of food banks and shelters.[39] And there is fragmentary evidence of increased psychological stress and maternal depression in women subject to welfare-to-work programs, especially among women who had preexisting risk factors, such as low reading scores, and preexisting problems of depression.[40] Another worrying trend is a post-PRWORA decline in Medicaid coverage of low-income children, despite the efforts of policymakers to prevent this from occurring by de-linking Medicaid eligibility and TANF eligibility in the PRWORA legislation.[41] Medicaid coverage declines among children have resulted both from individuals' being "diverted" from public assistance to jobs before they get onto welfare, and thus never getting enrolled for Medicaid either, and parents' getting sanctioned for not meeting work requirements in TANF and being automatically removed from Medicaid as well unless they reestablish eligibility for that program separately.[42] Administrative difficulties in disentangling TANF and Medicaid eligibility also contributed to a substantial drop in Medicaid receipt by low-income families in the immediate post-PRWORA period, but states appeared to have made some progress in addressing this problem by 1999.[43]

The Long-Term Prognosis

The long-term effects of welfare reform on child welfare and dependency are unlikely to become clear for some time. Most states do not have the capacity to effectively trace families who have left the rolls, even to find out if they have been able to remain employed.[44] Even if the labor market were able to absorb most welfare recipients, the low skill levels of many recipients and changing characteristics of the labor market itself suggest that (1) it is unlikely to provide uninterrupted employment; (2) many of them will not be able to move out of poverty and into self-sufficiency, since the jobs they obtain are mostly low paying; and (3) families that leave welfare are likely to remain very vulnerable to crises in child care, transportation, and illness.[45]

Our ability to judge the long-term effects of welfare reform will also have to wait until we have gone through at least one complete economic cycle. Indeed, what will happen when the nation's economy enters a downturn remains perhaps the most critical unknown about welfare reform. At present, low unemployment and a growing economy make states' task easier in a self-reinforcing "virtuous cycle": jobs for welfare low-skilled workers are relatively plentiful; caseload declines combined with fixed TANF federal funding have made it easier for states to spend more per recipient on transportation, child care, employment subsidies, training, intensive case management, and other activities to move welfare recipients into work and keep them there through the repeated crises in transportation, health care, and child care that characterize their lives. Overall economic growth has also lessened fiscal pressure on states to reduce spending on the poor.

When a recession hits, however, all elements of the virtuous cycle turn vicious, posing tougher choices for government and recipients. Problems of placing and retaining low-skill employees in jobs will grow when employers can be much pickier about whom they hire. States will also be fiscally stressed and reluctant to spend money on poor families, especially since increased state effort will no longer attract matching funds from the federal government, as it did under the AFDC program. Washington could bail the states out when this situation arises: indeed, at the time that welfare reform was being debated, proponents of reform argued that if more money were required later, Washington would likely supply it. But this was before passage of the 1997 balanced budget law, which firmly committed the Clinton administration and congressional Republicans to reaching and maintaining a balanced budget. It seems questionable at best that substantial new funding would be forthcoming from the federal government in this new fiscal environment.

Future directions in the well-being of low-income families, in short, depend on factors that are still largely question marks. Will the early diversity that has developed across states under TANF continue, or will a new uniformity emerge at some point? Will a race to the bottom develop among states during the next recession? Will effects of welfare reform on labor market behavior grow over time, will they plateau, or will they reverse direction? Will reproductive behavior, family formation, and self-investment in human capital show clear behavioral effects? When more families hit hard time limits, will states use the ways around those limits that Congress allowed? The long-term outcome for poor families is likely to be some shade of gray: some families will end up being better off, and others will end up being worse off. But we are a very long way from knowing how many will be in each group.

The Future of Welfare Politics

In 2002, Congress must reauthorize the Temporary Assistance to Needy Families program to keep it from expiring. After the political storm that surrounded welfare reform from 1993 to 1996, members of Congress have understandably been reluctant to address the issue again. Declining caseloads and a booming economy have made it unnecessary for them to do so.

In 2002, however, Congress will have no choice but to revisit TANF. And the political debate over welfare will likely be very conflictual and partisan once again. Liberals will want to revisit elements such as mandatory time limits for all states. Social conservatives will want to revisit illegitimacy provisions that were severely weakened in the final version of the Personal Responsibility and Work Opportunity Reconciliation Act. Fiscal conservatives will try to lower TANF spending levels, given the surpluses in most state accounts. States will seek to maintain current funding levels, and gain additional discretion in use of funds. Legislators from poor states will seek a reallocation of TANF block grant funds to give more money to states with higher rates of child poverty.

Ending welfare as we know it, in short, has sharply altered the substance of welfare policy, and thus the policy "default position" from which future policy debates will begin, but it has not altered the fundamental dynamics of welfare politics. The fundamental traps that bedevil welfare politics—dual clienteles, the iniquity of perverse incentives, reluctance to spend money on the "undeserving" poor, and federalism—will remain central in the new century. But falling caseloads and absence of evidence suggesting that PRWORA has had a catastrophic effect on poor children have weakened the salience of the welfare issue. Thus, while debate over TANF reauthorization is likely to be loud, the basic structure of the program will probably remain intact.

CHAPTER FOURTEEN

Welfare Reform and the Dynamics of American Politics

THIS VOLUME BEGAN with three sets of questions about welfare reform policymaking. Why have efforts at comprehensive welfare reform had such a high failure rate? What forces have driven changes in welfare reform agendas over time? And why did Republican-driven welfare reform succeed in 1996, after so many earlier failures? In reviewing the evidence on these questions, I will argue that welfare reform politics, while having many unique characteristics, also sheds light on the broader interplay of context and choice in American politics.

The Politics of Welfare Agenda Change

What causes welfare reform to emerge intermittently from the broad "discussion agenda" on which debate is occurring to move onto what Cobb and Elder have called government's "institutional agenda"—"that set of items explicitly up for the active and serious consideration of authoritative decisionmakers?"[1] And why has the content of the welfare reform agenda shifted over time—roughly speaking, away from income guarantees toward new paternalism, deterrence and devolution? Answers to the first question provide a useful framework and background for evaluation of the second.

From Discussion to Action

Chapter 4 argued that developments in what John Kingdon calls the "problem stream" were an important but insufficient catalyst for getting welfare from the discussion agenda onto government's institutional agenda. It is not that welfare was not seen as a problem. Precisely the opposite: welfare has *always* been seen as a problem, but not one that was necessarily susceptible to governmental action that was attractive in policy, electoral, and coalitional terms. While disturbing trends in key indicators (notably out-of-wedlock birth rates and caseloads) helped to increase support for welfare reform initiatives, catastrophic events did not catalyze action. Instead, awareness of "the welfare problem" was always a latent factor that favored getting welfare on the agenda, but perceptions of a welfare crisis needed to be joined to developments in the "policy stream" and the "political stream" to prompt intermittent welfare reform initiatives. In the policy stream, there had to be available a coherent and credible approach to reforming welfare that (1) appeared to offer to the political leaders supporting it an easy choice or a good choice in political, policy, and coalitional terms, and (2) had not been discredited by evaluation research. In the political stream, a presidential commitment to change was critical. Each of these elements is fragile: even if policy experts have reached a high degree of agreement on a particular direction to reform, legislators' views tend to be much more polarized. Once presidents realize that they may not be able to control outcomes, or indeed produce any final legislation at all, they tend to withdraw their limited political resources to concentrate on higher priorities.

The experience of the Clinton and Republican rounds is broadly similar to that of earlier times. In the Clinton round, the idea of a hybrid approach to welfare reform based on work incentives and obligations combined with training and universal health coverage and job guarantees had clear intellectual roots in David Ellwood's *Poor Support*. It had strong political roots in a broader New Democratic political project of making the Democratic party more attractive to Reagan Democrats and Perot voters, despite deep divisions among congressional Democrats on the issue. Clinton's campaign pledge to end welfare as we know it gave welfare reform an extraordinarily high profile, which bound the president to promote change even after he lost control of the legislative agenda after the 1994 election. But the high coalitional risks and budget costs and the uncertain returns of a welfare reform initiative kept pushing it to the back of the agenda queue during Clinton's first two years in office.

In the 1995–96 Gingrich round, things were a bit more complicated. President Clinton had already put welfare reform on the agenda. The inclusion of welfare reform in the Republicans' Contract with America in 1994 reflected the Republicans' desire to avoid losing the issue to Clinton and the

Democrats. The need to make good on their Contract promise gave the new congressional majority an additional stake in delivering policy change. This was particularly true after June 1996, when it appeared that welfare reform was about the only major social policy change the new Republican majority could deliver before the 1996 election.

Evolution of the Welfare Reform Agenda

The *content* of policy proposals for AFDC has also changed enormously over time, however. The Nixon and Carter administration proposals focused primarily on incentive approaches combined with minimum income guarantees. The Reagan administration decisively shifted the agenda away from an incentive approach toward a "proto-version" of the work-oriented new paternalism approach. It stressed devolution as well. In his last year in office, President Reagan signed the Family Support Act of 1988, which focused primarily on prevention/rehabilitation but also contained new paternalist and devolutionary elements. The policy agenda shifted again under the Clinton administration to an eclectic blend of policies drawn primarily from the incentives, prevention/rehabilitation, new paternalism, and devolution approaches. The Republican majority in the 104th Congress primarily stressed the new paternalism, deterrence, and devolution approaches.

The evolving content of the welfare agenda has multiple, complex roots, which again can be roughly divided into the problem, policy, and politics streams. In the problem stream welfare was always seen as a serious problem. It was, moreover, a problem with a racialized cast. The racial composition of the AFDC rolls both lowered public identification with and empathy toward welfare recipients and increased concerns about public subsidies to a permanent, undeserving underclass. But the nature of the welfare "problem" changed over time as society changed and policy research produced disturbing new findings. Policy research that highlighted growing out-of-wedlock birth rates, the long-term nature of much welfare receipt, and intergenerational patterns of welfare receipt all increased concerns over "welfare as a lure" and long-term dependency. Similarly, data on the low rates of child support receipt among single-parent families highlighted inadequacies in the child support system. In addition, public expectations about women working when they had young children helped lead to an increased focus on promoting work among AFDC mothers. The overall effect was to gradually shift the perception of the "welfare problem" held by many political and policy elites away from the resources available to poor families to the behavior of poor families (including fathers not part of the

AFDC support unit) and the ways in which government policy influenced and failed to influence their behavior.

In the policy stream, two factors stand out as driving change of the agenda. The evidence in chapters 4 and 6 suggests that evaluation research helped to drive old approaches off the agenda in most rounds of welfare reform and, in so doing, to create openings for new initiatives.[2] It did so because neither existing policies nor a variety of tested alternatives emerged from evaluation research as "silver bullet" solutions to "the welfare problem." Evidence suggesting significant problems with a particular approach (such as a guaranteed annual income) was frequently sufficient to move a proposal off the list of items under serious consideration by policymakers, while stimulating a search for new panaceas. The broadening of the welfare reform discussion agenda in the 1990s to include new paternalism, deterrence, and devolution approaches, for example, was triggered in part by the findings of evaluation research on the incentives and prevention/rehabilitation approaches, which suggested that both would make only modest improvements in the "welfare problem." The absence of supporting evidence (on teen mother exclusions and hard time limits, for example) did not keep a proposal off government's institutional agenda, however, although it did help to put the brakes on its adoption. Political competition between President Clinton and the Republicans to appear tough on welfare in the wake of Clinton's promise to end welfare as we know it, combined with leading policymakers' condemnation of the welfare status quo as an intolerable failure and their endorsement of new approaches, further legitimized those new approaches, despite a paucity of evidence suggesting that they would be effective.

A second key factor promoting agenda change in the policy stream is the role of policy intellectuals like Daniel Patrick Moynihan, Martin Anderson, David Ellwood, Charles Murray, and Lawrence Mead in articulating both powerful critiques of the policy status quo and policy recommendations that flow from those critiques. Crystallizing a new approach (or linked bundle of approaches, in Ellwood's case) to welfare is helpful in making the case to policymakers that they should bring the issue onto the agenda again: it provides, in effect, a new panacea. The role of these policy intellectuals is less important in some rounds than in others. The Carter round largely recycled ideas from the Nixon round, and the welfare-to-work research conducted by the Manpower Demonstration Research Corporation (MDRC) was a substitute in the Family Support Act round. In general, however, the cogent exposition of a distinctive approach to welfare reform matters plays a critical role in moving to the top of the agenda ideas that may always have been present in some form among groups of policymakers.

New approaches to welfare reform also need powerful supporters among the political class to move them from discussion agendas to government's institutional agenda. Politicians with the power to change the institutional agenda—generally presidents, but in the Family Support Act and Republican rounds, congressional leaders following a political opening created by presidents—played a critical role. Once again, it is not enough that a problem exists; if the welfare reform agenda is to shift, a politician with agenda-setting power must make the calculation that investing scarce political resources in putting a new set of welfare reform proposals on the agenda is a "good choice" in political, policy, and coalitional terms. In the 1995–96 Republican round, an important role in changing the welfare reform agenda was also played by a small group of activist Republican governors, who perceived that change was very likely and sought to move devolution to the center of the agenda to ensure that when change occurred, it worked to their advantage.

The Political Barriers to Comprehensive Welfare Reform

The failure of the Clinton administration to get its welfare reform package through in its first two years in office and the failure of the Republican initiative in 1995 before its revival the next year are both consistent with a long history of failed welfare reform initiatives. To understand this history, it is important to move beyond monocausal explanations (for example public opinion *or* racial divisions *or* political institutions) to understand how multiple forces combined to form a particularly deadly set of policymaking traps. The defining characteristic of these traps is that virtually any change from the status quo is almost certain to leave some policymakers perceiving themselves to be significantly worse off in policy terms than under the status quo. But the discussion in this volume also suggests that the contours and the salience of individual traps vary over time. Several of these traps had latent weaknesses that were not exposed until the policy agenda and balance of political forces on welfare issues shifted in the early 1990s.

The most profound and persistent of the traps inhibiting welfare reform is the dual clientele trap: the political difficulty of helping poor children, who are viewed sympathetically, without providing aid to their "undeserving" parents, or conversely, requiring more "responsible" behavior from parents without risking the welfare of children. The dual clientele trap has deep roots in American values stressing the importance of self-reliance and work. In the case of AFDC, these concerns have been exacerbated by the racialized hue of American poverty, AFDC rolls, and data on out-of-wedlock births. All of the major approaches to welfare reform are likely to promote concerns either about rewarding parents of questionable "deservingness" and creating long-term dependence, or concerns about the welfare of children—or both. Negative income tax proposals like Nixon's Family Assistance Plan were particularly likely to give rise to concerns about incentives for parents, while new paternalism and (especially) recent deterrence approaches raised concerns about children.

Two conclusions about the dual clientele trap emerge quite clearly from the history of welfare reform initiatives, including the most recent rounds in the 1990s. First, not only were individual policymakers (and members of the public) torn by conflicting concerns for the welfare of children and fears of increasing dependency, but liberals and conservatives weighed these concerns very differently. This aggravated the difficulty of finding a package of reforms acceptable to both political camps. A package including only benefit guarantees and incentives, for example, would be strongly opposed by conservatives, and a package consisting solely of work requirements and deterrence measures would be similarly opposed by liberals. A package containing a mix of changes appealing to conservatives and liberals was likely to be seen by both sides as conceding too much to the other side for too little gain. It is easiest to reform welfare, as the 1988 Family Support Act showed, when (1) there is widespread agreement on the nature of the problem and the proper direction for reform; (2) the nature of reform proposals is incremental; and (3) the reform options on the table do not pose strong threats to the core concerns of either liberals or conservatives. The increasing commitment of many conservatives in recent years to deterrence-oriented proposals such as teen mother exclusions and hard time limits, which liberals continued to reject, exacerbated the dual clientele trap by increasing the policy distance that must be bridged in any compromise. Given the multiple barriers to reform posed by American political institutions, a polarization of policymakers adhering to intransigent positions is usually the kiss of death for comprehensive welfare legislation.

A second conclusion is that the dual clientele trap had a fundamental weakness as a barrier to AFDC policy change. That weakness is racial composition of the AFDC program and the program's image with the public and policymakers. Race seldom appears in the narrative chapters of this book because it is a relative "constant." Whites and blacks composed roughly equal shares of the AFDC caseload from the early 1970s through the demise of the program in 1996 (the caseload share of both groups declined after the mid-1980s as the share of Hispanics rose). Racial antagonisms are also a relative constant in the period covered by this study. Open racial references with respect to the program are almost never made by key policymakers after the early 1970s, even in the 104th Congress. Thus the role of race is difficult to state with certainty. It must instead be inferred from research on the role that race plays in public attitudes toward public assistance programs and from the relative ease with which the public seems to have accepted repeated priming messages from politicians (Democrats as well as Republicans) in the 1990s that behavior of adults was a more important concern than the welfare of children and that almost any alternative was preferable to the status quo. This latent weakness remained hidden as long as proponents of policies that posed high potential risks to poor children (especially deterrence approaches) lacked sufficient control over government's institutional agenda to secure them more than a toehold there and opponents of such policies had enough control to obstruct such proposals. But when these relationships changed after 1994, the extent to which the strength of the dual clientele trap relied on the capacity of liberals to keep proposals they abhorred off the government's action agenda was laid bare.

The money trap—the desire of the public and policymakers to reform welfare without spending any more money on it—has also played a key role in contributing to the failure of welfare reform initiatives. All of the major approaches to welfare reform except deterrence and devolution are likely to cost more money in the short run than the AFDC program already in place—and the unpopularity of the AFDC program made spending more money on welfare recipients a tough sell politically among moderates as well as conservatives. The Budget Enforcement Act of 1990, by requiring that changes in entitlement programs pose no net deficit increase in the medium-term, made the money trap even more deadly. Its effects were especially clear in both the process of developing the Clinton welfare reform package of 1994 and the final substance of that package. The 1990s also revealed a potential weakness in the money trap as well, however. A welfare reform approach that appears attractive to a group of policymakers on other grounds (as deterrence and devolution were to Republican legislators in the 104th Congress) can be made even more attractive if it also holds the lure of saving money.

Two other traps also play important though less central roles in blocking welfare policy change. The perverse incentives trap (the difficulty of making a welfare policy change that does not pose new perverse incentives for recipients or exacerbate old ones) appears most clearly in the rounds of welfare reform that rely heavily on incentives and prevention/rehabilitation approaches to welfare reform (the Nixon, Carter, and Clinton rounds). Its contribution to the demise of welfare reform proposals was particularly important in the Nixon and Carter rounds. In other cases, these concerns proved surmountable, however. In the Family Support Act round, conservative concerns about work disincentive effects of minimum benefit standards and AFDC-UP expansion were assuaged by eliminating the former and limiting the latter. In the 1981 Reagan cuts, concerns that eliminating earnings disregards and lowering earnings limits could cause mothers to reduce work effort in order to maintain their eligibility for AFDC and Medicaid were simply brushed aside in the hurried debate over a large legislative package. Similarly, in the 1995–96 round, some Republicans had real concerns that family caps and teen mother exclusions could increase abortions. These concerns may have contributed to those provisions' being made state options rather than mandatory in the final legislation.

The main lesson is that the new paternalism, deterrence, and devolution approaches may have less difficulty with the perverse incentives trap than other approaches, but may differentially strengthen other traps (notably the dual clientele trap). A second lesson is that conflicts over alleged perverse incentives are especially likely to lead to stalemate (1) when they pit liberals against conservatives rather than compelling one group to make a trade-off within itself; (2) when the provisions that spark concern about perverse incentives lie at the core of the welfare reform initiative and thus cannot be jettisoned to make a reform package more politically palatable; and (3) when a group opposing a trade-off controls a veto point and sees exercising that control as a politically viable strategy. In the Nixon and Carter rounds, conflicts over the work effects of income guarantees were central to administration proposals, pitted liberals against conservatives, and were subject to veto by the Senate Finance Committee. In the 1995–96 Republican round, conflicts over abortion largely pitted conservatives against themselves. Moreover, most conservatives who supported deterrence approaches were willing to accept a risk of increased abortions as the price of deterrence measures, were unwilling to block an overall bill on those grounds, and were willing to accept less intrusive measures to reduce the number of out-of-wedlock births as a substitute.

The federalism trap (inability to increase state flexibility without sacrificing national standards valued by some policymakers, or to increase national standards without raising opposition and demands for compensation from some states) also plays an intermittent role in obstructing welfare policy change. Efforts to increase national standards in the Nixon and Carter rounds and to weaken them in the Reagan New Federalism round clearly complicated reform negotiations, contributing to the ultimate demise of those initiatives. They were also a centerpiece of the 1995–96 Republican round in welfare reform. The inability of the opponents of dramatic devolution to control any veto points where reform could be blocked was a critical weakness in the federalism trap that allowed reform to proceed.

As this discussion makes clear, each of these policymaking traps has been exacerbated by cross-cutting institutional features of the U.S. system, notably the multiple veto points, committee autonomy, and weak party discipline in the U.S. legislative process. These institutional characteristics facilitate the use of agenda limitation strategies to prevent controversial reform proposals from moving forward and make it difficult to hold fragile coalitions together when those options do come up for votes. Thus U.S. institutions create a strong bias toward the status quo, especially when there are deep divisions among political elites. The fact that welfare reform has most often broken down in the Senate, where the rights of political minorities are most deeply entrenched, further suggests the importance of institutional constraints. The Nixon and Carter rounds of welfare reform both show the power that entrenched "policy outliers" in congressional committees can exert to keep off the agenda alternatives that they strongly oppose. In the Family Support round, however, Senator Moynihan acted as a force to build a very broad consensus on a package of welfare reforms and to frame the debate in terms of that package rather than the "broken" status quo, making it politically difficult for a suspicious White House to block change.

The history of welfare reform also suggests several opportunities to maneuver around the multiple veto points in the U.S. constitutional system. The most important legislative path is use of budget reconciliation procedures. Since 1980 these procedures have provided a vehicle for forcing through AFDC changes with limited debate and minimal procedural vetoes. However, the very contentiousness of AFDC has made policymakers reluctant to include comprehensive welfare reform legislation in a reconciliation bill, both because they felt that a more extensive debate on those provisions was needed and because they feared that including controversial welfare procedures could endanger the fragile coalitions of support for always-controversial reconciliation legislation. As noted in chapter 12, moreover, the 1995 Republican reconciliation legislation, which included welfare provisions, illustrates the risks of bundling many pieces of controversial legislation. This bundling made all provisions subject to being sunk by the politically weakest ones with a presidential veto.

Two other pathways around multiple vetoes do not, significantly, involve the legislative process, and both have their own limitations.[3] The first is the role of the courts, visible especially in the expansion of welfare rights in the 1960s and 1970s. This unilateral expansion set a new policy default that was very difficult to undo legislatively, because the mechanisms to overturn court policy decisions in the short run—new legislation that will pass muster with the courts, or constitutional amendments—are themselves subject to all the usual procedural obstacles in the legislative process (and more, for constitutional amendments). Efforts by congressional conservatives to overturn court-imposed liberalization of AFDC, for example, were stymied in the House of Representatives.[4] But the courts' power to set a major new policy direction in AFDC or any other policy area is likely to be exercised intermittently and idiosyncratically, since it requires a legislative or a constitutional opening (such as ambiguous legislative language), plus judges (and especially a Supreme Court majority) who have strong policy views and are willing to assert them. Indeed, by the mid-1970s, the courts were retreating from their activist role in setting AFDC policy.

Another potential pathway around multiple vetoes in the U.S. system is the use of administrative discretion, seen here in the granting of AFDC waivers by the Reagan, Bush, and Clinton administrations. Again, limitations on this strategy are evident. There must be a legislative opening for discretion (for example, the section 1115 waiver process) as well as a clear policy direction within the administration; a willingness on the part of the administration to incur potential wrath from Congress for what some legislators will inevitably see as an abuse of that direction; and acquiescence by the courts if the use of discretion is challenged by those who are affected by it. While legislative action to overturn administrative actions encounters the usual multiple vetoes in the legislative process, it can be propelled by a perception that congressional prerogatives rather than simply policy preferences are being trampled on.

Enacting Welfare Reform, 1995–96

The third question posed at the beginning of this book was why comprehensive welfare reform passed in 1996 after the failure of many past initiatives, including that of the Clinton 1994 plan. The most obvious answer to this question is the 1994 election, which gave the Republican party control of both chambers of Congress and a majority of governorships and dramatically weakened President Clinton's bargaining leverage to resist Republican initiatives. But this change in partisan control is clearly an inadequate explanation for two reasons. First, it is unclear why dramatic policy change would occur in a period of divided party control of the presidency and Congress, an institutional arrangement that is more frequently associated with stalemate than with dramatic policy change. Even if we accept David Mayhew's argument that divided party control makes little difference in the amount of legislative activity, why should welfare reform pass in 1996 after failing in the previous two years, when President Clinton had Democratic majorities in both chambers of Congress?[5]

A second shortcoming of the party change hypothesis is that it cannot explain why the transformation of AFDC was enacted, with very heavy majorities on the final legislative votes, while other major elements of the Republican agenda failed. In particular, the record of the new Republican congressional majority in enacting their own proposals for changes in programs aimed at low-income Americans in the 104th Congress is a decidedly mixed one. The Republicans proposed significant reductions in the Earned Income Tax Credit (EITC), for example, which were bolstered by studies from the Internal Revenue Service and General Accounting Office suggesting that the program had widespread problems of fraud and abuse. However, President Clinton issued a strong threat to veto any bill that substantially reversed his 1993 expansion of the Earned Income Tax Credit. Proposals for substantial cuts in the EITC in the 104th Congress died with President Clinton's veto of the Republican budget reconciliation package and the party's decision in 1996 not to pursue a major tax reduction package. The EITC also emerged almost unscathed from the 1997 budget balancing package negotiated between the president and the Republicans in Congress.[6] The 1996 welfare reform legislation contained substantial cuts in Food Stamp program eligibility (especially for noncitizens) and benefits and a work requirement for most able-bodied adults. But Food Stamps were not folded into a single giant block grant in combination with school nutrition programs, the Special Supplemental Feeding Program for Women, Infants and Children (WIC), and other nutrition programs, as had been proposed in the Contract with America. And, as noted in chapter 12, Republican proposals to turn Medicaid—the biggest means-tested program of all—into a block grant were dropped in the summer of 1996.[7]

In short, to understand why comprehensive AFDC reform passed in 1996 after many previous failures, and when most other major Republican domestic policy initiatives in the 104th Congress failed, it is necessary to look both at a broader range of contextual factors than the 1994 change of party control in Congress and at the effects of those factors on the four policymaking traps, on cross-cutting institutional barriers to policy change, and on strategic choices made by politicians.

Contextual Factors and Policy Traps

Table 14-1 provides a "scorecard" for arguments about how contextual forces contributed to the enactment of welfare policy change in 1996. It suggests that multiple changes simultaneously weakened all four of the policymaking traps that had traditionally bedeviled welfare reform initiatives, made agenda limitation strategies less tenable as a mechanism for liberals to block reforms, and shaped repositioning choices by leading all but the most liberal policymakers to shift their "zones of acceptable outcomes" to the right.

On the public opinion front, the data presented in chapter 7 suggest a complex pattern of beliefs that had the overall effect of weakening the barriers to a reform initiative. Neither the Clinton administration nor Republican leaders in Congress enjoyed public trust and deference on the issue; indeed, the longer each was seen to be in the "driver's seat" without producing change, the less trust they enjoyed. The most important characteristic of public opinion was the unpopularity of the existing AFDC program. Because the public viewed almost any alternative as preferable to the status quo, as along as Republican elites could maintain agenda control and frame a political choice on welfare reform as one of change versus the status quo, they would be in a very strong position to get the support of many legislators (and the president) who did not agree with their proposal but did not want to be seen as defenders of the existing system. The unpopularity of the status quo gave Republican leaders an incentive to press for legislation that included not only "lowest common denominator" provisions that enjoyed broad public support (stronger work requirements and child support enforcement and increased funding for child care, for example), but also deterrence-oriented policies that were less popular with the public. In doing this, Republicans could help to preserve the general public perception that they were the party of "real" welfare reform by outbidding (or engaging in strategic disagreement on) any Democratic welfare reform proposal.[8] The combination of an overwhelming public desire for policy change ("primed" by both the president and Republican leaders in Congress) and absence of strong public consensus on a single approach or to the details of policy also meant that the Republican congressional majority would have substantial leeway to revise its package in response to shifting coalitional concerns—as it did repeatedly in 1995 and 1996—as long as it was perceived as producing real change. But public opinion only provided an opportunity for a welfare reform initiative by weakening the dual clientele trap rather than ensuring that such an initiative would succeed.

In other respects, the environment for a successful welfare reform initiative was more mixed. While there was a consensus among policy elites on increasing work effort by welfare recipients and child support, there was no elite consensus on a particular policy paradigm on how to do it; a variety of different approaches were pressed by rival policy elites. Policy research did not produce universally accepted consensus on a specific approach to reform. Indeed, policy research itself became increasingly contested, with multiple purveyors and limited agreement among policy elites on "whom you can trust" in the policy research community. But policy research did produce a number of broadly accepted "fire alarms" that further weakened the dual clientele trap.

The interest group environment also shifted in ways that provided opportunities for, but did not make inevitable, a major change in AFDC policies. The neutralization of the National Governors' Association in 1995 effectively silenced a potentially pivotal opponent, and allowed its place to be taken by supportive Republican governors. The growing importance of social conservative groups added an important new voice for deterrence-oriented reform, although it was unclear until late in the game whether they would be willing to make the compromises needed to get a reform package through Congress. The Democratic Leadership Council, increasingly visible, was an important voice close to Clinton urging the president to agree to welfare reform on almost any terms.

As noted earlier, the overall role of political institutions was at best mixed with respect to passing a welfare reform package: divided government made a purely one-party welfare initiative impractical, meaning that the president would have to be brought on board somehow. But the fact that the Republicans controlled the agenda throughout the congressional process meant that if Republicans could agree, they could confront the president with a "bad choice" between reform on their terms and the status quo. Moreover, as shown in table 14-1, the micro institutional conditions were far more favorable to reform: budget reconciliation procedures offered a

Table 14-1. *Contextual Arguments about Why Welfare Reform Succeeded in 1996 but Not Earlier*

Arguments	Evidence suggests	Implications for welfare policymaking traps and bargaining process
	Public opinion arguments	
Increased public unity on particular approaches to welfare reform overcomes any reservations by politicians; leads them to follow public opinion in adopting those solutions ("opinion change" hypothesis)	Partially true. Public support for work requirements, child care spending, job training, and stricter child support enforcement was strong; opinion more ambivalent on deterrence provisions such as family caps and time limits; support for continued AFDC entitlement status weak	Absence of consensus on single approach to welfare reform shaped by public opinion increases range of alternatives considered, but growing support for work requirements makes such requirements more likely
Increased salience of welfare issue and public opposition to status quo force political elites to adapt positions to preexisting public consensus on work-based approaches ("elite dissensus" hypothesis)	Partially true. Liberal elites faced increased public support for work-based approaches; conservative elites continued to press new approaches to welfare reform that did not enjoy public consensus	Unless agenda limitation strategies prevented open vote on work requirements, legislators' blame-avoiding instincts would give work requirements very broad support in Congress, even from legislators who did not agree with them
Public confidence in specific political leaders or parties high enough to allow accepting their prescriptions about welfare ("public deference" hypothesis)	False. Public quickly lost confidence in Clinton administration and Republican congressional leaders as managers of welfare reform	Ability of political elites to control agenda and maintain coalitional unity critical to holding together fragile coalitions and implementing policy preferences
Public discontent with program so high any change from the status quo would have been seen as improvement, or at least no worse ("public anger" hypothesis)	Largely true. Public discontent with program very high, primed by messages from President Clinton and Republicans that status quo was unacceptable. Most alternatives seen by public as improvement	Unpopularity of status quo and Republicans' use of welfare as a "wedge" issue gives policymakers strong incentives to support almost any change from status quo (broad "zone of acceptable outcomes"); Democrats thus have strong incentive to erase public

	Race and gender	

Race and gender

AFDC's clientele, disproportionately female heads of families and racial minorities, especially vulnerable to cutbacks

Partially true. AFDC widely disliked, but other programs serving low-income families had grown since 1980s

perceptions that they are "soft on welfare" through triangulation, strategic pursuit, and matching; facilitates building stable majority coalition for reform, but also gives Republicans strong incentives to maintain policy distance through strategic disagreement, if they can do so without appearing to block lesser change; gives politicians controlling legislative agenda leverage to revise their "bid" without forfeiting public support

AFDC vulnerable to cutbacks if its opponents could pose choices as their alternative versus status quo and its proponents could not block proposals they did not like

Policy paradigms and elite ideology

Elites reach agreement on policy paradigm with shared understanding of problems and solutions

Largely false. Multiple contending approaches to welfare in early 1990s, none clearly dominant; conservatives divided in emphasis on new paternalism, deterrence, and devolution

Elite agree on strengthening work and child support enforcement, but not on how to increase work and whether that is adequate response; distribution of policymakers' preferences and range of alternatives considered thus broad and support coalition for reform fragile

continued

Table 14-1. (*Continued*)

Arguments	Evidence suggests	Implications for welfare policymaking traps and bargaining process
	Policy research arguments	
Policy research leads to agreement on common definition of and response to problems of low-income families ("technocratic hypothesis")	Largely false. Skepticism about value of work-based approaches to welfare reform increasing; experts disagree on how to increase work among AFDC recipients and whether increased work was adequate response to child poverty and welfare dependency	Consensus on work-based approaches based more on value preferences and political posturing than on evaluation research
Policy research prevents adoption of alternatives that appear not to work or that appear risky and have not been tested ("circuit breaker hypothesis")	Partially true. Negative evidence killed negative income tax proposals, but absence of evidence did not prevent adoption of family caps (as state option) or hard time limits in PRWORA	Range of alternatives remains broad, including those that have not been tested
Evaluation research leads to concern about nature of problems but does not necessarily suggest a solution ("fire alarm hypothesis")	True. Social science information and its interpretations increased concern about nature of problems	Research on length of welfare spells, illegitimacy, etc., heightens concerns about dependency; focusing debate on parents' behavior more than children's welfare and weakening dual clientele trap
Policymakers favor research that agrees with their views and ignore the rest; policy research has no independent effect on outcomes ("ammunition hypothesis")	Partially true. Multiple sources of conflicting advice and policymakers' increasing tendency to see them as partisan compromised their usefulness	Range of alternatives remains broad

Liberal interest groups either had declining resources that weakened ability to be heard or lost access to political leaders	Partially true. Liberal interest groups did not have declining resources or lack access to Clinton administration, but they had limited access to congressional majority party setting the agenda after 1994 and could not mobilize grassroots to pressure Congress or president once their allies lost control of agenda; breadth of Republican reform agenda limited ability of liberals to draw support from potential allies in advocacy community; and liberals lacked reliable allies at legislative choke points	Liberal interest groups and their legislative allies unable to use agenda limitation to prevent open votes on welfare reform packages they dislike
Existing groups shifted positions to right	Partially true. Intergovernmental groups largely stalemated in 1995, but NGA pressed for devolution-oriented reform in 1996; interests of Republican governors not compatible with preferences of congressional Republicans for forcing conservative mandates on states	Stalemate within NGA allowed Republican governors to take lead on welfare reform
New conservative entrants in interest group environment counterbalanced liberal groups	Partially true. Social conservative groups acted cohesively in alliance with conservative think tanks to press for deterrence-focused policies and enjoyed strong leverage with Republican legislators; Democratic Leadership Council pressed Clinton to accept welfare reform on almost any terms	Insistence of social conservative groups on strong deterrence measures widened range of options and pushed welfare reform debate to the right but also potentially weakened Republican support for packages that do not include strong deterrence measures

continued

Table 14-1. (Continued)

Arguments	Evidence suggests	Implications for welfare policymaking traps and bargaining process
	Institutional and procedural arguments	
1994 congressional election brought Republican critics of AFDC into power with electoral commitment to dramatic change in program	True, but divided government generally increases prospects for policy gridlock and stalemate rather than policy change; critical impact of change in party control more on agenda control than prospects for gridlock	Divided government makes it more difficult to enact welfare reform on a partisan basis, but Republicans' desire to be seen as effective gives them strong incentives to act cohesively; Republican agenda control throughout the congressional process dramatically weakens power of liberal Democrats to keep proposals they do not like off legislative agenda and gives President Clinton choice of accepting welfare reform on Republican terms or appearing to support status quo
Budget Enforcement Act of 1990 made expansionary social policy initiatives and "privileged" initiatives that cut spending almost impossible	Mostly true. BEA made expansionary initiatives more difficult, but did not compel policy change in 1996	Budget Enforcement Act provisions on budget neutrality essentially exclude from moving forward options that were not more conservative than the status quo
Budget reconciliation provided mechanism to force through controversial measures by limiting debate and minority filibuster power in Senate	Mostly true	Reconciliation mechanism allows a cohesive congressional majority to force up-or-down choices between its preferred alternative and status quo, strengthening Republican reform coalition and weakening institutional basis for minority vetoes

Policy legacies and commitments

State-level experiments after 1988 created momentum for further reform, especially for devolutionary approaches	True. Governors began to see political credit-claiming opportunities in welfare reform, while devolution experience appealed to congressional Republicans	Resistance to devolution weakened for both federal and state policymakers
Clinton came into office with strong commitment to "end welfare as we know it"	Partially true. Clinton's endorsement of welfare reform did not guarantee passage of welfare reform any more than it did health care reform	Clinton's election pledge and constant criticisms of status quo reinforced growing perception among both political elites and ordinary citizens that nothing could be worse than AFDC policy status quo, which made it politically more difficult to mount defense of current AFDC program or veto welfare reform legislation

Political learning

Political learning from past rounds of welfare reform increased capacity of policymakers to overcome political and institutional barriers to welfare reform	Largely false. Capacity to learn from past rounds of reform limited by previous policy commitments made with limited time horizons, weak institutional memory, tendency to underestimate historical parallels, and tendency of newly empowered political leadership to overestimate capacity to produce change	Little or no impact

way to get around multiple roadblocks in the congressional approval process, and the money-saving nature of the Republicans' welfare package meant that provisions of the Budget Enforcement Act did not pose a major obstacle to reform, as they had for Clinton.

Perhaps the two most important contextual developments weakening the welfare policymaking traps, however, fit loosely within the rubric of "policy legacies." The first is the legacy of state welfare experiments in the 1980s and early 1990s. The positive (but hardly overwhelming) results of those experiments generally helped lower resistance to increased state discretion (the federalism trap) and, more important, convinced a core group of Republican governors that substantially increased discretion could have both financial and political rewards. The second key development is in fact a policy commitment rather than a true policy legacy: President Clinton's strong condemnation of the existing welfare system and promise to end welfare as we know it. This commitment helped to weaken the dual clientele trap and raised the political costs to the president of rejecting all but the most radical deterrence-oriented Republican welfare initiatives—and even then only if he could make (or be pushed by others into making) a strong case that those provisions were too "tough on kids."

In short, contextual developments weakened both traditional policy-making traps and agenda limitation strategies as barriers to comprehensive welfare reform during the first Clinton administration. But in so doing, they widened the opportunities for enactment of a welfare reform initiative rather than ensuring that such an initiative would succeed. To understand how this opportunity was turned into policy reality, we must turn to the micro world of policymakers' preferences and strategic choices.

Policymakers' Preferences

The policy preferences and commitments and political interests of key policymakers provided additional opportunities for policy change. President Clinton's oft-declared (and very gubernatorial) preference for increased state flexibility in welfare helped to weaken the federalism trap. The presidential ambitions of Senators Dole and Gramm ultimately weakened the multiple institutional barriers to reform: Dole had strong incentives to show that he could get a welfare bill through the Senate, and although Gramm had incentives to position himself to Dole's right, being an obstructionist to the point of blocking passage of a Senate welfare reform bill ultimately did not serve Gramm's presidential ambitions well. More broadly, the concentration of Republicans on some combination of new paternalism, deterrence, and devolution approaches meant that the perverse incentives trap (with the exception of the abortion issue) was a relatively modest obstacle once they gained the policy initiative. In addition, Republican preferences in the 104th Congress for extremely ambitious deficit and tax reduction targets helped to facilitate their hanging together to pass welfare reform because they needed the money. And the weak constituency interest of most House Republicans in welfare issues and their collective interest in appearing to govern effectively by passing the Contract with America (or something that could be said to be consistent with the Contract) gave them wide zones of acceptable outcomes as party leaders adjusted the legislative package in response to conflicting pressures from Republican governors and social conservatives.

Strategic Repositioning

The "ideal points" (preferred policy positions) of key participants remained far apart, however, and their political incentives were not necessarily in the direction of accommodating their political competitors. Welfare reform happened in 1996 because the positions taken by most of the major participants were political and relational—that is, they were determined in large part in relation to the positions of other participants. Relational considerations and short-term political calculations are critical to explaining both why key actors, especially the president and moderate and conservative Democrats, chose repositioning strategies that expanded their "zone of acceptable outcomes" to the right and why Republicans abandoned their strategy of strategic disagreement and came to an accommodation with them.

Figure 14-1 shows the key strategic choices and countermoves in this process in a very schematic form. It does not show all of the major developments in the process (for example, the role of the governors' initiative in February of 1996 that restarted a stalled reform process). It focuses instead on developments that led to important changes in participants' zones of acceptable outcomes. To simplify the presentation visually, the president's and various groups of legislators' positions on the multiple policy dimensions of welfare reform have been reduced in figure 14-1 to a single left-right dimension. The horizontal line represents a rough estimate of the range of different participants' zone of acceptable outcomes at a particular stage in the process. The bottom of the figure shows how these zones relate to specific legislative benchmarks (for example, the Contract with America welfare reform bill, or the Senate-passed welfare reform bill of 1995), and whether there exists a zone of agreement on which two-chamber legislative

Figure 14-1. *Positional Bargaining on Welfare Reform, 1992–96*

Step 1: 1992–94—Clinton *triangulates* vis-à-vis both liberal Democrats in Congress and congressional Republicans, then engages in *strategic pursuit* of House Republican positions in June 1994 administration bill

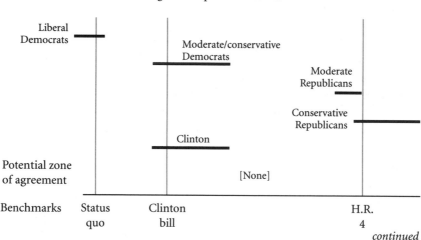

Step 2: Summer 1994—House Republicans move to right in H.R. 4 bill included in Contract with America, pursuing *strategic disagreement* strategy vis-à-vis Democrats and *splitting the difference* with respect to their internal disagreements

continued

Figure 14-1. *(Continued)*

Step 3: March 1995—Clinton and House Democrats move to right in supporting Deal alternative to H.R. 4, following *strategic pursuit* and *matching* strategies to hold Democrats together and avoid defections to H.R. 4

Range of acceptable outcomes

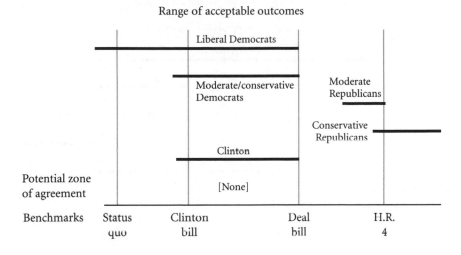

Step 4: September 1995—Clinton endorsement of Senate Republican bill pulls moderate Democrats to the right as they *match* Clinton; passage of Senate bill creates new default position in bargaining to which Republicans can return

Range of acceptable outcomes

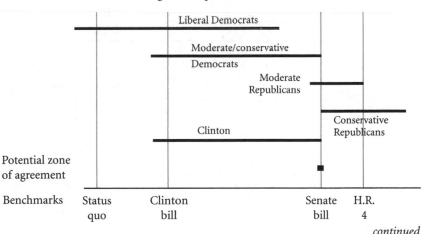

continued

Figure 14-1. *(Continued)*

Step 5: December 1995—House and Senate Republicans *split the difference* with respect to differences between their two bills, but Clinton rejects it both as part of reconciliation bill and as separate legislation; Senate welfare bill remains in place as a new default position in bargaining to which Republicans can return

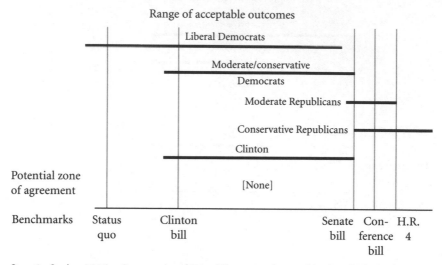

Step 6: Spring 1996—Congressional Republicans on the one hand and administration and congressional Democrats on the other pursue *strategic disagreement* on Medicaid reform

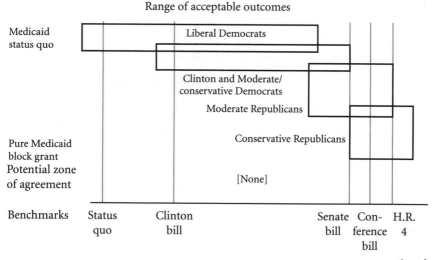

continued

Figure 14-1. *(Continued)*

Step 7: Summer 1996—House and Senate Republicans drop Medicaid provisions and *split the difference* with the administration between the conference bill and 1995 Senate bills; president and many congressional Democrats agree to support it

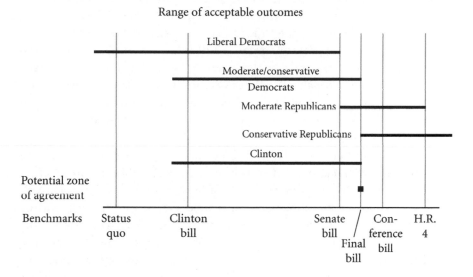

Range of acceptable outcomes

majorities and presidential assent can be based. Estimates of the breadth of these zones of acceptable outcomes are necessarily rough because (1) many dimensions of welfare policy have been collapsed into a single summary dimension; (2) the group categories, such as "Moderate/conservative" Democrats in Congress collapse the diverse groups of legislators with disparate individual preferences together; and (3) perhaps most important, the outer boundaries of policymakers' zones of acceptable outcomes are rarely known with certainty until policymakers have been presented with concrete choices on which they have to make a decision. Chapter 3 noted that policymakers may have strong incentives to be undecided about how far away from their ideal points they can be pushed, and the narrative chapters showed that President Clinton and others did use this strategy of ambiguity.

As figure 14-1 shows, the key initial step in the welfare reform process was taken by Bill Clinton during his first presidential campaign and the first eighteen months of his presidency. By pledging to end welfare as we know it and move to a system that placed a time limit on benefits after which work would be required, Clinton sought to place himself to the right of traditional Democratic positions on welfare reform but (by stressing child care, work incentives, and a public-sector job backstop) to the left of Republicans—a classic triangulation repositioning move with strong policy and electoral roots. It also threatened to create coalitional problems within the Democratic party, especially among the party's liberals. But the "New Democratic" outsider candidate and his staff viewed these considerations as a minor problem for the future at worst, and a potential political bonus (because it demonstrated Clinton's rejection of traditional Democratic positions and constituencies) at best, when they were initially formulating the campaign's welfare positions. It was not clear just how far to the right Clinton would move if pressed—but it also seemed unlikely until the Republicans took control of Congress that he would be pressed very hard or very far.

By the summer of 1994, with the Clinton administration's legislative agenda and political support collapsing, House Republicans under Newt Gingrich tried to set out a bold alternative agenda in the Contract with America.[9] Once again, a mixture of incentives can be seen at work: skirting unpopular social issues like abortion and school prayer while embracing broadly popular ones like welfare reform, attempting to solidify an alliance with social conservative groups, trying to reclaim the welfare issue for Republicans, and attempting to advance an agenda that most Republicans would agree was "good policy" and would unite the legislative caucus rather than dividing it. The party's move to the right (vis-à-vis both the Clinton administration and the party's earlier H.R. 3500 proposal) represented elements of both strategic-disagreement and splitting-the-difference strategies: the former in relation to the Clinton administration (in order to reclaim an image as the "real reformers") and the latter in relation to differences within the Republican party between supporters of H.R. 3500 and the more conservative Talent-Faircloth bill (H.R. 4544) on how much to stress deterrence strategies. The new Republican bid meant that policymakers no longer had a zone of agreement on which to enact welfare reform legislation. The question of how far President Clinton's and congressional Democrats' zones of acceptable outcomes could be pushed to the right was posed more starkly than before.

Two further steps in 1995 provided preliminary answers to the question of how far Democrats could be pushed. In March even liberal Democrats in the House of Representatives signed on to the Deal welfare reform bill, which was extraordinarily conservative by traditional Democratic standards (step 3). This strategic pursuit was motivated by a melding of electoral concerns (providing Democrats with a politically defensible alternative to the Republican bill to help in avoiding blame from the electorate when they voted against the Republican welfare bill) and coalitional concerns (avoiding massive defections by Democratic legislators to support the Republican bill). It also involved elements of matching. The rightward boundary for House Democrats' collective position "matched" the farthest left position that conservative Democrats would accept as a price of not swinging over to support the Republican bill. There still was no zone of agreement acceptable to a winning coalition of legislators and the president, however. That re-emerged in September 1995, when President Clinton endorsed the Senate-passed bill in principle (step 4). Moderate and conservative Democrats matched the president's move, creating a potentially winning zone of agreement around that bill—and a new default position to which Republicans could return if they failed to move the president's zone of acceptable outcomes further to the right. Thus Democrats' hopes for preventing the passage of Republican-oriented welfare reform legislation turned largely on (1) preventing a bill from getting to the president—a difficult task, since they controlled neither chamber of Congress; or (2) a House-Senate conference agreement significantly to the right of the Senate bill, combined with presidential unwillingness to extend his zone of acceptable outcomes any further to the right.

Although the first of these possibilities did not pan out, the second initially did. The Republican reconciliation bill sent to President Clinton in December 1995 roughly split the difference between the House and Senate bills (step 5). It also contained many other provisions (notably major Medicare and Medicaid cuts) that made it veto bait: the president's zone of acceptable outcomes was apparently not infinitely elastic, at least on non-welfare issues. Indeed, his veto of a separate welfare reform bill in January 1996 suggested real limits on what he would accept on school lunches and Food Stamps as well, although the rightward boundary of his zone of acceptable outcomes on AFDC remained fuzzy. An initiative from the governors to devolve both AFDC and Medicaid started and sputtered in the spring of 1996: strategic disagreement on the part of the Republicans regarding devolution of Medicaid (shown in two dimensions in step 6) was intended to draw President Clinton into agreeing to massive changes in that program as well as AFDC, but he signaled clearly that he would not agree. When polling data suggesting possible Republican losses in the upcoming fall elections gave Republicans an additional incentive to pass legislation, they dropped Medicaid provisions and roughly split the difference between the 1995 Senate-passed bill and the reconciliation bill, winning presidential assent (step 7).

The Centrality of Choice

This brief review of the repositioning choices made over the course of the Republican round in welfare reform supports and refines the arguments developed in this book about the importance of strategic choice in American politics. First, the breadth of policymakers' zones of acceptable outcomes are at least as important as their "ideal points" in explaining whether policy change is likely to occur. What made welfare reform possible in 1996 was not a convergence of preferences around a specific package of policy changes, but rather that (1) the zone of acceptable outcomes of many Democrats (including President Clinton) was stretched to become extraordinarily broad since they did not want to be perceived as defenders of the status quo, and (2) opponents of policy change did not control any points at which they could block open votes on proposals for change.

Second, rather than being based solely on electoral concerns, repositioning choices were generally based on a mixture of electoral, policy, and coalitional considerations. No clear hierarchy of concerns is visible across all of these choices. In large part, the absence of a clear hierarchy of concerns results from the fact that some considerations (for example, coalitional concerns in the case of Clinton's initial position to "end welfare as we know it") did not seem salient at the time that those repositioning choices were made. But it does seem clear that politicians constantly sought "good choices" (options that would make them better off on multiple dimensions and worse off on none) and that they tried to avoid "hard choices" (better off on some or all dimensions, worse off on others) and "bad choices" (worse off on some dimensions, better off on none). Avoiding blame was an especially high priority. When options that appeared to be "good choices" were available, politicians were likely to use political resources to press them on the agenda, as Clinton did with welfare reform in his presidential campaign. We also saw in the discussion of the earlier rounds of welfare reform that when politicians pressed options that were "good choices" for themselves but appeared to be "bad choices" for political competitors, those competitors typically responded by using agenda limitation to try to prevent consideration of those measures—a strategic option not open to liberal Democrats in the 1995–96 round, since they controlled no veto points at which such initiatives could be blocked.

A third conclusion is that policymakers' zones of acceptable outcomes are set relationally—that is, in relation to the positions taken by other policymakers as well as their own preferences and those of the electorate. These zones can change substantially over time within a single round of policymaking. In the last two rounds of welfare reform, the key role in redefining other policymakers' zones of acceptable outcomes was clearly played by President Clinton: many Democrats set the rightward boundary of their zone of acceptable outcomes wherever the president set his, in order to avoid being seen as to his left on welfare issues, while Republicans throughout most of the Clinton and Republican rounds tried to set their leftward boundary to the right of Clinton's rightward boundary, in order to prevent Clinton from getting the credit for reforming welfare, and to position themselves as tougher on the issue.

Fourth, policymakers' repositioning choices, and the range of their zone of acceptable outcomes, were heavily influenced by contextual factors. In particular, overwhelming public hostility toward the status quo and the racialized image of the AFDC program meant that most policymakers' zones of acceptable outcomes would be very wide if they were confronted with a choice between "change" and the status quo. Policy research helped move zones of acceptable outcomes to the right, especially among Republicans, as discouraging findings on welfare spells and illegitimacy and the inability of prevention/rehabilitation and work-based approaches to improve those trends were absorbed by policymakers. And partisan changes—in particular Republican control of the congressional agenda—meant that the nature of the "bids" to which other policymakers had to respond would be uniformly conservative ones. Partisan change also had a critical effect on agenda control: congressional Democrats could not prevent votes on Republican welfare bills, which forced them to expand their own zone of acceptable outcomes. But in analyzing how contextual factors shape policymaking in specific sectors, it may be less helpful to examine individual factors (ideology, race, public opinion) than the interaction of several factors, as in the case of welfare policymaking traps. Similarly, understanding policy change may require understanding the interaction of some factors that did change (elite and public opinion) with others that did not (racial composition of caseloads).

Fifth, repositioning choices were influenced by short-term political considerations and miscalculations as well as long-term developments in contextual factors. Politicians have short time horizons, tending to discount both costs and benefits that are highly uncertain and far off in the future.

The Republican decision to abandon strategic disagreement on welfare and Medicaid in the summer of 1996, for example, was influenced by polling data showing that congressional Republicans might face substantial potential losses in the 1996 congressional elections. Failure to anticipate future political developments also affected repositioning choices. Bill Clinton's strident antiwelfare rhetoric, for example, failed to anticipate a Democratic loss of control in Congress in 1994. The point here is not that these choices were "irrational"—on the contrary, they were rational responses to the situation at hand, given the information that policymakers had at the time. The point is rather that such choices, and the eventual outcome, might not be predicted a priori by a neutral observer looking just at broad contextual influences even a few months in advance.

The limitations of looking just at broad contextual factors—and hence the limitations of a priori prediction—are underscored by a sixth conclusion, that while the repositioning choices made by policymakers in the Clinton and Republican rounds of welfare were rational (and thus explainable) choices, they were not the only plausible choices. Rarely were policymakers in the situation where they had only an "easy choice" (a single alternative so attractive that no alternative could be plausibly imagined) or "no choice" (no plausible alternative to a single unattractive option). Bill Clinton's decision to stress welfare reform in his 1992 presidential campaign can probably be best characterized as politically easy given the combination of his own policy priorities, the availability of the Ellwood mixed approach to reforming welfare, and its fit with other elements of the Clinton platform. But the stress on "ending welfare as we know it" was only one of several plausible "good choices" for a welfare campaign theme. Alternative formulations such as including "making work pay," or "two years and then work" might have primed public hostility to welfare somewhat less, and thus had a less expansive impact on Democrats' (especially President Clinton's) zone of acceptable outcomes. The Republican leadership decision in the summer of 1994 to develop a new welfare reform bill rather than simply endorse the H.R. 3500 bill was a hard choice, but probably no more difficult than the alternative. In the summer of 1996, delinking Medicaid and AFDC reform and reaching an accommodation with President Clinton on the latter (and thus allowing him to share political credit for it) was by no means the only plausible choice for Republican congressional leaders, and they were not united on the subject.

Would the final outcome have been different if these plausible alternatives had been chosen? The answer is almost certainly yes, although how different, and in what ways it would have been different, we can never know. Making difficult choices from diverse alternatives—sometimes good choices, often hard choices or bad choices—is what politics is all about. But the plethora of alternatives and choices in the process, the multitude of short- and long-term factors that influenced those decisions, and the centrality of these decisions in the final outcomes, suggest that the tendency of social scientists retrospectively to view outcomes as inevitable and move from there to explanations that are seen as necessary, sufficient, and parsimonious may be a misreading of history. It may in fact be more accurate to say that in most choice situations, politicians face a limited number of options to which they are almost indifferent because each is a hard choice offering differing packages of costs and benefits with a similar overall value. They face hard choices because their political opponents work hard to make their choices as unappealing as possible. The centrality of choice—and hard choices—makes explanations of political events complex and incomplete and makes prediction less a science than an art that political scientists undertake only at the risk of embarrassing themselves.

A final conclusion is that choices have consequences; they can never be undone. These impacts can be immense, even if they are not immediately felt or even recognized. Clinton's promise to end welfare as we know it and his backing of the September 1995 Senate welfare bill clearly stand out as choices that limited his room to maneuver and ultimately broadened the zone of acceptable outcomes both for him and for many other Democratic policymakers. But other choices, notably the decision of Republicans to come to terms with Clinton in the summer of 1996 and President Clinton's decision not to veto the resulting bill, also had critical, permanent effects. Collectively these choices, and the cascade of repositioning by other policymakers that they inspired, turned "ending welfare as we know it" from political possibility into a policy reality.

Notes

Chapter One

1. The litany of failed comprehensive welfare initiatives includes President Nixon's Family Assistance Plan, President Carter's Program for Better Jobs and Incomes, President Reagan's abortive New Federalism, and President Clinton's Work and Responsibility program of 1994. Important AFDC reforms were enacted in 1981 and 1988 under President Reagan, but they were far less comprehensive than the initiatives just cited. Reform initiatives before the 1990s are discussed in more detail in chapter 4.

2. David T. Ellwood, "Welfare Reform as I Knew It," *American Prospect*, vol. 26 (May–June 1996), p. 22.

3. The argument here is not that the positions acceptable to various participants were *purely* relational, but rather that they were largely so. If they were purely relational, the interaction of the relational dynamics posed here would, in repeated iterations, push the positions of all parties infinitely far to the ideological right.

Chapter Two

1. Mary Ann Petri's story is from Jeff Israely, "Kids at Risk," *Oakland Tribune*, October 19, 1997.

2. Louisa Blue's story is told in Judith Havemann, "In Childbearing Choices, Many Motives Prove More Powerful than Money," *Washington Post*, March 30, 1997, p. A4.

3. Sandi Szabrowicz is profiled in the *Milwaukee Journal Sentinel*, May 31, 1998.

4. Kitty Funchess's story was told in Michael H. Hodges, "Grandmother Pays High Price for a Career—Her Family," *Detroit News*, September 21, 1997.

5. In 1995 there was a monthly average of 13,619,000 AFDC recipients, of whom 9,225,000 were children. House Ways and Means Committee, *1998 Green Book* (Government Printing Office), p. 413.

6. For overviews of the condition of children and issues in family policy see David Ellwood, *Poor Support: Poverty in the American Family* (Basic Books, 1988); Robert Haveman and Barbara Wolfe, "Children's Prospects and Children's Policy," *Journal of Economic Perspectives*. vol. 7 (Fall 1993), pp. 153–74; and Haveman and Wolfe, *Succeeding*

Generations: On the Effects of Investments in Children (Russell Sage Foundation, 1994). *The Green Book* is the definitive data source on the condition of children and family support policies.

7. House Ways and Means Committee, *1996 Green Book* (GPO), p. 1178.

8. A decline in birthrates among married women also contributed to the increase in the percentage of births that occur outside marriage.

9. R. Kent Weaver and William T. Dickens, eds., *Looking Before We Leap: Social Science and Welfare Reform* (Brookings, 1995), p. 29.

10. House Ways and Means Committee, *1996 Green Book*, pp. 1183–85.

11. Daniel Patrick Moynihan, *Family and Nation* (San Diego: Harvest HBJ, 1986), p. 46.

12. House Ways and Means Committee, *1996 Green Book*, p. 1217.

13. See Haveman and Wolfe, *Succeeding Generations*, chap. 1.

14. In addition to the approaches discussed here, some countries have provided universal flat-rate child benefits to all children. This avoids stigmatization, but it is also very expensive and is inefficient in its targeting. A large share of payments will go to families that do not need them. Universal family allowances have never been seriously on the policy agenda in the United States. A variant on this approach, targeting within universalism, is discussed in chapter 5.

15. The 1990 budget agreement phased out these deductions for the highest-income taxpayers.

16. Unfortunately, it is difficult to find out just how much child tax exemptions cost the federal treasury because they are considered part of the normal tax code rather than tax expenditures, and the resulting revenue losses are therefore not listed in the annual budget listing of tax expenditures. Irwin Garfinkel has estimated that the federal child tax exemption cost the federal treasury $22 billion in 1996, with only $2 billion going to (disproportionately poor) single-parent families. "Economic Security for Children: From Means-Testing and Bifurcation to Universality," in Irwin Garfinkel, Jennifer L. Hochschild, and Sara S. McLanahan, eds., *Social Policies for Children* (Brookings, 1996), p. 38. Similarly, Steven Pressman has estimated the federal revenue loss from child exemptions at $16 billion in 1984, with virtually none of that amount going to the poor. See "Child Exemptions or Child Allowances: What Sort of Antipoverty Program for the United States?" *American Journal of Economics and Sociology,* vol. 51 (July 1992), pp. 257–72.

17. The SSI program provides a uniform federally funded benefit, but many states supplement SSI benefits.

18. On the origins of SSI, see Martha Derthick, *Agency under Stress: The Social Security Administration in American Government* (Brookings, 1990); and Bob Woodward and Benjamin Weiser, "Costs Soar for Children's Disability Program," *Washington Post,* February 4, 1994, p. A1.

19. *Sullivan* v. *Zebley,* 493 U.S. 521. See also Woodward and Weiser, "Costs Soar for Children's Disability Program"; and General Accounting Office, *Social Security: Rapid*

Rise in Children on SSI Disability Rolls Follows New Regulations, HEHS-94-225, September 1994. The SSI program has also experienced rapid growth in recipiency by two groups not reflected in figure 2-1. Adult noncitizens who are legal residents of the United States increased from 3 percent of all SSI recipients in 1982 to almost 12 percent in 1993. Disabled SSI recipients whose diagnoses include addiction to drugs or alcohol increased eightfold from 1988 to 1994. Sixty-nine percent of legal immigrant recipients were at least sixty-five years old, while 31 percent were disabled. General Accounting Office, *Supplemental Security Income: Growth and Changes in Recipient Population Call for Reexamining Program,* HEHS-95-137 (GPO, 1995), p. 19.

20. In 1995, 87.2 percent of AFDC households received food stamps, 24.7 percent received WIC benefits, and 63.1 percent received free or reduced-price school lunches. House Ways and Means Committee, *1996 Green Book,* p. 856.

21. About half of food stamp households are headed by a woman and include children. House Ways and Means Committee, *1996 Green Book,* p. 880.

22. See Theda Skocpol, *Protecting Soldiers and Mothers: The Political Origins of Social Policy in the United States* (Harvard University Press, 1992), chap. 8.

23. Skocpol, *Protecting Soldiers and Mothers,* pp. 465–76. Skocpol notes (p. 471) that only 3 percent of mothers' pension recipients in a 1931 Children's Bureau survey were African American.

24. For a history of the creation of the AFDC program, see Linda Gordon, *Pitied but Not Entitled: Single Mothers and the History of Welfare 1890–1935* (Free Press, 1994).

25. For an excellent review of the law and politics of entitlements, see R. Shep Melnick, *Between the Lines: Interpreting Welfare Rights* (Brookings, 1994), chap. 3. This section draws heavily on Melnick's analysis.

26. States were also required to have a single state agency administering the state's plan. Melnick, *Between the Lines,* p. 69.

27. Ibid., pp. 68–72; and Gilbert Y. Steiner, *Social Insecurity: The Politics of Welfare* (Chicago: Rand McNally, 1966), chap. 4.

28. For analyses focusing on racial exclusion see, for example, Robert C. Lieberman, "Race and the Organization of Social Policy," in Paul E. Peterson, ed., *Classifying by Race* (Princeton University Press, 1995), pp. 156–87. For an analysis focusing more on fiscal capacity see Gareth Davies and Martha Derthick, "Race and Social Welfare Policy: The Social Security Act of 1935," *Political Science Quarterly,* vol. 112, no. 2 (1997), pp. 217–35. Davies and Derthick point out that not all southern legislators favored a decentralized public assistance system; some favored a nationalized system.

29. Melnick, *Between the Lines,* pp. 68–69; and Steiner, *Social Insecurity,* p. 246. On the role of southern Democrats in Congress in this period see Ira Katznelson, Kim Geiger, and Daniel Kryder, "Limiting Liberalism: The Southern Veto in Congress, 1933–1950," *Political Science Quarterly,* vol. 108, no. 2 (1993), pp. 283–306.

30. Melnick, *Between the Lines,* pp. 94–97; and Steiner, *Social Insecurity,* p. 246.

31. Need standards were used to determine program eligibility. In 1996 both applicants and enrollees had to have a gross income below 185 percent of the need standard,

and applicants had to have a net income no higher than 100 percent of the need standard. House Ways and Means Committee, *1996 Green Book*, p. 436.

32. Ibid.

33. Because food stamp benefits vary inversely with cash income, the interstate variation in AFDC benefits plus food stamps is less than that for AFDC benefits alone: in this
example the combined maximum food stamp and AFDC benefit would be $935 in New
York and $433 in Mississippi. Ibid., pp. 437–38.

34. All or part of three of the forty-eight contiguous states had combined
AFDC–food stamp benefits for a family of three at or above 80 percent of the federal
poverty guideline in January 1996. Ibid.

35. House Ways and Means Committee, *1993 Green Book*, pp. 665, 1240.

36. Jason DeParle, "Panel Urges Expanding Aid for Two-Parent Homes," *New York
Times*, December 10, 1993, p. A1; and Iris L. Lav and others, *The States and the Poor: How
Budget Decisions Affected Low Income People in 1992* (Washington: Center on Budget
and Policy Priorities, and Albany, N.Y.: Center for the Study of the States, 1993).

37. The program was first enacted in 1961 as a temporary antirecession measure
and made permanent in 1962. For a brief summary of AFDC-UP, see House Ways and
Means Committee, *1996 Green Book*, pp. 394–96.

38. Even in 1993, almost 90 percent of AFDC benefits were paid to single-parent
families. Ibid., p. 458.

39. Ibid., p. 385.

40. On the "withering away" fallacy, see Steiner, *Social Insecurity*, chap. 2.

41. House Ways and Means Committee, *1994 Green Book*, p. 325; and *Budget of the
United States Government, Fiscal Year 1997: Supplement*, p. 71.

42. See the discussion by William Dickens, "Why Has the AFDC Caseload
Increased?" in Weaver and Dickens, *Looking Before We Leap*, pp. 42–47.

43. For a recent review, see Martin Gilens, "'Race Coding' and White Opposition to
Welfare," *American Political Science Review*, vol. 90 (September 1996), pp. 593–604; and
Gilens, "Racial Attitudes and Opposition to Welfare," *Journal of Politics*, vol. 57, no. 4
(November 1995), pp. 994–1014. See also Paul M. Sniderman and Thomas Piazza, *The
Scar of Race* (Harvard University Press, 1993). On the role of race in anti-poverty pro-
grams generally, see Jill Quadagno, *The Color of Welfare: How Racism Undermined the
War on Poverty* (New York: Oxford University Press, 1994).

44. House Ways and Means Committee, *1994 Green Book*, p. 402.

45. Charles Murray, "New Welfare Bill, New Welfare Cheats," *Wall Street Journal*,
October 13, 1988, p. A22.

46. Elijah Anderson, *Streetwise: Race, Class and Change in an Urban Community*
(University of Chicago Press, 1990), p. 131.

47. Thomas Byrne Edsall and Mary D. Edsall, *Chain Reaction: The Impact of Race,
Rights, and Taxes on American Politics* (Norton, 1992), p. 176. See also Will Marshall and
Elaine Ciulla Kamarck, "Replacing Welfare with Work," in Will Marshall and Martin
Schram, eds., *Mandate for Change* (Berkley Books, 1993), pp. 217–36.

Chapter Three

1. See in particular Hugh Heclo, "The Political Foundations of Anti-Poverty Policy," in Sheldon H. Danziger and Daniel H. Weinberg, eds., *Fighting Poverty: What Works and What Doesn't* (Harvard University Press, 1986), pp. 312–40.

2. Robert A. Moffitt, "Explaining Welfare Reform: Public Choice and the Labor Market," Johns Hopkins University, April 1999. As will be discussed later, welfare case-loads had begun a rapid decline by the time the Personal Responsibility and Work Opportunity Reconciliation Act of 1996 (PRWORA) legislation was enacted.

3. See in particular Steven M. Teles, *Whose Welfare? AFDC and Elite Politics* (University Press of Kansas, 1996).

4. For differing views of the influence of race on American social policy, see Jill S. Quadagno, *The Color of Welfare: How Racism Undermined the War on Poverty* (Oxford University Press, 1994); Theda Skocpol, "African Americans in U.S. Social Policy," in Paul E. Peterson, ed., *Classifying by Race* (Princeton University Press, 1995), pp. 129–55; and Gareth Davies and Martha Derthick, "Race and Social Welfare Policy: The Social Security Act of 1935," *Political Science Quarterly*, vol. 112, no. 2 (1997), pp. 217–35.

5. Frances Fox Piven and Richard A. Cloward, *Regulating the Poor: The Functions of Public Welfare* (Pantheon, 1971).

6. Jill Quadagno, "From Old-Age Assistance to Supplemental Security Income: The Political Economy of Relief in the South, 1935–1972," in Margaret Weir, Ann Orloff, and Theda Skocpol, eds., *The Politics of Social Policy in the United States* (Princeton University Press, 1988), pp. 235–63.

7. Hugh Heclo, "Clinton's Health Reform in Historical Perspective," in Henry J. Aaron, ed., *The Problem That Won't Go Away: Reforming U.S. Health Care Financing* (Brookings, 1996), pp. 15–33.

8. See in particular Christopher Leman, "Patterns of Policy Development: Social Security in the United States and Canada," *Public Policy*, vol. 25, no. 2 (1977), pp. 261–91; and Sven H. Steinmo and Jon Watts, "It's the Institutions, Stupid! Why Comprehensive National Health Insurance Always Fails in America," *Journal of Health Policy, Politics and Law*, vol. 20, no. 2 (Summer 1995), pp. 329–72.

9. On state discretion in policymaking and the race to the bottom see Paul E. Peterson and Mark C. Rom, *Welfare Magnets: A New Case for a National Welfare Standard* (Brookings, 1990).

10. See especially Paul Pierson, *Dismantling the Welfare State? Reagan, Thatcher, and the Politics of Retrenchment* (Cambridge University Press, 1994).

11. As is discussed in chapter 6, recent research suggests that many AFDC-TANF recipients do work but do not report their income.

12. For an excellent introduction to the choice perspective see Kenneth A. Shepsle and Mark S. Bonchek, *Analyzing Politics: Rationality, Behavior, and Institutions* (Norton, 1997).

13. Depending on the diversity of opinion within the group, such informal structures may lead either to stalemate or to a groupthink that inhibits rational, comprehensive

decisionmaking. The classic study is Irving L. Janis, *Victims of Groupthink* (Houghton Mifflin, 1972).

14. On the reelection motive see, for example, David Mayhew, *Congress: The Electoral Connection* (Yale University Press, 1974); and R. Douglas Arnold, *The Logic of Congressional Action* (Yale University Press, 1990).

15. Arnold, *Logic of Congressional Action,* pp. 64–65.

16. See especially R. Kent Weaver, "The Politics of Blame Avoidance," *Journal of Public Policy,* vol. 6, no. 4 (1986), pp. 371–98.

17. See, for example, John Kingdon, *Congressmen's Voting Decisions* (Harper and Row, 1973), pp. 60–68; and Arnold, *Logic of Congressional Action,* chap. 4.

18. This process need not necessarily involve a truly new proposal; a reframing of old proposals that makes new claims about old policy ideas may do. The key is that it presents politicians with a win on political, policy, and coalitional terms.

19. Even if several good choices are available, however, policymakers may have to make trade-offs (for example, greater value congruence but fewer political rewards or less political feasibility). Moreover, particular options may offer greater rewards to some elements of a political coalition than to others. Thus even good choices may cause tension within a coalition.

20. The same alternatives may be perceived quite differently by different groups of politicians with different ideal points, of course. If the welfare options on the agenda are limited to policies more conservative than the status quo, for example, they will probably seem good choices to conservative Republicans, but bad choices to liberal Democrats.

21. John Kingdon, *Agendas, Alternatives, and Public Policies,* 2d ed. (HarperCollins, 1995). See also Frank Baumgartner and Bryan D. Jones, *Agendas and Instability in American Politics* (University of Chicago Press, 1993).

22. On problem definition as a component of the policymaking process and as a political process see Deborah Stone, "Causal Stories and the Formation of Policy Agendas," *Political Science Quarterly,* vol. 104, no. 2 (Summer 1989), pp. 281–300.

23. Kingdon, *Agendas, Alternatives, and Public Policies,* pp. 131–39. These survival tests in the policy stream are roughly equivalent to the welfare policymaking traps discussed later in this chapter: technical feasibility (the perverse incentives and federalism traps), affordability (money trap), value congruence (dual clientele and federalism traps), and political viability (cross-cutting institutional barriers).

24. Indeed, Kingdon argues that "advocates lie in wait, in and around government with their solutions in hand, waiting for problems to float by to which they can attach their solutions, waiting for a development in the political stream they can use to their advantage." *Agendas, Alternatives, and Public Policies,* p. 165.

25. See James Enelow, "Saving Amendments, Killer Amendments and an Expected Utility Theory of Sophisticated Voting," *Journal of Politics,* vol. 43, no. 4 (November 1981), pp. 1062–89; and John D. Wilkerson, "'Killer' Amendments in Congress," *American Political Science Review,* vol. 93, no. 3 (September 1999), pp. 535–52.

26. Working in multiple policy and political arenas simultaneously also forces policymakers to make consistent moves across games: it is difficult, for example, to undertake a welfare reform initiative that will cost significantly more money in the short run while tightening federal spending generally. See Robert D. Putnam, "Diplomacy and Domestic Politics: The Logic of Two-Level Games," *International Organization*, vol. 42 (Summer 1988), pp. 427–60; and George Tsebelis, *Nested Games: Rational Choice in Comparative Politics* (University of California Press, 1990).

27. In the jargon of political science, politicians' preferences are endogenous to the bargaining game. For a contrary argument see David W. Brady and Craig Volden, *Revolving Gridlock: Politics and Policy from Carter to Clinton* (Boulder, Colo.: Westview Press, 1998), chap. 1.

28. John B. Gilmour, *Strategic Disagreement: Stalemate in American Politics* (University of Pittsburgh Press, 1995).

29. See Thomas Schelling, *The Strategy of Conflict* (New York: Oxford University Press, 1963), p. 22; and Robert D. Putnam, "Diplomacy and Domestic Politics: The Logic of Two-Level Games," *International Organization*, vol. 42 (Summer 1988), pp. 427–60.

30. On strategic disagreement and bidding wars see the excellent analysis by John Gilmour in *Strategic Disagreement*. Gilmour defines strategic disagreements as "disagreements [that] result not from the absence of feasible agreement, but from tactics calculated to maintain political advantage." Strategic disagreement can take two forms: moving one's announced position further away from that of opponents, or shrinking the range of acceptable outcomes around one's policy ideal point. In either case the effect is to eliminate the zone of agreement in which acceptable outcomes overlap.

31. On selling out see, in particular, Gilmour, *Strategic Disagreement*, pp. 26–32.

32. Ibid., p. 56.

33. On this point, see Carolyn Hughes Tuohy, *Accidental Logics: The Dynamics of Change in the Health Care Arena in the United States, Britain, and Canada* (Oxford University Press, 1999), p. 12.

34. On the importance of the factors that constrain choices and shape preferences, see in particular Donald P. Green and Ian Shapiro, *Pathologies of Rational Choice Theory: A Critique of Applications in Political Science* (Yale University Press, 1994).

35. The "historical institutionalist" approach, for example, draws on uneven democratization, late development of a bureaucracy, and policy feedbacks to explain the character of the U.S. welfare state. See "Introduction: Understanding American Social Politics," pp. 3–27; and Ann Shola Orloff, "The Political Origins of America's Belated Welfare State," in Weir, Orloff, and Skocpol, *Politics of Social Policy in the United States*, pp. 37–80.

36. In *Poor Support*, Harvard economist (and later cochair of the Clinton administration's task force on welfare reform) David Ellwood similarly spoke of welfare's "helping conundrums," or problems that have no satisfactory solution. His focus, however, was primarily on the incentive structure for recipients, while the focus here is on the

political dilemmas faced by policymakers. David Ellwood, *Poor Support: Poverty in the American Family* (Basic Books, 1988).

37. On the dual clientele trap in welfare reform, see also Hugh Heclo's argument in "Poverty Politics" in Sheldon Danziger and Daniel Weinberg, eds., *Confronting Poverty: Prescriptions for Change* (Harvard University Press and Russell Sage, 1994), pp. 396–437. He makes the point that Americans simultaneously feel a responsibility to help those who cannot help themselves, want to promote self-sufficiency, and seek to reduce poverty without explicitly embracing redistribution. The ambivalence in American attitudes toward social policy is addressed in Jennifer L. Hochschild, *What's Fair: American Beliefs about Distributive Justice* (Harvard University Press, 1981); and Stanley Feldman and John Zaller, "The Political Culture of Ambivalence: Ideological Responses to the Welfare State," *American Journal of Political Science*, vol. 36 (February 1992), pp. 268–307.

38. The main effect is probably more in preventing efficient emigration than in fostering inefficient immigration. See Peterson and Rom, *Welfare Magnets*.

39. In addition, a decentralized, uneven benefit structure can create difficulties in moving to a national standard, should there ever be a will to do so. Given very different state payment levels, it would be hard to avoid making persons in high-benefit states worse off with a single benefit. Martha Derthick's discussion of the creation of Supplemental Security Income in 1972 shows the difficulties that very uneven baseline benefits can create in trying to move to a national system, at least in the short term. See *Agency under Stress: The Social Security Administration in American Government* (Brookings, 1990).

40. See Judith M. Gueron, "A Research Context for Welfare Reform," *Journal of Policy Analysis and Management*, vol. 15 (1996), p. 550.

Chapter Four

1. On the Family Assistance Plan, see Henry Aaron, *Why Is Welfare So Hard to Reform?* (Brookings, 1973); Theodore R. Marmor and Martin Rein, "Reforming the 'Welfare Mess': The Fate of the Family Assistance Plan, 1969–1972," in Alan Sindler, ed., *Policy and Politics in America* (Boston: Little, Brown, 1975); Daniel Patrick Moynihan, *The Politics of a Guaranteed Income: The Nixon Administration and the Family Assistance Plan* (Vintage, 1973); and Gilbert Y. Steiner, *The State of Welfare* (Brookings, 1971), chap. 3.

2. On the Carter initiative, see Laurence E. Lynn Jr. and David de F. Whitman, *The President as Policymaker: Jimmy Carter and Welfare Reform* (Temple University Press, 1981); and Christopher Leman, *The Collapse of Welfare Reform: Political Institutions, Policy and the Poor in Canada and the United States* (MIT Press, 1980).

3. Leman, *The Collapse of Welfare Reform*, p. 173.

4. On the 1981 experience, see Edward D. Berkowitz, "Changing the Meaning of Welfare Reform," in John C. Weicher, ed., *Maintaining the Safety Net: Income*

Redistribution Programs in the Reagan Administration (Washington: American Enterprise Institute, 1984), pp. 23–42.

5. *Social Security Bulletin Annual Statistical Supplement, 1997*, p. 340. Both expenditure and recipient figures are on a calendar year basis.

6. Edward D. Berkowitz, *America's Welfare State from Roosevelt to Reagan* (Johns Hopkins University Press, 1991), p. 118. In some major cities, the trends were even more dramatic. In New York City, by 1970 one in seven residents was on welfare, and public assistance expenditures composed more than one-quarter of the municipal budget, far exceeding education expenditures. Moynihan, *The Politics of a Guaranteed Annual Income*, pp. 26–27; Steiner, *The State of Welfare*, p. 296. About 44 percent of New York City's public assistance payments were for AFDC.

7. Among black children living with a single parent, the percentage whose parent had never married rose from 9.6 percent in 1960 to 14.1 percent in 1970, while the percentage living with a widowed parent fell from 21.3 to 14.6 percent. Among white children, the percentage living with a single parent rose from 7.1 percent in 1960 to 8.7 percent in 1970. The percentage of white children living with a single parent who had never married rose from 1.6 to 2.6 percent over this period, while the percentage living with a widowed parent fell from 29.0 to 22.7 percent. See House Ways and Means Committee, *1996 Green Book* (Government Printing Office, 1996), pp. 1183–84. See also Steiner, *The State of Welfare*, pp. 40–43.

8. On the role of the courts, see especially R. Shep Melnick, *Between the Lines: Interpreting Welfare Rights* (Brookings, 1994), chaps. 4–6; and Steven M. Teles, *Whose Welfare? AFDC and Elite Politics* (University Press of Kansas, 1996), chap. 6.

9. See Steiner, *The State of Welfare*, pp. 77–80.

10. On WIN, see Leman, *The Collapse of Welfare Reform*, pp. 71–72.

11. Steiner, *The State of Welfare*, pp. 44–48, 80, 329. Congress also rejected an administration request that would have required individual states to raise benefit levels to meet their own definitions of subsistence. *1967 Congressional Quarterly Almanac*, p. 897.

12. Other perverse incentives may also arise. A negative income tax could, for example, increase incentives to have a first child if it were limited to families with children.

13. Moynihan, *The Politics of a Guaranteed Annual Income*, p. 126.

14. Steiner (*The State of Welfare*, pp. 318–19) argued that while "AFDC served a clientele almost evenly divided between black and white, family assistance [Nixon's FAP] will serve 38 percent black and 62 percent white families."

15. See Leman, *The Collapse of Welfare Reform*, pp. 70–71; and Martin Anderson, *Welfare: The Political Economy of Welfare Reform in the United States* (Stanford, Calif.: Hoover Institution Press, 1978), chap. 3.

16. On the development of the Family Assistance Plan within the Nixon administration, see Moynihan, *The Politics of a Guaranteed Annual Income*; Vincent Burke and Vee Burke, *Nixon's Good Deed: Welfare Reform* (Columbia University Press, 1974); and

Kenneth Bowler, *The Nixon Guaranteed Income Proposal* (Cambridge, Mass.: Ballinger, 1974).

17. Leman, *The Collapse of Welfare Reform*, p. 78.

18. See the discussion in Marmor and Rein, "Reforming the 'Welfare Mess.'"

19. See Leman, *The Collapse of Welfare Reform*, pp. 80–81.

20. The National Welfare Rights Organization, which was based primarily in high-benefit states in the Northeast, was particularly concerned about the administration's 1970 revisions to the bill, which eliminated the guarantee that AFDC-UP families would not be cut below current levels. See Leman, *The Collapse of Welfare Reform*, p. 80.

21. Moynihan, *The Politics of a Guaranteed Annual Income*, p. 455.

22. On Long's agenda, see Melnick, *Between the Lines*, pp. 119–24.

23. See Leman, *The Collapse of Welfare Reform*, pp. 85-88.

24. On Nixon's withdrawal of active support for FAP, see Lynn and Whitman, *The President as Policymaker*, pp. 30–31.

25. On the 1973–76 period, see Leman, *The Collapse of Welfare Reform*, pp. 90–94. See also Linda E. Demkovitch, "Making Some Sense out of the Welfare 'Mess,'" *National Journal*, January 8, 1977, pp. 44–55; and "Welfare Policy," *1976 Congressional Quarterly Almanac*, pp. 605–06.

26. See Joseph A. Califano Jr., *Governing America: An Insider's Report from the White House and the Cabinet* (Simon and Schuster, 1981), pp. 320–21; Lynn and Whitman, *The President as Policymaker*, pp. 44–46; and Kathryn Waters Gest, "Welfare Reform: Carter Studying Options," *Congressional Quarterly Weekly Report*, April 30, 1977, pp. 792–96.

27. Lynn and Whitman, *The President as Policymaker*, pp. 45–46.

28. See, for example, Linda E. Demkovitch, "Carter Gets Some Outside Advice for His Welfare Reform Package," *National Journal*, vol. 9, no. 18 (April 30, 1977), pp. 673–75.

29. For a detailed discussion of the politics of the zero net cost constraint, see Califano, *Governing America*, pp. 334–50.

30. See Lynn and Whitman, *The President as Policymaker*, pp. 221–26; Linda E. Demkovitch, "Welfare Reform: Can Carter Succeed Where Nixon Failed?" *National Journal*, vol. 9, no. 33 (August 27, 1977), pp. 1328–34.

31. Some individuals would move between tiers based on the availability of work and on whether those individuals expected to work in fact met job search and work requirements. Benefit reduction rates for earned income were to be higher in states that supplemented benefits. In contrast to FAP, PBJI covered single people and childless couples as well as families with children, although with low benefit guarantees and stiffer work requirements. For details of the administration's PBJI proposal, see Kathryn Waters Gest, "Carter, Congress and Welfare: A Long Road," *Congressional Quarterly Weekly Report*, August 13, 1977, pp. 1699–1706.

32. State minimum wage rates would be paid where those were higher than the federal minimum wage. For a discussion of the PBJI job provisions, see James W. Singer,

"The Welfare Package: 1.4 Million Jobs, 1.4 Million Questions," *National Journal,* vol. 9, no. 46 (November 12, 1977), pp. 1764–68.

33. These figures omit an additional $3.4 billion for an expanded Earned Income Tax Credit for persons not receiving PBJI cash benefits. The administration also assumed that lower unemployment would make most of the $5.5 billion Comprehensive Employment and Training Act (CETA) countercyclical employment program available for PBJI job slots. See Singer, "The Welfare Package."

34. Congressional Budget Office, *The Administration's Welfare Reform Proposal: An Analysis of the Program for Better Jobs and Incomes* (GPO, April 1978), p. 40. See also Linda E. Demkovitch, "Carter's Welfare Reform Package Is Being Re-Formed on the Hill," *National Journal,* vol. 9, no. 51 (December 17, 1977), p. 1961; Kathryn Waters Gest, "Ullman Unveils Own Welfare Reform Plan," *Congressional Quarterly Weekly Report,* February 4, 1978, p. 268.

35. Lynn and Whitman, *The President as Policymaker,* pp. 232–40.

36. Martin Donsky, "Compromise Talks Open in Effort to Salvage Some Welfare Reform," *Congressional Quarterly Weekly Report,* April 29, 1978, pp. 1064–68.

37. See Gest, "Ullman Unveils Own Welfare Reform Plan."

38. Califano, *Governing America,* p. 323.

39. Demkovitch, "Welfare Reform."

40. See Demkovitch, "Carter's Welfare Reform Package Is Being Re-Formed on the Hill," pp. 1958–61.

41. See, for example, Kathryn Waters Gest, "Will Congress Kill Food Stamp Program?" *Congressional Quarterly Weekly Report,* January 21, 1978, pp. 128–30. Moreover, Congress had overhauled the Food Stamp program in 1977 to eliminate the purchase requirement and thus expand program participation—actions that would be rendered obsolete if Congress "cashed out" food stamps.

42. Kathryn Waters Gest, "Carter, Congress and Welfare." O'Neill refused to set up a special ad hoc committee that would bypass standing committees entirely, as was done for the Carter administration's energy package.

43. On the problems of the subcommittee, see, for example, Kathryn Waters Gest, "House Begins Work on Welfare Reform," *Congressional Quarterly Weekly Report,* December 3, 1977, p. 2512, and Demkovitch, "Carter's Welfare Reform Package Is Being Re-Formed on the Hill."

44. See Kathryn Waters Gest, "Senate Finance Committee Doing Its Own Thing on Welfare Reform," *Congressional Quarterly Weekly Report,* September 3, 1977, pp. 1865–69; Gest, "Finance Committee Reports Controversial Welfare Measure," *Congressional Quarterly Weekly Report,* November 19, 1977, pp. 2449–52; *Public Finance Amendments of 1977,* S. Rept. 95-573, 95 Cong. 1 sess., November 1, 1977.

45. See, for example, Califano, *Governing America,* p. 361.

46. See Kathryn Waters Gest, "Subcommittee Approves Welfare Reform Measure," *Congressional Quarterly Weekly Report,* February 11, 1978, p. 360.

47. On Carter's declining commitment to welfare reform, see Califano, *Governing America,* p. 356–64.

48. See Martin Donsky, "Congress Could Approve Welfare Reform Bill in 1978, Key Figures in Debate Say," *Congressional Quarterly Weekly Report,* May 20, 1978, p. 1250; Donsky, "Compromise Talks Open in Effort to Salvage Some Welfare Reform"; Harrison H. Donnelley, "Administration, House Leaders Agree on Basics of Welfare Reform Bill," *Congressional Quarterly Weekly Report,* June 10, 1978, p. 1514; and Linda E. Demkovitch, "State and Local Officials Rescue Welfare Reform—Too Late," *National Journal,* vol. 10, no. 25 (June 24, 1978), pp. 1007–09.

49. See especially Califano, *Governing America,* pp. 360–62.

50. See Demkovitch, "State and Local Officials Rescue Welfare Reform"; "Welfare Reform Stalled," *1978 Congressional Quarterly Almanac,* pp. 600–03.

51. See Harrison H. Donnelly, "Carter Welfare Reform Plan Faces Competition as House Markup Begins," *Congressional Quarterly Weekly Report,* July 14, 1979, pp. 1416–17; Donnelly, "House Passes Welfare Reform Bill, 222-184," *Congressional Quarterly Weekly Report,* November 10, 1979, p. 2534.

52. On political reactions to the negative income tax experiments, see, for example, Linda E. Demkovitch, "Good News and Bad News for Welfare Reform," *National Journal,* vol. 10, no. 51/52 (December 30, 1978), pp. 2061–63.

53. Harrison H. Donnelly, "Food Stamp Costs Head for $10 Billion Mark," *Congressional Quarterly Weekly Report,* January 26, 1980, pp. 191–92.

54. For Reagan administration views on the ineffectiveness of earnings disregards, see Bernard Weinraub, "Welfare Trims Expected to Affect 17% in Program," *New York Times,* June 30, 1981, p. D21; and Robert Pear, "Shift for Social Welfare," *New York Times,* October 28, 1981, p. A22. Stockman is quoted in David E. Rosenbaum, "Reagan's Thesis: Issue Is Entitlement," *New York Times,* March 24, 1981.

55. Berkowitz, "Changing the Meaning of Welfare Reform."

56. To lower political opposition to its program, the Reagan administration announced soon after taking office that it would not (at least in the short term) touch seven popular programs—including Social Security, Medicare, veterans' benefits, and school lunches—that constituted a "social safety net." But these safety net programs appear to have been chosen more for their political appeal than for their focus on the "truly needy." See Howell Raines, "Reagan Won't Cut 7 Social Programs That Aid 80 Million," *New York Times,* February 11, 1981, p. A1; Steven R. Weisman, "Sparing of Social Programs: Reagan Bids for a Consensus," *New York Times,* February 12, 1981, p. A24; David E. Rosenbaum, "Reagan's 'Safety Net' Proposal: Who Will Land, Who Will Fall?" *New York Times,* March 17, 1981, p. A1. On the administration's failed Social Security initiative, see Paul C. Light, *Still Artful Work: The Continuing Politics of Social Security Reform,* 2d ed. (McGraw-Hill, 1995), chap. 10.

57. Office of Management and Budget, *Fiscal Year 1982 Budget Revisions* (GPO, March 1981). See also Bernard Weinraub, "Reagan to Seek Job Requirement Tied to Welfare for up to 800,000," *New York Times,* March 11, 1981, p. A1. Many of the details

of the administration's proposed cuts in AFDC were not unveiled until after the House and Senate had passed their overall deficit reduction targets for the programs. See Weinraub, "Reagan Calls for Sharp Cuts in Welfare in Detailed Plan Sent to Congress," *New York Times*, May 5, 1981, p. B12.

58. On budget reconciliation, see John B. Gilmour, *Reconcilable Differences? Congress, the Budget Process, and the Deficit* (University of California Press, 1990), chap. 3.

59. See Martin Tolchin, "Senate Rejects Bid to Restore Welfare Funds," *New York Times*, April 1, 1981, p. A24; Tolchin, "Cut of $36.9 Billion in Social Programs Is Voted by Senate," *New York Times*, April 3, 1981, p. A1.

60. States were prohibited from requiring more hours of work than would result from dividing the monthly AFDC grant by the minimum wage, or from requiring participation by a parent caring for a child under age six (or age three if child care was provided).

61. Legislated changes to AFDC during 1981 are summarized in "Welfare Benefits Cut by Reconciliation," *1981 Congressional Quarterly Almanac*, pp. 473–74; and House Ways and Means Committee, *Background Material and Data on Major Programs within the Jurisdiction of the Committee on Ways and Means*, WMCP 98-2, 98 Cong. 1 sess., February 8, 1983, pp. 444–47.

62. In September 1981, the Department of Health and Human Services estimated that out of a caseload of 3.9 million families, a total of 408,000 families would lose benefits entirely and 279,000 would receive reduced benefits. See Harrison H. Donnelly, "Millions of Poor Face Losses Oct. 1 as Reconciliation Bill Spending Cuts Go into Effect," *Congressional Quarterly Weekly Report*, September 26, 1981, p. 1837; and Robert Pear, "Rules Would Remove 10 Percent of Families Now on Welfare Rolls," *New York Times*, September 22, 1981, p. A26. In January 1992 the Congressional Budget Office estimated that earnings disregards alone would result in reduced benefits for 7 percent of the caseload, with another 8 percent losing their benefits entirely. The latter were anticipated to lose an average of $1,950 per family, as well as eligibility for Medicaid. See House Ways and Means Committee, *Background Material and Data*, pp. 426–31. The budgetary effects of the Reagan administration's cutbacks in AFDC are still being debated. A General Accounting Office study found short-term savings from the 1981 cuts on the order of $1.1 billion a year, with a caseload reduction of 493,000—and substantially reduced incomes and rates of health insurance among those who left the rolls. See *1993 Green Book*, pp. 738–39. Some retrospective analyses have suggested that while the 1981 OBRA changes reduced AFDC caseloads, they may have had negligible budgetary impact because reduced earnings disregards caused those remaining on the rolls to reduce their labor supply. See Fred Englander and John Kane, "Reagan's Welfare Reforms: Were the Program Savings Realized?" *Policy Studies Review*, vol. 11, no. 2 (Summer 1992), pp. 3–23. And on the implementation of the 1981 reforms, see Robert Pear, "Delay by 24 States on Welfare Cuts Trims U.S. Savings," *New York Times*, November 29, 1981, p. A1.

63. For details of welfare cut proposals included in the Reagan administration's fiscal year 1983 budget, see Harrison H. Donnelly, "More Cuts Proposed in Social

Programs," *Congressional Quarterly Weekly Report,* February 13, 1982, pp. 240–41. Cuts initially considered by the administration included limits on benefits to two-parent families and a freeze on federal payments to high-benefit states. See Robert Pear, "Welfare Cutbacks Proposed for 2-Parent Families," *New York Times,* October 8, 1981, p. B9.

64. On the New Federalism proposal, see generally Timothy Conlan, *From New Federalism to Devolution: Twenty-Five Years of Intergovernmental Reform* (Brookings, 1998), chap. 9; and the special issue of the *National Journal,* February 27, 1982. The following paragraphs draw heavily on these accounts.

65. See for example Rochelle L. Stanfield, "Ready for 'New Federalism,' Phase II? Turning Tax Sources Back to the States," *National Journal,* August 22, 1981, pp. 1492–97; Linda E. Demkovitch, "Political, Budget Pressures Sidetrack Plan for Turning AFDC Over to States," *National Journal,* September 19, 1981, pp. 1671–73.

66. Harrison H. Donnelly, "Reagan Changes Focus with Federalism Plan," *Congressional Quarterly Weekly Report,* January 30, 1982, pp. 147–54; Conlan, *From New Federalism to Devolution,* p. 176.

67. Some conservatives worried that a later liberal administration might use a federalized Medicaid program as the basis for a national health insurance program. See Linda E. Demkovitch, "Medicaid for Welfare: A Controversial Swap," *National Journal,* vol. 14, no. 9 (February 27, 1982), p. 367.

68. Conlan, *From New Federalism to Devolution,* p. 189; Rochelle L. Stanfield, "'Turning Back' 61 Programs: A Radical Shift of Power," *National Journal,* vol. 14, no. 9 (February 27, 1982), pp. 369–74.

69. If Congress cut the two programs by the $3.7 billion requested by the Reagan administration for fiscal year 1983, the states would save a projected $2.6 million from the swap; if it did not, they would lose about $1.5 billion. See Demkovitch, "Medicaid for Welfare," pp. 362–69; Donnelly, "Reagan Changes Focus with Federalism Plan."

70. On divisions among the governors, see, for example, Adam Clymer, "Governors Split over Reagan Proposals," *New York Times,* January 28, 1982, p. B9; and more generally, Conlan, *From New Federalism to Devolution.*

71. States that had been relatively generous in offering optional services and services to optional clienteles under Medicaid would be especially likely to suffer from cuts in a federalized Medicaid program. States also worried that the Reagan administration might later try to separate the fast-rising costs of nursing home care from the Medicaid program and return them to the states as a block grant, again increasing the burden on the states. See Demkovitch, "Medicaid for Welfare," p. 367; and Conlan, *From New Federalism to Devolution,* p. 185–90.

72. Richard E. Cohen, "Meanwhile, in Congress, the Long Knives Are Out," *National Journal,* vol. 14, no. 9 (February 27, 1982), pp. 381–83.

73. Linda E. Demkovitch, "Missing the Trading Deadline," *National Journal,* vol. 14, no. 15 (April 17, 1982), p. 688; "Washington, States Move a Bit Closer on New Federalism," *National Journal,* vol. 14, no. 18 (May 1, 1982), pp. 751, 781.

74. For details, see "Welfare Spending Cuts," *1982 Congressional Quarterly Almanac,* pp. 476–79; *1983 Green Book,* appendix H. The largest share of anticipated savings came from "error rate" sanctions to be imposed on the states, which in fact proved politically impossible to implement.

75. On the proposals, see Robert Pear, "Reagan Asks Wide Cuts in Programs to Aid Poor," *New York Times,* January 29, 1983, p. A6.

76. See the discussion in Melnick, *Between the Lines,* pp. 126–30.

77. See House Ways and Means Committee, *1985 Green Book* (GPO, 1985), pp. 373–76, 380; "Deficit Reduction Act of 1984: Provisions Relating to the AFDC Program," *Social Security Bulletin,* vol. 47 (December 1984), pp. 3–6.

78. George J. Church, "Fixing Welfare," *Time,* February 16, 1987, p. 20. See also Robert D. Reischauer, "The Welfare Reform Legislation: Directions for the Future," in Phoebe H. Cottingham and David T. Ellwood, eds., *Welfare Policy for the 1990s* (Harvard University Press, 1989), pp. 16–17.

79. Robert D. Reischauer, "Welfare Reform: Will Consensus Be Enough?" *Brookings Review,* vol. 5 (Summer 1987), pp. 3–8.

80. See, for example, Michael Novak and others, *The New Consensus on Family and Welfare: A Community of Self-Reliance* (American Enterprise Institute, 1987); and Reischauer, "Welfare Reform: Will Consensus Be Enough?" See also Julie Kosterlitz, "Reexamining Welfare," *National Journal,* vol. 18, no. 49 (December 6, 1986), pp. 2926–31.

81. See Julie Rovner, "Congress Takes Ball and Runs after State of the Union Punt," *Congressional Quarterly Weekly Report,* January 31, 1987, pp. 206–08. See also Erica B. Baum, "When the Witch Doctors Agree: The Family Support Act and Social Science Research," *Journal of Policy Analysis and Management,* vol. 10, no. 4 (Fall 1991), pp. 603–15; and Ron Haskins, "Congress Writes a Law: Research and Welfare Reform," *Journal of Policy Analysis and Management,* vol. 10, no. 4 (Fall 1991), pp. 616–31.

82. Julie Rovner, "Governors Jump-Start Welfare Reform Drive," *Congressional Quarterly Weekly Report,* February 28, 1987, pp. 376–78.

83. Provisions requiring all states to adopt the AFDC-UP program were included by the Democratic majority House in its fiscal year 1986 and 1987 budget packages, but dropped because of strong opposition from Senate Republicans, Senator Russell Long, and President Reagan that could not be overcome. See "$11.7 Billion Deficit-Reduction Bill Cleared," *Congressional Quarterly Almanac 1986,* pp. 575–76.

84. "After Years of Debate, Welfare Reform Clears," *Congressional Quarterly Almanac 1988,* pp. 349, 360; and Julie Rovner, "Governors Press Reagan, Bentsen on Welfare," *Congressional Quarterly Weekly Report,* February 27, 1988, pp. 512–13.

85. Rovner, "Governors Press Reagan, Bentsen on Welfare"; and Haskins, "Congress Writes a Law," p. 627.

86. In February 1987 the National Governors' Association released a proposal that called for mandatory participation in work or training activities for mothers of children

aged three and over. The plan also called for maximum state flexibility and for the federal government to cover most of the added program costs. See Rovner, "Governors Jump-Start Welfare Reform Drive." See also David S. Broder, "Governors Group Falters on Welfare Revision," *Washington Post,* July 27, 1987, p. A3; and Rovner, "Governors Press Reagan, Bentsen on Welfare," p. 513.

87. See, for example, Spencer Rich, "Debate Opens on Welfare Overhaul amid Negotiations with White House," *Washington Post,* June 14, 1988, p. A5

88. For a discussion, see Reischauer, "Welfare Reform: Will Consensus Be Enough?"

89. Rovner, "Governors Press Reagan, Bentsen on Welfare"; and "After Year of Debate, Welfare Reform Clears," *1988 Congressional Quarterly Almanac.*

90. Under the Omnibus Reconciliation Act of 1981, AFDC recipients who lost eligibility for that program because of tightened earnings disregards after four months also lost Medicaid eligibility. Federal legislation passed in 1994 and 1995 provided such families with transitional eligibility for Medicaid for nine months, with an additional six months at state option. See House Ways and Means Committee, *1985 Green Book* (GPO, 1985), p. 373; House Ways and Means Committee, *1989 Green Book* (GPO, 1989), p. 535.

91. An ad hoc task force was created to deal with jurisdictional disputes as the committees developed their legislation. See Julie Rovner, "House Democrats Unveil Welfare Blueprint. Senate Also Has Overhaul on Fast Track," *Congressional Quarterly Weekly Report,* March 21, 1987, pp. 504–05.

92. For conservatives, there was a requirement that states have education, training, and work programs. Participation in these programs was to be mandatory for parents of children over age three if programs and day care were available locally. For liberals, there was expanded transitional Medicaid for AFDC recipients who began to work, a requirement that states provide benefits equal to 15 percent of their own median income (which would increase benefits in eighteen states, mostly in South) within five years, enhanced earnings disregards in AFDC benefit calculations, and mandatory AFDC-UP for all states.

93. Mark Willen, "Modified Welfare Reform Bill OK'd by House Subcommittee," *Congressional Quarterly Weekly Report,* April 11, 1987, pp. 682–84.

94. Spencer Rich, "Welfare-Overhaul Plan Cut by Almost $1 Billion," *Washington Post,* June 10, 1987, p. A3; Rich, "House Panel Approves Welfare Bill Stressing Jobs," *Washington Post,* June 11, 1987, p. A24.

95. The House Republican bill had an estimated additional cost of $1.4 billion over five years. It included tougher child support provisions and money for child care and training, but neither mandatory AFDC-UP nor minimum benefit provisions. See Julie Rovner, "Reagan Endorses Revised GOP Welfare Plan," *Congressional Quarterly Weekly Report,* August 8, 1987, p. 1811. See also Mark Willen, "Republicans Offer Alternative Welfare Plan," *Congressional Quarterly Weekly Report,* April 11, 1987, p. 683.

96. The reconciliation bill passed the House after welfare provisions and other controversial measures were excised. Elizabeth Wehr, "Wright Finds a Vote to Pass Reconciliation Bill," *Congressional Quarterly Weekly Report,* October 31, 1987,

pp. 2653–55; and Patrick L. Knudsen, "House Will Try Again on Welfare Reform," *Congressional Quarterly Weekly Report,* October 31, 1987, p. 2655.

97. Patrick L. Knudsen, "After Long, Bruising Battle, House Approves Welfare Reform Bill," *Congressional Quarterly Weekly Report,* December 19, 1987, p. 3157–59.

98. The shaved-down alternative was originally estimated to cost $5.7 billion over five years. The Congressional Budget Office later re-estimated the costs of the House bill at $7.1 billion over five years. The Rules Committee did not allow a vote on a substitute bill drafted by Democratic representatives Stenholm (Texas) and Carper (Delaware) that would have cut expenditure growth further—although less than the Republican alternative. The original rule approved by the House Rules Committee allowed only the Republican substitute. The second alternative was added to give conservative Democrats a middle-ground alternative between the bill backed by the Democratic leadership and the Republican alternative. For a discussion of the rules disputes, see Patrick L. Knudsen, "House Leaders Still Pressing Welfare Revision," *Congressional Quarterly Weekly Report,* November 14, 1987, pp. 2805–08; Knudsen, "Once-Burned House Leaders Shy Away from Welfare Fight," *Congressional Quarterly Weekly Report,* November 21, 1987, pp. 2876–77; Knudsen and Julie Rovner, "Amid Democratic Dissension, Welfare Bill Is Delayed Again," *Congressional Quarterly Weekly Report,* December 12, 1987, p. 3036; and Spencer Rich, "Welfare Overhaul Bill Passes Big Test," *Washington Post,* December 16, 1987, p. A10.

99. See Spencer Rich, "House Passes Welfare Plan That Stresses Job Training," *Washington Post,* December 17, 1987, p. A1; and Knudsen, "After Long, Bruising Battle, House Approves Welfare Reform Bill."

100. For a summary of the House bill provisions, see Patrick L. Knudsen, "Provisions, House Welfare-Revision Legislation," *Congressional Quarterly Weekly Report,* December 19, 1987, pp. 3160–65.

101. S.1511, *Family Security Act of 1987,* 100 Cong. 1 sess., July 21, 1987. Moynihan's plan included work or training requirements for mothers with children aged three and over (or aged one and over at state option) if child care were available, transitional child care and Medicaid benefits, federal funding for state welfare-to-work programs, and mandatory AFDC-UP for all states, but no incentives to states to raise benefits. See Spencer Rich, "Moynihan Unveils Welfare-Overhaul Plan," *Washington Post,* July 19, 1987, p. A5; and Julie Rovner, "Dole Not Ready to Join Moynihan on Welfare," *Congressional Quarterly Weekly Report,* July 25, 1987, p. 1674. At the insistence of Finance Committee chair Lloyd Bentsen, the AFDC-UP provision was later modified to allow states that did not previously offer the program to limit receipt of benefits to six months of every twelve. On Moynihan's views generally, see Spencer Rich, "Welfare Revision: Moynihan Tries Again," *Washington Post,* June 13, 1988, p. A9. For the administration's position on the bill see Senate Committee on Finance, *Welfare Reform,* S. Hrg. 100-450, 100 Cong. 2 sess. (GPO, 1988), part 2, pp. 127–55.

102. However, the funding cap was intentionally set at a much greater amount than the bill's authors thought (and the CBO estimated) states would actually draw down,

effectively making it an open-ended entitlement to the states, free from Appropriations Committee control.

103. Julie Rovner, "Child-Support Provisions Are the 'Engine' Pulling Controversial Welfare Reform Bill," *Congressional Quarterly Weekly Report,* June 18, 1988, pp. 1648–49. Moynihan also mentioned welfare-to-work programs as "a legislative freight train to haul the rest of this" welfare reform initiative. See Rovner, "Governors Jump-Start Welfare Reform Drive," p. 378.

104. Rovner, "Governors Press Reagan, Bentsen on Welfare." The Finance Committee adopted a Republican-sponsored amendment that increased the number of states allowed to conduct demonstration projects under waivers from ten to fifty. See Rovner, "Senate Finance Endorses Modified Welfare Bill," *Congressional Quarterly Weekly Report,* April 23, 1988, pp. 1068–70.

105. The AFDC-UP work requirement passed by a voice vote after opponents failed to table it by a 41-54 vote. Julie Rovner, "Deep Schisms Still Imperil Welfare Overhaul," *Congressional Quarterly Weekly Report,* June 18, 1988, pp. 1647–50.

106. For provisions of the bill as passed by the Senate, see *Congressional Quarterly Weekly Report,* June 25, 1988, pp. 1765–69.

107. Julie Rovner, "Difficult Conference Likely on Welfare Bill," *Congressional Quarterly Weekly Report,* June 25, 1988, p. 1764.

108. Debates on the House side were also complicated by jurisdictional battles over the number of conferees from each committee and which of them would have exclusive or shared jurisdiction over particular elements of the bill. Julie Rovner, "House Orders Its Conferees to Slash Cost of Welfare Bill," *Congressional Quarterly Weekly Report,* July 9, 1988, p. 1916.

109. On the Bentsen factor, see Julie Rovner, "Welfare Conference Begins, Buoyed by Bentsen's Selection," *Congressional Quarterly Weekly Report,* July 16, 1988, p. 1981.

110. For details of the changes, see Spencer Rich, "House Offers to Cut Back Welfare Bill," *Washington Post,* July 29, 1988, p. A4; Julie Rovner, "House Offer on Welfare Bill Pares Total Costs Somewhat," *Congressional Quarterly Weekly Report,* July 30, 1988, p. 2080; Rovner, "Welfare Conferees Narrow Their Differences," *Congressional Quarterly Weekly Report,* August 6, 1988, p. 2202; Rovner, "Accord Near on Welfare Bill, but White House May Resist," *Congressional Quarterly Weekly Report,* August 13, 1988, p. 2288.

111. P.L. 100-485, 102 Stat. 2343, October 13, 1988. For detailed provisions of the legislation, see the *1988 Congressional Quarterly Almanac,* pp. 351–58; and House Ways and Means Committee, *1989 Green Book* (GPO, 1989), pp. 590–613. See also Reischauer, "The Welfare Reform Legislation."

112. Section 406 of the Family Support Act did require the Department of Health and Human Services to contract with the National Academy of Sciences for a study of a national minimum benefit—a face-saving sop to House liberals.

113. Other added federal costs in FSA include $735 million for transitional child care assistance; $430 million for extended transitional Medicaid; $1,153 million for man-

dating the AFDC-UP program nationwide; and $165 million for expanded earnings disregards. Added state and local costs were estimated at $700 million for the same period. See *1989 Green Book,* p. 601–02.

114. The FSA required that child support awards enforced by a state child support agency be withheld from the paycheck of the noncustodial parent in all cases, rather than only when a parent fell behind with payments. These new procedures were to be phased in between 1990 and 1994. Judges were generally required to use guidelines (that states had been required to create under 1984 legislation) in setting child support payment levels, unless extraordinary circumstances dictated otherwise.

115. Among the exempt groups were individuals who were ill, in the second or third trimester of pregnancy, working more than thirty hours per week, under age sixteen or attending school full time, or parents of a child under age three (or age one, at state option) who were personally caring for that child. Parents caring for a child under age six could not be required to participate for more than twenty hours per week. States had to require custodial parents under age twenty who had not completed high school to engage in full-time education. States were also permitted, but not mandated, to require JOBS participants to negotiate a contract detailing the reciprocal obligations of the client and the state agency. To focus JOBS on current or likely long-term AFDC dependents, states were required to spend 55 percent of JOBS funds on high-risk populations, such as very young mothers who had not completed high school and those for whom the youngest child was within two years of ineligibility. The wage rate for working off "workfare" jobs was set at the higher of the state or federal minimum wage in most cases. After nine months in a workfare position, the wage rate used to calculate hours of work was required to be "the same as for a regular employee doing the same or similar work for the same employer, at the same site." *1989 Green Book,* p. 595

116. The basic earnings disregard in determining AFDC eligibility was increased, as were earnings disregards for child care. In addition, the EITC was not to be counted in determining AFDC eligibility or benefits after October 1, 1989.

117. Federal funding for child care was provided in the form of an open-ended entitlement at a matching rate of 50 to 80 percent (the same as for Medicaid).

118. Both transitional child care and Medicaid provisions were to "sunset" at the end of fiscal year 1998, after which transitional Medicaid would be limited to the prior law standard of four months.

119. Christopher Howard, *The Hidden Welfare State: Tax Expenditures and Social Policy in the United States* (Princeton University Press, 1997), p. 139.

120. On the origins of the EITC, see Howard, *The Hidden Welfare State,* chap. 3, and Leman, *The Collapse of Welfare Reform,* p. 94. My account draws heavily on Howard.

121. Howard, *The Hidden Welfare State,* p. 72.

122. On the 1986 and 1990 expansions of the EITC, see Howard, *The Hidden Welfare State,* chap. 7; and Sandra Hofferth, "The 101st Congress: An Emerging Agenda for Children in Poverty," in Judith Chafel, ed., *Child Poverty and Public Policy* (Washington: Urban Institute, 1993), pp. 203–43.

123. For an analysis of the expansion of the EITC, see Christopher Howard, "Happy Returns: How the Working Poor Got Tax Relief," *American Prospect*, no. 17 (Spring 1994), pp. 46–53.

124. See Timothy Noah and Laurie McGinley, "Advocate for the Poor, Respected on All Sides, Secures a Pivotal Place in Expanding Tax Credit," *Wall Street Journal*, July 26, 1993, p. A12.

125. On the EITC as an alternative to increasing the minimum wage and its appeal to moderate Republicans and centrist Democrats, such as the Democratic Leadership Council, see in particular Howard, *The Hidden Welfare State*, pp. 150–52.

126. For an excellent analysis of the EITC's "basic ambiguity" and its contribution to program growth, see Howard, "Happy Returns."

127. *1998 Green Book*, p. 867.

128. See R. Kent Weaver, "Ending Welfare as We Know It," in Margaret Weir, ed., *The Social Divide: Political Parties and the Future of Activist Government* (Brookings, 1998), pp. 361–416.

129. See Robert D. Behn, "How to Terminate a Public Policy: A Dozen Hints for the Would-be Terminator," *Policy Analysis*, vol. 4 (Summer 1978), pp. 393–413.

130. Interview with author, April 1994.

131. Personal communication from Erica Baum, August 1999.

132. Interview with author, April 1994.

133. Interview with author, August 1994.

134. Interview with author, August 1994.

135. Interview with author, February 1996.

136. Interview with author, April 1994.

137. Interview with author, April 1994.

138. Haskins did attempt to inject historical lessons into Republicans' political calculations on welfare strategy in the 104th Congress, repeatedly warning House Republicans against overreaching by citing the example of liberals who failed to accept the half-loaf of an "inadequate" minimum benefit in Nixon's Family Assistance Plan in hopes of getting a better deal later on, only to lose a historic opportunity that never recurred. This argument did not have a major impact, however.

139. For an early example of conservative frustration at states' foot-dragging in the implementation of work requirements, see Melnick, *Between the Lines*, p. 116.

Chapter Five

1. House Ways and Means Committee, *1993 Green Book: Overview of Entitlement Programs* (Government Printing Office, 1993), p. 641.

2. On Bush's lack of interest in the welfare issue until the 1992 presidential campaign, see Steven M. Teles, *Whose Welfare? AFDC and Elite Politics* (University Press of Kansas, 1996), pp. 130–34.

3. House Ways and Means Committee, *1996 Green Book* (GPO, 1996), pp. 1215–17. For a more detailed discussion of the data in this paragraph, see chapter 1 above.

4. See Michael O'Higgins, "The Allocation of Public Resources to Children and the Elderly in OECD Countries," in John L. Palmer, Timothy Smeeding, and Barbara Boyle Torrey, eds., *The Vulnerable* (Washington: Urban Institute, 1988), pp. 201–28.

5. Unpublished data from the Office of Family Assistance, Department of Health and Human Services. Includes AFDC–Unemployed Parent cases.

6. House Ways and Means Committee, *1996 Green Book: Background Material and Data on Programs within the Jurisdiction of the Committee on Ways and Means* (GPO, 1996), p. 471.

7. Ibid., p. 458.

8. National Center for Health Statistics, "Health, United States, 1999, with Health and Aging Chartbook" (Hyattsville, Md., 1999), p. 8.

9. Charles Murray, "The Coming White Underclass," *Wall Street Journal*, October 29, 1993, p. A14.

10. Greg J. Hill, Martha S. Duncan, and Sal D. Hoffmann, "Welfare Dependence within and across Generations," *Science*, January 29, 1988. See also House Ways and Means Committee, *1992 Green Book: Background Material and Data on Programs within the Jurisdiction of the Committee on Ways and Means* (GPO, 1992), pp. 689–91.

11. *1994 Green Book*, p. 402.

12. An early published version of this research by Kathryn Edin appears in a chapter co-authored with Christopher Jencks, "Welfare," in Jencks, ed., *Rethinking Social Policy: Race, Poverty, and the Underclass* (Harvard University Press, 1992), chap. 6.

13. See, for example, Mary Jo Bane and David T. Ellwood, *Welfare Realities: From Rhetoric to Reform* (Harvard University Press, 1994), chap. 2. See also *1992 Green Book*, pp. 685–88.

14. See especially Charles Murray, *Losing Ground: American Social Policy, 1950–1980* (Basic Books, 1984).

15. Murray, "The Coming White Underclass."

16. For contrasting views on the role of conservative foundations, see Sally Covington, *Moving a Public Policy Agenda: The Strategic Philanthropy of Conservative Foundations* (Washington: National Committee for Responsive Philanthropy, 1997); David Callahan, "Liberal Policy's Weak Foundations," *The Nation*, November 13, 1995, pp. 568–72; and Leslie Lenkowsky, "The Paranoid Perspective in Philanthropy," *Chronicle of Philanthropy*, June 12, 1997, pp. 61–62. On the role of conservative policy entrepreneurs, see Martin Rein and Christopher Winship, "Policy Entrepreneurs and the Academic Establishment: Truth and Values in Social Controversies," in Elliott White, ed., *Intelligence, Political Inequality, and Public Policy* (Westport, Conn.: Praeger, 1997), pp. 17–47.

17. See Robin Toner, "New Politics of Welfare Focuses on Its Flaws," *New York Times*, July 5, 1992, p. A1. On the importance of focusing on children to avoid a racialized welfare

debate, see Julie Rovner, "Daniel Patrick Moynihan: Making Welfare Work," *Congressional Quarterly Weekly Report,* March 21, 1987, p. 507.

18. See Amy Dominguez-Arms and Meeghan Prunty, "What's Missing from Welfare Coverage? How to Put Children into Your Welfare Stories," *The Children's Beat,* vol. 5, no. 3 (Spring 1998) pp. 11–13.

19. A more inclusive definition of welfare has a much longer history among conservatives. An early version, listing forty-four federal "welfare" programs, appears in Charles D. Hobbs, *The Welfare Industry* (Washington: Heritage Foundation, 1978). A list of fifty-nine federal welfare programs was published by the Reagan administration. See George J. Church, "Fixing Welfare," *Time,* February 16, 1987, p. 19.

20. See, for example, Robert Rector, "Welfare Is the 800-Pound Gorilla," *Los Angeles Times,* July 11, 1995, p. B9; and Rector and W. F. Lauber, *America's Failed $5.4 Trillion War on Poverty* (Washington: Heritage Foundation, 1995). See also the listing of the programs in House Ways and Means Committee, *1996 Green Book,* pp. 1321–24; and Cheryl Wetzstein, "How to Reform Welfare If You Can't Define It? What the System Includes Is Still a Matter of Dispute," *Washington Times,* December 19, 1994, p. A8. For a critique, see Sharon Parrott, *What Do We Spend on Welfare?* (Washington: Center on Budget and Policy Priorities, February, 1995).

21. On problem definition as a component of the policymaking process—and as a political process—see Deborah A. Stone, "Causal Stories and the Formation of Policy Agendas," *Political Science Quarterly,* vol. 104 (Summer 1989), pp. 281–300.

22. Murray, *Losing Ground,* p. 212.

23. On the 1962 amendments, see Gilbert Y. Steiner, *The State of Welfare* (Brookings, 1971), chap. 2; Martha Derthick, *Uncontrollable Spending for Social Services Grants* (Brookings, 1975), chaps. 1–2.

24. Lisbeth B. Schorr, with Daniel Schorr, *Within Our Reach: Breaking the Cycle of Disadvantage* (Anchor/Doubleday, 1989).

25. See, for example, Schorr, *Within Our Reach,* chap. 10.

26. See, in particular, William Julius Wilson, *The Truly Disadvantaged: The Inner City, the Underclass and Public Policy* (University of Chicago Press, 1987), and his more recent *When Work Disappears: The World of the New Urban Poor* (Alfred A. Knopf, 1996).

27. Theda Skocpol, "Targeting within Universalism: Politically Viable Policies to Combat Poverty in the United States," in Christopher Jencks and Paul E. Peterson, eds., *The Urban Underclass* (Brookings, 1991), pp. 411–36; and Wilson, *The Truly Disadvantaged.*

28. Hugh Heclo, "The Political Foundations of Anti-Poverty Policy," in Sheldon H. Danziger and Daniel H. Weinberg, eds., *Fighting Poverty: What Works and What Doesn't* (Harvard University Press, 1986), pp. 312–40.

29. See, in particular, Skocpol, "Targeting within Universalism"; and Irwin Garfinkel, "Economic Security for Children: From Means Testing and Bifurcation to Universality," in Irwin Garfinkel, Jennifer L. Hochschild, and Sara S. McLanahan, eds., *Social Policies for Children* (Brookings, 1996), pp. 33–82. See also Theda Skocpol and

William Julius Wilson, "Welfare as We Need It," *New York Times*, February 9, 1994, p. A21.

30. On child support assurance, see especially Irwin Garfinkel, *Assuring Child Support: An Extension of Social Security* (New York: Russell Sage, 1992); and Garfinkel, "Bringing Fathers Back In: The Child Support Assurance Strategy," *The American Prospect*, no. 9 (Spring 1992), pp. 75–76.

31. Garfinkel, *Assuring Child Support*, pp. 51–52.

32. For a liberal critique of universalistic approaches, see Robert Greenstein, "Universal and Targeted Approaches to Relieving Poverty: An Alternative View," in Jencks and Peterson, *The Urban Underclass*, pp. 437–59. Greenstein argues that a program's strength in resisting cutbacks depends on more than whether they are targeted on the poor. Social Security benefits from the fact that its benefits are perceived as earned. Moreover, targeted WIC and Head Start grew more than any other social programs in the 1980s; and the principal Medicaid cuts expired in 1984, after which it was expanded, as were the Food Stamp and Supplemental Security Income programs. He argues that program growth is possible in targeted programs where (a) the program primarily helps the working poor who are not on welfare, and therefore it is seen as encouraging work; (b) the program avoids a race-specific image, for example, Medicaid and Food Stamps; (c) benefits are seen as earned, as with the Earned Income Tax Credit; and (d) the program is funded solely at federal level, as with Food Stamps. He argues that a mixed approach is needed, with some universal programs (for example, health care and refundable child tax credit) as well as targeted programs like Head Start, WIC, and child immunization.

33. Lawrence M. Mead, *Beyond Entitlement: The Social Obligations of Citizenship* (Free Press, 1986), p. 3. See also Mead, *The New Politics of Poverty: The Nonworking Poor in America* (Basic Books, 1992).

34. Mead, *Beyond Entitlement*, p. 49.

35. Mead agrees that "the belief recipients have that their fate turns on forces outside themselves" is a serious impediment to self-sufficiency on the part of the nonworking poor, but he argues that those beliefs are in large part a result of government programs that encourage dependency. Mead, *Beyond Entitlement*, p. 145. In *The New Politics of Poverty*, Mead argues that the poor are "dutiful but defeated. There is a culture of poverty that discourages work, but the poor will work more regularly if government enforces the work norm" (p. 24).

36. See Mead, *Beyond Entitlement*, chap. 6.

37. Ibid., p. 13.

38. Ibid., p. 4 (italics in the original).

39. See Mead's critique of these approaches in *The New Politics of Poverty*, chap. 8.

40. Ibid., p. 183.

41. See, for example, David Wessel, "Rep. Weber's Plan for a Time Limit on Welfare Draws Criticism from Some of His Usual Allies," *Wall Street Journal*, June 17, 1992, p. A18.

42. Murray, "The Coming White Underclass."

43. William J. Bennett, "The Best Welfare Reform: End It," *Wall Street Journal,* March 30, 1994, p. A19.

44. Nancy Gibbs, "The Vicious Cycle," *Time,* June 20, 1994, p. 25.

45. Bennett, "The Best Welfare Reform."

46. For a review of arguments for and against devolution, see Robert D. Reischauer, "The Welfare Reform Legislation: Directions for the Future," in Phoebe H. Cottingham and David T. Ellwood, eds., *Welfare Policy for the 1990s* (Harvard University Press, 1989), pp. 31–35.

47. State discretion can also be linked to the expected benefits and costs of devolving authority from specific types of innovation. A 1995 Brookings study, for example, recommended that where there is strong evidence that proposed reforms are effective, they should be required by the federal government, and where they are clearly harmful, they should be prohibited; where prospects for success are good and risks to vulnerable families low, states should be permitted to experiment without receiving a federal waiver, and where the risks are higher, a waiver should be required. R. Kent Weaver and William T. Dickens, "Looking Before We Leap: An Introduction," in Weaver and Dickens, eds., *Looking Before We Leap: Social Science and Welfare Reform* (Brookings, 1995), pp. 1–12.

48. Reischauer, "The Welfare Reform Legislation," p. 33.

49. See, for example, Paul E. Peterson, "State Response to Welfare Reform: A Race to the Bottom?" in Isabel V. Sawhill, ed., *Welfare Reform: An Analysis of the Issues* (Washington: Urban Institute, 1995), pp. 7–10.

50. Wilson, *The Truly Disadvantaged,* p. 160.

51. Skocpol, "Targeting within Universalism," pp. 433–34.

52. David T. Ellwood, *Poor Support: Poverty in the American Family* (Basic Books, 1988).

53. Ibid., pp. 178–83.

54. Ibid., p. 241.

55. See R. Kent Weaver, Robert Y. Shapiro, and Lawrence R. Jacobs, "The Polls— Trends: Welfare," *Public Opinion Quarterly,* vol. 59, no. 4 (December 1995), p. 611; and chapter 7 below. Public opinion specialists have long noted that wording has a tremendous effect on responses, however: pluralities of the public consistently believe that too much is being spent on "welfare" while too little is being spent on "assistance to the poor" and "poor children." See Weaver, Shapiro, and Jacobs, "The Polls," pp. 618–19; and Tom W. Smith, "That Which We Call Welfare by Any Other Name Would Smell Sweeter: An Analysis of the Impact of Question Wording on Response Patterns," *Public Opinion Quarterly,* vol. 51, no. 1 (1987), pp. 75–83.

56. Weaver, Shapiro, and Jacobs, "The Polls," p. 614.

57. In the same poll, respondents simultaneously said that "families getting more welfare benefits than they need" was "a more serious problem in America" than (31 percent) "families not getting enough welfare to get by," while equal percentages (45 per-

cent) thought that "most people who receive money from welfare could get along without it if they tried" and that "most of them really need this help." Weaver, Shapiro, and Jacobs, "The Polls," p. 613.

58. Ibid., p. 625.

59. A Hart/Teeter survey for NBC News and the *Wall Street Journal* asked, "What would you say are the two or three most important issues or problems facing the nation today that you personally would like to see the federal government in Washington do something about?" In a May 1991 survey, 3 percent mentioned welfare abuse; in October 1991 and November 1991 surveys, 4 percent did so.

60. In a November 1991 *Los Angeles Times* poll asking how important it was that "abuses and fraud in the welfare system" be discussed in the upcoming presidential election, 21 percent of respondents said that it might be the most important issue, 53 percent thought that it was very important, and 19 percent thought it somewhat important. In a September 1992 poll by Yankelovich Clancy Shulman for *Time* and the Cable News Network that asked whether "reforming the nation's welfare system [was] one of the most important problems facing the country today," 19 percent said that it was one of the most important, 56 percent said it was "very important," and 18 percent said it was "somewhat important."

61. Bill Clinton and Al Gore, *Putting People First: How We Can All Change America* (Times Books, 1992), pp.164–68. See also Richard L. Berke, "The Ad Campaign; Clinton: Getting People off Welfare," *New York Times*, September 10, 1992, p. A20.

62. See Jason DeParle, "To Aid Those Most in Need, Clinton Wants to Help the Middle Class First," *New York Times*, November 10, 1992, p. A20. Guy Gugliotta, "Clinton Mixes Strategies for Anti-Poverty Strategy: Initiative Could Cost up to $7.5 Billion a Year," *Washington Post*, December 3, 1992, p. A9.

63. On Clinton's record in Arkansas, see Jason DeParle, "Arkansas Pushes Plan to Break Welfare Cycle," *New York Times*, March 14, 1992, p. A10; and David Whitman, with Dorian Friedman, "His Unconvincing Welfare Promises," *U.S. News and World Report*, April 20, 1992, p. 42. See also Daniel Friedlander, *Employment and Welfare Impacts of the Arkansas WORK Program: A Three-Year Follow-Up Study in Two Counties* (New York: Manpower Demonstration Research Corporation, 1988); and Daniel Friedlander and Gary Burtless, *Five Years After: The Long-Term Effects of Welfare-to-Work Programs* (New York: Russell Sage, 1995).

64. On Bill Clinton and his connections to the "New Democratic" Democratic Leadership Council, see Jon F. Hale, "The Making of the New Democrats," *Political Science Quarterly*, vol. 110, no. 2 (1995) pp. 207–32. On differences between the Clinton and DLC visions, see Margaret Weir, "Political Parties and Social Policymaking," in Weir, ed., *The Social Divide: Political Parties and the Future of Activist Government* (Brookings and Russell Sage, 1998), pp. 27–28.

65. Toner, "New Politics of Welfare Focuses on Its Flaws."

66. See Stanley B. Greenberg, *Middle Class Dreams: The Politics and Power of the New American Majority*, rev. ed. (Yale University Press, 1996), especially pp. 206–07.

67. See Toner, "New Politics of Welfare Focuses on Its Flaws"; Jason DeParle, "Talk of Cutting Welfare Rolls Sounds Good, but Progress Is Far from Sure," *New York Times,* October 17, 1992, p. A9.

68. "Remarks at a Breakfast with Community Service Clubs in Riverside, California," and "White House Fact Sheet: The President's Welfare Reform Strategy," *Weekly Compilation of Presidential Documents,* vol. 28, no. 31 (July 31, 1992), pp. 1359–64.

69. Ibid.; Andrew Rosenthal, "Bush Backs Wisconsin Attempt at Welfare Reform," *New York Times,* April 9, 1992, p. D20; Michael Wines, "Bush Outlines Welfare Plan before California Audience," *New York Times,* August 1, 1992, p. A8.

70. See, for example, Robin Toner, "Vulnerable, Bush Makes a Last Effort to Connect," *New York Times,* October 23, 1992, p. A20.

71. Sixteen percent of respondents thought that "neither of them" would do a good job, 10 percent said that "both of them" would, and 4 percent were not sure. Hart and Breglio telephone survey of 1,506 registered voters for NBC News and the *Wall Street Journal,* conducted September 12–15, 1992. In an ABC News/*Washington Post* telephone poll of 1,269 adults conducted October 4, 1992, 55 percent thought that Clinton "would do the best job dealing with poverty," compared with 21 percent who chose Bush and 11 percent who chose Perot; 6 percent said neither or no difference (volunteered response), and 7 percent did not know or had no opinion.

72. CBS News/*New York Times* telephone survey of 2,737 adults nationwide, October 29–November 1, 1992. This figure is the percentage of probable voters who planned to vote for Clinton, including leaners.

73. In a Louis Harris and Associates election night poll, only 1 percent of those surveyed said that welfare was one of the "two issues . . . most important to you in determining who you voted for in the presidential election." In a survey conducted the same week by the Wirthlin Group for the Family Research Council, fewer than 1 percent said that either too much or too little welfare assistance was "most important to you in making up your mind which candidate to support."

74. In a Louis Harris and Associates election night poll, only 2 percent of respondents cited welfare among the "two issues . . . most important for the newly elected president and Congress to deal with during the first 100 days of their term," well below respondents' concerns with the economy (52 percent), jobs and employment (25 percent), the federal deficit and the federal budget (23 percent), health care (20 percent), or a variety of other issues.

75. Norman J. Ornstein, Thomas E. Mann, and Michael J. Malbin, *Vital Statistics on Congress 1995–96* (Congressional Quarterly Press, 1996), p. 67. The figure was 65.6 percent in 1992 and an even lower 64.5 percent in 1994.

76. See, for example, Julie Rovner, "New Cries for Welfare Reform Target Able-Bodied Poor," *Congressional Quarterly Weekly Report,* March 28, 1992, pp. 809–10; Kitty Dumas, "States Bypassing Congress in Reforming Welfare," *Congressional Quarterly*

Weekly Report, April 11, 1992, pp. 950–53; and Dumas, "Welfare Reforms Get Backing from Ways and Means," *Congressional Quarterly Weekly Report,* June 27, 1992, p. 1886.

77. See Dumas, "States Bypassing Congress in Reforming Welfare."

78. Provisions making it easier for states to access JOBS funds were included in a Democratic-backed omnibus tax bill vetoed by President Bush. "Welfare-Related Bills," *1992 Congressional Quarterly Almanac,* p. 465.

79. Teles, *Whose Welfare?* chap. 7. The discussion here draws heavily on Teles's analysis.

80. Ibid., pp. 129–31.

81. Ibid., pp. 130–34.

82. See, in particular, Dumas, "States Bypassing Congress in Reforming Welfare."

83. State AFDC and AFDC-Unemployed Parent benefit and administrative costs rose from $8.697 billion in fiscal year 1988 to $11.371 in fiscal year 1992. State Medicaid costs more than doubled, from $23,654 million to $50,339 million, over the same period. *1998 Green Book,* pp. 411, 969.

84. The rankings were the same whether calculated by child AFDC recipients as a percentage of all children in the state or by all AFDC recipients as a percentage of total state population. See House Ways and Means Committee, *1992 Green Book,* pp. 667–68.

85. See Wayne King, "Maverick Democrat Confronts Trenton's Welfare Rules," *New York Times,* September 4, 1991, p. B1.

86. See Ted George Goertzel and John Hart, "New Jersey's $64 Question: Legislative Entrepreneurship and the Family Cap," in Donald F. Norris and Lyke Thompson, eds., *The Politics of Welfare Reform* (Beverly Hills, Calif.: Sage, 1995), pp. 109–45.

87. Lou Cannon, "Wilson Proposes 25% Welfare Cut," *Washington Post,* December 16, 1991, p. A6.

Chapter Six

1. See, for example, Allen Schick, "Informed Legislation: Policy Research versus Ordinary Knowledge," in William Robinson and Clay Wellborn, eds., *Knowledge, Power and Congress* (Congressional Quarterly Press, 1991), pp. 99–119. See also Charles E. Lindblom and David K. Cohen, *Usable Knowledge: Social Science and Social Problem Solving* (Yale University Press, 1979).

2. The series by Leon Dash ran between September 18 and 25, 1994; Charles Murray, *Losing Ground: American Social Policy, 1950–1980* (Basic Books, 1984).

3. John W. Kingdon, *Agendas, Alternatives, and Public Policies,* 2d ed. (HarperCollins, 1995), pp. 90–94.

4. The ammunition metaphor is used by Carol H. Weiss, "Congressional Committees as Users of Analysis," *Journal of Policy Analysis and Management,* vol. 8, no. 3 (1989), p. 412. Weiss offers a fourfold categorization of congressional uses of policy research that overlaps with the schema offered here.

5. For detailed reviews of the policy research available during this period, see Rebecca M. Blank, *It Takes a Nation: A New Agenda for Fighting Poverty* (Princeton University Press and Russell Sage, 1997); and William M. Epstein, *Welfare in America: How Social Science Fails the Poor* (University of Wisconsin Press, 1997). See also Isabel Sawhill, ed., *Welfare Reform: An Analysis of the Issues* (Washington: Urban Institute, 1995); and R. Kent Weaver and William T. Dickens, eds., *Looking Before We Leap: Social Science and Welfare Reform* (Brookings, 1995), especially chap. 3.

6. On the role of CRS, see especially Weiss, "Congressional Committees as Users of Analysis," p. 419; William H. Robinson, "The Congressional Research Service: Policy Consultant, Think Tank, and Information Factory," in Carol H. Weiss, ed., *Organizations for Policy Analysis: Helping Government Think* (Newbury Park, Calif.: Sage, 1992), pp. 181–200. Weiss's volume also contains profiles of other congressional research support agencies.

7. See, for example, Mark A. Peterson, "How Health Policy Information Is Used by Congress," in Thomas E. Mann and Norman J. Ornstein, eds., *Intensive Care: How Congress Shapes Health Policy* (Brookings, 1995), pp. 79–125; and R. Kent Weaver, "The Changing World of Think Tanks," *PS: Political Science and Politics,* vol. 22, no. 3 (Fall 1989) pp. 563–78.

8. See Sawhill, *Welfare Reform;* and Weaver and Dickens, *Looking Before We Leap.* Sawhill's volume appeared first as a series of four- to six-page policy briefs. Both volumes received funding from the Annie E. Casey Foundation, which focuses heavily on children's issues.

9. Peter Huber and others have criticized the growth of what they call "junk science" by "experts-for-sale," especially in tort litigation. See, for example, Peter W. Huber, *Galileo's Revenge: Junk Science in the Courtroom* (Basic Books, 1991); and Kenneth R. Foster and Peter W. Huber, *Judging Science: Scientific Knowledge and the Federal Courts* (MIT Press, 1997).

10. Andrew Rich and R. Kent Weaver, "Advocates and Analysts: Think Tanks and the Politicization of Expertise in Washington," in Allan J. Cigler and Burdett A. Loomis, eds. *Interest Group Politics,* 5th ed. (Congressional Quarterly Press, 1998), pp. 235–53.

11. A contrary view is offered by Weiss, who argues that congressional committee staff "seem to prefer to get their analysis from interest groups than from objective academic analysts. They know the position that the interest group is promoting, and they can gauge what kind of 'correction factor' they have to apply. With an academic analyst, they are not sure." Weiss, "Congressional Committees as Users of Analysis," p. 420.

12. See Bruce Bimber, "Information as a Factor in Congressional Politics," *Legislative Studies Quarterly,* vol. 16, no. 4 (November 1991), pp. 585–605.

13. See especially Weiss, "Congressional Committees as Users of Analysis." For a similarly pessimistic view of the use of policy research in the executive, see Walter Williams, *Mismanaging America: The Rise of the Anti-Analytic Presidency* (University Press of Kansas, 1990); and Walter Williams, *Honest Numbers and Democracy: Social*

Policy Analysis in the White House, Congress, and the Federal Agencies (Georgetown University Press, 1998).

14. Erica B. Baum, "When the Witch Doctors Agree: The Family Support Act and Social Science Research," *Journal of Policy Analysis and Management,* vol. 10, no. 4 (Fall 1991), pp. 609–10. In addition, participants attribute MDRC's success to making that research "user-friendly" in form, doing its best to disseminate and "sell" the research broadly, being well tied in to policy networks, and entering directly into policy debates—although this last did raise questions of objectivity and checks on quality control. MDRC's use of "random assignment," assigning some welfare recipients to programs and others to a control group that did not receive program services, increased researchers' and policymakers' confidence that observed increases in earnings by program participants were not simply artifacts of "cream-skimming" and self-selection. The fact that research results were consistent in direction, if not intensity, across multiple sites that varied in their approaches, resource inputs, and administrative capacities also increased confidence in MDRC studies. See also Ronald Haskins, "Congress Writes a Law: Research and Welfare Reform," *Journal of Policy Analysis and Management,* vol. 10, no. 4 (Fall 1991), pp. 616–32.

15. See Peter L. Szanton, "The Remarkable 'Quango': Knowledge, Politics, and Welfare Reform," *Journal of Policy Analysis and Management,* vol. 10, no. 4 (Fall 1991), pp. 590–602.

16. Baum, "When the Witch Doctors Agree."

17. Haskins, "Congress Writes a Law."

18. See especially Murray, *Losing Ground.*

19. Barbara Ventura and others, "Advance Report of Final Natality Statistics, 1993," *Monthly Vital Statistics Report,* National Center for Health Statistics, vol. 44, no. 3 (September 21, 1995) supplement, pp. 1–2.

20. See Sara McLanahan and Gary Sandefur, *Growing Up with a Single Parent: What Hurts, What Helps* (Harvard University Press, 1994). For a more recent study focusing on problems associated with teenage childbearing, see Rebecca Maynard, *Kids Having Kids: Economic Costs and Social Consequences of Teen Pregnancy* (Washington: Urban Institute, 1997).

21. Freya L. Sonenstein and Gregory Acs, "Teenage Childbearing: The Trends and Their Implications," pp. 47–50, in Sawhill, ed., *Welfare Reform,* p. 48.

22. The absolute number of births to teens also declined by nearly one-quarter from 1970 to 1997. See Stephanie Ventura, T. J. Mathews, and Sally Curtin, "Declines in Teenage Birth Rates, 1991–1997: National and State Patterns," *National Vital Statistics Report,* vol. 47, no. 12 (December 17, 1998), p. 3. For press coverage of declines in birth rates during the welfare reform debates, see Barbara Vobejda, "Teen Births Decline; Out-of-Wedlock Rate Levels Off," *Washington Post,* September 22, 1995, p. A1; and "Rate of Births for Teen-Agers Drops Again," *New York Times,* September 22, 1995, p. A1.

23. See Ventura, Mathews, and Curtin, "Declines in Teenage Birth Rates," pp. 2–3.

24. For critiques in this vein, see, for example, David Blankenhorn, *Fatherless America: Confronting Our Most Urgent Social Problem* (Basic Books, 1995); and David Popenoe, *Life without Father: Compelling New Evidence That Fatherhood and Marriage Are Indispensable for the Good of Children and Society* (New York: Martin Kessler, 1996). See also Charles Murray's testimony in Senate Finance Committee, *Welfare Reform Wrap-Up,* 104 Cong. 1 sess., April 27, 1995, Senate Hearing 104-327 (Government Printing Office, 1995). An alternative perspective is provided by Kristin Luker, *Dubious Conceptions: The Politics of Teenage Pregnancy* (Harvard University Press, 1996).

25. See, for example, Arline T. Geronimus and Sanders Korenman, "The Socio-Economic Consequences of Teen Childbearing Reconsidered," *Quarterly Journal of Economics,* vol. 107 (November 1992), pp. 1187–1214; and Geronimus, "Teenage Childbearing and Personal Responsibility: An Alternative View," *Political Science Quarterly,* vol. 112, no. 3 (Fall 1997) pp. 405–30. See also the testimony and prepared statement of Frank E. Furstenberg in House Ways and Means Committee, Subcommittee on Human Resources, *Causes of Poverty, with a Focus on Out-of-Wedlock Births,* March 5, 1996, House Serial 104-52 (GPO, 1996), pp. 73–77. For a comprehensive recent review and assessment, see Maynard, *Kids Having Kids.*

26. The picture is more complicated when Medicaid benefits are factored in, for they have risen in real terms on a per capita basis. But most scholars argue that the real value of Medicaid benefits is heavily discounted by recipients because these benefits are not disposable income that recipients can spend as they choose.

27. For reviews of evidence on the incentive effects of welfare, see Robert Moffitt, "Incentive Effects of the U.S. Welfare System: A Review," *Journal of Economic Literature,* vol. 30 (March 1992), pp. 1–61; Gregory Acs, "Do Welfare Benefits Promote Out-of-Wedlock Childbearing?" in Sawhill, *Welfare Reform,* pp. 51–54; and Weaver and Dickens, *Looking Before We Leap,* pp. 30–34. A more recent review appears in Robert Moffitt, "The Effect of Welfare on Marriage and Fertility: What Do We Know and What Do We Need to Know?" in Moffitt, ed., *Welfare, the Family, and Reproductive Behavior: Research Perspectives* (Washington: National Research Council, 1999). See also the testimony and prepared statement of Rebecca Blank in Subcommittee on Human Resources of the House Ways and Means Committee, *Contract with America—Welfare Reform,* 104 Cong. 1 sess., Committee Serial 104-43 (GPO, 1995), pp. 196–209.

28. For a powerful ethnographic study by a journalist challenging the idea that teen pregnancies are unintentional, see Leon Dash, *When Children Want Children: An Inside Look at the Crisis of Teenage Parenthood* (Penguin, 1990).

29. Elijah Anderson, *Streetwise: Race, Class, and Change in an Urban Community* (University of Chicago Press, 1990), p. 112. See more generally chapter 4 in Anderson.

30. For press coverage, see, for example, Mike Males, "Why Blame Young Girls?" *New York Times,* July 29, 1994, p. A26.

31. For a liberal critique of the Murray analysis, see Sharon Parrott and Robert Greenstein, *Welfare, Out-of-Wedlock Childbearing, and Poverty: What Is the Connection?* (Washington: Center on Budget and Policy Priorities, January 1995).

32. For this critique, see Charles Murray, "What to Do about Welfare?" *Commentary*, vol. 98, no. 6 (December 1994), pp. 26–34.

33. Peter Gottschalk, "The Intergenerational Transmission of Welfare Participation: Facts and Possible Causes," *Journal of Policy Analysis and Management*, vol. 11, no. 2 (1992), pp. 254–72.

34. Furstenberg, Testimony, in House Ways and Means Committee, *Causes of Poverty*, pp. 75–76.

35. See, in particular, William Julius Wilson, *When Work Disappears: The World of the New Urban Poor* (Knopf, 1996), chap. 4; a brief review of the literature on the "marriageable male" thesis appears on pp. 95–97. For an early critique, see Maris A. Vinovskis, "Teenage Pregnancy and the Underclass," *The Public Interest*, no. 93 (Fall 1988), pp. 87–96.

36. See Murray, "What to Do about Welfare?" See also Murray, "Does Welfare Bring More Babies?" *The Public Interest*, no. 114 (Spring 1994), pp. 17–30.

37. It is unlikely that liberal writers and researchers found their arguments entirely plausible, either. As Christopher Jencks has noted, "Although liberals scoff publicly at these [conservative] arguments, few really doubt that changing the economic consequences of single motherhood can affect its frequency." Jencks, "Foreword," in Kathryn Edin and Laura Lein, *Making Ends Meet: How Single Mothers Survive Welfare and Low-Wage Work* (New York: Russell Sage, 1997), p. xxiv.

38. See Subcommittee on Human Resources, *Contract with America*, pp. 157, 161.

39. See Thomas Gabe, "Demographic Trends Affecting Aid to Families with Dependent Children (AFDC) Cascload Growth," 93-7 EPW, Congressional Research Service 93-7, December 1992. See also Gabe's testimony in House Ways and Means Committee, Subcommittee on Human Resources, *Trends in Spending and Caseloads for AFDC and Related Programs*, March 13, 1993, Committee Serial 103-2 (GPO, 1993).

40. See the analysis by William T. Dickens in Weaver and Dickens, *Looking Before We Leap*, pp. 42–47.

41. See the prepared statement of Robert C. Granger of the Manpower Demonstration Research Corporation, pp. 79–85, in Senate Finance Committee, *Teen Parents and Welfare Reform*, March 14, 1995, Senate Hearing 104-349 (GPO, 1995); and Douglas Kirby and others, "School-Based Programs to Reduce Sexual Risk Behaviors: A Review of Effectiveness," *Public Health Reports*, vol. 109, no. 3 (May–June 1994), pp. 339–59. For a more recent review, see Rebecca A. Maynard, "Paternalism, Teenage Pregnancy Prevention, and Teenage Parent Services," in Lawrence M. Mead, ed., *The New Paternalism: Supervisory Approaches to Poverty* (Brookings, 1997), pp. 89–129.

42. See the prepared statement of Rebecca A. Maynard in Senate Finance Committee, *Teen Parents and Welfare Reform*, p. 89. More recent reviews of the few existing studies suggest that abstinence-only interventions are not effective in delaying intercourse. See Douglas Kirby, *No Easy Answers: Research Findings on Programs to Reduce Teen Pregnancy* (Washington: National Campaign to Prevent Teen Pregnancy, March 1997); and National Campaign to Prevent Teen Pregnancy, *Evaluating Abstinence-Only Interventions* (Washington: August 1998).

43. For a review of the New Jersey experience and an argument that the experiment's control group methodology understated the effects of the family cap, see Ted G. Goertzel and Gary S. Young, "New Jersey's Experiment in Welfare Reform," *The Public Interest*, no. 125 (Fall 1996), pp. 72–80; and Goertzel, "Why Welfare Research Fails," paper presented at the 1998 meetings of the Eastern Evaluation Research Society, Cape May, N.J. (www.crab.rutgers.edu/~goertzel/fail2.html).

44. Iver Petersen, "Abortions Up Slightly for Welfare Mothers," *New York Times*, May 17, 1995, p. B7.

45. Senator Bradley referred to evaluation studies carried out by Rutgers University, arguing that the data were too preliminary to make a decision mandating family caps. Senator Nickles referred to a Heritage Foundation policy brief arguing that the family cap had led to a decline in births in AFDC control and experimental groups. Nickles argued that this reflected a broader moral message influencing the behavior of women in both groups. The Senate debate is in the *Congressional Record*, daily ed., vol. 141, no. 142 (September 13, 1995), pp. 13486–89. The Heritage policy brief is Robert Rector, "The Impact of New Jersey's Family Cap on Out-of-Wedlock Births and Abortions," F.Y.I. 59 (Washington: Heritage Foundation, September 6, 1995).

46. House Ways and Means Committee, *1994 Green Book* (GPO, 1994), p. 411.

47. See the discussion in Mary Jo Bane and David Ellwood, *Welfare Realities: From Rhetoric to Reform* (Harvard University Press, 1994), pp. 55–60.

48. Ibid., p. 28.

49. Ibid.; and the contributions of LaDonna Pavetti to Weaver and Dickens, *Looking Before We Leap*, pp. 36–41.

50. Bane and Ellwood, *Welfare Realities*, p. 39. This research is also discussed in the House Ways and Means Committee's *Green Book*; see, for example, *1992 Green Book*, pp. 685–88, and *1994 Green Book*, pp. 440–447.

51. For alternative explanations of "negative duration dependence" in exits from AFDC, see Moffitt, "Incentive Effects of the U.S. Welfare System," pp. 25–26.

52. For a skeptical view of child care costs as a barrier, see Lawrence M. Mead, *The New Politics of Poverty: The Nonworking Poor in America* (Basic Books, 1992), pp. 119–24.

53. For recent reviews of the "spatial mismatch" literature, see Christopher Jencks and Susan E. Mayer, "Residential Segregation, Job Proximity, and Black Job Opportunities," in Lawrence E. Lynn and Michael G. H. McGeary, eds., *Inner-City Poverty in the United States* (Washington: National Academy Press, 1990); and Paul A. Jargowsky, *Poverty and Place: Ghettoes, Barrios, and the American City* (New York: Russell Sage, 1997), pp. 123–26.

54. See, for example, Katherine S. Newman and Chauncy Lennon, "The Job Ghetto," *The American Prospect*, no. 22 (Summer 1995), pp. 66–67.

55. Mead, *The New Politics of Poverty*, p. 91. See more generally chapter 5.

56. Robert Greenstein, "Losing Faith in 'Losing Ground,'" *The New Republic*, March 25, 1985, pp. 12–17.

57. See, for example, Moffitt, "Incentive Effects of the U.S. Welfare System"; and Bane and Ellwood, *Welfare Realities*, pp. 70–71. See also Douglas Besharov, "Escaping the Dole," *Washington Post*, December 12, 1993, p. C3.

58. Robert Moffitt and Barbara Wolfe, "The Effect of the Medicaid Program on Welfare Participation and Labor Supply," *Review of Economics and Statistics*, vol. 74, no. 4 (November–December 1992), pp. 615–26.

59. See Michael Tanner, Stephen Moore, and David Hartman, *The Welfare versus Work Trade-Off: An Analysis of the Total Level of Welfare Benefits by State*, Policy Analysis 240 (Washington: Cato Institute, September 19, 1995). For press coverage, see Michael Tanner and Stephen Moore, "Why Welfare Pays," *Wall Street Journal*, September 28, 1995, p. A20; and Cheryl Wetzstein, "Why Work, Asks Study, If Welfare Is More Lucrative?" *Washington Times*, September 19, 1995, p. A6.

60. See Sharon Parrott, *The Cato Institute's Report on Welfare Benefits: Do the Numbers Add Up?* (Washington: Center on Budget and Policy Priorities, April 22, 1996). Parrott's critique focused especially on the inclusion of Medicaid benefits and housing subsidies in the Cato calculation. See also Michael Tanner and Naomi Lopez, "The Value of Welfare: Cato vs. CBPP," Cato Institute Briefing Paper 27, June 12, 1996. For press coverage, see Bob Herbert, "Poison Numbers," *New York Times*, April 22, 1996, p. A13; and Stephen Moore and Michael Tanner, "Welfare Reform vs. the Minimum Wage," *Washington Times*, May 10, 1996, p. A20.

61. Early versions of the research appears in Christopher Jencks and Katherine Edin, "The Real Welfare Problem," *The American Prospect*, vol. 1, no. 1 (Spring 1990), pp. 31–50; and Kathryn Edin, "Surviving the Welfare System: How AFDC Recipients Make Ends Meet in Chicago," *Social Problems*, vol. 38, no. 4 (1991) pp. 462–74. Comprehensive results are reported in Kathryn Edin and Laura Lein, "Work, Welfare, and Single Mothers' Economic Survival Strategies," *American Sociological Review*, vol. 61 (February 1996), pp. 253–66; and Edin and Lein, *Making Ends Meet*. In the latter, Edin and Lein argued that almost all poor mothers forgo more lucrative criminal activities such as prostitution or selling drugs in favor of low-wage work because they view the former as incompatible with good mothering (p. 8).

62. Lawrence M. Mead, "The Decline of Welfare in Wisconsin," *Journal of Public Administration Research and Theory*, vol. 9 (October 1999).

63. For a review, see Moffitt, "Incentive Effects of the U.S. Welfare System," pp. 15–19; see also Ellwood and Bane, *Welfare Realities*, pp. 101–02. And for a slightly more optimistic view, see Robert Lerman, "Increasing the Employment and Earnings of Welfare Recipients," in Sawhill, *Welfare Reform*, pp. 17–20.

64. For overviews, see Gary Burtless, "When Work Doesn't Work: Employment Programs for Welfare Recipients," *Brookings Review*, Spring 1992, pp. 26–29; Judith M. Gueron, "Work and Welfare: Lessons on Employment Programs," *Journal of Economic Perspectives*, vol. 4, no.1 (Winter 1990), pp. 79–98; Judith M. Gueron and Edward Pauly, *From Welfare to Work* (New York: Russell Sage Foundation, 1991); Richard P. Nathan,

Turning Promises into Performance: The Management Challenge of Implementing Workfare (Columbia University Press, 1993); and Daniel Friedlander and Gary Burtless, *Five Years After: The Long-Term Effects of Welfare to Work Programs* (New York: Russell Sage, 1995).

65. See Judith M. Gueron, "A Research Context for Welfare Reform," *Journal of Policy Analysis and Management,* vol. 15, no. 4 (1996), p. 552. Earnings results are after three years of follow-up. Riverside also increased the percentage of AFDC single-parent recipients ever employed in the three-year period from 53.4 percent for those who did not participate in GAIN compared with 67.1 percent for those who did participate (p. 551).

66. Gueron, "Work and Welfare," p. 94.

67. In a welfare-to-work project in San Diego, for example, benefits dropped 8 to 14 percent over those paid to the control group; the biggest income gain for any demonstration group was $1,800 per participant, in a program with costs that were twelve times that much. See Burtless, "When Work Doesn't Work," p. 28. See also Friedlander and Burtless, *Five Years After.*

68. Haskins, "Congress Writes a Law," pp. 616–31.

69. See, for example, Lawrence M. Mead, "An Administrative Approach to Welfare Reform," in Sawhill, *Welfare Reform,* pp. 21–24. For press coverage, see Paul Taylor, "Gain in Earnings Seen in Modified Work Program," *Washington Post,* April 23, 1992, p. A3; and Jason DeParle, "Counter to Trend, a Welfare Program in California Has One Idea: Get a Job!" *New York Times,* May 16, 1993, p. A14.

70. See, in particular, Gary Burtless, "Are Targeted Wage Subsidies Harmful? Evidence from a Wage Voucher Experiment," *Industrial and Labor Relations Review,* vol. 39, no. 1 (October 1985), pp. 105–14. See more generally the discussion by Burtless, "A Primer," in Weaver and Dickens, *Looking Before We Leap,* pp. 52–57.

71. Rebecca M. Blank, "Policy Watch: Proposals for Time-Limited Welfare," *Journal of Economic Perspectives,* vol. 8, no. 4 (Fall 1994), pp. 183–93.

72. Many critics, including Judith Gueron of MDRC, warned that even the most "highly mandatory" JOBS sites had achieved the work participation rates anticipated in Republican welfare bills and that, as a result, "states might simply choose to accept financial penalties for failing to do so and cut back on their welfare-to-work programs." See Gueron, "A Research Context for Welfare Reform," p. 556.

73. Evelyn Z. Brodkin, "Administrative Capacity and Welfare Reform," in Weaver and Dickens, *Looking Before We Leap,* pp. 75–90.

74. One prominent researcher estimated that the "number of welfare recipients who cannot work, or who could work only with special support, is probably less than 25 percent." Gueron, "A Research Context for Welfare Reform," p. 555. See also James Riccio and Stephen Freedman, *Can They All Work? A Study of the Employment Potential of Welfare Recipients in a Welfare-to-Work Program* (New York: Manpower Demonstration Research Corporation, 1995).

75. Henry Aaron, *Politics and the Professors: The Great Society in Perspective* (Brookings, 1978), p. 98.

76. For a parallel argument, see Martin Rein and Christopher Winship, "Policy Entrepreneurs and the Academic Establishment: Truth and Values in Social Controversies," in Elliott White, ed., *Intelligence, Political Inequality, and Public Policy* (Westport, Conn.: Praeger, 1997), pp. 17–47.

77. Interview with author, April 1995.

78. See, for example, Harwood, "Think Tanks Battle to Judge the Impact of Welfare Reform."

79. Interview with author, April 1994.

Chapter Seven

1. This chapter draws heavily on the author's collaborative work with Robert Y. Shapiro and Lawrence R. Jacobs on public opinion toward welfare reform, which was part of a larger collaborative project on the Clinton administration and social policy supported by the Russell Sage Foundation and a project on welfare reform funded by the Annie E. Casey Foundation. See R. Kent Weaver, Robert Y. Shapiro, and Lawrence R. Jacobs, "The Polls—Trends: Welfare," *Public Opinion Quarterly*, vol. 59, no. 4 (December 1995), pp. 606–27; and R. Kent Weaver, Robert Y. Shapiro, and Lawrence R. Jacobs, "Public Opinion on Welfare Reform: A Mandate for What?" in Weaver and William T. Dickens, eds., *Looking Before We Leap: Social Science and Welfare Reform* (Brookings, 1995), pp. 109–28. Jim Abrams provided valuable research assistance in preparing this chapter.

2. The best overall treatment of the relationship between public opinion and welfare policy is Steven M. Teles, *Whose Welfare? AFDC and Elite Politics* (University Press of Kansas, 1996).

3. On Republican efforts, see, in particular, John Harwood, "GOP, Given Power by Voters Angry over Welfare, Seeks a Compassionate Image in Reform Debate," *Wall Street Journal*, March 22, 1995, p. A18; and Mona Charen, "High Ground on Welfare," *Washington Times*, March 22, 1995, p. A20.

4. Representative Jan Meyers of Kansas in Ronald Brownstein, "Welfare Debate Puts Blame for Poverty Mainly on the Poor," *Los Angeles Times* (Washington ed.), March 24, 1995, pp. A1, A8.

5. David Binder, "Children Crusade against Proposed Republican Budget Cuts," *New York Times*, March 20, 1995, p. A13.

6. The focus here is on examining modal positions of the public at large rather than differences among specific subgroups of the American population. For an analysis that stresses the views of particular subgroups, see Geoffrey Garin, Gary Molyneux, and Linda DiVall, *Public Attitudes toward Welfare Reform: A Summary of Key Research Findings* (Peter D. Hart Research Associates, American Viewpoint).

7. Kaiser-Harvard Program on the Public and Health-Social Policy, *Survey on Welfare Reform: Basic Values and Beliefs; Support for Policy Approaches; Knowledge about Key Programs* (Henry J. Kaiser Family Foundation, January 1995).

8. See Natalie Jaffe, "Attitudes toward Public Welfare Programs and Recipients in the United States," in Lester Salamon, *Welfare: The Elusive Consensus* (Praeger, 1978); Tom W. Smith, "That Which We Call Welfare by Any Other Name Would Be Sweeter: An Analysis of the Impact of Question Wording on Response Patterns," *Public Opinion Quarterly,* vol. 51, no. 1 (1987), pp. 75–83; and Kenneth A. Rasinski, "The Effect of Question Wording on Public Support for Government Spending," *Public Opinion Quarterly,* vol. 53 (Fall 1989), pp. 388–94.

9. On the public's distinctions among recipients of income transfer programs, see Fax Lomax Cook, *Who Should Be Helped? Public Support for Social Services* (Beverly Hills, Calif.: Sage, 1979); and Cook and Edith J. Barrett, *Support for the American Welfare State: The Views of Congress and the Public* (Columbia University Press, 1992).

10. As Teles (*Whose Welfare?* p. 44) notes, the biggest drop in support for increased welfare spending was between 1961 and 1973, when the percentage of the population believing that too little was being spent on welfare fell from 60 to 20 percent. At least some of this change probably resulted from "a shift in the public's impression of how much the government was actually spending rather than underlying support for any given level of welfare spending."

11. On the determinants of public attitudes toward welfare spending over time, see James Kluegel, "Macro-Economic Problems, Beliefs about the Poor and Attitudes toward Welfare Spending," *Social Problems,* vol. 34, no. 1 (February 1987), pp. 82–99; and Teles, *Whose Welfare?* chap. 3.

12. In the Kaiser-Harvard welfare reform survey conducted in December 1994, 57 percent of Democrats and 78 percent of Republicans said that too much was being spent on welfare. Kaiser-Harvard Program, *Survey on Welfare Reform,* table 5. Teles (*Whose Welfare?* pp. 46–47) notes that the substantial increase in hostility to welfare spending between 1991 and 1993 was not accompanied by similar increases in opposition in aid to blacks or aid to big cities, suggesting that it was opposition to welfare in particular rather than increases in racial hostility that were at work.

13. Two percent of respondents thought that the welfare system worked very well, 14 percent fairly well. Comparable figures were 1 percent and 19 percent for the criminal justice system; 4 percent and 32 percent for the health care system; 5 percent and 34 percent for the education system; 3 percent and 36 percent for the tax system; and 9 percent and 49 percent for the social security system. Telephone poll of 1,020 respondents conducted between November 12 and 15, 1993, by Peter D. Hart Research Associates.

14. This figure is drawn from two polls of 1,000 adults conducted by Yankelovich Partners for *Time*/CNN in May 1994 and September 1995. In the first poll 81 percent favored fundamental reform over minor changes; in the second poll, 79 percent.

15. In the May 1995 Hart/Teeter poll for NBC and the *Wall Street Journal*, 5 percent of respondents said that the welfare system had both good and bad consequences, 2 percent said neither, and 1 percent was not sure. An identically worded poll conducted in January 1994 received very similar responses: 19 percent said the welfare system "does more good than harm," 71 percent said it "does more harm than good," 5 percent said some of both, 2 percent said neither, and 1 percent was not sure. Both polls were conducted by Hart/Teeter for NBC and the *Wall Street Journal*.

16. *Los Angeles Times* poll, Survey 334, "National Issues," April 1994, question 75. In an April 1995 CBS/*New York Times* poll of 1,089 respondents, only 15 percent of respondents felt that "most people on welfare are using welfare for a short period of time and will get off it eventually," whereas 79 percent felt that "most people on welfare are so dependent on welfare that they will never get off it." Six percent had no opinion.

17. See Weaver, Shapiro, and Jacobs, "Poll Trends," for a detailed presentation of poll data. See also the discussion in Harvard/Kaiser, "Survey Shows 'Two Faces' of Public Opinion on Welfare Reform," news release (Washington: The Henry J. Kaiser Family Foundation, January 12, 1995).

18. Six percent of those surveyed said that neither was a problem, and 5 percent were unsure. Peter D. Hart Research Associates, "American Viewpoint," Study 3805B, p. 4.

19. For an examination of the role of beliefs and values in public opinion, see Stanley Feldman, "Structure and Consistency in Public Opinion: The Role of Core Beliefs and Values," *American Journal of Political Science*, vol. 32, no. 2 (May 1998), pp. 416–38.

20. When asked, "Of the people currently on welfare in the United States, how many would you say deserve to be receiving welfare benefits?" 4 percent of respondents said "nearly all"; 14 percent said "most, but not all"; 42 percent said "about half"; 32 percent said "less than half"; 5 percent said "almost none at all"; and 3 percent were not sure. Telephone poll of 1,020 respondents conducted between November 12 and 15, 1993, by Peter D. Hart Research Associates, question 6b.

21. See Hugh Heclo, "Poverty Politics," in Sheldon Danziger and Daniel Weinberg, eds., *Confronting Poverty: Prescriptions for Change* (Harvard University Press and Russell Sage, 1994), pp. 396–437. When asked in December 1994 whether "it is the responsibility of government to take care of people who can't take care of themselves," 65 percent agreed, 29 percent disagreed, and 65 did not know. See Maureen Dowd, "Americans Like GOP Agenda but Split on How to Reach Goals," *New York Times*, December 15, 1994, p. A1. In the Harvard/Kaiser survey the same month, only 14 percent of respondents felt that government should have the primary responsibility for ensuring that nonworking low-income people have a minimum standard of living; while 26 percent believed that people themselves, their friends, and voluntary agencies should be responsible; and 57 percent said that responsibility should be shared. Most (71 percent) of those who believed that responsibility should be shared felt that government's obligation should be limited in duration, however. See Harvard/Kaiser, "Survey Shows 'Two Faces,'" table 23.

22. When asked in December 1994 in a *New York Times*/CBS News poll, "Which is better for the children of unmarried mothers under 21 who have no income: to be placed in foster care or an orphanage or to remain with their mothers on welfare?" 20 percent said foster care or orphanage, 72 percent said to remain with their mother, and 8 percent did not know. Dowd, "Americans Like GOP Agenda." When asked, somewhat differently, if they favored "a proposal that would end all welfare benefits for unmarried mothers and their children, even if it means that some of the children would have to be cared for in group homes or orphanages," 25 percent favored such a proposal, 66 percent opposed it, and 9 percent did not know or refused to answer. Kaiser-Harvard Program, "Survey on Welfare Reform," table 22.

23. Heclo, "Poverty Politics." For an argument emphasizing Americans' support for a work-based approach to supporting poor families, see, in particular, Teles, *Whose Welfare?*

24. A CBS/*New York Times* survey in December 1994 asked the question, "Which is closer to your view: welfare recipients should continue to get benefits as long as they work for them, or after a year or two welfare recipients should stop receiving all benefits?" Seventy-one percent of respondents chose getting benefits, 24 percent chose ending benefits, and 5 percent did not know. Dowd, "Americans Like G.O.P. Agenda."

25. When asked what the government should do if it were "to cut off AFDC . . . or welfare benefits after a specific period of time and after it provides education, training, health benefits, and child care to those families," 10 percent of respondents chose "simply end the families' benefits, including Aid to Families with Dependent Children," 56 percent chose "make the parent or parents do community service work in exchange for welfare benefits," 25 percent chose "guarantee jobs to the parent or parents after they are cut off welfare," 10 percent did not know or refused to answer. Harvard/Kaiser/KRC Communications research, December 27–29, 1994, summarized in Kaiser-Harvard Program, "Survey on Welfare Reform," table 18. These results are similar to those of a 1993 Hart/Teeter poll that asked (question 13d), "Which one of these two approaches to welfare reform would you say is better: (1) after two years, benefits would be ended for all able-bodied recipients, and the government would not provide any job; or (2) after two years, welfare recipients who have not found other employment would be required to work at a public service job?" Twelve percent of respondents chose cutting off benefits, 83 percent preferred requiring recipients to work at a public service job, and 2 percent answered each of both the same, neither, and not sure.

26. Data for December 1994 are from Harvard/Kaiser Program, *Survey on Welfare Reform.* In an identically worded question in a November 1993 poll for *U.S. News and World Report,* 37 percent of respondents chose experiment at the state level, 43 percent, reform at the national level.

27. Richard Morin, "Public Growing Wary of GOP Cuts," *Washington Post,* March 21, 1995, pp. A1, A6.

28. The April 1995 CBS/*New York Times* survey stated: "Republicans in Congress have passed a number of changes to federal programs that serve the poor. Do you think

the changes they have made go too far, do not go far enough, are about what is needed, or haven't you heard enough about these changes to say." "Too far" was chosen by 12 percent of respondents, 23 percent said "not far enough," 12 percent said "about what is needed," 48 percent had not heard enough to say, and 5 percent did not know or did not answer. The May 1995 results are from a Hart/Teeter poll for NBC and the *Wall Street Journal.*

29. See, for example, Shanto Iyengar, "Television News and Citizens' Explanations of National Affairs," *American Political Science Review,* vol. 81, no. 3 (September 1987), pp. 815–32.

Chapter Eight

1. Gilbert Y. Steiner, *The Children's Cause* (Brookings, 1976), p. 143.

2. See Jill Quadagno, *The Color of Welfare: How Racism Undermined the War on Poverty* (Oxford University Press, 1994).

3. See Richard Cloward and Frances Fox Piven, *Regulating the Poor: The Functions of Public Welfare* (Vintage Books, 1971).

4. On the National Welfare Rights Organization, see Gilbert Y. Steiner, *The State of Welfare* (Brookings, 1971), chap. 8; and Richard Cloward and Frances Fox Piven, *Poor People's Movements: Why They Succeed, How They Fail* (Vintage Books, 1977), chap. 5.

5. On liberal advocacy groups, see Douglas R. Imig, "Resource Mobilization and Survival Tactics of Poverty Advocacy Groups," *Western Political Quarterly,* vol. 45, no. 2 (1992), pp. 501–20; and Douglas R. Imig, *Poverty and Power: The Political Representation of Poor Americans* (University of Nebraska Press, 1996).

6. See, for example, Andrew S. McFarland, *Public Interest Lobbies: Decision Making on Energy* (Washington: American Enterprise Institute, 1976); and Jeffrey M. Berry, *Lobbying for the People* (Princeton University Press, 1977).

7. See Allan J. Cigler and Anthony J. Nownes, "Public Interest Entrepreneurs and Group Patrons," pp. 77–99, in Cigler and Burdett A. Loomis, eds., *Interest Group Politics,* 4th ed. (Congressional Quarterly Press, 1995).

8. Generally speaking, 501(c)(3) organizations may devote only an "insubstantial" share (interpreted by the courts to mean no more than 5 percent) of their expenditures to efforts to influence legislation. But organizations that file a lobbying report with the IRS can spend up to 20 percent of their first $500,000 for lobbying; 15 percent of the next $500,000; 10 percent of the third $500,000; and 5 percent of all expenditures over $1.5 million. However, the limits on "grassroots" lobbying to influence public opinion on legislation are more strict: no more than 25 percent of allowable lobbying expenses. Organizations that receive federal funds are not allowed to use those funds for lobbying. See Children's Defense Fund, *Lobbying and Political Activity for Nonprofits: What You Can (and Can't) Do under Federal Law* (Washington, 1983); and John R. Wright, *Interest Groups and Congress: Lobbying, Contributions, Influence* (Boston: Allyn and Bacon, 1996), p. 31.

9. Wright, *Interest Groups and Congress,* pp. 65–73.

10. See Children's Defense Fund, *Lobbying and Political Activity for Nonprofits,* pp. 6–9.

11. See Kay Lehman Schlozman and John T. Tierney, *Organized Interests and American Democracy* (Harper and Row, 1986), pp. 209–14.

12. See, in particular, Kevin Hula, "Rounding Up the Usual Suspects: Forging Interest Group Coalitions in Washington," in Cigler and Loomis, *Interest Group Politics,* pp. 239–58; and Hula, *Lobbying Together: Interest Group Coalitions in Legislative Politics* (Georgetown University Press, 1999).

13. On the increasingly blurred boundaries between research and advocacy groups, see Andrew Rich and R. Kent Weaver, "Analysts and Advocations: Think Tanks and the Politicization of Expertise," in Alan J. Cigler and Burdett A. Loomis, eds., *Interest Group Politics,* 5th ed. (Congressional Quarterly Press, 1998), pp. 235–53.

14. Jeff Shear, "Tightfisted Liberals," *National Journal,* September 3, 1994, pp. 2021–25.

15. Interview with author, May 1994.

16. See, for example, Christopher Howard, "Happy Returns: How the Poor Got Tax Relief," *American Prospect,* no. 17 (Spring 1994), pp. 46–53; and Greenstein's testimony in *Selected Aspects of Welfare Reform,* Hearing before the Subcommittees on Select Revenue and on Human Resources of the House Committee on Ways and Means, 103 Cong. 1 sess., serial 103-29 (Government Printing Office, 1993), pp. 116–26.

17. Interview with author, April 1996.

18. Robert Fersh, quoted in Barbara Vobejda and Judith Havemann, "Traditional Welfare Constituencies Put Out by Lack of Input in Reform," *Washington Post,* May 21, 1995, p. A4.

19. Interview with author, April 1996.

20. "A Historical Perspective on the Center for Law and Social Policy," in *CLASP: Twenty-Five Years of Change* (Washington: Center for Law and Social Policy, 1995).

21. After welfare reform legislation passed in 1996, Greenberg and other CLASP lawyers were also very active in advising state welfare agencies about their obligations and options under the new law. See Dana Milbank, "Lawyer Helps States See the Loopholes in Welfare Law," *Wall Street Journal,* March 14, 1997, p. A18.

22. On the early years of CDF, see Steiner, *The Children's Cause,* pp. 98–101, 172–75.

23. Interview with author, July 1998.

24. CDF has also been subject to increasing criticism, even within the child advocacy community, for being a top-down organization and inattentive to the views of state and local activists. For recent profiles of the CDF, see Dana Milbank, "Children's Defense Fund and Its Lauded Leader Lose Clout as Social Policy Shifts to the States," *Wall Street Journal,* May 28, 1996, p. A28; and Elizabeth Gleick, "The Children's Crusade," *Time,* June 3, 1996, pp. 31–35.

25. Bill Clinton had promised to name Peter Edelman to a federal judgeship when he became president, but backed down in the face of Republican opposition. On the

friendship between the Edelmans and the Clintons, see Neil A. Lewis, "A Friendship in Tatters, over Policy," *New York Times,* September 13, 1996, p. A26.

26. Interview with author, April 1996.

27. Megan Rosenfeld, "They All Call Themselves Christians, but in the Battle over Welfare Reform They're Preaching Two Gospels," *Washington Post,* August 9, 1995, p. D1.

28. Perceptions of child advocacy groups as liberal and Democratic are also widespread among state legislative leaders, limiting their effectiveness. See State Legislative Leaders Foundation, *State Legislative Leaders: Keys to Effective Legislation for Children and Families* (Centerville, Mass., 1995).

29. Robin Toner, "War over an Overhaul Appears to Be No Contest," *New York Times,* January 13, 1995, p. A13.

30. Daly is quoted in Jeff Shear, "Looking for a Voice," *National Journal,* March 16, 1996, p. 591–95.

31. On the history of the Democratic Leadership Council, see Jon F. Hale, "The Making of the New Democrats," *Political Science Quarterly,* vol 110, no. 2 (1995), pp. 207–32. Hale notes that many of the early members of the DLC were liberals more interested in changing the party's image to make it palatable to voters than in changing the substance of policy (p. 216).

32. Dan Balz, "Moderate, Conservative Democrats Buck 'Constraints,' Form Think Tank," *Washington Post,* June 30, 1989, p. A21.

33. See Elaine Ciulla Kamarck and William A. Galston, "A Progressive Family Policy for the 1990s," in Will Marshall and Martin Schram, eds., *Mandate for Change* (Berkley Books, 1993), pp. 153–78; and Marshall and Kamarck, "Replacing Welfare with Work," in Marshall and Schram, *Mandate for Change,* pp. 217–36.

34. See Al From, "Hey Mom—What's a New Democrat?" *Washington Post,* June 6, 1993, p. C1; Dan Balz, "'New Democrats' Promise New Pressure on Clinton," *Washington Post,* December 5, 1993, p. A4; and William Claiborne, "Dueling Ideologies May Redefine Clinton's Vision of Welfare Reform," *Washington Post,* March 18, 1994, p. A8.

35. See Will Marshall, "Putting Work First," *New Democrat* (January–February 1995), pp. 43–46; Will Marshall, Ed Kilgore, and Lyn A. Hogan, "Work First: A Proposal to Replace Welfare with an Employment System," Progressive Policy Institute Policy Briefing, March 2, 1995; and Al From, "How Democrats Can Seize the Initiative on Welfare Reform," Democratic Leadership Council, July 17, 1995, http://epn.org/ ppi/ppfrom.htm.

36. In PPI's proposal, the federal government would provide $20 million in seed money for three years. Individual "second-chance home" programs would be designed by local community-based organizations. See Kathleen Sylvester, "Second-Chance Home: Breaking the Cycle of Teen Pregnancy," Progressive Policy Institute policy briefing, June 23, 1995.

37. "Ending Welfare as We Know It: The President's Done His Job, Now Let's Do Ours," *DLC Update,* August 1, 1996.

38. For a description of the Big Seven, see Beverly A. Cigler, "Not Just Another Special Interest: Intergovernmental Representation," in Cigler and Loomis, *"Interest*

Group Politics, 4th ed., pp. 131–53. See also Anne Marie Cammissa, *Governments as Interest Groups: Intergovernmental Lobbying and the Federal System* (Westport, Conn.: Praeger, 1995).

39. Interview with author, March 1995.

40. If a proposed new policy has not been transmitted to all members fifteen days in advance of an NGA plenary, it requires approval by three-quarters of all governors present and voting at the plenary to suspend the rules and consider that policy, and three-quarters' approval is again required to adopt the policy and for any amendments to the policy. See National Governors' Association, "Adoption of Policy Statements in Plenary Sessions," no date. Both the Medicaid and the welfare reform policies adopted by the NGA at its winter 1996 meeting were adopted under the three-quarters requirement.

41. Interview with author, March 1995.

42. On conservative groups and welfare policymaking, see, for example, Hilary Stout, "GOP's Welfare Stance Owes a Lot to Prodding from Robert Rector," *Wall Street Journal,* January 23, 1995, pp. A1, A10.

43. For brief profiles of these organizations, see Clyde Wilcox, *Onward Christian Soldiers? The Religious Right in American Politics* (Boulder, Colo.: Westview Press, 1996). The classic study of religious lobbies in Washington is Allen D. Hertzke, *Representing God in Washington: The Role of Religious Lobbies in the American Polity* (University of Tennessee Press, 1988).

44. On the Christian Coalition, see, for example, Ralph Reed Jr., *Active Faith: How Christians Are Changing the Soul of American Politics* (Free Press, 1996); and Dan Balz and Ronald Brownstein, *Storming the Gates: Protest Politics and the Republican Revival* (Boston: Little, Brown, 1996), chap. 7.

45. On the Family Research Council and Focus on the Family, see Peter H. Stone, "All in the Family," *National Journal* (October 28, 1995), pp. 2641–45; Elizabeth Kolbert, "Politicians Find a Window into the Heart of the Christian Right," *New York Times,* November 1, 1995, p. A14; and Marc Fisher, "The GOP, Facing a Dobson's Choice," *Washington Post,* July 2, 1996, p. D1.

46. On the Traditional Values Coalition, see Gregg Zoroya, "Flying Right," *Los Angeles Times,* October 1, 1995, p. E1.

47. See, for example, Gary Bauer's views in Kolbert, "Politicians Find a Window."

48. See, in particular, Ralph Reed Jr., "Casting a Wider Net," *Policy Review,* no. 65 (Summer 1993), pp. 31–35. On efforts by the Christian Coalition to broaden its political appeal, see for example Jonathan Peterson, "Christian Group Adds Budget Items to Agenda," *Los Angeles Times,* October 30, 1996.

49. See, for example, Fisher, "The GOP, Facing a Dobson's Choice"; Benjamin Domenech, "Why the Conservative Outsider's Agenda Worries GOP Leaders," *Washington Post,* April 19, 1998, p. C2.

50. Fisher, "The GOP, Facing a Dobson's Choice."

51. Reed, "Casting a Wider Net," p. 35.

52. See, for example, Marvin N. Olasky, *The Tragedy of American Compassion* (Washington: Regnery, 1995). The leading congressional advocate of increased reliance on charitable organizations, including churches, in administering welfare is Senator John Ashcroft (Republican, Missouri). See Viveca Novak, "Fight Looms over Welfare Provisions That Funnel Aid through Churches," *Wall Street Journal,* September 7, 1995, p. A16; and Eliza Newlin Carney, "Bodies and Souls," *National Journal,* vol. 27 (October 28, 1995), pp. 2651–55.

53. Stout, "Behind the Scenes: GOP's Welfare Stance Owes a Lot to Prodding from Robert Rector."

54. See Robert Rector, "Welfare Reforms on the Sidelines," *Washington Times,* May 31, 1996, p. A16.

55. Marilyn Werber Serafini, "Not a Game for Kids," *National Journal,* September 21, 1996, p. 2013.

56. Kolbert, "Politicians Find a Window."

57. The policy briefs listed here were all written by Jennifer E. Marshall. The first four were published by the Family Research Council in March 1995, and the fifth in May 1995.

58. Gary L. Bauer, "New Welfare Poll Shows Strong Support for Combating Illegitimacy" (Washington: Family Research Council, November 1995).

59. Sandy Hume, "Christian Coalition Touts Its Electoral Clout," *Hill,* March 13, 1996, pp. 1, 18.

60. On exaggerated membership and organizational claims by the Christian Coalition, see Laurie Goodstein, "Coalition's Woes May Hinder Goals of Christian Right," *New York Times,* August 2, 1999, p. A1.

61. On distribution methods see Wilcox, *Onward Christian Soldiers?* p. 80.

62. Interview with author, March 1996.

63. On the relationship between Dole and conservative Christian groups and the Republican right, see Jason DeParle, "Sheila Burke Is the Militant Feminist Commie Peacenik Who's Telling Bob Dole What to Think," *New York Times,* November 12, 1995, p. 32; and DeParle, "A Fundamental Problem," *New York Times Magazine,* July 14, 1996, p. 10.

64. See David Hosansky, "The GOP's House Divided: Social Activists vs. Business," *Congressional Quarterly Weekly Report,* May 30, 1998, pp. 1447–48.

65. See the testimony submitted by the U.S. Chamber of Commerce in Subcommittee on Human Resources of the House Ways and Means Committee, *Contract with America—Welfare Reform,* 104 Cong. 1 sess., Committee Serial 104-43 (GPO, 1995), pp. 1706–08.

66. Schlozman and Tierney (*Organized Interests and American Democracy,* p. 206) note that when the Reagan administration came into office, 67 percent of liberal organizations they surveyed said that their influence had decreased, compared with 14 percent of "middle-of-the-road" and only 2 percent of conservative organizations.

67. Gerald F. Seib, "Religious Right Unveils Contract for the Family," *Wall Street Journal*, May 18, 1995, p. A4. See also Thomas B. Edsall, "Religious Right Ready to Press GOP on Its Own Social Contract," *Washington Post*, May 14, 1995, p. A4; and Ronald Brownstein, "GOP Leaders Embrace Christian Coalition's 'Contract,'" *Los Angeles Times*, May 18, 1995, p. A7. The Contract with the American Family included a pilot program of school vouchers, new restrictions on late-term abortions, provisions potentially allowing increased leeway for prayer in public schools, and an end to public funding for the National Endowment for the Humanities and the Corporation for Public Broadcasting.

68. See, for example, Richard Berke, "Conservative Christian Group Ends Conference with a Dual Identity," *New York Times*, September 10, 1995, p. A25; David Brooks, "Social Issues Strike Back," *Weekly Standard*, February 26, 1996, pp. 13–14; and David Hosansky, "Christian Right's Electoral Clout Bore Limited Fruit in 104th," *Congressional Quarterly Weekly Report*, vol. 54 (November 2, 1996), pp. 3160–62.

Chapter Nine

1. For a critique of the Clinton administration's rhetoric by one of its own officials, see David T. Ellwood, "From Social Science to Social Policy? The Fate of Intellectuals, Ideas and Ideology in the Welfare Debate in the Mid-1990s," Distinguished Public Lecture Series, Center for Urban Affairs and Public Policy, Northwestern University, 1996, pp. 20–22.

2. See Douglas J. Besharov, "A Monster of His Own Creation," *Washington Post*, November 2, 1995, p. A31.

3. See, for example, Jeffrey H. Birnbaum, *Madhouse: The Private Turmoil of Working for the President* (Times Books, 1996), p. 135.

4. Although no separate figure was given for welfare reform, the Clinton campaign manifesto, *Putting People First* (Times Books, 1992), gave the total cost for "rewarding work and families" in fiscal year 1995 as $6.5 billion (p. 27), far less than the estimates by Ellwood and others for a fully implemented work program.

5. Bob Woodward, *The Agenda: Inside the Clinton White House* (Simon and Schuster, 1994), p. 109. The first two promises were to provide more jobs and to reform health care.

6. See David T. Ellwood, "Welfare Reform as I Knew It," *American Prospect*, no. 26 (May–June 1996), p. 24.

7. Interview with author, April 1994.

8. See David Broder, "A Party Split," *Washington Post*, August 7, 1996, p. A19.

9. Through fiscal year 1993, separate caps on discretionary spending were set for the domestic, international affairs, and defense accounts. Since fiscal year 1994, there has been a single spending cap for discretionary spending.

10. For details of the Budget Enforcement Act and its development, see James Edwin Kee and Scott V. Nystrom, "The 1990 Budget Package: Redefining the Debate," *Public Budgeting and Finance*, vol. 11 (Spring 1991), pp. 3–24; and Richard Doyle and

Jerry McCaffery, "The Budget Enforcement Act of 1990: The Path to No-Fault Budgeting," *Public Budgeting and Finance,* vol. 11 (Spring 1991), pp. 25–40.

11. Woodward, *The Agenda,* p. 132; Ellwood, "Welfare Reform as I Knew It," p. 26. For an account from Bruce Reed's perspective, see Birnbaum, *Madhouse,* pp. 109–10.

12. On the importance of setting priorities for the president, see, for example, Paul C. Light, *The President's Agenda* (Johns Hopkins University Press, 1982), especially chaps. 2 and 3.

13. See, for example, James P. Pfiffner, *The Strategic Presidency: Hitting the Ground Running,* 2d ed. (University Press of Kansas, 1996), chap. 6.

14. Woodward, *The Agenda;* and Ann Devroy, "How the White House Runs and Stumbles; Staff's Power Is Diffuse, Agenda Suffers," *Washington Post,* November 9, 1993, p. A1.

15. For an overview of the immigration issue, see Roberto Suro, "Fortress America? Suddenly the Golden Door Is Closing," *Washington Post,* November 6, 1994, p. C3.

16. Sixty-nine percent said that immigration was a major problem, 17 percent a moderate problem. In addition, 25 percent of respondents said that *legal* immigration was a major problem, and 22 percent a moderate problem. Immigration was the third most commonly cited as the "most important problem" facing California, behind the economy and crime. Dianne Klein, "Majority in State Are Fed Up with Illegal Immigration," *Los Angeles Times,* September 19, 1993, p. A1.

17. See Pete Wilson, "Washington Must Act Now on Immigrants," *Washington Post,* May 6, 1994, p. A25; and Theresa A. Parker, "The California Story," *Public Welfare,* vol. 52, no. 2 (Spring 1994), pp. 16–20. In 1993 the State of Texas estimated its annual revenues from illegal aliens at $290 million and its annual costs at $456 million. See Sam Howe Verhovek, "Stop Benefits for Aliens? It Wouldn't Be That Easy," *New York Times,* June 6, 1994, p. A1.

18. See Larry Rohter, "Florida Opens New Front in Fight on Immigration Policy," *New York Times,* February 11, 1994, p. A14; Seth Mydans, "Move in California to Bar Service to Aliens," *New York Times,* May 27, 1994, p. A18; Sam Howe Verhovek, "Texas Plans to Sue U.S. over Illegal Alien Costs," *New York Times,* May 27, 1994, p. A10; and Mireya Navarro, "Florida's Plea for Immigration Relief Fails," *New York Times,* December 21, 1994, p. A20.

19. The measure also required state agencies that deal with illegal immigrants to report them to state and federal authorities. See Kenneth B. Noble, "California Immigration Measure Faces Rocky Legal Path," *New York Times,* November 11, 1994, p. B20.

20. On the popular media, see, for example, Randy Fitzgerald, "Welfare for Illegal Aliens?" *Reader's Digest,* June 1994, pp. 35–40. For scholarly studies, see, for example, George J. Borjas and Stephen J. Trejo, "Immigrant Participation in the Welfare System," *Industrial and Labor Relations Review,* vol. 44, no. 2 (January 1991), pp. 195–211; Borjas and Lynette Hilton, "Immigration and the Welfare State: Immigrant Participation in Means-Tested Entitlement Programs," *Quarterly Journal of Economics,* vol. 111, no. 2

(May 1996), pp. 575–604; Michael Fix and Wendy Zimmerman, *Immigrant Families and Public Policy: A Deepening Divide* (Washington: Urban Institute, 1995); and Fix and Jeffrey Passell, *Immigration and Immigrants: Setting the Record Straight* (Washington: Urban Institute, 1994). Congressional hearings included *Impact of Immigration on Welfare Programs*, Hearing before the Human Resources Subcommittee of the House Ways and Means Committee (Government Printing Office, 1993); and *Access to Public Assistance Benefits by Illegal Aliens*, Hearing before the Subcommittee on International Law, Immigration, and Refugees of the House Committee on the Judiciary, 103 Cong. 2 sess (GPO, 1994).

21. House Ways and Means Committee, *1996 Green Book* (GPO, 1996), p. 1305.

22. Ibid., p. 1306. Michael Fix and Wendy Zimmerman argue that the higher rate of SSI participation is probably due to a combination of insufficient work experience to gain eligibility for Social Security benefits and a desire to gain access to Medicaid benefits, which are automatically available to those who qualify for SSI. Fix and Zimmerman, "When Should Immigrants Receive Public Benefits?" in Isabel Sawhill, ed., *Welfare Reform: An Analysis of the Issues* (Washington: Urban Institute, 1995), pp. 69–72. The SSI statute also contained a deeming period of three years (five years after 1993) for immigrants brought in as "sponsored aliens" for five years.

23. Of a total of 738,140 noncitizen recipients of federally administered SSI benefits in 1994, the most frequent countries of origin were Mexico (123,240), former Soviet republics (70,800), Cuba (53,980), Vietnam (48,290), China (39,960), and the Philippines (39,200). *1996 Green Book*, p. 1306.

24. Viveca Novak, "What If . . . ?" *National Journal*, vol. 26 (January 22, 1994), pp. 165–69. Gibbons had never served on the Ways and Means Subcommittee on Human Resources (nor its predecessor, the Subcommittee on Public Assistance and Unemployment Compensation), since that subcommittee was formed in 1975, although he was involved in floor-managing antipoverty legislation in the 1960s.

25. Kenneth J. Cooper, "Rep. Ford Finds New Faces, Old Issues: Long-Absent Subcommittee Chairman Retakes Helm and Tackles Welfare Overhaul," *Washington Post*, April 22, 1993, p. A21.

26. Two other potential leaders for compromise on the Human Resources subcommittee were Thomas Downey and Robert Matsui. Downey, the acting chair through most of Ford's legal troubles, was now out of Congress, having lost his bid for re-election in 1992. And Matsui, perhaps the leading liberal Democrat on welfare reform issues and the acting chairman after Downey's defeat, became acting chairman of the Trade subcommittee of Ways and Means after Rostenkowski's indictment, replacing Gibbons in that role. For a profile of Matsui, see Bruce Stokes, "The Odd Couple," *National Journal*, vol. 26 (July 30, 1994), pp. 1798–801.

27. William Claiborne, "Moynihan Presses Welfare Reform: White House Warned Not to Defer Issue because of Health Care Debate," *Washington Post*, January 10, 1994, p. A6. On the conflict between Moynihan and the Clinton administration on health care

and welfare reform, see Eleanor Clift and Tom Brazaitis, *War without Bloodshed: The Art of Politics* (Scribner, 1996), chap. 3.

28. Clift and Brazaitis, *War without Bloodshed,* pp. 174–75.

29. Several overviews of the Clinton administration's efforts to craft a welfare reform proposal have been published in the media. See, in particular, Jason DeParle, "The Clinton Welfare Bill Begins Trek in Congress," *New York Times,* July 15, 1994, p. A18; Jeff Shear, "Pulling in Harness," *National Journal,* June 4, 1994, pp. 1286–90; and David Whitman with Matthew Cooper, "The End of Welfare—Sort of," *U.S. News and World Report,* June 20, 1994, pp. 28–37.

30. Two of the other key administration players, Wendel Primus and Isabel Sawhill, were also professional economists and recognized experts on human resources policy. Primus, the deputy assistant secretary of health and human services for planning and evaluation who headed the almost daily early morning meetings in which detailed provisions of the Clinton initiative were developed, had come from the House Ways and Means Committee, where he had developed the *Green Book,* used as the virtual Bible of social policy information in the human services area. Primus had also served as staff director of the Human Resources Subcommittee of Ways and Means, which has jurisdiction over the AFDC program. And Sawhill had written widely on human resources programs at the Urban Institute before joining the Clinton administration in the Office of Management and Budget. For a detailed discussion of the use of policy research by the Clinton administration task force, see David Richard Nather, "Social Science, Policy Research and the Clinton Welfare Reform Plan," M.A. thesis, George Washington University, January 1995, esp. chap. 3.

31. For a profile of Reed, see Stephen Barr, "Linking Politics and Policy: Reed Is at Center of Clinton Initiative," *Washington Post,* May 17, 1993, p. A19; and Birnbaum, *Madhouse,* chap. 3. Ellwood is profiled in Barbara Vobejda, "HHS Nominee Is Right at Home as Point Man in Welfare Debate," *Washington Post,* May 28, 1993, p. A21.

32. Interview with author, April 1994.

33. See, for example, Jason DeParle, "Clinton Planners Facing a Quiet Fight on Welfare," *New York Times,* March 18, 1994, p. A18; and DeParle, "The Clinton Welfare Bill Begins Trek in Congress."

34. In the early stages of the planning process, there were also a series of task forces that dealt with particular welfare reform issues.

35. Interview with author, March 1995.

36. Ibid.

37. H.R. 3500, "Responsibility and Empowerment Support Program Providing Employment, Child Care and Training," 103 Cong. 1 sess., November 10, 1993.

38. The spending cap provisions were in Title VII of the bill, the nutrition block grant in Title VIII, restrictions on alien benefits in Title VI, and the optional state AFDC block grant in section 301. On the Republican welfare bill, see Jeffrey L. Katz, "GOP's Two-Year Welfare Limit Sends Message to Clinton," *Congressional Quarterly Weekly*

Report, November 13, 1993, p. 3131; Guy Gugliotta, "House GOP Welfare Plan Would Limit Benefits to Two Years," *Washington Post*, November 11, 1993, p. A4; and Jason DeParle, "House G.O.P. Proposes 'Tough Love' Welfare Requiring Recipients to Work," *New York Times*, November 11, 1993, p. B19.

39. William Claiborne, "Dueling Ideologies May Redefine Clinton's Vision of Welfare Reform," *Washington Post*, March 18, 1994, p. A8.

40. A discharge petition signed by a majority of members of the House can be used to force a committee to discharge a bill on which it has not acted. If a discharge resolution carries, consideration of that bill then receives expedited consideration. See Walter J. Oleszek, *Congressional Procedures and the Policy Process*, 4th ed. (Congressional Quarterly Press, 1996), p. 338.

41. For conservative critiques, see James A. Barnes, "Waiting for Clinton," *National Journal*, March 5, 1994, pp. 516–20.

42. H.R. 4566, *Real Welfare Reform Act of 1994*, June 10, 1994. See also Eric Pianin, "Formerly United House Republicans Split over Welfare Reform Package," *Washington Post*, April 29, 1994, p. A37.

43. Laurie McGinley, "Clinton Faces Daunting Task in Turning Welfare Rhetoric into Reality," *Wall Street Journal*, December 29, 1992, p. A12.

44. Paul Offner, "Target the Kids," *New Republic*, January 24, 1994, pp. 9–11. It should be noted that Offner's proposal was somewhat different from the one eventually adopted by the Clinton administration. Offner focused on teen parents; women who waited until after age twenty to have children could potentially avoid work requirements. The administration's plan avoided this potential by using the mother's date of birth as the cut-off.

45. Interview with author, August 1994. Another central participant similarly recalled, "We liked the idea of targeting on the young because it sent the right message to the younger cohort and, you know, there were just a zillion discussions of these issues and a consensus would sometimes just emerge around a topic like that. This is one where my recollection is that most of us said, 'Yes, that's right. That's a great idea.'" Interview with author, March 1995. See also William Claiborne, "Panel Urges Phased-in Aid Cutoffs," *Washington Post*, February 25, 1994, p. A1.

46. See Jason DeParle, "Proposal for Welfare Cutoff Is Dividing Clinton Officials," *New York Times*, May 22, 1994, p. A20.

47. See Eric Pianin, "Tenet of Clinton Welfare Plan Faces Test," *Washington Post*, May 20, 1994, p. A6.

48. Interview with author, August 1994.

49. Interview with author, December 1994.

50. See, for example, Ron Suskind, "Scaled-Back Welfare-Reform Proposals Are Outlined by Clinton Administration," *Wall Street Journal*, March 3, 1994, p. A18.

51. Ellwood, "From Social Science to Social Policy?" p. 2.

52. Interview with author, March, 1995.

strict AFDC assets test, a more generous federal match in JOBS, a variety of demonstration projects, four-year time limits, child support assurance, and increased earnings disregards. The report also indirectly expressed skepticism about the effectiveness of deterrence policies in reducing out-of-wedlock birth rates, arguing that "no known public policy will subdue or reduce these rates." See Shaw, Johnson, and Grandy, "Moving Ahead: How America Can Reduce Poverty through Work," U.S. House of Representatives, Committee of the Ways and Means, June 1992, p. ii.

20. On the development of the Contract with America, see Dan Balz, "GOP 'Contract' Pledges 10 Tough Acts to Follow," *Washington Post,* November 20, 1994, pp. A1, A10.

21. Jeffrey L. Katz, "Welfare Issue Finds Home on the Campaign Trail," *Congressional Quarterly Weekly Report,* October 15, 1994, p. 2956.

22. The Contract's agenda was also intended to appeal in particular to Perot voters who did not give a high priority to social issues but cared a lot about deficits. On the calculus involved in formulating the Contract and the role of religious conservatives, see Ralph Reed, *Active Faith: How Christians Are Changing the Soul of American Politics* (Free Press, 1996), pp. 184–87. Reed's book mentions welfare only tangentially, however—much more attention is devoted to the family tax credit proposal also contained in the Contract.

23. Balz and Brownstein, *Storming the Gates,* p. 39. On the criteria used in developing the Contract, see also Balz, "GOP 'Contract' Pledges 10 Tough Acts to Follow." After the 1994 election, Christian Coalition executive director Ralph Reed promised an unprecedented lobbying effort on behalf of the Contract with America, with welfare reform as the coalition's top priority. See Richard L. Berke, "The 'Contract' Gets New Ally on the Right," *New York Times,* January 18, 1995, p. D19; Nancy E. Roman, "Christian Coalition Gets Call to Pray from Gingrich," *Washington Times,* January 19, 1995, p. A12.

24. These provisions included a "sense of the Congress" preamble on the harmful effects of illegitimacy, a Food Stamp workfare program, and a tax credit for married couples. Ron Haskins, "Requested Changes in Republican Leadership Bill, " memorandum to Rick Santorum, Dave Camp, and others, September 12, 1994.

25. H.R. 4, *The Personal Responsibility Act of 1995,* 104 Cong. 1 sess., January 4, 1995. For a critical summary, see Mark Greenberg, *Contract with Disaster: The Impact on States of the Personal Responsibility Act* (Washington: Center for Law and Social Policy, November 1994).

26. H.R. 4, section 601.

27. For example, H.R. 3500 would have denied AFDC benefits both to additional children born while the mother was receiving AFDC and to the children of teen mothers, but states could opt out of these requirements. The Talent-Faircloth bill had a teen mother exclusion that initially applied to mothers until age twenty-one—longer at state option—and would rise to age twenty-six after four years; had no opt-out provision; and applied to Food Stamps and housing assistance as well as AFDC, barring excluded children from benefits until they turned eighteen. The Contract Bill included family caps and applied teen mother exclusions until age eighteen, had no state opt-

53. Jason DeParle, "Paying for Welfare Promises Proves the Hard Part," *New York Times,* February 22, 1994, p. A16; DeParle, "Welfare Plan May Require New Taxes," *New York Times,* February 25, 1994, p. A16; DeParle, "Welfare Planners Struggle over Final Sticking Points," *New York Times,* March 21, 1994, p. B6; DeParle, "Clinton Planners Facing a Quiet Fight on Welfare."

54. Jason DeParle, "Casinos Become Big Players in the Overhaul of Welfare," *New York Times,* May 9, 1994, p. A1.

55. Interview, June 1994.

56. Details of the administration's proposal are given in two documents released by the Department of Health and Human Services, *Work and Responsibility Act of 1994: Detailed Summary,* and *Work and Responsibility Act: Costs,* and a document released by the Office of Management and Budget, *Financing the President's Welfare Reform Plan.* Detailed plan specifications and legislative language are provided in *Proposed Legislation—Work and Responsibility Act of 1994,* H. Doc. 103-273, 103 Cong. 2 sess., June 21, 1994.

57. *Work and Responsibility Act of 1994,* H.R. 4605, 103 Cong. 2 sess., June 21, 1994.

58. Department of Health and Human Services, *Work and Responsibility Act of 1994: Detailed Summary,* p. 13.

59. The bill provided that "the plan must be reasonable in light of the individual's literacy, skills, and needs, and the resources and opportunities for employment (including self-employment) within the community where the individual resides, and shall, to the maximum extent possible, reflect the preferences of such individual." See section 102(a), creating section 482(a)(2)(a)(2) of the Social Security Act.

60. H.R. 4605, section 103(j), amending section 484 of the Social Security Act.

61. H.R. 4605, section 104, creating new section 417(a)(2)(A) of the Social Security Act.

62. The bill also authorized limited demonstration projects to test whether incentive payments to parents could be helpful in establishing paternity. Demonstration projects were authorized in up to three states, with a federal matching rate of 90 percent and a total federal expenditure of no more than $1,000,000. H.R. 4605, section 643.

63. H.R. 4605, section 667.

64. H.R. 4605, sections 668 and 665.

65. H.R. 4605, section 673.

66. By limiting eligibility for child support assurance payments to children for whom paternity had been established, the administration's bill provided another incentive for mothers to cooperate in establishing paternity. H.R. 4605, title H, sections 681 and 682.

67. In addition, sponsored aliens would continue to be ineligible for the three programs after five years if the sponsor's income was above the median family income for U.S. families (then $39,500). Smaller savings—almost 10 percent—came from further tightening and standardizing eligibility standards for these three programs and Medicaid

for those who are not legal permanent residents. For a more detailed description of the bill's financing provisions, see *Work and Responsibility Act of 1994: Financing.*

68. H.R. 4605, section 903. These changes did not affect eligibility for Medicaid, however, and current recipients were "grandfathered" into the program. Nor did the restrictions apply to asylum seekers or refugees; and immigrants who became citizens could then apply for benefits on their own.

69. See, for example, Ron Suskind, "Labor Is Pushing Clinton to Make Sure Changes in Welfare System Won't Threaten Union Jobs," *Wall Street Journal,* February 9, 1994, p. A16.

70. Dan Balz and Ronald Brownstein describe "derailing Clinton's agenda for the rest of the year and then framing the election around his failures as President" as one of the three key strategies of the House Republican leadership in the run-up to the 1994 election (along with presenting a positive agenda through the Contract with America and ensuring that all viable Republican candidates had enough resources to mount adequate campaigns). See Balz and Brownstein, *Storming the Gates: Protest Politics and the Republican Revival* (Boston: Little, Brown, 1996), p. 36. On welfare as a campaign issue in 1994, see Jeffrey L. Katz, "Welfare Issue Finds Home on the Campaign Trail," *Congressional Quarterly Weekly Report,* vol. 52, no. 38 (October 15, 1994), pp. 2956–58.

71. Mickey Kaus, "They Blew It," *New Republic,* December 5, 1994.

72. David Ellwood, in his own retrospective on the Clinton welfare reform round, notes that if money for welfare reform had remained in the 1993 budget package, "the administration would have been forced to submit its welfare reform proposal by late spring in 1993 . . . and our search for dollars would not have been necessary." But he goes on to show that welfare reform faced many other obstacles in the administration and Congress. Ellwood, "From Social Science to Social Policy?" p. 18.

73. Ibid., p. 19.

Chapter Ten

1. On the Contract with America, see Jeff Shear, "The Santa Clauses," *National Journal,* October 22, 1994, pp. 2451–53; and Dan Balz and Ronald Brownstein, *Storming the Gates: Protest Politics and the Republican Revival* (Boston: Little, Brown, 1996), pp. 37–46.

2. See R. Kent Weaver, "Deficits and Devolution in the 104th Congress," *Publius: The Journal of Federalism,* vol. 26, no. 3 (Summer 1996), pp. 45–87.

3. Respondents were asked, "I'd like to read you a list of seven legislative priorities. Please tell me which *one* or *two* you feel are the most important issues for Congress to address." Welfare reform was mentioned by 46 percent, health care reform by 29 percent, a middle-class tax cut by 28 percent, a balanced budget amendment by 24 percent, an increase in the minimum wage by 18 percent, and a capital gains tax cut by 8 percent. But when asked, "What would you say are the two or three most important issues or problems facing the nation today that you personally would like to see the federal gov-

ernment in Washington do something about," without priming for specific answers, 25 percent of respondents mentioned welfare, up from only 6 percent in January 1994, but still less than health care (35 percent) and crime and violence (30 percent). Hart/Teeter Study 4056, pp. 3–4, 11.

4. See, for example, Elizabeth Drew, *Showdown: The Struggle between the Gingrich Congress and the Clinton White House* (Simon and Schuster, 1996), pp. 26, 84.

5. Robert Carleson, "Can Welfare Reform Survive Friendly Fire?" *Washington Times,* February 29, 1996, p. A21; and the statement by Peter J. Ferrara of the National Center for Policy Analysis in *Contract with America—Welfare Reform,* Hearings before the Subcommittee on Human Resources of the House Ways and Means Committee, 104 Cong. 1 sess. (Government Printing Office, 1996), pp. 852–60.

6. See, for example, Robert Rector, "Stringing Along," *National Review,* April 17, 1995, pp. 50–53.

7. Eric Pianin, "5 Years of GOP Tax Cuts Total $196 Billion," *Washington Post,* February 2, 1995, p. A4; see also testimony of Assistant Secretary of the Treasury Leslie R. Samuels in House Ways and Means Committee, *Contract with America—Overview,* Committee Serial 104-20 (GPO, 1995), p. 261.

8. See Weaver, "Deficits and Devolution"; and Drew, *Showdown.*

9. Reconciliation also offers important procedural advantages in the Senate. These are discussed in chapter 11.

10. On this point, see Weaver, "Deficits and Devolution."

11. See especially Donald F. Norris and Lyke Thompson, eds., *The Politics of Welfare Reform* (Beverly Hills, Calif.: Sage, 1995); and chapter 5.

12. The classic study is Jack L. Walker, "The Diffusion of Innovations among the American States," *American Political Science Review,* vol. 63, no. 3 (September 1969), pp. 880–99.

13. Thomas J. Corbett, "Welfare Reform in Wisconsin: The Rhetoric and the Reality," in Norris and Thompson, *The Politics of Welfare Reform,* p. 42.

14. On the Wisconsin experience, see Corbett, "Welfare Reform in Wisconsin"; Michael Wiseman, "State Strategies for Welfare Reform: The Wisconsin Story," *Journal of Policy Analysis and Management,* vol. 15, no. 4 (1996), pp. 515–46; Paul E. Peterson and Mark C. Rom, *Welfare Magnets: A New Case for a National Welfare Standard* (Brookings, 1990), pp. 24–49.

15. See Barbara Vobejda, "Most States Are Shaping Their Own Welfare Reform," *Washington Post,* February 3, 1996, p. A1.

16. Interview with author, January 1997.

17. Interview with author, 1998.

18. See Mark Greenberg, Steve Savner, and Rebecca Schwartz, *Limits on Limits: State and Federal Policies on Welfare Time Limits* (Washington: Center for Law and Social Policy, June 1996), pp. 10–12.

19. A June 1992 report released by Clay Shaw, Nancy Johnson, and Fred Grandy called for much more modest policy changes, including broader waiver authority, a less

out, and applied only to AFDC. See Center for Law and Social Policy and Center on Budget and Policy Priorities, "Welfare Bills and Proposals: A Family Focus" (Washington: June 17, 1994).

28. States were to be given grants equal to the amount by which federal expenditures were reduced by excluding families of teen mothers. These grants could be used for teen pregnancy prevention programs, "to establish and operate orphanages," "to establish and operate closely supervised residential homes for unwed mothers," and for related services. These provisions are discussed in more detail below.

29. In H.R. 3500, states had the option of denying assistance after a total of five years, either permanently or temporarily. The Talent-Faircloth bill had given states the option of using hard time limits for AFDC, housing assistance, and Food Stamps, while providing that those who lost AFDC due to the time limits would continue to be eligible for Medicaid.

30. H.R. 4, section 401.

31. Elizabeth Shogren, "Key Republican Retreats on Welfare Reform," *Los Angeles Times,* December 2, 1994, p. A34. On the threat to Shaw, see Balz and Brownstein, *Storming the Gates,* p. 286. See also Hilary Stout, "Some GOP Congresswomen, Uneasy with Parts of Welfare Plan, May Play a Moderating Role," *Wall Street Journal,* February 14, 1995, p. A24.

32. Nancy Johnson, memorandum to colleagues, September 26, 1994.

33. See, for example, Lori Montgomery, "In Welfare Debate, Engler Is Both a Model and a Maverick," *Detroit Free Press,* January 20, 1995, p. A1.

34. See Robert Pear, "Republicans' Philosophical Discord Stalls Plan for Changes," *New York Times,* January 12, 1995, p. A20.

35. Interview with author, April 1995.

36. Interview with author, April 1995.

37. See for example Dan Balz, "GOP Governors Seek Shift in Power," *Washington Post,* November 21, 1994, p. A1.

38. See Robert Pear, "Governors Deadlocked on Replacing Welfare Programs with Grants to States," *New York Times,* January 31, 1995, p. A14. At its winter 1995 meeting, the NGA adopted a new policy statement that "governors have not yet reached consensus on whether cash and other entitlement assistance should remain available as Federal entitlements to needy families or whether it should be converted to a state entitlement block grant. Governors do agree, however, that in either case states should have the flexibility to enact welfare reforms without having to request federal waivers." See Robert Pear, "Governors Agree Children Must Be Protected No Matter What Shape Welfare Takes," *New York Times,* February 1, 1995, p. A19.

39. See, for example, Dan Balz, "Governor Assails GOP Welfare Proposal," *Washington Post,* January 9, 1995, p. A6.

40. See especially Jeffrey L. Katz, "Governors' Group Sidelined in Welfare Debate," *Congressional Quarterly Weekly Report,* May 20, 1995, pp. 1423–25. The NGA was able to take institutional positions on some issues where governors were in bipartisan agreement.

For example, the NGA asked that any block grant of family assistance payments include provisions to increase funding in times of recession, and it opposed stiffer work requirements and other mandates or transfers of obligations to the states. See Robert Pear, "G.O.P. Leaders Halt Abolition of Food Stamps," *New York Times,* February 25, 1995, p. A1; and Judith Havemann and Barbara Vobejda, "Food Stamp Program Survives in Break with GOP 'Contract,'" *Washington Post,* February 25, 1995, p. A1.

41. Barbara Vobejda, "GOP Outlines Broad Welfare Reform," *Washington Post,* January 7, 1995, p. A1.

42. Pear, "Republicans' Philosophical Discord Stalls Plan for Changes."

43. For an early version of this argument from Republican National Committee chair Haley Barbour, see Ann Devroy and Kevin Merida, "President Hits GOP as Callous," *Washington Post,* February 23, 1995, pp. A1, A12.

44. Two caveats are in order here. First, Congress can, of course, go back and change the authorizing legislation to lower funding for the block grant, but the strong political presumption would be against such action, at least in the short term. Second, once the authorization has expired (in five years) and the block grant requires reauthorization, falling caseloads could cause Congress to lower its funding level.

45. Interview with author, April 1995.

46. See Dennis Farney, "Have Liberals Ignored 'Have-Less' Whites at Their Own Peril?" *Wall Street Journal,* December 14, 1994, p. A1.

47. See, for example, R. W. Apple, "Clinton's Grip on '96 Ticket Not So Sure," *New York Times,* November 21, 1994, p. A1.

48. See David Broder, "2 Years in Office Have Washed Away Clear Image of 'New Democrat' Clinton," *Washington Post,* October 2, 1994, p. A1.

49. Interview with author, January 1997.

50. Interview with author, February 1997.

51. Executive Office of the President, Office of Management and Budget, *Budget of the United States Government, Fiscal Year 1996* (GPO, 1995), pp. 25–30.

52. Elizabeth Shogren and Paul Richter, "White House Plans Bipartisan Summit to Create Strategy for Welfare Reform Policy," *Los Angeles Times,* December 9, 1994, p. A18.

53. See Hilary Stout, "Democrats and GOP Fail to Narrow Rift on Welfare, Hurting Chances for a Bill," *Wall Street Journal,* January 30, 1995, p. A5.

54. On Republican efforts, see, in particular, John Harwood, "GOP, Given Power by Voters Angry over Welfare, Seeks a Compassionate Image in Reform Debate," *Wall Street Journal,* March 22, 1995, p. A18; Mona Charen, "High Ground on Welfare," *Washington Times,* March 22, 1995, p. A20; and Rochelle L. Stanfield, "The Kiddie Card," *National Journal,* February 11, 1995, pp. 353–56. On debate framing generally, see, for example, Walter J. Oleszek, *Congressional Procedures and the Policy Process,* 4th ed. (Congressional Quarterly Press, 1996), pp. 39–42.

55. Representative Jan Meyers of Kansas, in Ronald Brownstein, "Welfare Debate Puts Blame for Poverty Mainly on the Poor," *Los Angeles Times* (Washington ed.), March 24, 1995, pp. A1, A8.

56. David Binder, "Children Crusade against Proposed Republican Budget Cuts," *New York Times*, March 20, 1995, p. A13.

57. H.R. 4, section 108.

58. Tom Morgenthau and others, "The Orphanage," *Newsweek*, December 12, 1994, pp. 28–32.

59. Both quotations are from "Gingrich Offers Defense of Plan for Orphanages," *New York Times*, December 5, 1994.

60. For public opinion data and a discussion of GOP backpedaling on the orphanage issue, see Ronald Brownstein, "Clinton Sharply Attacks GOP's Orphanage Plan," *Los Angeles Times*, December 11, 1994, p. A1.

61. See House Ways and Means Committee, *Contract with America—Overview*, pp. 80–84. The exchange was reported in Nancy E. Roman, "Orphanages Fit into Clinton's Welfare Reform," *Washington Times*, January 11, 1995, p. A1.

62. Ann Devroy, "House Republicans Get Talking Points," *Washington Post*, February 2, 1995, p. A9.

63. See Randall Strahan and R. Kent Weaver, "Subcommittee Government and the House Ways and Means Committee," paper presented at the annual meeting of the Southern Political Science Association, Memphis, November 1989.

64. As a staff aide to one Ways and Means Republican put it, "It's appalling how some members of the Ways and Means Committee just don't care. These are poor people and thank you very much, I do taxes and trade, I don't do poor people issues. . . . You have a lot of members who just could not give a damn." Interview with author, March 1995.

65. On members new to the Ways and Means Committee, see *Congressional Quarterly Weekly Report*, March 25, 1995, p. 98.

66. Marcia Gilbert, "Ensign and Nethercutt Find Being Rookies on Prized Committees Isn't Easy," *Hill*, February 1, 1995, p. 50.

67. In the original markup document, individual states' shares were set as the percentage of total AFDC funding that they received in 1991 through 1993. This formula was later modified to give states several options for their base time periods. Subcommittee on Human Resources of the House Ways and Means Committee, "Markup Documents for Welfare Reform, February 13, 1995, Personal Responsibility Act Title I, Temporary Family Assistance Block Grant," p. 5.

68. To transfer accounts to the general fund, a state first had to establish an account for the purpose of paying emergency benefits, which could be carried over from year to year. In any year in which the funds in that account reached 120 percent of the state's share of the block grant, it could transfer funds over that amount to its general account. Ibid., p. 6.

69. Ibid., p. 3. For a critique, see Mickey Kaus, "Workfare Wimp-out," *New Republic*, March 13, 1995, p. 4.

70. Immigrants would remain eligible for means-tested benefits that fostered individual improvement (for example, student loan programs, Job Corps, the Earned

Income Tax Credit) rather than transfers. See Subcommittee on Human Resources of the House Ways and Means Committee, "Markup Documents for Welfare Reform, February 13, 1995, Personal Responsibility Act, Title III, Restricting Welfare for Aliens."

71. See, for example, Robert Pear, "Republicans Advance Proposal to Replace Welfare System," *New York Times*, February 10, 1995, p. A16.

72. See, for example, Devroy and Merida, "President Hits GOP as Callous"; and Barbara Vobejda and Ann Devroy, "Republicans Get a Full Plate of Blame on School Lunch Plan," *Washington Post*, March 9, 1995, p. A23.

73. Rangel is quoted in Barbara Vobejda and Judith Havemann, "Democrats' Welfare Plan Demands Immediate Work," *Washington Post*, February 11, 1995, p. A1. For the views of the House Democratic leadership on AFDC entitlement, see Robert Pear, "House Panels Back Changes for Welfare," *New York Times*, March 9, 1995, p. A21.

74. Vobejda and Havemann, "Democrats' Welfare Plan Demands Immediate Work"; Judith Havemann, "White House Says GOP Welfare Plan Is Too Lenient in Work Requirement," *Washington Post*, February 14, 1995, p. A5; and Judith Havemann, "Democrats Forge New Welfare Role," *New York Times*, March 7, 1995, p. A16.

75. Quoted in Judith Havemann, "Prominent Conservative Faults GOP Welfare Plan," *Washington Post*, February 19, 1995, p. A14.

76. Ford and Shaw are quoted in Elizabeth Shogren, "House Panel Backs GOP Welfare Plan," *Los Angeles Times* (Washington ed.), February 16, 1995, p. A1. See also Robert Pear, "House Panel Takes Step 1 in Plan to Revamp Welfare," *New York Times*, February 16, 1995, p. D22.

77. The subcommittee did approve by voice vote an amendment offered by Republican John Ensign that would allow the secretary of health and human services to penalize a state by up to 3 percent of its block grant for failing to meet work requirements. For a detailed discussion of debates and votes on amendments in the subcommittee, see Jeffrey L. Katz, with Alissa J. Rubin and Peter MacPherson, "Major Aspects of Welfare Bill Approved by Subcommittee," *Congressional Quarterly Weekly Report*, February 18, 1995, pp. 525-29.

78. The compromise would allow states that had electronic benefit transfer (EBT) systems in place to receive food stamp funds as a block grant. On the food stamp battles in this period, see, for example, Robert Pear, "GOP Leaders in House Agree on Alternatives to Food Stamps," *New York Times*, March 2, 1995; Judith Havemann and Barbara Vobejda, "Governors Offered Control of Food Stamps," *Washington Post*, March 2, 1995, p. A4; Nancy E. Roman, "GOP Targets Fraud in Laying Out New Food-Stamp Plan," *Washington Times*, March 1, 1995, p. A12. The House Agriculture Committee ultimately rejected a block grant approach to food stamps, but did give states additional leeway for harmonizing the eligibility standards for food stamps with those of other means-tested programs. See David Hosansky, "Bill to Set Food Stamps Cuts, Work Rules OK'd by Panel," *Congressional Quarterly Weekly Report*, March 11, 1995, pp. 756-58.

79. House Ways and Means Committee, "Markup Document for Welfare Reform, Chairman's Mark, February 28, 1995, Personal Responsibility Act, Title I, Temporary Family Assistance Block Grant," pp. 3–6.

80. Ibid., p. 12.

81. See Robert Pear, "Heeding Criticisms, Republicans Alter Some Parts of Welfare Overhaul Plan, *New York Times,* March 1, 1995, p. A17; and Barbara Vobejda, "Abortions, Out-of-Wedlock Births Targeted," *Washington Post,* March 1, 1995, p. A14.

82. "Unwed Teen Mothers," *Washington Times,* March 2, 1995; Jeffrey L. Katz and Alissa J. Rubin, "House Panel Poised to Approve GOP Welfare Overhaul Bill," *Congressional Quarterly Weekly Report,* March 4, 1995, pp. 689–92.

83. Child support provisions had not been included in the Contract or the subcommittee bill. The Ways and Means Committee's proposals borrowed heavily from the Clinton administration's 1994 proposal and generally won praise from Ways and Means Democrats. On the child support provisions, see Judith Havemann and Barbara Vobejda, "GOP Drops Child Support Penalties from Bill," *Washington Post,* March 3, 1995, p. A17; Havemann, "Clash Delays Ways and Means Vote on GOP Welfare Reform Proposal"; Cheryl Wetzstein, "Provisions for Welfare Reform Friendly to Fathers," *Washington Times,* March 7, 1995, p. A10; and Wetzstein, "House Eyes Licenses of Deadbeat Parents," *Washington Times,* March 13, 1995, pp. A1, A10.

84. The child support amendment on license revocations and an amendment that would have prohibited welfare recipients from replacing current workers failed on 17-17 tie votes, with Republican members changing their votes or abstaining to prevent passage. Also defeated was a Democratic substitute bill that foreshadowed provisions of the Deal bill offered during floor debate in the full chamber. Its provisions, including a four-year hard time limit in most cases, are outlined in "Rationale for and Explanation of the Democratic Substitute Offered by Rep. Sam Gibbons and Rep. Harold Ford to the Republican Welfare Bill," March 3, 1995. The committee did approve an amendment by Republican Nancy Johnson requiring that states maintain their spending efforts on child protection (foster care, adoption assistance, child abuse prevention, and so forth) in 1996 and 1997 relative to 1994 spending levels. See Katz and Rubin, "House Panel Poised to Approve GOP Welfare Overhaul Bill," for a detailed discussion of amending activity at the full committee level.

85. The lone Democrat to support the bill, Gerald Kleczka of Wisconsin, did so because it included provisions to revise the SSI program that he had helped to devise. See Katz and Rubin, "House Panel Poised to Approve GOP Welfare Overhaul Bill." The Ways and Means Committee provisions of the welfare reform bill were reported as H.R. 1157, *Welfare Transformation Act of 1995,* 104 Cong 1 sess., March 8, 1995.

86. See "Remarks of the President to the National Association of Counties," *Weekly Compilation of Presidential Documents,* March 7, 1995, Office of the Federal Register; and "Letter from President Clinton to Congress on Welfare Reform," *Weekly Compilation of Presidential Documents,* March 20, 1995. See also John F. Harris and Judith Havemann,

"Clinton to Push Child-Support Enforcement Idea," *Washington Post,* March 7, 1995, p. A4; John F. Harris, "Clinton: GOP Welfare Reform Efforts Aim to Cut Budget, Not Promote Work," *Washington Post,* March 9, 1995, p. A4; Elizabeth Shogren, "House Panel Approves Final Piece of Welfare Reform," *Los Angeles Times* (Washington ed.), March 9, 1995, p. A1; and Shogren, "Clinton Calls for Tougher Child Support Enforcement," *Los Angeles Times* (Washington ed.), March 19, 1995, p. A1.

87. Shogren, "House Panel Approves Final Piece of Welfare Reform," p. A8. On the administration's efforts to distance itself from the current AFDC system, see, for example, Secretary Shalala's statement at the March 10, 1995, Senate Finance Committee hearing, "Administration's Views on Welfare Reform," 104 Cong. 1 sess., S361-59, March 10, 1995.

88. See Elizabeth Shogren, "GOP Troops to Seek Softer Welfare Bill," *Los Angeles Times* (Washington ed.), March 20, 1995, p. A1.

89. Personal interview with the author, May 1995.

90. Another amendment, offered by Judiciary Committee chair Henry Hyde, forbade the use of block grant funds to fund abortions. On the opposition of Catholic bishops and the National Right-to-Life Committee to the Republican bill, and especially to its potential impact on abortion, see Robert Pear, "Catholic Bishops Challenge Pieces of Welfare Bill," *New York Times,* March 19, 1995, p. A1; and Judith Havemann and Ann Devroy, "Bishops Win Concessions on Welfare Bill," *Washington Post,* March 21, 1995, p. A6.

91. The amendments on vouchers and a funding increase for child care were adopted, as was an amendment requiring states to suspend occupational, professional, and recreational licenses for noncustodial parents who did not meet child support obligations. See Robert Pear, "House Bill Links Licenses to Child-Support Payment," *New York Times,* March 24, 1995, p. A22.

92. See David Rogers, "House Opens Welfare Debate amid Jockeying," *Wall Street Journal,* March 22, 1995, p. A18; Kenneth J. Cooper, "Welfare Overhaul Survives Abortion Dispute," *Washington Post,* March 23, 1995, p. A12; and Robert Pear, "Debate in House on Welfare Bill Splits G.O.P. Bloc," *New York Times,* March 23, 1995, p. A1.

93. Wetzstein, "House GOP Welfare Reform Creeps Slowly Ahead." The rule allowed votes on a total of thirty-one amendments, as well as two Democratic substitutes. The rules for debate are outlined in House Ways and Means Committee, *Providing for the Further Consideration of H.R. 4, The Personal Responsibility Act of 1995,* H. Rept. 104-85, 104 Cong. 1 sess., March 21, 1995.

94. On the strategic dilemmas involved in building and getting liberal and leadership support for the Deal bill, see especially Nancy E. Roman, "Conservative Democrats Face Intraparty Struggle on Welfare," *Washington Times,* March 14, 1995, p. A10. See also Robert Pear, "Democrats See Virtue in Shift to the Right on Welfare," *New York Times,* March 17, 1995, p. A18.

95. See H.R. 1267, *Individual Responsibility Act of 1995,* 104 Cong. 1 sess., March 21, 1995. For a summary and discussion of the bill, see Office of Congressman Nathan

Deal, "Summary of the Individual Responsibility Act of 1995 (The Deal-Clement-Tanner-Stenholm-Lincoln-Thurman-Payne Substitute)," March 21, 1995; and Office of Congressman Nathan Deal, "Responses to Anticipated Criticisms of the Individual Responsibility Act of 1995 (Deal-Clement-Tanner-Stenholm-Lincoln-Thurman-Payne Substitute)," no date.

96. The lone Republican to vote for the Deal substitute was Representative Connie A. Morella of Maryland. See Kenneth J. Cooper, "House Rejects Democrats' Welfare Plan to Promote Work," *Washington Post,* March 24, 1995, p. A14.

97. Conservative Democrats objected in particular to school lunch provisions and the bill's failure to concede more to pro-life forces. See Nancy E. Roman, "Conservative Democrats Abandon GOP on Welfare," *Washington Times,* March 23, 1995, p. A10. Five Republicans voted against H.R. 4 on final passage, while nine Democrats voted for it. Of the five Republicans, two were Cuban Americans, and one opposed it because of concerns that it would increase abortion. See Robert Pear, "House Backs Bill Undoing Decades of Welfare Policy," *New York Times,* March 25, 1995, p. A1.

98. Edwin Chen, "Clinton Veto Threat Raised by Panetta," *Los Angeles Times* (Washington ed.), March 27, 1995, p. A1.

99. Pear, "House Bill Links Licenses to Child Support Payment."

100. See Harwood, "GOP, Given Power by Voters Angry over Welfare, Seeks a Compassionate Image in Welfare Debate."

101. June E. O'Neill, Director, Congressional Budget Office, letter to Honorable Bill Archer, March 31, 1995. The Clinton administration estimate was almost $70 billion in expenditure reductions over five years. See Department of Health and Human Services and other departments, *The Work Opportunity Act of 1995, S. 1120: Senate Republican Leadership Plan; Impacts and Provisions; Children and Family Effects; State and Federal Program Effects,* section I, August 7, 1995, p. 10.

102. Jeffrey L. Katz, "GOP Moderates Central to Welfare Overhaul," *Congressional Quarterly Weekly Report,* March 18, 1995, p. 813.

103. On Whitman, see Michelle Ruess, "Whitman Breaks with GOP over Welfare Reform, Backs Aid to Aliens, Teen Moms," *Record* (Bergen, N.J.), February 10, 1995, p. A7; Kelly Richmond, "GOP Bill Takes N.J.'s Reforms a Step Further: Whitman Criticizes Some Cuts," *Record,* March 25, 1995, p. A10; and Michelle Ruess, "Welfare Reform Costly to N.J.: $1.5B Loss Seen: Whitman Silent," *Record,* March 31, 1995, p. A3. On Voinovich, see Gerald F. Seib, "Welfare Reform: Can Washington Simply Let Go?" *Wall Street Journal,* March 8, 1995, p. A22; and Laura R. Hamburg, "Welfare Plan Penalizes Ohio, Voinovich Says," *Plain Dealer* (Cleveland), March 24, 1995, p. A6.

104. On the governors' national political aspirations, see Richard L. Berke, "Four Midwestern Governors Angle for an Offer from Dole," *New York Times,* March 18, 1996, p. A1; Donald Lambro, "Engler Runs Hard for No. 2 Spot on Ticket," *Washington Times,* March 18, 1996, p. A1; and Hilary Stout, "Midwest GOP Governors Emerge as Key Forces for Dole's Chances to Defeat Clinton in the Fall," *Washington Times,* March 18, 1996, p. A20.

Chapter Eleven

1. *Broad Policy Goals of Welfare Reform,* Hearings before the Senate Finance Committee, 104 Cong. 1 sess., March 9, 1995 (Government Printing Office, 1995); and *Welfare to Work,* Hearings before the Senate Finance Committee, 104 Cong. 1 sess., March 20, 1995 (GPO, 1995).

2. See Robert Pear, "Welfare Bill Gets Key Endorsement by G.O.P. Senators," *New York Times,* March 28, 1995, p. A1; Elizabeth Shogren, "Packwood: Senate to Reject Welfare as Entitlement," *Los Angeles Times* (Washington ed.), March 28, 1995, p. A4; Nancy E. Roman, "Senate Stiffens on Welfare Reform as Term Limits Face House Defeat," *Washington Times,* March 29, 1995, pp. A1, A16.

3. See, for example, "Republican Welfare Turmoil," *Washington Post,* June 16, 1995, p. A24.

4. On Chafee's role, see Marilyn Weber Serfani, "Mr. In-Between," *National Journal,* December 16, 1995, pp. 3080–84.

5. Adam Clymer, "Ethics Panel in Senate Accuses Packwood of Sexual Misconduct," *New York Times,* May 18, 1995, p. A1.

6. On the relationship between Dole and Packwood in 1995, see David S. Cloud, "Abrupt End to Packwood Drama Leaves Void at Key Moment," *Congressional Quarterly Weekly Report,* September 9, 1995, pp. 2699–2703.

7. Philip D. Duncan and Christine C. Longworth, *Politics in America, 1996* (Congressional Quarterly Press, 1995), pp. 1171–72.

8. On Chafee and other Senate Republican moderates, see Serafini, "Mr. In-Between"; David S. Cloud, "GOP Moderates Refusing to Get in Line," *Congressional Quarterly Weekly Report,* September 30, 1995, pp. 2963–65; and Jennifer Senior, "Sen. Jeffords Walks Moderate High Wire," *Hill,* March 20, 1996, p. 1.

9. On forces for bipartisanship in the 1995 Senate, see David S. Broder, "Shift to the Senate," *Washington Post,* April 12, 1995, p. A25.

10. Rick Wartzman, "Clinton Lobbyist Focuses on Senate as Best Bet for the White House to Moderate Legislation," *Wall Street Journal,* June 15, 1995, p. A16.

11. On the nonmajoritarian nature of floor decisionmaking in the Senate and the budget process exception, see Stephen S. Smith, *Call to Order: Floor Politics in the House and Senate* (Brookings, 1989), chap. 4.

12. See the statement by Senator Olympia Snowe in Cloud, "GOP Moderates Refusing to Get in Line," p. 2963.

13. On the rules for reconciliation bills in the Senate, see Allen Schick, *The Federal Budget: Politics, Policy, Process* (Brookings, 1995), pp. 85–86.

14. Precisely this argument was made in a letter sent to Majority Leader Dole in a letter from Senator Joseph Lieberman and forty-one other Senate Democrats on June 28, 1995.

15. On Dole's patronage of food stamps, see Linda E. Demkovitch, "The 'Odd Couple' Is Whipping Up a New Dish on Food Stamps," *National Journal,* vol. 9, no. 12 (March 19, 1977), pp. 428–29.

16. Bill McAllister, "Dole Criticizes House Plan: Teen Mothers' Welfare Cutoff Called Unlikely," *Washington Post,* January 23, 1995, p. A4.

17. See generally Ronald Brownstein, "Dole Walks Fine Political Line in Bid for Presidency," *Los Angeles Times* (Washington ed.), April 4, 1995, p. A6; R. W. Apple, "Dole Defending Middle Ground in G.O.P. Race," *New York Times,* August 13, 1995, p. A1; and Jason DeParle, "A Fundamental Problem," *New York Times Magazine,* July 14, 1996.

18. See Kevin Merida, "Dole Takes 180-Degree Turn on Affirmative Action," *Washington Post,* March 17, 1995; Fay Fiore, "Dole Mounts Drive to Repeal Gun Ban," *Los Angeles Times,* March 18, 1995, p. A1; Jerry Gray, "Dole, in a 2nd Nod to the Right, Pledges to Fight Gun Ban," *New York Times,* March 18, 1995, p. A1. Gun owners are a particularly powerful political block in New Hampshire, site of the first presidential primary.

19. See Paul A. Gigot, "Dole Bows to GOP's New Powers," *Wall Street Journal,* April 14, 1995, p. A8.

20. Jon M. Broder, "Wilson Aims Double-Barrel on Clinton, Dole for Welfare," *Los Angeles Times,* September 7, 1995, p. A16.

21. Senator Paul Coverdell (Republican, Georgia), memorandum to Majority Whip Trent Lott, quoted in Rich Lowry, "The Big Squeeze," *National Review,* April 17, 1995, pp. 25–26.

22. See, for example, Eric Pianin, "Budget Compromise Doesn't Appear Easy," *Washington Post,* June 5, 1995, p. A4.

23. Quoted in Robert Pear, "Moynihan Joins Welfare Fray with Bill of His Own," *New York Times,* May 14, 1995, p. A22.

24. On Moynihan's role in the Senate debate, see Barbara Vobejda, "Moynihan, Observing from the Wings," *Washington Post,* June 4, 1995, p. A1; Mickey Kaus, "Pat Answers," *New Republic,* June 5, 1995, p. 4; Robin Toner, "Moynihan Battles View He Gave Up on Welfare Fight," *New York Times,* June 18, 1995, p. A1; and Ian Fisher, "Moynihan Stands Alone in Welfare Debate," *New York Times,* September 27, 1995, p. B1.

25. Pear, "Welfare Bill Gets Key Endorsement by G.O.P. Senators"; Shogren, "Packwood: Senate to Reject Welfare as Entitlement"; and Roman, "Senate Stiffens on Welfare Reform as Term Limits Face House Defeat."

26. See Ronald F. King, "Welfare Reform: Block Grants, Expenditure Caps, and the Paradox of the Food Stamp Program," *Political Science Quarterly,* vol. 114, no. 3 (1999), pp. 359–85. The draft bills under discussion in the Senate did not convert the school lunch program into a block grant—an element of the House bill that had been highly controversial. Both governors and senators wished to avoid a repeat of this controversy. On negotiations between the Republican governors and Senate Republicans, see Elizabeth Shogren, "Senators, Aided by Governors, Drafting Milder Welfare Reforms," *Los Angeles Times* (Washington ed.), April 12, 1995, p. A4; Robert Pear, "G.O.P. Governors Urge Big Changes for Welfare Bill," *New York Times,* April 13, 1995, p. A4; Judith Havemann and Barbara Vobejda, "Senate Welfare Draft Splits with House," *Washington Post,* April 13, 1995, p. A4; Vobejda and Havemann, "Traditional Welfare Constituencies Put Out by Lack of Input in Reform," *Washington Post,* May 21, 1995. On food stamps

and the school lunch program, see R. Kent Weaver, "Deficits and Devolution in the 104th Congress," *Publius: The Journal of Federalism,* vol. 26, no. 3 (Summer 1996), pp. 45–87.

27. Elizabeth Shogren, "Senate Welfare Reform Proposal Goes Easier on the States," *Los Angeles Times* (Washington ed.), May 16, 1995, p. A4; Judith Havemann, "Senate Plan Turns Welfare Over to States," *Washington Post,* May 16, 1995, p. A4.

28. States were also required to submit an annual report detailing how they intend to reduce the incidence of out-of-wedlock pregnancies. Details of the Packwood bill are given in the Senate Finance Committee markup document, "The Family Self-Sufficiency Act of 1995: Brief Summary," May 1995.

29. See Douglas J. Besharov, "The Welfare Balloon," *Washington Post,* June 11, 1995, p. C11.

30. See Robert Pear, "Senate Welfare Plan Cuts $41 Billion over 7 Years," *New York Times,* May 26, 1995, p. A18. Revised CBO estimates showed savings of $38.6 from fiscal years 1996 through 2002. See *The Family Self-Sufficiency Act of 1995,* S. Rpt. 104-96, 104 Cong. 1 sess. (GPO, 1995), p. 42.

31. For a critique of the Moynihan plan, see Kaus, "Pat Answers."

32. The committee rejected, following party lines, a Rockefeller (Democrat, West Virginia) amendment that would give states the option of exempting individuals in areas of high unemployment from the five-year time limit if they participated in workfare or community service jobs. A state maintenance of effort proposed by Senator Breaux (Democrat, Louisiana) was defeated on a party line vote; an amendment by Senator Graham (Democrat, Florida) to allocate block grant funds based on the number of poor children in a state rather the state's historical spending patterns lost on a 12-8 vote. An amendment offered by Senator Don Nickles (Republican, Oklahoma) that would have added to the committee bill's requirement that states "take action to prevent and reduce the incidence of out-of-wedlock pregnancies" (without saying how they should do so) a clause stating that this should be accomplished "without increasing the incidence of pregnancy terminations" lost on a 10-9 vote. The closest vote (a tie) came not on AFDC, but on an amendment contained in the Packwood bill that would ease the restrictions on the receipt of SSI by children. The Moynihan substitute lost and the bill cleared the committee by identical 12-8 votes, with Senator Max Baucus (Democrat, Montana) voting with the Republicans. Roll call votes in the committee are reported in *The Family Self-Sufficiency Act of 1995,* pp. 35–41. Details of amendments offered are contained in Senate Finance Committee, "Mark Up on H.R. 4, The Personal Responsibility Act of 1995," May 26, 1995. The text of the bill as reported by the Senate Finance Committee is H.R. 4 [Report 104-96], June 9, 1995. On the Nickles amendment, see Cheryl Wetzstein, "Fight over Illegitimacy Rules Snags Senate Welfare Reform," *Washington Times,* June 26, 1995, p. A6.

33. Robert Pear, "Senate Committee Approves a Vast Overhaul of Welfare," *New York Times,* May 27, 1995, p. 1.

34. Pear, "Senate Welfare Plan Cuts $41 Billion over 7 Years"; and Todd S. Purdum, "Republicans' Welfare Plan Is Again Attacked by Clinton," *New York Times,* June 7, 1995, p. A25.

35. Vobejda, "Moynihan, Observing from the Wings."

36. Pear, "Senate Committee Approves a Vast Overhaul of Welfare."

37. Ibid.; Cheryl Wetzstein, "Welfare Bill Advances: Senate Panel Sends Bill to Floor, 12-8," *Washington Times,* May 27, 1995, p. A1; and Jeffrey L. Katz, "Senate's Plan Falls in Line, Shifts Welfare to the States," *Congressional Quarterly Weekly Report,* May 27, 1995, pp. 1503–06. See also *The Family Self-Sufficiency Act of 1995.*

38. Senators Faircloth, Santorum, Lott, and Gramm, letter to Senator Packwood, May 18, 1995. See also Senator Faircloth's bill, S. 834, "Real Welfare Reform Act of 1995," 104 Cong. 1 sess., introduced on May 19, 1995.

39. Katz, "Senate's Plan Falls in Line, Shifts Welfare to the States"; Barbara Vobejda and Judith Havemann, "To Save Welfare Reform, Dole Faces GOP Peers in Senate," *Washington Post,* June 28, 1995, p. A4.

40. Faircloth is quoted in Hilary Stout, "Senate GOP Leaders Delay Welfare Vote as Party Unity Splinters over the Issue," *Wall Street Journal,* June 15, 1995, p. B4; and Judith Havemann and Helen Dewar, "Heated Debate on Welfare Reform Threatens to Melt GOP Solidarity," *Washington Post,* June 19, 1995, p. A4.

41. See Wetzstein, "Fight over Illegitimacy Rules"; Wetzstein, "Family-Friendly Welfare Bill Ready," *Washington Times,* July 26, 1995, p. A8; and Elizabeth Shogren, "Welfare Debate Focusing on Out-of-Wedlock Births," *Los Angeles Times,* August 3, 1995, p. A14.

42. Vobejda and Havemann, "To Save Welfare Reform Measure."

43. On the conflict between Dole and Gramm, see Richard L. Berke, "Dole and Gramm Clash on Revising Laws on Welfare," *New York Times,* July 16, 1995, p. A1.

44. See Barbara Vobejda and Judith Havemann, "Senate Welfare Debate Opens on Solemn Note," *Washington Post,* May 25, 1995, p. A7; Laura R. Hamburg, "Welfare Reform Plan Penalizes Ohio, Voinovich Says," *Plain Dealer* (Cleveland), March 24, 1995, p. A6; Paul Offner, "GOP Welfare Scam," *New Republic,* May 29, 1995, p. 11.

45. Voinovich, for example, also criticized President Clinton for attacking Republicans' motivations and supported a block grant with few restrictions on the states and a cash grant "rainy day fund." See William Hershey, "Clinton Blasts GOP Plans to Cut Welfare," *Beacon-Journal* (Akron), June 7, 1995, p. A4; Tom Diemer, "Voinovich, Clinton Agree, Disagree," *Plain Dealer* (Cleveland), June 7, 1995, p. A10; William Hershey, "Voinovich Spoils Party for the GOP," *Beacon-Journal* (Akron), June 12, 1995, p. C1.

46. Senator Kay Bailey Hutchinson, letter to Senators Robert Packwood and Daniel P. Moynihan, May 23, 1995. These concerns had been raised earlier by Democratic governor Lawton Chiles of Florida. See Judith Havemann, "Chiles Raps Florida's Cut of Welfare Pie," *Washington Post,* May 2, 1995, p. A17.

47. Gerald Miller, director of Michigan's Department of Social Services, who as Governor Engler's representative was a key player in negotiations between the Republican governors and congressional Republicans, charged that defenders of the status quo "in desperation . . . threw [the formula issue] up as a smokescreen" to prevent

conversion of AFDC. See Hilary Stout, "After Early Success, GOP's Effort to Overhaul Welfare System May Be Derailed in Senate," *Wall Street Journal,* July 6, 1995, p. A10. Of course, many of the key advocates of a formula change were Republican advocates of a block grant for AFDC.

48. "Welfare Overhaul Plans," *Congressional Quarterly Weekly Report,* June 24, 1995, p. 1843.

49. On the formula fights in welfare reform and their implications for Medicaid, see especially Jeffrey L. Katz, "Sunbelt Senators Revolt over Welfare Formula," *Congressional Quarterly Weekly Report,* June 24, 1995, pp. 1842–44; and Robin Toner, "Drive for Block Grants Pitting State against State," *New York Times,* June 28, 1995, p. A1.

50. On the Agriculture Committee's actions, see Judith Havemann and John F. Harris, "Clinton Backs Limit on Welfare Benefits," *Washington Post,* June 15, 1995, p. A1. On the Gramm-Faircloth initiative, see Havemann and Barbara Vobejda, "Food Stamp Block Grant Eyed as Way of Breaking Welfare Reform Stalemate," *Washington Post,* July 13, 1995, p. A6; Cheryl Wetzstein, "Welfare Bill Gets Senate Rewrite," *Washington Times,* July 17, 1995, p. A6; Havemann, "Gramm Proposes Tough Welfare Plan Designed to Appeal to GOP Conservatives," *Washington Post,* July 21, 1995; Wetzstein, "Seven GOP Senators Join Gramm's Welfare Reform," *Washington Times,* July 24, 1995, p. A8; Vobejda and Havemann, "Key GOP Senators Agree on Division of Welfare Funds," *Washington Post,* July 29, 1995, p. A6.

51. Among the hardship exemptions from the sixty-month time limit specified in the Daschle bill were persons living in areas of greater than 7.5 percent unemployment, child-only cases, teen parents still in school and making significant progress, persons who were ill or caring for an incapacitated parent or child, and parents of children under one year of age. In addition to these hardship categories, states could exempt up to 15 percent of their caseloads. An outline of the bill's provisions appears in U.S. Senate, Democratic Policy Committee, "The Democratic Welfare Reform Plan: 'Work First,'" DPC Information Packet, June 8, 1995. The text of the bill appears in *Work First Act of 1995,* S. 1117, 104 Cong. 1 sess., August 3, 1995.

52. Senator Moynihan's minority staff director on the Senate Finance Committee argued that because of unity among Republicans, the Daschle bill was unlikely to win, and thus "the Democrats may not be doing much more than choosing the way they will lose." Robert Pear, "From Democrats, a New Welfare Plan," *New York Times,* June 9, 1995, p. A21. See also Hilary Stout, "Senate Democrats Unveil Welfare Bill Requiring Work, Pledges to Keep Jobs," *Wall Street Journal,* June 9, 1995, p. 5A; and Havemann and Harris, "Clinton Backs Limit on Welfare Benefits." By mid-June, however, Moynihan was saying that he was "on board" with the Daschle bill. See Toner, "Moynihan Battles View He Gave Up on Welfare Fight."

53. See Robert Pear, "Republican Squabble Delays Welfare Debate," *New York Times,* June 16, 1995, p. A19; Cheryl Wetzstein, "Welfare Reform Has GOP Family Feuding," *Washington Times,* June 19, 1995, p. A5.

54. See Vobejda and Havemann, "To Save Welfare Reform Measure"; Jackie Calmes, "Conservatives Bash GOP Congressional Staffers as Moderates out of Step with the Revolution," *Wall Street Journal,* July 18, 1995, p. A16; Kevin Merida and Helen Dewar, "Dole's Chief of Staff Is Magnet for Criticism," *Washington Post,* July 21, 1995, p. A4; and Lloyd Grove, "Sheila Burke, on the Wrong Side of the Right," *Washington Post,* August 11, 1995, p. F1; Jason DeParle, "Sheila Burke Is the Militant Commie Peacenik Who's Telling Bob Dole What to Think," *New York Times Magazine,* November 12, 1995, sec. 6, p. 32.

55. Christopher Georges, "GOP Senators Want $25 Billion More to Be Slashed from Welfare Programs," *Wall Street Journal,* July 13, 1995, p. B8.

56. See "The President's Radio Address, July 1, 1995," *Weekly Compilation of Presidential Documents,* vol. 31, no. 27 (July 10, 1995), pp. 1186-87; and "The President's Radio Address, July 8, 1995," *Weekly Compilation of Presidential Documents,* vol. 31, no. 28 (July 17, 1995), pp. 1209–11.

57. The administration also allowed states to deny a partially offsetting increase in Food Stamp benefits to recipients who had their AFDC benefits cut for refusing to take jobs. See "Remarks to the National Governors' Association in Burlington, Vermont, July 31, 1995," *Weekly Compilation of Presidential Documents,* vol. 31, no. 31 (August 7, 1995), pp. 1342–47.

58. See for example Berke, "Dole and Gramm Clash on Revising Laws on Welfare."

59. High-benefit states remained vulnerable to risks of increases in welfare caseloads, however. See the provisions in *Work Opportunity Act of 1995,* S. 1120 creating a new Section 403(a)(3) of the Social Security Act, and Senator Hutchinson's defense of the compromise in *Congressional Record,* daily ed., September 12, 1995, pp. S13317, S13357.

60. States that chose to convert Food Stamp funds into a block grant would have their funding frozen, and the choice was irrevocable; they could not switch back to entitlement funding later.

61. On the negotiations, see Vobejda and Havemann, "Key GOP Senators Agree on Division of Welfare Funds."

62. Cheryl Wetzstein, "Gramm, Faircloth Scoff at Dole's Welfare Reform," *Washington Times,* August 3, 1995, p. A10.

63. The administration called for state maintenance of effort incentives, earmarked funding for child care and employment, rewards for incentives that moved more recipients into work, and increased funds for states that experienced increases in population or unemployment. See Robert Pear, "White House Seeks Areas of Welfare Accord with G.O.P.," *New York Times,* August 6, 1995, p. A24; Pear, "Dole Offers Welfare Bill, but Conservatives Reject It," *New York Times,* August 5, 1995, p. A8.

64. Barbara Vobejda, "Dole Faces GOP Rifts on Welfare," *Washington Post,* September 6, 1995, p. A15. The Dole bill's maintenance of effort provisions were also criticized in editorials in both the *Washington Post* and the *New York Times.* See "Welfare: Two Kinds of Compromise," *Washington Post,* September 7, 1995, p. A18; and "Mr. Dole's Bogus Welfare Safeguards," *New York Times,* September 8, 1995, p. A26.

65. See Judith Havemann, "Governors Push Welfare Reform," *Washington Post,* August 11, 1995, p. A5; and Havemann, "Dole Offers Concessions on Welfare Plan," *Washington Post,* August 12, 1995, p. A8; see also Senator Dole's statement in the *Congressional Record,* daily ed., August 11, 1995, pp. S12510–11.

66. Republicans replied, as they had on the issue of block grants for welfare reform, that there was no reason to believe that governors would be less sympathetic than the federal government to claims made by specific groups. See Judith Havemann, "A New Welfare Bill Complication," *Washington Post,* August 24, 1995, p. A17.

67. See Cheryl Wetzstein, "Few Debate Democratic Welfare Plan," *Washington Times,* September 7, 1995, p. A6.

68. The Daschle substitute was defeated by a 45-54 margin, with all Republicans voting against it and all but one Democrat (Baucus of Montana) voting for it.

69. The stricter maintenance of effort provision would have excluded state expenditures for Medicaid, but counted state expenditures for any other legislation established or altered by the Dole welfare reform bill, including Food Stamps, foster care, and SSI supplementary benefits. The family cap provision, like its House counterpart, would have allowed states to give vouchers for particular goods and services, but did not require them to do so. The maintenance of effort requirements would have applied only for fiscal years 1997 through 1999. For the text and a summary of the Dole amendment package, see *Congressional Record,* daily ed., September 8, 1995, pp. S12911–13.

70. See Barbara Vobejda and Judith Havemann, "Dole Concedes Some Major Points to Gain Support for Welfare Bill," *Washington Post,* September 9, 1995, p. A8. For a list of amendments, see *Congressional Record,* daily ed., September 8, 1995, pp. D1056–65.

71. See "President's Radio Address, September 16, 1995," in *Weekly Compilation of Presidential Documents,* vol. 31, no. 38 (September 25, 1995), pp. 1573–75. On the preliminary poverty estimates, see Gerald F. Seib and Michael K. Frisby, "As Welfare Reform Bill Moves to the Middle, Concerns Arise Whether the Center Can Hold," *Wall Street Journal,* September 19, 1995, p. A24.

72. One Republican, Senator Lauch Faircloth of North Carolina, voted against the bill on final passage.

73. Interview with author, January 1997.

74. Marian Wright Edelman, "'Say No to This Welfare Reform,'" *Washington Post,* November 3, 1995, p. A23.

75. Ann Devroy and Barbara Vobejda, "Clinton Faces 'Huge Heat' on Welfare," *Washington Post,* November 4, 1995, p. A1.

Chapter Twelve

1. For a summary of the differences, see *Personal Responsibility and Work Opportunity Reconciliation Act of 1995,* H. Conference Rept. 104-430, December 20, 1995.

2. Jeffrey L. Katz, "Outlines of Agreement Emerge as Conference Convenes," *Congressional Quarterly Weekly Report,* October 28, 1995, p. 3313; and Jeffrey L. Katz and David Hosansky, "Welfare Bills Compared," *Congressional Quarterly Weekly Report,* October 28, 1995, p. 3324.

3. A procedural problem also emerged in the period after Senate passage of welfare reform. The House and Senate Republican leadership planned to fold the conference version of welfare reform into the reconciliation bill that was expected to go through Congress in the late fall of 1995; indeed, if welfare did not pass Congress before or concurrently with the reconciliation bill, the Republicans could not hope to meet their deficit reduction targets. But under an obscure Senate rule (known as the Byrd rule) designed to prevent attracting extraneous amendments to "must pass" legislation, reconciliation bills cannot include provisions that do not have a significant effect on spending or revenues. Under the then-existing system of AFDC entitlement, many of the conservative mandates in the House-passed bill, such as teen mother exclusions, family caps, and hard time limits (also in the Senate bill), would have met this test, because they would have lowered federal expenditures. But because both Republican bills turned AFDC into a fixed block grant, any savings generated by these conservative mandates would accrue to the states, not to the federal government. Thus when Senate Democrats challenged forty-six elements of the Senate reconciliation bill, including hard time limits in state welfare programs, the Senate parliamentarian ruled that these provisions should be stricken from the bill. This ruling was certain to be applied to the broader range of mandates in the House-passed bill as well, if they were included in a conference agreement that would have to come back through the Senate for final passage. The application of the Byrd rule to welfare reform legislation changed bargaining leverage and strategies in several ways. Most obvious, it increased Democratic leverage to get rid of the mandates; the Byrd rule can be overridden with sixty votes in the Senate, but only the five-year time limit had a plausible chance of getting that many votes. On the "Byrd rule" generally, see Allen Schick, *The Federal Budget: Politics, Policy, Process* (Brookings, 1995); and George Hager, "Reconciliation Now a Major Tool," *Congressional Quarterly Weekly Report,* October 28, 1995, p. 3286.

4. Robert Pear, "President Draws Line on Welfare," *New York Times,* October 10, 1995, p. A18.

5. Shaw is quoted in ibid.; Judith Havemann, "Governors Oppose Welfare Bill's Ban on Aid to Mothers," *Washington Post,* October 11, 1995, p. A8.

6. Havemann, "Governors Oppose Welfare Bill's Ban on Aid to Mothers."

7. See Pear, "President Draws Line on Welfare"; and Judith Havemann, "Women in Congress, Others Appeal to Welfare Conferees," *Washington Post,* October 17, 1995, p. A10.

8. See Judith Havemann and Ann Devroy, "Democrats Seek Senate Welfare Plan Study," *Washington Post,* October 27, 1995, p. 7.

9. "Message to the House of Representatives Returning without Approval the Personal Responsibility and Work Opportunity Reconciliation Act of 1995, January 9,

1996," *Weekly Compilation of Presidential Documents*, vol. 32, no. 2 (January 15, 1996), pp. 30–32.

10. For example, the NGA proposal would have allowed states to count recipients who left assistance for work as long as they remain employed, and cut the work participation requirement to twenty-five hours for most workers and twenty hours for parents with children under age six. The NGA also recommended that Food Stamps remain an uncapped entitlement, that foster care and adoption assistance remain open-ended entitlements, and that cuts in the Earned Income Tax Credit be limited. See National Governors' Association, "Welfare Reform" (Washington, February 6, 1996). The NGA modified its February proposal in early March to require a state match for additional child care funds and to include a maintenance of effort requirement to be eligible for recession-related contingency funds. For a discussion of why the NGA was able to reach an agreement, see R. Kent Weaver, "Deficits and Devolution in the 104th Congress," *Publius: The Journal of Federalism*, vol. 20, no. 3 (Summer 1996), pp. 45–87.

11. Paul Cullinan, memorandum, Congressional Budget Office, Budget Analysis Division, February 16, 1995.

12. See Barbara Vobejda, "Government's Fiscal Impasse Leaves State Budgets in Limbo," *Washington Post*, January 14, 1996, p. A4; and Judith Havemann, "Governors Counting Cash before Reform Is Passed," *Washington Post*, February 26, 1996, p. A6. On state welfare reform initiatives taken in anticipation of a block grant system, see Center for Law and Social Policy, "Racing to the Bottom? Recent State Welfare Initiatives Present Cause for Concern" (Washington, February 21, 1996). On New York, see James Dao, "Budget Sails before Federal Winds," *New York Times*, December 16, 1995, p. A1; "New York State's Proposed Budget Reveals Sharp Spending Cuts, Significant Federal Risks, and Challenges Ahead," *Moody's Municipal Credit Report*, January 11, 1996.

13. See Ron Scherer, "Unsettled Budget Leaves State Plans on Shaky Ground," *Christian Science Monitor*, December 26, 1995, p. 1; Linda Feldmann, "America's Governors Emerge as 'Third House of Congress,'" *Christian Science Monitor*, February 8, 1996, p. 1.

14. For a conservative critique of the governors' proposal, see Robert Rector, "Welfare Reform and the Death of Marriage," *Washington Times*, February 23, 1996, p. A20.

15. Interview with author, February 1996.

16. Donna E. Shalala, Testimony before the Senate Finance Committee, 104 Cong. 1 sess., February 28, 1996. See also Jeffrey L. Katz, "Shalala: Governors' Proposals Give States Too Much Power," *Congressional Quarterly Weekly Report*, March 2, 1996, pp. 558–60.

17. See John B. Gilmour, *Strategic Disagreement: Stalemate in American Politics* (University of Pittsburgh Press, 1995), chap. 2.

18. On Republican divisions on welfare strategy, see Patrice Hill, "GOP Has New Strategy for Getting Welfare-Medicaid Bill to Clinton," *Washington Times*, March 7, 1996, p. A4; and Jeffrey L. Katz and David S. Cloud, "Welfare Overhaul Leaves Dole with

Campaign Dilemma," *Congressional Quarterly Weekly Report,* April 20, 1996, pp. 1023–26.

19. See Jeffrey L. Katz, "Voter Call for Revamped Welfare Poses Problem for Democrats," *Congressional Quarterly Weekly Report,* April 20, 1996, pp. 1027–29.

20. See, for example, Michael K. Frisby and John Harwood, "Clinton Steals Republicans' Thunder by Moving to the Right on Some Controversial Social Issues," *Wall Street Journal,* May 7, 1996, p. A24.

21. On the intertwined political calculus of Clinton and congressional Democrats, see Jeffrey L. Katz, "GOP's New Welfare Strategy Has Democrats Reassessing," *Congressional Quarterly Weekly Report,* July 13, 1996, pp. 1969–70.

22. On the Clinton administration's executive actions imposing additional requirements on the states, see, for example, Barbara Vobejda, " President Limits Teens on Welfare," *Washington Post,* May 5, 1996, p. A1; and John F. Harris and Judith Havemann, "Clinton Vows Tougher Rules on Finding Welfare Fathers," *Washington Post,* June 19, 1996, p. A2.

23. Republicans introduced congressional legislation to give automatic approval to the Wisconsin waiver request. See Judith Havemann, "President Backs Proposal to Scrap Welfare," *Washington Post,* May 19, 1996, p. A1; John E. Yang and Judith Havemann, "House, Bypassing Clinton, Votes to Grant Wisconsin Welfare Waiver," *Washington Post,* June 7, 1996, p. A8; and Robert Pear, "Clinton Wavers after Backing Welfare Plan," *Washington Post,* June 15, 1996, p. A1.

24. See Jeffrey L. Katz, "Ignoring Veto Threat, GOP Links Welfare, Medicaid," *Congressional Quarterly Weekly Report,* May 25, 1996, pp. 1465–67; Robert Pear, "G.O.P. Submits New Bill to Revamp Welfare and Medicaid," *New York Times,* May 23, 1996, p. B9; Cheryl Wetzstein, "GOP Takes Offensive on Welfare," *Washington Times,* May 23, 1996, p. A4; Judith Havemann and John F. Harris, "Governors' Welfare, Medicaid Deal Blows Up amid Charges of Partisanship," *Washington Post,* May 30, 1996, p. A7.

25. "A Study in Evasion," *Washington Post,* July 3, 1996, p. A24.

26. *New York Times*/CBS and *Washington Post*/ABC polls published in June asking about "generic" (that is, without naming candidates) preferences for the House of Representatives showed Democratic candidates favored over Republicans by margins of 45 percent to 38 percent and 50 to 38 percent, respectively. Richard L. Berke, "Poll Indicates Stable Ratings for President," *New York Times,* June 5, 1996, p. A1; and Richard Morin and Mario Brossard, "Key Voters Are Fleeing House GOP," *Washington Post,* June 17, 1996, p. A1.

27. See Janet Hook, "GOP Pares Legislative Wish List in Run-Up to Elections," *Los Angeles Times* (Washington ed.), July 8, 1996, p. A6. Differences between the House and Senate versions of Medicaid reform also contributed to the decision to separate Medicaid and welfare reform. See Cheryl Wetzstein, "GOP to Split Welfare, Medicaid Reforms?" *Washington Times,* July 11, 1996, p. A10.

28. Congressmen John Ensign and Dave Camp, letter to Speaker Gingrich and Majority Leader Lott, June 26, 1996. See also Jeffrey L. Katz, "GOP May Move to Split

Medicaid, Welfare," *Congressional Quarterly Weekly Report,* June 22, 1996, pp. 1761–62; and Laurie Kellman, "GOP Lawmakers Urge Welfare Split from Bill," *Washington Times,* June 28, 1996, p. A10.

29. Jeffrey L. Katz, with Steve Langdon, "Committee Gives Partisan Vote to Welfare, Medicaid Plans," *Congressional Quarterly Weekly Report,* June 29, 1996, pp. 1877–78. Senate Finance Committee chair William Roth referred to Medicaid reform as a "poison pill" that was blocking welfare reform by preventing bipartisan support and a presidential signature. See Cheryl Wetzstein, "Clinton May Sign Welfare Measure," *Washington Times,* July 12, 1996, p. A4.

30. Katz, "GOP's New Welfare Strategy Has Democrats Reassessing"; and Judith Havemann, "GOP Calls President's Bluff on Welfare," *Washington Post,* July 12, 1996, p. A20.

31. House Majority Leader Richard Armey said that Republicans wanted to force the president to decide whether "to sign this bill and satisfy the American people while he alienates his left-wing political base, or if he's going to veto the bill in order to satisfy the left wing of the Democrat Party, and thereby alienate the American people." E. J. Dionne, "Clinton's Choice," *Washington Post,* July 23, 1996, p. A17.

32. On the signals sent by the administration, see Robert Pear, "White House Is Optimistic about Chances of Welfare Bill with New G.O.P. Moves," *New York Times,* July 13, 1996, p. 10; Dan Balz, "Clinton Prods Congress on Welfare Overhaul Bill," *Washington Post,* July 17, 1996, p. A6; Elizabeth Shogren, "House Opens Debate on Welfare Reform," *Los Angeles Times* (Washington ed.), July 18, 1996, p. A8; Robert Pear, "House Approves Shift on Welfare," *New York Times,* July 19, 1996, p. A1.

33. The overall vote on final passage was 256-170, with thirty Democrats voting yes and four Republicans and one Independent voting no. A bipartisan alternative crafted by Representatives John Tanner and Mike Castle and backed by President Clinton failed by a vote of 168-258. See H.R. 3734, Personal Responsibility Act, *Congressional Record— Daily Digest,* July 18, 1996. The most complete coverage of House consideration is Jeffrey L. Katz, "Conferees May Determine Fate of Overhaul Bill," *Congressional Quarterly Weekly Report,* July 20, 1996, pp. 2048–51.

34. See Barbara Vobejda, "White House Hoping for More 'Progress' as Welfare Bills Head to Conference," *Washington Post,* July 25, 1996, p. A4.

35. See Isabel Sawhill and Sheila Zedlewski, "A Million More Poor Children," *Washington Post,* July 26, 1996, p. A27, and Elizabeth Shogren, "Study Warns about Effects of Proposed Welfare Changes," *Los Angeles Times,* July 26, 1996, p. A6.

36. See, for example, Barbara Vobejda, "Welfare Bill Opponents Turn Up Pressure," *Washington Post,* July 27, 1996, p. A4; Elizabeth Shogren, "Welfare Panel Heeds Clinton on Food Stamps," *Los Angeles Times,* July 30, 1996, p. A1.

37. See, for example, Barbara Vobejda, "Controversy Hits March for Children," *Washington Post,* March 31, 1996, p. A1; Robert Pear, "Thousands to Rally in Capital on Children's Behalf," *New York Times,* June 1, 1996, p. A10; Tim Weiner, "A Capital Rally Attracts Groups from across the Nation to Focus on Children's Needs," *New York Times,*

June 2, 1996, p. A30. For the conservative viewpoint, see, in particular, Robert Rector, "Welfare Reform on the Sidelines," *Washington Times*, May 31, 1996, p. A16.

38. See Vobejda, "Welfare Bill Opponents Turn Up Pressure"; and Joyce Price, "Panetta: Welfare Bill Is Doomed without Presidential Changes," *Washington Times*, July 29, 1996, p. A4.

39. See Lawrence D. Longley and Walter J. Oleszek, *Bicameral Politics: Conference Committees in Congress* (Yale University Press, 1989), especially chap. 9.

40. Elizabeth Shogren, "House and Senate Conferees Approve Welfare Overhaul," *Los Angeles Times*, July 31, 1996, p. A1.

41. For accounts of the meeting, see John Broder, "Decision Was Difficult for Clinton, Tough on Dole," *Los Angeles Times*, August 1, 1996, p. A16; and Todd Purdum, "Clinton Recalls His Promise, Weighs History, and Decides," *New York Times*, August 1, 1996, p. A1. First-hand accounts of the meeting appear in Robert B. Reich, *Locked in the Cabinet* (Knopf, 1998), pp. 319–22; and George Stephanopoulos, *All Too Human: A Political Education* (Boston: Little, Brown, 1999), pp. 419–22.

42. The House passed the bill by a margin of 328-101, with Democrats split 98-98. The Senate passed the bill 78-21, with Democrats split 25-21 in favor of passage. Only one of seven Democratic senators up for reelection, Paul Wellstone (Minnesota) voted against the conference report. *Congressional Quarterly Weekly Report*, July 20, 1996, pp. 2074–75.

43. Section 401(b) of the Personal Responsibility and Work Opportunity Reconciliation Act of 1996 states "NO INDIVIDUAL ENTITLEMENT—This part shall not be interpreted to entitle any individual or family to assistance under any State program funded under this part."

44. I am indebted to R. Shep Melnick for this analysis.

45. Congressional Budget Office, *Federal Budgetary Implications of H.R. 3734, The Personal Responsibility and Work Opportunity Reconciliation Act of 1996* (August 9, 1996), p. 1. These figures do not take into account the effects of falling caseloads, which would have lowered actual AFDC spending and thus reduced budgetary savings.

46. See David A. Super and others, *The New Welfare Law* (Washington: Center on Budget and Policy Priorities, August 14, 1996), p. 13.

47. Ellwood had left HHS in the summer of 1995 to return to Harvard's Kennedy School of Government.

48. Survey of 761 national registered voters conducted by Princeton Survey Research Associates for *Newsweek*, August 8–9, 1996. Seven percent of respondents thought that he had done so for both reasons equally, and 8 percent said that they did not know.

49. See Jeffrey L. Katz, "Changes in New Law Hinge on Budget Deal," *Congressional Quarterly Weekly Report*, November 23, 1996, pp. 3310–11; and Robert Pear, "Clinton Considers Move to Soften Cuts in Welfare," *New York Times*, November 27, 1996, p. A1. On divisions within the Republican ranks, see Sandy Hume, "Welfare Plan Splits Republicans," *Hill*, vol. 3, no. 48 (December 4, 1996), pp. 1, 9.

50. See, for example, Judith Havemann, "GOP Governors Reject Reopening of Welfare Bill but May Seek Some Aid," *Washington Post,* February 2, 1997, p. A7; Dan Balz and Barbara Vobejda, "Under GOP Pressure, Governors Soften Welfare Stance," *Washington Post,* February 3, 1997, p. A4; Robert Pear, "Governors Limit Revisions Sought in Welfare Law," *New York Times,* February 3, 1997, p A1; Janet Hook, "Wilson Joins Call to Help Immigrants Facing Cuts," *Los Angeles Times,* February 3, 1997, p. B1.

51. See Robert Pear, "Clinton Will Seek Tax Break to Ease Path off Welfare," *New York Times,* January 28, 1997, p. A1. See also Rochelle Sharpe, "A Tax Credit Designed to Spur Hiring Seems Promising—at First," *Wall Street Journal,* August 21, 1997, p. A1.

52. For a detailed summary and explanation of these provisions, see Mark Greenberg, *Welfare to Work Grants and Other TANF-Related Provisions in the Balanced Budget Act of 1997* (Washington: Center for Law and Social Policy, August 1997). Opponents of minimum wage laws argued that these would limit states' capacity to move recipients into work activities. Moreover, they argued that such laws would make it difficult for low-benefit states to comply with PRWORA requirements that a specified percentage of a state's caseload be engaged in work for twenty or more hours per week (for single-parent families), increasing to thirty hours from 2000—unless those states increased their benefit levels. See Steve Savner, *The Implications of Applying Federal Minimum Wage Standards to TANF Work Activities* (Washington: Center for Law and Social Policy, April 1997); Marilyn Werber Serafini, "Wimping Out," *National Journal,* October 18, 1997, pp. 2072–75; Barbara Vobejda, "GOP Backs Off in Fight against Workforce Protections," *Washington Post,* October 10, 1997, p. A17.

Chapter Thirteen

1. See Richard P. Nathan and Thomas L. Gais, *Implementing the Personal Responsibility Act of 1996: A First Look* (Albany, N.Y.: Nelson A. Rockefeller Institute of Government, 1999). Nathan and Gais refer to the "three S's: signals, services, and sanctions," p. 4.

2. Sanctions may also affect eligibility for Food Stamps and Medicaid. For a summary of mandatory and optional sanctions under TANF, see General Accounting Office, *State Sanction Policies and Number of Families Affected,* HEHS-00-44, march 2000, pp. 7–11.

3. Administration for Children and Families, *Changes in TANF Caseloads* (U.S. Department of Health and Human Services, December 1999).

4. Administration for Children and Families, *Changes in TANF Caseloads.*

5. Jason DeParle, "Shrinking Welfare Rolls Leave Record High Share of Minorities," *New York Times,* July 27, 1998, p. A1.

6. In August 1998, the urban counties containing the nation's thirty largest cities were home to 39 percent of TANF cases: almost twice those counties' 20 percent share of the population and an increase from 33 percent of AFDC cases only four years earlier. Bruce Katz and Katherine Allen, "Survey: The State of Welfare Caseloads in America's

Cities, 1999" (Brookings Center on Urban and Metropolitan Studies, February 1999), p. 1. See also Katz and Kate Carnevale, "The State of Welfare Caseloads in America's Cities" (Brookings Center on Urban and Metropolitan Studies, May 1988). There has also been a very large increase in the number of "child only" TANF cases: cases in which only the child is receiving benefits because the mother is absent, is ineligible for benefits (for example, because she is not a legal resident of the United States or she receives SSI payments), or has been sanctioned for noncompliance with work requirements or other state TANF requirements. Child-only cases are now estimated to make up more than 20 percent of TANF cases, and more than 40 percent in some states, mostly in the South. Barbara Vobejda and Judith Havemann, "'Child-Only' Cases Rise on Welfare Roles," *Washington Post,* January 2, 1999, p. A1.

7. A May 1997 report by the Council of Economic Advisers (CEA) attributed 44 percent of the caseload decline through 1996 to improvement in the economy, with another 31 percent due to the effects of state welfare reform experiments under federal waivers, and the rest due to other factors, such as enrichment of the EITC and improved child support enforcement. A later CEA report attributed one-third of the decline in caseloads from 1996 to 1998 to TANF program reforms, 8–10 percent to an improved labor market, about 10 percent to a higher minimum wage, and 1–5 percent to reduced cash benefits. See Council of Economic Advisers, *Explaining the Decline in Welfare Receipt, 1993–1996* (Washington, May 9, 1997); Council of Economic Advisers, *Technical Report: Explaining the Decline in Welfare Receipt, 1993–1996* (Washington: May 9, 1997); and Council of Economic Advisers, *The Effects of Welfare Policy and the Economic Expansion on Welfare Caseloads: An Update* (Washington, August 3, 1999). For a critical evaluation of the earlier CEA report, see Alberto Martini and Michael Wiseman, "Explaining the Recent Decline in Welfare Caseloads: Is the Council of Economic Advisers Right?" *Challenge,* vol. 40, no. 6 (November–December 1997), pp. 6–20. David N. Figlio and James P. Ziliak, "Welfare Reform, the Business Cycle, and the Decline in AFDC Caseloads," in Sheldon Danziger, ed., *Economic Conditions and Welfare Reform* (Kalamazoo, Mich.: W.E. Upjohn Institute for Employment Research, 1999), pp. 17–48. Figlio and Ziliak attribute 75 percent of caseload declines through 1996 to macroeconomic conditions, with a negligible role for welfare reform. Republicans have stressed both the role of activist governors from their own party and recipients' anticipation—and later experience—of the 1996 PRWORA. See Barbara Vobejda, "Welfare Drop Attributed to Economic Rise," *Washington Post,* May 10, 1997, p. A9.

8. See, for example, Barbara Vobejda and Judith Havemann, "Welfare Clients Already Work, off the Books," *Washington Post,* November 3, 1997, p. A1.

9. Jason DeParle, "Success, and Frustration, as Welfare Rules Change," *New York Times,* December 30, 1997, p. A1; Timothy Egan, "As Idaho Prospers, Prisons Fill Up While Spending on the Poor Lags," *New York Times,* April 16, 1998, p. A1.

10. Judith Havemann, "Welfare Reform Still on a Roll as States Bounce It Down to Counties," *Washington Post,* August 29, 1997, p. A19.

11. U.S. Department of Health and Human Services, Administration for Children and Families, Office of Planning, Research and Evaluation, *Temporary Assistance to Needy Families Program, First Annual Report to Congress, August 1998*, section 9 (hereafter *TANF, First Annual Report*)(Government Printing Office, 1998); and *TANF, Second Annual Report, August 1999*, section 13 (GPO, 1999).

12. One regional cluster may exhibit these interstate causal effects, however: the triad of Wisconsin, Illinois, and Indiana, where concerns over welfare migration have been politically sensitive for many years.

13. Fifteen states had family caps when PRWORA was passed, and four others had received permission to implement them but had not yet done so. L. Jerome Gallagher and others, *One Year after Federal Welfare Reform: A Description of State Temporary Assistance for Needy Families (TANF) Decisions as of October 1997* (Washington: Urban Institute, May 1998), p. VI-8, VI-9. See also *TANF, First Annual Report*, section 9.

14. Nathan and Gais, *Implementing the Personal Responsibility Act of 1996*, pp. 8–12.

15. For example, California disregards the first $225 of earnings and 50 percent of earnings beyond that, while New Hampshire, Pennsylvania, and Washington disregard 50 percent of all earnings. *TANF, First Annual Report*, section 9. Sixteen states phase out earnings disregards as TANF recipients remain on the rolls for a longer period. See General Accounting Office, *States Are Restructuring Programs to Reduce Welfare Dependence*, HEHS-98-109 (June 17, 1998), p. 46; and Gallagher and others, *One Year after Federal Welfare Reform*, sections 3 and 6 for a complete list.

16. This represents an increase from 1998, when thirty-eight states had relaxed resource limits and one had tightened them. See *TANF, First Annual Report*, section 9; *TANF, Second Annual Report*, section 13.

17. *TANF, Second Annual Report*, section 13.

18. Ibid.

19. States with the most stringent sanctions policies are concentrated in the Plains states and the South. See General Accounting Office, *State Sanction Policies and Number of Families Affected*, pp. 14–15.

20. General Accounting Office, *States' Experiences in Providing Employment Assistance to TANF Clients*, HEHS-99-22 (February 1999).

21. The General Accounting Office estimates that if states' available resources are calculated as their 1997 TANF allocation plus their 80 percent maintenance-of-effort level compared with what their 1997 expenditures would likely have been under the old AFDC law (taking into account caseload declines), Wisconsin enjoyed a whopping 65 percent bonus in resources under PRWORA, compared with 48 percent for Louisiana, 43 percent for Oregon, 32 percent for Texas, 8 percent for California, and only 1 percent for Connecticut. General Accounting Office, *States Are Restructuring Programs to Reduce Welfare Dependence*, pp. 78–79.

22. These figures are based on September 1997 Department of Health and Human Services estimates of TANF grants for fiscal year 1997 and TANF family caseloads in June 1997.

23. Judith Havemann, "Some States Are Hobbled in Race to Welfare Reform," *Washington Post,* October 22, 1996, p. A4.

24. See Carol S. Weissert, "Welfare Reform in Michigan: Beyond the Headline and the Hype," *Rockefeller Institute Bulletin 1999* (Albany, N.Y.: 1999). An expanded version was presented as a paper at the 1998 annual meeting of the Midwest Political Science Association, April 23–25, 1998.

25. For a discussion of the weak employment focus and "process" (that is, enrollment) rather than "outcome" focus of most AFDC offices under the JOBS program, see General Accounting Office, *Welfare to Work: Most AFDC Training Programs Not Emphasizing Job Placement,* HEHS-95-113 (May 1995).

26. A 1997 Department of Health and Human Services report suggests that two-thirds of states are not making adequate progress in tracking cases against time limits within their own borders; progress in tracking recipients who move across state lines is even more rudimentary. See General Accounting Office, *States Are Restructuring Programs to Reduce Welfare Dependence,* pp. 54–55.

27. See Nathan and Gais, *Implementing the Personal Responsibility Act of 1996,* pp. 7, 22–23. They argue that program managers often use independent job search requirements as a sorting method to eliminate cases that do not in fact need help: once such a job search fails, they then assess what else is needed to make an applicant job ready.

28. General Accounting Office, *States Are Restructuring Programs to Reduce Welfare Dependence,* pp. 30–33.

29. See, in particular, Northeast Region Food Stamp Program, *New York Program Access Review, November–December 1998* (U.S. Department of Agriculture, Food, and Nutrition Service, February 5, 1999); and *Reynolds v. Giuliani,* Southern District of New York, February 1, 1999.

30. Both quotes from Nathan and Gais, *Implementing the Personal Responsibility Act of 1996,* p. 46. This paragraph draws heavily on pp. 45–51.

31. For recent data on cross-state variations in sanctioning activity, see General Accounting Office, *State Sanction Policies and the Number of Families Affected,* pp. 52–53.

32. General Accounting Office, *Welfare Reform: States' Early Experiences with Benefit Termination,* HEHS-97-74 (May 1997), p. 7.

33. Ibid., p. 9.

34. Dan Bloom, "Welfare Time Limits: An Interim Report Card," paper presented at the annual research conference of the Association for Public Policy Analysis and Management, New York, November 1999. Gordon L. Berlin, *Encouraging Work, Reducing Poverty: The Impact of Work Incentive Programs* (New York: Manpower Demonstration Research Corporation, March 2000), pp. 44–45. See also Judith Havemann and Barbara Vobejda, "The Welfare Alarm That Didn't Go Off," *Washington Post,* October 1, 1998, p. A1.

35. Gary Burtless, "Can the Labor Market Absorb Three Million Welfare Recipients?" in *The Low-Wage Labor Market: Challenges and Opportunities for Economic Self-Sufficiency* (Department of Health and Human Services, December 1999), p. 65.

36. Dan Bloom and others, *The Family Transition Program: Implementation and Interim Impacts of Florida's Initial Time-Limited Welfare Program* (New York: Manpower Demonstration Research Corporation, March 1998).

37. Custodial teen parents were also required to "participate" in education. See Jodie Levin-Epstein, *Teen Parent Provisions in the Personal Responsibility and Work Opportunity Reconciliation Act of 1996* (Washington: Center for Law and Social Policy, November 1996).

38. A recent study suggests that slight increases in contraceptive use and a shift toward more reliable methods of contraception may account at least in part for the lower teen birth rates. See Rebekah Saul, "Teen Pregnancy: Progress Meets Politics," *Guttmacher Report on Public Policy,* vol. 2, no. 3 (June 1999), pp. 6–9.

39. See, for example, Melissa Healey, "Shelters Budge in Wisconsin, a Welfare Vanguard," *Los Angeles Times,* March 3, 1997, p. A8.

40. Martha Zaslow and others, "Welfare Reform and Children: Potential Implications," New Federalism Series A-23 (Washington: Urban Institute, June 1998).

41. See, for example, Leighton Ku and Teresa A. Coughlin, "How the New Welfare Reform Law Affects Medicaid," New Federalism Series A-5 (Washington: Urban Institute, February 1997).

42. See, for example, Nina Bernstein, "State's Medicaid Rolls Have Declined since '95," *New York Times,* August 17, 1998, p. B1.

43. On the TANF-Medicaid linkage, see Marilyn Ellwood, *The Medicaid Eligibility Maze: Coverage Expands, but Enrollment Problems Persist* (Menlo Park, Calif.: Kaiser Family Foundation, September 1999). See also Eileen Ellis and Vernon K. Smith, *Medicaid Enrollment in Twenty-One States: June 1997 to June 1999* (Menlo Park, Calif.: Kaiser Commission on Medicaid and the Uninsured, April 2000).

44. See, for example, Wendy Wedland, "Welfare Rolls Slashed, Many People Find Jobs," *Free Press* (Detroit), August 12, 1997.

45. Families that are sanctioned for failure to comply with work requirements more frequently have multiple barriers to work (for example, difficulties with health and transportation) than those who are not sanctioned. General Accounting Office, *State Sanction Policies and the Number of Families Affected,* p. 34.

Chapter Fourteen

1. Roger W. Cobb and Charles D. Elder, *Participation in American Politics: The Dynamics of Agenda-Building* (Johns Hopkins University Press, 1972), p. 86.

2. The positive role played by the Manpower Demonstration Research Corporation's evaluations of welfare-to-work experiments in the Family Support Act round is an exception to this pattern.

3. I am indebted to R. Shep Melnick for much of this analysis.

4. See R. Shep Melnick, *Between the Lines: Interpreting Welfare Rights* (Brookings, 1994), chap. 6.

5. David R. Mayhew, *Divided We Govern: Party Control, Lawmaking, and Investigations, 1946–1990* (Yale University Press, 1991). Mayhew notes several possible countervailing tendencies that could explain why unified party control does not result in more legislation, including randomly distributed differences in presidential skill, constancy in demands for legislation, heightened legislative activity by presidential aspirants during periods of divided government, and changes in the public mood. Of these, only the activity of presidential aspirants and changes in public mood seem applicable to the welfare reform case. The latter clearly is not an institutional explanation, but a public opinion explanation. The former is relevant to the Republican decision in the summer of 1996 to pursue a "split the difference" strategy with President Clinton rather than continue "strategic disagreement." This is discussed below in the context of strategic repositioning.

6. See R. Kent Weaver, "Ending Welfare as We Know It," in Margaret Weir, ed., *The Social Divide: Political Parties and the Future of Activist Government* (Brookings, 1998), pp. 397–400.

7. For a comparison of the politics of AFDC with those of Food Stamps, Medicaid, and school nutrition programs, see R. Kent Weaver, "Deficits and Devolution in the 104th Congress," *Publius: The Journal of Federalism*, vol. 20, no. 3 (Summer 1996), pp. 45–87.

8. In addition, those policies were a closer fit with Republicans' own preferences and those of their social conservative political base—that is, they were a "good" choice on policy and coalitional grounds, if they could in fact be enacted and did not have negative electoral consequences.

9. For the sake of simplicity, I do not discuss two intermediate steps in the text. First, the Republican development of H.R. 3500 before the Clinton administration's still-unannounced welfare reform package represents a form of strategic disagreement with the administration, intended to stake out a more conservative position for the GOP—but not so conservative that H.R. 3500 did not have a chance of winning away conservative Democrats. Second, the Talent-Hutchinson bill represented a form of strategic disagreement within Republican ranks. It was intended to demonstrate conservative discontent with H.R. 3500 in order to move the overall welfare reform debate and the debate within the Republican party to the right, while lowering the odds that Republicans would agree to welfare reform on Clinton's terms.

Index

Aaron, Henry, 162

Abortion: conservative interest groups, 212, 215; Contract with America, 261, 263; counseling, 264; deterrence strategies, 121, 152, 213, 214; H.R. 4, 285–86

ACLU. *See* American Civil Liberties Union

ADC. *See* Aid to Dependent Children

AFDC. *See* Aid to Families with Dependent Children

AFDC–Unemployed Parent (AFDC-UP): Family Support Act, 93; reform, 71, 73; state option, 19, 56, 58, 77–78; work issues, 75, 101, 144

Affirmative action, 298–99

African Americans: AFDC, 20–21, 105; marriage, 150; mothers' and widows' pensions, 16; out-of-wedlock births, 11, 103, 149; poverty rates, 11; single-parent families, 11, 55; TANF, 343; work ethic, 26

Aid to Dependent Children (ADC), 16, 28

Aid to Families with Dependent Children (AFDC): abolition, 1; caseloads, 68, 103, 129, 146, 151, 154, 173, 322, 343; changes, 1, 14, 20, 55, 92, 224–25, 328; costs and funding, 17, 20, 51, 55, 105, 132, 173, 226, 295; critiques and

controversies, 21–22, 55–56, 91–92, 100, 171–72; dependency, 103, 104, 105, 150; dual clientele trap, 360; EITC, 21, 81–84; effects, 104; eligibility, 17, 49, 70; employment, 21; entitlement status, 16–20, 101, 183, 203, 284, 303, 304, 313, 317; fraud, 222; means and asset testing, 13; Old Age Insurance, 20; origins, 16, 20; participation rates, 55; policy agenda, 28; public opinion, 191; racial issues, 4, 26, 28, 45, 48, 57; reasons, 10, 12, 19; role of the courts, 364; Social Security, 12; state issues, 28–29, 122; structure, 25; two-parent families, 19; welfare reform, 1, 3, 16, 20, 91–92, 328; welfare traps, 4–5, 86–87; work participation and requirements, 67, 68, 70, 71, 78, 103–04, 118, 153, 155–57, 242. *See also* AFDC–Unemployed Parent; Medicaid; Welfare reform, *1996*

Aid to Families with Dependent Children, benefits: amounts, 21, 27, 70, 71, 78–79; calculations, 68; children, 10; entitlement, 18; family caps, 1; Food Stamps, 19; increases, 103; indexing to inflation, 19, 28; magnet states, 27–28; recipients, 10, 20–21, 45, 48, 55, 68, 84; shared federal-state system, 28; spending on, 14, 15f; standards for, 18–19; state requirements, 18, 49; termination of, 18; women, 68; work requirements, 1

American Civil Liberties Union (ACLU), 203

American Prospect, 140, 164

American Public Welfare Association, 60, 75, 197, 208

Americans for Tax Reform, 299

Anderson, Martin, 358

Arkansas, 127

Archer, Bill, 252, 265, 326

Arizona, 350

Armey, Richard, 210, 262, 263

Balanced Budget Act of *1997* (BBA), 337, 353

Balanced Budget Amendment, 299

Bane, Mary Jo, 153–54, 233, 234–35, 239, 272, 335–36

Bauer, Gary, 211, 214

Baum, Rikki, 74

BBA. *See* Balanced Budget Act of *1997*

BEA. *See* Budget Enforcement Act of *1990*

Bennett, William, 120–21, 151

Bentsen, Lloyd, 76, 232

Big Seven, 208

Births, out-of-wedlock: *1996* welfare reforms, 329, 350, 351; AFDC, 55; benefits for, 48–49, 56, 149; conservative and liberal views, 148–51, 212; deterrence, 178–79, 212, 213, 264; effects, 121; evaluation research, 151–52; explanations, 149–51; H.R. *4*, 264, 285, 287–88, 304; numbers, 11, 103, 146, 148, 161; public opinion, 25; teenage mothers, 148, 179–80, 213, 264

Blank, Rebecca, 159

Blue, Louisa, 9, 10

Boston, 9

Breaux, John, 306

Bryant, Wayne, 132

Budget Enforcement Act of *1990* (BEA): *1996* welfare reforms, 374; Clinton

welfare reforms, 250; EITC, 81; financing welfare reform, 51; money trap, 45, 361; rules, 226, 361; work programs, 238

Budget issues: *104*th Congress, 291; AFDC, 105; budget reconciliation process, 257, 297, 321–22, 339, 363–64, 367, 374; fast track, 227; new budget rules, 226–28, 257; welfare reform and, 92, 114–15, 188, 226–29, 249, 297–98, 321–22; WORK program, 243. *See also* Congress; *individual presidents and administrations*

Burke, Sheila, 99, 307–08

Bush, George, 102, 129, 220

Bush administration, 20, 102, 129, 131

Califano, Joseph, 63

California: AFDC, 132; caseloads, 343; GAIN program, 158–59; illegal immigration, 230; Proposition *13*, 65; SSI, 231; welfare reform, 132, 305, 321

Camp, Dave, 262

Carter, Jimmy, 60–61, 62. *See also* Program for Better Jobs and Incomes

Carter administration; agenda, 64; health insurance reform, 62; welfare reform, 61, 65, 66, 87, 90, 94–95, 357, 358, 362, 363

Castle, Mike, 127, 262

Catholic Charities, 197

Cato Institute, 156–57

CBO. *See* Congressional Budget Office

CBRICA. *See* Congressional Budget Reform and Impoundment Control Act of *1974*, 67

CDF. *See* Children's Defense Fund

Center on Budget and Policy Priorities (CBPP), 156, 197, 199–201, 202–03

Center for Law and Social Policy (CLASP), 143, 197, 201, 202–03

CETA. *See* Comprehensive Employment and Training Act

Chafee, John, 295, 296, 302–03

Chicago, 104

Child Exclusion Task Force, 203

Children: advocacy groups, 199–205; AFDC recipients, 10, 77; child care, 80, 107, 116, 154–55, 240, 244, 329, 335, 345; child support, 116–17, 125, 244–45; in dual clientele trap, 45–46, 48, 274–75; Family Support Act, 76; guaranteed income, 58; long-term prognosis, 352–53; orphanages, 274–76; paternity, 244, 264, 324, 350; political issues, 80, 191, 194, 196; poll results, 179–80; poverty rates, 103; Program for Better Jobs and Incomes, 62, 63; public opinion, 191, 194; spiritual vs. material poverty, 213–14; SSI recipients, 13, 286, 317–18, 335; welfare reform, 105, 312, 313, 319, 327, 351–52. See also Families; Interest and advocacy groups; Women's issues

Children's Defense Fund (CDF), 143, 197, 202–03, 233–34, 327

Christensen, Jon, 277

Christian Coalition, 27; congressional testimony, 143; Contract with the American Family, 220; political strategy, 211–12; sympathy for, 25; and welfare issues, 197; welfare reform, 211, 304, 322

CLASP. See Center for Law and Social Policy

Clinton, Bill: 1992 platform, 271, 290–91; AFDC, 32, 248, 339; as chair of National Governor's Association, 210; effect of campaign pledge, 166, 171, 224–25, 250, 356; EITC, 365; executive orders, 324; family caps, 240; Family Support Act, 127; incremental reform, 94, 97–98; interest and advocacy groups, 217, 220; Medicaid, 323; political positioning and, 379–80; presidential campaign, 127–30; public opinion, 188, 191, 270; repositioning Democratic Party, 7; "to end welfare as we know it," 2, 127, 384; welfare reform, 4, 94–96, 127, 129–30, 174, 235, 249, 286, 292–93, 312, 318, 319, 324, 327–28, 340–41; Work First

program, 307, 308; zones of acceptable outcomes, 312, 313, 381, 383, 384

Clinton, vetoes: causes, 320, 381; Democratic Party, 288, 324; Edelman, Marian Wright, and, 315; effects, 224, 273, 307, 340; Moynihan and, 303; Republican Party, 286–87, 323, 324

Clinton administration: agenda, 228, 235–37, 248; budget issues, 80, 81, 226–28, 272–73; Center on Budget and Policy Priorities, 200; Children's Defense Fund, 202; Democratic Leadership Council, 206–07; EITC, 1, 80–81; health care reform, 37, 228–29; policy research, 151–52; policy sectors, 205

Clinton administration, welfare reform: 1996, 171, 270–73, 283–84, 303, 314–15; AFDC, 224, 238, 239, 303; budget issues, 227, 229–30, 239–42, 243, 249, 250; children's issues, 240, 244–45, 322; closure, 237–42; coalitions, 231; costs and funding, 244, 245–46, 271; dual clientele trap, 194, 239; effects of Clinton campaign pledge, 50, 97–98, 224–25; elections of 1996, 336; Ellwood and, 223; failure, 51, 97–99, 133, 194–95, 246–51; final 1994 proposal, 242–48; guaranteed and subsidized jobs, 194, 243; health care reform, 229–30, 270–71; interagency task force, 233–34; interest and advocacy groups, 217; limits on benefits and jobs, 239, 243, 244; money trap, 231, 238, 251; Moynihan and, 2; political issues, 51, 335–36, 356; priority, 37; teenage pregnancy, 238, 239–40, 245; policy research, 94–96, 162, 165–66; politics and policy choice, 232–37, 245, 246–51, 273; public opinion, 186–88, 192–193; Republican program, 270–73; state programs and waivers, 260, 308; strategic issues, 248–49, 251, 272–73; work issues, 165–66, 183, 232–33, 237–39, 242–44; zones of acceptable outcomes, 289, 380. See also Decisionmaking

Clinton, Hillary, 202, 233–34, 275
Coalition on Human Needs, 205
Coalitions, political: *1994* elections, 290;
   Carter administration, 61, 63, 65; child
   development issues, 202; Clinton
   administration, 231, 246, 247;
   coalitional unity, 30; compromise and,
   93; conservative groups, 214, 215–16;
   Contract with America, 274, 277,
   284–85; in decisionmaking, 33, 34;
   Democratic, 225–26, 380; devolution
   and, 123; hand-tying and, 40–41;
   H.R. *4*, 264–65; interest and advocacy
   groups, 198, 214, 218, 221; Nixon
   administration, 58; Reagan administration, 67, 73; Republican and Clinton
   administration, 272–73; Republican
   governors, 267, 277; strategic pursuit
   and, 41–42; threats to Republican, 257;
   welfare reform, 51–52, 87, 90, 92,
   119–20, 121, 134, 291, 303–13
Committee for Economic Development,
   60
Comprehensive Employment and
   Training Act (CETA), 119, 194
Concerned Women of America, 143, 211
Congress: *95*th, 65; AFDC, 56; agenda, 27,
   90, 101; budget process, 27, 87, 322;
   committees, 27, 36, 144, 287, 327, 363;
   family caps, 240; guaranteed income,
   57; hearings, 141–43; institutional
   memory, 98–99; jurisdictional splits,
   72–73; policymaking authority, 27;
   Reagan welfare reforms, 72–76, 90;
   rules, 27, 59, 65, 74, 90, 327; state
   interests and, 28; use of policy
   research, 144; welfare reform, 91, 130,
   359. *See also* House of Representatives;
   Policymaking; Senate
Congress, *103*d: hearings, 141, 143; H.R.
   3500, 236; polls, 247; welfare reform,
   130, 228, 231–32, 241
Congress, *104*th: budget issues, 291;
   Clinton reform proposals, 272–73;
   hearings, 141, 143; H.R. *3500*, 262–63;
   institutional memory, 99; interest and

advocacy groups, 200–01, 212, 217–18;
   overestimation of political capacity, 99;
   policy and political objectives, 260–61;
   policy research, 168; public opinion,
   191; Republican governors, 217; Ways
   and Means Committee membership,
   277; zones of acceptable outcomes,
   375. *See also* Contract with America
Congress, *104*th, welfare reform: AFDC,
   263, 264; block grants, 263; Clinton
   administration and, 252–53;
   decisionmaking, 263; deterrence, 357;
   Family Support Act, 98; interest groups
   and, 27, 204; policy preferences, 375;
   political issues, 260–65, 96; spending
   caps, 263; state issues, 194; traps, 253;
   vetoes and passage, 2, 4; working
   group, 262–63. *See also* Contract with
   America; House of Representatives
Congressional Black Caucus, 225
Congressional Budget Office (CBO):
   costs of welfare reform, 87; H.R. *4*, 291,
   303–04, 318, 321; policy research, 140;
   Program for Better Jobs and Incomes,
   62; PRWORA, 335
Congressional Budget Reform and
   Impoundment Control Act of *1974*
   (CBRICA), 67
Congressional Research Service, 140, 151,
   163–64, 265
Connecticut, 346, 348, 350
Conservatives and conservatism:
   abortion, 121, 264; AFDC, 60, 71, 105;
   block grants, 269; children's issues,
   194, 245, 269, 275; deterrence, 360,
   362, 367; devolution, 123; EITC, 80, 81;
   energizing issues, 263; Family
   Assistance Plan, 59; H.R. *4*, 284,
   285–86, 309, 311; H.R. *3500*, 237;
   incentives, 111, 114, 145, 156–57;
   income distribution, 123–24; interest
   and advocacy groups, 211–21, 225;
   limits, 322; multiple sources of
   expertise, 163–64; negative income tax
   proposals, 57; New Federalism, 69;
   out-of-wedlock births, 148–49,

150–51, 152, 322; penalties for failure to work, 58; prevention and reha-bilitation, 114; Program for Better Jobs and Incomes, 63; religious rights, 211; renaissance of, 104–05; Social Security, 60; state welfare discretion, 50; targeted universalism, 117; welfare reform, 6, 26–27, 32, 87, 100, 104–05, 106, 133–34, 164–65, 256, 313; WORK program, 247; work requirements, 57, 58, 59, 61, 65, 160, 164. *See also* Political issues; Republican Party

Constitutional issues, 265, 345, 363

Contract with America; agenda, 255–58, 380; budget issues, 256, 257–58, 264, 283; Clinton administration and, 270–73; conservative interest groups, 216; Dole and, 299; federalism trap, 265–66; H.R. *4*, 252, 262–70, 275, 277, 283, 295–300, 301–03, 304, 314; H.R. *3500*, 262–63, 283, 380; Murray, Charles, 123; One Hundred Days, 209–10, 252, 287, 291, 295; positional bargaining, 380; schedule of, 277; taxa-tion issues, 257; welfare reform, 2, 94, 237, 255–56, 261, 274, 283, 356–57. *See also* Congress, *104*th; Republican Party

Contract with the American Family, 220

Council of State Governments, 208

Courts, 364; Federal, 17–19, 55, 328; U.S. Supreme, 13, 17–18

Cuban Americans, 288, 291

Cunningham, Rosa Lee, 135

Daly, Sharon, 205

Danforth, John, 295

Daschle, Tom, 306, 312

Deal, Nathan, 288, 293

Deal welfare bill, 288, 289, 380

Dean, Howard, 267, 322

Decisionmaking: *104*th Congress, 263; Clinton administration, 234–35, 237, 250–51; congressional rules, 29; position options, 32–35, 37–40, 45; trade-offs, 30–32, 33–34. *See also* Policymaking

Democratic Caucus, 254, 284, 293

Democratic Leadership Council (DLC), 197, 199, 206–07, 217, 220–21, 270, 367

Democratic Party: AFDC, 22, 71, 93, 171, 288; child advocacy groups, 199, 204, 216; Clinton repositioning, 7; Clinton welfare proposals, 246–48, 249–50; coalitions, 225–26, 380, 381; Deal welfare bill, 380–81; devolution, 122; Family Assistance Plan, 59; Family Support Act, 130; H.R. *4*, 286, 288; New Democrats, 119, 122, 128, 206, 207, 224, 233, 270, 356, 380; policy sectors, 205; positional bargaining, 379–81; public opinion, 188; Reagan programs, 67, 71, 74; in South, 18, 206; welfare reform, 32, 71, 90, 93, 128, 206, 258–59, 273, 284, 313–14, 323–24, 336; zones of acceptable outcomes, 293, 323–24, 381, 382, 383, 384. *See also* Clinton, Bill

Deterrence: child advocacy groups, 203–04; Clinton administration reforms, 239; conservatives, 164, 212, 213, 216; dual clientele trap, 124; effectiveness, 152–53, 163, 166–67; Republican reforms, 264, 269, 290; in welfare reform, 120–21

Detroit News, 9–10

Devolution. *See* Federalism

Disincentives. *See* Incentives and disincentives

DLC. *See* Democratic Leadership Council

Dobson, James, 211, 212

DOL. *See* Labor, Department of

Dole, Robert; conservative interest groups, 216; Dole welfare reform bill, 308–09; Gramm and, 304, 323; political positioning, 298–99, 307; presidential politics, 374; welfare reform passage, 309–12; workfare programs, 75

Domenici, Pete, 312

Downey, Tom, 76

Dukakis, Michael, 76

Durenberger, David, 295

Eagle Forum, 211

Earned Income Tax Credit (EITC): abuse, 241–42, 365; AFDC, 21, 81–84, 100; compared to welfare reform, 5; costs, 80, 81, 83; effects, 80, 83–84; expansion, 1, 14, 15f, 28, 54, 62, 78–84, 80, 83, 84, 100, 125, 227; Family Support Act, 107; funding, 80–81; Greenstein, Robert, 200; limits on, 246; as major family credit, 13, 79; passage, 79–80; political issues, 81, 83–84, 100, 241–42; Program for Better Jobs and Incomes, 62; Republican proposals, 365; shortcomings, 84; workfare earnings, 337; WORK program, 243

Earnings. *See* Income and earnings

Economic issues; decreasing caseloads, 343–44; inflation, 19, 283, 328; Law of Unintended Rewards, 111; recessions, 17, 20, 69, 126, 230, 306, 353; revenue sharing, 60; slowdowns, 79; welfare reform, 352-353; working mothers, 351

Edelman, Marian Wright, 202, 203, 315

Edelman, Peter, 202, 335–36

Edgar, Jim, 301

Edin, Katherine, 157

Education and training, 72, 75, 175

EITC. *See* Earned Income Tax Credit

Ellwood, David: attack on poverty, 125, 127; Center on Budget and Policy Priorities, 200; Clinton administration welfare reforms, 94, 95, 233, 234–35, 272; costs of welfare reform, 240; limits on AFDC benefits, 223; phase in of work requirements, 239; welfare dependency, 153–54; in welfare reform, 358. *See also Poor Support*

Emmanuel, Rahm, 271, 328

Employment issues: AFDC, 20, 22, 56; barriers, 118; benefits, 21, 73, 107, 111; costs, 238; income notches, 57; job availability, 155, 183; labor market barriers, 155–56; penalties, 58, 59; poll results, 181–83; public opinion, 190–91; public service jobs, 61–62, 63, 237–38; skills, 155, 352; time limits,

161, 183–85, 190, 264, 283; welfare, 48–49, 61, 64, 70–71, 100–01, 181–83, 207. *See also* Income and earnings

Employment requirements: *1994* welfare reforms, 234, 237–39, 242–44; *1996* welfare reforms, 194, 264, 284, 285; AFDC, 77; costs, 127; Family Assistance Plan, 57, 58; Family Support Act, 3, 75; H.R. *4,* 264, 283, 284, 285; Job Opportunities and Basic Skills Training Program, 77; past efforts, 70, 119; paternalism and, 119; PRWORA, 343; Work Incentives Program, 56; WORK program, 234, 243

Empower America, 237

End of Equality, The (Kaus), 248

Engler, John, 258, 266, 267, 268, 292, 301

Ensign, John, 277

Entitlement programs: *1996* welfare reforms, 328; AFDC, 16–20, 101, 183, 203, 284, 303, 304, 313, 317, 328; Budget Enforcement Act, 226–27; Clinton welfare reform proposals, 245; devolution, 122; Food Stamps, 284; government expenditures, 16–17; H.R. *4,* 263; JOBS program, 77; predictability, 17; public opinion, 183, 185t; Reagan reforms, 72; removal of benefits, 17; service programs, 114

Ethics. *See* Morality and ethical issues; Values

Executive branch, 141, 218, 229

Faircloth, Lauch: conservatism, 299; deterrence of teen mothers, 312; devolution, 306, 309; filibuster threat, 304, 313. *See also* Talent-Faircloth bill

Families: benefits for working poor, 100, 125, 156; breakup, 55, 57; Clinton proposals for working poor, 240; health care issues, 229, 230; income guarantees, 58; income needs, 12–13; interest and advocacy groups, 211; marriage, 57, 115, 148, 150; paternal obligations, 70, 71, 72, 76; poll results, 178–80; PRWORA, 330–34; reports,

199; sanctions, 118, 119; single-parent, 11, 45, 48–49, 55, 62, 77, 78, 146; two-parent, 11, 56, 62, 107; welfare reform initiatives, 91–92; work issues, 163. *See also* Children; Earned Income Tax Credit; Employment issues; Women's issues
Family caps: child advocacy groups, 203; Clinton welfare proposals, 239, 245; conservative groups, 215; effects, 152, 153, 161; goals, 350; H.R. *4*, 283; national poll, 214–15; public opinion, 178, 179t, 191; right-to-life groups, 247; in welfare debate, 3
Family Assistance Plan (FAP): failure, 54; focus, 3; funding, 58–59; income guarantee, 58; negative income tax, 360; policy streams, 85; presidential support, 85; work requirements, 58
Family Research Council, 211, 212, 214–15, 304
Family Support Act of *1988* (FSA): background, 70–72, 92; benefits for two-parent families, 19–20, 107; changes in AFDC policy, 20, 72–77, 78; children's issues, 76–77, 93–94, 107, 244; compromises, 76, 93, 145; Congress, 72–76, 90; costs, 51, 74, 76; focus, 3, 77, 357; lessons, 92–92, 98; policy formulation, 72–76; policy streams, 85; presidential support, 85; state issues, 102, 130, 144; teenage mothers, 239; traps, 78, 362; unemployed parents, 77–78; use of policy research, 144–45; welfare-to-work programs, 102, 144, 145, 158
Federalism: New Federalism, 3, 54, 68–69, 100; welfare policies, 27–28, 29, 322. *See also* Trap, federalism
Florida, 230, 258, 291, 351
Focus on the Family, 211, 212
Food Research and Action Center, 201
Food Stamps Program: AFDC, 14, 19; Balanced Budget Act of *1997*, 337; agriculture committees and, 73; block grants, 201, 306, 308, 365; low-income

families, 13–14; New Federalism, 54, 69, 70; Program for Better Jobs and Incomes, 63; PRWORA, 335; purchase requirement, 66; spending on, 226; state responsibilities, 69, 306; welfare reform, 61, 284
Ford Foundation, 201
Ford administration: EITC, 79; negative income tax proposal, 60
Ford, Harold, 73, 231–32, 284
Friedman, Milton, 57
From, Al, 206–07
FSA. *See* Family Support Act of *1988*
Funchess, Kitty, 9–10

GAIN. *See* Greater Avenues to Independence
Galston, William, 207
General Accounting Office (GAO), 140, 158, 348, 349
Gibbons, Sam, 231, 252
Gilmour, John, 37, 42
Gingrich, Newt: abortion, 261, 263; Contract with America, 252, 380; Dole and, 323; orphanages, 275–76; school lunches, 289; school prayer, 263; welfare reform, 94, 152, 171, 268, 269–70, 356. *See also* Contract with America; Republican Party
Gore, Al, 81, 233, 241, 328
Government, federal: AFDC, 17, 18, 20, 22, 68; divided, 27, 365, 367; as employer of last resort, 116; responsibility to the poor, 66; welfare benefits, 60
Government, state. *See* States
Governors. *See* Republican Party; States
Gramm, Phil: block grant allocations, 305; conservative mandates, 309; devolution, 306; filibuster threat, 313; presidential politics, 323, 374; welfare reform legislation, 299, 304
Gramm-Rudman-Hollings Act of *1985*, 72, 76, 225
Grants, block: AFDC, 203, 207, 210, 263–64, 268–69; child protection

funds, 286; effects, 339; Food Stamps, 201, 284–85, 308; foster care programs, 317; governors, 302; proposals, 90, 122, 268; school lunches, 287, 289, 317, 320; Senate Republican view, 294–95, 301; Work First program, 307. *See also* Temporary Assistance for Needy Families

Grassroots support, 205, 215, 220

Greater Avenues to Independence (GAIN, Calif.), 158–59

Greenberg, Mark, 201–02

Greenstein, Robert, 199, 200

Greenwood, Jim, 291

Haskins, Ron, 99

Health and Human Services, Department of (HHS): AFDC programs, 17; Clinton administration welfare task force, 234, 235; provision of statistics, 140; welfare reform, 229, 242, 271–72, 311, 329, 335–36; welfare waivers, 1, 131, 259–60

Health, Education, and Welfare, Department of (HEW), 61, 95

Health care and insurance issues; Carter administration, 62; Clinton reforms, 128, 228–30, 241, 249, 270–71; failure, 27; politics, 37; universal, 116; welfare reform and, 73, 125

Heclo, Hugh, 116

Heritage Foundation, 105, 143, 213, 237

HHS. *See* Health and Human Services, Department of

Hispanic Caucus, 231, 247

Hispanics, 11, 343, 361

House of Representatives: Agriculture Committee, 276, 287; Carter welfare reform, 65–66; child advocacy groups, 201; Clinton welfare reform, 247; Contract with America, 254–55; discharge petitions, 236–37; Economic and Educational Opportunities Committee, 276, 287; Family Assistance Plan, 54, 59; Family Support

Act, 72–74, 76; H.R. *4*, 254, 276–93, 318; H.R. *3500*, 236–37, 261; Human Resources Subcommittee, 231–32; New Federalism, 69–70; policy and political objectives, 260–65; Rules Committee, 287, 290. *See also* Congress

House Republican Conference, 262

House Ways and Means Committee: *1996* welfare reforms, 276–77, 285–86, 287; bottlenecks, 229; Clinton welfare proposals, 248; hearings, 141, 142; partisanship, 232

Howard, Christopher, 79–80

H.R. *4*. *See* Personal Responsibility Act

Hutchinson, Kay Bailey, 305

Hutchinson, Tim, 261–62, 268

ICMA. *See* International City/County Management Association

Idaho, 344, 347

Immigration issues: benefits and services, 230–31; Clinton welfare reform proposals, 245–46; employment, 155; H.R. *4*, 291; illegal, 230; Jewish groups, 231; PRWORA, 335, 336; sponsors, 230–31, 245–46; welfare reform, 132, 228, 264, 337

Incentives and disincentives: *1990s* welfare reforms, 107, 111, 118, 120–21, 150–51, 156–57; AFDC, 21, 48, 76–77, 83, 101, 104, 158; EITC, 83–84; Family Assistance Plan, 59; Family Support Act, 76; policy research and, 149; Program for Betters Jobs and Incomes, 63; Work Incentives Program, 56

Income and earnings: earnings disregards, 21, 54, 68, 70, 77, 101, 107, 259, 329; guaranteed, 25, 57, 60, 62, 66, 79, 90; income notches, 57, 59, 61, 63; minimum wage, 62, 63, 80, 81, 83, 84, 111, 125, 225, 337; off the books, 157; welfare-to-work, 351; working mothers, 104, 351. *See also* Earned Income Tax Credit

Indexing to inflation, 19, 28

Indiana, 347
Interest and advocacy groups: *501*(c)(*4*) organizations, 198, 202; abortion issues, 218, 220, 256, 285, 290; children, 196, 199–205, 216, 220, 246, 295, 302–03, 315, 327; coalitions, 198, 214, 218, 221; effects, 217–21; congressional testimony, 141; Democratic Party, 206–07; elections of *1994*, 217; funding, 197–98; intergovernmental, 207–11; lobbying activities, 198; mobilization, 31; in policy formulation, 197–99, 217, 218, 219; politicians and, 219; power, 218–19; representing state and local officials, 197; Republican Party, 256; resources, 204t, 219; social conservative groups, 211–17; social science techniques, 143–44; techniques, 198, 202, 220; welfare reform, 26–27, 91–92, 171, 197, 207–11, 217–21, 319, 367; welfare rights, 26, 196–97
International City/County Management Association (ICMA), 208

Jackson, Jesse, 270
Job Opportunities and Basic Skills Training Program (JOBS): Family Support Act, 107; funding, 77; participation rate, 101; policy research, 154; state participation, 102; welfare dependency, 104; welfare reform, 302, 309, 328
Johnson, Lyndon, 56
Johnson, Nancy, 261, 262, 265, 287

Kaiser Family Foundation, 172
Kamarck, Elaine, 207
Kansas, 349
Kantor, Mickey, 328
Kaus, Mickey, 248–49
Kerner Commission on Civil Disorders, 57
Kerrey-Danforth Commission, 200
Kingdon, John, 35, 36, 103, 136, 355

Labor issues: Clinton welfare proposals, 225, 247; minimum wage, 337; unions, 68, 197, 205; WORK program, 243. *See also* Employment issues
Labor, Department of (DOL), 61, 95
Legal issues, 18, 22, 55. *See also* Courts
Legislation, 93: bundling, 363–64; Clinton welfare proposals, 247; H.R. *3500*, 236–37, 261, 262–63; legislative process, 363; overturning court decisions, 364. *See also* Policymaking; *individual acts and plans*
LaHaye, Beverly, 211
LaHaye, Tim, 211
Lein, Laura, 157
Liberals and liberalism: AFDC, 71–72; criticism of Clinton, 220; devolution, 122, 123; EITC, 80; Family Assistance Plan, 58; Family Support Act, 76; interest and advocacy groups, 216, 217, 225; new paternalism, 119; out-of-wedlock birthrates, 149, 150–51, 152; prevention and rehabilitation approach, 111–15; Program for Better Jobs and Incomes, 63, 64, 65; state welfare discretion, 50; time limits on benefits, 239; welfare reform, 61, 87, 90, 101, 106, 164–65, 225–26; welfare-to-work, 157, 160, 164. *See also* Democratic Party; Political issues
Long, Russell: Carter welfare reform initiative, 64, 65; control of legislation, 59, 65, 90; EITC, 79; guaranteed income, 90; replacement of AFDC, 60; work issues, 62, 63, 105–06
Los Angeles Times, 230
Losing Ground (Murray), 111, 120, 135, 156
Louisiana, 348
Luntz, Frank, 276

MacArthur Foundation, 199
Maine, 347
Mandate for Change (Democratic Leadership Council), 206, 207

Manpower Demonstration Research Corporation (MDRC), 140, 144, 159, 351, 358

Marshall, Will, 222

Massachusetts, 9, 305

Matsui, Robert, 327

Mayhew, David, 365

MDRC. *See* Manpower Demonstration Research Corporation

Mead, Lawrence, 117, 118, 119, 124, 156, 358

Means- and asset-tested programs, 13, 15f, 28. *See also* Aid to Families with Dependent Children; Earned Income Tax Credit; Food Stamps Program; Medicaid; Supplemental Security Income; Temporary Assistance to Needy Families

Media: child advocacy groups and, 205, 327; Contract with America, 299; and public opinion, 194; welfare, 105, 135–36;

Medicaid: AFDC and, 3, 19, 21, 54, 68–69, 77, 78, 107, 230; block grant proposal, 365; changes, 321; conversion to block grant, 305; costs, 62; coverage of children, 352; Family Assistance Plan, 59; Family Support Act, 107; income notches, 59, 61, 62; labor unions, 205; low-income families, 14; move from welfare to work, 116, 156, 228–29; New Federalism, 54; Program for Better Jobs and Incomes, 62; as a welfare program, 105; welfare reforms, 321, 322, 326, 345, 381–82

Medicare, 16, 116, 205, 226

Michigan, 10, 132, 258, 305, 346–47, 349

Mikulski, Barbara, 306

Miller, Gerald, 268

Mills, Wilbur, 59

Mink, Patsy, 288

Mississippi, 19, 346

Missouri, 347

Mondale, Walter, 206

Morality and ethical issues: *1996* welfare reform, 315; AFDC payments to unwed mothers, 121; family caps, 239; policymaking, 21; Reagan administration, 70; social conservative groups, 212; state concerns, 18; teenage pregnancy, 151; unreported income, 104. *See also* Values

Morris, Dick, 324, 328

Moynihan, Daniel Patrick: AFDC, 56, 301, 303; Clinton administration and, 98–99, 300; costs of welfare reform, 238, 240; Family Assistance Plan, 60; Family Support Act, 232, 300; Finance Committee, 61, 232, 294; health care reform, 232; negative income tax, 58; out-of-wedlock births, 103; poverty and family structure, 11; view of Senate Finance Committee, 59; welfare reform, 2, 74–75, 92, 93, 98–99, 222, 232, 300, 307, 313, 358, 363; working mothers, 70; work requirements, 190–91

Murray, Charles; AFDC, 104; deterrence, 124, 212; out-of-wedlock births, 150–51; role in change, 358; social philosophy, 123; welfare dependency, 70; white illegitimacy rate, 103. *See also* *Losing Ground*

National Association of Counties (NACo), 197, 208, 319

National Center for Health Statistics, 140

National Conference of State Legislatures (NCSL), 197, 209, 210

National Governor's Association (NGA): *1987–88* welfare reform, 267; *1994* welfare reform, 127, 211; *1996* welfare reform, 319, 324, 340, 367; Family Support Act, 207-08; bipartisanship, 267; immobilization, 217; officers, 210; policy positions, 209; supermajority decision rules, 218–19, 267; task force on welfare reform, 262

National Governor's Conference, 60

National Journal, 140

National League of Cities (NLC), 197, 208, 319

National Organization of Women (NOW), 203

National Review, 104

National Right to Life Committee, 213, 215, 265

National Welfare Rights Organization, 55-56, 59, 63, 197

NCSL. *See* National Conference of State Legislatures

Negative income tax (NIT). *See* Family Assistance Plan; Taxation issues

New Democrats. *See* Democratic Party

New Jersey: family caps, 152, 203, 214; welfare reform, 132, 258, 347

New Mexico, 343

New Republic, 238

Newsweek, 275

New York State: maximum family benefit, 19; welfare offices, 348–49; welfare reform, 305, 321

New York Times, 140, 318

NGA. *See* National Governor's Association

Nixon, Richard, 56, 58, 220. *See also* Family Assistance Plan

Nixon administration: federal welfare spending, 58; negative income tax plan, 58, 60; welfare reform, 90, 101, 357, 362, 363

NLC. *See* National League of Cities

Nutrition, 13–14. *See also* Food Stamp Program

Oakland Tribune, 9

OBRA. *See* Omnibus Budget Reconciliation Act of *1981*

Office of Management and Budget (OMB), 140, 200, 229, 242

Offner, Paul, 238

Old Age Assistance program, 16

Old Age Insurance, 16, 20, 116

Omnibus Budget Reconciliation Act of *1981* (OBRA), 54, 68, 90

O'Neill, Tip, 64

Oregon, 346

Orphanages. *See* Children

Packwood, Bob, 294-96, 301, 302, 303, 305, 311

Panetta, Leon, 242, 289, 328

Paternalism. *See* Welfare reform

PBJI. *See* Program for Better Jobs and Incomes

Penalties. *See* Employment issues

Personal Responsibility Act (H.R. 4). *See* Contract with America; Welfare reform, *1996*

Personal Responsibility and Work Opportunity Reconciliation Act of *1996* (PRWORA): abolition of AFDC, 1; caseload declines, 343–44; children, 344; incentive structures, 342–343; limits, 161, 346; political issues, 344; provisions, 328–35; race to the bottom, 347; Republican coalitions, 167; state program design, 344–47; work requirements, 344, 345–46. *See also* Welfare reform, *1996*

Petri, Mary Ann, 9, 10

Policymaking: changes, 24; contextual forces in welfare reform politics, 24–29, 44, 366, 368–73, 383; Contract with America, 284–85; bottlenecks, 229; divided government, 27; evaluation research, 151–53; federal courts, 17–18; feedbacks and past policy choices, 28–29, 44, 91; hand-tying, 38, 40–41; inclusion in other legislation, 73–74; incremental, 92, 96; indicators, 136, 139, 146–49; "killer amendments," 311; mechanisms and strategies, 12, 29–43; moral hazard, 21–22; movement from status quo, 43; policy paradigms, 25; policy streams, 35, 85, 124, 356, 358; political choices, 29–43, 228, 232–37, 250–51, 374–75; positional strategies, 37–43, 45; 382–85; public opinion, 170; relational bargaining, 8; repositioning, 37–40, 293, 375–82; secrecy, 227; stalemate, 25, 39; strategic pursuit and disagreement, 7–8, 39, 41–42, 52, 65, 76, 375, 384; traps, 24, 43–51, 91–99,

100, 128; triangulation, 7, 38, 41, 324, 380; welfare reform, 194–95. *See also* Decisionmaking; Interest and advocacy groups; Policy research; Welfare reform, *1994*; Welfare reform, *1996*

Policy research: boom in, 140–43; Clinton welfare proposals, 250; contested, 166–67; effects, 167–68, 357, 358, 383; evaluatory, 158–60; explanatory, 155–57; information types, 136–39; lacking, 162–63; negative lessons, 163; out-of-wedlock pregnancy, 151–53, 167; program entry, 145–53; social sciences, 25–26, 44; sources, 140, 141; use and limitations, 137–39, 143–45, 160–62, 358, 367; welfare-to-work, 153–55

Political issues: AFDC, 22, 24–25, 28, 86–87, 105, 196–97; blame or credit, 31, 37, 40, 41, 76, 90, 274, 293, 323–24, 382; budget reconciliation, 257–58; children, 80, 191, 194, 196; Clinton welfare reform proposals, 127–28, 246–48; constituencies, 28, 30, 37, 40; culture, 24; EITC, 81, 83–84, 100; economic growth, 79; fragmentation of political institutions, 27–28; guaranteed income, 66; interest and advocacy groups, 209, 219, 221; learning, 91–99; manipulating agendas, 35–37; political streams, 356; presidential leadership, 40, 85–86, 97, 173–74; public opinion, 188; resources of the poor, 26; state innovations and waivers, 258, 260; strategic repositioning, 375–82; taxes, 80; trade-offs, 30–32, 33–34, 42–43; zones of acceptable outcomes, 24, 34–35, 37, 40, 41, 42, 43, 93, 121, 289, 382–83. *See also* Policymaking

Political issues, welfare reform: *1969–88*, 87, 90; *1990*s, 126–33, 162–63, 170; *1994*, 223–28, 232–37, 239, 243–44; *1996*, 254–55, 268, 286, 292–93, 313–15; AFDC, 80; agenda change, 103–06, 355–59; bipartisanship, 324;

block grants, 268; Clinton commitment to welfare reform, 374; commitments and research, 165–66; conservative approaches, 6, 86-87, 104–05; contextual forces in welfare reform, 24–29, 368–73; costs and funding, 241–42; EITC, 80; health care reform, 229–30; income guarantees and supplements, 57; interest and advocacy groups, 203–04, 207, 217–21; learning, 91–99; liberal approaches, 150–51; magnet effects, 27–28, 50; polarization, 44, 254, 356; policymaking traps, 43–52, 86–90; positional bargaining, 376–84; previous commitments, 97–98; public opinion, 190; Reagan administration, 67, 72–73, 115; support, 29, 67, 85, 169–70; traps, 362; voter score cards, 215; waivers, 132–33; War on Poverty, 115; zones of acceptable outcomes, 254, 289, 383

Political parties, 6, 30, 37, 189, 254. *See also* Democratic Party; Republican Party

Politics and the Professors (Aaron), 162

Polls and polling: *104*th Congress, 247; *1996* elections, 325, 381–82, 384; Contract with the American Family, 220; family caps, 214–15; orphanages, 276; polling organizations, 176; PRWORA, 336, 338; question formulation, 172, 175, 177, 183, 186, 214; welfare reform, 225, 254. *See also* Public opinion

Poor Support (Ellwood), 125–26, 133, 356

Poverty: *1996* welfare reform, 312, 314–15, 327; AFDC plus Food Stamps, 19; causes, 126; children, 11, 312, 313, 319, 327; culture of, 117–18; effectiveness of welfare, 117–20; families, 5, 10-11, 159, 163; hopes to change 124; poll results, 177, 178; poverty line, 63, 68; public opinion, 175, 188; teen mothers, 238. *See also* Families; Medicaid

Primus, Wendell, 99, 234–35, 335–36
Program for Better Jobs and Incomes
   (PBJI), 3, 54, 60-62, 63
Progressive Policy Institute (PPI), 197,
   206, 207
PRWORA. *See* Personal Responsibility
   and Work Opportunity Reconciliation
   Act of *1996*
Public Interest, 104, 140, 164
Public opinion: AFDC, 6, 20–21, 22, 45,
   51, 126, 170, 366, 383; causes of
   poverty and welfare dependence,
   175–77, 194; Clinton welfare reform
   agenda, 224; Clinton versus Bush, 129;
   conservative views of welfare, 161; elite
   convergence hypothesis, 170; elite
   priming, 171–72; guaranteed income,
   57; importance of work, 70–71;
   orphanages, 276; political blame or
   credit, 31, 34, 318–19; politicians and
   parties, 30, 35, 170–71; shifts in, 25; use
   of policy research, 144; welfare and
   welfare recipients, 9, 25, 124, 169–70,
   172–75, 186. *See also* Polls and polling
Public opinion, welfare reform, 177–95,
   366–67; changing agendas, 29; Clinton
   welfare proposals, 249–50; mandates,
   6; policy change and, 169–71, 126–33,
   162; PRWORA, 336, 338; Republican
   Party, 262; role in political culture,
   24–26
Public Service Employment Program,
   119

Racial and minority issues: AFDC
   recipients, 4, 26, 28, 45, 48, 357, 360;
   employment, 155; negative income tax,
   57; TANF, 343; welfare policy, 26–27;
   white out-of-wedlock births, 11. *See
   also* African Americans; Hispanics;
   Social structures
RAND Corporation, 143
Rangel, Charles, 284
Reagan, Ronald: agenda, 71; changes in
   AFDC, 54; conservatism, 104;
   reconciliation process, 339; shrinking

of government, 69. *See also* Family
   Support Act; Federalism
Reagan administration: AFDC cutbacks,
   20, 66, 67, 103–04; agenda, 66–67, 69,
   70, 71; Budget Reform and Impound-
   ment Control Act, 67; budget requests,
   67; CETA, 194; veto threats, 72, 75, 76;
   waivers, 72, 131; welfare reform, 21, 54,
   67, 90, 92, 107, 357, 363. *See also*
   Family Support Act
Real Welfare Reform Act of *1994*, 237
Rector, Robert, 105, 213, 214, 216, 237,
   256, 266, 284
Reed, Bruce, 128, 206, 233, 234–35, 271,
   328
Reed, Ralph, 211–12, 220
Reich, Robert, 200
Reid, Harry, 241
Religious right. *See* Conservatives and
   conservatism
Republican Caucus, 254, 291, 304
Republican Governors' Association, 219,
   267
Republican Party: *1994* elections, 26;
   1996 elections, 325–26; AFDC, 171;
   agenda, 253; block grants, 339; budget
   issues, 305; Clinton veto threat,
   286–87; Clinton welfare reforms, 246,
   253; conservative interest groups, 6,
   216; costs of welfare, 105–06;
   deterrence, 121, 124, 216, 253, 256;
   devolution, 122–23, 256, 322;
   governors, 216, 217, 265–70; gridlock
   and governance, 290; interest and
   advocacy groups, 205, 217, 225; limits,
   322; minimum wage, 84; National
   Governors' Association, 211; policy
   research, 168; pro-life constituency,
   256; public opinion, 187, 188, 192;
   Reagan programs, 67, 73, 74; strategic
   disagreement with Clinton, 7–8, 375;
   work requirements, 101, 165, 253;
   zones of acceptable outcomes, 383. *See
   also* Coalitions
Republican Party, welfare reform: *103*d
   Congress, 130; Carter administration,

65; Clinton administration, 32, 188, 365, 367; Clinton welfare reform, 235–36; consensus, 25; conservatism, 6, 27; Contract with America, 98; enactment, 96, 364–75; Family Support Act, 93, 99; H.R. *3500,* 236–37; polls, 186, 325; state innovation, 258–59. *See also* Congress, *104*th; Contract with America; Personal Responsibility Act; Personal Responsibility and Work Opportunity Reconciliation Act

Rhode Island, 343, 346–47
Ribicoff, Abraham, 60
Rich, Andrew, 143
Robertson, Pat, 211
Rockefeller Institute of Government, 348, 349
Roosevelt, Franklin, 16
Roosevelt (Franklin) administration, 18
Rostenkowski, Dan, 73, 231
Rubin, Robert E., 328

Sanctions. *See* Families; Temporary Assistance for Needy Families
Santorum, Rick, 262
Sawhill, Isabel, 235
Schlafly, Phyllis, 211
Schick, Allen, 135, 136
Schools: lunch programs, 14, 306, 317, 320; prayer in, 215, 263
Schorr, Lisbeth, 114
Senate: *1996* welfare reforms, 254, 289, 294–315; bipartisanship, 255, 295; blocking change, 52, 232; budget reconciliation, 297–98; child advocacy groups, 201; Clinton welfare reform, 232; committees, 296–97, 308; Democrats, 297–87, 300–301; coalitions, 295; conservative interest groups, 216; Contract with America, 254–55; debate in, 296–97; Earned Income Tax Credit, 81; energy taxes, 81; Family Assistance Plan, 54, 59, 60; Family Support Act, 74–75, 92; Finance Committee hearings, 141, 142, 294; political issues, 296–300; Program for

Better Jobs and Incomes, 65; Reagan welfare reform, 74–75; welfare reform, 65, 67, 229, 232, 296, 303, 308. *See also* Congress

Shalala, Donna, 202, 233–34, 276, 283, 312, 328, 336
Sharpton, Al, 232
Shaw, Clay, 261, 265, 284, 286–87, 318, 323
Sheldon, Louis, 211
Skocpol, Theda, 124
Social issues: Law of Unintended Rewards, 111; out-of-wedlock births, 104; policy feedbacks and, 44; race, ethnicity, and class, 26–27; teenage pregnancy, 149; welfare system, 249–50; work, 118. *See also* Abortions; Conservatives and conservatism
Social Security Act of *1935*: *1962* amendments, 56, 131; adequacy of payments, 18; AFDC, 16, 56; minimum standards, 18
Social Security Act of *1972,* 60
Social Security: as entitlement, 16; Reagan administration, 67; as social insurance, 12; spending on, 226; survivors benefits, 14, 20; as targeting within universalism, 115–16
Social sciences, 25–26, 44
Social services, 18, 114–15, 212–13
Social Service Amendments of *1962,* 114
Southern states: AFDC, 17, 26, 73; benefit levels, 69; Family Assistance Plan, 59; family caps, 345; resistance to public assistance, 18; Southern Democrats, 206; welfare reforms, 273, 347
Special Supplemental Feeding Program for Women, Infants and Children (WIC), 14, 92
SSI. *See* Supplemental Security Income
States: *1994* elections, 258, 260; alternatives to AFDC, 75; benefits, 230, 259; budgets, 50, 87, 132, 321–22; caseloads, 343, 349, 350; devolution, 122; earnings disregards, 259; emergency assistance to, 246; experimentation and

innovation, 130–33, 161, 162, 212, 245, 258–60, 374; Family Assistance Program, 58, 60; family caps, 1, 153, 161, 259; Family Support Act, 102, 130; governors, 28, 69, 71, 72, 75, 77, 135, 216, 374; guaranteed income programs, 58, 66; magnet states and race to the bottom, 27–28, 50, 122, 132, 264, 335, 344, 347; mothers' and widows' pensions, 16; needs standards, 19; policy discretion, 100; Program for Better Jobs and Incomes, 62, 63; rules and requirements, 77; sanctions, 349; training and work programs, 72, 75, 77; waivers, 1, 131–33, 153, 258, 259, 322, 324, 345; welfare benefits, 87; welfare offices, 128, 348–50; welfare-to-work programs, 119, 120, 348–49; welfare reform, 131–33, 216

States, AFDC programs: AFDC-UP, 19–20, 56, 71; benefits, 14, 49, 55, 73; changes in, 1, 28–29; compromises, 100; constitutional issues, 17–18; JOBS program, 77; local conditions, 49–50; Reagan reforms, 68–69, 71, 75; rules and obligations, 49, 55, 56, 71–72, 75; state discretion, 27–28; workfare, 78, 159. See also Medicaid; Southern states

States, welfare reform, 1994: children's issues, 244–45; costs and funding, 246; family caps, 245; immigration, 231; teenage pregnancy, 245; welfare-to-work programs, 242–44

States, welfare reform, 1996: abortion, 285; AFDC, 268, 328, 329, 342; Balanced Budget Act of 1997, 337; devolution, 253; block grants, 266, 268–69, 283, 292, 295, 302, 305, 306, 320, 322, 328–29, 337; budget issues, 321, 335; children's issues, 305, 321; deterrence, 346; entitlements, 322, 328; exemptions, 161; family caps, 218, 283, 317, 320, 321, 345; Food Stamps, 306, 312; funding and costs, 283, 292, 295, 305, 321, 328–29; governors, 256–57, 258, 265–66, 292, 321–24; H.R. 4,

263–64; immigrants, 283, 345; limits, 320, 335, 346–47, 350; maintenance of effort, 312, 317; out-of-wedlock births, 218, 285, 287–88, 312, 320; PRWORA, 344–47; state issues, 265–70, 305, 320, 344–47; SSI access, 283; teenage mothers, 218, 283, 320, 345; time limits, 283, 302; work issues, 264, 285, 302, 311, 312, 317, 320, 321, 329, 337, 345–46, 348–49. See also Personal Responsibility and Work Opportunity Reconciliation Act; Temporary Assistance for Needy Families

Steiner, Gilbert, 196

Stephanopoulos, George, 297

Stockman, David, 66, 69

Supplemental Security Income (SSI): Clinton reform proposals, 246; H.R. 4, 286, 317–18; immigrants, 231; low-income families, 13; PRWORA, 335

Szabrowicz, Sandi, 9, 10

Talent-Faircloth bill, 237, 263, 380

Talent, James, 237, 261–62, 263, 268, 380

TANF. See Temporary Assistance for Needy Families

Taxation issues: 501(c)(4) organizations, 198, 202; charity deductions, 198; Contract with America, 257; credits, 13, 337; cuts, 216, 257, 264, 271, 274, 299; energy, 80; excise, 69; exemptions and deductions, 12–13, 14, 28; on gambling, 241; incentives and disincentives, 59; increases, 51, 183, 226, 227, 238, 241; interest and advocacy groups, 198; Internal Revenue Code, 14, 198; negative income tax, 57, 85, 360. See also Earned Income Tax Credit; Family Assistance Plan

Teenage pregnancy: AFDC, 147; benefits for, 191; Clinton administration reform proposals, 238, 239–40, 245; conservative and liberal views, 114, 147, 149, 213; deterrence, 120, 213; evaluation research, 163; executive orders, 324; H.R. 4, 264, 283; numbers

and trends, 146, 148, 351; public
opinion, 179–80, 191. *See also* Births,
out-of-wedlock

Teles, Steven M., 131

Temporary Assistance for Needy Families
(TANF): *1996* welfare reforms, 328–29;
AFDC, 328; changes to, 336–37;
children recipients, 10, 352; debates,
336; establishment, 1; incentives, 343;
Medicaid, 352; means and asset testing,
13; number of recipients, 343; political
issues, 336–37, 354; sanctions, 342–43,
349; Social Security, 12; state programs, 345. *See also* Aid to Families
with Dependent Children

Texas, 230, 305, 346

Think tanks, 140, 142, 143, 164, 198, 237

Thompson, Tommy; *1996* welfare
reforms, 301; National Governors'
Association proposals, 267, 322;
presidential politics, 292; welfare
proposal, 324; Wisconsin welfare
reforms, 132, 258-59; work issues, 119

Transitional Employment Assistance
(TEA), 306

Traditional Values Coalition, 211, 214,
304, 307–08, 309

Trap, dual clientele: AFDC, 4–5, 45–46,
48, 66, 71, 81; block grants, 268–69;
child advocacy groups, 204; Clinton
administration, 224, 239, 290, 374;
definition, 359; deterrence, 121; EITC,
81; failure of welfare reform, 86-87, 88,
359–61; Family Assistance Plan, 58;
Family Support Act, 78, 93; H.R. *4*,
264, 283; policy research, 164;
PRWORA, 339; weakening of, 105, 119,
122, 214; welfare reform, 52, 119, 274,
275, 319, 367

Trap, federalism: AFDC, 50; block grants,
269, 294–95; Clinton preference for
state flexibility, 374; Contract with
America welfare bill, 265–66;
definition, 362–63; devolution, 123;
failure of welfare reform, 363; H.R. *4*,
290; state innovation, 374; weakening

of, 52; welfare reform, 47, 49–50, 87,
89, 119

Trap, money: AFDC, 4; benefits for
immigrants, 231; Budget Enforcement
Act, 226; Carter administration, 61;
Clinton administration, 224;
definition, 361; EITC, 82, 83; Family
Assistance Plan, 58; Family Support
Act, 78; H.R. *4*, 283, 290; universalism,
117; weakening of, 52; welfare reform,
47, 87, 114-15, 119, 145, 361

Trap, perverse incentives: Carter
administration proposals, 63;
definition, 361–62; ETIC, 81, 82, 83;
Family Assistance Plan, 59; Family
Support Act, 78; H.R. *4*, 285; negative
income tax, 57; Republican policy
preferences, 374–75; welfare reform,
46, 87, 111, 361–62

Traps, policymaking: AFDC, 82;
avoidance, 91–99; context, 44–45,
88–89; effects, 4, 359; public opinion,
190, 367; specific welfare reform
approaches, 111–12, 253. *See also*
Welfare reform; *individual traps*

Ullman, Al, 63, 64, 79

Unemployment insurance, 12, 16, 17

Unions. *See* Labor issues

Universalism. *See* Welfare reform

Urban Institute, 94–95, 140, 327

Urban issues, 56, 115, 155, 343

USCM. *See* U.S. Conference of Mayors

U.S. Catholic Conference, 319

U.S. Conference of Mayors (USCM), 208,
319

Values: Clinton welfare proposals, 128,
234; core American, 21, 44; dual
clientele trap, 360; out-of-wedlock
births, 152; policy research, 164–65;
sense of responsibility, 49; welfare, 174,
175; work ethic, 25, 26, 58, 128

Vasiloff, Jennifer, 205

Vermont, 347

Virginia, 350
Voinovich, George, 292, 304
Voters: *1994* elections, 253–54; interest and advocacy groups, 220; voter guides, 198, 215, 322; knowledge of party stance, 37. *See also* Public opinion

Waivers, 1, 72, 131–33, 153, 364. *See also* States
Wall Street Journal, 103, 254
War on Poverty, 115
Warren, Earl, 18. *See also* Courts
Washington Post, 135, 140, 315
Washington Research Project Action Council, 202
Way, Kathi, 235
Weaver, Kent, 143
Weld, William, 258, 267
Welfare: benefits, 26, 125–26, 149; caseloads, 25, 68; as child abuse, 274; costs, 105–06; dependency, 70, 118, 126, 153–54, 194, 346; fraud, 135; included programs, 105–06; limits, 351; reasons, 10; recipient behavior, 350–52, 357–58, 361; rules, 55; welfare offices, 347–50; work participation, 156–60. *See also* Incentives and disincentives; *individual programs*
Welfare reform: *1970s*, 25; *1990s*, 106–34, 161, 163, 170, 191, 194; agenda, 3–4, 26, 85–86, 357–59, 363, 367, 382; coalitions, 53; costs, 51, 73, 74, 87, 105, 124–25; devolution, 122–23, 125, 362; failure and success, 26, 27, 28–29, 51–52, 94, 97, 313–15; family caps, 152–53; history, 2, 3, 54, 60–61; incentives, 107, 111; interest and advocacy groups, 198, 207, 210, 213, 216–17; issues, 2, 3–5, 26, 106, 212; lessons and patterns, 84–99; paternalism, 117–20, 124, 181, 191, 335, 346, 362; policy stream, 106–26, 356, 358; political issues, 36–37, 359–64; poll results, 176, 178; proposals, 106–07; prevention and

rehabilitation, 111–15, 152, 181; racial issues, 360–61; Reagan administration, 70–78; state role, 183, 185; time limits, 161, 183–85; universalism, 115–17, 124; work-oriented, 70, 128
Welfare reform, *1994*, 222–23; budget issues, 226–28; failure, 194–95, 246–51, 359; final proposal, 242–48; interest and advocacy groups, 198–99, 200, 225; money trap, 361; policy choices, 232–42; political environment, 223–28, 230–32, 356; program phase-in, 227–30. *See also* Clinton, Bill
Welfare reform, *1996*: amendments to legislation, 287–88; block grants, 263–64, 268, 284–85, 286, 301, 302, 304, 305, 306, 308–09, 317, 320; budget issues, 297–98, 303, 305, 308, 318, 320, 322–23, 336–37; children's issues, 203–04, 283, 302, 305, 309, 312, 313, 319, 326–27, 329, 335; Clinton administration, 171, 270–73, 292–93, 300–301; coalitions, 303–13, 316; comparison of House and Senate provisions, 302–03, 317–28; contextual arguments, 368–73; Deal bill, 288, 289, 293, 306; Democrats, 297–98, 306–07, 309, 311, 312, 381; deterrence, 317, 318, 329; economic factors, 283; enactment, 364–85; entitlements, 277, 283, 317, 322; evolution, 278–82, 337–41; family caps, 161, 218, 302, 312, 317, 320, 329; Food Stamps, 306, 308, 326; governors, 256–57, 258, 265–66, 292, 301–02, 304, 310, 321–24, 340, 359; House, 274–93; interest and advocacy groups, 220–21; limits, 161, 191, 317, 320, 329, 335; long-term prognosis, 352–53; Medicaid, 322, 325, 326, 341; out-of-wedlock births, 287, 304, 311, 312, 313, 320, 329; political issues, 171–72, 190, 292, 300–01, 304, 313–15, 317–28, 340; political learning, 101; positional bargaining, 376–82; presidential politics, 298–300, 323, 328, 340, 374; public opinion, 169–95, 336,

338; reconciliation and final legislation, 191, 316–35, 339–40; Republican issues, 171, 194, 307–09, 340; Senate, 294–315; state issues, 283, 312, 317; success, 4, 23–24, 26, 27, 28, 29, 289–93, 364–82, 385; teenage mothers, 161, 218, 302, 317, 329; traps, 290, 319, 339, 340–41, 362, 363; vetoes, 320; Work First program, 306–07; work issues, 302, 309, 311, 312, 317, 320, 326, 329; zones of acceptable outcomes, 309, 312, 375–79, 382. *See also* Personal Responsibility and Work Opportunity Reconciliation Act of *1996*

Welfare-to-work. *See* Employment requirements

Western states, 59

West Virginia, 347

Whites. *See* Racial and ethnic issues

Whitman, Christine Todd, 292

WIC. *See* Special Supplemental Feeding Program for Women, Infants and Children

Williams, John, 59, 63

Wilson, Pete, 132, 230, 258, 292, 299

Wilson, William Julius, 115, 123, 150

Wisconsin: AFDC, 258–59; caseloads, 343; sanctions, 349; welfare reform, 132, 157, 258–59, 305; work issues, 348

Women's issues; AFDC, 68, 147, 150, 154–55, 265; employment, 16, 48, 103–04, 107, 111, 164; establishment of paternity, 244; JOBS program, 78; "man in the house" rules, 18, 55; working mothers, 62, 63, 104, 183, 227–28, 238, 350–51, 357; WORK program, 243, 244. *See also* Births, out-of-wedlock; Children; Families; Teenage pregnancy

Work and Responsibility Act of *1994*, 242–48

Work First Program, 306–07

Work Incentives Program (WIN), 56, 76, 130

WORK program, 234, 243

Wright, James, 73

Wyoming, 343